ELIJAH M. JAMES • SANDRA J. WELLMAN
Dawson College Seneca College

MACROECONOMICS

SECOND EDITION

PEARSON
Toronto

To my granddaughter, Baby Sabrina, who will some day learn to read this book, and to Jennifer (Jen), my daughter-in-law who is doing a fabulous job in raising her.
Elijah James

To my mother, Barbara Keene-MacMillan, unquestionably the greatest teacher I have ever had.
SandraWellman

To my mother, Wongel Alemu, who instilled in me the importance of education.
Worku Aberra

Vice-President, Editorial Director: Gary Bennett
Editor-in-Chief: Nicole Lukach
Acquisitions Editor: Claudine O'Donnell
Marketing Manager: Leigh-Anne Graham
Supervising Developmental Editor: Suzanne Schaan
Developmental Editor: Toni Chahley
Project Manager: Richard di Santo
Manufacturing Coordinator: Susan Johnson
Production Editor: Susan Bindernagel
Copy Editor: Susan Bindernagel
Proofreader: Leslie Saffrey
Compositor: Hermia Chung
Permissions Researcher: Natalie Barrington
Art Director: Julia Hall
Interior and Cover Designer: Anthony Leung
Cover Image: Shutterstock

Credits and acknowledgments borrowed from other sources and reproduced, with permission, in this textbook appear on the appropriate page within text, and on page C1.

10 9 8 7 6 5 4 3 2 1 CKV

Library and Archives Canada Cataloguing in Publication

James, Elijah M.
Macroeconomics / Elijah M. James, Sandra J. Wellman, Worku Aberra.—2nd ed.

Includes index.
ISBN 978-0-13-801096-6

1. Macroeconomics—Textbooks. I. Wellman, Sandra II. Aberra, Worku, 1951– III. Title.

HB172.5.J345 2011a 339 C2011-906260-7

ISBN 978-0-13-801096-6

Brief Contents

Contents

Preface

Writing textbooks does not necessarily get easier with each revision. When a textbook is well received, great effort must be expended in trying to retain and even improve on its strengths and eliminate its weaknesses. It is a constant challenge to incorporate in the new edition the changes suggested by users of the previous edition. Additionally, explanations and passages that students find difficult or unclear must be reworked and simplified.

The primary objective of *Macroeconomics*, Second Edition, has remained unchanged, namely, to assist beginning students in economics to understand the fascinating subject of economics and to motivate them to make a serious study of it. In the process, we hope that the book will convey the power and excitement of economic analysis.

Macroeconomics, Second Edition, continues to use students' intuitive knowledge of economics as a stepping stone to present basic economic concepts, ideas, and principles. The dialogical approach that proved to be quite successful in engaging students in the previous edition has been retained in this new edition. Like its predecessor, this book is completely interactive. Our survey of students who have used the previous edition revealed that this is one of the features of the book that students find helpful. Many claimed that this approach has actually taught them how to answer questions.

Revisions, additions, extensions, and deletions have been made in order to improve the book and increase its appeal. Where pruning was necessary, it was done without robbing the student of essential material. In preparing this second edition of *Macroeconomics*, we made a concerted effort to ensure that students continue to find this book easy to read and understand. Much would be lost if this book that was designed specifically to be student-friendly were placed beyond the readability comfort of the very people for whom it was written. It is hoped that such a tragedy has been averted.

As is the case with its predecessor, *Macroeconomics*, Second Edition, is written specifically for students taking their first course in economics. Such a course should provide a solid foundation in economic ideas and principles, and in the basic tools used to analyze economic behaviour. Economics is an interesting and important subject, and those who make a serious study of it often find it useful in their personal lives. Such a course should also encourage and motivate students by presenting the subject in a manner they consider relevant. This textbook tries to achieve these objectives. Words and diagrams are the main tools used in presenting economic ideas to students. No mathematics beyond elementary algebra is used in this book, and even then, math is used sparingly or relegated to the MyEconLab, where instructors and students who need to use it can find it. Care has been taken to ensure that the use of mathematics facilitates rather than impedes the learning of basic economic concepts and principles.

This book recognizes that many students will not continue their formal study of economics beyond this introductory level. This fact is demonstrated in the material covered in the text.

Responding to Students' Needs

This text is specially designed to help students succeed. Before writing this book, one of the authors conducted a survey to determine the features that students find most helpful in textbooks. In writing this new textbook, we incorporated students' expressed needs as follows:

1. **A preview of what is to be learned**. The student survey revealed that students want to know what they will learn in a chapter before reading the chapter. Each chapter begins with clearly stated Learning Objectives in the form of numbered statements of what students should be able to do after studying the chapter. NEW! Each of the major sections in the book is associated with a learning objective, and this theme carries through to the Key Points to Remember, and the Problems and Exercises.
2. **Assess Your Knowledge questions.** As indicated earlier, most students taking their first course in economics have some knowledge of the subject. Many students will be motivated to test their knowledge of the material in the chapter even before studying the chapter. Short self-test questions at the beginning of each chapter provide this opportunity. Answers are provided on the MyEconLab.
3. **In-text explanations of graphs.** Students expressed a desire for graphs to be explained within the text. In this book, detailed explanations of all graphs are given within the text. Thus, graphs become an integral part of the explanation being offered or of the concept or principle being presented. NEW! All of the key graphs in each chapter have been placed on quad paper.
4. **Concept citation.** According to the survey, students want basic concepts and ideas to be emphasized in the text. This is done in Macroeconomics, Second Edition. NEW! At the beginning of each major section, a key concept or idea is expressed, and this key concept or idea is tied to a learning objective for the chapter.
5. **Definitions and important terms emphasized in the text.** Students indicated that they want definitions and important terms to be accentuated in the text. In this book, all important terms are bolded and the terms and definitions are repeated in the margin. Important material or principles are highlighted, because students often highlight material that they consider to be important. NEW! The Second Edition of Macroeconomics also includes a complete glossary at the end of the book.
6. **Review.** Students want a textbook that contains a review of the material studied. Review is an important component of this book. At the end of each chapter, students are asked to review the learning objectives with a view to determining the extent to which they have accomplished the objectives. Additionally, this section contains key points for students to remember. NEW! In keeping with the organization of major sections in each chapter by learning objective, we have also organized key sections in the chapter review by learning objective.
7. **Important terms collected at the end of each chapter.** Students have identified this as a desirable feature of a textbook. In Macroeconomics, Second Edition, a section at the end of each chapter entitled Economic Word Power satisfies this need. Under Economic Word Power, all economic terms introduced in the chapter and included in the margins are listed alphabetically with page references to where they are defined in the chapter.
8. **Questions that challenge comprehension of the material.** The survey revealed that students want the textbook to contain review questions that challenge their understanding of the material they have studied. Accordingly, each major section of the

book is followed by key Reading Comprehension questions, in which students are asked to answer questions based on the material contained in the preceding section and its associated learning objective.

9. **Problems and Exercises.** Students want a textbook that allows them to practise problems and exercises based on the material covered in the text. Responding to this expressed need, Macroeconomics, Second Edition, contains a Problems and Exercises section in which students can practise applying key concepts in the book. The problems and exercises are grouped into three categories: Basic, Intermediate, and Challenging. Answers to these are not given in the text, but students can consult their instructors for the answers. NEW! Basic questions are now tied to the learning objectives in the chapter.
10. **Self-assessment and use of economic resources on the internet.** An important aspect of the teaching–learning relationship is self-assessment. This textbook contains a Study Guide that uses multiple-choice questions as an effective way for students to assess themselves. Answers are provided in the textbook. In addition, the Study Guide contains another set of Problems and Exercises, the answers to which are on the MyEconLab. Students then have an opportunity to strengthen any weaknesses revealed by the self-assessment. The MyEconLab also includes Economics Online Exercises which list websites where students can augment their study of the material in the chapter.

What's Different about This Book?

This question has been partially answered by the 10 points outlining the responses to students' expressed needs and by the dialogical approach taken in this book. However, other differences remain between this and other introductory economics textbooks.

1. *Macroeconomics*, Second Edition, draws on the strengths of its predecessors (*Economics: A Problem-Solving Approach*; *Macroeconomics: Basic Concepts, Questions and Answers*; and *Introduction to Economics*). The text is easy to read and understand, it is student friendly, and it focuses on basic principles and concepts that students at the introductory level need to know.
2. This book employs a results-oriented learning-by-objective (LBO) approach. Learning objectives are established at the beginning of each chapter, and at the end of the chapter, the objectives are reviewed to determine whether students accomplished those objectives.
3. Graphs are large and clear and are fully integrated and explained in the body of the text rather than being curtained off in potentially distracting boxes outside the main body of the text. Thus, all graphs form an integral part of the explanation of the concepts and ideas they are used to represent or depict. Graphs illustrating key concepts are also presented on quad paper to enhance student understanding.
4. A huge number of interesting macroeconomic topics can be included in an introductory economics text. For example, this textbook contains an entire chapter on the aggregate demand–aggregate supply model in the long run. In discussing fiscal policy, the supply side is given due consideration. Also, the effects of the 2008–2009 recession on the Canadian economy and policymakers' responses receive adequate attention. These topics are presented at an elementary level that is suitable for comprehension by introductory students. To keep this book within a reasonable length, we have chosen topics with care. The result is a text that covers a suitable range of macroeconomic topics that are relevant to present-day students.

5. Most macroeconomics textbooks, in discussing macroeconomic models of equilibrium income determination, ignore the injections-withdrawals approach or accord it only passing reference. The injections-withdrawals model is a powerful tool for presenting the concept of equilibrium income to beginning students. *Macroeconomics*, Second Edition, devotes a great deal of space to this model, incorporating it with the Keynesian expenditure model.
6. Many of the students who will use this book are business students. Business and economics share a close relationship. In fact, many business decisions are grounded in economics. Business examples, called Business Situations, are scattered throughout the book to give students an opportunity to apply the economic theory they are learning to a variety of business situations.
7. *Macroeconomics*, Second Edition, uses visual aids liberally to complement verbal explanations. This feature will be particularly helpful to students whose first language is not English.
8. *Macroeconomics*, Second Edition, uses colour judiciously and effectively to enhance understanding of graphs and charts. For example, in demand-supply graphs, the downward-sloping demand curve is always shown as a blue curve, while the upward-sloping supply curve is always shown as a red curve.

Organization of the Book

This book is divided into six parts. Part I introduces the subject matter of economics and discusses the economic problem. It also deals with the important topic of demand and supply. Part II deals with national income, unemployment, and inflation. Part III incorporates macroeconomic models of income determination and economic growth. Short-run and long-run models of income determination and the price-level are discussed here, along with the Keynesian expenditure model. Part IV discusses economic fluctuations and fiscal policy, while Part V deals with money, banking, and monetary policy. Part VI discusses other macroeconomic issues: inflation and unemployment, the international economy, and the balance of payments and exchange rates.

New to the Second Edition

In **Chapter 1**, the material on the importance of understanding economics has been substantially rewritten to include more recent events; a new section on where economists work and what they do has been included in this edition; the concept of time as a resource has been included; leadership has been added as an example of entrepreneurial ability; and the concept of financial capital has been further clarified. A short list of Canadian entrepreneurs and the companies and products associated with them has been added.

In **Chapter 2**, the discussion on opportunity cost has been expanded and more examples have been added. More relevant examples are used in **Chapter 3**. For example, USB flash drives, Blu-rays, and iPhones replace older examples, and profit has been made explicit as a motivator for producers. We have also added a new mathematical appendix, in which the basic demand/supply model is presented algebraically.

In **Chapter 4**, the discussion on the gross domestic product for Canada now contains the effect of the 2008–2009 recession. Data on unemployment and inflation have been updated.

Chapter 5 contains increased use of examples to illustrate concepts and ideas, and the discussion of the Human Development Index has been expanded. Of course, all data have been updated.

A number of changes have been introduced in **Chapter 6**. These include the capacity utilization rate, the employment rate, stocks and flows in the labour market, redefinition of full employment to reflect current usage and to achieve greater clarity and accuracy, construction of the consumer price index (CPI), calculation of the rate of inflation, and the core rate of inflation.

Chapter 7 deals with the Aggregate Demand/Aggregate Supply model in the short run. The fallacy of composition is used to distinguish between market demand and aggregate demand. There is an expanded explanation of the three ranges of the short-run aggregate supply curve.

Chapter 8 now discusses the effects of recent natural disasters on the economy's long-run aggregate supply (*AS*) curve. Economic growth and sustainability are now added to this chapter.

In **Chapter 9** we have incorporated the material on injections and withdrawals from Chapter 8 of the first edition. In **Chapter 11**, the 2008–2009 recession is discussed and Canada's response is used as an example of fiscal policy in action.

In **Chapter 12**, the discussion of business cycles has been enriched by the addition of a section with detailed discussion of the sectoral impact of business cycles, and in **Chapter 13**, we have added a section on the characteristics of money.

Chapter 14 now contains an extended treatment of the Bank of Canada. A discussion of Schedule I, Schedule II, and Schedule III banks is also contained in this chapter.

Chapter 15 has a new discussion of the asset demand for money, and here also, the Bank of Canada's response to the 2008–2009 recession is used as an example of monetary policy in action.

New topics discussed in **Chapter 16** include the natural rate of unemployment in Canada, the phenomenon of a low rate of unemployment and a low rate of inflation in the early 2000s, and the impact of minimum wages on employment.

Chapter 17 now includes a discussion of the United Nations Conference on Trade and Development, and the International Monetary Fund (IMF). The data in **Chapter 18** have been updated.

Pedagogy

- **Learning Objectives:** Each chapter starts with a list of learning objectives directly related to the key concepts presented in the chapter. These learning objectives are in turn tied to each major section of the book, associated reading comprehension questions, and key elements of the chapter review.
- **Assess Your Knowledge:** These questions at the beginning of each chapter cover the main objectives of the chapter and can be used to review for tests and exams. Answers to these questions are provided on the MyEconLab.
- **Key terms:** Key terms are bolded within the text and defined. The terms and definitions are repeated in the margins as well. Terms are also listed with page references at the end of each chapter in the section entitled Economic Word Power, and all terms are included in the comprehensive glossary at the end of the book.

- **Business Situation boxes:** These brief vignettes give students an opportunity to apply economic theory to a variety of business situations. Each business scenario is followed by a question about the relevance of the example to the chapter topic. Answers to the questions are found in an appendix at the end of the book.
- **Highlighted sections of the text:** These are used to emphasize important concepts.
- **Figures:** All figures are explained in the body of the text and thus form an integral part of the concepts and ideas they are used to represent or depict.
- **End-of-chapter materials:** These sections provide students with multiple opportunities for review (Key Points to Remember), Problems and Exercises for instructors to assign, and opportunities for student self-assessment (embedded Study Guide).

Supplements

A comprehensive supplements package accompanies the text.

Instructor's Resource CD-ROM: This resource CD includes the following instructor supplements:

- **Pearson TestGen** is a testing software that enables instructors to view and edit the existing questions, add questions, generate tests, and distribute the tests in a variety of formats. Powerful search and sort functions make it easy to locate questions and arrange them in any order desired. TestGen also enables instructors to administer tests on a local area network, have the tests graded electronically, and have the results prepared in electronic or printed reports. TestGen is compatible with Windows and Macintosh operating systems, and can be downloaded from the TestGen website located at www.pearsoned.com/testgen. Contact your local sales representative for details and access.
- The **Instructor's Resource Manual** is designed to help the instructor make the best possible use of his or her limited time. Each chapter includes a list of important terms and concepts introduced in the chapter, the objectives of the chapter, a brief overview of its contents, and teaching suggestions and possible topics for class discussion. The Manual also contains solutions to the Problems and Exercises. The Instructor's Manual is available for downloading from a password-protected section of Pearson Education Canada's online catalogue (www.pearsoned.ca/highered). Navigate to your book's catalogue page to view a list of those supplements that are available. See your local sales representative for details and access.
- **PowerPoint Presentations** reflect the main topics featured in the text, along with graphic depictions of important economic ideas discussed in the book.
- The **Image Library** contains all of the numbered figures and tables in the textbook.

The moment you know.
Educators know it. Students know it. It's that inspired moment when something that was difficult to understand suddenly makes perfect sense. Our MyLab products have been designed and refined with a single purpose in mind—to help educators create that moment of understanding with their students.
MyEconLab delivers proven results in helping individual students succeed. It provides engaging experiences that personalize, stimulate, and measure learning for each student. And, it comes from a trusted partner with educational expertise and an eye on the future.

MyEconLab can be used by itself or linked to any learning management system. Visit MyEconLab to learn more about how it combines proven learning applications with powerful assessment.

MyEconLab—the moment you know.

For more information on MyEconLab, please visit www.myeconlab.com.

Technology Specialists. Pearson's Technology Specialists work with faculty and campus course designers to ensure that Pearson technology products, assessment tools, and online course materials are tailored to meet your specific needs. This highly qualified team is dedicated to helping schools take full advantage of a wide range of educational resources, by assisting in the integration of a variety of instructional materials and media formats. Your local Pearson Education sales representative can provide you with more details on this service program.

CourseSmart for Instructors. CourseSmart goes beyond traditional expectations—providing instant, online access to the textbooks and course materials you need at a lower cost for students. And even as students save money, you can save time and hassle with a digital eTextbook that allows you to search for the most relevant content at the very moment you need it. Whether it's evaluating textbooks or creating lecture notes to help students with difficult concepts, CourseSmart can make life a little easier. See how when you visit www.coursesmart.com/instructors.

CourseSmart for Students. CourseSmart goes beyond traditional expectations—providing instant, online access to the textbooks and course materials you need at an average savings of 60 percent. With instant access from any computer and the ability to search your text, you'll find the content you need quickly, no matter where you are. And with online tools like highlighting and note-taking, you can save time and study efficiently. See all the benefits at www.coursesmart.com/students.

Pearson eText. Pearson eText gives students access to the text whenever and wherever they have access to the internet. eText pages look exactly like the printed text, offering powerful new functionality for students and instructors. Users can create notes, highlight text in different colours, create bookmarks, zoom, click hyperlinked words and phrases to view definitions, and view in single-page or two-page view. Pearson eText allows for quick navigation to key parts of the eText using a table of contents and provides full-text search. The eText may also offer links to associated media files, enabling users to access videos, animations, or other activities as they read the text.

ACKNOWLEDGMENTS

This new edition of *Macroeconomics* has increased our indebtedness to instructors, colleagues, and students whose comments, suggestions, and questions have contributed significantly to improving the quality of the book. To them we say a heartfelt thank you. In this regard, we would like to single out Ahmad Banki and Charles-Albert Ramsay who pointed out areas where clarification was needed, and we thank them sincerely. Matlub Hussain continues to be generous with his comments and suggestions. Thank you, Mat.

Elijah's students at Concordia University, John Molson School of Business, McGill University, John Abbott College, and particularly Dawson College continue to influence his writing. Worku's students at Dawson College and Sandra's students at Seneca College have also had an impact on their writing. By our students' questions, they demanded clarity and precision. Without their contributions, the tone of the book would have been vastly different. We thank them from the bottom of our hearts.

Just when we thought we had done the most incredible job with this second edition, we were summoned back to the drawing board by the reviewers. Their comments, constructive criticisms, and suggestions were discerning, incisive, and occasionally even caustic. The result? A much improved textbook. We owe them a debt of gratitude. They are:

Mohammad Akbar, Kwantlen Polytechnic University
Sarah Arliss, Seneca College
Michael Bozzo, Mohawk College
John Cavalliere, Sault College
David Desjardins, John Abbott College
Geoffrey Prince, Centennial College
Sheila Ross, SAIT

The skills and professionalism of the Pearson team that worked on this book must be acknowledged. It is tempting to believe that Pearson Canada once again went out of its way to assemble the best possible team for this project, including Acquisitions Editor, Claudine O'Donnell; Developmental Editor, Toni Chahley; Project Manager, Richard di Santo; and Production Editor and Copyeditor, Susan Bindernagel.

We have exerted a great deal of effort into making Macroeconomics, Second Edition, an enjoyable and student-friendly text from which to learn introductory economics. We hope we have achieved this objective.

Finally, we would like to thank some other people who cannot remain nameless.

From Worku: I am grateful to my children Adam and Rebecca, my wife Arlyle, and, my sister Martha for their support, inspiration, and encouragement. Without their consistent support I would not have been able to make my contribution to the book.

From Sandra: I would like to thank my dear husband John and my children Alexandra, Lucas, and Gabrielle for their enduring patience and unflinching support without which I would not have been able to write this book.

From Elijah: I would like to thank my children, Ted and Andrea, for their unwavering support and sacrifice throughout the years. You have given so much and have required nothing in return. You are both terrific and I love you beyond measure. Connie, I am still thinking of ways to thank you for your unparalleled support. My indebtedness to you is so great that I am beginning to think that I will never be able to thank you enough. I must agree with Robert Byrne that "The purpose of life is a life of purpose." I thank you all.

Elijah M. James
Sandra Wellman
Worku Aberra

TO THE STUDENT

How to Study Economics

The study of economics requires time and serious concentration. Study habits vary from student to student, and what works for one student may not work for all. This course in economics is designed to provide you with some insight into the functioning of an economy and into some of the policy issues that are being hotly debated.

Interest in economics varies. Some students aspire to a career in economics, while others are concerned merely with acquiring a basic understanding of the subject. Whatever your interest might be, here are some general guidelines that you will find helpful as you study this book.

1. Study the Assess Your Knowledge section to determine your prior knowledge.
2. As you read through the various sections of the text, make sure that you are equipped with paper and pencil to make your own notes. Do not rush through the material. You are learning economics, not reading a story book.
3. Practise drawing the diagrams on the basis of the arguments presented. This way, you will learn much more than if you merely tried to study the completed diagram as it is presented in the book.
4. As concepts are presented, try to provide examples, if possible, from your own experience. Your ability to provide examples is a measure of your understanding.
5. The Reading Comprehension questions at the end of each major section are designed to assess your comprehension of the material covered in the section. Try to answer all of these and then check the accuracy of your answers in MyEconLab.
6. Make sure that you understand the terms and concepts introduced in each chapter by reviewing them in the Economic Word Power section at the end of each chapter.
7. The Problems and Exercises are designed to help you to apply what you have learned. Try to work through as many of these as you can.
8. Form study groups if you can. By discussing economics (answering questions and solving problems) in groups, your understanding will be enhanced.
9. Finally, a Study Guide is included in the text. Use the questions for self-assessment. Answers are provided at the end of the book for your guidance.

Chapter 1

The Subject Matter of Economics

Learning Objectives

After studying this chapter, you should be able to

1.1 Explain the importance of understanding economics

1.2 Discuss economics as a profession

1.3 Discuss the subject matter of economics

1.4 Define resources, classify them into categories, and discuss the incomes derived from each category of resources

1.5 Explain the scientific method and discuss economic methodology

1.6 Identify positive and normative economics and explain why economists sometimes disagree

1.7 Recognize different types of variables and cause-effect relations

1.8 Distinguish between microeconomics and macroeconomics

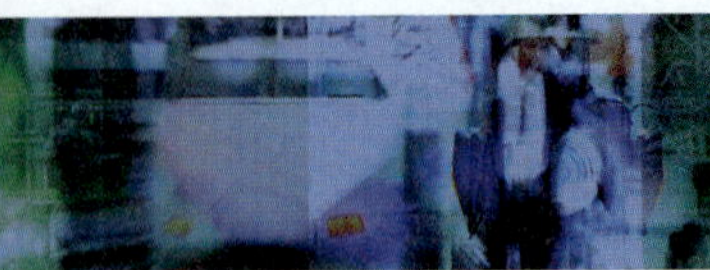

Assess Your Knowledge

MyEconLab

Answers to these questions can be found on MyEconLab at **www.myeconlab.com.**

1. Identify two topics that you would expect to study in economics.
2. Identify one resource that is not scarce.
3. Why do people have to make choices?
4. Can someone make a choice without giving up something?
5. Identify two social science disciplines.

LO 1.1 Explain the importance of understanding economics

Why Study Economics?

Why is having an understanding of economics important?

These are indeed exciting times to be studying economics. Recent events have turned the spotlight on the economy and on economists. News about economic matters can be read in the newspapers, heard on the radio, and seen on television; all over the internet and the World Wide Web, a great deal of information exists on important economic topics. Governments, large corporations, small business enterprises, and consumers are turning to economists for answers to our economic problems.

Whether it is forest fires in California, the H1N1 virus, unusually frequent federal elections in Canada, accusations of price fixing among the gasoline companies, a tsunami in Samoa, government bailouts of failing companies, the so-called *economic stimulus*, or violent protests in Egypt, they all are related in some way to economics. Economics is involved directly or indirectly with whether you decide to go to summer school or take a vacation in the Dominican Republic, to purchase a used car for transportation to and from school or take public transportation, to live at home with your patents or rent an apartment close to school, or to purchase some U.S. dollars to shop in the United States this weekend. On April 14, 2010, and again on October 14, 2010, the Canadian dollar rose above the U.S. dollar in value. On November 4, 2010, the Canadian dollar was on par with the U.S. dollar, and on January 24, 2011, one Canadian dollar was worth 1.0054 U.S. dollars. Why did these changes occur and who benefits from them? The fact is, economic issues and problems are all around us; we cannot escape them.

Economic analysis can shed light on these and many other issues that are of great significance for many of us because they affect our lives in important ways. Once we accept this simple fact, then economic understanding assumes great importance.

Let us consider the following benefits derived from understanding economics.

Understanding the Economy and Society Understanding the operation of our economic system enables us to improve its performance and helps us to deal with many of the problems that our country faces. The economy is such an important part of society that it is impossible to understand society without a basic knowledge of economics. Our relationships with one another, our environment, the manner in which our collective wealth is distributed, the types of work we do, and the amount of money we earn are all related to our economy. Our lives are shaped by the myriad economic decisions that have been made in the past by others and that are being made by us today. A decision to build more warplanes instead of providing more educational and health facilities will affect us not only today but also for a long time in the future.

The better our understanding of our economy and our society, the better the control that we are likely to have over our destiny. It can be argued that the recent global and economic crisis would have been longer and more severe if economists did not have such a good understanding of how the economy works.

Understanding World Affairs Change is occurring rapidly in the world. Just pick up a newspaper, turn on the radio or television, or go to a news agency on the internet, and you will get an idea of the many important changes that are taking place in the world. The political face of the Middle East has already assumed a different appearance, and the war in Afghanistan still rages on. Many countries of the world are engaged in important negotiations, and North Korea continues to defy the United Nations sanctions by testing its missiles. The economy of Zimbabwe was in shambles with an estimated unemployment rate of 95% in 2010 and an estimated inflation rate of 231 000 000% in 2008. After Zimbabwe abandoned the Zimbabwean dollar in 2009, the rate of inflation fell dramatically to about 5.3% in July 2010.

The G-20—finance ministers and central bankers from a group of 19 countries and the European Union—holds meetings to discuss global economic stability. Their deliberations are important because they hold significant economic power. According to the *African Sun News,* as of August 27, 2010, about 15 African countries were at war or were experiencing postwar tensions. Among other factors at the root of these wars were the rich natural resources owned by each of these countries. Thus, the cause of many of these wars was economic in nature. Portugal, Ireland, Greece, and Spain have all recently experienced economic difficulties. Economics as a discipline may be able to offer some solutions. Our way of life has been changed drastically by terrorist threats, and national security is now on the list of top priorities for most countries. During January and February 2011, demonstrations, protests, and social unrests in Tunisia, Egypt, Yemen, Bahrain, and Libya, engaged the world's attention. Economics will help us to understand many of these important world events and how they affect our country, our governments, and us as individuals.

Being an Informed Citizen As consumers, it is important for us to know how to spend our income so that we can derive maximum satisfaction from our purchases. It is also important for us to use our labour services and other resources wisely. Not only should people be wise consumers, but as citizens in a democracy, they must also be able to visualize and evaluate the consequences of different courses of action to determine which ones are most likely to lead to improvements in economic and social well-being.

What are the issues involved in the federal government's decision to run a deficit during a period of severe economic slow-down? Will such a policy achieve its intended goal? Did our government make the right decision in its dealings with the automakers? Will Canadians benefit from this arrangement? What are the costs? General Motors offered $3000 to anyone who scrapped an old car and bought a new one. Was General Motors' offer of this $3000 scrap incentive a wise economic move? During the global recession, the Bank of Canada lowered its interest rate drastically. Was that policy initiative a good one? Can the government do anything about unemployment? Should Canada pursue a policy of protectionism as a means of supporting its domestic industries?

Can subsidies to farmers be justified on economic grounds? In an election, citizens often vote for a party on the basis of its political platform, which, to a significant degree, contains issues and intended policies that are essentially economic in nature. A knowledge of economics enables citizens to replace emotional judgment with reasoned analysis in the decision-making process.

Thinking Logically One of the most important reasons for studying economics is that it develops a particular way of thinking and making decisions. Good decision making requires a careful evaluation of the benefits (advantages) and costs (disadvantages) associated with the decision or the choice. Actually, economic analysis is, to a large extent, an exercise in logic and thus helps to sharpen our common sense.

Getting Personal Satisfaction People may have a more personal reason for studying economics. Because the study of economics can be intellectually exciting and stimulating, it yields great personal satisfaction. If you happen to become a great economist, you could end up being the president or chief executive officer (CEO) of a corporation, or an economic consultant to one of our levels of government, with an annual salary in the six-figure range.

Reading Comprehension

The answers to these questions can be found on MyEconLab at www.myeconlab.com. MyEconLab

1. Present an argument to support the claim that economics is worth studying.
2. If you were to purchase a car, what benefits would you consider? What costs would you consider?
3. Describe a recent world affair that you believe to be related to economics.

 Discuss economics as a profession

Economics as a Profession

Where do economists work and what do they actually do?

Economists are employed in many different places, including the following:

- Private firms, such as banks, insurance companies, large manufacturing companies, unions, and telephone companies
- High schools, colleges, and universities
- Government departments and government agencies
- Research institutions
- Nonprofit organizations
- Independent consultancies
- International organizations and agencies, such as the United Nations, the World Bank, and the International Monetary Fund

You may even find economists serving as ministers of government.

Let us turn to the second part of the question: What do economists actually do? Certainly, you have a good idea of what your economics instructor does. But what other kinds of jobs do economists do? A large corporation, such as Wal-Mart, General Motors, Costco, or your telephone company, might hire economists to estimate the demand for its products or to figure out what effects a change in price will have on its profits. A bank might employ economists to forecast interest rates or the demand for loans. The federal government might hire economists to determine the effects of certain taxes on the government's revenue and on the level of economic activity within the country. Finally, a union might employ economists to study matters relating to wages and employment. Economists serve as presidents, vice-presidents, general managers, and executives of a wide variety of organizations. Clearly, economists can add value to an organization in a variety of contexts.

Reading Comprehension

The answers to these questions can be found on MyEconLab at www.myeconlab.com. MyEconLab

1. What opportunities exist for economic graduates?
2. What kinds of work do economists do?
3. Why might an electrical power generating company hire an economist?

LO 1.3 Discuss the subject matter of economics

What Is Economics All About?

What do we mean by scarcity? Isn't Canada a land of plenty?

We live in a world where our wants vastly outstrip the means available to satisfy those wants. Society wants automobiles, homes, clothes, computers, entertainment centres, schools, roads, food, telecommunication systems, health services, books, symphony orchestras, amusement parks, libraries, and so on. Indeed, our wants seem to be limitless. But the means available to satisfy all these wants are severely limited. Suppose every Canadian is given a month to list all the things that he or she would like to have, not considering cost. At the end of the month, the lists are collected, and the economy embarks on a massive production effort to produce everything on all the lists. Will the Canadian economy be capable of producing all the things on those lists? The answer is emphatically and resoundingly "no." We just don't have enough factories, natural resources, machinery, and workers to produce all the things we would like to have. **Scarcity** is the situation that exists when resources are inadequate to produce all the goods and services that people want. So although Canada is a land of plenty (we are well-endowed with resources, and we have a relatively high standard of living), we still have the problem of scarcity.

scarcity the situation that exists when resources are inadequate to produce all the goods and services that people want

Now we know what scarcity means, but what does that have to do with choice?

If we could have everything that we want, then we would not have to choose. We would simply take it all. If you have $200, you cannot purchase a Kindle wireless reading device

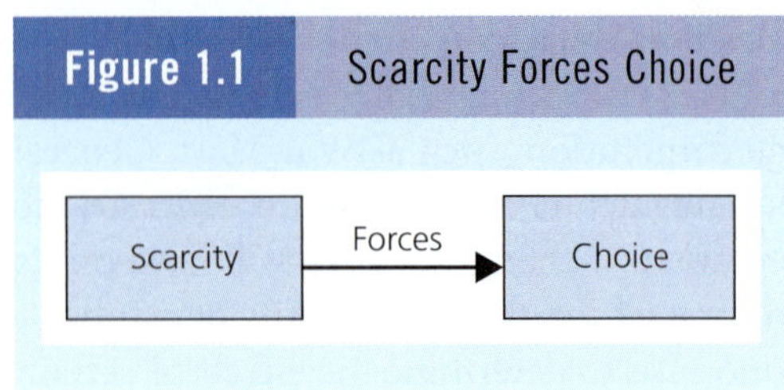

Figure 1.1 Scarcity Forces Choice

that costs $200 and two jackets that cost $100 each. You are confronted with scarcity and you will have to choose between the Kindle and the two jackets. Your parents have a strict budget of $10 000. They cannot take the Caribbean cruise that costs $10 000 and buy you that red used car for $10 000. They are confronted with scarcity and must therefore choose between your dream car and their cruise. Guy Laliberté can afford to spend several millions of dollars as a space tourist, but he cannot physically attend a hockey game at the same time that he is in space. Even people as wealthy as Laliberté and Bill Gates face scarcity and are forced to choose, since they have a limited amount of time. We see, therefore, that choice is a direct result of scarcity. Figure 1.1 highlights the relationship between scarcity and choice.

Does society as a whole also have to make choices?

Yes. For the same reason that individuals must make choices, society as a whole must also make choices. Society is equally confronted with scarcity and must therefore choose between different alternatives that are available. Society must choose between more schools or more hospitals, better roads or more recreational facilities, more submarines or more environmental protection, and so on. As long as scarcity exists, choices must be made.

BUSINESS SITUATION 1.1

John Adams owns a corner grocery store. He has just obtained a loan of $25 000 from his bank. He is thinking of using this money to increase the size of his stock.

What element of economics does this situation illustrate?

The answer to this Business Situation can be found in Appendix A.

What is economics?

economics the social science that studies how people use limited means to satisfy their unlimited wants

We have indicated that scarcity and choice are at the heart of economics. They are the most basic economic concepts. In fact, economics has everything to do with the way we choose among available alternatives—the way we use our scarce means to satisfy our unlimited wants. We can define economics this way: **Economics** is the social science that studies how people use limited means to satisfy their unlimited wants.

Economics reminds you that you cannot have everything you want. You cannot go to a movie and study for your economics test at the same time. If you think that the movies will benefit you more than studying for the test, then you will give up studying for the test. Conversely, if you believe that studying for the test will benefit you more than going to the movie, then you will give up going to the movies. Economics is at work in your decision.

What is a social science?

social science any discipline that studies human behaviour

A **social science** is any discipline that studies human behaviour. Many disciplines study different aspects of human behaviour. Psychology deals with the mental characteristics associated with a particular kind of behaviour; sociology is the study of society and its institutions; anthropology studies the origin and development of humans as social beings; and political science is concerned with the nature and functions of the state and the way we are governed. All these disciplines, along with economics, are social sciences. These disciplines often overlap. For example, economics and political science both study the functions of the state, but they may do so from different perspectives.

Reading Comprehension

The answers to these questions can be found on MyEconLab at www.myeconlab.com. MyEconLab

1. Why do individuals, businesses, and governments all have to make choices?
2. Economics is the study of scarcity and choice. Do you consider this to be an adequate definition of economics?
3. Would you personally be confronted with scarcity if you could buy all the goods and services you want?
4. What makes economics a social science?

LO 1.4 Define resources, classify them into categories, and discuss the income derived from each category of resources

Resources

What are the limited means referred to in the definition of economics?

resources the things used to produce goods and services

goods tangible things that satisfy wants

services intangible things that satisfy wants

Limited means are the things that are needed to produce the items to satisfy our wants. They are more generally referred to as **resources** or factors of production and include trees in British Columbia, rivers in Quebec, lakes in Ontario, parliament buildings in Ottawa, the oil sands of Alberta, potash in Saskatchewan, the productive efforts of human beings all over Canada, time, factories, highways, nuclear power plants, and all things used in the process of production.

Figure 1.2 shows that resources produce not only goods and services to satisfy consumer wants, but they also produce other resources that can, in turn, be used to produce goods and services.

Figure 1.2 Resources Produce Goods, Services, and Other Resources

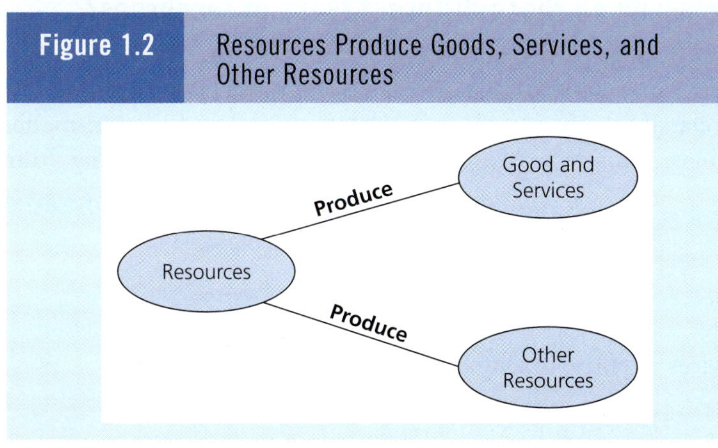

For example, we use trees to produce paper, rivers for navigation and fishing, buildings as dwellings and warehouses, human effort to operate machines and to load and unload trucks, and nuclear power plants to generate electricity. We produce factories and then use them to produce shoes and clothing.

What is the difference between goods and services?

The main difference between goods and services is that **goods** are tangible things (you can touch them) that satisfy wants, and **services** are

Water is an important resource that Canada is well endowed with.

intangible things that satisfy wants. Examples of goods are computers, iPads, television sets, shoes, and textbooks. Examples of services are teaching, banking, transportation services, and garbage collection. Goods and services both give satisfaction and are therefore wanted. Goods and services are collectively referred to as **commodities**. Such items as garbage and pollution that are unwanted and do not give any satisfaction are called **bads**. People are willing to pay money to obtain goods and services; they are also willing to pay money to get rid of bads.

Does the economy produce bads?

Yes, but not deliberately. That is, people do not use the economy's resources with the main objective of producing bads, but in the process of producing goods and services, bads are sometimes produced. For example, in the process of producing automobiles, steel, and many other products, our factories spew out large amounts of environmental toxins. And even in driving our cars and heating our homes, we pollute the environment. We see, therefore, that human activity often results in the production of bads.

commodities goods and services together

bads things that are unwanted and do not give any satisfaction

Are all resources scarce?

No. Not all resources are scarce; a few resources are available in sufficiently large quantities to satisfy our wants for them. Air and sunlight come readily to mind. They are abundant, not scarce. Of course, air and sunlight are scarce to miners trapped in a mine. We don't have to economize on the use of limitless resources; consequently, economics does not focus on them. Canada is fortunate in that it has large amounts of different types of resources, yet they are insufficient to allow us to produce all the goods and services that we desire.

Is there any way to classify all these different types of resources?

We can classify resources in many ways. For example, we could use a two-way classification and divide them into resources that are scarce and those that are abundant. Alternatively, we could classify them into two categories: natural and human-made. However, economists have chosen to classify resources into the following four categories:

1. Land
2. Labour
3. Capital
4. Entrepreneurial services or entrepreneurship

As you continue your study of economics, you will find that some terms do not have quite the same meanings as they have in everyday language. This will seem strange at first, but you will get accustomed to it.

land all natural resources

Land All natural resources are referred to as **land**. It includes much more than the solid portion of the earth on which you can grow crops, erect a building, or use as a parking lot. In economics, any non-human resource that is made available by nature is called land. Thus, land includes minerals embedded in the earth; fish in the seas, rivers, and lakes; the vast expanse of oceans; the natural waterfalls; wildlife; oxygen in the air; time; and even the space within which economic activity takes place. The term *natural resources* is often used as a synonym for land.

labour human physical and mental efforts

Labour **Labour** as a factor of production refers to human physical and mental efforts that people contribute to the production process. It is not difficult to visualize the labour expended by craftspeople as they mould materials into works of art, farmers as they cultivate their crops, or assembly-line workers as they contribute to the production of an item. But the services rendered by sales representatives, lawyers, teachers, doctors, musicians, and actors are all classified under the category of labour.

capital produced means of production

human capital education, training, skills, health, and so on, that improve the quality of labour

Capital **Capital** is any produced means of production, that is, any manufactured item that can be used to produce goods and services or other resources. Buildings, roads, manufacturing plants, equipment, and tools are examples of capital, or *capital goods* as they are also called. Actually, there are different types of capital. The physical manufactured resources listed above are called *real capital.* Businesses invest in these capital goods to produce things. **Human capital** refers to the education, training, skills, health, and so on, that improve the quality of labour. Skilled, educated, experienced, and healthy workers are more productive than unskilled, uneducated, inexperienced, and unhealthy workers. Thus, many businesses are willing to invest in their workers to increase their human capital. People take the time to build their human capital to improve the quality of their labour. Students at colleges and universities at all levels are building their human capital as they pursue their studies. They are making an investment in themselves.

entrepreneurship the organization of land, labour, and capital into production; the risk-taking aspect of business decision making

Entrepreneurship The mere existence of land, labour, and capital will not cause the production of goods and services to take place. Someone must make the decision to organize these human and non-human resources into the production process. The individual who brings these factors of production together and organizes them into production is called an *entrepreneur.* **Entrepreneurship** (or entrepreneurial services) is the organization of land, labour, and capital into the production of goods and services. Entrepreneurs come up with innovative ways of doing things, are willing to assume the risks associated with their decisions, and are risk-takers. Entrepreneurial skills include managerial skills, organizational skills, decision-making skills, innovative skills, leadership skills, and risk-taking.

Canada has many entrepreneurs. You may be familiar with some of their products. The following is a short list of some of Canada's entrepreneurs and the company or product with which they are associated:

Entrepreneur	Company or Product Association
Jason Goncalves	Permabrand Corporation
Scott Abbott	Trivial Pursuit
J. A. Bombardier	Snowmobile
Tim Horton	Tim Hortons
Heather Reisman	Chapters/Indigo
Edwin Mirvish	Honest Ed's
Christine Magee	Sleep Country Canada
Sam Sniderman	Sam the Record Man
Denise Meehan	Licks
Henry Woodward	Electric light bulb
Linda Lundstrum	Fashion designer

How can we discuss capital without including money?

financial capital money, as opposed to real capital (machinery, equipment, tools, etc.)

In economics, we distinguish between money and real capital. In everyday language and in many areas of business, money and capital are used synonymously. **Financial capital** is defined as funds available to purchase real capital. They are tangible assets that can be used as money. In economics however, the emphasis is on real capital, which refers to the productive agents produced by people to be used in conjunction with other productive factors to produce goods and services. So, to be inclusive, we could say that there are really three types of capital: real capital (machines, tools, etc.), human capital (education, training, etc.), and financial capital (money).

What incomes are generated by the factors of production?

rent income from land

wages and salaries income from labour

interest and dividends income from capital

profit income from entrepreneurship

The factors of production generate incomes for their owners. For example, if you sell your labour services by taking a part-time job while you are at college or university, your employer will pay you for your labour services. Landowners receive income from their land if they use it or if they lease it out to others. The income generated by each category of resources has a special name. Owners of land receive **rent**, and owners of capital receive **interest and dividends**, while those who provide labour services receive **wages and salaries**, and individuals with entrepreneurial skills obtain **profit**. The incomes derived from the four categories of resources are summarized in Table 1.1.

Note that resources are the source of all income. If we total all the rent, wages and salaries, interest and dividends, and profits in an economy, we obtain total income in

Table 1.1 Factors of Production and Their Earnings

Factors	Earnings
Land	Rent
Labour	Wages and salaries
Capital	Interest and dividends
Entrepreneurship	Profits

that economy. Thus, if we use R to denote rent; W to denote wages and salaries; i to indicate interest and dividends; and π to denote profits, we obtain the following equation for total income:

$$\text{Total income} = R + W + i + \pi$$

For example, if rent amounts to $80 billion, wages and salaries add up to $500 billion, interest and dividends add up to $40 billion, and profits total $100 billion, then total income is $80 + 500 + 40 + 100 = $720 billion.

Reading Comprehension

The answers to these questions can be found on MyEconLab at www.myeconlab.com. MyEconLab

1. Scarcity of resources is an economic reality. What are these resources and how are they broadly classified?
2. Give two examples each of land, labour, capital, and entrepreneurship.
3. What is the difference between real capital and financial capital?
4. Why can oil revenues from Alberta tar sands be classified as rent?

LO 1.5 Explain the scientific method and discuss economic methodology

Economics and the Scientific Method

In the definition of economics introduced earlier, the word *science* was used. What is science?

science or the scientific method a particular method of acquiring knowledge that includes observation, measurement, and testing; also refers to the knowledge acquired through the process

The word *science* conjures up images of people in white laboratory coats, test tubes, spacecraft, microscopes, and telescopes. But when we speak of science, we are referring to a particular method of acquiring knowledge that includes observation, measurement, and testing. **Science** can be defined as a branch of study, especially one concerned with facts, principles, and methods. Science refers not only to a method of acquiring knowledge but also to the knowledge produced by the approach. For our purposes, we define science or the **scientific method** as follows:

> The scientific method or approach is the systematic investigation and observation of phenomena and the formulation of general laws or tendencies there from, after testing and verifying hypotheses.

We can discuss the main elements of the scientific approach under the headings of observation and measurement, hypotheses, and verification.

Observation and Measurement One of the basic tasks of scientists is to observe and record facts about the phenomena they are investigating. This is the descriptive or empirical aspect of science. To facilitate this aspect of their work, scientists use certain technical terms that have very precise meanings. The development of such a particularized vocabulary is an important step in the development of any field of scientific inquiry.

hypothesis a statement of suspected relationships among two or more variables

Hypotheses The process of observation often leads to ideas, hunches, or guesses about relationships among the things observed. A **hypothesis** is a statement of suspected relationships among two or more variables or factors. It does not state some fact that is already known but something to be tested. For example, consider the following two statements:

> **Statement 1:** The average grade of students who took economics last term was 70%.
> **Statement 2:** Students who attend classes regularly and do their homework will get better grades than those who don't attend regularly and do no homework.

The first statement is not a hypothesis; it merely expresses a fact that is already known. The second statement, however, is a hypothesis because the statement expresses a relationship among students' performance in economics, their attendance, and whether or not they do their homework. Hypotheses should be stated in a verifiable manner so that they can be confirmed or disproved.

Verification Verification through testing is the heart of the scientific procedure. Once scientists have formulated their hypotheses, they proceed to test these hypotheses to determine the extent to which they are supported by empirical evidence. Relating questions to evidence sets scientific inquiry apart from other types of inquiry.

To what extent does economics follow the scientific approach?

Economics is not a science in the same sense that physics, chemistry, and biology are sciences. Such disciplines as chemistry and biology are called *natural* sciences. Physicists, chemists, zoologists, and biologists can conduct controlled laboratory experiments. They deal with the physical and material world, such as minerals, gases, liquids, and plants. Social scientists, such as economists and sociologists, deal with people and therefore cannot conduct experiments in traditional laboratories. No laboratory instruments can measure human behaviour with any degree of precision. Nevertheless, economics follows the scientific procedure as faithfully as do the natural sciences. In attempting to explain economic phenomena, economists follow the scientific approach. They gather information, analyze it, and select what they consider to be the most relevant facts. They formulate and test hypotheses and thus arrive at general statements or laws concerning economic phenomena. Economics, therefore, has a legitimate claim to be considered a science.

What methodology do economists use in studying economic phenomena?

The factors involved in studying real-world economic events are often quite complex. The scientific economist comes to grips with these complexities by constructing models. An **economic model** is a simplification of the real economy or some aspect of it, and it consists only of the factors that appear to pertain most to what is being studied. Details that do not pertain directly to the question being studied are simply stripped away in the model. The principle of stripping away irrelevant detail is often referred to as the principle of Occam's razor, named after the fourteenth-century philosopher William Occam.

economic model a simplification of economic reality

Economists use models in much the same way that engineers use them. An engineer who has the job of building a bridge would, most likely, design a model before building the real thing. The model allows the engineer to study certain aspects of the bridge before it actually exists. For example, the model bridge could give information about how the actual bridge would look, how it would accommodate traffic, and what modifications might be necessary to make it safe. Similarly, economists construct and use economic models to understand how the real economy works. Several economic models will be introduced and used in this book.

What are the parts of a model?

An economic model can be expressed verbally, mathematically, or graphically. Whatever form an economic model takes, it has the following components:

- Definitions
- Assumptions
- Hypotheses
- Predictions

definition a set of words that explain the meaning of a term or concept

Definitions All economic terms used in the model must be clearly defined. A **definition** is a set of words that explain the meaning of a term or concept. Economists have developed an impressive number of terms and concepts that form a part of the specialized language or *jargon* of the discipline. You have already encountered a few of these terms (land, capital, scarcity, rent). As you work through this book, many of the other terms and concepts that are a part of the economist's vocabulary will become familiar to you. The main purpose of the set of definitions in a model is to identify the variables of the model so that measurement can be facilitated. For example, if the term *interest rates* were used in an economic model without any clear definition, it would be difficult to determine whether the reference was to long-term rates, short-term rates, mortgage rates, or interest rates on loans or on savings deposits.

assumptions statements of the conditions under which a model will work

Assumptions An economic model is intended to explain the economy or some aspect of it under certain conditions. These conditions are stated as **assumptions**. Assumptions, then, are statements of the conditions under which the model is supposed to work. Basically, we usually make two types of assumptions in economics. One type of assumption relates to what motivates economic behaviour. For example, we assume that consumers are motivated by the desire to maximize their satisfaction, whereas businesses are motivated by the desire to maximize their profits. Another type of assumption made in economics is aimed at simplifying the complexities of the actual economy so that the task of the economist is made much easier. For example, if economists are not currently concerned with an economy's external trade relations, they may simplify their analyses by assuming that the country does not engage in trade with the rest of the world. Abstractions of this nature are necessary because of the complexities of the actual economy. Admittedly, economic assumptions are sometimes quite unrealistic, but often what is lost in realism is more than compensated for in understanding.

ceteris paribus other things being equal; allows for the investigation of the effects of one variable while assuming that others remain constant

An assumption of particular importance in economics is the **ceteris paribus** assumption, which is a Latin phrase that means "other things being equal." This assumption allows economists to investigate the effects of one variable while assuming that others remain constant. Suppose we are interested in finding out the effect of a fall in the price of iPhones on the quantity of iPhones that people will buy. Some of these factors include peoples' incomes and their preference for iPhones over other types of smart phones. We can hypothesize that if the price of iPhones falls, people will buy more of them. If we observe that a fall in the price of iPhones is accompanied by an increase in the quantity purchased, can we conclude that the increase in quantity purchased results from a fall in price? Is it not possible that the increase in quantity purchased results from an increase in income or some other factor?

To determine how a change in one factor affects other factors, we must find some way of isolating the effects of other factors. In the above example, we must isolate income, preference, and other factors (except the price of iPhones) that can affect the quantity of iPhones that people will purchase. We can accomplish this task by using the ceteris paribus assumption. This assumption allows us to keep other factors constant while we examine the effects of the factor that currently interests us. Thus, we can investigate how a change in price affects the quantity purchased by assuming that income, preference, and all other factors except the price of iPhones remain unchanged throughout the process of investigation. We can emerge with such a statement as "If the price of a product falls, other things being equal, the quantity purchased will increase."

Hypotheses We have already mentioned hypotheses in an earlier section. You will recall that they are statements about suspected relationships among factors. Hypotheses greatly advance our knowledge of economics because they can be tested and shown to be true or false. Economists have formulated a number of important hypotheses, many of which will be introduced throughout this book. When hypotheses are tested and determined to be correct, we can summarize the results into economic theories. An *economic theory* is a summary statement of what we believe to be true about the operation of an economy or some part of it.

Predictions Testing a hypothesis results in the ability to predict. If the predictions of the model are consistent with the facts, we can predict with some degree of certainty (though not with perfect certainty) what will happen in the economy. Economic predictions usually take the form of "if you do this, then such and such will result." An economic prediction should not be confused with an economic forecast. An **economic prediction** is a statement about the general direction of a variable resulting from the fulfillment of certain conditions. An **economic forecast** is the assignment of a future value to a variable. The following examples should help to illustrate the difference between the two concepts.

economic prediction a statement of the general direction of a variable resulting from the fulfillment of certain conditions

economic forecast the assignment of a future value to a variable

Economic prediction: If the government lowers personal income taxes, total spending on consumer goods and services will rise, other things being equal.
Economic forecast: By next spring, the rate of unemployment will fall to 7%.

Can we determine the "goodness" of an economic model?

Yes. The whole purpose of an economic model is to help us explain some aspect of economic reality and to predict certain outcomes. An economic model that does this well is a good model. If model A explains and predicts economic phenomena better than the competing model B, then model A is judged to be better than model B. For example:

Model A's prediction: If peoples' wages and salaries increase by 10%, they will increase their purchases of goods and services by 8%.
Model B's prediction: If peoples' wages and salaries increase by 10%, they will increase their purchases of goods and services by 5%.
Reality (from actual observation): When wages and salaries increase by 10%, people increase their purchases of goods and services by 7.5%.

Under these circumstances, we would accept model A as the better model.

If an economic model fails to explain what we observe (that is, economic reality), then it may be rejected. At one time, greater attention was paid to the realism of the assumptions of a model than to the model's power of prediction. It is now generally accepted that the "goodness" of a model should be based primarily on its ability to explain and predict.

The use of high-speed computers has enabled economists to manipulate huge amounts of data in an incredibly short time. Thus, it is now relatively easy to test economic hypotheses against observed phenomena. The branch of economics that deals with the use of statistical methods to test economic hypotheses is called **econometrics**. This has become such an important branch of economics that most schools require their economics majors to take at least one course in economic statistics or econometrics.

econometrics the use of statistical methods to test economic hypotheses

Reading Comprehension

The answers to these questions can be found on MyEconLab at www.myeconlab.com. MyEconLab

1. What are the fundamental elements in scientific inquiry and to what extent do economists follow the scientific approach?
2. What is an economic model? Why do economists find it useful to construct models?
3. What are the components (parts) of an economic model?
4. Explain the role of assumptions in economic models.

LO 1.6 Identify positive and normative economics and explain why economists sometimes disagree

Positive and Normative Economics and Disagreement among Economists

What is the difference between positive economics and normative economics?

An understanding of the difference between positive statements and normative statements will help you to understand the difference between positive economics and normative economics. **Positive statements** are statements about some fact. They express what is, was, or will be, and they can be verified. Verification is achieved by referring to the relevant facts. An example of a positive statement is "There are 50 students in your economics class." This is a positive statement even if the actual number of students in your economics class is only 35. The point is that it is a statement about some fact—the number of students in a class. Note that a positive statement can be true or false. Because a positive statement relates to facts, it can be verified or disproved by checking it against the facts. The statement "An increase in average income levels will lead to higher consumption levels" is an example of a positive economic statement.

positive statements statements about what is

Normative statements, conversely, are value judgments or statements of opinions about what ought to be. They cannot be tested for verification by referring to facts because there are no facts. An example of a normative statement is "Every student at college or university should take at least one course in economics."

normative statements statements about what ought to be

Obviously, normative statements are not scientific because they cannot be subjected to empirical testing. This does not suggest that the scientific economist is never concerned with normative issues. In fact, concern with the normative aspects of economics is a major focus of disagreement among economists, as you will see shortly. Even though value judgments are not scientific, they are nevertheless important.

positive economics explains or describes how the economy works

normative economics explains how the economy should work

Now that you are familiar with the difference between positive statements and normative statements, it is easier to understand the distinction between positive economics and normative economics. **Positive economics** explains or describes how the economy actually works and the behaviour of economic units. Positive economics attempts to explain what will happen under certain conditions, but it does not explain what the economic situation ought to be. It does not seek to make any judgments about whether the result of any economic action is good or bad. The concern of positive economics is to describe the economic system as it is and how it actually works. What causes the price of oil to rise? What was the economic impact of the terrorist attack of 9/11? Why has the value of the Canadian dollar risen or fallen in terms of the U.S. dollar? How will an overall increase in taxes affect the Canadian economy? Such questions relate to positive economics.

Normative economics is concerned with explaining how the economy should work. It attempts to judge whether economic outcomes are good or bad and to what extent they can be improved. Should the Government of Canada lend or give money to Air Canada to prevent it from going bankrupt? Should the provincial governments reduce their tax on gasoline? Should governments grant subsidies to farmers? Should the government reduce the tax on cigarettes to reduce the amount of smuggling? Should Canadian banks be allowed to merge? Should the Canadian government have offered greater financial assistance to Haiti following the earthquake on January 12, 2010? Normative economics deals with answers to such questions. Note that the issues of normative economics are policy oriented.

Not surprisingly, normative economics relies heavily on positive economics. Let us consider the following normative economic issue: Should Canada remain a part of the North American Free Trade Agreement (NAFTA)? We could conceivably answer this question on the basis of emotion, but an answer based on an economic analysis of the situation would be preferable. What are the likely benefits of this agreement? What are the costs? Answers to such questions will help up to answer the normative question about the trade agreement.

Why is there so much disagreement among economists?

There is much more agreement among economists than disagreement. This fact may surprise you in view of all the stories of disagreement among economists. Physicists disagree among themselves; so do biologists, geologists, and chemists. Scientists don't always see eye to eye. But let us see why economists disagree. Economists have different values, and they judge economic situations and events differently. When economists are asked to make judgments about some economic action, they may try to be objective, but their objectivity might be coloured by their own moral sentiments. One economist might argue that cigarette smoking is bad for your health; hence, a heavy tax should be imposed on cigarettes to discourage smoking. Another economist might take the position that there are other products that are also hazardous to your health and dangerous to your life—why single out cigarettes? The same economist might argue, moreover, that if people want to smoke cigarettes, it is their business and that the government has no right to interfere with a person's lifestyle; such intrusions should be resisted.

It is not only on normative issues, however, that economists disagree. They disagree on the positive, scientific aspects as well. Often, different explanations exist for how the economy actually operates, and it is not always clear which explanation is best. In other words, economists may disagree over the appropriate model of the economy. It would seem that it should be easy to settle the disagreement simply by confronting the theory with the empirical data. Unfortunately, the available data might not be such as to allow for definitive conclusions.

Economists may disagree even though they use the same economic model. They may agree on the qualitative aspects but disagree on the quantitative aspects. For example, two economists might agree that a fall in interest rates will result in an increase in investment. They might disagree, however, over the magnitude of the increase, one claiming that the increase will be negligible, and the other claiming that the increase will be significant. Again, this type of disagreement can be prolonged because of the inadequacy of relevant data.

Reading Comprehension

The answers to these questions can be found on MyEconLab at www.myeconlab.com. MyEconLab

1. What is the difference between positive and normative economics?
2. Give two examples each of positive and normative statements. Give one example each of positive and normative economics.
3. Do you agree with the statement that normative propositions have no place in scientific economics? Give reasons for your opinion.
4. George Bernard Shaw joked, "If all economists were laid end to end, they would not reach a conclusion." Is this a fair assessment of disagreement among economists? Why or why not?
5. Economists disagree over normative economics but not over positive economics. Is this statement true or false? Explain.

LO 1.7 Recognize different types of variables and cause-effect relations

Variables and Cause-Effect Relations

What is a variable?

variable anything that changes

constant anything that remains unchanged

The work of economists consists largely of establishing relationships among different factors that can have an effect on economic behaviour. When they construct models, they use variables. In fact, an economic model is a system of relations among economic variables. A **variable** is anything that can change and assume different values under different circumstances. In simpler terms, a variable is anything that changes. Examples of economic variables are prices, income, consumer spending, interest rates, exports, imports, government spending, taxes, total production, the number of people unemployed, the unemployment rate, and the level of savings. A **constant**, as opposed to a variable, is anything that remains unchanged. If in the course of analysis we *assume* that government spending does not change, then that variable becomes a constant. Whether or not we consider something to be a variable or a constant depends on what we are investigating.

What is the difference between an endogenous variable and an exogenous variable?

When economists construct models to explain real-world economic phenomena, some variables used will be explained within the model, while others will be determined by

endogenous variable a variable whose value is determined within a given model

exogenous variable a variable whose value is determined by factors outside a given model

factors outside the model. An **endogenous variable** is one whose value is determined within the model. An **exogenous variable** is one whose value is determined by factors outside the model. The exogenous variables affect the endogenous variables. Let's look at an example to show the difference between endogenous and exogenous variables. Suppose we are trying to determine students' grades in an economics class. We could say that students' grades depend on their attendance of classes, suggesting that the more classes they attend, the better will be their grades. In this case, students' grades and their attendance are endogenous variables. But we know that their grades will also be affected by the amount of time they spend studying economics, whether or not they do their assignments, whether they pay attention in class, and so on. All these variables other than their attendance are exogenous variables.

A set of variables labelled endogenous and another set labelled exogenous do not exist. Whether a particular variable is endogenous or exogenous depends on the problem being studied. Needless to say, we cannot determine whether or not a particular variable is endogenous or exogenous without a model.

What is the difference between stocks and flows?

stock a quantity existing at a particular time

flow a change in a stock over time

An important distinction should be noted between stocks (or stock variables) and flows (or flow variables). A **stock** is the quantity of anything existing at a particular time. You may have a stock of five Blu-ray movies beside your Blu-ray player. That's the quantity that exists at that time. As time progresses, your stock of Blu-ray movies will likely change. A **flow** is a measure of the change in the stock over time. If you decide to purchase one Blu-ray movie each month, then the flow would be one Blu-ray movie per month. Note that a flow is a rate and has a time dimension: It is measured per unit of time (per day, per week, per month, per year, etc.). A stock has no time dimension: It is measured at a particular time (on October 11, 2012; at 11:30 a.m. on November 6, 2011; etc.). Note also that stocks and flows are both variables. Examples of stock variables and flow variables are given in Table 1.2.

Is correlation the same as causation?

No. They are not the same, and we must be careful not to confuse them. Two variables can be correlated, which means only that they move together. The fact that variables are correlated does not necessarily mean that a change in one causes a change in the other. The change could be a chance occurrence, or it could be the effect of a third variable. If you obtained a good grade on an economics examination that you wrote on a rainy day, you would not conclude that the good grade was the result of rain. If it can be

Table 1.2 Examples of Stocks and Flows

Stocks	Flows
• The balance in your savings account	• The monthly deposits to your account
• The amount of money in your wallet or purse at this moment	• The amount you spend each week for lunch
• The amount of equipment owned by a firm on April 14, 2005	• The amount a firm spends each year on equipment
• The number of people who watched the presidential debates in the United States on a particular night	• The number of people who watch *Dr. Phil* on TV each week
• The number of cars produced on November 1, 1981	• The number of cars sold in Canada each year

determined that a change in one variable causes a change in another, then we know that changing one will change the other. This conclusion may not hold if only a correlation exists between the variables. We must remember the age-old warning that correlation does not imply causation.

What is the post hoc fallacy?

post hoc fallacy the erroneous conclusion that one event causes another simply because it precedes the other

When two events occur in sequence, it is tempting to conclude that the first event caused the second to occur, which may not be the case. This erroneous conclusion is called the post hoc, ergo propter hoc fallacy (**post hoc fallacy**), which is a Latin phrase meaning, "after this, therefore because of this." This fallacy is also referred to as sequential fallacy. Let us assume that you began to read your economics textbook and then it began to rain. If you concluded that it rained because you started to read your textbook, then you would have fallen into the post hoc fallacy. It could very well be that you were planning to go out with your friends, but you listened to the weather forecast and heard that rain was expected, so you decided to read instead of going out. In that case, you would be reading because of the expected rain.

Reading Comprehension

The answers to these questions can be found on MyEconLab at www.myeconlab.com. MyEconLab

1. Give an example of each to show that you understand the difference between endogenous and exogenous variables.
2. Give an example of each to show that you understand the difference between a stock variable and a flow variable.
3. Give an example of the post hoc fallacy.
4. A seller of stained glass windows noticed that when she lowered the price of her windows, she sold a greater quantity of windows. Is anything wrong in concluding that the increase in sales was due to the lower price? Explain.

LO 1.8 Distinguish between microeconomics and macroeconomics

Microeconomics versus Macroeconomics

What is the difference between microeconomics and macroeconomics?

microeconomics the branch of economics that studies the behaviour of individual economic units

price theory another name for microeconomics

macroeconomics the branch of economics that studies the behaviour of broad economic aggregates

Economics is divided into two main branches: microeconomics and macroeconomics. **Microeconomics** studies the behaviour of individual economic units and focuses on the allocation of resources. It concerns itself with what determines the composition of total output and analyzes such topics as the behaviour of consumers and firms, the determination of relative prices, and the distribution of the economy's output among various groups. Microeconomics is also called **price theory**. An investigation into the causes of changes in the price of gasoline would be a microeconomic study.

Macroeconomics studies the economy as a whole rather than the individual units—the whole flock, so to speak, rather than the individual sheep that make up

income and employment theory another name for macroeconomics

that flock. Macroeconomics concerns itself with the total or aggregate behaviour of consumers and producers, and it analyzes such topics as inflation, unemployment, and economic growth. Macroeconomics is also called **income and employment theory**. A study that attempts to explain the causes of severe unemployment in Canada would be a macroeconomic study. A thorough understanding of the operation of the economic system requires knowledge of both microeconomics *and* macroeconomics. Both study choices that individuals, businesses, and governments make, and the effects of those choices on our economic lives.

Reading Comprehension

The answers to these questions can be found on MyEconLab at www.myeconlab.com. MyEconLab

1. What is the difference between microeconomics and macroeconomics?
2. To which branch of economics (microeconomics or macroeconomics) is a study of the recent global economic crisis more closely related?
3. Why should we study both microeconomics and macroeconomics?

BUSINESS SITUATION 1.2

A company is contemplating the introduction of a new product. To do so will require a loan. Among the factors to consider are the following:

- The price at which the product will be sold
- The level of economic activity and how it will affect the sale of the product
- The quantity of the product to produce
- The general level of interest rates that will affect the company's ability to repay the loan

Which of these considerations relate to microeconomics and which relate to macroeconomics?

The answer to this Business Situation can be found in Appendix A.

Review

1. Review the learning objectives listed at the beginning of the chapter.
2. Have you accomplished all the objectives? One way to determine this is to answer the Reading Comprehension questions at the end of each section. They will help you assess the extent to which you have accomplished the learning objectives
3. If you have not accomplished an objective, review the relevant material before proceeding.

Key Points to Remember

1. LO 1.1 A knowledge of economics is important because it enables us to understand the economy, society, and world affairs; it helps us to be better informed citizens and to think logically.It gives great personal satisfaction.
2. LO 1.2 Economists are employed in almost every facet of economic life. They are employed in industry, govern-

ment, and education. Economists are also self-employed as consultants.

3. LO 1.3 Scarcity is a fact of life. It is the situation that exists when the means to produce all the things that society would like to have to satisfy all wants are insufficient. Everyone faces scarcity—the rich, the poor, everyone.
4. LO 1.3 Economics can be defined as the study of scarcity and choice. It is the social science that studies how people make choices in the face of limited resources and unlimited wants. Economics, psychology, sociology, political science, and anthropology are all social science disciplines.
5. LO 1.4 All the various resources can be classified into four categories. Land refers to all natural resources, such as minerals in the earth, rivers, lakes, and so on. Labour refers to human effort, such as the work of farmers in cultivating land and the services provided by sales representatives. Capital refers to manufactured items, such as machinery, factories, and tools that businesses use to produce goods and services. Human capital refers to education, training, skills, and experience that enhance the quality of labour. Entrepreneurship refers to the organization of land, labour, and capital into the production process. Money is financial capital as opposed to real capital.
6. LO 1.4 Owners of land earn a form of income called rent; owners of labour earn wages and salaries; owners of capital earn interest and dividends; and providers of entrepreneurial services earn profits. Any form of income can be traced back to its source—a resource. The sum of the incomes derived from resources is total income.
7. LO 1.5 Economics is a science in the sense that it deals with facts and principles, and follows a particular method of inquiry. It follows the scientific approach of observation, measurement, and verification by confronting theory with empirical evidence. Because of the complexities of economic phenomena, economists construct economic models, which are simplifications of reality.
8. LO 1.6 Positive economics deals with how an economy actually functions, while normative economics deals with how an economy should function. Economists disagree about normative economics because they have different values. They disagree about positive economics because they may use different models. They may also disagree over quantitative aspects.
9. LO 1.7 Variables can be classified as endogenous (determined inside a model) or exogenous (determined by factors outside a model). They can also be classified as stocks (existing at a particular time) or flows (change per unit of time).
10. LO 1.7 Correlation between two variables does not establish a cause-effect relationship between them.A post hoc fallacy is the error of concluding that one event caused another because it preceded the other.
11. LO 1.8 Microeconomics examines the behaviour of individual economic units, while macroeconomics examines the behaviour of broad economic aggregates. Both microeconomics and macroeconomics help us understand economic behaviour and the functioning of the economic system.

Economic Word Power

Assumptions (p. 13)
Bads (p. 8)
Capital (p. 9)
Ceteris paribus (p. 13)
Commodities (p. 8)
Constant (p. 17)
Definition (p. 13)
Econometrics (p. 15)
Economic forecast (p. 14)
Economic model (p. 12)
Economic prediction (p. 14)
Economics (p. 6)
Endogenous variable (p. 18)
Entrepreneurship (p. 9)
Exogenous variable (p. 18)
Financial capital (p. 10)
Flow (p. 18)
Goods (p. 7)
Human capital (p. 9)
Hypothesis (p. 11)
Income and employment theory (p. 20)
Interest and dividends (p. 10)
Labour (p. 9)
Land (p. 9)
Macroeconomics (p. 19)
Microeconomics (p. 19)
Normative economics (p. 16)
Normative statements (p. 15)
Positive economics (p. 16)
Positive statements (p. 15)
Post hoc fallacy (p. 19)
Price theory (p. 19)
Profit (p. 10)
Rent (p. 10)
Resources (p. 7)
Scarcity (p. 5)
Science (p. 11)
Scientific method (p. 11)
Services (p. 7)
Social science (p. 6)
Stock (p. 18)
Variable (p. 17)
Wages and salaries (p. 10)

Problems and Exercises

Basic

1. **LO 1.1** A proper study of economics is quite time-consuming. Do you think studying economics is worth the time involved? Explain why or why not.
2. **LO 1.2** Give three reasons why a career as an economist might be of interest to a student.
3. **LO 1.3** What do economists mean when they describe something as being scarce?
4. **LO 1.3** If you won $50 million in the lottery, would you personally still have an economic problem?
5. **LO 1.3** Scarcity is an economic constraint. Discuss.
6. **LO 1.4** Indicate the category of resources to which each of the following belongs:
   a. A freezer in a supermarket
   b. A hospital
   c. Fish in a lake
   d. Mineral deposits in northern Ontario
   e. The services provided by a neurosurgeon
   f. The driver of a taxicab
   g. The risk taken by an individual who buys resources to establish a business
7. **LO 1.4** Beside each resource category in column 1 of Table 1.3, place the income category associated with the resource category.

Table 1.3 Resources and Associated Income

Resource Category	Income Category
Land	______
Labour	______
Capital	______
Entrepreneurial ability	______

8. **LO 1.5** Economics is an interesting subject. Unfortunately, it cannot be studied scientifically. Discuss briefly.
9. **LO 1.6** Give two reasons why economists might disagree.
10. **LO 1.7** Using *S* for stock and *F* for flow, indicate whether each of the following is a stock or a flow:
    a. The amount of money a bus driver earns per week
    b. The number of students who were in class at 11:30 a.m. on Wednesday
    c. The amount of money in your purse/wallet at this moment
    d. Your average expenditure per week in the cafeteria
    e. The total annual sales of a furniture manufacturer
    f. The total value of merchandise in a department store on February 1, 2011, at 10:30 a.m.
11. **LO 1.8** It has been observed that the price of gasoline sometimes fluctuates greatly. A study has been launched to determine the possible causes. To which of the main branches of economics would such a study fall?

Questions in the Intermediate and Challenging Sections cover several different concepts, and have not been organized by learning objectives.

Intermediate

1. Would personal computers still be scarce if all computer manufacturers produced so many computers that to sell them, they had to lower the price to $100?
2. Economics cannot be a science. If it were, economists would not disagree to the extent that they do. Discuss.
3. Alberta and Ontario both have relatively high average incomes; Newfoundland and Labrador and Prince Edward Island have relatively low average incomes. Do you think that scarcity of resources can help to explain these income differentials?
4. Economists can increase the usefulness of a model by including every conceivable variable. After all, the greater the number of variables, the more useful the model. Discuss.

Challenging

1. I have a model that explains students' grades in economics. The model states that regular attendance improves students' grades. One student attends every class, yet his grades have not improved. Does this observation invalidate my model? Explain.
2. One of your friends is contemplating taking either an economics course or some other course. What arguments could you use to persuade him or her to take the economics course? For each argument, indicate whether it is positive or normative and give reasons.
3. Write up a list of five social, economic, or political problems or issues facing Canada today. For each problem or issue, discuss its economic aspects (if any). What role can economics play in helping us to understand the problem or issue, or in finding solutions?
4. In constructing a simple model of the Canadian economy, an economist assumed that only two kinds of goods are produced and that all the goods are used within Canada. Can such a model have any use at all in terms of explaining certain economic events in Canada?

MyEconLab Visit the MyEconLab website at **www.myeconlab.com.** This online homework and tutorial system puts you in control of your own learning with study and practice tools directly correlated to this chapter's content.

Study Guide

Self-Assessment

The answers to the Study Guide questions can be found in Appendix B.

What's your score?

Circle the letter that corresponds with the correct answer.

1. A knowledge of economics is important because
   a. It guarantees perpetual employment
   b. It ensures that we will always make decisions that are in our own self-interest
   c. It helps us to understand many of the issues that affect our lives directly and indirectly
   d. All of the above

2. Today, economists work:
   a. Only as civil servants in government offices
   b. Only in profit-seeking organizations
   c. Only in certain large corporations
   d. In practically every aspect of business and government

3. Scarcity exists
   a. When things are available only in small quantities
   b. When resources are insufficient to produce all the desired goods and services
   c. Only among poor people who cannot afford to buy the things they want
   d. In underdeveloped countries but not in advanced countries

4. Choice is a direct result of
   a. Ambition
   b. Scarcity
   c. Extravagance
   d. None of the above

5. Choice is a matter of free will and is quite unrelated to economics.
   a. True
   b. False

6. Which of the following is the primary concern of economics?
   a. How people vote in an election
   b. How people make choices when faced with scarcity
   c. The mental processes involved in making a decision regarding the purchase of an expensive item
   d. None of the above

7. Which of the following aspects of human behaviour *most* concerns the economist?
   a. The methods used to select leaders in a society
   b. The public's attitude toward certain social issues
   c. The behaviour of individuals and groups engaged in using scarce resources
   d. The behaviour of people trying to understand the origin of civilization

8. Economics is
   a. An exact science
   b. A social science
   c. A physical science
   d. Not a science

9. Economists work on the premise that
   a. Resources are unlimited but wants are limited
   b. Resources are limited but wants are unlimited
   c. Both resources and wants are unlimited
   d. Both resources and wants are limited

10. Factors of production are
   a. All the factors that must be considered when making a decision to start a business
   b. The monetary costs involved in setting up a business to produce goods
   c. Gifts of nature, not anything that we produce
   d. Things that can be used to produce goods and services

11. Things like cigarettes and alcohol are
   a. Not goods because they are harmful
   b. Goods because they are scarce
   c. Goods because people want them
   d. Goods because the government has not placed a ban on their use

12. Illegal substances and chemicals, and goods smuggled into a country, are classified as
   a. Bads because they are illegal
   b. Bads because taxes are not paid on them

c. Goods, provided that they are wanted
d. Goods because someone produced them

13. Economists classify resources into the following categories:
a. Available, scarce, expensive, and natural
b. Land, labour, capital, and entrepreneurship
c. Artificial, financial, human, and manufactured
d. Natural, imported, limitless, and personal

14. Capital generates a type of income known as
a. Money
b. Interest
c. Profit
d. None of the above

15. The scientific approach involves
a. Total reliance on values and moral sentiments
b. Observation, measurement, and testing of hypotheses
c. The formulation of theories without confronting theory with evidence
d. All of the above

16. An economic model is
a. An exact replica of a real economic situation, faithfully reproducing every single detail
b. Always expressed graphically because graphs are easy to read and understand
c. A simplification of a real economy or some aspect of it, with irrelevant details omitted
d. None of the above

17. Economists construct models in order to
a. Impress non-economists
b. Prevent entry into the economics profession
c. Make it easier to understand how the economy works
d. Introduce as many variables as possible into their analyses

18. Assumptions
a. Have no place in scientific economics
b. Simply complicate the economic reasoning process
c. Convert positive statements into normative statements
d. Indicate the conditions under which a given model is intended to work

19. The Latin phrase ceteris paribus means
a. No changes should be made because all is well
b. Sometime in the future
c. The outcome is certain
d. Other things being equal

20. An economic hypothesis is
a. An assumption about how the economic system actually works
b. An assumption about how the economic system ought to work
c. An expression of suspected relations among economic variables
d. A statement that is generally accepted but cannot be proved

21. The main difference between positive statements and normative statements is that
a. Positive statements can be verified by testing, while normative statements cannot be verified
b. Positive statements are always true, while normative statements may be true or false
c. Positive statements are a part of economic study, while normative statements are not
d. Positive statements are based on emotion, while normative statements are based on facts

22. Disagreement among economists is due to
a. The fact that economics is not a science
b. The fact that economic models are often expressed verbally instead of mathematically
c. The fact that some economists just don't understand the complexities of modern mathematics used in economic models
d. The fact that economists have different values, or they may use different economic models to explain the same economic phenomenon

23. The values of exogenous variables
a. Are determined inside the given model
b. Have no effect on variables within the given model
c. Are predetermined by factors outside the given model
d. Are of no concern to the economist

24. Endogenous variables are those variables whose values
a. Are determined within the given model
b. Have no effect on variables within the given model
c. Are predetermined by factors outside the given model
d. None of the above

25. The main difference between a flow and a stock is that
a. A flow has a time dimension while a stock does not
b. A stock has a time dimension while a flow does not
c. A flow is a variable while a stock is a constant
d. None of the above

26. Two variables, *A* and *B*, are related in such a way that when *A* rises, *B* also rises. From this we can correctly conclude that
a. The increase in *B* is caused by the increase in *A*
b. *A* and *B* are influenced by a common factor
c. There is a correlation between *A* and *B*
d. None of the above

27. Microeconomics
a. Deals only with small changes in economic variables, while macroeconomics deals only with large changes in economic variables
b. Is scientific in its approach, while macroeconomics is not
c. Deals with the behaviour of individual economic units, while macroeconomics deals with the behaviour of broad economic aggregates
d. Deals only with the positive aspects of economics, while macroeconomics deals only with the normative aspects of economics

28. Considering both microeconomics and macroeconomics, the tools of microeconomics are more useful when predicting
   a. The rate of increase in the average level of all prices
   b. The effects of investment on total income and total employment
   c. The effects of changes in the money supply on national output
   d. The price that will maximize a firm's profits

Problems and Exercises (Use Quad Paper for Graphs)

Answers to these questions can be found on MyEconLab at www.myeconlab.com. MyEconLab

1. Look through one or more recent newspapers and highlight four headlines that deal with economics. Then, on the basis of your findings, complete Table 1.4, indicating (1) the name of the newspaper, (2) the date of publication, (3) the headlines selected, and (4) the economic issue being addressed.

Table 1.4 Newspaper Information

Name of Newspaper	Date Published	Headline	Economic Issue

2. Indicate what might be the scarce element in each of the following situations. (For example, time is the scarce element preventing you from attending an economics class at 8:30 a.m. and sleeping in until 9:00 a.m. that same day).
   a. A farmer is unable to produce more corn and more wheat at the same time.
   b. A retailer is unable to carry larger inventories (stocks) of both computers and DVD players.
   c. Tiger Woods cannot play golf at 2:30 p.m. today and appear live as a guest on a popular television program.
   d. You cannot buy all your required textbooks for this term at the same time.
   e. Your parents must choose between taking a cruise and buying a new refrigerator.
3. Indicate whether each of the following should be classified as land, labour, capital, or entrepreneurship.
   a. Oil deposits in Alberta
   b. Highway 401 between Montreal and Toronto
   c. The services provided by administrative assistants in an insurance company
   d. Wildlife in the Prairie Provinces
   e. Forests in British Columbia
   f. Banff National Park in Alberta
   g. The Great Lakes of Canada and the United States
   h. John Henry's efforts in acquiring labour and capital to establish a manufacturing plant
   i. The services provided in establishing and running an electronic boutique
   j. Chemical fertilizer used by Ontario farmers in growing their crops
4. Canada is well endowed with a wide variety of natural resources, a highly skilled and educated adult population, and vast amounts of capital goods. In what sense are these resources scarce in Canada?
5. Indicate whether each of the following types of income would be classified technically as rent, wages and salaries, interest and dividends, or profit.
   a. The compensation (payment) that administrative assistants receive for their services
   b. The money Josh pays each month for living accommodation in an apartment building
   c. The payment Susan receives from her part-time job at the supermarket
   d. The annual amount that a Canadian bank pays its shareholders
   e. The amount of money that Mr. Johnson receives each year for the use of his parking lot
   f. The money that Mr. Johnson pays his parking lot attendant
   g. The net income that John Henry receives for his effort in acquiring labour and capital to establish a manufacturing plant
   h. The net earnings of $200 000 received by a group of innovators for developing and marketing a product
6. In Table 1.5, rearrange the items in the second column, and place the correct arrangement in the third column so that they correctly match the items in the first column.

Table 1.5 Factors and Earnings

Column 1	Column 2	Column 3
Labour	Rent	______
Land	Wages	______
Entrepreneurship	Interest and dividends	______
Capital	Profits	______

7. Categorize each of the following as either positive or normative statements:
   a. An increase in the price of oil will result in higher prices for other products.
   b. If the price of oil rises, people will buy less oil.

c. The government should impose a ceiling on the price of gasoline.
d. The sale of cigarettes should be illegal.
e. Lower interest rates on mortgages will increase the purchases of new homes.
f. Interest rates should be kept as low as possible so that the economy can produce more jobs.

8. Indicate whether each of the following falls under the heading of positive economics or normative economics:
a. A study of the relationship between investment spending and the rate of interest
b. The observation that when average income rises, consumers increase their purchases of most goods and services
c. The conclusion that the amounts of money allocated to education and health in Canada are much too small
d. The assertion that hockey and baseball players should never go on strike, because they earn enough money
e. A program designed to reduce poverty based on the opinion that poverty levels are too high
f. A description of how the money supply affects the performance of the economy
g. The notion that taxing the wealthy to give welfare payments to the poor is unfair
h. The assertion that the accumulation of debts is bad both for individuals and for governments

9. Classify each of the following as a stock or a flow:
a. The annual salary of your economics professor
b. The number of washing machines owned by the Quick Clean Laundromat on December 30, 2011
c. The annual interest payable on a bank loan
d. The number of new homes available for sale in November 2012
e. The quantity of merchandise sold each month by a department store
f. The unpaid balance on a bank loan as of February 23, 2010
g. Consumers' expenditure on goods and services over a six-month period
h. The number of workers who showed up for work at 7:30 this morning

10. Indicate whether each of the following falls under microeconomics or macroeconomics:
a. A study of the relationship between employment and total production
b. A model explaining why, on average, actors earn more than doctors
c. An explanation of the factors that affect total spending in the Canadian economy
d. A theory explaining how the level of investment spending affects aggregate employment
e. A model explaining how many workers a firm should hire to produce a desired volume of output
f. An explanation of the effect of a tax on cigarettes on the price of cigarettes
g. A model showing that when the price of gold rises, the price of silver also rises, other things being equal
h. A model that explains why the prices of home computers have fallen over the past few years

Appendix 1A

Some Useful Tools

Learning Objectives

After studying this appendix, you should be able to

1A.1 Use functional notation to express relationships among variables

1A.2 Use graphs to show relationships among variables

1A.3 Define and calculate the slopes of linear and non-linear curves

1A.4 Calculate the percentage change in variables

Assess Your Knowledge

MyEconLab

Answers to these questions can be found on MyEconLab at **www.myeconlab.com**.

1. Why are graphs so useful in studying economics?
2. If one line is relatively steep while another is relatively flat, which one has the bigger slope?
3. The price of an item rises from $15.00 to $18.00. Calculate the percentage increase in the price.

LO 1A.1 Use functional notation to express relationships among variables

Functional Notation

Do we need to know a great deal of mathematics to understand introductory economics?

Advanced courses in economics do require a good knowledge of mathematics. However, in this book, you will not be required to know a great deal of mathematics, so you need not fear the mathematics. Graphs are used liberally in this book, but they are explained in simple and understandable terms. The production possibilities diagrams that you will study in Chapter 2 are examples of the use of graphs in economics. In this book, you will learn the basic principles and concepts of economics, and they will be presented by using words, examples, and graphs that help to clarify the ideas. Even when *simple* mathematical tools are used, words, not mathematics, will be the main communication medium. You can therefore feel comfortable with the mathematics you already know.

What exactly is a function?

functional notation a mathematical tool for expressing relations among variables

function an expression of a relation among variables

Economics involves establishing and studying relationships among variables. Such relationships can be expressed by using a **functional notation**, which is a very convenient mathematical tool. A **function** expresses a relationship among two or more variables. Consider the following statement: "The amount of money that people spend on consumer goods and services depends on their income." Another way of expressing the same idea is as follows: "The amount of money that people spend on consumer goods and services *is a function of* their income." Both statements mean exactly the same thing—namely, if income changes, the amount of money that people spend on consumer goods and services will change (other things being equal, of course). We have used the concept of a function to express a relationship between the amount of money that people spend on consumer goods and services (i.e., consumption) and their income.

How can functional notation be used to express the idea that consumption depends on income?

The first step in using functional notion is to symbolize (i.e., use symbols instead of words). Let us use C to denote the amount of money that people spend on consumer goods and services, and y to denote income. Note that the use of these symbols has already simplified our task of expressing the relationship between the variables of interest to us. Instead of writing "the amount of money that people spend on consumer goods and services," we simply write C, and instead of writing "income," we simply write y. The idea that consumption depends on income can now be expressed as

$$C = f(y)$$

and is read "$C = f$ of y" or "consumption is a function of income" or "consumption depends on income."

> **Example:** When air fares increase, people take fewer vacations in foreign countries. We can use the functional notation to express this idea. Let us symbolize as follows:
>
> $$A = \text{air fare}; \; V = \text{number of vacations}$$
>
> We can now express the idea in the functional form as follows:
>
> $$V = f(A)$$
>
> which means that the number of vacations depends on airfares.

What is the difference between a dependent variable and an independent variable?

dependent variable the variable that is being explained

independent variable the variable that provides the explanation; it causes changes in the dependent variable

We'll answer this question with reference to the first example above, in which consumption depends on income. Hence, in the above function, C is the **dependent variable**. The variable on which it depends is called the **independent variable**. The dependent variable, then, is the variable that we are trying to explain, and the independent variable is the one that provides the explanation. In economics, it is customary to modify the form of the above functional notation. Instead of using f, we replace it with the dependent variable. The above function would therefore appear as

$$C = C(y)$$

How is functional notation written when there is more than one independent variable?

Quite often, we need to express the idea that one variable depends on two or more other variables. For example, suppose we want to express the idea that consumption depends not only on income but also on the rate of interest. Using C for consumption and y for income as before, and using r to symbolize the rate of interest, we can express the idea as

$$C = C(y, r)$$

Note that the independent variables, y and r, are separated by a comma, with no space between them.

Reading Comprehension

The answers to these questions can be found on MyEconLab at www.myeconlab.com. MyEconLab

1. What is the main use of the functional notation in economics?
2. What is the difference between dependent and independent variables?
3. How is the functional notation used when the idea involves more than one independent variable?

LO 1A.2 Use graphs to show relationships among variables

The Use of Graphs

Why are graphs used in economics?

You have probably heard that a picture is worth a thousand words. The same can be said of graphs. Graphs are indeed an effective way of showing relations among variables. They add clarity to ideas that we try to express—they actually *show* the changes that take place. For example, when population growth takes place in a country, we can use a graph to show the growth in population. This type of graphic, visual presentation makes concepts and ideas come alive.

How do we plot points on a graph?

Let us begin at the beginning, as it were, with an elementary introduction to the use of graphs. Consider the diagram shown as Figure 1A.1. The two lines (called *axes*) intersect at a 90-degree angle. The point of intersection is called the **origin**. We give this point a value of 0 and from it measure all distances. Note that the two intersecting lines divide the plane into four quadrants, numbered as shown in Figure 1A.1. In quadrant II, the x value is negative; in quadrant III, both x and y are negative; and in quadrant IV, the y value is negative.

origin the point of intersection of the vertical and horizontal axes

Suppose we want to plot the point for the $x = 3$ and $y = 4$, usually indicated as (3, 4). First, we locate the value 3 along the x axis. Then, we move vertically up to the value 4 measured along the $y$axis. This locates the desired point (3, 4). Now consider Table 1A.1, which gives values of x and y. We can plot these values on a graph, such as Figure 1A.2. Note that points will appear in quadrants II, III, or IV only when a negative value is involved.

In general, economic variables have either positive values or a value of zero. For most of our graphs, therefore, we will need only the first quadrant. Most graphs will appear without the negative parts of the axes.

Figure 1A.1 Axes, Origin, Quadrants, and a Point on a Graph

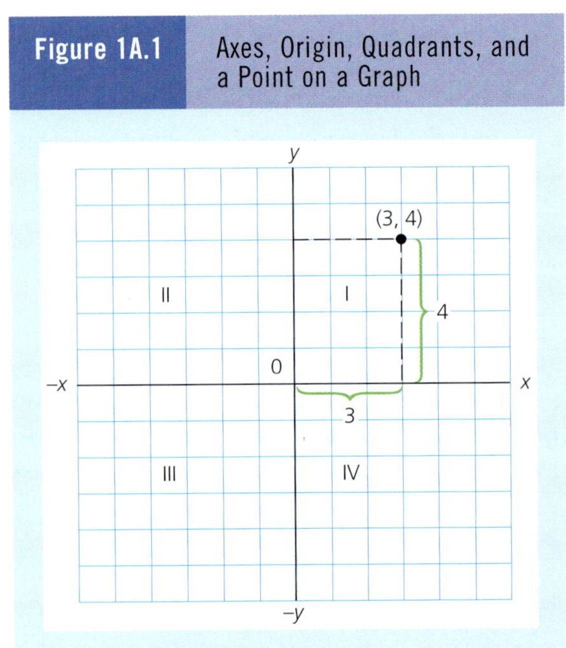

Table 1A.1 Values of x and y

x Values	y Values
1	−3
2	4
−3	2
4	1

How do we graph data contained in tables?

Once we know how to plot points on a graph, we can graph data contained in tables. The process is exactly the same. Suppose we have the information shown in Table 1A.2 for income and consumption in a hypothetical economy for a year.

From this table, we can see that as income increases, consumption also increases; however, we cannot quite see it *at a glance*. Let us graph the information contained in Table 1A.2. This is done in Figure 1A.3.

When income is 0, consumption is 30. This is represented by point A on the graph. When income is 20, consumption is 40. This is shown as point B on the graph. When income is 40, consumption is 50. This is point C on the graph. The other combinations of income and consumption are plotted in the same way and illustrated by points D, E, F, and G on the graph. By connecting the points, we obtain a graph that shows clearly and easily that as income rises, consumption also rises.

Figure 1A.2 Points Plotted on a Graph

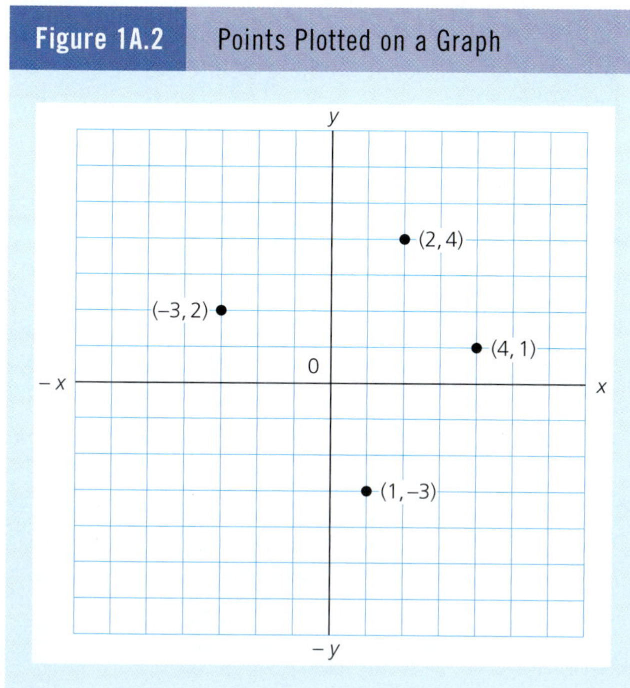

Figure 1A.3 The Graphic Representation of the Relation between Income and Consumption

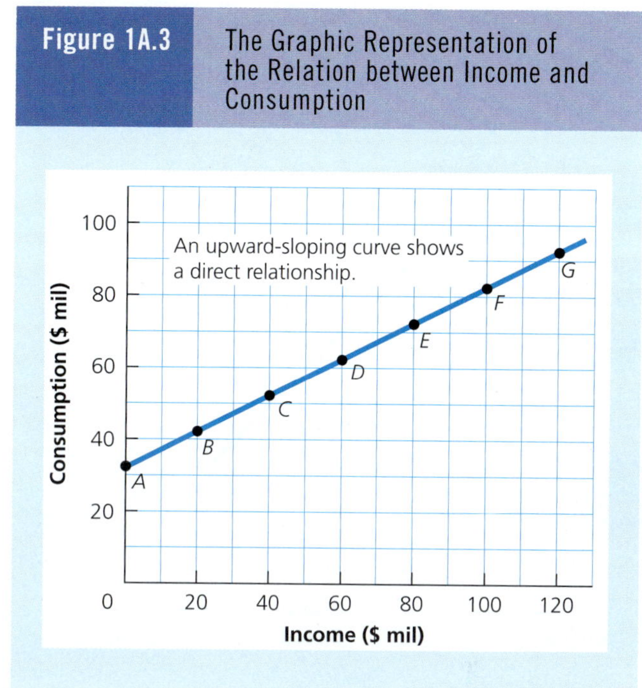

Table 1A.2 Income and Consumption Data for a Hypothetical Economy

Income ($ mil)	Consumption ($ mil)
0	30
20	40
40	50
60	60
80	70
100	80
120	90

How are direct and inverse relationships shown on graphs?

Consider the following statement: "As the rate of interest rises, people save more; as the rate of interest falls, people save less." Here we have two variables: the rate of interest and the volume of saving. They rise and fall together. When variables move up or down together, we say that there is a **direct relation** between them. A graph showing a direct relationship between two variables is upward sloping, like the graph in Figure 1A.3. Variables that are likely to have a direct relationship are people's height and their weight; age and experience; level of education and income; and class attendance and grade.

Now consider the following statement: "The faster a person travels, the less time it takes to cover a certain distance." Here we have two variables: speed and time; when one increases, the other decreases. They move in opposite directions. When variables move in opposite directions, we say that there is an **inverse relation** between them. A graph showing an inverse relationship between two variables is downward sloping, like the graph in Figure 1A.4.

direct relation the relation that exists between variables that increase or decrease together; the variables move in the same direction

inverse relation the relation that exists between variables such that as one increases, the other decreases, and vice versa; the variables move in opposite directions

What are some typical graphs used in economics?

The graph shown in Figure 1A.4 is a good example of the graphs used in economics. Some other examples follow. Consider the relationship between the rate of interest and the level of investment. As the rate of interest falls, the level of investment increases. Investment here refers to expenditure on manufacturing plants, equipment, buildings, and so on—real capital investment. We can get a very clear picture of this relation by using a graph. Note that these two variables move in opposite directions; in other

Figure 1A.4 An Inverse Relation between Two Variables

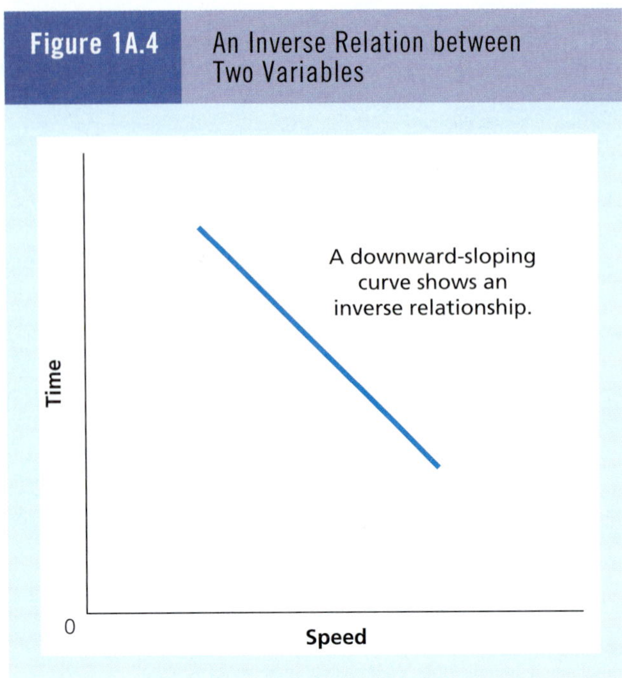

Figure 1A.5 The Relation between Investment and the Rate of Interest

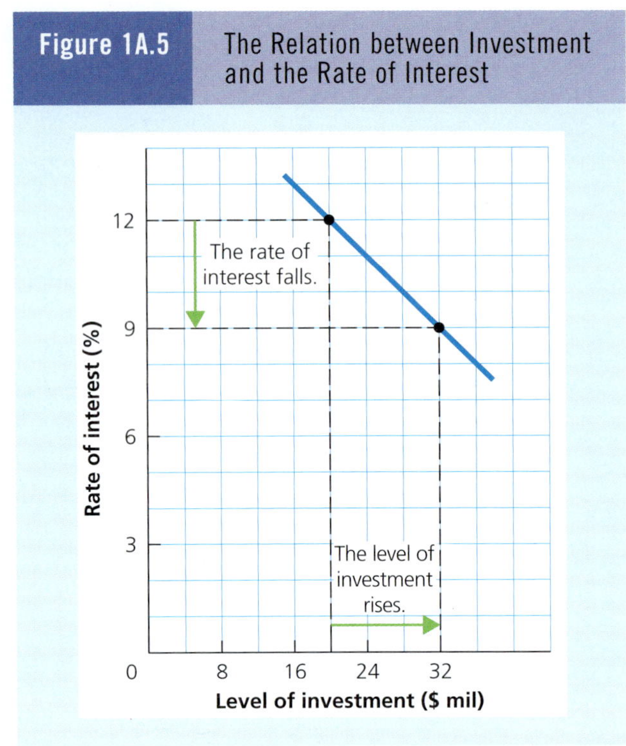

Figure 1A.6 The Relation between the Tax Rate and Tax Revenue

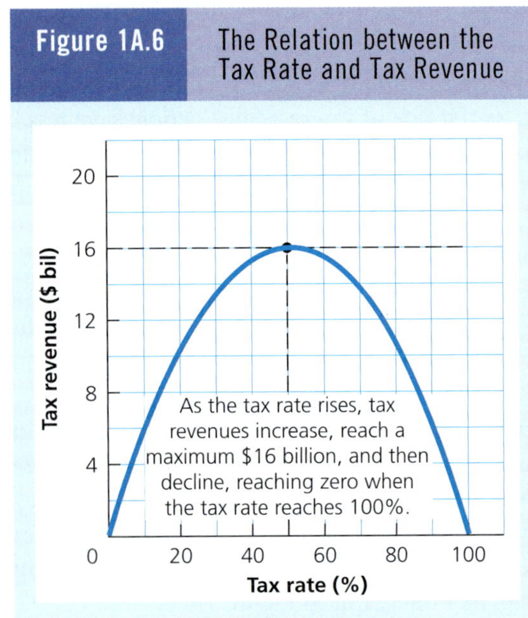

words, there is an inverse relation between the rate of interest and the level of investment. This inverse relation is illustrated graphically by the downward-sloping (falling) curve shown in Figure 1A.5. This figure shows that as the rate of interest falls from 12% to 9%, the level of investment increases from $20 million to $32 million. Two very popular graphs in economics are ones that show (1) the relation between the price of an item and the quantity of that item that people would be willing to buy, and (2) the relation between the price of an item and the quantity of that item that firms would be willing to sell.

A graph might show a relationship starting at zero, rising to a maximum, and then falling to zero. Such might be the case between tax revenue and tax rates, as shown in Figure 1A.6.

When the tax rate is zero, the government receives no tax revenue. As the tax rate increases, tax revenue rises, reaching a maximum of $16 billion at a tax rate of 50%. But as the tax rate continues to rise, it may be that the incentive to earn extra income decreases and so tax revenue falls. If the tax rate increases to 100%, no one will willingly earn any income because it would all be taxed away. The government's revenue from income tax would be zero if no one earns any income.

In economics, we also encounter relationships that start at a certain point, fall to a minimum, and then rise. An example of such a relationship is the cost of making photocopies, shown in Figure 1A.7.

As the number of copies increases from zero, the cost per copy falls. At a volume of 1000 copies per day, the cost per copy is minimized at $0.03 per copy. But as the volume

Figure 1A.7 The Relation between Cost per Copy and Number of Copies

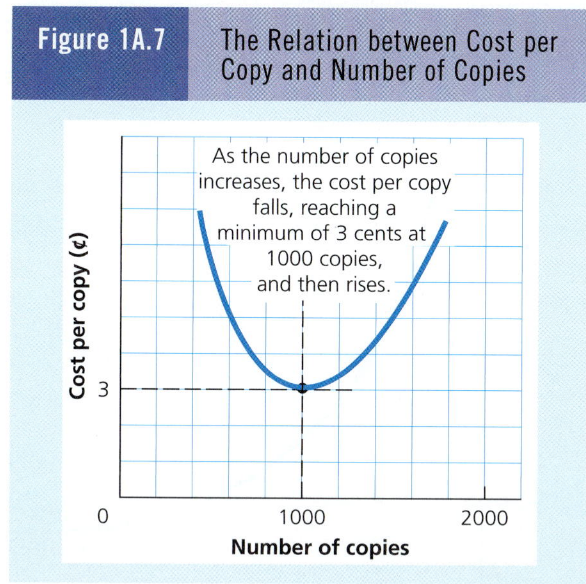

increases beyond 1000 copies per day, the cost per copy rises, perhaps because the photocopy machine is pushed beyond its most efficient operating capacity.

Quite often, it is necessary to graph data that are unrelated. For example, no relation exists between inflation and the distance a person travels each day. Such a situation is shown in Figure 1A.8.

In Diagram A of Figure 1A.8, the rate of inflation is 1.5% whether the distance travelled is 20, 40, 60, or 80 km per day. The graph is therefore a horizontal straight line. Consider now the situation shown in Diagram B. The price of fish in Canada has no effect on the number of briefcases sold in an Australian department store each month. When the price of fish changes, the sale of briefcases remains the same, namely, 40. There is no relationship between the two variables, so the graph is a vertical line.

What is the difference between a concave and a convex curve?

concave curve a curve bowed outward from the origin

convex curve a curve bowed toward the origin

Students often confuse these two concepts. A **concave curve** is bowed outward, as shown in Diagram A of Figure 1A.9, while a **convex curve** is bowed toward the origin, as shown in Diagram B of Figure 1A.9.

Are other types of graphs used in economics?

bar graph a vertical or horizontal graph with categories on one axis and the value assigned to each category measured on the other axis

Two other types of graphs are quite commonly used in economics: bar graphs and pie charts. A **bar graph** is a vertical or horizontal graph with categories on one axis and the value assigned to each category measured along the other axis. Let us look at the information contained in Table 1A.3. It shows sales for a firm for the first six months of the year.

Figure 1A.8 Graphs of Unrelated Data

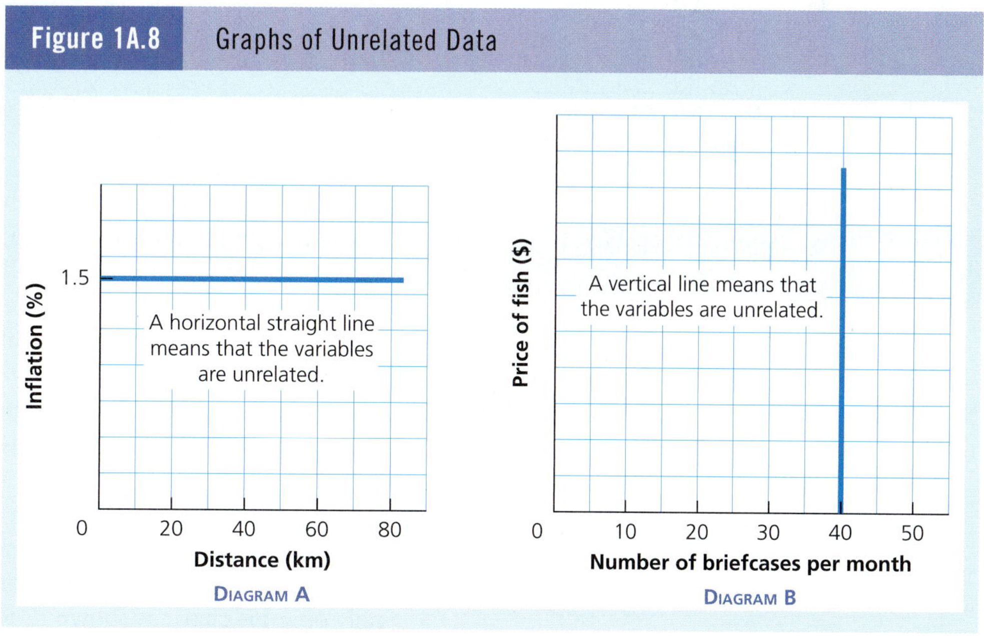

Figure 1A.9 Concave and Convex Curves

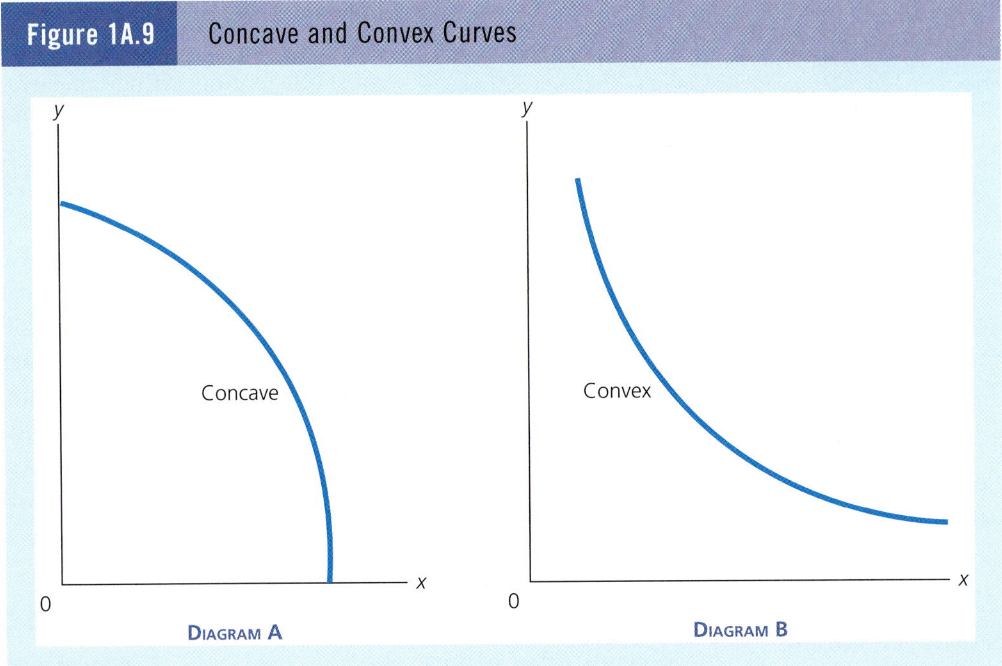

pie chart a circular graph whose pieces add up to 100%

Figure 1A.10 A Bar Chart for Sales from January to June

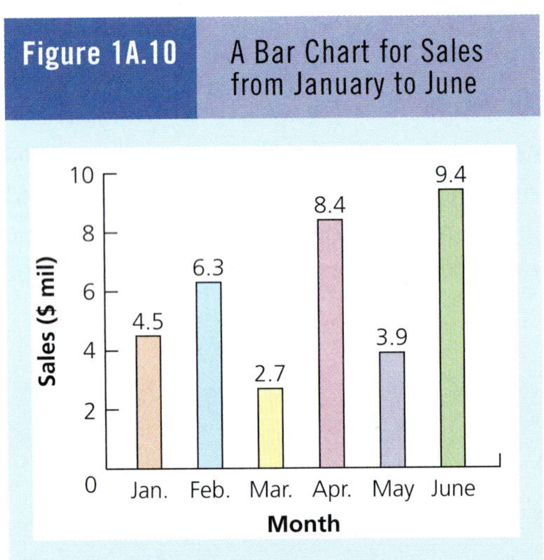

Figure 1A.11 A Pie Chart for Payroll Shares

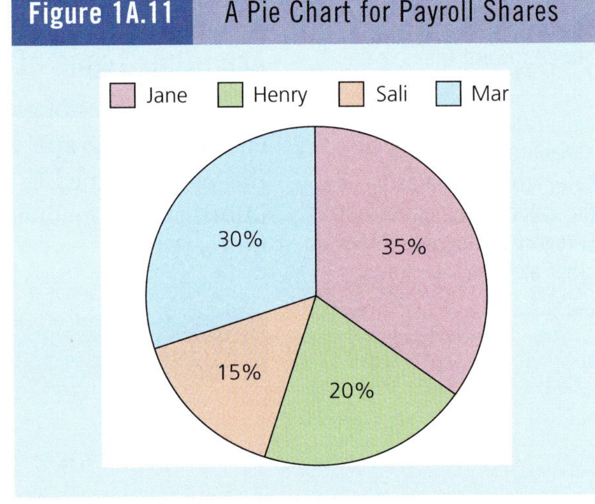

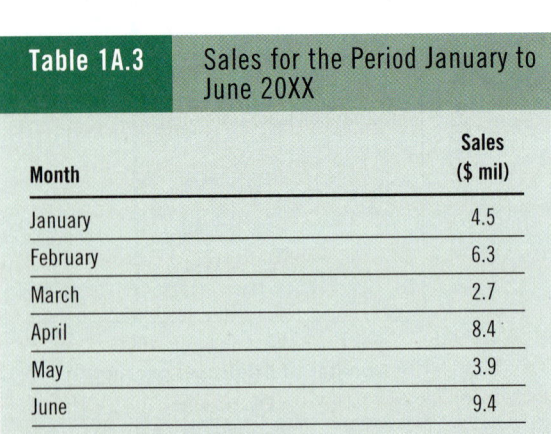

Table 1A.3 Sales for the Period January to June 20XX

Month	Sales ($ mil)
January	4.5
February	6.3
March	2.7
April	8.4
May	3.9
June	9.4

A bar graph can be used to effectively show these sales figures. Such a graph is illustrated in Figure 1A.10. This graph is a vertical bar graph, with the category of month on the horizontal axis, and the sales value assigned to each month on the vertical axis.

A pie chart is another useful device for showing information. A **pie chart** is a circular graph whose pieces add to 100%. Let's assume that a small business has four employees: Jane, Henry, Sali, and Mark. The share of the payroll going to each employee is as follows: Jane (35%), Henry (20%), Sali (15%), and Mark (30%). This information can be presented graphically on a pie chart, as shown in Figure 1A.11.

BUSINESS SITUATION 1A.1

Table 1A.4 The Relation between Number of Calls and Number of Orders

Number of Calls per Quarter	Quarterly Sales ($)
15	250 000
20	300 000
23	320 000
25	350 000
32	400 000
35	425 000

A sales manager observes that the more calls her salespeople make on potential clients, the larger the orders from clients. She gathered the data shown in Table 1A.4. She wants to motivate her salespeople to make more calls by illustrating this link between calls and sales in a graphic manner.

How can she show this relation?

The answer to this Business Situation can be found in Appendix A.

Is there any limitation to the use of graphs?

Yes, there is. Clearly, the economist can make good use of graphs in presenting certain economic relations. Despite their great advantage, however, the use of graphs is limited to cases with few variables. As the number of variables increases, our ability to graph relations among them decreases. How would we graph the idea that consumption varies with current income, the rate of interest, and consumer expectations? This is indeed a formidable, if not impossible, exercise. Models that involve relations among several variables are usually presented verbally or algebraically rather than geometrically or graphically.

Reading Comprehension

The answers to these questions can be found on MyEconLab at www.myeconlab.com. MyEconLab

1. Discuss the importance of graphs in the study of economics.
2. If two variables are directly related, what would a graph depicting the relationship look like?
3. If two variables are inversely related, what would a graph depicting the relationship look like?
4. Explain the difference between a concave and a convex curve.
5. Discuss the limitation to the use of graphs in economics.

LO 1A.3 Define and calculate the slopes of linear and non-linear curves

The Slope: Concept and Measurement

We understand the terms *upward sloping* and *downward sloping*, but what is slope?

slope (of a curve) the steepness or flatness of a curve; the upward or downward inclination of a curve

In your study of economics, you will find the concept of a slope and its measurement of the utmost importance. Economists are interested in knowing the rates at which the curves they draw rise or fall. Measuring the slopes of these curves provides the answer. The **slope** of a

Figure 1A.12 The Relation between Income and Consumption

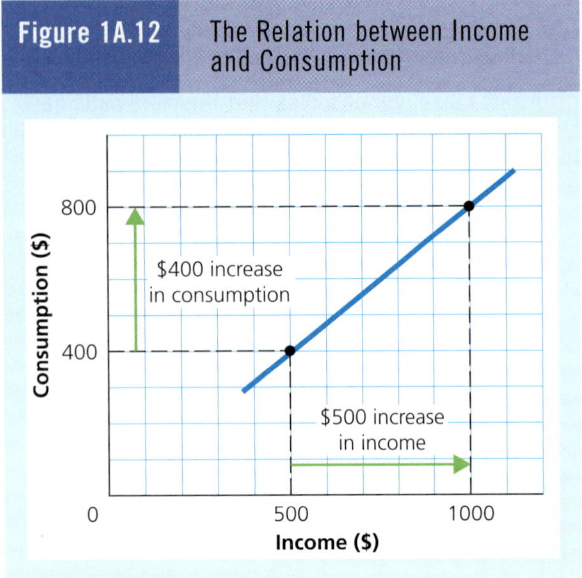

curve refers to its steepness or flatness; it is the upward or downward inclination of the curve. Suppose you observe or believe that as people's incomes rise, they spend more money on consumer goods and services. You could show this relationship on a graph, as depicted in Figure 1A.12. The relationship is similar to the one shown in Figure 1A.3 on page 31.

Consumption is measured along the vertical axis while income is measured along the horizontal axis. The graph shows that as income rises, consumption also rises. It would be interesting and useful, however, to know the degree to which consumers respond to changes in their incomes. We could say, for example, that a \$500 increase in income (from \$500 to \$1000) results in a \$400 increase in consumption (from \$400 to \$800). The slope of the line gives us that information. The slope provides information on the steepness or flatness of the curve and is measured by the ratio of the vertical distance (rise) to the horizontal distance (run).

Consider Figure 1A.13. Because the curve is a linear curve (that is, a straight line), it has the same slope at every point. The slope of the line in Figure 1A.13 is

Figure 1A.13 The Slope of a Straight Line

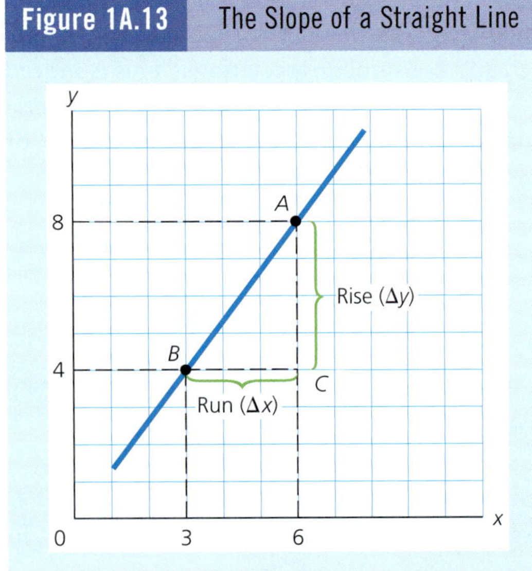

$$\text{Slope} = \frac{\text{Vertical distance}}{\text{Horizontal distance}} = \frac{AC}{BC}$$

The slope, then, is the change in the y value divided by the change in the x value when y is on the vertical axis and x is on the horizontal axis. The change in the y value can be written as Δy, while the change in the x value can be written as Δx. The symbol Δ is the Greek letter *delta*, used here to mean "a change in." Thus,

$$\text{Slope} = \frac{\Delta y}{\Delta x} = \frac{\text{Rise}}{\text{Run}}$$

In Figure 1A.13, $\Delta y = 8 - 4 = 4$; $\Delta x = 6 - 3 = 3$; therefore, the slope of the line in Figure 1A.13 is $4 \div 3 = 1^1/_3$.

Let us calculate the slope of each line shown in Figure 1A.14. First, consider Diagram A. If we move from point A to point B, y falls from 9 to 4. Hence, $\Delta y = -5$. At the same time, x rises from 2 to 5; so $\Delta x = 3$. Therefore,

$$\text{Slope} = \frac{\Delta y}{\Delta x} = \frac{-5}{3} = -1\tfrac{2}{3}$$

If we move from point B to point A, y rises from 4 to 9. Hence, $\Delta y = 5$. But x falls from 5 to 2; so $\Delta x = -3$. Therefore,

$$\text{Slope} = \frac{\Delta y}{\Delta x} = \frac{5}{-3} = -1\tfrac{2}{3}$$

A declining curve has a negative slope.

Figure 1A.14 Linear Curves with Positive and Negative Slopes

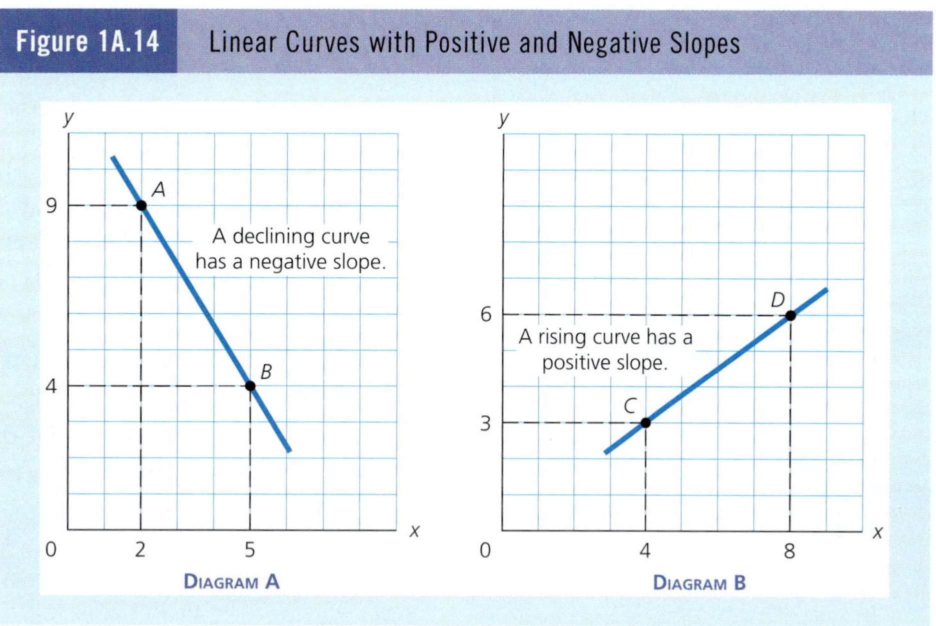

Let us now consider Diagram B. If we move from point C to point D, y rises from 3 to 6. Hence, $\Delta y = 3$. At the same time, x rises from 4 to 8; so $\Delta x = 4$. Therefore,

$$\text{Slope} = \frac{\Delta y}{\Delta x} = \frac{3}{4}$$

If we move from point D to point C, y falls from 6 to 3. Hence, $\Delta y = -3$. At the same time x falls from 8 to 4; so $\Delta x = -4$. Therefore,

$$\text{Slope} = \frac{\Delta y}{\Delta x} = \frac{-3}{-4} = \frac{3}{4}$$

A rising curve has a positive slope.

There seems to be some relationship between inverse relations and direct relations and slope. Is that the case?

If two variables have an inverse relation, the slope of the curve showing that relationship will be negative. The curve will be downward sloping. If two variables have a direct relation, the slope of the curve showing that relationship will be positive. The curve will be upward slopping.

We can calculate the slopes of linear curves, but what about non-linear curves?

A non-linear curve has a different slope at each point on the curve. We can calculate the slope of a non-linear curve at any point on the curve if we know the following fact:

Figure 1A.15 The Slope of a Non-linear Curve

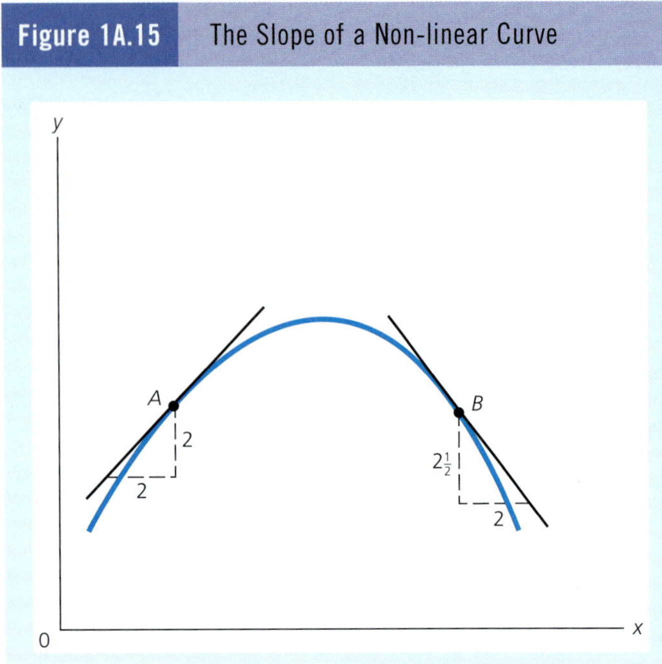

The slope of a non-linear curve at a particular point is the slope of the straight line drawn tangent to the curve at that particular point..

Figure 1A.15 shows a non-linear curve. Tangent lines are drawn at points *A* and *B* on the curve. The slope of the curve at point *A* is the slope of the tangent line at *A*, which is

$$\frac{\Delta y}{\Delta x} = \frac{2}{2} = 1$$

The slope of the curve at *B* is the slope of the tangent line at *B*, which is

$$\frac{\Delta y}{\Delta x} = \frac{-2\frac{1}{2}}{2} = -1\frac{1}{4}$$

Reading Comprehension

The answers to these questions can be found on MyEconLab at www.myeconlab.com. MyEconLab

1. What is the meaning of slope?
2. How is the slope of a straight line measured?
3. How is the slope of a non-linear curve measured?
4. It is meaningful to talk about the slope of a straight line, but not the slope of a non-linear curve. Explain.

Calculate the percentage change in variables

Percentage Change

What is the importance of percentage change in economics?

In economics, it is often necessary to calculate the percentage change in a quantity. Percentages often give us a clearer sense of the magnitude of the change and facilitate comparisons of the size of change. For example, is an increase in price from \$115 to \$135 relatively larger or smaller than an increase from \$120 to \$140? In each case, the absolute increase is the same, namely, \$20, but the relative or percentage change in price may be different.

Is there a formula that we can use to calculate percentage change?

There is. If x is the original quantity and x_1 is the new quantity, the formula for calculating the percentage or relative change from x to x_1 is

$$\frac{100(x_1 - x)}{x}$$

In words, this means that we subtract the original quantity from the new quantity, multiply the result by 100, and divide by the original quantity. The following illustrative example will demonstrate how the formula is used.

Example: The price of an item increased from \$90 to \$95. What is the percentage increase in the price of the item?

Solution: The original price (x) = \$90 and the new price (x_1) = \$95.

The percentage change in price is

$$\frac{100(x_1 - x)}{x} = \frac{100(95 - 90)}{90} = \frac{100 \times 5}{90} = 500 \div 90 = 5.56\%$$

Let us now answer the question raised at the beginning of this section: "Is an increase in price from \$115 to \$135 relatively larger or smaller than an increase in price from \$120 to \$140?"

The percentage increase in price from \$115 to \$135 is

$$\frac{100(x_1 - x)}{x} = \frac{100(135 - 115)}{115} = \frac{100 \times 20}{115} = \frac{2000}{115} = 17.39\%$$

The percentage change in price from \$120 to \$140 is

$$\frac{100(x_1 - x)}{x} = \frac{100(140 - 120)}{120} = \frac{100 \times 20}{120} = \frac{2000}{120} = 16.67\%$$

Therefore, an increase in price from \$115 to \$135 is relatively larger than an increase in price from \$120 to \$140. Note that the absolute differences between the prices were the same, that is, \$20, but they are not meaningfully comparable. The percentage changes, conversely, are comparable.

The formula used for an increase in a variable applies also to a decrease. For example, if the population of a small town fell from 2000 to 1500 over two years, what was the percentage change in the population?

In this example, $x = 2000$ and $x_1 = 1500$. The percentage change is

$$\frac{100(x_1 - x)}{x} = \frac{100(1500 - 2000)}{2000} = \frac{100 \times -500}{2000} = -25\%$$

The population fell by 25%.

It should be clear that a 10% increase on \$1500 is significantly different from a 10% increase on \$150 000. A 10% increase on \$1500 is \$150, whereas a 10% increase on \$150,000 is \$15 000. Although the percentage change is the same (10%), the magnitudes are different.

Is there also a formula for expressing one number as a percentage of another number?

Yes. Suppose we know that a household has an income of \$3000 per month and spends \$800 a month on rent. What percentage of this household's income is spent on rent? We can use the following formula to answer this question.

To express one number, x, as a percentage of another number, y, we divide the first number by the second number and then multiply the result by 100. Thus, x expressed as a percentage of y is

$$\frac{x}{y} \times 100$$

Can we do an example?

Let us assume that the population of a certain small country is 80 000. Assume also that 16 000 of these people are more than 60 years old. Express the number of people over age 60 as a percentage of the total population.

In the example above,

$$x = \text{population over } 60 = 16\,000$$
$$y = \text{total population} = 80\,000$$
$$\frac{x}{y} \times 100 = \frac{16\,000}{80\,000} \times 100 = 20\%$$

Thus, we know that 20% of the population is over 60 years old.

Reading Comprehension

The answers to these questions can be found on MyEconLab at www.myeconlab.com. MyEconLab

1. Explain the importance of the concept of percentage change in economics.
2. Explain how you would convert a ratio into a percentage.

BUSINESS SITUATION 1A.2

A businessperson can invest $100 000 at 7% interest annually or he can purchase inventories that he can resell for $107 500. Before making a decision, he consults his accountant.

What advice should his accountant give?

The answer to this Business Situation can be found in Appendix A.

Review

1. Review the learning objectives listed at the beginning of the appendix.
2. Have you accomplished all the objectives? One way to determine this is toanswer the Reading Comprehension questions at the end of each section. They will help you assess the extent to which you have accomplished the learning objectives.
3. If you have not accomplished an objective, review the relevant material before proceeding.

Key Points to Remember

1. **LO 1A.1** A function expresses a relationship among two or more variables. Functional notation is a very efficient way of expressing relationships among variables. Because much of economics has to do with relations among variables, functional notation is a very useful tool.
2. **LO 1A.1** If A and B are two variables, and if changes in B cause changes in A, then A is a function of B, written as

$A = A(B)$. Here, A is the dependent variable (the variable we are trying to explain), and B is the independent variable (the variable that provides the explanation).

3. **LO 1A.2** Graphs allow us to depict relations among economic variables clearly and vividly so that the relations can be seen at a glance. A rising curve shows a direct relation between the variables under consideration, a declining curve shows an inverse relation, and a vertical or horizontal line shows that the graphed variables are not related—changes in one have no effect on the other.
4. **LO 1A.3** The slope of a straight line is measured by the ratio of the vertical distance to the horizontal distance (rise over run). A straight line has a constant slope. The slope of a non-linear curve at a point on the curve is the slope of the straight line drawn tangent to the curve at that point. The slope is different at every point on a non-linear curve. A rising curve has a positive slope, while a declining curve has a negative slope.
5. **LO 1A.4** Percentages allow us to compare the relative magnitudes of changes in variables. They give a clear sense of the magnitudes involved.

Economic Word Power

Bar graph (p. 33)
Concave curve (p. 33)
Convex curve (p. 33)
Dependent variable (p. 29)
Direct relation (p. 31)
Function (p. 28)
Functional notation (p. 28)
Independent variable (p. 29)
Inverse relation (p. 31)
Origin (p. 30)
Pie chart (p. 34)
Slope (of a curve) (p. 35)

Problems and Exercises

Basic

1. **LO 1A.1** Use functional notation to express each of the following relations:
   a. Coffee consumption (C) depends on the atmospheric temperature (T).
   b. Students' academic performance (P) is a function of their professors' qualifications (Q).
   c. If the quantity of personal computers (Q) sold increases, the quantity of ink cartridges (I) sold will also increase.
   d. An increase in the number of immigrants (M) migrating to Canada will cause the quantity of furniture (F) bought to increase.
   e. An increase in income (y) in Canada will cause an increase in exports (x) from the United States.
   f. The rate of interest (r) influences the use of credit cards (C).
   g. Tax revenues (T) vary with the level of income (y) and the tax rate (t).
2. **LO 1A.1** Use words to express the idea contained in the following notation: $N = N(P,r,y)$ where N is the number of international trips, P is the price of airline tickets, r is the rate of interest, and y is income.
3. **LO 1A.1** For each of the relations in Question 1, indicate the dependent variable and the independent variable(s).
4. **LO 1A.2** Use graphs to show the relationship that you would expect to find between each of the following variables:
   a. The price of grapes and the quantity of grapes bought
   b. The duration of a deep freeze in Florida and the quantity of oranges brought to the market
   c. The rate of interest and the amount of money people put in their savings accounts
   d. The number of students attending a college and the quantity of textbooks bought and sold at the college bookstore
5. **LO 1A.2** Referring to Question 4, indicate whether each relationship is direct or inverse.
6. **LO 1A.2** What kind of graph would you use to illustrate each of the following?
   a. The monthly rainfall for 2010
   b. The proportion of total sales attributable to four retail outlets
   c. A comparison of the populations of 10 different countries
   d. The percentage of total sales attributable to five different products sold by a company
7. **LO 1A.2** Indicate whether each of the following is true or false:
   a. An upward-sloping straight line has an increasing slope.
   b. If two variables are directly related, the graph showing the relationship between them will be upward sloping.

c. A downward-sloping straight line has a negative but constant slope.
d. Concave curves are never used in economics.

Questions in the Intermediate and Challenging Sections cover several different concepts, and have not been organized by learning objectives.

Intermediate

1. Consider Figure 1A.16.
   a. Calculate the slope of line *A* at point *P*.
   b. Calculate the slope of line *A* at point *Q*.
   c. Calculate the slope of line *B* at point *R*.
   d. Calculate the slope of line *B* at point *S*.
   e. What can you conclude about the slope of a straight line at different points on the line?

Figure 1A.16 The Slope of a Straight Line

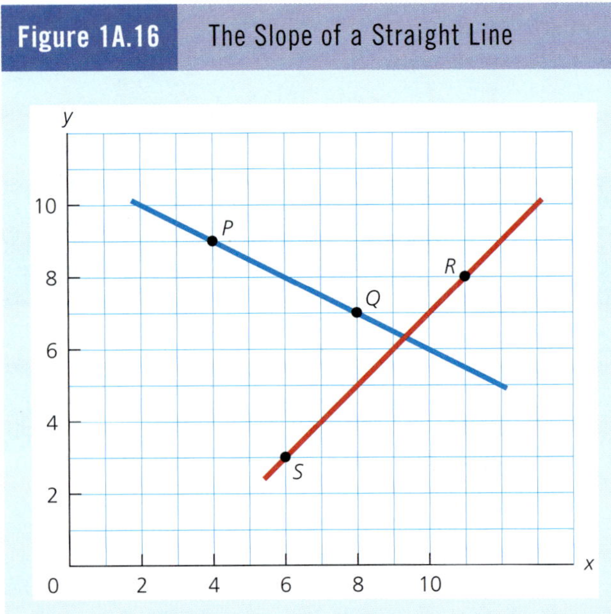

2. Consider Figure 1A.17.
   a. Calculate the slope of the curve at point *A*.
   b. Calculate the slope of the curve at point *B*.
   c. What can you conclude about the slope of a non-linear curve at different points on the curve?
3. Carefully explain the procedure for obtaining the slope of a non-linear curve at a point on the curve.
4. The population of a certain town grew from 150 000 to 195 000 in 10 years. During the same time, the population of another town grew from 250 000 to 320 000. Calculate the rate of growth in each town.
5. At a hockey game, the spectators consisted of 11 000 men and 7000 women.
   a. What was the ratio of women to men?
   b. What percentage of the total spectators were women?

Figure 1A.17 The Slope of a Non-linear Curve

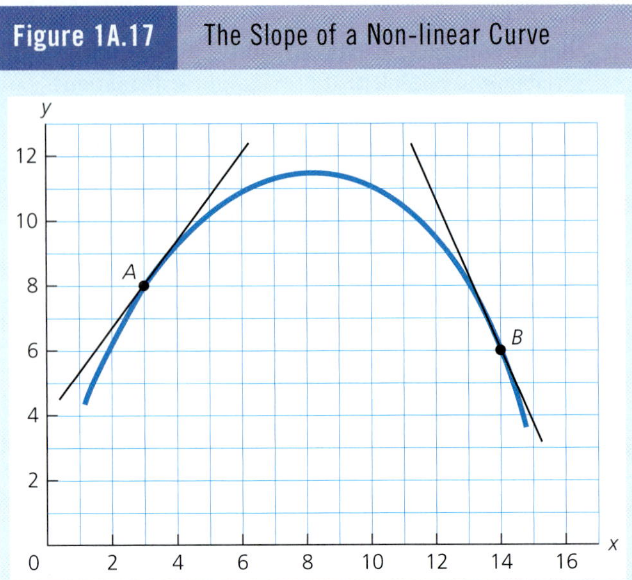

Table 1A.5 Total Cost and Quantity

Q	*TC*
0	4 + 2(0) = 4 + 0 = 4
1	4 + 2(1) = 4 + 2 = 6
2	
3	
4	
5	
6	

Challenging (Use Quad Paper for Graphs)

1. a. Between 2007 and 2011, average house prices in one province rose from \$180 000 to \$205 000. During the same period, in another province, average house prices rose from \$235 000 to \$260 000. Under these conditions, will average house prices in both provinces ever be equal?
   b. Draw a diagram to illustrate what is happening here.
2. The relationship between total cost (*TC*) and total quantity produced (*Q*) is given by the equation $TC = 4 + 2Q$.
   a. Complete Table 1A.5 by calculating *TC* for each quantity produced.
   b. With *TC* on the vertical axis and *Q* on the horizontal axis, graph the data contained in the completed table. Let us refer to the graph as a cost curve.
   c. At what value does your graph cut the vertical axis? That is called the intercept.
   d. Use your graph to calculate the slope of your cost curve.

MyEconLab Visit the MyEconLab website at visit www.myeconlab.com. This online homework and tutorial system puts you in control of your own learning with study and practice tools directly correlated to this appendix's content.

Study Guide

Self-Assessment

The answers to the Study Guide questions can be found in Appendix B.

What's your score?

Circle the letter that corresponds with the correct answer.

1. The statement that the volume of production is a function of the state of technology means that
   a. Changes in the volume of production will cause changes in the state of technology
   b. Changes in the state of technology will cause changes in the volume of production
   c. The volume of production defines the state of technology
   d. We cannot know the state of technology without first knowing the volume of production
2. The expression $Q = Q(P)$, where Q represents quantity and P represents price, means
   a. Quantity must always be multiplied by price
   b. Price and quantity are equal
   c. If price changes, quantity will also change
   d. If quantity changes, price will also change
3. In the expression $Q = Q(P)$,
   a. P is the dependent variable and Q the independent variable
   b. Both Q and P are dependent variables
   c. Both Q and P are independent variables
   d. Q is the dependent variable and P the independent variable
4. In the expression $I = I(y, r)$, I is
   a. The lead variable
   b. The independent variable
   c. The product of y and r
   d. None of the above
5. If a change in one variable has no effect on another variable, a graph showing the relationship between them will be
   a. A straight line through the origin
   b. Impossible to draw
   c. Either vertical or horizontal
   d. Drawn cutting both axes
6. The statement that changes in the volume of output (Q) and the state of technology (T) will cause changes in the cost of production (C) can be expressed as
   a. $C = C(Q + T)$
   b. $Q = Q(C, T)$
   c. $C = C(Q, T)$
   d. $C = Q + T$
7. Graphs enable us to show
   a. Inverse relations but not direct relations
   b. Direct relations but not inverse relations
   c. Both direct and inverse relations
   d. Dependent but not independent variables
8. When we say that two variables are directly related, we mean that
   a. One is derived from the other
   b. One is a multiple of the other
   c. They appear side by side in functional notation
   d. Both variables change in the same direction
9. A downward-sloping curve means that the variables are
   a. Inversely related
   b. Directly related
   c. Not closely related
   d. None of the above
10. When interest rates fall, businesses invest more. This relationship between investment and the rate of interest would be shown on a graph as
    a. An upward-sloping curve
    b. A downward-sloping curve

c. A vertical line
d. A horizontal line

11. A graph of two unrelated variables
a. Can be a vertical or a horizontal line
b. Cannot be drawn
c. Can only be a vertical line
d. Can only be a horizontal line

12. The difference between a convex curve and a concave curve is that
a. One is horizontal and the other is vertical
b. A concave curve is linear while a convex curve is non-linear
c. A convex curve is linear while a concave curve is non-linear
d. None of the above

13. Bar graphs and pie charts
a. Are useful in statistics but not very useful in economics
b. Are just embellishments that add nothing to data presentation
c. Are effective and vivid means of presenting data
d. Can be used only when the data involve percentage changes

14. One serious limitation of using graphs in economics is that
a. They are too difficult to understand
b. They can be used only when several variables are involved
c. Our ability to use graphs decreases as the number of variables increases
d. None of the above

15. The concept of slope refers to
a. Only straight lines
b. Only non-linear curves
c. Both linear and non-linear curves
d. Concave curves but not convex curves.

16. The slope of a line can be measured by
a. The ratio of the vertical distance to the horizontal distance
b. The ratio of the horizontal distance to the vertical distance
c. The difference between the vertical distance and the horizontal distance
d. The sum of the vertical and horizontal distances

17. An upward-sloping curve has
a. A negative slope
b. A positive slope
c. Zero slope
d. None of the above

18. A linear curve always has
a. A positive slope
b. A negative slope
c. A constant slope
d. A variable slope

19. The formula for calculating percentage change from x to x_1 is
a. $\frac{100(x - x_1)}{x}$
b. $\frac{100(x_1 - x)}{x}$
c. $\frac{100(x - x_1)}{x_1}$
d. $\frac{100(x_1 - x)}{x_1}$

20. Percentages are useful because
a. They are easy to calculate
b. They facilitate comparisons of relative changes in variables
c. Numbers always give more information than do words
d. None of the above

Problems and Exercises (Use Quad Paper for Graphs)

Answers to these questions can be found on MyEconLab at www.myeconlab.com. MyEconLab

1. Use functional notation to express each of the following statements:
a. The level of saving (S) depends on the rate of interest (r).
b. If the money supply (M) changes, the rate of interest (r) will also change.
c. Changes in income (y) will cause changes in the demand for money (Md).
d. If the demand for money (Md) changes, the rate of interest (r) will change.
e. Changes in income (y) and the rate of interest (r) will cause the level of investment (I) to change.

2. In each of the following functions, identify the dependent and independent variables:
a. $C = C(P, i)$
b. $Q = Q(p, y, T)$
c. $x = x(R, y)$
d. $y = y(r, W)$
e. $I = I(y, r, E)$

3. In each of the following relations, indicate the dependent and independent variables:
   a. If the price (*P*) of computers changes, the quantity (*Q*) that people will buy will also change.
   b. Changes in the quantity (*Q*) of VCRs that people will buy are due to changes in the price (*P*) of VCRs and people's income (*y*).
   c. A change in the average income (*y*) of Canadians will result in a change in the amount of imported goods (*M*).
   d. Changes in income (*y*) and the rate of interest (*r*) will cause investment (*I*) to change.
4. a. Construct a table with hypothetical values to show the relation you would expect between the rate of interest and the frequency of use of credit cards. (Use six different rates.)
   b. Plot the information from your table on a graph.
5. Draw graphs (without plotting) to illustrate the relationship you would expect between the following pairs of variables:
   a. Class attendance and grade in your economics course.
   b. The price of movies and movie attendance.
   c. Air fare and vacations abroad.
   d. Income and the amount of income tax a person pays.
6. Table 1A.6 contains information on combinations of corn and wheat that a farmer can grow on a given area of land.

Table 1A.6 Combinations of Corn and Wheat

Corn (tonnes)	**Wheat** (tonnes)
0	20
1	16
2	12
3	8
4	4
5	0

   a. With wheat on the vertical axis and corn on the horizontal axis, draw a graph showing the various combinations of corn and wheat that the farmer can grow.
   b. Calculate the slope of your graph.

7. Table 1A.7 shows combinations of two goods, x and y, that an economy can produce. With y on the vertical axis and x on the horizontal axis,

Table 1A.7 Combinations of *X* and *Y*

Combinations	***X***	***Y***
A	0	15
B	1	14
C	2	12
D	3	9
E	4	5
F	5	0

   a. Plot the curve from Table 1A.7.
   b. Calculate the slope at point *D* on the graph.
8. With reference to Figure 1A.18, calculate the slope of the curve at points *A* and *B*.

Figure 1A.18 A Slope Calculation

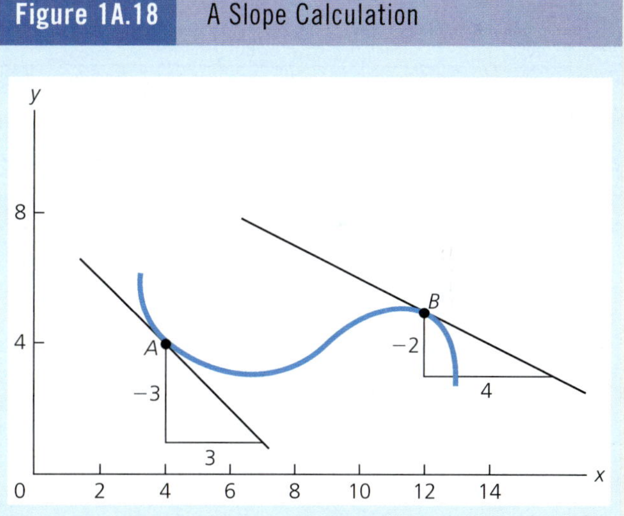

9. Table 1A.8 contains data on total income and government spending for a hypothetical economy for 1985, 1990, 1995, and 2000.

a. Calculate the percentage change in total income from 1985 to 1990, from 1990 to 1995, and from 1995 to 2000. Complete column (3).

b. Express government spending as a percentage of total income for each year shown in the table and complete column (5).

10. In 2000, the number of students enrolled in economics at a certain Canadian college was 1500. This figure grew to 2500 by 2004. At the same time, the number of economics professors increased from 10 to 15.

a. Calculate the percentage change in the number of students enrolled in economics over the period 2000 to 2004.

b. How does the percentage change in the number of economics professors compare with the percentage change in the number of students enrolled in economics?

c. Express the number of economics professors as a percentage of the number of economics students in 2000 and 2004.

Table 1A.8 Hypothetical Data for Total Income and Government Spending

Year (1)	Total Income ($) (2)	% Change (3)	Government Spending ($) (4)	Government Spending as % of Total Income (5)
1985	12 400 000	______	3 500 000	______
1990	15 000 000	______	3 750 000	______
1995	20 500 000	______	5 637 000	______
2000	24 900 000	______	5 851 500	______

Chapter 2

The Economic Problem: Scarcity and Choice

Learning Objectives

After studying this chapter, you should be able to

2.1 Explain the relationship among scarcity, choice, and opportunity cost

2.2 Discuss and use the concepts of production possibilities schedules and production possibilities curves

2.3 Discuss and illustrate graphically shifts in the production possibilities curve

2.4 Explain the fundamental economic questions and classify them as microeconomic or macroeconomic issues

2.5 Construct a circular flow model and explain the flow of goods, services, and resources in the economy

Assess Your Knowledge

MyEconLab

Answers to these questions can be found on MyEconLab at **www.myeconlab.com.**

1. Think of cost as whatever you give up when you make a choice. On graduation from high school, you decided to go to college instead of going to work. Using this concept of cost, what did the decision to go to college cost you?
2. Which of the following will enable a country to produce more goods and services?
   a. An increase in the country's workforce
   b. A general increase in the prices of goods and services
   c. Neither a nor b
   d. Both a and b
3. What is a firm?
4. What is economic growth?

LO 2.1 Explain the relationship among scarcity, choice, and opportunity cost

Scarcity and Choice Again

Is there still more to say about scarcity and choice?

Yes, there is. We have already established a relationship between scarcity and the necessity to choose. But there is more to the concept of choice or choosing than you might expect. When you are asked to make a choice between two things, you naturally think of taking one of them. That's how most people see choice—the act of taking. But think about it this way. If you were confronted with a choice between a two-week vacation in Paris and an expensive new television set, and you chose the television set, then you actually gave up the vacation in Paris. If you choose to go to a movie with your friends, you must give up something that you could have done during that time—something like studying economics. If you choose to attend a class at 8:30 a.m., you must give up some extra sleep that you could have enjoyed. The point should be clear: you cannot choose without giving up something.

Let's state it another way. The television set that you chose cost you the vacation in Paris. Going to the movies with your friends may have cost you a better grade on your economics test. And what is the cost of attending your 8:30 a.m. class? That's right! It's the extra sleep that you could have had.

Is there a technical term for the alternative that is given up when we choose?

opportunity cost the next-best alternative that is sacrificed when a choice is made

Not surprisingly, there is. It is a very important economic concept called opportunity cost or alternative cost. **Opportunity cost** is the next-best alternative that is sacrificed when a choice is made. Note that this cost is not necessarily expressed in terms of money but rather in terms of whatever is sacrificed or given up.

If Canada decides to buy new submarines instead of spending the money on health care, then the opportunity cost of the submarines would be the loss of the health services that could have been bought instead. If you decide to go to the movies, the admission ticket is part of the opportunity cost, but if you buy dinner at a restaurant before the movie instead of having dinner at home, then the money you spend for dinner is not part of the opportunity cost. You would have had dinner anyway.

We can measure opportunity cost per unit of the alternative chosen. If John gives up 10 kilograms of potatoes in order to get 20 kilograms of corn, then the opportunity cost of the 20 kilograms of corn is 10 kilograms of potatoes. This means that the opportunity cost of 1 kilogram of corn is 0.5 kilograms of potatoes. If John has to give up 20 kilograms of corn in order to get 10 kilograms of potatoes, then the opportunity cost of 10 kilograms of potatoes is 20 kilograms of corn. This means that the opportunity cost of 1 kilogram of potatoes is 2 kilograms of corn.

We can see from this example that opportunity cost is what we give up divided by what we get in its place.

$$\text{Opportunity cost} = \frac{\text{What we give up}}{\text{What we get}}$$

In John's case, the opportunity cost of corn is

$$\frac{\text{10 kilograms of potatoes}}{\text{20 kilograms of corn}} = \frac{\text{0.5 kilogram of potatoes}}{\text{1 kilogram of corn}}$$

On the other hand, the opportunity cost of potatoes is

$$\frac{\text{20 kilograms of corn}}{\text{10 kilograms of potatoes}} = \frac{\text{2 kilograms of corn}}{\text{1 kilogram of potatoes}}$$

Example: In order to get 3 more Blu-ray movies, you have to give up 6 USB flash drives. Calculate the opportunity cost of Blu-ray movies.

Solution:

$$\frac{\text{What we give up}}{\text{What we get}} = \frac{\text{6 USB flash drives}}{\text{3 Blu-ray movies}} = \frac{\text{2 USB flash drives}}{\text{1 Blu-ray movie}}$$

The opportunity cost of a Blu-ray movie is 2 flash drives.

A relationship seems to exist among scarcity, choice, and opportunity cost. Is there?

Most certainly. We are forced to choose only because of scarcity; and whenever we choose, we incur a cost, that is, an opportunity cost. Figure 2.1 illustrates the relationship well.

Can you give a practical example of the use of the opportunity cost concept in real life?

We make all kinds of decisions in our daily lives. Should I take a part-time job while I am in college? If scheduling conflicts prevent me from registering for both economics and mathematics, which one should I take? Should I skip my economics class today? Let's see how the concept of opportunity cost can help us to arrive at a decision regarding attending (or not attending) an economics class. Let us assume that you have already arrived at school. You attend classes because you believe that you will derive certain benefits from

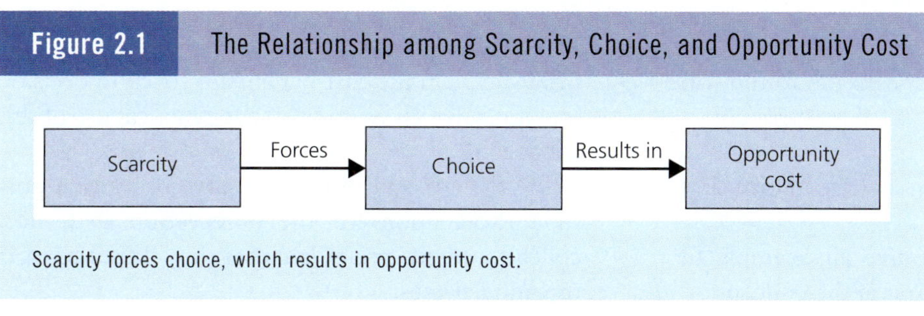

Scarcity forces choice, which results in opportunity cost.

doing so. What are these benefits? Possible benefits are a good attendance record that will improve your grade; better understanding of how the central bank tries to control interest rates (that's what is being discussed in class and you've always been fascinated by it); and being with your friends who are also taking the course. But attending class also has costs associated with it. These may include playing a game of cards with some friends, going to the nearby mall, or taking this last opportunity to watch that movie that you've been waiting to see. Notice that these costs are what you will give up by attending the class. They are the opportunity cost of going to class.

To make the decision, you weigh the benefits against the costs. If, in your own subjective evaluation, the benefits of going to class outweigh the costs, then you will decide in favour of attending the class. If, in your estimation, the costs outweigh the benefits, then you will decide against attending the class. This is the cost-benefit approach to decision making. The **cost-benefit approach** is an analysis in decision making that involves the comparison of costs and benefits. The decision rule is simple: if the benefits outweigh the costs, then do the activity; otherwise, don't.

cost-benefit approach an analysis in decision making that involves the comparison of costs and benefits

Can we apply this approach to more complicated decisions?

This way of thinking, using the concept of opportunity cost, can be applied to the simplest decisions as well as to very complex decisions involving the expenditure of a great deal of money. Let us consider the decision to go to college or take a full-time job. David has just completed his secondary-school education. He can get a job that pays $25 000 per year. However, he would like to go to college to obtain a diploma. This will take two years. Tuition, books, and other things, such as transportation and supplies, that are directly related to attending college will cost $35 000 for the two-year period. What is the full cost to David of a diploma? How should David decide whether or not to go for the diploma?

If David makes his decision on the basis of the $35 000 only, he would severely underestimate his cost. The full cost of his degree must include the $25 000 per year (or $50 000 for the two-year period) that he could have received as salary from his employment. That is the opportunity cost. Thus, the full cost of the diploma is ($35 000 + $50 000) = $85 000. To decide whether or not to go for the diploma, David must consider the benefits of having a diploma. These may include a higher-paying job, better working conditions, greater job security, and the prestige of having a college diploma. If these benefits outweigh the $85 000 cost, then David would sacrifice the job and attend college. Otherwise, he would take the job for $25 000 per year.

Reading Comprehension

The answers to these questions can be found on MyEconLab at www.myeconlab.com. MyEconLab

1. What is the relationship among scarcity, choice, and opportunity cost?
2. Define opportunity cost and give an example to demonstrate your understanding of the concept.
3. Briefly explain the cost-benefit approach to decision making. Give an example of the practical use of this approach.
4. Using the concept of opportunity cost, give a possible explanation for the observation that most college students prefer late morning classes to early morning classes.

LO 2.2 Discuss and use the concept of production possibilities schedules and production possibilities curves

Production Possibilities

What are production possibilities?

An economy's production possibilities show its potential to produce goods and services with the resources at its disposal. Let us construct a simple model to explain an economy's production possibilities. Assume that our hypothetical economy devotes all its resources to the production of only two goods: smart phones and personal computers. Several possible combinations of smart phones and personal computers are illustrated in Table 2.1.

Table 2.1 A Production Possibilities Schedule Showing Constant Cost

Possibilities	Number of Smart Phones (000 000)	Number of Computers (000 000)
A	15	0
B	12	1
C	9	2
D	6	3
E	3	4
F	0	5

If the economy uses all its resources to produce only smart phones, it can produce a maximum of 15 000 000 smart phones (possibility *A*). If it uses all its resources to produce only personal computers, it can produce 5 000 000 computers (possibility *F*). Between these two extreme cases are many combinations of smart phones and computers that the economy can produce. For example, Table 2.1 shows that the economy can produce 12 000 000 smart phones and 1 000 000 computers (possibility B); or it can produce 3 000 000 smart phones and 4 000 000 computers (possibility *E*). Note that for every 1 000 000 computers produced, the economy has to give up 3 000 000 smart phones. Thus, the opportunity cost of 1 000 000 computers is 3 000 000 smart phones. In this example, the opportunity cost remains constant throughout.

production possibility (p-p) schedule a table showing various combinations of goods and services that can be produced with full utilization of all resources and a given state of technology

Table 2.1 is referred to as a **production possibilities (p-p) schedule**, which is a tabular representation of an economy's production possibilities. It shows the various combinations of goods and services (in this case, smart phones and computers) that an economy can produce with a given state of technology if it uses all its resources.

Note that the economy can produce 6 000 000 smart phones and 1 000 000 computers; but in so doing, it will not be using all its resources. Note also that if it is producing 6 000 000 smart phones, it cannot at the same time produce 4 000 000 computers. Why not? Because it does not have enough resources.

What is a production possibilities curve?

The information contained in the production possibilities schedule can be shown on a graph. With smart phones on the vertical axis and computers on the horizontal axis, we can plot all six combinations of smart phones and computers represented by possibilities *A* to *F* in Table 2.1. This is done in Figure 2.2. The curve shows the maximum number of smart phones and the maximum number of computers that this hypothetical economy can produce with given technology at a particular time. The curve is a **production possibilities curve (p-p curve)** or production possibilities frontier (p-p frontier), which is a graphical representation of an economy's production possibilities. It shows all combinations of commodities that can be produced if all resources are fully employed and technology is constant.

production possibilities (p-p) curve a graph showing all combinations of goods and services that can be produced if all resources are fully employed and technology is constant

The curve in Figure 2.2 is linear (a straight line) because we have assumed a constant opportunity cost; each unit of computers costs exactly the same quantity of smart phones. In other words, the production of computers could be traded off for the production of smart phones at a fixed rate of three smart phones for one computer. A linear production possibilities curve illustrates constant opportunity cost.

Figure 2.2 A Production Possibilities Curve Showing Constant Opportunity Cost

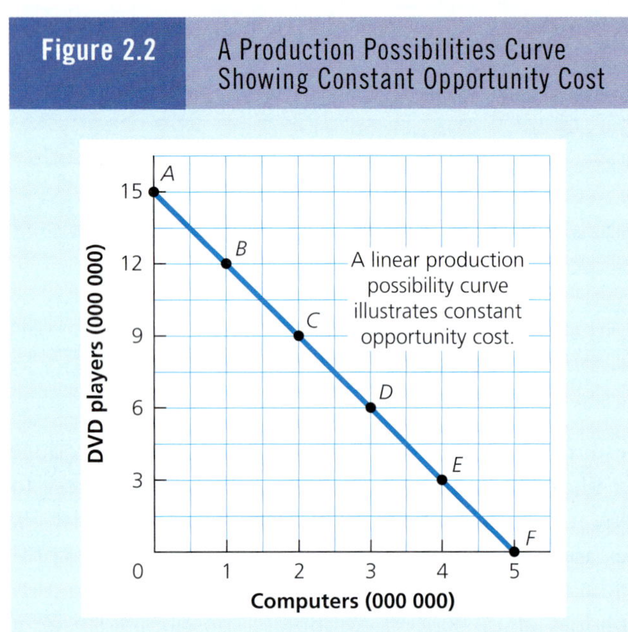

Are production possibilities curves always linear?

No. In fact, in the real world, we are unlikely to encounter situations of constant opportunity cost in production. Constant opportunity cost in production would occur only if all resources were equally efficient in all uses. This clearly is not the case. Some human resources, for example, are better equipped to perform technical work than mental work; and some parcels of land are more suitable for agricultural purposes than are others. In reality, resources are not all equally efficient in all lines of production. Some resources will produce smart phones more efficiently than they will computers. As we continue to shift resources from smart phone production to computer production, we are likely to experience increasing cost. This happens because these resources are likely to become less efficient in the production of computers. For example, it may be relatively easy at first to shift workers from smart phone production to computer production. As the process continues, however, it will become increasingly difficult to find smart phone workers who are efficient in computer production. After all, the number of excellent workers in the production of smart phones who are just as efficient in computer production is limited. For this reason, p-p curves are unlikely to be linear.

BUSINESS SITUATION 2.1

A manufacturer of neckties has a given amount of money that can be used to produce silk ties and polyester ties. Producing more silk ties is possible only at the expense of polyester ties.

What tool can this manufacturer use to illustrate this trade-off situation?

The answer to this Business Situation can be found in Appendix A.

What is the likely shape of a production possibilities curve?

Table 2.2 will help to answer the question. We retain the assumptions that the economy uses all its resources and that it has a given technology.

Table 2.2 A Production Possibilities Schedule Showing Increasing Cost

Possibilities	Number of Smart Phones (000 000)	Number of Computers (000 000)
A	15	0
B	14	1
C	12	2
D	9	3
E	5	4
F	0	5

Table 2.2 shows that if the economy produces 15 000 000 smart phones it cannot produce any computers. To produce the first 1 000 000 computers, it must shift resources from smart phone production to computer production. In so doing, the quantity of small phones produced falls to 14 000 000. The economy has to give up 1 000 000 smart phones for 1 000 000 computers. To produce another 1 000 0000 computers, the economy must give up 2 000 000 smart phones this time. (The quantity of smart phones falls from 14 000 000 to 12 000 000.) So the opportunity cost of the second 1 000 000 computers is 2 000 000 smart phones. The third 1 000 000 computers can be obtained at an additional cost of 3 000 000 smart phones. According to Table 2.2, the fourth 1 000 000 computers cost 4 000 000 smart phones, and the fifth 1 000 000 computers cost 5 000 000 smart phones. Table 2.3 summarizes the cost of computers in terms of smart phones.

Clearly, as the economy increases its production of computers, the cost of additional computers (in terms of smart phones) rises. Just about any productive activity that you can think of will display increasing opportunity cost.

Is there a name for this phenomenon of increasing cost?

law of increasing opportunity cost the phenomenon of increasing unit cost as an economy increases its production of a commodity

Economists refer to this phenomenon of increasing cost as **the law of increasing opportunity cost**, which states that as an economy increases its production of a commodity, the cost per unit of production rises.

Table 2.3 The Opportunity Cost of Computers in Terms of Smart Phones

Computer	Opportunity Cost in Smart Phones
First 1 000 000 computers	1 000 000 smart phones
Second 1 000 000 computers	2 000 000 smart phones
Third 1 000 000 computers	3 000 000 smart phones
Fourth 1 000 000 computers	4 000 000 smart phones
Fifth 1 000 000 computers	5 000 000 smart phones

Figure 2.3 A Production Possibilities Curve Showing Increasing Opportunity Cost

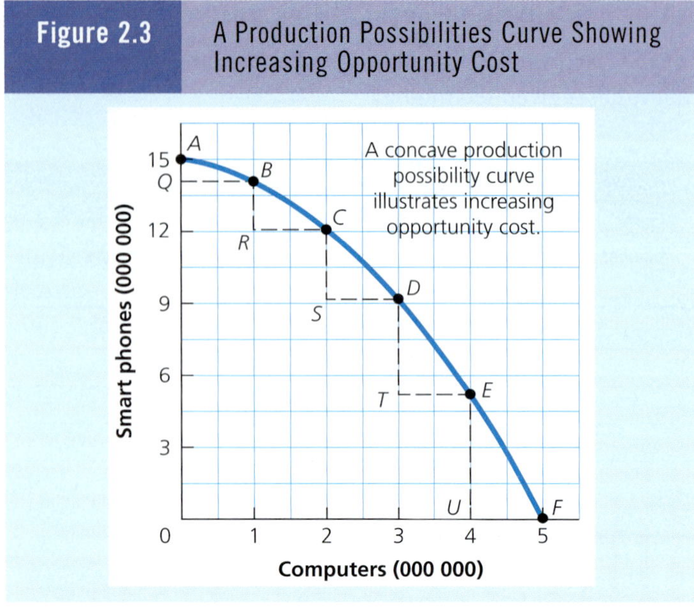

Figure 2.4 A Production Possibilities Diagram Illustrating Scarcity and Choice

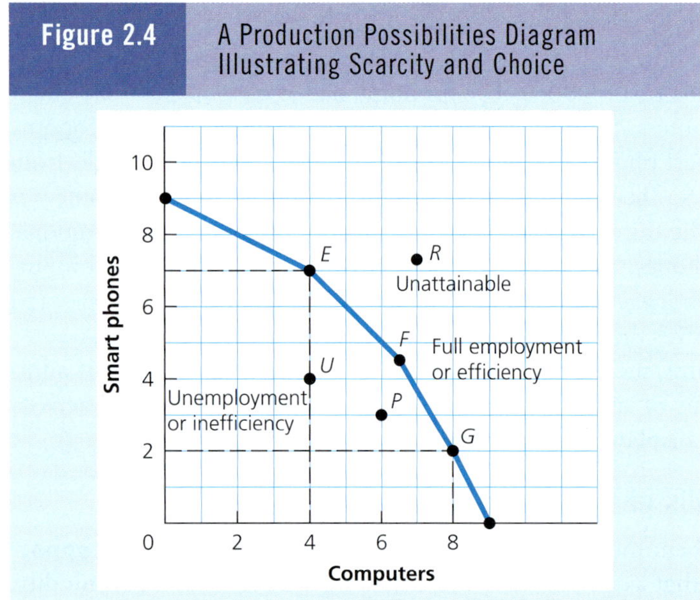

We have established that production will display increasing cost, but we still have not answered the question: What is the likely shape of the production possibilities curve?

We can answer that right now. Let us plot the information in Table 2.2 on a graph. The resulting graph is shown as Figure 2.3.

Note that the horizontal segments *QB*, *RC*, *SD*, *TE*, and *UF* are all equal, representing equal increases in units of computers. The vertical segments *QA*, *BR*, *CS*, *DT*, and *EU* represent the units of smart phones that must be sacrificed to obtain the additional units of computers. Thus, to increase the production of computers from 1 000 000 to 2 000 000 (*RC*), the economy must give up 2 000 000 smart phones (*BR*). To increase the production of computers from 2 000 000 to 3 000 000 (*SD*), the economy must give up 3 000 000 smart phones (*CS*); and to increase the production of computers from 4 000 000 to 5 000 000 (*UF*), the economy must give up 5 000 000 smart phones (*EU*). Note that $EU > DT > CS > BR$. This means that the opportunity cost of a unit of computers increases as the economy increase its production of computers. A curve that is bowed outward like the curve in Figure 2.3 is said to be concave. A concave production possibilities curve illustrates increasing opportunity cost. Because of the prevalence of increasing opportunity cost, the p-p curve is likely to be concave.

Now we know that the production possibilities model can be used to illustrate opportunity cost. Can it be used also to illustrate scarcity and choice?

productive efficiency the situation that exists when an economy cannot increase its production of one commodity without reducing its production of some other commodity

productive inefficiency the situation that exists when it is possible to produce more of one commodity without producing less of some other commodity

Consider the production possibilities diagram in Figure 2.4. All points on the curve, such as *E*, *F*, and *G*, represent combinations of smart phones and computers that the economy can produce with full employment of all available resources and with its current state of technology. Therefore, points on the p-p curve represent full employment.

Notice that once the economy is operating on its p-p curve, it cannot increase its production of one commodity without reducing its production of some other commodity. Economists use the term **productive efficiency** to describe this situation. Such points as *U* and *P*, which lie below the p-p curve, represent unemployment of resources. An economy that is operating below its p-p curve is not producing its maximum output of goods and services. Economists use the term **productive inefficiency** to describe an economy in which it is possible to produce more of one commodity without producing less of some other commodity. Such a point as *R* represents a combination of smart phones and computers that lies beyond the economy's productive capacity. Such a combination is currently unattainable. The diagram illustrates scarcity. If the economy is operating at point *E*, producing seven units of smart phones and four units of computers, and decides to increase its production of computers to eight units, it can do so only by reducing its production of smart phones, moving from point *E* to point *G*. The necessary reduction in the production of smart phones is a result of scarcity, as is the fact that combination *R* is unattainable. With more resources, the economy could conceivably attain combination *R*. Scarcity forces the economy to choose among various production alternatives that are available. With full use of its resources and given technology, the economy must choose among points along the p-p curve.

free lunch the additional output produced without sacrificing the production of any other good or service

Can the economy ever be in a situation where it can produce more of one item without giving up any of another item?

Figure 2.5 Free Lunch: Getting Something for Nothing

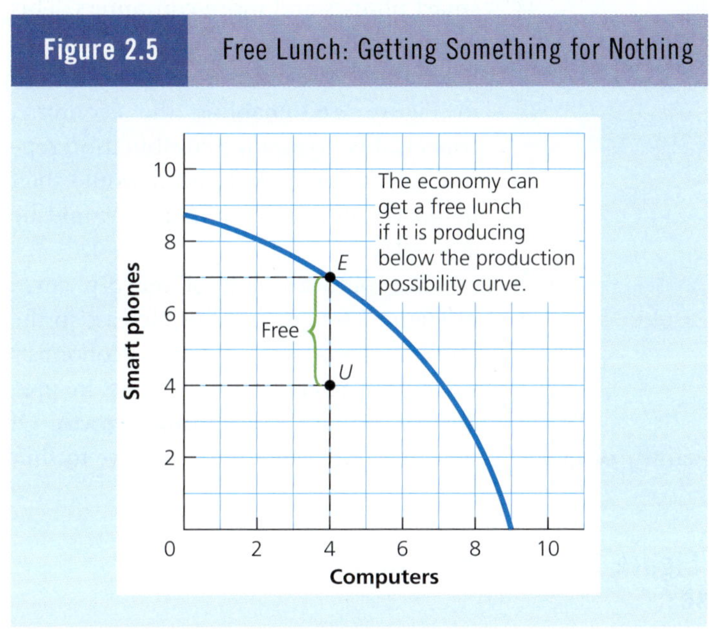

That is an interesting question. Let us answer it with the help of Figure 2.5. Assume that the economy is operating at point *U*, producing four units of smart phones and four units of computers. At *U*, there is unemployment. By using unemployed resources, the economy can move to point *E* on the p-p curve, producing seven units of smart phones and still four units of computers. Thus, the economy produces three additional units of smart phones without sacrificing any computers. The economy manages to obtain three smart phones at zero opportunity cost. This is a case of a **free lunch**—getting something for nothing or, more formally, having additional output produced without sacrificing the production of any other good or service. Because the increased output associated with the move from *U* to *E* does not involve sacrificing any output, we can conclude that the opportunity cost of unemployed resources is zero.

Reading Comprehension

The answers to these questions can be found on MyEconLab at www.myeconlab.com. MyEconLab

1. What does a linear p-p curve tell us about opportunity cost?
2. Explain why p-p curves are more likely to be concave than linear.
3. State the law of increasing opportunity cost.
4. Define the following:
   a) Productive efficiency
   b) Productive inefficiency
5. In economics, there is no way of getting something for nothing (no free lunch). Do you agree? Explain fully.

LO 2.3 Discuss and illustrate shifts in the production possibilities curve

Shifts in the Production Possibilities Curve

How will an increase in the quantity or quality of resources, or an increase in technology, affect an economy's p-p curve?

Figure 2.6 The Effect of an Increase in the Quantity or Quality of Resources, or an Increase in Technology

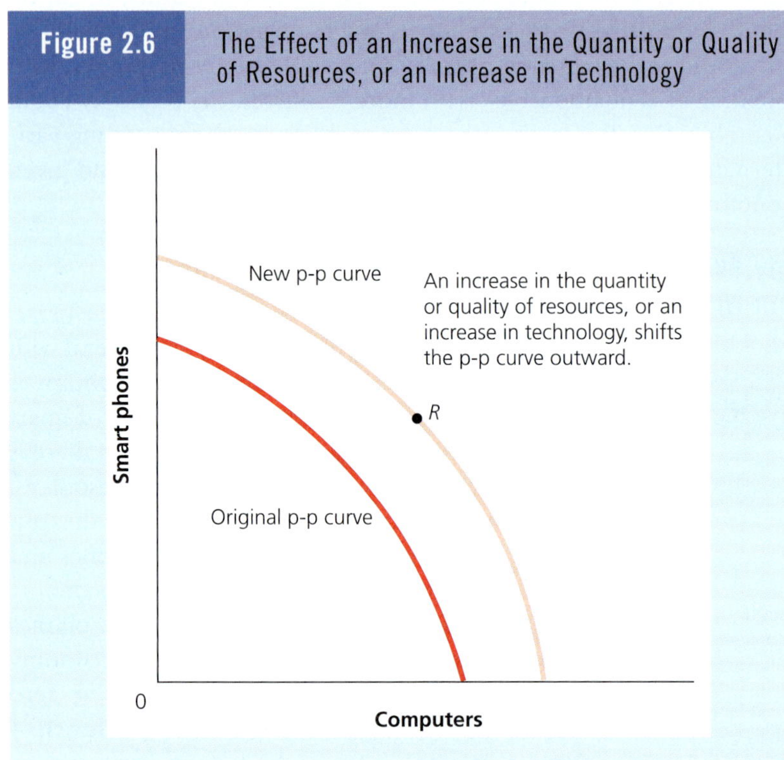
Smart phones
New p-p curve
An increase in the quantity or quality of resources, or an increase in technology, shifts the p-p curve outward.
R
Original p-p curve
0
Computers

Let's look at Figure 2.6. Point *R* lies beyond the original p-p curve and is therefore currently unattainable. It represents a combination of smart phones and computers that this economy cannot produce with its available resources and its current state of technology. Should technology advance or should the quantity or quality of its resources increase, then the economy could produce more smart phones and more computers. This would result in a new p-p curve lying to the right of the original curve as shown in Figure 2.6, enabling the economy, conceivably, to attain a combination represented by point *R*. Point *R* would then lie on the new p-p curve, and would be attainable.

The outward shift of the p-p curve in Figure 2.6 represents an increase in the economy's productive capacity. Economists sometimes refer to this increase in productive capacity as **economic growth**. Of course, a decrease in the quantity or quality of resources will cause the p-p curve to shift inward, to the left.

economic growth an increase in the economy's productive capacity

The new p-p curve in Figure 2.6 is parallel to the original curve. Is this usually the case?

The parallel shift of the p-p curve implies that the increase in the quantity or quality of resources or the technological advance that caused the curve to shift affected the production of smart phones and the production of computers to the same extent. It will more often be the case that technology and changes in the quantity and quality of resources will affect different industries differently. For example, the introduction of robotics into the manufacturing of automobiles will affect that industry while having no impact on agriculture.

How will the production possibilities curve relating to the manufacturing industry and the fishing industry be affected by technological advance in only manufacturing or only fishing?

If the technological advance occurred only in the manufacturing industry, then the ability to produce manufactured goods would increase while the ability to produce fish and fish products would remain unchanged. The p-p curve would shift out in a non-parallel

Figure 2.7 A Technological Advance in Only One Industry

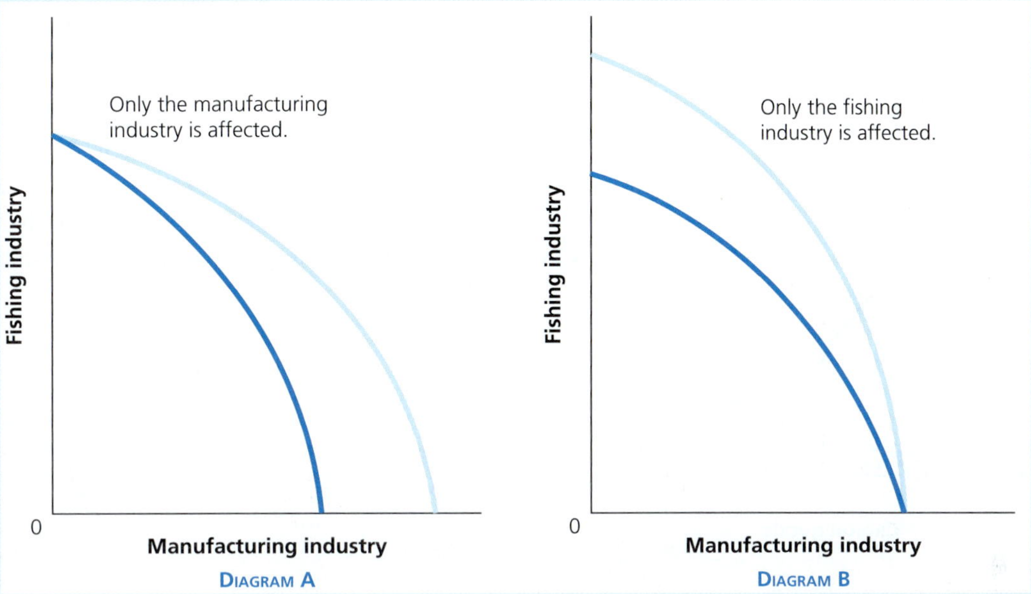

Only the manufacturing industry is affected.

Fishing industry

0

Manufacturing industry

DIAGRAM A

Only the fishing industry is affected.

Fishing industry

0

Manufacturing industry

DIAGRAM B

Diagram A: Technological advance in manufacturing only

Diagram B: Technological advance in fishing only

manner, as shown in Diagram A of Figure 2.7. Similarly, if the technological advance occurred only in the fishing industry, then the growth attributed to the technological advance would occur only in the fishing industry. The p-p curve would again shift out in a non-parallel manner, as illustrated by Diagram B of Figure 2.7.

Does an increase or a decrease in actual production shift the economy's production possibilities curve?

No. Only a change in the quantity or quality of the economy's resources or a change in technology will shift the p-p curve. A shift in the production possibilities curve means that the economy's productive capacity has changed. If, for example, new resources are discovered but not yet used, the p-p curve will shift to the right, because the economy now has the potential to produce more goods and services, even though it is not using that potential. If, however, existing resources that were previously not used are now being utilized, then actual production will increase, but the economy's p-p curve would not shift because there would be no increase in the economy's productive capacity.

How does an economy's decision to increase its current production of capital goods at the expense of consumer goods affect its p-p curve in the future?

The decision to produce more capital goods and fewer consumer goods means that the economy is sacrificing current consumption while building up its capital stock. With a

Figure 2.8 A Sacrifice in Current Consumption for Future Consumption

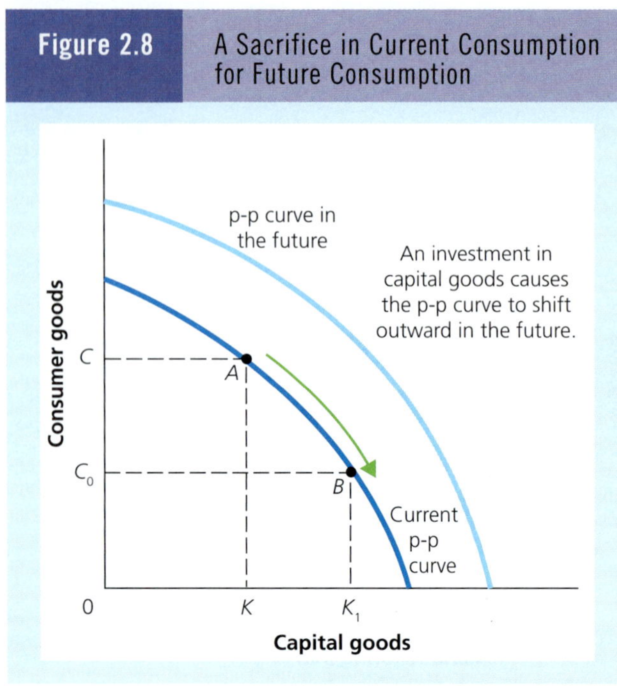

larger capital stock in the future, the economy would be able to produce more capital goods *and* more consumer goods. In other words, the economy's p-p curve will shift out to the right in the future. Figure 2.8 illustrates the point. Let us assume that the economy decides to move from point A to point B, reducing its production of consumer goods from $0C$ to $0C_0$ and increasing its production of capital goods from $0K$ to $0K_1$. Because of the increase in capital resources in the future, the p-p curve would shift out in the future, enabling the economy to produce both more consumer goods and more capital goods.

Reading Comprehension

The answers to these questions can be found on MyEconLab at **www.myeconlab.com**. MyEconLab

1. Give three examples of specific events that would cause Canada's p-p curve to shift out to the right.
2. How can economic growth be illustrated on a p-p diagram?
3. Explain why a fall in prices will not shift an economy's p-p curve.
4. Explain why p-p curves are unlikely to shift in or out in a parallel manner.

LO 2.4 Explain the fundamental economic questions and classify them as microeconomic or macroeconomic issues

Fundamental Economic Questions

What are the fundamental questions of microeconomics?

The fundamental microeconomic questions can be stated quite briefly as

- What?
- How?
- For whom?

What does the "What" refer to?

What refers to what goods and services will the economy produce and in what quantities. Will the economy produce automobiles, houses, grapes, milk, computers, musical instruments, television sets, oil, electricity, roads, and so on? In what quantities will it produce them? Because of the ever-present problem of scarcity, more of one thing means less of some other thing. If more hospital beds are provided, fewer classrooms might be the consequence. What to produce and how much are important decisions that every economy has to make.

What does the "How" refer to?

Once the decisions have been made regarding the types and quantities of goods and services that will be produced, a decision has to be made regarding how the goods and services will be produced. How will apples be harvested? Will it be done manually or with the help of specialized machinery? What method of production will be used in producing automobiles? Will robotics be used instead of labour for certain activities? *How* refers to the method of production that will be used in producing the goods and services that have been decided on. The economy's scarce resources can be combined in many ways to produce goods and services. The economy must decide which to use.

What does "For whom" refer to?

For whom refers to who gets the goods and services after they have been produced. Once the "what" and the "how" questions have been addressed, a decision must be made regarding the distribution of the goods and services among the various members of the community. Should all the available goods and services produced be divided equally among all members of society, or should some people get a larger share than others?

What are some of the important issues of macroeconomics?

The list of macroeconomic problems and issues is arbitrary, but we can identify five issues that are fundamental to macroeconomics.

aggregate output the total volume of goods and services produced in the economy

Aggregate Output First, macroeconomics is concerned with **aggregate output**, the total volume of goods and services produced in the economy. This is an important issue because our standard of living is directly related to the volume of goods and services that our economy produces. The standard of living refers to the volume of goods and services available for consumption. If a society can keep the total output of goods and services close to the economy's potential, its citizens will be better off. Closely associated with the volume of goods and services produced are fluctuations in the total output of goods and services. Economists refer to these alternating periods of ups and downs in aggregate production as **business cycles**. Economic fluctuations can result in unemployment and inflation—two other important macroeconomic problems that policymakers often have to deal with.

business cycles fluctuations in the aggregate output of goods and services

unemployment the condition that exists when people who are willing and able to work at prevailing wage rates are unable to find jobs

Unemployment Second is **unemployment**, the condition that exists when people who are willing and able to work at prevailing wage rates are unable to find jobs. If an economy is operating at a high level of efficiency, at a point near to its p-p curve, then unemployment will be low. If the economy is operating at a low level of efficiency and output, then unemployment will likely be high. Clearly, unemployment is tied to people's income and hence to their ability to purchase the goods and services required to satisfy their wants. Why does our economy often fail to generate full employment?

inflation a sustained increase in the average level of prices over time; a persistent increase in the cost of living

Inflation The third crucial macroeconomic issue is the problem of **inflation**: a sustained increase in the average level of prices over time. In your lifetime, you have noticed that a dollar does not buy as much as it used to 10 years ago. Your parents have noticed even more substantial losses in the value of a dollar. When the dollar loses

Economic growth enables Canadians to enjoy high living standards.

value or purchasing power, it means that the cost of living rises. The **cost of living** is the amount of money you have to spend to obtain goods and services. Inflation is a persistent increase in the cost of living. Most people dislike inflation because they realize that they have to spend more money to acquire a given amount of goods and services.

Some countries have lived with rates of inflation of 200% and higher. In general, developed countries tend to have low inflation, while developing counties tend to have high inflation. It is reported that the rate of inflation in Zimbabwe in 2008 was 24 000%. In Canada, we have not had to cope with inflationary situations of the magnitude that many developing countries experience. Yet economists are aware of the dangers of high rates of inflation and are constantly seeking a better understanding of the inflationary process.

cost of living the amount of money that must be paid to obtain goods and services

Economic Growth Fourth is economic growth. The Canadian economy has experienced economic growth over the past several decades. Our economy is now producing more goods and services than it did in the 1960s and 1970s; consequently, our standard of living has increased. Economic growth requires not only that we use our resources efficiently but also that we increase our productive capacity over time. What are the factors that contribute most to economic growth? What can be done to achieve and maintain a prolonged period of economic growth? Clearly, economic growth has important benefits, but what are the costs? These are important questions that macroeconomics tries to answer.

The International Economy Last is the international economy. The Canadian economy does not exist in isolation. In fact, almost every economy in the world is affected by factors outside its own borders. The world economies have become more interdependent than ever before. Trading blocks have been formed and new trading blocks continue to be created. Globalization is now an economic reality. How do events in the rest of the world affect the Canadian economy? For example, when the price of crude oil hits a record high, does it have any effect on the Canadian economy? Will Canadian businesses be able to compete with businesses elsewhere in the world? Will Canadian producers be able to find markets in the rest of the world? Macroeconomics tries to find answers to such questions.

BUSINESS SITUATION 2.2

On October 27, 2006, Toronto-based Maple Leaf Foods Inc. blamed its third-quarter loss of $22.3 million in part on the higher Canadian dollar.

How might a strong Canadian dollar adversely affect Maple Leaf Foods?

The answer to this Business Situation can be found in Appendix A.

Reading Comprehension

The answers to these questions can be found on MyEconLab at www.myeconlab.com. MyEconLab

1. What are the fundamental microeconomic questions?
2. What do the following microeconomic questions refer to: what? how? and for whom?
3. Identify four important macroeconomic questions or issues and explain briefly why each is important.
4. Why would ordinary Canadians be interested in the cost of living?

LO 2.5 Construct a circular flow model and explain the flow of goods, services, and resources in the economy

The Simple Circular Flow Model

What is the circular flow model?

Businesses (we can call them firms) purchase resources (land, labour, capital, and entrepreneurship) and use them to produce goods and services for sale to their customers. The sellers of the resources receive income in the form of rent, wages and salaries, interest and dividends, and profits, which they use to purchase goods and services from the firms. The expenditures of the firms' customers accrue to the firms as their income or revenue, which they use to purchase resources; and the process continues. This flow of resources, goods and services, expenditures, and income between sectors of the economy is referred to as the **circular flow**.

circular flow an economic model that shows the flow of resources, goods and services, expenditures, and income between sectors of the economy

Can the circular flow model be illustrated by a diagram?

Let us make the following simplifying assumptions:

1. The economy consists of only two sectors: households and firms. **Households** make decisions about what resources to sell and what goods and services to buy. **Firms** make decisions about what resources to purchase and how the resources will be used to produce goods and services for sale to the households.
2. All the economy's resources are owned by the households.
3. Money is used in all exchanges. That is, firms use money to buy the factors of production, and households use money to buy goods and services.
4. The income received by households is spent in purchasing goods and services, and the income (revenue) received by firms is spent in purchasing resources.

households the economic sector that makes decisions about what resources to sell and what goods and services to buy

firms the economic sector that makes decisions about what resources to purchase and how the resources will be used to produce goods and services

Figure 2.9 illustrates the circular flow model. The sale of resources and the sale of goods and services take place in markets. A **market** is a mechanism that facilitates the buying and selling of resources and goods and services. You probably think of a market as a place where people buy and sell things. For example, you may have purchased your new Nike or Brooks running shoes in a market, and you purchased your last movie ticket in a market. Similarly, firms, such as the Bay, buy labour services in a market. But a market is not necessarily a geographic location. Today, many buying and selling activities take place without any physical meeting of the buyers and sellers. A great deal of buying and selling is done via airmail, telephone, and the internet. Let's study Figure 2.9.

market the mechanism that facilitates the buying and selling of resources and goods and services

Figure 2.9 The Circular Flow Diagram

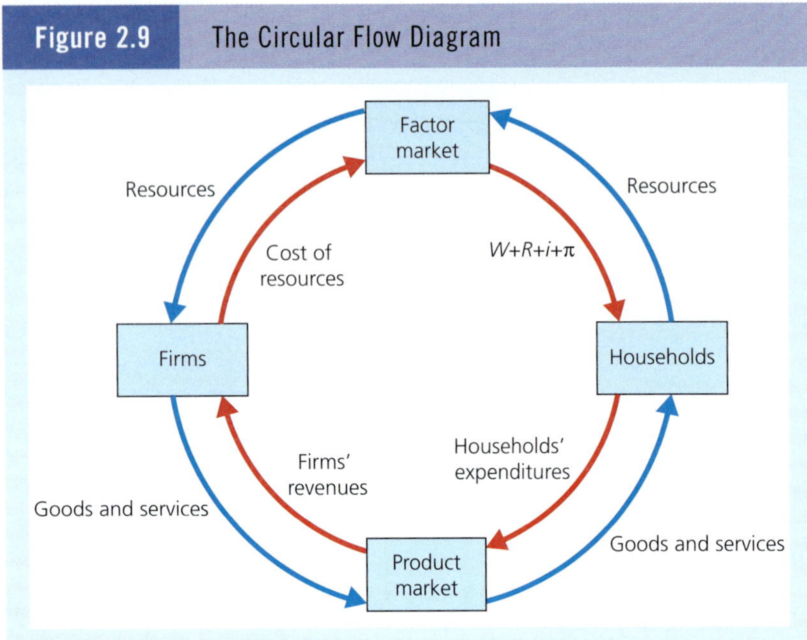

We can begin with the households because we have assumed that they have the resources. You will notice that resources flow from the households to the factor market. The direction of flow is indicated by arrows. The **factor market**, also called the **resource market**, is the market in which factors of production are traded (bought and sold). For example, firms buy steel and raw materials and labour services in the factor market.

Firms buy and households sell resources in the factor market. After the exchange of resources for money, we see a flow of resources from the factor market to the firms, and a flow of income from the factor market to the households. The flow of income from the factor market to the households consists of wages (W), rent (R), interest and dividends (i), and profits (π).

factor market or resource market the market in which factors of production are bought and sold

product market or goods and services market the market in which goods and services (products) are bought and sold

Now the firms have resources and the households have income (money). By the process of production, the firms convert the resources into goods and services, which they sell to households in the **product market**, also called the **goods and services market**, the market in which goods and services are bought and sold. For example, consumers buy clothes, vacations, furniture, and automobiles in product markets. You will notice a flow of goods and services from the firms to the product market, and a flow of expenditures from the households to the product market.

Firms sell and households buy goods and services in the product market. After the exchange of goods and services for money in the product market, we see a flow of goods and services from the product market to the households, and a flow of income (revenues) from the product market to the firms.

Note that the roles of buyers and sellers are reversed in the product and factor markets. In the factor market, the sellers are the households, while the buyers are the firms. In the product market, the sellers are the firms, while the buyers are the households.

What is the difference between real flows and money flows?

Let us look again at Figure 2.9. Look specifically at the flow of land, labour, capital, and entrepreneurship from households to the factor market, and at the flow of these resources from the factor market to the firms. Look also at the flow of goods and services from the firms to the product market, and at the flow of these goods and services from the product market to the households. Such flows are referred to as **real flows** and are the flows of real, physical goods and services, such as Blackberries, laser jet printers, refrigerators, and medical services, and resources such as plastic, water, machinery, and raw materials. Because of the way in which this diagram is arranged, these flows happen to be the outer flows in this model.

real flows flows of real, physical goods and services and resources

Look now at the flow of expenditure from the firms to the factor market, and at the flow of income (rent, wages and salaries, interest and dividends, and profits) from the factor market to the households. Look also at the flow of expenditures from the households to the product market, and at the flow of income or revenues from the product market to the firms. Such flows are referred to as **money flows** and are the flows of income and expenditures in monetary terms. Examples of money flows are $600 a week on groceries for a family, $6000 a year for college fees, $5000 a week that a firm spends in wages and $100 000 a year for office space. Because of the way in which this diagram is arranged, these flows happen to be the inner flows in this model. In this particular model, the money flows are the values of the real flows, or alternatively, the real flows are what can be bought with the money flows.

money flows flows of income and expenditures in monetary terms

Reading Comprehension

The answers to these questions can be found on MyEconLab at www.myeconlab.com. MyEconLab

1. Explain the roles of households and firms in the factor market and the product market. Give one example each of a product market and a factor market.
2. In the real world, earning a profit is associated with firms. Why, in the circular flow model, do households earn profits?
3. Distinguish between real flows and money flows. Give an example each of a real flow and a money flow in the circular flow model.

Review

1. Review the learning objectives listed at the beginning of the chapter.
2. Have you accomplished all the objectives? One way to determine this is to answer the Reading Comprehension questions at the end of each section. They will help you assess the extent to which you have accomplished the learning objectives.
3. If you have not accomplished an objective, review the relevant material before proceeding.

Key Points to Remember

1. LO 2.1 Because of scarcity, we are forced to choose, and when we choose, we give up something. Whatever it is that we give up when we make a choice is referred to as opportunity cost.
2. LO 2.2 Productive efficiency is the term used to describe the situation that exists when the economy is operating on its p-p curve. Productive inefficiency describes the situation that exists when the economy is operating below its p-p curve. A point beyond the p-p curve represents an unattainable combination of goods and services.
3. LO 2.2 If an economy is operating below its p-p curve and then moves to a point on the curve, it will produce additional commodities without having to give up any output. The additional output will be obtained at zero opportunity cost to the economy. That is the case of a free lunch.
4. LO 2.3 The p-p curve will shift if the quantity or quality of resources or the level of technology changes. An outward shift of the p-p curve is referred to as economic growth.
5. LO 2.4 The fundamental questions of microeconomics are (1) what goods and services are to be produced and in what quantities? (2) how will the goods and services be produced? That is, what method of production is to be employed in producing goods and services? (3) who will get the goods and services that the economy produces?
6. LO 2.4 Important macroeconomic questions include the following: What are the factors that determine the volume of goods and services that the economy produces and why does the economy sometimes experience wide fluctuations in aggregate output? Why does the economy

often fail to generate full employment? What causes inflation? What are the factors that contribute to economic growth? What is the relationship between the domestic economy and the international economy?

7. **LO 2.5** The circular flow model is an economic model that shows the flow of resources, goods and services, expenditures, and income between sectors of the economy. Households are the economic sector that makes decisions about what resources to sell and what goods and services to purchase. Firms are the economic sector that makes decisions about what resources to purchase and how to use them to produce goods and services.

Economic Word Power

Aggregate output (p. 59)
Business cycles (p. 59)
Circular flow (p. 61)
Cost of living (p. 60)
Cost-benefit approach (p. 50)
Economic growth (p. 56)
Factor market or resource market (p. 62)
Firms (p. 61)
Free lunch (p. 55)
Households (p. 61)
Inflation (p. 59)
Law of increasing opportunity cost (p. 53)
Market (p. 61)
Money flows (p. 63)
Opportunity cost (p. 48)
Product market or goods and services market (p. 62)
Production possibilities (p-p) curve (p. 52)
Production possibilities (p-p) schedule (p. 51)
Productive efficiency (p. 54)
Productive inefficiency (p. 54)
Real flows (p. 62)
Unemployment (p. 59)

Problems and Exercises

Basic

1. **LO 2.1** If you did not give up anything, you did not choose; hence, you did not incur any opportunity cost. Discuss.
2. **LO 2.1** Name an opportunity cost associated with each of the following choices:
   a. You decided to go to Europe during your vacation.
   b. You chose to purchase a used car for $8000.
   c. You watched a two-hour movie on television.
   d. You decided to eat out at a restaurant.
   e. You chose to spend two years at college.
3. **LO 2.2** Table 2.4 has information about an economy that produces only books and cartons with its available resources.

Table 2.4 A Production Possibilities Schedule for Books and Cartons

Combinations	Books (000)	Cartons (000)
A	0	10
B	1	9
C	2	7
D	3	4
E	4	0

   a. If the economy is producing only cartons and then decides to produce 1000 books, what is the opportunity cost of the 1000 books in terms of cartons?
   b. On the basis of the data contained in the table, draw the economy's production possibilities curve.
   c. On your diagram, indicate a point of productive inefficiency with the letter *U*.
   d. Indicate a point of full employment with the letter *F*.
   e. Indicate an unattainable combination of books and cartons with the letter *O*.
4. **LO 2.3** Show how each of the following events will affect a country's production possibilities curve:
   a. A large number of people emigrate from the country.
   b. The country discovers new resources.
   c. A more efficient method of production is discovered but not yet implemented.
   d. Unemployed workers are hired.
5. **LO 2.5** Indicate whether each of the following is true or false as it relates to the simple circular flow model with only households and firms:
   a. Firms sell resources to the households.
   b. The firms' income includes wages, rent, and interest.
   c. Firms sell their output in the product market.
   d. Households sell resources in the factor market.
   e. Households operate only in the product market, buying goods and services.
   f. Firms operate in both product and factor markets.

6. LO 2.3 An economy is producing only two goods, apples and butter, under conditions of increasing opportunity cost. Use diagrams to illustrate how each of the following will affect the economy's production possibilities curve:
   a. A technological improvement in the production of apples that does not affect butter production
   b. The discovery of new resources that affect the production of apples and butter equally
   c. A technological improvement in the production of butter that does not affect apple production
7. LO 2.5 Using *P* for the product market and *F* for the factor market, indicate the market in which the exchanges in Table 2.5 are likely to occur.

Table 2.5 Product and Factor Markets

Exchange	Market
a. A book publisher sells books to bookstores.	______
b. A book publisher buys paper from a firm.	______
c. The government buys furniture from a firm.	______
d. Businesses borrow money from banks.	______
e. A government employs new civil servants.	______
f. Households buy electrical appliances.	______

Questions in the Intermediate and Challenging Sections cover several different concepts, and have not been organized by learning objectives.

Intermediate

1. In the circular flow diagram in Figure 2.10, the inner flows are money flows, while the outer flows are real flows. The arrows indicate the direction of the flows. *H* represents households and *F* represents firms.
   a. In the spaces below, list the items that make up the inner flow from the factor market to the households.

   ____

   ____

   ____

   ____

   b. On the diagram, label the flows shown by the letters.
2. An economy produces only two goods: capital goods and consumer goods. Its production possibilities curve is shown in Figure 2.11. The economy has a choice of operating at point A or point B. At which point should this economy operate if economic growth is a high priority?
3. Use the concept of opportunity cost to explain why attendance at colleges and universities might increase during periods of high unemployment and job shortages.
4. There would be no need to choose if scarcity did not exist. Discuss.
5. Indicate whether the following statement is true or false and give the reason for your choice: "An outward shift of an economy's p-p curve means that the economy is actually producing a greater quantity of goods and/or services."

Figure 2.10 A Simple Circular Flow Model

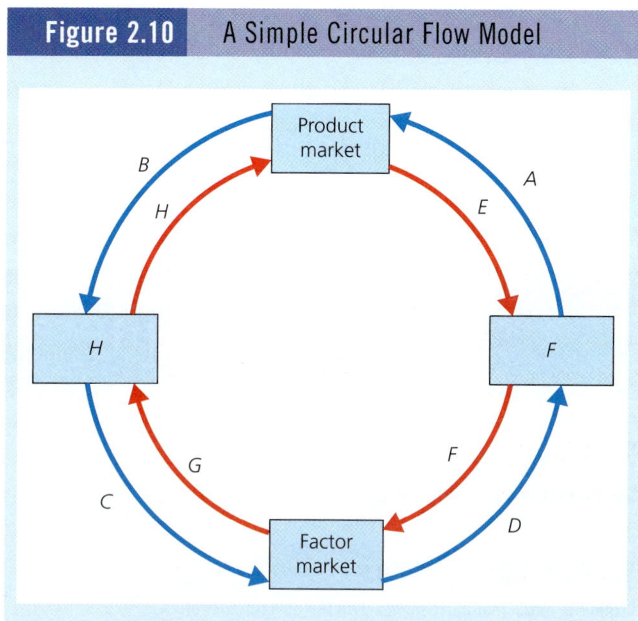

Figure 2.11 A Production Possibilities Curve

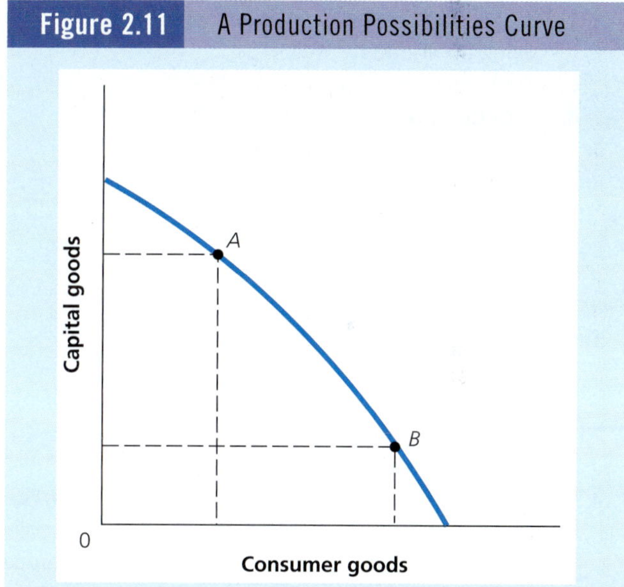

Challenging

1. Explain why, other things being equal, a business executive would be less willing than would his or her administrative assistant to stand in line at a supermarket for 10 minutes. (Hint: Use the concept of opportunity cost.)
2. Use production possibilities curves to illustrate the effect of capital formation now and five years in the future, for two countries, one with a relatively high and the other with a relatively low rate of capital formation.

MyEconLab Visit the MyEconLab website at **www.myeconlab.com.** This online homework and tutorial system puts you in control of your own learning with study and practice tools directly correlated to this chapter's content.

Study Guide

Self-Assessment

The answers to the Study Guide questions can be found in Appendix B.

What's your score?

Circle the letter that corresponds with the correct answer.

1. Choice involves
   a. Taking something without giving up anything
   b. Giving up nothing
   c. Giving up something
   d. All of the above

2. The opportunity cost of an item is
   a. The market price of the item
   b. The monetary cost of the resources used to produce the item
   c. The profit realized from the sale of the item
   d. None of the above

3. Opportunity cost
   a. Exists in theory but not in practice
   b. Exists in practice but not in theory
   c. Exists both in theory and in practice
   d. Is always zero when it exists

4. The cost-benefit approach to decision making involves
   a. Adding together all benefits and costs
   b. Making sure that opportunity costs are not included in decision making
   c. Reducing opportunity costs to zero
   d. Comparing benefits and costs

5. A production possibilities curve shows
   a. All combinations of goods and services consumed in the economy
   b. The total value of all goods and services produced in the economy
   c. All possible ways of producing goods and services
   d. The boundary between combinations of goods and services that are attainable through production and those that are unattainable

6. A linear production possibilities curve implies
   a. Constant opportunity cost
   b. Increasing opportunity cost
   c. Zero opportunity cost
   d. None of the above

7. A production possibilities curve showing increasing opportunity cost is
   a. Linear and upward sloping
   b. Linear and downward sloping
   c. Convex and downward sloping
   d. None of the above

8. Which of the following will cause a country's p-p curve to shift to the right?
   a. The country acquires more resources
   b. The country increases production by hiring previously unemployed workers
   c. Prices in the country fall
   d. All of the above

9. The phenomenon of rising unit production cost as an economy produces more of an item is called
   a. The law of production possibilities
   b. The law of alternative production
   c. The law of no free lunch
   d. The law of increasing opportunity cost

10. A production possibilities diagram shows all of the following except
   a. Opportunity cost
   b. Price
   c. Scarcity
   d. Choice

11. A situation in which the economy cannot produce more of one commodity without producing less of some other commodity is labelled
   a. Production inability
   b. A state of unattainability
   c. Productive inefficiency
   d. Productive efficiency

Questions 12 and 13 refer to Figure 2.12.

12. According to the diagram, the economy is facing
   a. Constant opportunity cost
   b. Zero opportunity
   c. Increasing opportunity cost
   d. It is impossible to tell

Figure 2.12 A Production Possibilities Curve

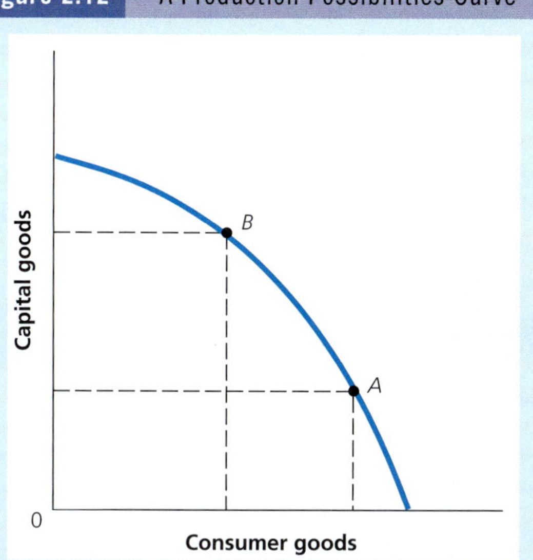

13. If the economy decides to move from point *A* to point *B*
   a. The opportunity cost would be zero
   b. The opportunity cost would be increased production of capital goods
   c. The production possibilities curve would shift to the right in the future
   d. The production possibilities curve would shift to the left in the future

14. The *what* in what, how, and for whom refers to
   a. The price to charge for an item to make the most money
   b. The technology to use to produce goods and services
   c. What to do with the goods and services that have been produced
   d. None of the above

15. The microeconomic questions of *what, how,* and *for whom* arise because of
   a. Scarcity
   b. Poor economic decisions
   c. An overabundance of resources in the economy
   d. All of the above

16. The microeconomic question of *what* refers to
   a. What cost will be incurred in producing goods and services
   b. What method of production will be used in producing goods and services
   c. What resources are available to produce goods and services
   d. What goods and services will be produced and in what quantities

17. Which of the following is not a macroeconomic question?
   a. What determines the aggregate output of goods and services produced in an economy?
   b. What prices should a firm charge for its product to maximize its profits?
   c. What determines the level of unemployment in the economy?
   d. Why does aggregate output fluctuate?

18. When the dollar loses value
   a. The cost of living rises
   b. The cost of living falls
   c. Most people are better off
   d. Only the poor are adversely affected

19. Which of the following is a true statement?
   a. The factor market is the market in which firms buy goods and services
   b. The product market is the market in which firms sell resources
   c. The product market is the market in which households buy resources
   d. The factor market is the market in which firms buy resources

20. Flows of income and expenditures are
   a. Real flows
   b. Money flows
   c. Normative flows
   d. None of the above

Problems and Exercises (Use Quad Paper for Graphs)

Answers to these questions can be found on MyEconLab at www.myeconlab.com. MyEconLab

1. Table 2.6 shows various combinations of television sets and radios that an economy can produce with a given technology and full utilization of all its resources.

Table 2.6 The Possible Production of Maximum Quantities of TV Sets and Radios

Quantity of TV Sets (000)	Quantity of Radios (000)
0	37
1	35
2	32
3	29
4	20
5	11
6	0

   a. On the basis of Table 2.6, complete Table 2.7 showing the opportunity cost of TV sets in terms of radios.
   b. Determine whether this economy faces constant or increasing opportunity cost in producing TV sets. Explain.

2. a. Draw a production possibilities curve showing increasing opportunity cost.
   b. On your diagram, indicate a point of unemployment with the letter *U*.

c. Indicate a point of productive efficiency with the letter *E*.
d. Indicate an unattainable production combination with the letter *x*.

Table 2.7 The Opportunity Cost of TV Sets

TV Sets	Opportunity Cost in Radios
First 1 000 TV sets	________
Second 1 000 TV sets	________
Third 1 000 TV sets	________
Fourth 1 000 TV sets	________
Fifth 1 000 TV sets	________
Sixth 1 000 TV sets	________

3. An economy produces only two goods: furniture and tours around the country. Assume that the economy operates under conditions of increasing opportunity cost. Use graphs to show how each of the following events will affect the country's production possibilities curve:
   a. A number of immigrants take up residence in the country
   b. A fall in prices causes consumers to buy more goods and services
   c. People migrate to the country but are unable to find work
   d. Research leads to the discovery of a more efficient method of production
   e. Employment increases because firms hire more workers to meet increasing demand for their products
4. Referring to Question 3, draw a production possibilities diagram illustrating the effect of a technological advance that affects only the furniture industry.
5. An economy hires five previously unemployed workers and pays them $400 per week each. What is the opportunity cost of the extra output produced by these five new workers?
6. Table 2.8 shows production possibilities for a hypothetical economy.

Table 2.8 Production Possibilities

Number of Word Processors (000)	Number of Calculators (000)
0	15
1	14
2	12
3	9
4	5
5	0

   a. What is the table called?
   b. Plot the points on a graph and connect them.
   c. What is the graph called?
   d. Does this economy face constant or increasing opportunity cost?
7. A small country produces only two goods: shoes and corn. Various combinations of maximum quantities of shoes and corn that the country can produce are shown in Table 2.9.

Table 2.9 The Production Possibilities for Corn and Shoes

Quantities of Corn (000 metric tons)	Quantities of Shoes (000 pairs)
100	0
90	10
70	20
40	30
0	40

   a. With thousands of metric tons of corn on the vertical axis and thousands of pairs of shoes on the horizontal axis, plot the data in the table on a graph.
   b. What is the opportunity cost of the first 10 000 pairs of shoes?
   c. What is the opportunity cost of the third 10 000 pairs of shoes?
   d. What is the opportunity cost of 40 000 pairs of shoes?
8. Complete Table 2.10 by indicating whether each of the following is a major microeconomic or macroeconomic issue.

Table 2.10 Major Microeconomic and Macroeconomic Issues

Issue	Classification
What to produce	________
Fluctuations in total output	________
How to combine resources in production	________
Increases in the cost of living	________
The level of employment in the economy	________
The distribution of output among consumers	________

9. Construct a simple circular flow model with only households and firms. Indicate the following:
   a. The product market
   b. The factor market
   c. The flow of resources
   d. The flow of expenditures
   e. The flow of income
   f. The flow of products (goods and services)

Chapter 3

Demand, Supply, and Prices: Basic Concepts

Learning Objectives

After studying this chapter, you should be able to

- **3.1** Describe the market process and distinguish between demand and quantity demanded
- **3.2** State the law of demand and explain the shape of the demand curve
- **3.3** Identify the factors affecting quantity demanded
- **3.4** Distinguish between a change in demand and a change in quantity demanded
- **3.5** Distinguish between supply and quantity supplied
- **3.6** State the law of supply and explain the shape of the supply curve
- **3.7** Identify the factors affecting quantity supplied
- **3.8** Distinguish between a change in supply and a change in quantity supplied
- **3.9** Explain market price determination and the effects of changes in demand and supply

Assess Your Knowledge

MyEconLab

Answers to these questions can be found on MyEconLab at **www.myeconlab.com.**

1. A large segment of the population wants small, fuel-efficient cars. Does this constitute a demand for small, fuel-efficient cars?
2. Indicate whether the following statement is true or false: "The lower the price of an item, the greater the quantity that sellers will offer for sale."
3. Which of the following factors will affect the quantity of an item that people will buy?
   a. The cost of producing the item
   b. The average income of the buyers
   c. The technology used to produce the item
   d. All of the above
4. What is a shortage?
5. If the demand for an item increases and nothing else changes, then we can expect
   a. A fall in the price
   b. An increase in the price
   c. No change in the price
   d. The price to rise and then fall

LO 3.1 Describe the market process and distinguish between demand and quantity demanded

The Market Process

In Chapter 2, we defined a market as a mechanism that facilitates the exchange of goods and services between buyers and sellers. For a market to exist, the following must be present:

- At least one buyer
- At least one seller
- A product (good or service)
- A price

Buyers and sellers are the players in the market. The buying and selling decisions of the players are reflected in their behaviour in the market. This chapter discusses behaviour in markets that are competitive; these markets have so many buyers and sellers that no one can individually exert any influence on the price.

The market process is the process by which buyers and sellers exchange goods and services. In a free enterprise system, such as ours, prices play a crucial role in determining the flow of goods and services between buyers and sellers. You will see shortly that demand and supply are at the heart of the market process.

Demand analyzes the behaviour of buyers. It deals with the buyers' side of the market.

What exactly do economists mean by *demand*?

Think of something for which you are ready to pay a lot of money. Your demand for that thing would be high. If you are not ready to pay any money for something, then you have no demand for that thing. Thus, it is possible to desire or want something without having a demand for it.

Are you saying there is a difference between demand and want?

demand the various quantities of a good or service that people are willing and able to buy at various prices during a specific period

There is a difference between demand and want. No matter how much you want something, if you are not willing and able to spend money to buy it, then your wants will be ineffective. In economics, demand has a very specific meaning. Let us look at the economic definition of **demand**: the various quantities of a good or service that people are willing and able to buy at various possible prices during a specific period.

We should note the following points in this definition:

1. Demand is not a particular *quantity* that people will buy at a specific price. Rather, it is a series of quantities with their associated prices.
2. Demand is a *flow* rather than a stock concept. It has a time dimension.
3. Demand requires both the willingness and the ability to buy, not just the desire.

It sounds as if you are saying that demand is a functional relationship between price and quantity. Is that correct?

demand schedule a table showing the inverse relationship between price and quantity demanded

That is correct. In economics, demand is a functional relationship between the various possible prices of an item and the various quantities of the item that people would buy. We can show this relationship in a **demand schedule**, a table showing the inverse relationship between price and quantity demanded. It shows the various quantities of a good or service that people will be willing and able to buy at various prices during a specific period, and it is a tabular representation of demand.

Table 3.1 shows the various quantities of USB flash drives per week that people will be willing and able to buy at various prices.

So it is the entire schedule that represents demand?

That's right. Demand is not a specific quantity that people will be willing and able to buy at a specific price. It is all the quantities with their associated prices—the entire schedule.

OK. It's clear so far. But what is the name given to a particular quantity that people will be willing and able to buy at a specific price? For example, at a price of $8, people will be willing and able to buy 60 000 flash drives per week. What do we call the 60 000 if it is not demand?

quantity demanded the quantity that people will be willing and able to buy at a specific price

The quantity that people will be willing and able to buy at a specific price is referred to as **quantity demanded**. Thus, at a price of $8, the quantity demanded (not the demand) is 60 000, and at a price of $4, the quantity demanded (not the demand) is 100 000. We will return several times to this very important distinction between demand and quantity demanded. While we are discussing quantity demanded, note the importance of the time period. For example, to say that the quantity of flash drives demanded at a price of $4 is 100 000 is somewhat unclear. To say that the quantity of flash drives demanded at a price of $4 is 100 000 a

Table 3.1 A Hypothetical Demand Schedule for USB Flash Drives

Price of USB Flash Drives ($)	Quantity demanded per week (000 packs)
10	40
9	50
8	60
7	70
6	80
5	90
4	100

week has much more meaning. Buying 100 000 flash drives at $4 each in one week is certainly not the same as buying the same quantity at the same price in a year. The quantities demanded at various prices are per unit of time (per week, per month, per year, etc.).

Are we talking about an individual's demand for an item or the total (market) demand for the item?

It is important to be able to distinguish between individual demand and market demand. Here, we are talking about the total or market demand for a good or service. It consists of all the buyers in the market for that particular good or service. The individual consumer's demand for a good or service is an important microeconomic topic.

BUSINESS SITUATION 3.1

An entrepreneur observed an increase in the number of people buying laptop computers. He concluded that this was evidence of an increase in demand for laptop computers and so thought of increasing his stock of laptops. His economic consultant cautioned that he could be mistaken.

What might the consultant have had in mind?

The answer to this Business Situation can be found in Appendix A.

Reading Comprehension

The answers to these questions can be found on MyEconLab at www.myeconlab.com. MyEconLab

1. List the four elements that must be present for a market to exist.
2. What is the market process?
3. What is the difference between demand and want?
4. "There can be want without demand, but there cannot be demand without want." Discuss briefly.
5. What is the difference between demand and quantity demanded?

LO 3.2 State the law of demand and explain the shape of the demand curve

The Law of Demand

It seems logical that as the price of an item falls, a greater quantity will be demanded. Is this characteristic of demand?

law of demand a statement of the inverse relationship between price and quantity demanded

In fact, it is. The fact that a greater quantity is demanded at a lower price is so universal that it is called the **law of demand** and can be stated as follows:

> As the price of a good or service falls, other things being equal, the quantity demanded increases; as the price of a good or service rises, other things being equal, the quantity demanded decreases.

Note that the law of demand does not say that if the price of an item falls, the quantity demanded will rise, and vice versa. It says that if the price falls and nothing else changes (other things being equal), then the quantity demanded will rise. So if the price of an item falls, and consumers' incomes also fall, they may not buy more of the item. This would not violate or negate the law of demand, because other things were not equal. This is an important point to remember. Price performs a rationing function, because higher prices discourage people from using scarce goods and services.

Can this response to a price change be explained beyond saying that it makes sense?

The inverse relationship between price and quantity demanded (as price goes up, quantity demanded goes down) has three explanations: (1) the market-size effect, (2) the income effect, and (3) the substitution effect. The specific question that we are trying to answer is this: Why do people buy more USB flash drives as the price falls? Let us examine each of the explanations.

The Market-Size Effect At a price of $10 per flash drive, some people would not buy any. But as the price of flash drives falls to $9, some of those people will enter the market and purchase some flash drives at the lower price. Thus, as the price falls, more and more people are drawn into the market. In other words, as the price falls, the size of the market increases, thus the quantity of flash drives demanded increases. More people buy the item as its price falls. We can call this the **market-size effect**, a term first introduced in 1994 by your author, Elijah James (1938–).

market-size effect the effect on quantity demanded caused by a change in the number of buyers in the market as a result of a change in price

The Real Income Effect Suppose you have $20 to buy flash drives this week. Suppose also that the price of a flash drive is $10. You will be able to buy two of them with your $20. If the price of flash drives falls to $5, you can now buy four instead of two. Your purchasing power (or **real income**) has increased. Even if you still have only $20, it can now buy more flash drives. When the price of an item falls, other things being equal, the people who buy that item experience an increase in purchasing power or real income, so they buy more—people buy more of the item as its price falls. This increase in quantity demanded resulting from an increase in the buyers' real income is referred to as the real income effect.

real income purchasing power

The real income effect also works in reverse. When prices rise, other things being equal, peoples' real income falls, so they buy a smaller quantity of the item whose price has risen. The real income effect, which is also called the **income effect**, is the effect on quantity demanded caused by the change in purchasing power resulting from a change in price.

income effect the effect on quantity demanded caused by the change in purchasing power resulting from a change in price

The Substitution Effect When the price of flash drives falls, some people will switch from other items (perhaps external hard drives) that they were previously purchasing but that have now become relatively more expensive. That is, some people will substitute the cheaper flash drive for some other data storage device. This change in quantity demanded caused by people switching to or from a product as its price changes is often referred to as the **substitution effect**.

substitution effect the effect on quantity demanded caused by people switching to or from a product as its price changes

Figure 3.1 The Demand Curve for Flash Drives

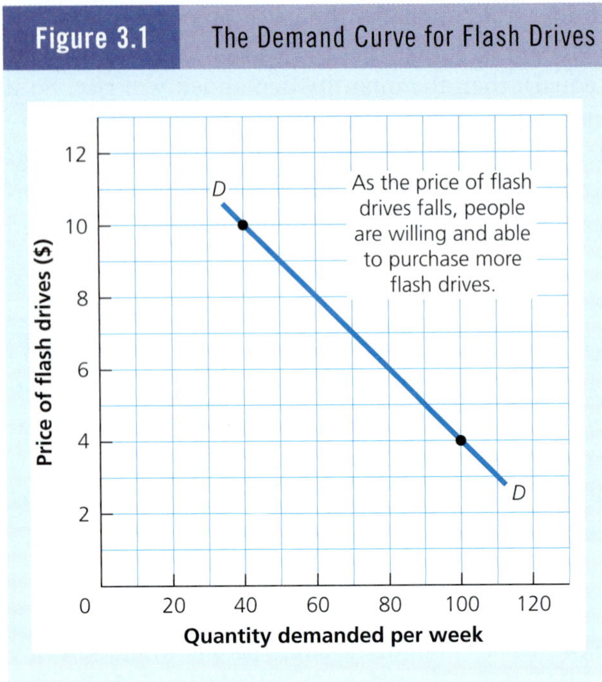

For these three reasons (the market-size effect, the real income effect, and the substitution effect), we might reasonably expect buyers to purchase a greater quantity of a good or service as its price falls, or alternatively, to buy less as its price rises, other things being equal.

What would be the result if we plot the information in Table 3.1 on a graph?

It has become common practice in economics to measure price on the vertical axis and quantity demanded per unit of time on the horizontal axis. The information in the demand schedule (Table 3.1) is plotted on a graph shown as Figure 3.1. Economists refer to this curve as a **demand curve**, which is a downward-sloping curve that shows the inverse relationship between price and quantity demanded, or the various quantities of a good or service that people will be willing and able to buy at various prices.

It is the inverse relationship between price and quantity demanded (the law of demand) that causes the demand curve to slope downward and to the right, as shown by *DD* in Figure 3.1.

The concept of demand can be illustrated graphically by a demand curve.

demand curve a downward-sloping curve showing the inverse relationship between price and quantity demanded

Can the demand curve be used to illustrate the difference between demand and quantity demanded?

When we studied the demand schedule earlier, we indicated that a particular quantity that people would be willing and able to buy at a particular price was called quantity demanded, while the entire schedule represented demand. Now let's look at Figure 3.1. At a price of $10 per flash drive, people would be willing and able to buy 40 000. This 40 000 is a quantity demanded at a price of $10. It is a point on the demand curve. Similarly, at a price of $4 per flash drive, the quantity demanded is 100 000. This 100 000 is a quantity demanded at a price of $4 and is another point on the demand curve. We can conclude that quantity demanded is represented by a point on the demand curve, while demand is represented by the entire demand curve.

In the demand curve and also in the demand schedule, the relationship between price and quantity is linear. Does this mean that demand curves are always linear?

No. The linear relationship is used for convenience only. In fact, it's unlikely that demand curves will be linear. People are unlikely to adjust their purchases in constant proportion to changes in price. Figure 3.2 shows a demand curve for cases of soap that is non-linear. When the price of a case of soap is $250, the quantity demanded is 20 cases. When the price falls to $125, the quantity demanded rises to 60 cases, and when the price falls to $50, the quantity demanded increases to 170 cases. At this point, the important thing to note about the shape of the demand curve is that it is downward sloping.

Figure 3.2 A Non-linear Demand Curve

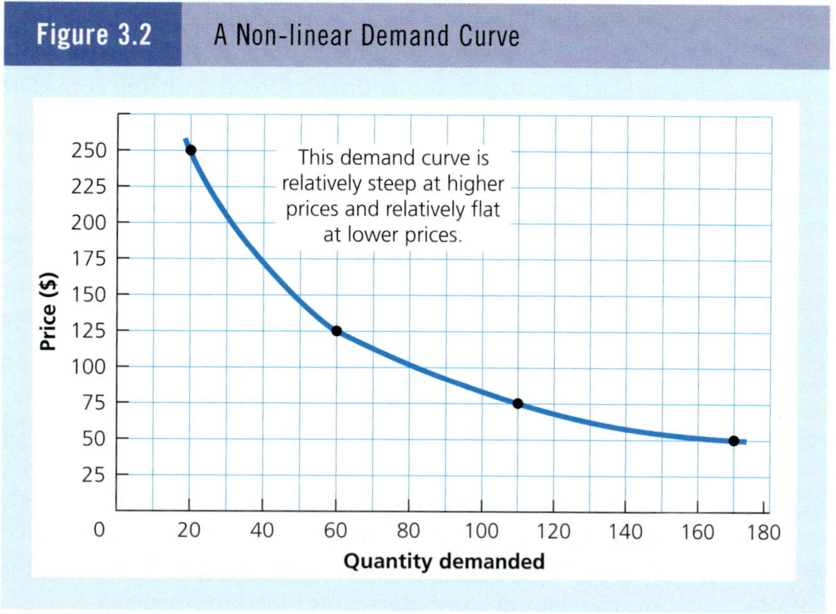

Reading Comprehension

The answers to these questions can be found on MyEconLab at www.myeconlab.com. MyEconLab

1. "A greater quantity of an item will be demanded at a lower price?" Is anything wrong with that statement of the law of demand? If something is wrong with it, restate it so that it is true.
2. Briefly explain each of the following:
   a) The market-size effect
   b) The real income effect
   c) The substitution effect
3. Why does a fall in price increase real income?
4. Why is the typical demand curve downward sloping?

LO 3.3 Identify the factors affecting quantity demanded

Factors Affecting Demand

What are the main factors that affect the demand for a good or service?

We have seen that when the price of a good or service changes, other things being equal, the quantity demanded (not demand) also changes. This is the law of demand. But we must deal with your question. What are the main factors that affect the demand for a good or service? They are as follows:

- Income
- Prices of related goods
- Tastes and preferences
- Expectations
- Population

Because the factors listed above do not include the price of the good or service under consideration, we can refer to them as *non-price determinants* of demand. *Non-price* means anything other than the price of the item being considered. Therefore, the prices of related goods are included in the category of non-price determinants, because they are factors other than the price of the item being considered.

How does each of these factors affect demand?

Let us deal with each in order.

Consumers' Income If consumers' incomes increase, they will tend to buy more goods and services than they did before the increase in their incomes. Think about it for a moment. Let's consider the effect that an increase in income will have on the demand for cellphones. Suppose people were buying 3000 cellphones each week when the price was $45 per cellphone. If their incomes increase, they may find that they can now afford to purchase 3500 cellphones at the same price without having to buy less of anything else. As income increases, then, it seems likely that more of a given item will be purchased at any given price. This is the case for most goods and services; hence, economists refer to goods for which demand increases as income increases and for which demand falls as income falls as **normal goods**. For most people, normal goods Blu-ray movies, laptop computers, and vacation packages.

normal goods good for which demand increases as income increases and for which demand falls as income falls

Are some goods not *normal*?

Although most goods are normal goods, for some goods, people do not buy more as their incomes rise. Instead, they may buy less. Let us consider regular ground beef. If the price of regular ground beef is $6.50 per kilogram, at any given level of income, people will buy a certain amount per week. If these people's incomes increase, they may actually reduce their purchases of regular ground beef and buy steaks or lean ground beef instead. Thus, as income rises, people may buy less, not more, regular ground beef. Economists refer to goods for which demand decreases as income increases and for which demand increases as income falls as **inferior goods**. Examples might be drink mixes, such as Kool-Aid (instead of real fruit juices), macaroni and cheese (instead of restaurant dinners), beans (instead of meat), and used clothing (instead of new clothes).

inferior goods goods for which demand decreases as income increases and for which demand increases as income falls

Is it accurate to say that normal goods are necessarily "better" than inferior goods?

Not really. The distinction made between normal and inferior goods does not imply any value judgment about the items. It is better to think of the terms normal and inferior as the economist's jargon for describing buyers' behaviour or reaction to a change in income rather than as descriptions of the goods per se.

How are goods related?

Prices of Related Goods Goods and services can be related to each other in two main ways: they may be substitutes or they may be complements. One good is said to be a **substitute** for a second good if it can be used in place of the second good. Examples of goods that are substitutes for each other are lemons and limes, sugar and honey, butter and margarine, tea and coffee, and e-readers such as Kindle or Kobo and paper books. Two goods are said to be **complements** if one is used in conjunction with the other (they are consumed or used together). Complementary goods are demanded jointly. If you buy more of one, you are likely to buy more of the other also. Examples of complementary goods (complements) are automobiles and gasoline, Blu-ray movies

substitute a good that can be used in place of another

complements goods that are consumed (used) together

and Blu-ray players, computers and flash drives, flashlights and batteries, and coffee and cream.

Think about goods that are substitutes (perhaps Pepsi and Coke). If the price of Pepsi were to increase, people would tend to switch to a substitute (Coke, for example). Hence, the demand for Coke would increase. In general, if the price of an item increases, the demand for its substitute will increase.

Let us now consider the case of complements and think of coffee and cream. If the price of coffee falls, people will buy more coffee and, as a consequence, the demand for cream will tend to increase. In general, if the price of an item falls, people will tend to purchase more of an item that is its complement.

Can we claim that all goods are related?

independent goods goods that are not related

That claim would be difficult to justify. Some goods are neither substitute goods nor complementary goods. For example, we would not expect any relationship between automobiles and oranges, computers and winter jackets, or cellphones and baseball bats. Goods, such as those just listed, that are not related are said to be **independent goods**. If the price of cellphones increases, we can hardly expect it to have any effect on the demand for baseball bats.

BUSINESS SITUATION 3.2

An office supply store sells computers and USB flash drives. One of the store's suppliers of computers has offered the store a large quantity of computers at a 30% discount on the regular cost.

How might this store use its inexpensive computers to boost its sales of flash drives?

The answer to this Business Situation can be found in Appendix A.

The more you like something, the more of it you will buy at any given price. Right?

Tastes and Preferences That's correct. Tastes and preferences refer to people's "liking" for things. For example, a more favourable attitude toward exercise is an increase in taste (or preference) for exercise. People will "buy" more exercise (more people will pay to use gym facilities) if their preference for exercise increases. If health concerns about eating meat cause people's tastes to change from meat to vegetable diets, then it is obvious that the demand for vegetables will increase. Businesses spend millions of dollars in advertising in an attempt to influence people's tastes and preferences in favour of their products. By so doing, these firms are trying to increase the demand for their products.

Expectations do influence behaviour, but what kind of expectations are we discussing?

Expectations Expectations are future oriented. In this particular context, we are discussing price and income expectations. People's expectations regarding the course of future prices will affect present demand for goods and services. If people expect the price of an item to rise, they are likely to increase their purchases of that item now to

As Canada's population grows, the demand for most goods and services also grows.

avoid paying the expected higher price in the future. They may even stock up on the item and thus postpone paying the ensuing higher price for as long as possible. Conversely, if the price of an item is expected to fall, people will attempt to delay their purchases of the item now to take advantage of the lower future price.

That's clear. How about expected future income now?

People's expectations about future changes in their incomes will also affect the present demand for goods and services. If people expect substantial raises in their salaries sometime in the near future, they are likely to buy more goods and services even before the increase in income materializes. If people expect decreases in their income (resulting from loss of employment, for example), they are likely to buy fewer goods and services. Thus, the demand for an item will increase if future income is expected to rise and fall if future income is expected to fall.

So with expectations, people respond to expected changes in future prices and expected changes in future incomes, rather than to actual changes in prices and income. Is that correct?

That is absolutely right. You have grasped the idea.

Now, this is common sense. The more people a market for an item has, the greater the demand for that item will be. Isn't that the idea?

Population That is the idea. The quantity of an item that people will buy depends on the number of buyers in the market for that particular item. Other things being equal, we would expect the demand for oranges in Toronto, Ontario, to be significantly higher than the demand for oranges in Corner Brook, Newfoundland and Labrador, because Toronto has many more buyers than does Corner Brook. If the number of buyers increases, the demand for an item will increase.

Reading Comprehension

The answers to these questions can be found on MyEconLab at **www.myeconlab.com.** MyEconLab

1. List the main factors that are likely to affect the quantity of home movies rented in a month.
2. What are normal goods? Give three specific examples of normal goods.
3. What are inferior goods? Give three specific examples of inferior goods.
4. What is the difference between substitutes and complements in consumption? What effect will a decrease in the price of inkjet printers have on the demand for inkjet cartridges?

LO 3.4 Distinguish between a change in demand and a change in quantity demanded

A Change in Demand versus a Change in Quantity Demanded

The terms change in demand and change in quantity demanded are used differently. Are they different concepts?

Yes, they are different concepts and we should be careful not to confuse them. When economists speak of demand, they are referring to the entire demand curve or schedule. It follows, then, that if demand changes, the entire demand curve will shift (that is, change its position). Suppose the demand for flash drives was as shown in the first two columns of Table 3.2, but that the demand for flash drives increases because the government has introduced a new program that makes it less costly for people to own computers.

Table 3.2 A Demand Schedule Showing an Increase in Demand

Price of Flash Drives ($)	**Original Quantity Demanded per Week** (000 packs)	**New Quantity Demanded per Week** (000)
10	40	60
9	50	70
8	60	80
7	70	90
6	80	100
5	90	110
4	100	120

Figure 3.3 An Increase in Demand

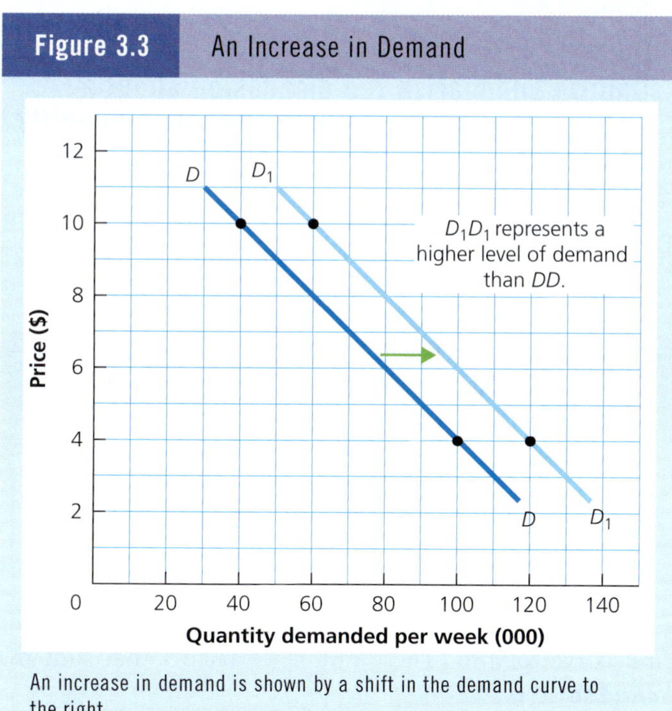

An increase in demand is shown by a shift in the demand curve to the right.

As a consequence of the government's program, we will obtain a new demand schedule showing that a greater quantity of flash drives will be purchased at each price. The new quantities are shown in the right-hand column of Table 3.2. Notice that people buy more flash drives not because of a fall in the price of flash drives, but because they are buying more computers. This is an increase in the demand for flash drives.

What would a graph of these demand schedules look like?

We can plot these two demand schedules on the same graph to illustrate the shift in demand brought about by the government's program. Figure 3.3 shows this.

An increase in demand is shown by a shift in the demand curve to the right. Is that correct?

DD is the original demand curve; D_1D_1 is the new demand curve. The increase in demand is shown

Figure 3.4 A Decrease in Demand

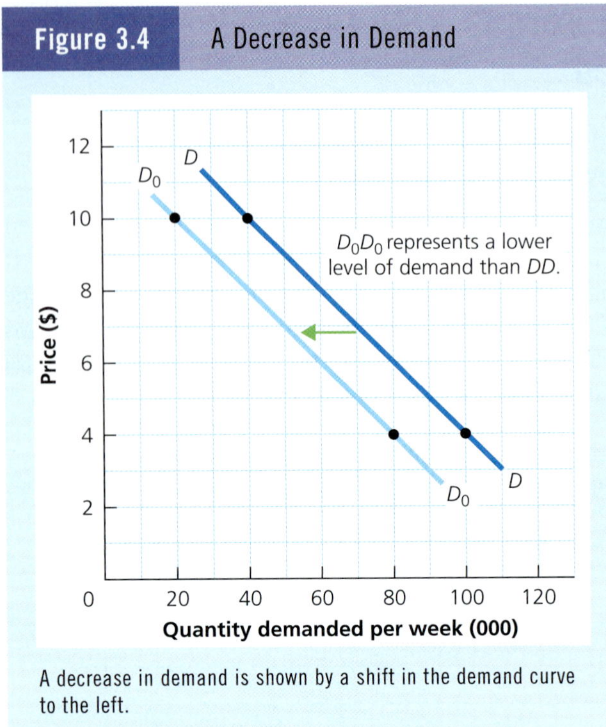

A decrease in demand is shown by a shift in the demand curve to the left.

Figure 3.5 A Change in Quantity Demanded

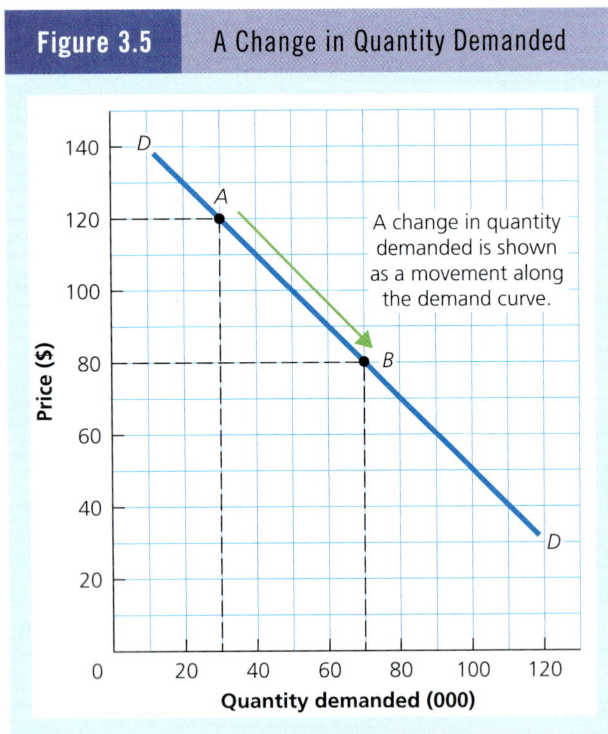

by shifting the entire demand curve to the right of the original demand curve. The location of the demand curve has now changed. Note that at any given price, a greater quantity is purchased. A decrease in demand for flash drives (caused perhaps by the development of a better data storage device for computers) would mean that at any given price for flash drives, a smaller quantity would be purchased. This decrease in demand would be represented by a leftward shift in the demand curve, as shown in Figure 3.4, where the demand curve shifts from DD to D_0D_0.

So a change in demand is shown by shifting the entire demand curve, either to the right (for an increase) or to the left (for a decrease). How do we show a change in quantity demanded on a graph?

A change in quantity demanded refers to the change in the quantity that would be bought as a result of a change in price. Let us examine the demand curve for cellphones shown in Figure 3.5.

At a price of $120 for cellphones, the quantity demanded is 30 000 per week. If the price falls to $80, a quantity of 70 000 per week will be demanded. This change in quantity demanded is represented by a movement along the same demand curve from point *A* to point *B* in Figure 3.5.

Can we summarize the discussion about a change in demand versus a change in quantity demanded?

> A change in the price of the commodity under consideration will not cause a change in the demand for the commodity; it will cause a change in quantity demanded, shown as a movement along the demand curve. Only a change in a non-price determinant can cause a change in the demand for that commodity. Such factors as a change in income, a change in taste, a change in population, a change in the price of a related good, or a change in expectations will cause a change in demand—that is, they will cause the entire demand curve to shift.

demand shifters the non-price determinants that shift the demand curve

Table 3.3 presents a convenient list of the major factors that cause the demand curve to shift. These non-price factors that shift the demand curve are called **demand shifters**.

Table 3.3 Demand Shifters: Non-price Factors That Change the Location of the Demand Curve

Demand Shifters	Illustrative Examples
1. A change in income	An increase in income increases purchasing power. The demand for most goods (normal goods) will increase, but the demand for inferior goods (used tires, for example) will decrease.
2. A change in the prices of related goods	An increase in the price of Coke will increase the demand for Pepsi because related goods of they are substitutes. A decrease in the price of computers will increase the demand for disks because they are complements.
3. A change in tastes and preferences	A successful advertising campaign for eggs increases the demand for eggs because it changes buyers' tastes in favour of eggs.
4. A change in expectations	The announcement of the imposition of a tax on DVDs produces expectations of higher future prices and this increases the current demand for DVDs.
5. A change in population	An increase in the number of immigrants entering Canada increases the demand for furniture.

Can you provide graphs showing the effects of some of the demand shifters?

Yes. Let's do so in Figure 3.6.

Figure 3.6 The Factors That Shift the Demand Curve (Demand Shifters)

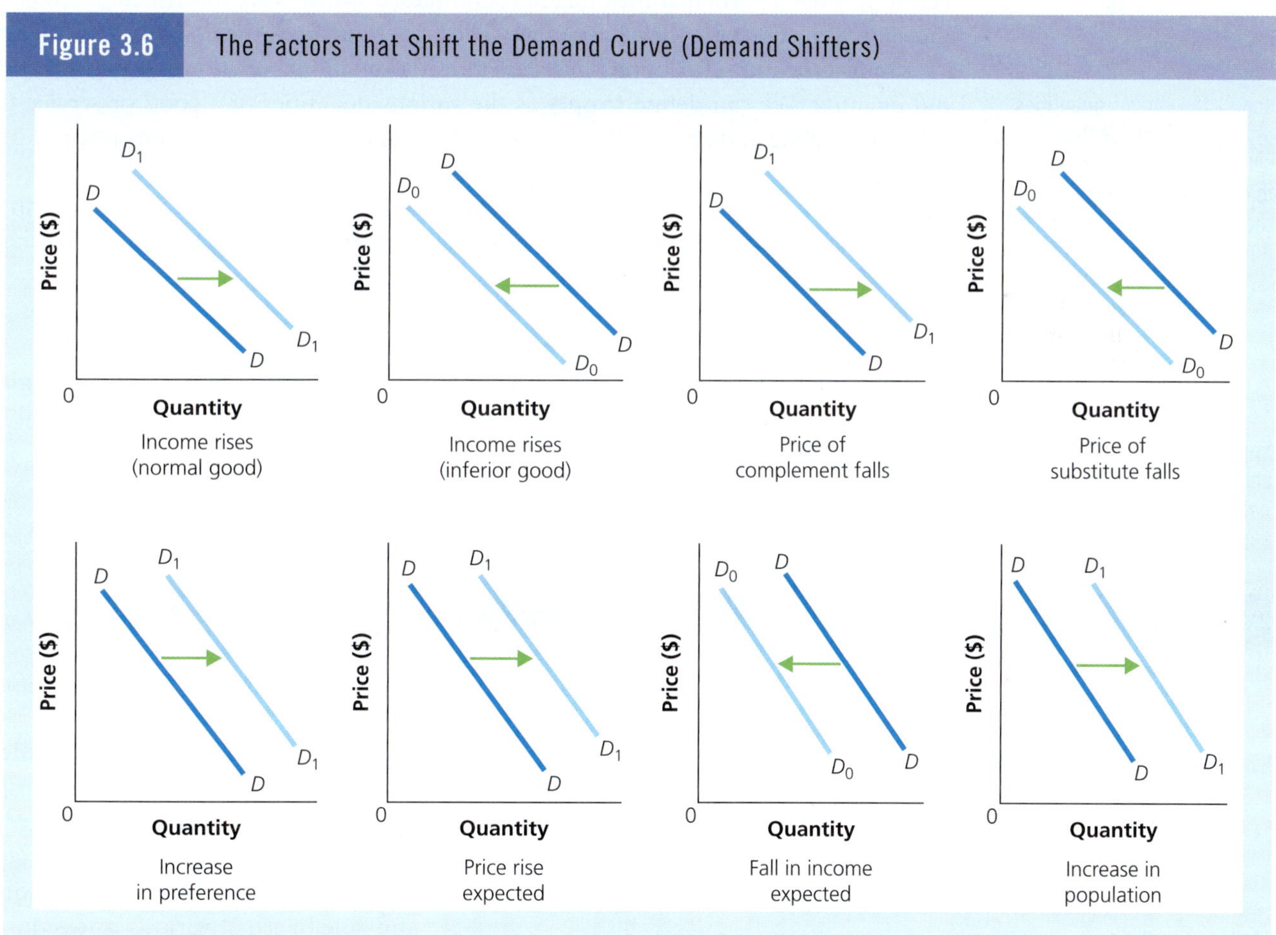

Reading Comprehension

The answers to these questions can be found on MyEconLab at www.myeconlab.com. MyEconLab

1. With the help of an appropriate diagram, explain the difference between a change in demand and a change in quantity demanded.
2. How is an increase in demand illustrated on a graph? How is a decrease in demand illustrated on a graph?
3. Other things being equal, people buy more of an item as its price falls. Is this an increase in demand? Explain briefly.
4. List three factors that will shift the demand curve to the left.

LO 3.5 Distinguish between supply and quantity supplied

Supply

Demand has a particular meaning in economics. Does *supply* also have a particular meaning?

Yes, supply has a particular meaning in economics. Producers are motivated to sell goods and services by the price they will receive. The higher the price, the more they will be willing to produce and sell. Supply, like demand, is a functional relationship between price and quantity. We can define **supply** as the various quantities of a good or service that sellers are willing and able to offer for sale (place on the market) at various prices during a specific period.

supply the various quantities of a good or service that sellers are willing and able to offer for sale (place on the market) at various prices during a specific period

As in the case of demand, supply refers not to a specific quantity that will be sold at some particular price, but to a series of quantities and a range of associated prices.

In the same way that we can have a table showing a functional relationship between price and quantity demanded, so too we can have a table showing the relationship between price and quantity supplied. Is that right?

supply schedule a table showing the direct relationship between price and quantity supplied

Yes, that is right. Let's construct such a table right now. Of course, you know what such a table is called.

Table 3.4 A Hypothetical Supply Schedule for USB Flash Drives

Price of Flash Drives ($)	Quantity Supplied per Week (000)
10	80
9	70
8	60
7	50
6	40
5	30
4	20

Yes. It's called a supply schedule. Is that correct?

Right again. Table 3.4 shows a supply schedule for USB flash drives.

We can define a **supply schedule** as a table showing the direct relationship between price and quantity supplied. It shows the various quantities of a good or service that producers will be willing and able to sell at various prices during a specific period, and is a tabular representation of supply.

Reading Comprehension

The answers to these questions can be found on MyEconLab at www.myeconlab.com. MyEconLab

1. What do economists mean by supply?
2. What is the difference between supply and quantity supplied?
3. What is a supply schedule?

LO 3.6 State the law of supply and explain the shape of the supply curve

The Law of Supply

There is a law of demand. Is there also a law of supply?

Table 3.4 shows that at a price of $10 per flash drive, producers will be willing to offer 80 000 of them for sale. As the price falls, they are willing to offer smaller quantities. Note that price and quantity supplied move in the same direction, that is, a direct relationship exists between them. This direct relationship between price and quantity supplied is called the **law of supply** and is stated as follows:

law of supply a statement of the direct relationship between price and quantity supplied

> As the price of a good or service falls, other things being equal, the quantity offered for sale decreases; as the price of a good or service rises, other things being equal, the quantity supplied increases.

supply curve an upward-sloping curve showing the direct relationship between price and quantity supplied

According to the law of supply then, there is a direct relationship between the price of a product and the quantity supplied.

The concept of supply can be illustrated graphically by a supply curve.

Why will producers offer more for sale as price rises?

Producers are motivated by profit. The main reason that producers will be willing to offer more for sale at a higher price is that higher prices serve as an incentive for producers to offer greater quantities and thus earn more profit. This is the function of price as a production motivator. Increases in price can also entice new producers into the market.

The following example will help to explain how producers respond to an increase in price. Suppose farmers have a certain amount of land on which they produce wheat and corn. If the price of wheat increases, farmers will find it profitable to shift land out of corn production and into wheat production. Also, it is conceivable that some farmers who were not previously producing wheat will now become wheat farmers. Hence, the quantity of wheat produced increases.

Figure 3.7 A Supply Curve for Flash Drives

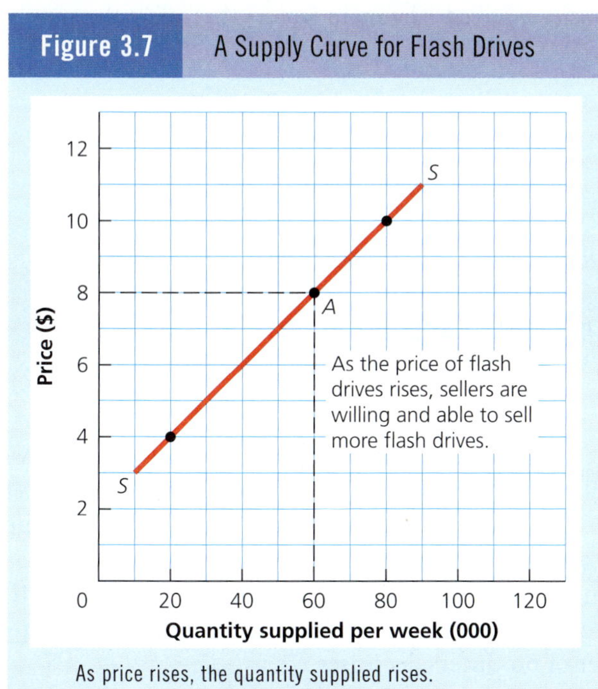

As price rises, the quantity supplied rises.

What would be the result if we plot the information in Table 3.4 on a graph?

Plotting the data in Table 3.4 on a graph results in Figure 3.7. The graph is called a **supply curve**, which is an upward-sloping curve showing the direct relationship between price and quantity supplied. It shows the various quantities of a good or service that producers are willing and able to offer for sale at various possible prices.

It is the direct relationship between price and quantity supplied that causes the supply curve to slope upward, as shown by *SS* in Figure 3.7.

Can the supply curve be used to illustrate the difference between supply and quantity supplied?

The entire supply curve represents supply, while a point on the supply curve represents quantity supplied at some specific price. In Figure 3.7, for example, the quantity supplied at a price of $8 is 60 000, represented by point *A* on the supply curve. The supply is represented by the entire supply curve.

Reading Comprehension

The answers to these questions can be found on MyEconLab at www.myeconlab.com. MyEconLab

1. State the law of supply.
2. Explain how price serves as a production motivator.
3. What is a supply curve?
4. Use a graph to show the difference between supply and quantity supplied.

LO 3.7 Identify the factors affecting quantity supplied

Factors Affecting Supply

What are the main factors that affect the supply of a good or service?

We have seen that the quantity of a good or service that producers are willing and able to offer for sale depends on the price of the good or service. In other words, the price of a good or service affects the *quantity supplied*. The main factors that affect the supply of a good or service are

- Number of producers
- Prices of related products
- Technology
- Expectations
- Cost of inputs

How does each of these factors affect supply?

Let's examine each one in turn.

Number of Producers The number of producers selling a product will obviously have some effect on total market supply of that product. This occurs because the market supply of a good or service is the sum of the quantities offered for sale by all of the individual sellers of that good or service. We can expect market supply to increase as the number of sellers increases, and to decrease as the number of sellers decreases. If, however, the average output of producers increases significantly, the total market supply can increase even if the number of producers decreases.

Are goods related in the same way in supply as in demand?

Prices of Related Products Yes, in pretty much the same way. You will recall our discussion of substitutes and complements on the demand side. As you suspect, goods can be substitutes or complements in production. Goods are **substitutes in production** (or production substitutes) if they are produced as alternatives to each other. Examples of substitutes in production are lettuce and tomatoes (a farmer can produce one or the other on the same piece of land), and leather bags and belts (both can be produced with the same type of resources). Goods are **complements in production** or **joint products** (or production complements) if they are produced together; the production of one implies the production of the other. Beef and hides are a classic example of goods that are complements in production.

substitutes (in production) goods that are produced as alternatives to each other

complements (in production) or joint products goods such that the production of one implies the production of the other

How does a change in the price of a substitute in production affect the supply of a product?

Let us consider the case of lettuce and tomatoes. If the price of lettuce increases, the supply of tomatoes will decrease as producers shift from tomato production to lettuce production. In general, if the price of a production substitute increases, producers will tend to reduce the supply of the item in question.

If two items are complements in production, an increase in the price of a production complement will increase the supply of the item in question. Is that correct?

That is correct. Let us consider beef and hides. If the price of beef rises, the quantity of beef supplied will rise but so will the quantity of hides as more cattle are slaughtered. In general, if the price of a complement in production rises, other things being equal, the supply of the good in question will increase, and if the price of a complement in production falls, the supply of the good in question will also fall.

It's not quite clear how changes in technology affect supply. Can you explain?

Technology Producers use inputs (factors of production) to produce goods and services. An increase in technology makes existing factors (inputs) more productive, and introduces new types of inputs that are more efficient than older types. Hence, an improvement in technology causes an increase in supply.

Expectations If producers of a certain item expect its price to rise in the future, they might begin now to expand their productive capacity and thus increase their present output levels of that particular item. This is particularly so in the case of products that cannot be stored easily. However, it is quite possible that expectations of a higher future price may lead producers into building stocks now so that they will have a larger quantity to sell at the future higher price. Such action will, of course, reduce current supply to the market. Therefore, generalizations should not be made about the effect of expected price changes on supply.

It seems as if the price of inputs affects the cost of production. Is this the case?

Cost of Inputs That is the case. Payment for factor inputs represents a significant part of production costs. The higher the prices of these inputs, the greater the costs of production will be, and the less will be produced. If wages rise, for example, other things being equal, the ability of businesses to produce an item will be reduced; thus, the supply will fall. A reduction in input prices will, of course, cause the supply to increase.

Reading Comprehension

The answers to these questions can be found on MyEconLab at www.myeconlab.com. MyEconLab

1. List three factors that will cause an increase in supply.
2. Give three examples of production substitutes.
3. What are joint products? Give two examples of joint products.
4. Explain how expectations can influence the quantity of an item offered for sale.
5. What is the relationship (if any) between cost of production and the prices of inputs?

LO 3.8 Distinguish between a change in supply and a change in quantity supplied

A Change in Supply versus a Change in Quantity Supplied

We studied the distinction between a change in *demand* and a change in *quantity demanded*. Does this distinction apply to supply?

Yes it does, and it should facilitate our understanding of the difference between a change in supply and a change in quantity supplied. When we speak of supply, we refer to the entire supply curve or schedule. It follows, then, that if supply changes, the entire supply curve will shift. Earlier in this chapter, we looked at a hypothetical supply schedule for flash drives. We reproduce that supply schedule here in the first two columns of Table 3.5. Let us now suppose that the supply of flash drives increases because of a

Table 3.5 A Hypothetical Supply Schedule for Flash Drives

Price of Flash Drives Supplied ($)	Original Quantity Supplied (000)	New Quantity Supplied (000)
10	80	100
9	70	90
8	60	80
7	50	70
6	40	60
5	30	50
4	20	40

Figure 3.8 An Increase in Supply

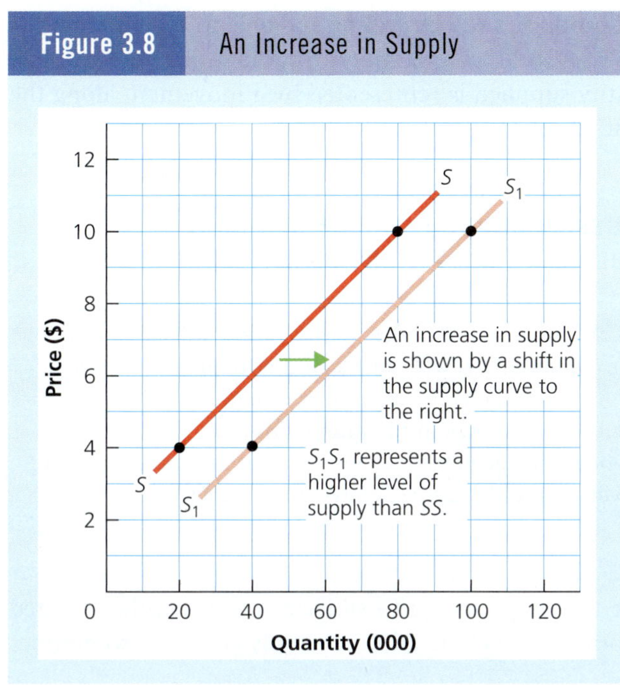

Figure 3.9 A Decrease in Supply

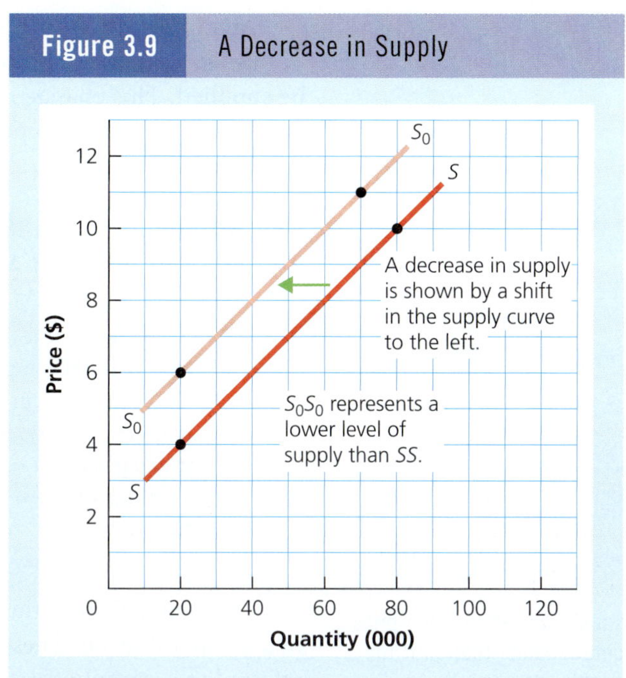

Figure 3.10 A Movement Along the Supply Curve Caused by a Change in Price

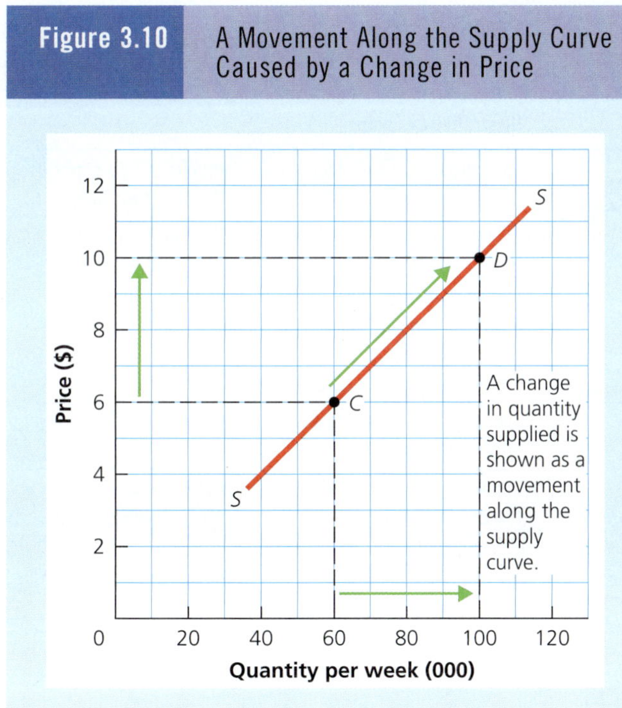

reduction in the cost of producing them. We will obtain a new supply schedule showing that a greater quantity of flash drives will be supplied at each price of flash drives. The new quantities supplied are shown in the right column of Table 3.5.

What would these supply schedules look like on the same graph?

Let's plot them and see. In Figure 3.8, *SS* is the original supply curve; S_1S_1 is the new supply curve. The increase in supply is shown by shifting the entire supply curve to the right of its original position. The location of the curve has now changed. Notice that at any given price of flash drives, a greater quantity is supplied. A decrease in supply would mean that at any given price of flash drives, a smaller quantity would be supplied, and would be represented by a leftward shift in the supply curve, as shown in Figure 3.9. The supply curve shifts from *SS* to S_0S_0.

Is a change in quantity supplied represented by a movement along the supply curve, as in the case of a change in demand?

Yes. A change in quantity supplied refers to the change in quantity that would be offered for sale as a result of a change in price. Let us examine the supply curve in Figure 3.10.

At a price of $6 for this item, producers will be willing and able to sell 60 000 units of this item per week. If the price rises to $10, a quantity of 100 000 units per week will be supplied. This change in quantity supplied is represented by a movement along the same supply curve from point *C* to point *D* in Figure 3.10.

Can we summarize the discussion about a change in supply versus a change in quantity supplied as we did with demand?

A change in the price of the commodity under consideration will not cause a change in the supply of the commodity; it will cause a change in quantity supplied. Only a change in a non-price determinant can cause a change in the supply of that commodity. Such factors as a change in the number of producers, a change in the price of a related good, a change in technology, a change in expectations, or a change in input prices will cause a change in supply—that is, they will cause the supply curve to shift.

supply shifters the non-price determinants that shift the supply curve

The major factors that cause the supply curve to shift are conveniently collected in a list in Table 3.6. These non-price factors that shift the supply curve are sometimes referred to as **supply shifters**.

Table 3.6 Supply Shifters: Non-price Factors That Change the Location of the Supply Curve

Supply Shifters	Illustrative Examples
1. A change in the number of producers	An increase in the number of manufacturers of DVD players increases the supply of DVD players. If many of the firms producing jeans go out of business, the supply of jeans falls.
2. A change in the prices of related goods	An increase in the price of lettuce reduces the supply of turnips because they are production substitutes. An increase in the price of refined cane sugar increases the supply of molasses because they are joint products.
3. A change in technology	The invention of high-speed computers increases the supply of computational services.
4. A change in expectations	Suppliers expect an increase in the price of coffee so they reduce present supplies with the intention of selling at the future higher price.
5. A change in the price of inputs	A substantial increase in the price of steel reduces the supply of chairs with steel frames.

Can we graph the effects of the supply shifters?

Yes. Figure 3.11 shows the effects of some of the supply shifters.

Figure 3.11 The Factors That Shift the Supply Curve (Supply Shifters)

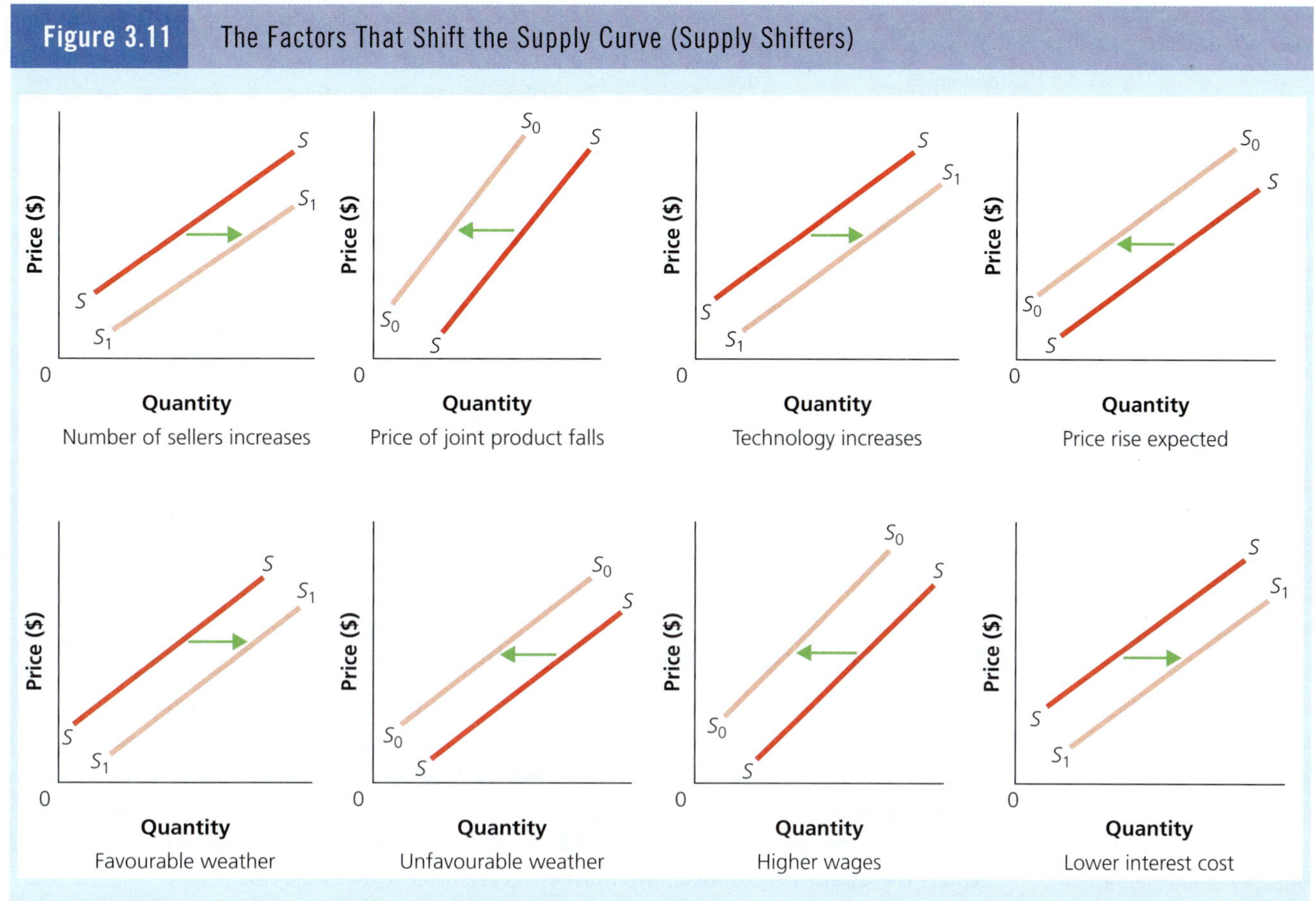

Reading Comprehension

The answers to these questions can be found on MyEconLab at www.myeconlab.com. MyEconLab

1. What is the difference between a change in supply and a change in quantity supplied?
2. What effect will an increase in the price of an item have on the supply of that item?
3. Mention three factors that will shift the supply curve to the right.
4. How is an increase in supply shown on a graph? How is a decrease in supply shown?

LO 3.9 Explain market price determination and the effects of changes in demand and supply

Determination of Equilibrium Price

Are we going to bring the buyers and sellers together?

Certainly—and this is the perfect time to do it; by so doing, we will see how market forces determine the price of a good or service. To help with the explanation, Table 3.7

Table 3.7 Hypothetical Demand and Supply Schedules for Flash Drives, and Market Price Determination

Price of Flash Disks ($)	Quantity Demanded (000 packs)	Quantity Supplied (000)	Market Condition	Pressure on Price	
10	40	80	Surplus	Downward	↓
9	50	70	Surplus	Downward	↓
8	60	60	Equilibrium	None	—
7	70	50	Shortage	Upward	↑
6	80	40	Shortage	Upward	↑
5	90	30	Shortage	Upward	↑
4	100	20	Shortage	Upward	↑

reproduces the hypothetical demand and supply schedules shown in Tables 3.1 and 3.4 (pages 71 and 82), respectively. We also show the market condition at each price-quantity combination and the effect on price.

What do you mean by market condition?

market condition the relationship between quantity demanded and quantity supplied

shortage or excess quantity demanded a situation in which quantity demanded exceeds quantity supplied

surplus or excess quantity supplied a situation in which quantity supplied exceeds quantity demanded

Market condition describes the situation of the market in terms of the relation between the quantity demanded and the quantity supplied. If the quantity demanded (Q_D) exceeds the quantity supplied (Q_S), a **shortage** (or **excess quantity demanded**) exists in the market. Conversely, if the quantity supplied exceeds the quantity demanded, a **surplus** (or **excess quantity supplied**) exists in the market. If the quantity demanded equals the quantity supplied, the market has neither a shortage nor a surplus. The market is then said to be in equilibrium.

We can summarize market conditions as follows:

1. If $Q_D > Q_S$, a shortage exists.
2. If $Q_D < Q_S$, a surplus exists.
3. If $Q_D = Q_S$, the market is in equilibrium.

Then we can use Table 3.7 to illustrate market conditions. Right?

That's right. Let us first consider the situation when the price is $4. At this price, buyers are willing and able to purchase 100 000 flash drives a week, but producers are willing and able to offer only 20 000 for sale. There will therefore be a shortage of 80 000 flash drives. At a price of $9, for example, buyers are willing and able to purchase only 50 000 flash drives a week, while sellers are willing to offer 70 000. There will therefore be a surplus of 20 000 flash drives in the market. Let us now consider a price of $8. At this price, buyers are willing to purchase 60 000 flash drives per week, and sellers are willing to offer 60 000 for sale. At this price, there is neither a surplus nor a shortage.

What happens when a market has a surplus or a shortage?

At any price other than $8, market forces are set in motion to raise or lower the price. Consider a price of $10. At this price, as the supply schedule shows, sellers are willing to put 80 000 on the market, but buyers are willing to buy only 40 000. A surplus or excess quantity supplied will result. Sellers will then attempt to dispose of this surplus by lowering the price. As the price falls, a greater quantity will be demanded. The price will settle at $8 because, at this price, the market will be cleared.

> Whenever a surplus exists in the market, it will exert a downward pressure on the price.

If the price happens to be $6, buyers will be willing to purchase 80 000 flash drives, but sellers will be willing to offer only 40 000 for sale. A price of $6 results in a shortage or excess quantity demanded. Unhappy with the shortage and wanting more flash drives, buyers will bid up the price. Sellers then will offer greater quantities at the higher prices. The price will again settle at $8 because, at this price, the quantity demanded equals the quantity supplied.

> Whenever a shortage exists in the market, it will exert an upward pressure on the price.

Note that the price of $8 is the only price that will prevail in the market. There will be no tendency for this price to change.

equilibrium price the price at which quantity demanded equals quantity supplied; there is no tendency for this price to change

equilibrium quantity the quantity traded (bought and sold) at the equilibrium price

Is there a special name for this price?

Indeed, there is. The price at which quantity demanded equals quantity supplied is referred to as the **equilibrium price**, and the quantity traded (exchanged) at this price is called the **equilibrium quantity**.

> Competitive market equilibrium occurs when the quantity of the product demanded equals the quantity supplied at a specific price.

Figure 3.12 Equilibrium Price and Quantity

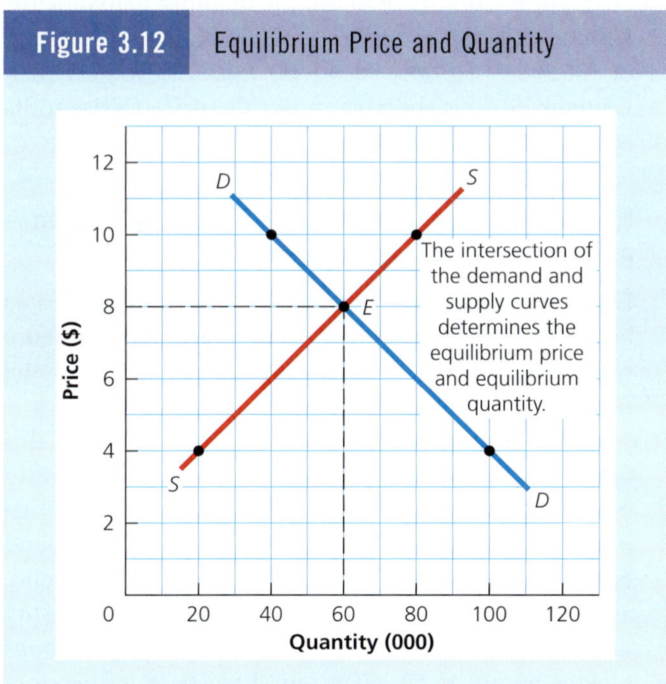

Can market equilibrium be illustrated graphically?

The market equilibrium condition is illustrated graphically in Figure 3.12. The demand curve *DD* and the supply curve *SS* are drawn from the schedules in Table 3.7. The two curves intersect at *E* to give an equilibrium price of $8 and an equilibrium quantity of 60 000.

Is the equilibrium price the price that makes buyers and sellers most happy?

This is a popular, but false, conclusion. It is more likely that neither buyers nor sellers will be completely satisfied with the equilibrium price. The buyers would prefer to pay a lower price for their flash drives, and the sellers would prefer to sell their flash drives at a higher price. But the buyers are purchasing all they want to buy at that price; and the producers are selling all they want to sell at that price.

Figure 3.13 Surplus and Shortage

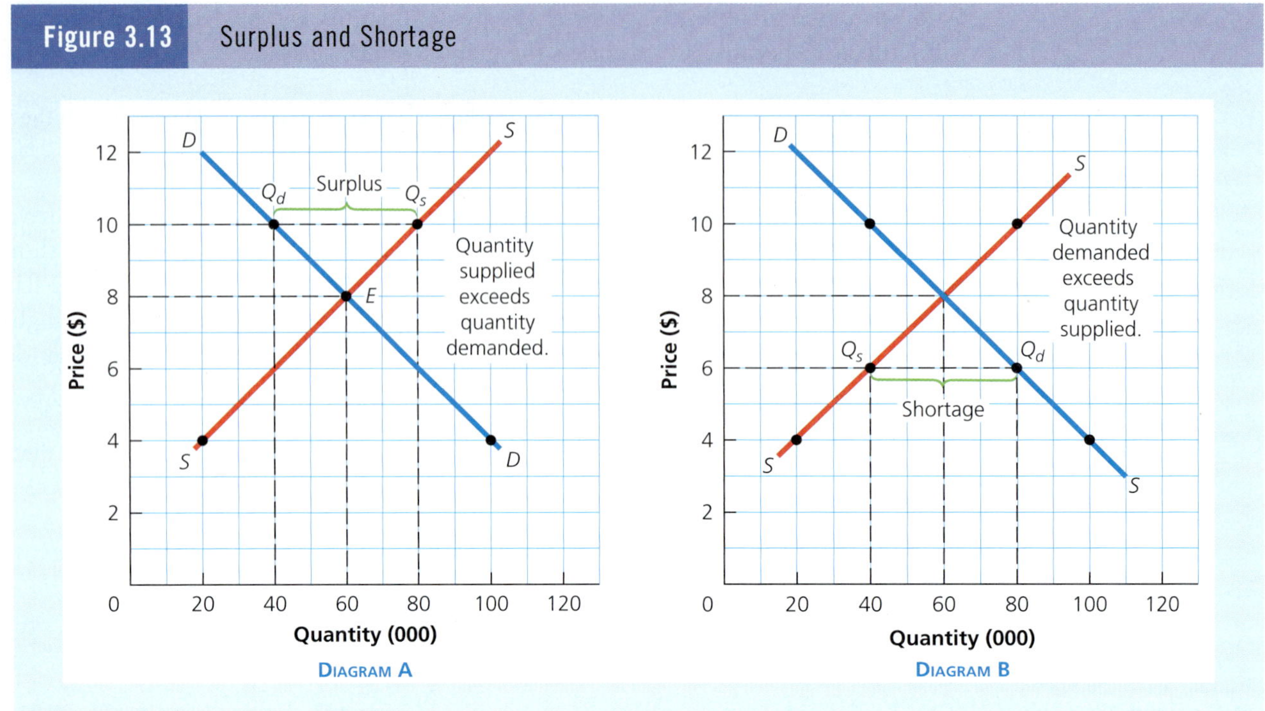

A change in demand, other things being equal, shifts the demand curve and changes the equilibrium price and quantity.

Can surpluses and shortages also be illustrated graphically?

The answer is yes. Let's look at Figure 3.13. In Diagram A we see that at a price of $10, the quantity supplied is 80 000, while the quantity demanded is 40 000. A surplus of (80 000 − 40 000) = 40 000 exists, as indicated in Diagram A. This surplus will cause the price to fall to the equilibrium level of $8. Look at Diagram B. At a price of $6, the quantity demanded is 80 000, while the quantity supplied is 40 000. A shortage of (80 000 − 40 000) = 40 000 exists, as indicated in Diagram B. This shortage causes the price to rise to its equilibrium level of $8.

Figure 3.14 The Effect of an Increase in Demand

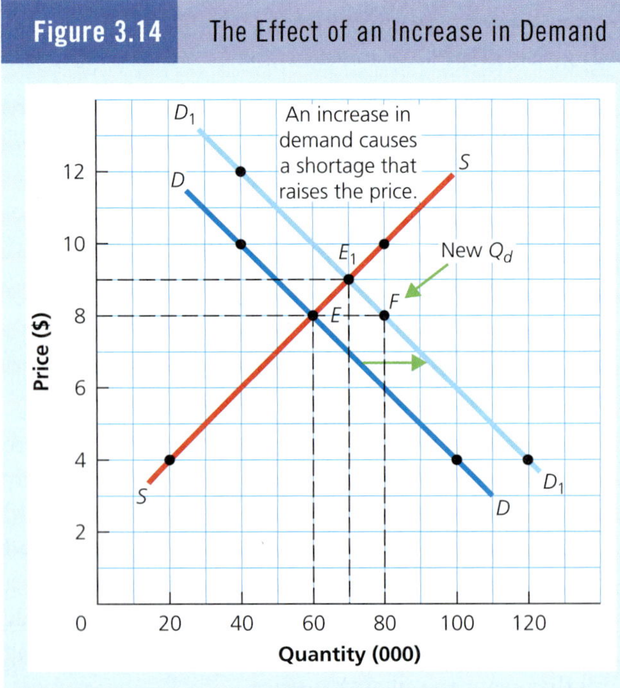

What is the effect of an increase in demand on equilibrium price and quantity?

Let us assume that the demand for flash drives increases because more people own computers and therefore require flash drives. Let us analyze the situation with the help of Figure 3.14.

The original demand and supply curves in this figure are *DD* and *SS*, respectively, and the equilibrium price and quantity are $8 and 60 000, respectively. An increase in demand is shown by a shift in the demand curve from *DD* to D_1D_1. With this new higher demand, and with the initial price of $8, the new quantity demanded is 80 000 (point *F*), while the quantity supplied remains at 60 000 (point *E*). There is therefore

Figure 3.15 The Effect of a Decrease in Demand

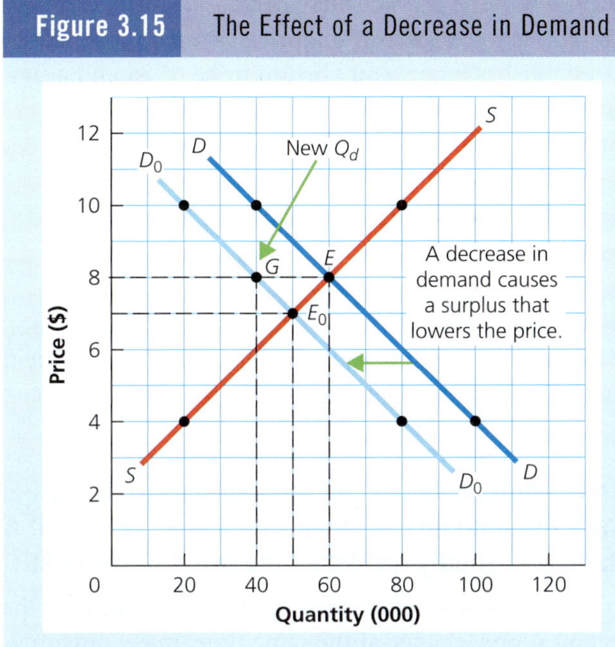

Figure 3.16 The Effect of an Increase in Supply

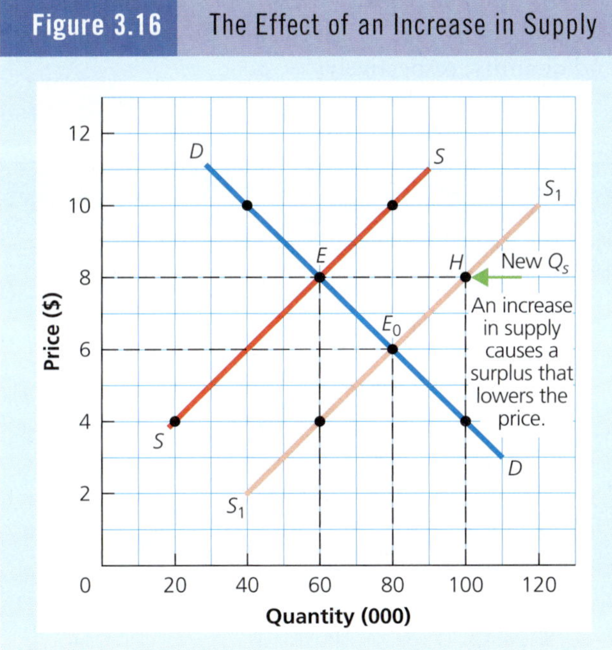

a shortage (excess quantity demanded) of 20 000 flash drives. The shortage will exert upward pressure on the price. The market establishes a new equilibrium price of \$9 and a new equilibrium quantity of 70 000. The result can be stated by the following proposition:

> An increase in demand, other things being equal, will cause the equilibrium price and quantity to increase.

Note that although the quantity bought and sold increases, supply does not increase; the location of the supply curve remains the same. There is, however, a movement along the supply curve *SS*, from point *E* to point E_1—an increase in quantity supplied.

Will a decrease in demand lower the equilibrium price and quantity?

Yes, but let's do the analysis. In Figure 3.15, the original demand and supply curves are *DD* and *SS*, respectively, and the equilibrium price and quantity are \$8 and 60 000. Now let's suppose that a new data storage device causes the demand for flash drives to fall. This fall in demand shifts the demand curve to the left of its original position, from *DD* to D_0D_0. With this new lower demand, and with the initial price of \$8, the new quantity demanded is 40 000 (point *G*), while the quantity supplied remains at 60 000 (point *E*). There is therefore a surplus (excess quantity supplied) of 20 000 flash drives. This surplus will exert downward pressure on the price. The market establishes a new equilibrium price of \$7 and a new equilibrium quantity of 50 000.

The result can be stated by the following proposition:

> A decrease in demand, other things being equal, will cause the equilibrium price and quantity to decrease.

Note again that although the quantity demanded and supplied fall, supply does not decrease; the location of the supply curve remains the same. There is, however, a movement along the supply curve *SS*, from point *E* to point E_0.

What is the effect of an increase in supply on equilibrium price and quantity?

Suppose the supply of flash drives increases because of a technological improvement in the production of flash drives. We can analyze the effect of this change with the help of Figure 3.16. The initial demand and supply curves are *DD* and *SS*, respectively; the equilibrium price is \$8, and the equilibrium quantity is 60 000. An increase in supply is shown by shifting the supply curve to the right of its initial position, from *SS* to S_1S_1. At the initial price of \$8, the new quantity supplied is 100 000 (point *H*), while the quantity demanded remains at 60 000. The market therefore has a surplus of flash drives. This surplus will exert a downward pressure on the price as sellers compete to sell their flash drives. The market establishes a new equilibrium price of \$6 and a new equilibrium quantity of 80 000 flash drives.

We can now state the following proposition:

> An increase in supply, other things being equal, will cause the price to fall and the quantity to rise.

A change in supply, other things being equal, shifts the supply curve and changes the equilibrium price and quantity.

Note again that although the quantity demanded has increased, demand has not; the location of the demand curve has not changed. Instead, there has been a movement along the demand curve, from E to E_0. The effect of a fall in supply is left as an exercise for you.

When demand and supply both change, equilibrium price and quantity can be affected in a variety of ways.

Now, we know that an increase in demand raises the equilibrium price and that an increase in supply lowers the equilibrium price. Does this mean that a simultaneous increase in demand and supply will leave the price unchanged?

Not necessarily. It depends on the relative size of the increase in demand and the increase in supply. When demand and supply change at the same time, many outcomes are possible, depending on the relative size and direction of the changes. Let us examine six of the possible outcomes. Figure 3.17 will help us with the analysis. In each case, *DD* and *SS* are the initial demand and supply curves, respectively, and \$8 and 60 000 flash drives are the equilibrium price and quantity, respectively.

Figure 3.17 The Effects of Changes in Demand and Supply

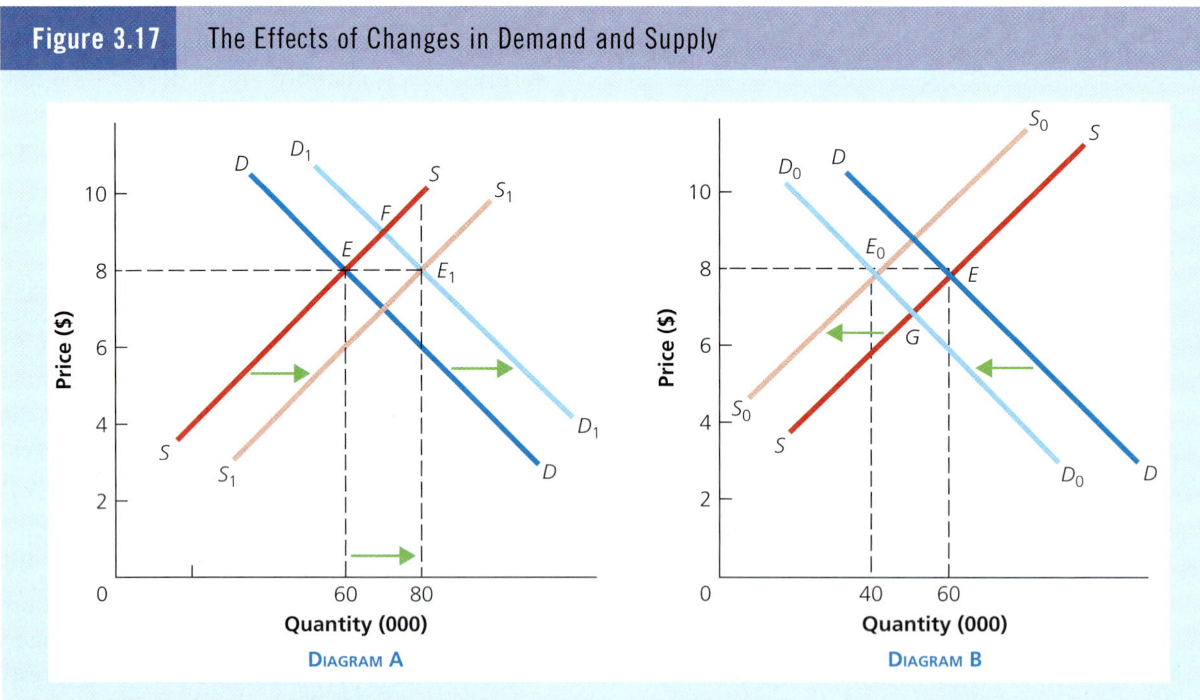

Diagram A: An increase in demand and an increase in supply of the same size leave the price unchanged but increase the quantity.

Diagram B: A decrease in demand and a decrease in supply of the same size leave the price unchanged but reduce the quantity.

Figure 3.17 The Effects of Changes in Demand and Supply (*cont'd*)

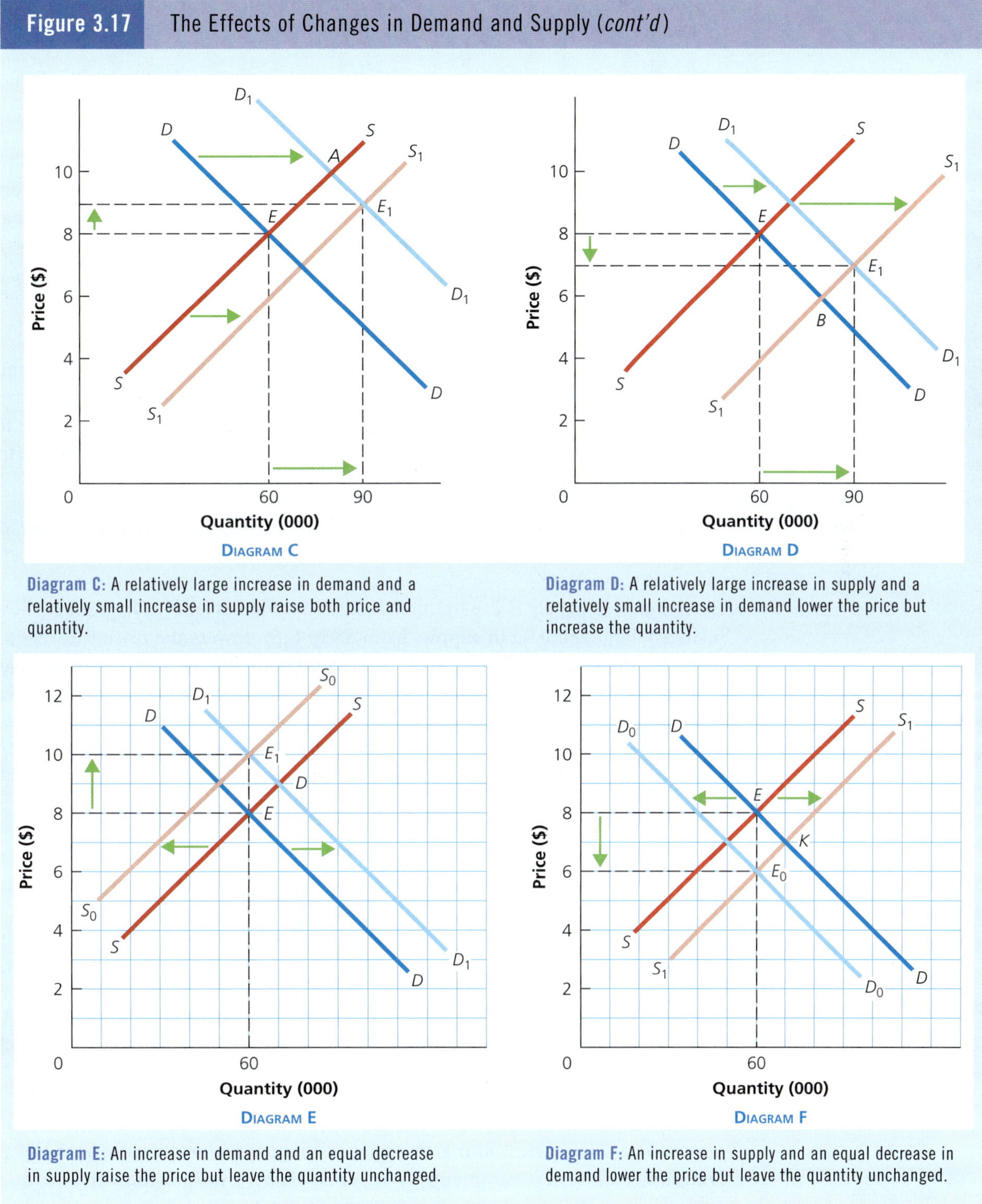

Diagram C: A relatively large increase in demand and a relatively small increase in supply raise both price and quantity.

Diagram D: A relatively large increase in supply and a relatively small increase in demand lower the price but increase the quantity.

Diagram E: An increase in demand and an equal decrease in supply raise the price but leave the quantity unchanged.

Diagram F: An increase in supply and an equal decrease in demand lower the price but leave the quantity unchanged.

The Increase in Demand Is Equal to the Increase in Supply In Diagram A of Figure 3.17, the increase in demand from *DD* to D_1D_1 raises the equilibrium price from \$8 to \$9 and increases the equilibrium quantity from 60 000 to 70 000 (point *F*). The increase in supply from SS to S_1S_1 lowers the price back to \$8 but increases the quantity from 70 000 to 80 000 (point E_1). We can conclude that

> If demand and supply increase equally, the equilibrium price will remain the same but the equilibrium quantity will increase.

The Fall in Demand Is Equal to the Fall in Supply In Diagram B, the decrease in demand from DD to D_0D_0 lowers the price from \$8 to \$7 and reduces the quantity from 60 000 to 50 000 (point G). The decrease in supply from SS to S_0S_0 raises the price back to \$8 but lowers the quantity even further to 40 000 (point E_0). Thus,

> If demand and supply decrease equally, the equilibrium price will remain the same but the equilibrium quantity will fall.

The Increase in Demand Is Greater than the Increase in Supply Diagram C shows that the relatively large increase in demand, from DD to D_1D_1, raises the price from \$8 to \$10 and increases the quantity from 60 000 to 80 000 (point A). The increase in supply from SS to S_1S_1 lowers the price from \$10 to \$9 and increases the quantity further from 80 000 to 90 000 (point E_1).

> If the increase in demand is larger than the increase in supply, both the equilibrium price and quantity will rise.

The Increase in Supply Is Greater than the Increase in Demand Diagram D shows that a relatively large increase in supply, from SS to S_1S_1, lowers the price from \$8 to \$6 and increases the quantity from 60 000 to 80 000 (point B). However, the relatively small increase in demand, from DD to D_1D_1, raises the price from \$6 to \$7 and raises the quantity from 80 000 to 90 000 (point E_1).

> If the increase in supply is larger than the increase in demand, the equilibrium price will fall, but the equilibrium quantity will rise.

An Increase in Demand and an Equal Decrease in Supply An increase in demand alone raises the price, and a decrease in supply alone also raises the price. In Diagram E, the increase in demand from DD to D_1D_1 raises the price from \$8 to \$9 and increases the quantity from 60 000 to 70 000 (point D). The decrease in supply from SS to S_0S_0 raises the price from \$9 to \$10 but reduces the quantity from 70 000 to 60 000 (point E_1).

> If an increase in demand is matched by an equal decrease in supply, the equilibrium price will rise, but the equilibrium quantity will remain the same.

An Increase in Supply and an Equal Decrease in Demand An increase in supply alone lowers the price, and a decrease in demand alone also lowers the price. In Diagram F, the increase in supply from SS to S_1S_1 lowers the price from \$8 to \$7 and increases the quantity from 60 000 to 70 000 (point K). The decrease in demand from DD to D_0D_0 lowers the price further to \$6 and reduces the quantity back to 60 000 (point E_0).

> If an increase in supply is matched by an equal decrease in demand, the equilibrium price will fall, but the equilibrium quantity will remain the same.

Can we summarize these results in a table?

That's a good idea. Table 3.8 summarizes the results.

Note that sometimes the effect on price is uncertain. For example, if demand and supply both increase, the price might rise, remain the same, or fall; it depends on the relative size of the change in demand and supply. But in this case, the effect on quantity is unambiguous. Quantity will increase. The effect of changes in demand and supply on price is certain, while the effect on quantity can be uncertain. For example, if demand increases and supply decreases, the price will definitely increase, but the quantity might increase, remain the same, or decrease. It depends again on the relative size of the changes.

Table 3.8 The Effects of Simultaneous Changes in Demand and Supply

Change in Demand and Supply	Effect on Price and Quantity
1. Demand and supply both increase equally.	Price remains the same but quantity increases.
2. Demand and supply both decrease equally.	Price remains the same but quantity decreases.
3. The increase in demand is greater than the increase in supply.	Both price and quantity increase.
4. The increase in supply is greater than the increase in demand.	Price falls but quantity increases.
5. Demand increases and supply decreases equally.	Price increases but quantity remains the same.
6. Demand decreases and supply increases equally.	Price falls but quantity remains the same.

Reading Comprehension

The answers to these questions can be found on MyEconLab at www.myeconlab.com. MyEconLab

1. Define the following terms:
   a) Shortage
   b) Surplus
2. What is the effect of a shortage on price? What is the effect of a surplus on price?
3. Define *equilibrium price* and *equilibrium quantity*.
4. The equilibrium price is the price at which demand and supply are equal. Is this statement correct?
5. What is the effect of an increase in demand on price, other things being equal?
6. What is the effect of a decrease in supply on price, other things being equal?

Review

1. Review the learning objectives listed at the beginning of the chapter.
2. Have you accomplished all the objectives? One way to determine this is to answer the Reading Comprehension questions at the end of each section. They will help you assess the extent to which you have accomplished the learning objectives.
3. If you have not accomplished an objective, review the relevant material before proceeding.

Key Points to Remember

1. **LO 3.1** Demand refers to the various quantities of a good or service that people are willing and able to buy at various prices during a specific period. Demand is a functional relationship between price and quantity demanded and can be represented by a table called a demand schedule or by a graph called a demand curve. Quantity demanded is the amount that will be demanded at a specific price.

2. LO 3.2 The law of demand states that, other things being equal, as the price of an item rises, the quantity demanded will fall; and as the price falls, the quantity demanded will rise. Because of this inverse relationship between price and quantity demanded, the demand curve is downward sloping.
3. LO 3.3 The main factors that affect the demand for a product are income, prices of substitutes and complements, tastes and preferences, buyers' expectations about future prices and future income, and the number of buyers.
4. LO 3.4 A change in the price of a product will cause the quantity demanded of that product to change and is illustrated by a movement along the demand curve from one point to another. A change in a non-price determinant will cause demand to change—this is illustrated by a shift in the entire demand curve.
5. LO 3.5, 3.8 Supply refers to the various quantities of a good or service that sellers (producers) are willing and able to offer for sale (i.e., place on the market) at various prices during a specific period. Supply can be represented by a supply schedule or by a supply curve. Quantity supplied is the amount that will be offered for sale at a specific price.
6. LO 3.6 The law of supply states that as the price of an item rises, other things being equal, the quantity supplied will also rise; and as the price falls, the quantity supplied will fall. Because of this direct relationship between price and quantity supplied, the supply curve is upward sloping.
7. LO 3.7 The factors affecting supply include the number of producers (sellers), the prices of related products, technology, sellers' expectations, and the prices of inputs (cost of production).
8. LO 3.9 The equilibrium price is the price at which quantity demanded and quantity supplied are equal. The equilibrium quantity is the quantity that will be bought and sold (traded) at the equilibrium price. The intersection of the demand and supply curves determines the equilibrium price and quantity. The equilibrium price is not necessarily the best price for buyers or sellers.
9. LO 3.9 A change in demand, other things being equal, will cause price and quantity to change in the same direction as the change in demand. A change in supply, other things being equal, will cause price to change in the opposite direction—and quantity to change in the same direction—as the change in supply.

Economic Word Power

Complements (in production) or joint products (p. 85)
Complements (p. 76)
Demand (p. 71)
Demand curve (p. 74)
Demand schedule (p. 71)
Demand shifters (p. 80)
Equilibrium price (p. 91)
Equilibrium quantity (p. 91)
Income effect (p. 73)
Independent goods (p. 77)
Inferior goods (p. 76)
Law of demand (p. 72)
Law of supply (p. 83)
Market condition (p. 90)
Market-size effect (p. 73)
Normal goods (p. 76)
Quantity demanded (p. 71)
Real income (p. 73)
Shortage or excess quantity demanded (p. 90)
Substitute (p. 76)
Substitutes (in production) (p. 85)
Substitution effect (p. 73)
Supply (p. 82)
Supply curve (p. 83)
Supply schedule (p. 82)
Supply shifters (p. 88)
Surplus or excess quantity supplied (p. 90)

Problems and Exercises

Basic

1. LO 3.1 Use a demand curve to illustrate the difference between demand and quantity demanded.
2. LO 3.3 Mention three factors that will increase the demand for a normal good.
3. LO 3.6 What is the meaning of an upward-sloping supply curve?
4. LO 3.7 With the help of a supply curve, explain the effect of rising costs on the supply of an item. Do rising costs also affect quantity supplied? Explain briefly.

5. LO 3.9 Draw hypothetical demand and supply curves for iPods in Canada. Show how each of the following events will affect the equilibrium price and quantity of iPods in Canada:
   a. A successful advertising campaign by producers of iPods
   b. Technological advance in the production of iPods
   c. A fall in the price of a portable media player that is a close substitute for an iPod
   d. The government offering tax incentives to all producers of portable media players, including iPods
6. LO 3.9 Consider apples and oranges to be substitutes as fruits. Unusually cold weather in Florida destroys a large portion of the orange crop. What would you expect to happen to the price and quantity of the following?
   a. Oranges
   b. Apples
   c. Orange juice

Questions in the Intermediate and Challenging Sections cover several different concepts, and have not been organized by learning objectives.

Intermediate

1. Indicate whether the following statement is true (T) or false (F): "An increase in demand implies an increase in quantity demanded, but an increase in quantity demanded does not necessarily imply an increase in demand."
2. Use demand and supply curves to show that an increase in demand, other things being equal, results in a shortage that forces the equilibrium price up. Indicate the shortage on your diagram.
3. Use demand and supply curves to show that an increase in supply, other things being equal, results in a surplus that forces the equilibrium price down. Indicate the surplus on your diagram.
4. Suppose you are given the following information: In 2007, partly because of media publicity, people's interest in physical exercise increased. Gym membership soared. Sales of exercise equipment skyrocketed, and many new gyms were opened. By 2010, it became extremely expensive to operate a gym because of increases in rent, heating, and electricity costs.
   a. Use a demand-supply diagram to show what happened to the demand for gym time.
   b. What effect did this demand shift have on the equilibrium price of gym time?
   c. Show the effect of the increase in cost in 2010 on the supply curve.
   d. What effect did this supply shift have on the price of gym time?

Challenging

1. During the ice storm in Eastern Ontario and Quebec in 1998, the prices of candles, flashlights, and batteries rose considerably. Some people claimed that the price increase was immoral because the higher prices could not induce a larger output; they merely gave extra profits to the sellers who just happened to own the highly demanded items. These people argued that prices should be prevented from rising or that the government should intervene to prevent unjust profits. Do you agree with this analysis? If so, why? If not, why not?
2. The tuition fee at Success College (a fictitious college) in 2000 was $10 000 per year, and in that year 6000 students enrolled. In 2010, when the college raised its tuition fees to $14 000 per year, 8000 students enrolled. Clearly, when the price (tuition fee) rose, the quantity of students increased. Can we then conclude, on the basis of this information, that the demand curve for places at Success College is upward sloping? Explain.
3. The price of gas rises and you immediately notice a line-up at the pumps. Is this a violation of the law of demand? If not, what possible explanation can you offer for this phenomenon?

MyEconLab Visit the MyEconLab website at **www.myeconlab.com.** This online homework and tutorial system puts you in control of your own learning with study and practice tools directly correlated to this chapter's content.

Study Guide

Self-Assessment

The answers to the Study Guide questions can be found in Appendix B.

What's your score?

Circle the letter that corresponds with the correct answer.

1. There is a demand for an item provided that
   a. People want the item
   b. People are able to purchase the item
   c. People are willing to purchase the item
   d. People are willing and able to purchase the item
2. In economics, demand refers to
   a. The amount of money that buyers spend on an item during a specific period
   b. The amount of an item that people will buy at a particular price
   c. The various quantities that people are willing and able to buy at various prices during a specific period
   d. All of the above
3. A demand schedule shows
   a. The demand for a good or service at a particular price
   b. Various quantities of a good or service demanded at various prices
   c. The relation between price and income when all other things remain equal
   d. People's preference to have more income than less
4. Demand can be represented by
   a. A demand curve
   b. A point on a demand curve
   c. A price-quantity combination in a demand schedule
   d. All of the above
5. The law of demand states that
   a. Price will fall as demand rises
   b. People will always buy more of a good or service when its price falls
   c. Quantity demanded will fall as price rises, other things being equal
   d. Demand will exist as long as people have money to buy things
6. Which of the following helps to explain the law of demand?
   a. The fact that demand and quantity demanded are related
   b. The fact that price is a production motivator
   c. The idea that buyers operate under consumer sovereignty
   d. The substitution effect
7. The demand curve is
   a. Upward sloping, showing a direct relationship between price and quantity demanded
   b. Upward sloping, showing an inverse relationship between price and quantity demanded
   c. Downward sloping, showing an inverse relationship between price and quantity demanded
   d. Downward sloping, showing an inverse relationship between income and quantity demanded
8. Which of the following is likely to increase the demand for cellphones?
   a. A fall in the price of cellphones
   b. A general increase in income
   c. Expectations of a fall in the price of cellphones
   d. All of the above
9. A normal good is
   a. A good of normal price and quality
   b. A good for which demand increases as price increases
   c. A good for which demand increases as income rises
   d. A good that causes abnormal people to exhibit normal behaviour
10. Tide and ABC are substitutes as detergents. If the price of ABC rises, other things being equal,
    a. The quantity of ABC demanded will fall
    b. The demand for ABC will not be affected
    c. The demand for Tide will increase
    d. All of the above
11. Cameras and batteries are complements. If the price of cameras falls, other things being equal,
    a. The demand for cameras will increase
    b. The quantity of batteries demanded will fall
    c. The demand for batteries will rise
    d. The demand for batteries will fall
12. An increase in the price of Kindle wireless reading device, other things being equal, will
    a. Increase the supply of Kindles
    b. Increase the quantity of Kindles supplied
    c. Reduce the demand for Kindles
    d. All of the above
13. Which of the following will not shift the supply curve for an item?
    a. A change in the price of the item
    b. An improvement in technology
    c. A change in production costs
    d. A change in the number of sellers

Questions 14–16 refer to Figure 3.18.

14. At a price of $8,
    a. There is a shortage that will exert upward pressure on the price
    b. Demand will increase to move the price to its equilibrium level

Figure 3.18 Demand and Supply

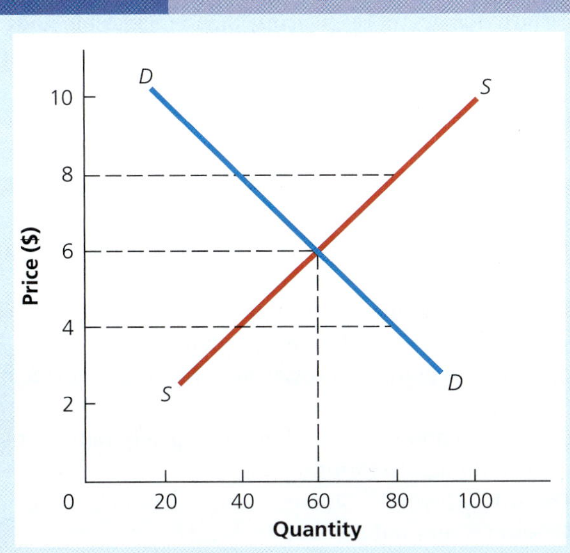

c. Quantity supplied is greater than quantity demanded; this will lower the price
d. The market has reached the highest price

15. At a price of $4,
    a. Demand is greater than supply
    b. The quantity demanded is greater than the quantity supplied; price will rise
    c. There is a surplus that will force the price up
    d. There is a shortage that will shift the supply curve to its equilibrium position
16. At a price of $6,
    a. Buyers and sellers are completely happy
    b. Buyers are willing to buy more, and sellers are willing to sell more
    c. Buyers are buying all they want to buy at that price, and sellers are selling all they want to sell at that price
    d. Buyers will adjust the amount they want to buy, and sellers will adjust the amount they want to sell until both are completely happy
17. In the market for a normal good, an increase in the average income of buyers, other things being equal, will
    a. Increase demand and raise both equilibrium price and quantity
    b. Increase demand and lower both equilibrium price and quantity
    c. Reduce demand and raise equilibrium price and quantity
    d. Reduce demand and lower both equilibrium price and quantity
18. Which of the following will lower equilibrium price and quantity, other things being equal?
    a. An increase in supply
    b. A decrease in supply
    c. An increase in demand
    d. A fall in demand
19. If demand and supply increase simultaneously, we can predict that
    a. Equilibrium price and quantity will rise
    b. Equilibrium price will rise, but equilibrium quantity will fall
    c. Equilibrium price will fall, but equilibrium quantity will rise
    d. Equilibrium quantity will rise, but equilibrium price might rise, fall, or remain the same
20. If demand increases and supply decreases at the same time, we can predict that
    a. Equilibrium price will rise, but equilibrium quantity might rise, fall, or stay the same
    b. Equilibrium price and quantity will fall
    c. Equilibrium price will fall, but equilibrium quantity might rise, fall, or stay the same
    d. Equilibrium quantity will rise, but equilibrium price might rise, fall, or stay the same

Problems and Exercises (Use Quad Paper for Graphs)

Answers to these questions can be found on MyEconLab at www.myeconlab.com. MyEconLab

1. Table 3.9 shows a hypothetical demand schedule for pizza per week in a small Canadian community. Fill in the third column with numbers to show how this schedule will be affected by a rapid movement of people into the community. You have to make up your own numbers.

Table 3.9 A Hypothetical Demand Schedule for Pizza

Price ($)	Original Quantity Demanded	New quantity Demanded
5	6000	______
6	5000	______
7	4000	______
8	3000	______
9	2000	______
10	1000	______

Draw a demand curve based on the data contained in the first two columns of Table 3.9. On the same diagram, draw the new demand curve resulting from the movement of people into the community.

2. Indicate whether the events in the left-hand column of Table 3.10 will affect the quantity demanded or the demand for the item specified in the middle column. Complete the third column. The first one is done as an example: If people expect the price of novels to rise, the demand for novels will increase as people will buy more novels now to avoid paying the higher future price. Because

Table 3.10 Events and Effects

Event	Item	Concept affected
a. Expectations of a higher price for novels	Novels	Demand
b. An increase in the price of apple juice	Orange juice	
c. An increase in income	Airline tickets	
d. An increase in the price of personal computers	Printers	
e. A fall in the price of personal computers	Personal computers	
f. Expectations of a higher price for colouring books	Crayons	

expectations are a non-price determinant, it is the *demand* (rather than *quantity demanded*) that will be affected.

3. With reference to Question 2, draw graphs to illustrate how each of the events in column 1 will affect the demand for or quantity demanded of the item in column 2.
4. In Table 3.11, you are given the demand and supply schedules for a particular item.
   a. Plot the demand and supply curves from these schedules.
   b. Indicate the equilibrium price and the equilibrium quantity.
   c. On your graph, show the effect of an increase in demand on the equilibrium price and the equilibrium quantity.
   d. On a new diagram, reproduce the demand and supply curves from (a), and show the effect of an increase in supply on the equilibrium price and equilibrium quantity.

Table 3.11 Demand and Supply Schedules

Price ($)	Quantity Demanded	Quantity Supplied
10	60	100
9	70	90
8	80	80
7	90	70
6	100	60
5	110	50

5. Explain, with the help of demand and supply graphs, the effect that each of the following events would have on the equilibrium price and quantity of oranges:
   a. Consumers believe a claim that oranges can cure acne.
   b. A new machine is developed that will automatically pick oranges more efficiently than previous methods.
   c. The price of grapefruit (a substitute for oranges) increases.
   d. Average income increases.
6. Use demand and supply diagrams to show the effect of the following events on the equilibrium price and quantity of shoes:
   a. A decision to eliminate the sales tax (that consumers pay) on shoes.
   b. An announcement that the price of shoes will increase by at least 25% within the next month.
   c. The immigration into Canada of a large number of people.
   d. The invention of a machine that greatly reduces the cost of manufacturing shoes.
7. The ABC Moving & Storage Company has the demand for storage bins indicated in Table 3.12.

Table 3.12 The Demand for Storage Bins

Price per Bin per Month ($)	Quantity of Bins Demanded per Month
50	500
45	550
40	600
35	650
30	700
25	750
20	800

The company has 625 storage bins available and currently charges $25 per month for each bin. It cannot obtain more bins.

   a. What problem does the ABC Company face in its current pricing policy?
   b. What might the company do to solve this problem?
   c. Suppose ABC increases its price. What effect will this price increase have on the demand for ABC bins?
   d. Now suppose other storage companies increase their prices while ABC price remains unchanged. What effect will this have on the demand for ABC bins?
8. Use demand and supply analysis (with graphs) to explain how each of the following events will affect the market (i.e., equilibrium price and quantity) for air travel:
   a. A decrease in landing fees.
   b. A marked increase in terrorist activity.
   c. Expectations of increases in the incomes of households.
   d. A substantial increase in the prices of bus fares.
   e. A big discount for round-trip train travel.

Appendix

3A

Elementary Mathematics of Demand and Supply

Learning Objectives

After studying this appendix, you should be able to

3A.1 Appreciate the mathematical approach to studying demand, supply, and equilibrium price and quantity determination

3A.2 Define the demand function and use functional notation to express demand

3A.3 Define the supply function and use functional notation to express supply

3A.4 Solve demand and supply equations to determine equilibrium price and quantity

3A.5 Use demand and supply equations to calculate the shortage or surplus at a particular price

3A.6 Use demand and supply equations to calculate the effect of a change in demand or supply on equilibrium price and equilibrium quantity

Assess Your Knowledge

MyEconLab

Answers to these questions can be found on MyEconLab at **www.myeconlab.com**.

1. What does a demand equation represent?
2. What does a supply equation represent?
3. What does it mean to say that an equation is linear?
4. If $x = 2$ and $y = 3$, what is the value of $2x + 3y$?

LO 3A.1 Appreciate the mathematical approach to studying demand, supply, and equilibrium price and quantity determination

The Mathematical Approach to Market Analysis

What is the purpose of the mathematical approach to demand-supply analysis?

The main purpose of this elementary mathematical approach to demand-supply analysis is to provide you with another type of tool that can be used to analyze demand, supply, and market price determination. You will have an opportunity to apply the functional notation introduced in Appendix 1A earlier in this book. The algebraic approach can give greater precision and is often easier than a tabular or graphical analysis.

Does this approach require a great deal of mathematical dexterity?

Not at all. No mathematics beyond elementary algebra is used. The actual mathematics used in more advanced economic analysis is much more complex and sophisticated than the simple algebra used here, but even this rudimentary presentation will give you a bit of the flavour of a mathematical approach to economic analysis.

Reading Comprehension

The answers to these questions can be found on MyEconLab at www.myeconlab.com. MyEconLab

1. How will you benefit from learning a mathematical approach to studying economics?
2. "Only sophisticated mathematics is useful in the study of economics." Do you agree with this statement?

LO 3A.2 Define the demand function and use functional notation to express demand

THE DEMAND FUNCTION

demand function an equation expressing the relationship between price and quantity demanded

What exactly is a demand function?

A **demand function** is a mathematical way of expressing the relationship between quantity demanded and the factors that affect quantity demanded. The demand function for a commodity can be expressed as follows:

$$Q_D = Q(P, Y, P_r, T, E_x, Po) \qquad \text{Equation (1)}$$

where Q_D = quantity demanded
P = price of the commodity
Y = income
P_r = prices of related goods
T = tastes (preferences)
E_x = expectations
P_o = population

The effect of each of the independent variables (the variables in the bracket) on quantity demanded was discussed in Chapter 3 in relation to demand and supply.

In the demand schedules and the demand curves in Chapter 3, we expressed quantity demanded as a function of price alone. Now we have so many variables other than price in the demand function. How do we deal with them?

That is a very important question. To simplify the demand function shown above, let us assume that income, the prices of related goods, tastes, expectations, and population are constant. That is, let's treat them as exogenous variables. The demand function now becomes a relation between price and quantity demanded and may be expressed as the simpler demand function shown in Equation (2):

$$Q_D = Q(P) \qquad \text{Equation (2)}$$

The independent variables in Equation (1) that have been assumed constant are called *shift parameters* (remember *demand shifters*?). If they change, they cause the demand curve to shift. According to the law of demand, the relation between price and quantity demanded is an inverse one. If we assume a linear relationship between price and quantity demanded, then we can express the demand function as follows:

$$Q_D = a - bP, a > 0, b > 0 \qquad \text{Equation (3)}$$

The value of a represents the quantity demanded at a price of zero, and $-b$ represents the slope of the demand function, which is appropriately negative since the demand curve is downward sloping (that is, it has a negative slope). A demand function, for example, could take the form of an equation such as this:

$$Q_D = 10 - 2P \qquad \text{Equation (4)}$$

What are the differences among a demand schedule, a demand curve, and a demand function?

They are all very closely related, but they are *technically* different. They all show the relationship between price and quantity demanded. But the demand schedule is a tabular representation, the demand curve is a graphical representation, and the demand function is an equation.

Reading Comprehension

The answers to these questions can be found on MyEconLab at www.myeconlab.com. MyEconLab

1. What is a demand function? How is it different from a demand curve?
2. Why does the demand equation have a negative sign before the price variable?
3. Suppose demand is expressed as a functional relationship between price and quantity demanded. List three exogenous variables in this relationship.

LO 3A.3 Define the supply function and use functional notation to express supply

The Supply Function

What exactly is a supply function?

supply function equation expressing the relationship between price and quantity supplied

A **supply function** is a mathematical way of expressing the relationship between quantity supplied and the factors that affect quantity supplied. The supply function for a commodity can be expressed as:

$$Q_S = Q(P, N, P_r, T_e, E_x, P_i) \qquad \text{Equation (5)}$$

where Q_S = quantity supplied
P = price of the commodity
N = number of sellers
P_r = prices of related goods
T_e = technology
E_x = expectations
P_i = prices of inputs

Can we simplify this function as we did with the demand function?

That is exactly what we are going to do. If we assume that the number of sellers (N), the prices of related goods (P_r), technology (T_e), expectations (E_x), and input prices (P_i) are constant, then we can express the supply function as follows:

$$Q_S = Q(P) \qquad \text{Equation (6)}$$

The independent variables in Equation (5) that have been assumed constant are also called *shift parameters* as in the case of demand (remember *supply shifters*?). If they change, they cause the supply curve to shift. A direct relation exists between price and quantity supplied. As in the case of the demand function, let us assume a linear relationship between price and quantity supplied. We can express the supply function as follows:

$$Q_S = c + dP, d > 0 \qquad \text{Equation (7)}$$

where c is a constant and d is the slope of the supply function. The positive slope means that the supply curve is upward sloping. A supply function could be of the following form:

$$Q_S = -5 + 3P \qquad \text{Equation (8)}$$

Assuming that the price is expressed in dollars, the negative sign here means that unless the price is above \$1.67 (\$5 ÷ 3), sellers will not offer the product for sale.

Reading Comprehension

The answers to these questions can be found on MyEconLab at www.myeconlab.com. MyEconLab

1. What is a supply function? How is it different from a supply curve?
2. Why does the supply equation have a positive sign before the price variable?
3. Suppose supply is expressed as a functional relationship between price and quantity supplied. List three exogenous variables in this relationship.

LO 3A.4 Solve demand and supply equations to determine equilibrium price and quantity

Market Equilibrium

Can we use equations to present a model of market price determination?

Yes, we can. To determine equilibrium price and quantity, we must bring the demand and supply functions together in a model of price determination. The demand and supply equations give us two equations in three unknowns (Q_D, Q_S, and P). We know that equilibrium in supply and demand analysis occurs when the price is such that there is neither a shortage nor a surplus in the market, hence the equilibrium condition is

$$Q_D = Q_S \qquad \text{Equation (9)}$$

This equation completes the model and allows us to obtain a unique solution. The complete model is

$$Q_D = a - bP \qquad \text{Equation (10)}$$

$$Q_S = c + dP \qquad \text{Equation (11)}$$

$$Q_D = Q_S \qquad \text{Equation (12)}$$

By solving this system of equations for P and Q, we will obtain the market equilibrium price and quantity.

Can we solve the demand and supply equations given in Equations (4) and (8)?

Let's do it. The system of equations that we need to solve is as follows:

$$Q_D = 10 - 2P$$

$$Q_S = -5 + 3P$$

Since in equilibrium $Q_D = Q_S$, we have

$$10 - 2P = -5 + 3P$$

Solving for P, we have $-5P = -15$, so $P = 3$.

Substituting $P = 3$ in either of the equations, we obtain

$$Q_D = 10 - 2(3) = 4 \qquad \text{or} \qquad Q_S = -5 + 3(3) = 4$$

Hence the equilibrium price is 3, and the equilibrium quantity is 4.

LO 3A.5 Use demand and supply equations to calculate the shortage or surplus at a particular price

Shortage or Surplus

Can we use these equations to determine the shortage or surplus at any given price?

Yes. Let us examine the market condition at a price of \$2. At this price, the quantity demanded is as follows:

$$Q_D = 10 - 2P = 10 - 2(2) = 6$$

and the quantity supplied is

$$Q_S = -5 + 3P = -5 + 3(2) = 1$$

Since the quantity demanded (6) is greater than the quantity supplied (1), there is a shortage of $(6 - 1) = 5$.

Let us now examine the market condition at a price of \$5. At this price, the quantity demanded is

$$Q_D = 10 - 2P = 10 - 2(5) = 0$$

and the quantity supplied is

$$Q_S = -5 + 3P = -5 + 3(5) = 10$$

Since the quantity demanded (0) is less than the quantity supplied (10), there is a surplus of $(10 - 0) = 10$.

LO 3A.6 Use demand and supply equations to calculate the effect of a change in demand or supply on equilibrium price and equilibrium quantity

EFFECTS OF A CHANGE

Can we use this algebraic model to determine the effect of a change in demand on equilibrium price and equilibrium quantity?

Yes, we can. Let us use the following demand and supply equations:

$$Q_D = 10 - 2P \text{ and } Q_S = -5 + 3P$$

Now let us suppose that demand increases by 2 units. This means that the quantity demanded increases by 2 units at each price. Thus, the new demand equation becomes

$$Q_D{}^1 = 12 - 2P$$

The supply equation remains

$$Q_S = -5 + 3P$$

We can calculate the new equilibrium price and new equilibrium quantity by solving the two equations:

$$Q_D{}^1 = Q_S\text{: } 12 - 2P = -5 + 3P$$

$$-5P = -17$$

The new equilibrium price is $-17 \div -5 = 3.4$.

The new equilibrium quantity is $-5 + 3(3.4) = (-5 + 10.2) = 5.2$.

What about a change in supply?

This can be done in a similar way. Using the same demand and supply equations as before, we can analyze the effects of an increase in supply on equilibrium price and on equilibrium quantity. Let us assume that supply increases by 3 units. This means that the quantity supplied increases by 3 units at each price. Thus the new supply equation becomes

$$Q_S^{\,1} = -2 + 3P$$

The demand equation remains

$$Q_D = 10 - 2P$$

We can calculate the new equilibrium price and equilibrium by solving the two equations:

$$Q_D = Q_S^{\,1}\text{: } 10 - 2P = -2 + 3P$$

$$-5P = -12$$

The new equilibrium price is $-12 \div -5 = 2.4$.
The new equilibrium quantity is $-2 + 3(2.4) = -2 + 7.2 = 5.2$.

Reading Comprehension

The answers to these questions can be found on MyEconLab at www.myeconlab.com. MyEconLab

1. The demand and supply equations are given as

   $$Q_D = 90 - 6P;\ Q_S = -20 + 5P$$

   Quantity demanded is in units and price is in \$. Calculate the equilibrium price and the equilibrium quantity.
2. Referring to the demand and supply equations in Question 1, calculate the shortage or surplus at a price of \$8.
3. Referring to the demand and supply equations in Question 1, calculate the shortage or surplus at a price of \$12.
4. Referring to the demand and supply equations in Question 1, calculate the new equilibrium price and quantity following an increase in demand of 11 units.

Review

1. Review the learning objectives listed at the beginning of the appendix.
2. Have you accomplished all the objectives? One way to determine this is to answer the Reading Comprehension questions at the end of each section. They will help you assess the extent to which you have accomplished the learning objectives.
3. If you have not accomplished an objective, review the relevant material before proceeding.

Key Points to Remember

1. **LO 3A.1** The algebraic approach to demand and supply analysis can give greater precision to the analysis and is sometimes easier than a tabular or graphical approach.
2. **LO 3A.2** A demand function is a mathematical expression of the relationship between quantity demanded and the variables that determine quantity demanded. By assuming that all influences on quantity demanded, except the

price of the item under consideration, are held constant, we can reduce the demand function to a simple functional relationship between price and quantity demanded.

3. LO 3A.2 Influences on quantity demanded that have been assumed constant are called shift parameters.
4. LO 3A.2 If the relationship between price and quantity demanded is represented by a table, it is called a demand schedule. If it is represented by a graph, it is called a demand curve; and if it is represented by an equation, it is called a demand function.
5. LO 3A.3 A supply function is a mathematical expression of the relationship between quantity supplied and the variable that determine quantity supplied. By assuming that all influences on quantity supplied, except the price of the item under consideration, are held constant, we can reduce the supply function to a simple functional relationship between price and quantity supplied.
6. LO 3A.3 The influences on quantity supplied that have been held constant are called shift parameters.
7. LO 3A.4 The market equilibrium price and quantity are determined by solving a system of equations consisting of the demand equation, the supply equation, and the equilibrium condition.
8. LO 3A.5 By using a given price in the demand and supply equations, we can determine whether there is a shortage or a surplus at the given price.
9. LO 3A.6 The effect of a change in demand or supply on equilibrium price and equilibrium quantity can be easily calculated by using the algebraic approach.

Economic Word Power

Demand function (p. 104)
Supply function (p. 106)

Problems and Exercises

Basic

1. LO 3A.4, 3A.5 You are given the following demand and supply equations:

$$Q_D = 600 - 2P$$
$$Q_S = 300 + 4P$$

   a. Calculate the equilibrium price and quantity.
   b. Calculate the shortage or surplus at $P = 40$
   c. Calculate the shortage or surplus at $P = 60$

2. LO 3A.4 The demand and supply curves are given as

$$P = 12 - 2Q_D \text{ and } P = 4Q_S$$

Find the equilibrium price and quantity.

3. LO 3A.4 Solve each of the following equations to determine the equilibrium price and the equilibrium quantity:
   a. $Q_D = 32 - 3P$
      $Q_S = -12 + 8P$
   b. $Q_D = 60 - 3P$
      $Q_S = -40 + 7P$
   c. $Q_D = 900 - 20P$
      $Q_S = -100 + 30P$
      $Q_D = 50 - 4P$
      $Q_S = -10 + 8P$

4. LO 3A.4 You are given the following demand and supply equations:

$$Q_D = 130 - 3P$$
$$Q_S = -20 + 12P$$

   a. Complete the demand and supply schedules in Table 3A.1 on the basis of the demand and supply functions.

Table 3A.1 Demand and Supply Schedules

Price	Quantity Demanded	Quantity Supplied
5	0	
10	0	
15	0	
20	0	

   b. From the demand schedule, determine the equilibrium price and quantity.
   c. Solve the demand and supply equations for P and Q and compare your answer with the answer obtained in part (b).

5. LO 3A.4 The demand and supply equations in the market for a certain item are:

$$Q_D = 28 - 2P$$
$$Q_S = 5P$$

   a. What are the equilibrium price and quantity?
   b. Set up demand and supply schedules based on these equations for these prices: \$7, \$6, \$5, \$4, \$3, \$2, and \$1.
   c. Use your demand and supply schedules to plot the demand and supply curves.

6. LO 3A.4 The market demand and supply equations are as follows:

$$Q_D = 18 - 2P$$
$$Q_S = -3 + 5P$$

a. By selecting prices ranging from $1 to $6, plot the demand and supply curves.
b. Solve the equations for the equilibrium price and the equilibrium quantity.

7. LO 3A.6 Referring to the demand and supply equations in Question 6, calculate the new equilibrium price and equilibrium quantity after an increase in demand of 7 units.

Chapter 4
An Overview of Macroeconomics

Austrian-British economist and political philosopher Friedrich Hayek (1899–1992) at the London School of Economics.

Learning Objectives

After studying this chapter, you should be able to

4.1 Sketch the major historical developments in macroeconomics

4.2 Discuss the developments in macroeconomics since Keynes, including supply-side approaches and the concept of stagflation

4.3 Discuss the importance of macroeconomics

4.4 Construct a circular flow model of the economy that includes households, businesses, and the government

4.5 Describe the performance of the Canadian economy, in terms of GDP, unemployment, and inflation, over the past few decades

Assess Your Knowledge

MyEconLab

Answers to these questions can be found on MyEconLab at **www.myeconlab.com.**

1. What does the *invisible hand* refer to?
2. When did the Great Depression occur?
3. What does *gross domestic product* (*GDP*) mean?
4. What does the unemployment rate measure?

LO 4.1 Sketch the major historical developments in macroeconomics

A Historical Sketch of Macroeconomics

When did macroeconomics originate?

In a sense, macroeconomics is as old as economics itself. Adam Smith (1723–1790), considered to be the grandfather of economics and author of *The Wealth of Nations,* was concerned with the factors that would contribute to a country's wealth. *The Wealth of Nations,* published in 1776, is recognized as a kind of "opus" which provided ground for equally as many unasked as unanswered economic queries. Adam Smith shifts focus away from the study of the individual to the study of the whole economy and provides insight into what constitutes the wealth of a nation. He advocates that what determines the wealth of a country is not the sum of individual wealth, nor the accumulation of money or gold, but rather a nation's capacity to produce an abundance of goods and services that underlies a nation's riches. Notwithstanding, his approach was not a *macroeconomic* approach as we know it today. Much of Adam Smith's work dealt with the market mechanism or, as he called it, the **invisible hand**. Before the 1930s, economics was essentially synonymous with microeconomics.

invisible hand the term used by Adam Smith to describe the market mechanism

Great Depression a period of severe economic slump lasting 10 years, from 1929 to 1939

The Great Depression of the 1930s led to a revival of thinking about economics and the economy. The **Great Depression** was a period of severe economic contraction, (some called it an *entrenched recession*), spanning a decade from 1929 to 1939. This was the longest and most severe economic slump ever experienced by the industrialized world. In 1929, only 116 000 Canadians were unemployed. By 1933, that number had jumped to 826 000. Whereas the unemployment rate was only 2.9% in 1929, it exceeded 19% by 1933. In 1933, the total output of goods and services in the Canadian economy fell by 7.2%. Bankruptcies were widespread and economic hardship occurred everywhere.

Classical Economics There were no macroeconomic models to explain the phenomenon of the Great Depression. The only models available were *microeconomic* models, which were, nevertheless, applied to the macroeconomy. These **classical economic models**, as they are called, were incapable of explaining prolonged periods of involuntary unemployment. As pre-Keynesian economic models, they emphasized the market forces of demand and supply.

classical economic models pre-Keynesian economic models that emphasized the market forces of demand and supply

The popular economic view at the time was as follows: If unemployment developed (perhaps because of a fall in output and consequently a fall in quantity demanded), there would be a surplus of workers in the labour market. This excess quantity of labour supplied would cause the wage rate (the price of labour) to fall. As wages fell, employers would be willing to hire more workers at the new, lower, wage rate. Workers would be hired until the excess labour was absorbed by the market.

> Classical economics predicted that unemployment would cause wages to fall. The fall in wages would be an incentive for employers to hire more workers until the unemployed workers were all hired.

But something was obviously wrong with this model because it did not explain the economic reality of the time. In that economic environment, *macroeconomics* was born.

What was the consequence of the failure of classical economic models to explain the Great Depression?

John Maynard Keynes

Keynesian Macroeconomics The failure of classical economic models to explain the Great Depression led economist John Maynard Keynes to formulate a new economic model that could explain the economic situation during the 1930s. In his classic work, *The General Theory of Employment, Interest, and Money*, published in 1936, Keynes developed a framework that was to become the foundation of macroeconomics. Instead of focusing on wages and prices, Keynes emphasized *total spending* as the major determinant of employment in the economy.

> Keynesian macroeconomics emphasizes total spending as the main determinant of the level of income and employment in the economy.

Keynes's ideas became quite popular as both economists and politicians embraced his views on the macroeconomy and formulated economic policies based on his theories. The Keynesian model was embraced mainly because it seemed to adequately address the pressing economic problem: the Great Depression that plagued the economy at the time. Largely as a result of Keynes's work, the idea that a government could use its spending and taxing powers to stabilize the economy gained widespread acceptance. In the 1960s, **fiscal policy**—the use of government spending and taxes to regulate economic activity—was in its prime. Many economists believed that the government could use this macroeconomic tool to achieve high employment and relatively stable prices *together*.

fiscal policy the use of government spending and taxes to regulate economic activity

Reading Comprehension

The answers to these questions can be found on MyEconLab at **www.myeconlab.com**. MyEconLab

1. What is the relationship between modern macroeconomics and the Great Depression?
2. Did classical economics adequately explain the Great Depression? Explain.
3. What was the classical economists' view of unemployment? How was this view different from the ideas of Keynes?
4. What accounted for the enormous popularity of Keynesian economics beginning in the 1930s and enduring up to the 1960s?

LO 4.2 Discuss the developments in macroeconomics since Keynes, including supply-side approaches and the concept of stagflation

The Development of Macroeconomics since Keynes

Have there been any developments in macroeconomics since Keynes's publication of the General Theory?

Keynesian economics economics based on the premise that total output is determined by total spending; it emphasizes the demand side of the economy

Developments since the 1970s **Keynesian economics** lost its appeal during the 1970s. One explanation for the failing zeal of Keynesian economics was that the economy was no longer responding to Keynesian prescriptions as it had in the past. There were significant fluctuations in output and employment, and the economy experienced inflation. For example, the rate of growth of output fell from 7.7% in 1973 to only 2.6% in 1975. Worse yet, output actually fell by 3.2% in 1982, when the economy experienced a serious recession. The rate of inflation remained high during much of the 1970s and into the early 1980s.

Stagflation the simultaneous occurrence of high rates of inflation and high rates of unemployment

Simple Keynesian economics called for increased spending to combat recession and reduced spending to combat inflation. Fiscal policy initiatives will be explored in greater depth in Chapter 11. For now, we can acknowledge that this prescription was appropriate before the 1970s, when inflation was observed only during periods of rapid economic growth *or* when the rate of unemployment was low. But in the 1970s, economists observed high rates of inflation *and* high rates of unemployment at the same time. This simultaneous occurrence of high rates of inflation and high rates of unemployment—called **stagflation**—was a new, complex phenomenon. It was a situation beyond the scope of the simple Keynesian model.

BUSINESS SITUATION 4.1

Suppose it is widely known that a pro-Keynesian government is in power. The unemployment rate, while it has been coming down from its peak of 8.7% in August, 2009 is still considered relatively high today (7.8% as of March 2011). A businesswoman has been contemplating hiring additional workers to increase her firm's output to satisfy increasing demand.

Should this businesswoman hire the additional workers now or should she wait?

The answer to this Business Situation can be found in Appendix A.

supply side the production or cost side of the economy

Since the mid-1970s, macroeconomists have been considering new macroeconomic theories that they hope will help better explain how the macroeconomy operates. Keynesian theory emphasized manipulation of total spending or demand. One of the "new" approaches is the **supply-side** approach, which emphasizes the production or cost side of the economy. This supply-side approach became quite popular in the 1980s during the administration of U.S. President Ronald Reagan.

new classical economists economists who emphasize wage and price flexibility and believe in rapid macroeconomic adjustment

Today, there are two leading schools of thought in macroeconomics: the new classical and the new Keynesian schools. **New classical economists**(also called *neoclassical economists*) place emphasis on wage and price flexibility and believe in rapid macroeconomic adjustment. They are called new classical economists because their views are somewhat similar to those of the classical (pre-Keynesian) economists.

new Keynesian economists economists who emphasize wage and price inflexibility and believe that markets can fail to adjust

New Keynesian economists, in contrast, attempt to explain why wages and prices fail to adjust to clear the labour market. Because their explanation closely resembles Keynesian ideas, they are called new Keynesians.

There is an important similarity between the two schools of thought: they both agree that macroeconomics should be based on microeconomic foundations.

Reading Comprehension

The answers to these questions can be found on MyEconLab at www.myeconlab.com. MyEconLab

1. Why did the popularity of Keynesian economics decline during the 1970s?
2. In what sense is Keynesian economics demand-side economics?
3. In what ways are new Keynesian economists different from new classical economists? What do they have in common in their approach to the study of macroeconomics?

LO 4.3 Discuss the importance of macroeconomics

The Importance of Macroeconomics

Why is macroeconomics important?

macroeconomic policy deliberate government action taken to achieve economic objectives

Before the development of macroeconomics, governments in free enterprise economic systems did not see themselves as being responsible for the way the economy functioned. In fact, there was no such thing as **macroeconomic policy**—deliberate government action to achieve macroeconomic objectives. Governments adopted a *laissez-faire* attitude toward the economy. Today, in contrast, governments have a significant responsibility for regulating macroeconomic activity and aiming to ensure a certain level of economic stability.

monetary policy action taken by the central bank to change the money supply and interest rates to achieve economic objectives

incomes policies actions taken by the government to control wages and prices to achieve economic objectives

Macroeconomic theory provides a basis for government (public) policy. Keynes suggested that government spending and taxes could be used to regulate the economy. Fiscal policy (government spending and taxation decisions) is now an important tool that governments use to try to stabilize the economy. In addition, governments have some control over the quantity of money and credit in the economy to bring about certain desired macroeconomic conditions. Action taken by the central bank to change the money supply and interest rates to achieve economic objectives is called **monetary policy**.

The government also uses macroeconomics when it imposes direct controls on wages and prices—an instrument known as **incomes policies**. Incomes policies can be defined as actions taken by the government to control wages and prices to achieve economic objectives.

Do economists generally support incomes policies?

Most economists believe in the general efficiency of the market system. Because incomes policies impede the price adjustment mechanism, they are not generally well regarded by most economists. These intervention policies prevent market clearing that would otherwise occur in an efficient market and as such they are received with a certain degree of suspicion.

The importance of microeconomics in the business environment is self-evident. Is macroeconomics also useful in decision making at the firm level?

Business decisions are made not only within a microeconomic framework but also with consideration for the macroeconomic environment in which these businesses operate. A firm's profitability depends not only on its pricing and output decisions, and on the performance of other firms in the industry, but also on the performance of the whole economy. For example, during a period of rapid economic growth, the demand for the firm's product might be expected to increase. The firm's decisions should reflect this possibility.

Reading Comprehension

The answers to these questions can be found on MyEconLab at www.myeconlab.com. MyEconLab

1. Briefly discuss the importance of macroeconomics.
2. Distinguish between fiscal policy and monetary policy.
3. Why is it that economists do not generally support incomes policies?

LO 4.4. Construct a circular flow model of the economy that includes households, businesses, and the government

The Circular Flow Revisited

In the simple circular flow model that we studied in Chapter 2, we saw the interaction between households and firms. Can we use the circular flow diagram to show the interaction among households, firms, and government?

The circular flow diagram enables us to see the flow of some important macroeconomic variables among these three major economic players. Careful consideration of Figure 4.1 will show that it retains the key features of the *simple* circular flow model; but because of the introduction of government, the model takes on a more complex appearance.

Our analysis begins with the factor market, with households as the owners of the factors of production. Households sell labour services and other resources to firms. This is illustrated in the upper part of the diagram by the flow of resources (land, labour, and capital) from the households to the firms. They also invest in firms by purchasing shares (stocks) and lend to firms by buying their bonds. Some households work for the government; thus, labour resources flow from the households to the government as well. Households may also purchase government bonds. From the firms, the households receive wages, rent, interest, and dividends as payment for the resources provided to the firms. From the government, households also receive wages, salaries, interest, and dividend payments. In addition, some households may receive other payments, such as welfare and employment insurance benefits. Such payments are called **transfer payments**—payments that do not represent compensation for goods or services.

transfer payments payments that do not represent compensation for goods or services

Let's summarize up to this point. Figure 4.1 shows resources flowing from the households to the firms and the government. It also shows wages, rent, interest, and

Figure 4.1 The Circular Flow of Income and Expenditure

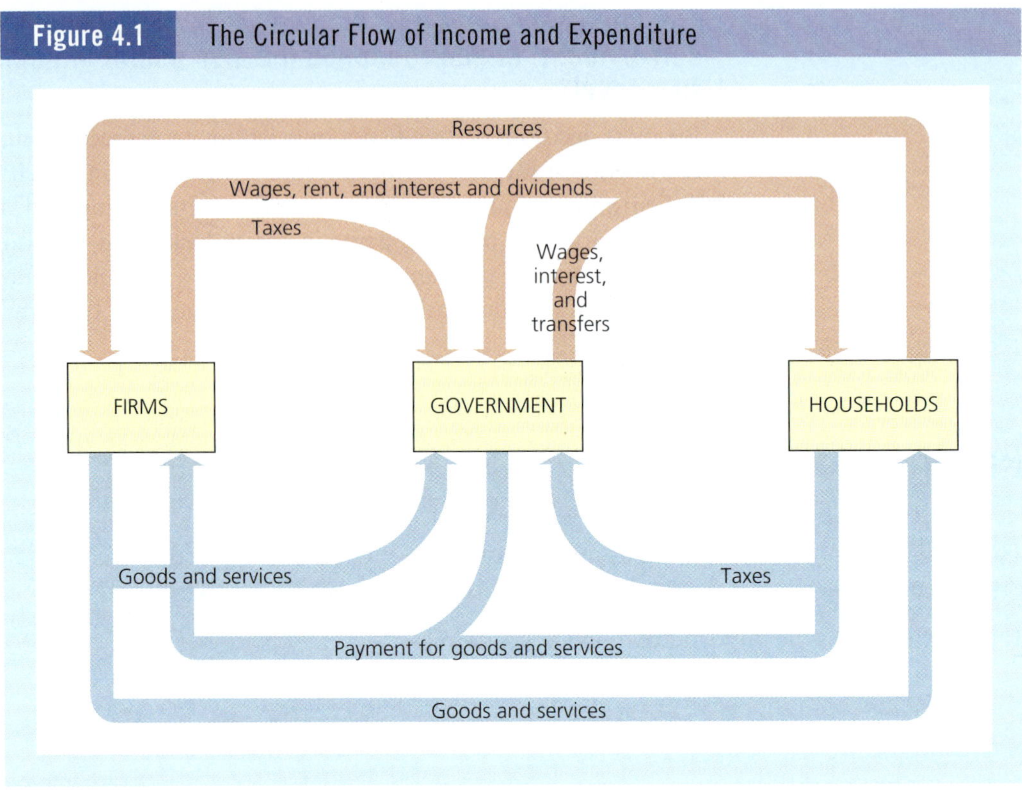

dividends flowing from firms to households; and it shows wages, interest, and transfer payments flowing from the government to the households.

With their income, households purchase goods and services from firms and pay taxes to the government. In addition to paying taxes, firms supply goods and services to the government, and they receive payment from the government. Figure 4.1 shows a flow of goods and services from firms to households, and a payment flow for goods and services from households back to firms. The diagram also shows a flow of taxes from households to the government, a flow of goods and services and taxes from firms to the government, and a flow of payment from the government to the firms.

It is important to note that the expenditure of any sector becomes the receipt of some other sector. This fact should not be surprising. If you purchase a car from General Motors, then the payment for the car becomes income to General Motors. Every economic transaction has two sides: a buyer and a seller. Any payment made must be received by someone. This is one of the main points illustrated by the circular flow model.

Reading Comprehension

The answers to these questions can be found on MyEconLab at www.myeconlab.com. MyEconLab

1. What roles do households, firms, and the government play in the macroeconomy? (Consider the circular flow model).
2. What resources are represented in the flow from households to firms?
3. What are transfer payments? Provide examples.

LO 4.5 Describe the performance of the Canadian economy, in terms of GDP, unemployment, and inflation, over the past few decades

The Behaviour of the Canadian Economy

How has the Canadian economy behaved over the past few decades?

We will attempt to answer this question by looking at the behaviour of three crucial macroeconomic variables: output, unemployment, and inflation. Let us begin with the growth of output.

Growth of GDP The total value of goods and services produced in the Canadian economy, or what is referred to as *gross domestic product* (*GDP*), grew from $13.9 billion in 1947 to $1622 billion in 2010.

Gross domestic product (GDP) is the market value of all the goods and services produced in a country during a specific period.

Figure 4.2 Growth Rate of GDP, 1962–2010

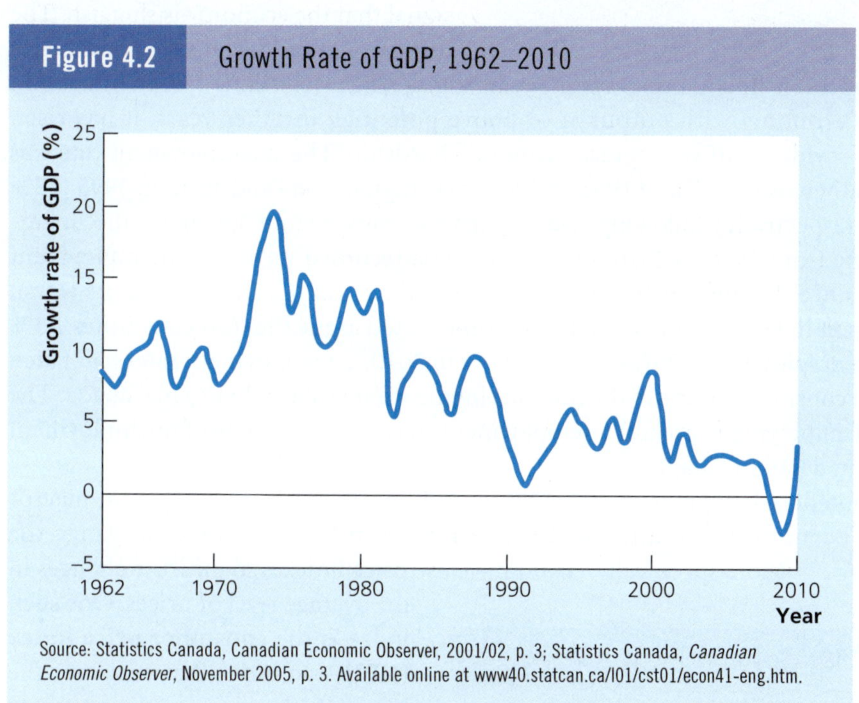

Source: Statistics Canada, Canadian Economic Observer, 2001/02, p. 3; Statistics Canada, *Canadian Economic Observer*, November 2005, p. 3. Available online at www40.statcan.ca/l01/cst01/econ41-eng.htm.

Throughout the period from 1962 to 2010, the average rate of growth of output was just under 8.0%. You should notice the short-term fluctuations throughout this period. In some years growth was considerable, more than 15% at times; in others, it was considerably more dismal, at less than 4%. Figure 4.2 gives you a clear picture of the growth rate of GDP in the Canadian economy in the years between 1962 and 2010. You'll notice the negative growth in 2009 (yes, a lower level of output in 2009 compared to that in 2008), a direct result of the most recent recession. In 2008, GDP was approximately $1599 billion. By 2009, GDP had fallen to $1527 billion. This represents a decline in the market value of output by 4.5%.

BUSINESS SITUATION 4.2

Since GDP is growing again, and it is widely anticipated that it will continue to grow into 2014, how should businesses react? Given the reduced level of aggregate demand, and the layoffs which followed during the recession in 2008–2009, do you think it is appropriate for business to respond in anticipation of this higher demand by hiring more labour and/or increasing production levels?

As a business owner, do you think it is wise to prepare for this anticipated demand by increasing production levels?

The answer to this Business Situation can be found in Appendix A.

Figure 4.3 Unemployment Rate, 1976–2010

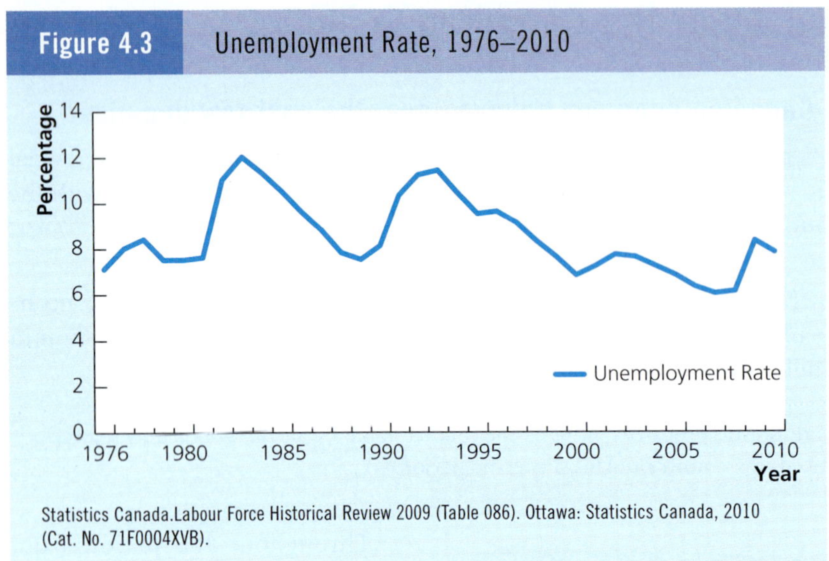

Statistics Canada.Labour Force Historical Review 2009 (Table 086). Ottawa: Statistics Canada, 2010 (Cat. No. 71F0004XVB).

The Unemployment Rate The **unemployment rate** is the number of working age Canadians actively seeking employment (yet currently unemployed) expressed as a percentage of the labour force. If the unemployment rate is high, then the economy is not operating at its potential. Given that our labour resources are idle, it makes sense that there must be forgone potential in the form of lost output. If the unemployed workers could be gainfully put to work, then the economy's total output would expand.

unemployment rate the number of working age Canadians actively seeking employment (yet currently unemployed) expressed as a percentage of the labour force

A high rate of unemployment is a signal that the economy is sluggish. The unemployment rate in Canada has shown considerable fluctuation. In some years, it has fallen well below 3%, an indication of an active economy with output at or above potential; in other years, it has risen above 11%—evidence of widespread economic hardship. The unemployment rate was relatively low between 1947 and 1953 and relatively high in 1983 and again in 1993 (12% and 11.4%, respectively) following two major recessions. Figure 4.3 shows the unemployment rate from 1976 to 2010. In 2007, Canada recorded its lowest unemployment rate (6.0%) since the mid-1970s. In 2008, another recession occurred and, at its worst, unemployment in Canada measured 8.3%. Some would argue that this constitutes 2.3% of cyclical unemployment. During the recovery in 2010, unemployment rates had fallen to 7.8%, still considerably above the full-employment rate (natural rate) in Canada. The topics of full employment, cyclical unemployment, and the natural rate of unemployment are covered in detail in Chapter 6.

consumer price index (CPI) an index that measures the level of the prices of consumer goods and services

As we noted earlier, price level stability is an important area of concern in macroeconomics. Economists are interested in the rate of inflation as a way to gauge the stability of prices. More specifically, economists use price indexes to measure changes in the average level of prices. One such index is the **consumer price index (CPI)**—an index that measures the level of the prices of consumer goods and services. (Price indexes will be discussed in detail in the next chapter).

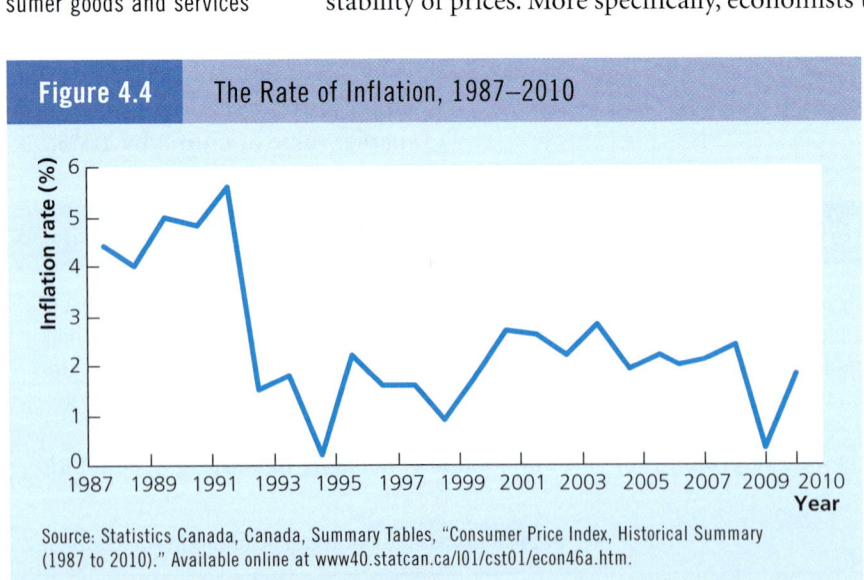

Figure 4.4 The Rate of Inflation, 1987–2010

Inflation rate (%): 0, 1, 2, 3, 4, 5, 6

Year: 1987 1989 1991 1993 1995 1997 1999 2001 2003 2005 2007 2009 2010

Source: Statistics Canada, Canada, Summary Tables, "Consumer Price Index, Historical Summary (1987 to 2010)." Available online at www40.statcan.ca/l01/cst01/econ46a.htm.

The Canadian economy experienced relative price level stability during the 20-year period from 1952 to 1971. The rate of inflation was particularly high in the mid-1970s, reaching nearly 11%.

Again, between 1980 and 1982, the rate of inflation was also relatively high, averaging 11.1% over the three-year period. As Figure 4.4

shows, prices have been fairly stable since 1990. Between 1990 and 2009, the average rate of inflation was 2.3%. As you will learn in Chapter 13, this is within the Bank of Canada's target range for inflation of 1%–3%. As GDP grew in 2010, the rate of inflation averaged 1.8%.

Reading Comprehension

The answers to these questions can be found on MyEconLab at www.myeconlab.com. MyEconLab

1. How would you describe the performance of the Canadian economy in terms of output?
2. Define the unemployment rate. Outline Canada's experience with unemployment over the past 30 years.
3. How successful has Canada been in managing inflation over the past few decades?

Review

1. Review the learning objectives listed at the beginning of the chapter.
2. Have you accomplished all the objectives? One way to determine this is to answer the Reading Comprehension questions at the end of each section. These will help you assess your understanding of the learning objectives.
3. If you have not accomplished an objective, review the relevant material before proceeding.

Key Points to Remember

1. **LO 4.1** Modern macroeconomics owes its origin to the work of John Maynard Keynes, who developed a macroeconomic model that explained the Great Depression of the 1930s. Before Keynes's work, economics was largely rooted in existing microeconomic theory.
2. **LO 4.2** The economic models that existed before Keynes's work were called classical models. According to classical economics, the economy could not experience prolonged periods of unemployment. The classical model failed to explain the entrenched recession experienced during the Great Depression of the 1930s.
3. **LO 4.2** New classical economics emphasizes wage and price flexibility and rapid macroeconomic adjustment. Conversely, new Keynesian economics emphasizes the failure of wages and prices to adjust and the consequences of such failure. New classical and new Keynesian economists agree that macroeconomics should be based on microeconomic foundations.
4. **LO 4.3** Macroeconomics provides a basis for public macroeconomic policy. Macroeconomics is also important in business decision making because the behaviour of the macroeconomy significantly influences private business decisions.
5. **LO 4.4** The circular flow model can be used to show the interaction among households, firms, and the government. The diagram illustrates that any payment made within the model must show up as a receipt within the same model.
6. **LO 4.5** In terms of the output of goods and services produced, the Canadian economy has performed reasonably well, with an annual average rate of growth of output of more than 8% over the past 40 years.
7. **LO 4.5** The Canadian economy has experienced fluctuations in the rate of unemployment, falling below 3% in some years and rising to as high as 11% in other years. The unemployment rate has averaged just more than 7% over the past six years.
8. **LO 4.5** In terms of price level stability, there has been fluctuation similar to that experienced with unemployment rates. In some years, the rate of inflation has been as high as 11%, while in other years, it has been as low as 0.2%.

Economic Word Power

Classical economic models (p. 113)
Consumer price index (CPI) (p. 120)
Fiscal policy (p. 114)
Great Depression (p. 113)
Incomes policies (p. 116)
Invisible hand (p. 113)
Keynesian economics (p. 115)
Macroeconomic policy (p. 116)
Monetary policy (p. 116)
New classical economists (p. 115)
New Keynesian economists (p. 116)
Stagflation (p. 115)
Supply side (p. 115)
Transfer payments (p. 117)
Unemployment rate (p. 120)

Problems and Exercises

Basic

1. LO 4.1 Identify each of the following statements as classical (C) or Keynesian (K):
   a. Flexible wage rates would eliminate unemployment
   b. Total spending is the main determinant of the level of employment
   c. Unemployment will cause wages to fall
   d. Unemployment results from wages that are too high
   e. Governments can use fiscal policy to reduce unemployment
2. LO 4.1 Indicate whether each of the following is true (T) or false (F):
   a. Keynesian economics emphasizes the supply side of the economy
   b. Keynesian economics is just the right medicine for stagflation
   c. New classical economics emphasizes wage and price flexibility and rapid economic adjustments
   d. New Keynesians believe that wages and prices are inflexible and that macroeconomic adjustment is slow
   e. Active fiscal policy is a product of new classical economics
3. LO 4.3 In the circular flow model with a government sector, give a specific example of each of the following:
   a. A resource flowing from households to government
   b. A resource flowing from households to firms
   c. Payment from government to households
   d. A flow from firms to households
   e. A flow from households to firms

Questions in the Intermediate and Challenging Sections cover several different concepts, and have not been organized by learning objectives.

Intermediate

1. Draw a graph with unemployment on the vertical axis and output on the horizontal axis to show the relationship that you would expect between unemployment and output.
2. Why would you expect output to be high during periods of low unemployment and low during periods of high unemployment?
3. Imagine that Statistics Canada has just announced that the rate of unemployment is expected to rise significantly in the near future. How might each of the following groups respond or react to this announcement? (What might each group do or not do?)
   a. Households
   b. Firms
   c. Government
   d. Labour unions
4. Suppose that Statistics Canada has recently announced that the rate of inflation is expected to fall significantly in the near future. How might each of the following groups respond or react to the announcement? (What might each group do or not do?)
   a. Households
   b. Firms
   c. Government
   d. Labour unions

Challenging

1. For some unknown reason, consumers and firms have become pessimistic about the future. Accordingly, they have reduced their current spending dramatically. What prediction would a Keynesian economist make about unemployment? What remedy would he or she prescribe?
2. Suppose that consumers and firms greatly curtail their spending because of pessimism about the economy in the near future. What prediction would a classical economist make about unemployment? What remedy would he or she prescribe?

Study Guide

Self-Assessment

What's your score?

Circle the letter that corresponds with the correct answer.

1. The "invisible hand" refers to
   a. The government's method of taxing us even before we receive our paycheques
   b. Supernatural powers that often save the economy from disasters
   c. The price adjustment mechanism
   d. The government's secret and invisible control of the macroeconomy

2. The Great Depression is recognized as a momentous period in the history of the Western world when
   a. A vast majority of the population experienced emotional depression
   b. The economy experienced severe unemployment and significant loss of output during the 1930s
   c. Because of overall shortages of most goods and services, the rate of inflation reached unprecedented high levels
   d. None of the above

3. Classical economists are
   a. Economists after Keynes who refined Keynes's ideas and formulated the first macroeconomic model
   b. Economists who believed that the economy would regularly experience prolonged periods of severe unemployment
   c. Economists who did not believe that the market mechanism (demand and supply) could explain the Great Depression
   d. Economists who believed that the market system would quickly solve any lapses from full employment

4. According to classical economics,
   a. Severe unemployment was a normal occurrence in a free enterprise economic system
   b. The solution to unemployment was higher wages
   c. The only macroeconomic problem that could be expected in a free enterprise economic system was unemployment
   d. If unemployment occurred, wages would fall until the unemployed were hired

5. Keynesian macroeconomics emphasizes
   a. Flexible wages and prices that would lead to full employment
   b. Total spending as the main determinant of income and employment
   c. The production side of the economy as the main determinant of employment
   d. None of the above

6. The origin of modern macroeconomics is most closely associated with
   a. Milton Friedman
   b. Alfred Marshall
   c. John M. Keynes
   d. John P. Hughes

7. A central idea in the General Theory is that
   a. The economy, if left alone, will produce desired outcomes
   b. Government has no role in a free market enterprise economic system
   c. Households and firms always have to be told what to do and how to do it
   d. Government spending and taxes could be used to control economic activity

8. Fiscal policy refers to
   a. Manipulation of the money supply by the central bank
   b. Direct controls on wages and prices to achieve certain economic objectives
   c. Non-involvement by government in the macroeconomy
   d. Changes in government spending and taxes as a means of effecting certain desired macroeconomic objectives

9. According to the simple Keynesian model of the economy,
   a. Increased spending can be used to control recessions
   b. Reduced government spending can combat recessions
   c. Increased spending can combat inflation
   d. Changes in spending have no effect on economic activity
10. High inflation along with high unemployment is called
   a. Deployment
   b. Conflation
   c. Stagflation
   d. None of the above
11. The simple Keynesian model had difficulty coping with
   a. Inflation
   b. Unemployment
   c. Stagflation
   d. All of the above
12. New classical economics places emphasis on
   a. The use of fiscal policy as a stabilization tool
   b. Non-economic determinants of economic activity
   c. The failure of the labour market to clear
   d. Rapid macroeconomic adjustment
13. New Keynesian economics places emphasis on
   a. The idea that wages and prices are flexible
   b. The notion that the economy adjusts rapidly
   c. The belief that wages and prices are inflexible
   d. None of the above
14. Which of the following is correct?
   a. Only governments use macroeconomics in decision making
   b. Only firms use macroeconomics in decision making
   c. Both governments and firms use macroeconomics in their decision making
   d. Only microeconomics can be used in private decision making
15. Macroeconomic policy may include
   a. Fiscal policy
   b. Monetary policy
   c. Incomes policy
   d. All of the above
16. Monetary policy is
   a. Another name for fiscal policy
   b. Conducted by the central bank
   c. The use of the government's budget to regulate the economy
   d. Identical to incomes policy
17. Incomes policies
   a. Enable the price system to function better
   b. Are conducted by the central bank
   c. Prevent the price system from functioning
   d. None of the above
18. The circular flow model shows that
   a. Transfer payments are payments for productive services
   b. Firms receive finished goods and services from households and provide households with resources
   c. The spending of one sector becomes an income receipt of some other sector
   d. All of the above
19. Gross domestic product refers to
   a. The value of goods and services produced by the economy
   b. The total amount of government spending in the economy
   c. The total value of all goods and services bought by all consumers during a specific period
   d. The sum of an economy's imports and its exports
20. The Canadian economy has experienced
   a. Inflation but not unemployment
   b. Unemployment but not inflation
   c. Both inflation and unemployment
   d. Economic growth without economic fluctuations

Problems and Exercises (Use Quad Paper for Graphs)

Answers to these questions can be found on MyEconLab at www.myeconlab.com. MyEconLab

1. Draw a circular flow diagram similar to Figure 4.1. Use your diagram to explain how the three sectors (households, firms, and government) interact.
2. Assume that wages are rigid and that there is neither a surplus nor a shortage of labour. Explain what is likely to happen to unemployment if a large number of immigrant workers enter the country.
3. Assume that wages are flexible and that there is neither a surplus nor a shortage of labour. Explain what is likely to happen to wages and unemployment if a large number of immigrant workers enter the country.
4. Briefly explain how a private individual could make use of the following macroeconomic information:
   a. The rate of unemployment
   b. The rate of change of output
5. Briefly explain how a firm could make use of the following macroeconomic information:
   a. The rate of inflation
   b. The rate of change of output

Chapter 5

National Income and Product Accounts

Learning Objectives

After studying this chapter, you should be able to

- **5.1** Explain national income accounting and its importance
- **5.2** Explain the concept of gross domestic product
- **5.3** Explain the two major approaches to measuring gross domestic product
- **5.4** Identify the main items included in the income approach to measuring GDP
- **5.5** Identify the main items included in the expenditure approach to measuring GDP
- **5.6** Discuss the shares of income and expenditure in the gross domestic product
- **5.7** Discuss the provincial and territorial gross domestic product
- **5.8** Discuss concepts related to the national income accounts
- **5.9** Explain how to use price indexes to deflate and inflate the gross domestic product
- **5.10** Discuss gross domestic product as a measure of economic well-being

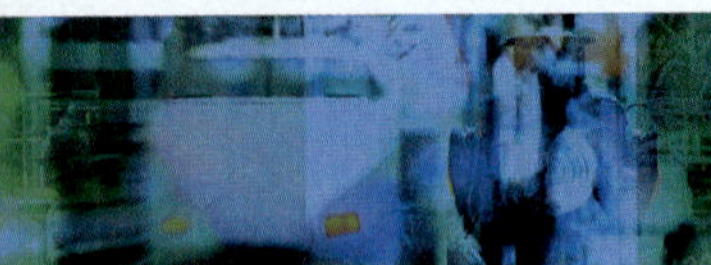

Assess Your Knowledge

MyEconLab

Answers to these questions can be found on MyEconLab at **www.myeconlab.com.**

1. What is the name of the federal government agency that is responsible for collecting and publishing statistics for Canada?
2. Indicate whether each of the following is true (T) or false (F):
   a. Imported goods are a part of Canada's gross domestic product because they increase our standard of living
   b. Exports must be subtracted from Canada's gross domestic product because the goods are sent out of the country
   c. Ontario is the largest producer of Canada's output
   d. A family is necessarily better off if it receives more income

LO 5.1 Explain national income accounting and its importance

National Income Accounting

What is national income accounting?

national income accounting the process of collecting, measuring, and recording data on the economy's output

Individuals who want to keep track of their income and expenditures over a given period do so by recording income and expenditure transactions. A business firm knows how well it is doing by keeping records that enable it to track its income and its expenditures. Similarly, to keep track of the performance of the economy as a whole, a country has to record a few aggregate measures that reflect the performance of its economy. The process of recording these aggregate measures is referred to as **national income accounting** and may be defined as the process of collecting, measuring, and recording data on the economy's output. It gives some indication of the health of the economy over time.

Who is responsible for measuring and recording these aggregate economic transactions?

Statistics Canada the special federal government agency responsible for collecting and publishing national economic and social statistics

A special federal government agency is responsible for collecting and publishing national income statistics. This agency is **Statistics Canada**, or *Statcan*, for short.

What is the importance of the statistics collected by Statistics Canada?

National income accounts provide much useful information about the pattern of economic activity. How is the economy performing this year compared with last year? What is the rate of growth of the economy's total output of goods and services? Clearly, these statistics are of great importance to economists and other researchers who are trying to explain economic and social phenomena. They are also important to policymakers in government and industry who need to formulate good economic policies. It is no wonder, then, that national income statistics are among the most closely watched figures collected by statisticians.

Reading Comprehension

The answers to these questions can be found on MyEconLab at www.myeconlab.com. MyEconLab

1. What is national income accounting and which government agency has the responsibility for Canada's national income accounting?
2. What is the importance of national income statistics?

LO 5.2 Explain the concept of gross domestic product

The Output of a Country

What is the relationship between a country's total output of goods and services and its standard of living?

Conceivably, a country's standard of living or economic well-being could be measured in a variety of ways. We could, for example, survey the members of the economy and come up with some standard-of-living index based on people's responses to certain questions. It is widely believed, however, that the economy's total production of goods and services is a relatively good measure of the country's standard of living. This measure, which is officially known as the **gross domestic product (GDP)**, is defined as the market value of all final goods and services produced in an economy during a specific period, usually one year.

gross domestic product (GDP) the market value of all final goods and services produced in an economy during a specific period

Are any particular points worth noting in the above definition of GDP?

Yes. There are a few points to note in the definition of GDP. First, GDP is a flow concept as opposed to a stock concept. GDP refers to the flow of output during the year and not to the stock of goods and services measured at some particular time in the year.

Second, GDP is expressed in monetary terms. The Canadian economy produces a large variety of goods and services annually. How do we add all these millions of different goods and services to arrive at a single number that indicates total output? We do it by using money as a common denominator and adding the value in monetary terms of all the items produced during the year. That is the meaning of the term *market value* in our definition. Imagine that you went grocery shopping and you bought 50 items. Instead of itemizing the 50 items—one loaf of bread, 1 dozen eggs, 1 litre of orange juice, 2 cans of peas, and so on—as is done on the cash register receipt, you could look at the total dollar value of these items, also shown on the cash register receipt. That is exactly how money is used to express the value of all goods and services produced in the economy.

Can this idea be illustrated by a simple example?

Let us assume that we are dealing with a very simple economy that produces only 100 000 kg of potatoes, 10 000 shirts, 8000 bottles of grape juice, and 500 bicycles in a year. Let us assume also that potatoes are sold at $0.50 per kg, shirts at $10 each, grape juice at $2 per bottle, and bicycles at $50 each. The total value of the goods produced in this simple economy (its GDP) would be calculated as in Table 5.1.

Table 5.1 GDP of a Simple Economy

Product/Service	Amount Sold	Average Price	Total Output
Potatoes	100 000 kg	$0.50	$50 000
Shirts	10 000 items	$10.00	$100 000
Grape juice	8000 bottles	$2.00	$16 000
Bicycles	500 items	$50.00	$25 000
TOTAL			**$191 000**

Thus, the GDP for this economy would be $191 000.

Is it possible to count an item more than once?

double counting counting an item more than once when measuring GDP

In adding the value of all goods and services produced in a year, we want to make sure that we count each good or service once and only once. The error that would be made by counting an item more than once when measuring GDP is called **double counting**.

The following example illustrates how double counting could arise. Suppose that farmers produce $60 million worth of wheat. The farmers then sell the wheat to flour mills. The flour mills produce flour, which they sell to bakeries for $100 million. The bakeries produce bread, which they sell to retail grocery outlets for $150 million. Table 5.2 illustrates the process.

value added the difference between the value of the output and the cost of the inputs

intermediate products the outputs of one firm or industry that are used as inputs by other firms or industries

final product a good or service intended for final use and not intended for resale or further processing

If we add the value of production at each stage of production, we arrive at a total of $490 million. This figure, however, overestimates the value of production in the economy because of double counting. The flour, for example, was made from $60 million worth of wheat that has already been counted. In fact, then, the flour producers added only $40 million to the production process. Similarly, the $150 million worth of bread sold by the bakeries contains $100 million worth of flour that has already been counted in the output of the flour mills, so the bakeries added only $50 million of production. This difference between the value of the output and the cost of the inputs is called **value added**. In other words, the value added by the flour producers is $40 million, and the value added by the bakeries is $50 million.

How can double counting be avoided in GDP calculations?

The wheat bought by the flour mills and the flour bought by the bakeries are called **intermediate products**, which are the outputs of one firm or industry that are used as inputs by other firms or industries. The bread sold by the retail grocers is a **final product**, a good or service intended for final use by the ultimate user, not intended for resale or further processing.

Table 5.2 Value Added in Production

Production	Value of Product ($ mil)	Value Added ($ mil)
Wheat production	60	60
Flour production	100	40
Bread production	150	50
Sales by retail outlets	180	30
TOTAL	**490**	**180**

So the steel and the fabric and the fibreglass used in the production of a car are intermediate products, whereas the car is the final product?

If we include the values of both intermediate and final products in our computation of GDP, we would be double counting.

I can see that, because the value of final goods includes all intermediate transactions.

Therefore, to avoid double counting, we must calculate only the values added at each stage of production or the total value of the final products. That's why the definition of GDP includes the phrase "final goods and services."

Some transactions do not reflect current production. How are they treated in national income accounting?

Treatment of Non-productive Transactions GDP measures the value of current production, not current sales. Thus, purely financial transactions that do not reflect current production are excluded from GDP. Examples of financial transactions that do not represent values of current production are government transfer payments, private transfer payments, and the sale and purchase of securities, such as bonds issued by corporations. **Government transfer payments** are payments made by the government that do not represent payments for productive services. Examples of government transfer payments are employment insurance benefits, welfare payments, old age security payments, and grants to students. **Private transfer payments** are transfers of purchasing power from one individual or group to another that do not represent payments for goods or services produced. For example, a grant from a private organization to a student would be a private transfer payment. Another example is an allowance that a parent gives to a child.

private transfer payments transfers of purchasing power from one individual or group to another for which no goods and services are produced

government transfer payments payments made by the government that do not represent payments for productive services (e.g., employment insurance payments, welfare payments, old age security payments)

Such transfers are not included in GDP because they do not represent payments for goods and services produced. The buying and selling of stocks (shares) and bonds are excluded from GDP because such transactions merely represent the exchange of financial instruments (certificates of debt) between people. They do not represent payments for production.

How does national income accounting treat the sale of used or second-hand goods?

If we focus on what the national account is measuring, the answer should be clear. Recall that the GDP attempts to measure the value of goods and services produced during a certain period. If we are measuring the GDP for 2009, then only goods and services produced in 2009 should be included. When a new car that is produced in 2009 is purchased in 2009, its value is included in the GDP for 2009. If the original purchaser of the new car sells it later, the amount obtained from that sale should not be included in the GDP. To include it would constitute double counting.

BUSINESS SITUATION 5.1

A Canadian manufacturer of automobile tires sells its products from coast to coast. It is now planning its production levels for the coming year.

How can national income accounting figures help with the production decision?

The answer to this Business Situation can be found in Appendix A.

Reading Comprehension

The answers to these questions can be found on MyEconLab at www.myeconlab.com. MyEconLab

1. What is the relationship between the total quantity of goods and services produced by an economy and its standard of living?
2. Define the gross domestic product (GDP) of a country.
3. Give an example of how double counting might occur. How can double counting be avoided?
4. Briefly explain the concept of value added.
5. Why are transfer payments not included in GDP?

Explain the two major approaches to measuring GDP

Measuring the Total Output of an Economy

How can the total value of all goods and services produced in an economy be measured?

The total value of goods and services produced in an economy can be measured in two main ways. We can measure income, or we can measure expenditure. Apart from statistical errors, both methods should give the same result since both methods measure the same thing. You will soon see why.

The two approaches can be illustrated by a simple circular flow diagram similar to the one shown as Figure 5.1.

We can measure the value of the goods and services produced in this simple model by measuring the total income earned by those who contribute to the production of the total output. This approach would be equivalent to measuring the inner flow in the top

Figure 5.1 The Circular Flow of Income and Expenditure

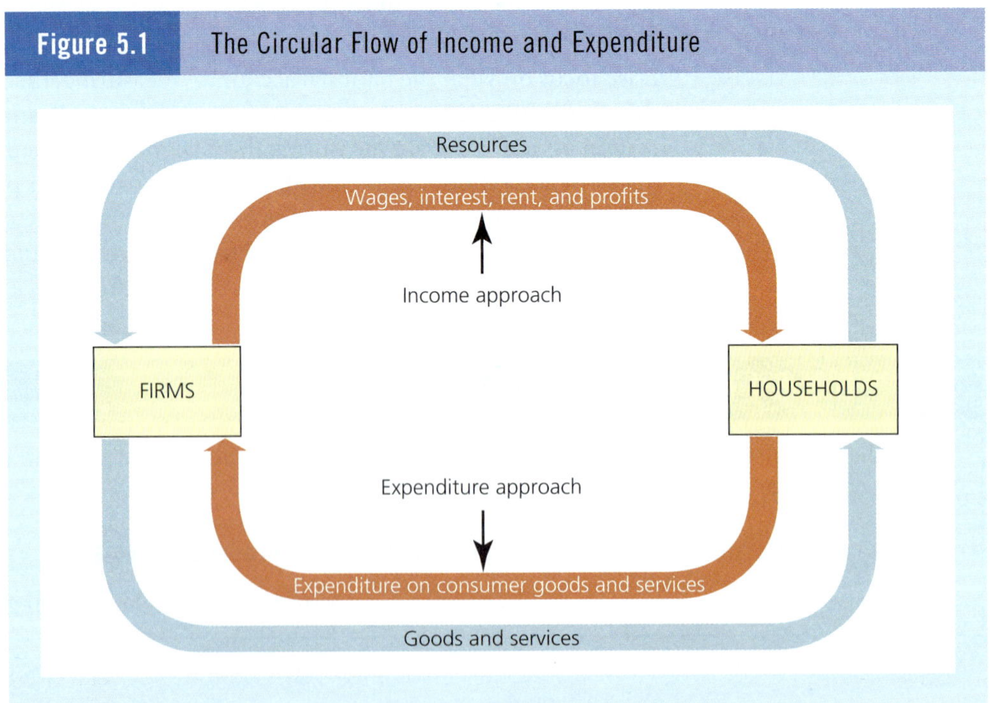

section of Figure 5.1. By so doing, we would be adding the incomes earned by the owners of the resources used in producing the total output. This method is called the **income approach**. The income approach is a method of calculating GDP that involves measuring the total income generated in the process of producing the economy's output of goods and services.

income approach a method of calculating GDP that involves measuring the total income generated in the process of producing the economy's goods and services

If a person earns an annual salary of $30 000, then this person's labour services contribute $30 000 to total output. Thus, the total amount earned by the factors of production and accruing to factor owners as income represents the total value of goods and services produced.

Alternatively, we can measure the value of the goods and services produced in the economy by measuring the total amount spent in purchasing the total output. This approach would be equivalent to measuring the inner flow in the bottom section of Figure 5.1. This method is called the **expenditure approach**. The expenditure approach is a method of calculating GDP that involves measuring the total amount spent on the economy's total output of goods and services.

expenditure approach a method of calculating GDP that involves measuring the total amount spent on the economy's total output of goods and services

The logic here is straightforward. If a total of $500 000 is spent in purchasing the economy's total output of goods and services, then the value of those goods and services must be $500 000.

Let us look a little more closely at these two approaches. All expenditures on goods and services are received as income by those who contribute to the production of the goods and services. Thus we arrive at the following identity:

$$\text{Total expenditure on the economy's output of goods and services} \equiv \text{Total income earned in producing the economy's output}$$

Reading Comprehension

The answers to these questions can be found on MyEconLab at www.myeconlab.com. MyEconLab

1. What are the two main approaches to measuring the total output of an economy? What does each approach measure?
2. Explain why total expenditure on the economy's output of goods and services equals the total income generated in producing that output.

LO 5.4 Identify the main items included in the income approach to measuring GDP

The Income Approach

What items are considered when using the income approach to measure the value of the economy's total output?

Recall that the incomes derived from labour, land, capital, and entrepreneurial services are wages and salaries, rent, interests and dividends, and profits, respectively. Thus, the income approach to measuring GDP involves totalling these various types of factor incomes. You will see later that an adjustment has to be made to arrive at GDP from summing the factor incomes. Table 5.3 shows the components of Canada's GDP in 2010 when using the income approach.

Table 5.3 Gross Domestic Product, Income-Based, 2010

Item	Value ($ mil)
Wages, salaries, and supplementary labour income	852 138
Corporation profits before taxes	173 908
Government business enterprise profits before taxes	15 929
Interest and miscellaneous investment income	69 433
Accrued net income of farm operators from farm production	843
Net income of non-farm unincorporated business, including rent	105 767
Inventory valuation adjustment	843
Taxes less subsidies on factors of production	74 143
Net domestic product at basic prices	1 293 004
Taxes less subsidies on products	99 002
Capital consumption allowances	229 057
Statistical discrepancy	466
Gross domestic product at market prices	1 621 529

Source: Statistics Canada, **http://www40.statcan.gc.ca/l01/cst01/econ03-eng.htm**

Let us examine the various categories in that table, beginning with wages, salaries, and supplementary labour income.

Wages, Salaries, and Supplementary Labour Income Wages and salaries are payments made to the hundreds of thousands of workers employed in the private and public sectors of the economy, including military personnel. Business executives, civil servants, nurses, teachers, engineers, computer programmers, salespeople, factory workers, administrative assistants, garbage collectors, and firefighters all earn wages and salaries. The number of people who earned wages, salaries, and supplementary labour income in Canada in 2010 totalled 17 041 000.

The concept of wages and salaries is clear, but what is supplementary labour income?

Wages and salaries are not the only payments that employers make for the labour services that they use. Supplementary labour income includes other payroll costs, such as employment insurance premiums and pension funds, which employers pay on behalf of their employees. In 2010, wages, salaries, and supplementary labour income amounted to $852 billion—about 70.0% of total income earned by all the factors of production.

Corporation Profits before Taxes The next item in the table is *corporation profits before taxes.* This income category can be best understood by considering the ways that corporations dispose of their total income (profits). First, they pay a portion to the government in taxes on profits. Second, they distribute a part of their profits to their shareholders as dividends. Third, they may withhold a part of the profits for reinvestment. Thus, this income category is the aggregate of three items: corporation income taxes, dividends paid to shareholders, and retained earnings or undistributed profits. In 2010, corporation profits before taxes amounted to almost $173.9 billion, representing just slightly more than 14% of total factor income. Between 2007 and 2009, corporate profits before taxes fell by almost 27%—another tale of the effect of the global recession.

Government Enterprise Profits Governments operate some business enterprises that may earn profits, such as Crown corporations. These operations use resources that produce income. The profits must be included as an income category. In this particular instance, you can think of the government as the entrepreneur, and the profits from government enterprises as the income (reward) for the entrepreneurial services provided by the government. Examples of Crown corporations in Canada are Canadian Broadcasting Corporation, Canada Post, Via Rail, SaskEnergy, and Hydro-Quebec. Crown corporations exist at the federal, provincial, and local levels of government. In 2010, profits from government business enterprises amounted to $15.9 billion, representing only about 1.3% of total factor income.

Interest and Miscellaneous Investment Income You must be careful not to confuse *interest and miscellaneous investment income* with investment, which is an expenditure item, not an income item. The focus here is on *income* from investment, not investment itself. Included in this income category are interest payments made by private businesses to individuals who provided financial capital. Interest payments made by the government are not included here because they are not payments for current goods and services. The interest that the government pays on its debt, for example, is considered a transfer payment and is therefore excluded from this income category. Miscellaneous investment income includes returns, such as royalties and dividends paid to individuals. Interest and miscellaneous investment income in 2010 was $69.4 billion, accounting for about 5.7% of total income from the factors of production.

Accrued Net Income of Farm Operators from Farm Production To arrive at the figure in the *accrued net income of farm operators from farm production* income category, the following items are added together: (1) total revenue from the sale of farm products, (2) the total value of farm products not sold but consumed on the farm, and (3) the value of the change in inventories of farm output. Because the figure we want to arrive at is net farm income, we subtract all expenses incurred in operating the farms and the depreciation of the real capital stock (farm machinery, equipment, and buildings) during the year. In 2010, this income category amounted to $843 million, or about 0.06% of total factor income.

Why do we include farm products not sold but consumed on the farm?

Well, let's focus on what we want to measure. We are trying to measure the value of all goods and services produced—whether sold or not—during the year. Because farm products consumed on the farm (perhaps by the farmers and their families) were produced during the period under consideration, they must be included. Of course, their value would have to be estimated, perhaps using the concept of opportunity cost.

Net Income of Non-farm Unincorporated Business, Including Rent The next category, *net incomes of non-farm unincorporated business, including rent*, includes incomes of single proprietorships, partnerships, self-employed people, and any other type of income other than corporation income and income derived from farm operations. (Corporation income and farm income are treated in separate categories.) Rent is included here as the income of landlords. Clearly, this category contains different types of income but no attempt is made to sort them into their respective classes as labour income or investment income. Net income of non-farm unincorporated business, including rent, was more than $105.7 billion, or roughly 8.7% of total factor income in 2010.

Inventory Valuation Adjustment During any period, the value of inventories (stocks of finished or semi-finished goods) may change because of changes in prices. Because the objective of national income accounting is to measure current production, an appropriate adjustment is made for so-called windfall profits resulting from valuing inventories at higher prices. In 2010, *inventory valuation adjustment* was $843 million.

Taxes Less Subsidies on Factors of Production Taxes are imposed on resources used in the production of goods and services. Examples are taxes on labour, land, buildings, and other assets used in the process of production. These taxes are viewed as costs to the firms that have to pay them. Also, subsidies are given on some of those factors of production. Examples are subsidies received by firms for labour, pollution abatement subsidies, and interest subsidies. To the extent that subsidies are granted to owners of resources used in production, they have the effect of reducing prices. *Taxes less subsidies on factors of production* amounted to $74.1 billion in 2010.

Net Domestic Product at Basic Prices This is an aggregate measure consisting of the sum of labour income; corporation profits before taxes; government business enterprise profits before taxes; interest and miscellaneous investment income; accrued net income of farm operators; unincorporated business income, including rent; inventory valuation adjustment; and taxes less subsidies on factors of production. *Net domestic product at basic prices* in 2010 amounted to $1293.0 billion.

Can we summarize the discussion up to this point?

Let us use W to denote the income category wages, salaries, and supplemental labour income; π to denote profits of corporations and government business enterprises; i to denote interest and miscellaneous investment income; R to denote net income of non-farm unincorporated business including rent; O to denote accrued net income of farm operators; and t_f for taxes less subsidies on factors of production. If we assume that inventory valuation adjustment is zero, then net domestic product at basic prices (NDP) can be expressed by the following summary equation:

$$\text{NDP} = W + \pi + i + R + O + t_f$$

Taxes Less Subsidies on Products Firms treat taxes imposed on their products as a part of their production costs. They take these taxes into consideration when pricing their products. Taxes on products include sales taxes, fuel taxes, import duties, and excise taxes on tobacco and alcohol. The government gives certain subsidies on products. Subsidies cause market prices to be lower than they would otherwise be. These subsidies must therefore be subtracted to arrive at market prices. Subsidies on products include those received by farmers on agricultural products, and subsidies received on transportation services such as Via Rail. *Taxes less subsidies on products* were estimated at $99 billion in 2010. We will use *tp* to denote taxes less subsidies on products.

Capital Consumption Allowances During any given year, the capital stock (plant, tools, equipment, etc.) used to produce the national output suffers some loss of value because of wear and tear. This loss of value in the economy's capital stock is called capital consumption because it measures the value of capital "consumed" (used up) during the year. The allowance made for this loss of capital is called **capital consumption allowance** or an allowance made for the depreciation of the economy's capital stock during production.

capital consumption allowance an allowance made for the depreciation of the economy's capital stock during production

By including capital consumption allowances, we convert our net figure to a gross figure. Capital consumption allowances amounted to $229.0 billion in 2010. We will use the letter *D* (for depreciation) to denote capital consumption allowances.

Statistical Discrepancy Although Statistics Canada tries to obtain accurate and reliable estimates of GDP, it is unlikely that both the income and the expenditure approaches to measuring GDP will produce the same result. The difference between the results obtained from using the two approaches is attributed to statistical error. We will return to the treatment of this discrepancy when we discuss the expenditure approach below. If we assume that there is no statistical discrepancy, and if we denote GDP income-based as GDP*Y*, then income-based GDP can be expressed as

$$GDP_Y = W + \pi + i + R + O + t_f + t_p + D$$

Reading Comprehension

The answers to these questions can be found on MyEconLab at www.myeconlab.com. MyEconLab

1. What are the main items included in the income approach to measuring GDP?
2. How can net domestic product be converted to gross domestic product?

 Identify the main items included in the expenditure approach to measuring GDP

The Expenditure Approach

Is the expenditure approach as complicated as the income approach?

In general, students find the expenditure approach a bit simpler than the income approach, probably because the expenditure approach contains fewer items.

What is the basic principle behind the expenditure approach?

If an economy produced only wheat, we could find the value of the wheat produced by finding out the total amount of money spent buying that wheat. The value of wheat bought logically equals the value of wheat produced. Similarly, by finding out the total expenditure on the economy's output of goods and services, we will arrive at the market

Table 5.4 Gross Domestic Product, Expenditure-Based, 2010

Item	Value ($ mil)
Personal expenditure on consumer goods and services	941 419
Government current expenditure on goods and services	352 698
Government gross fixed capital formation	67 312
Government inventories	–31
Business gross fixed capital formation	289 362
Business investment in inventories	2 048
Exports of goods and services	476 507
Imports of goods and services	507 320
Statistical discrepancy	–466
Final domestic demand	1 650 791
Gross domestic product at market prices	1 621 529

Source: Statistics Canada, **http://www40.statcan.gc.ca/l01/cst01/econ04-eng.htm**

value of total production—the GDP. This approach divides the economy's customers into four groups: consumers, government, firms, and foreigners. Table 5.4 shows how Statistics Canada classifies the groups that purchase the economy's output of goods and services to arrive at expenditure-based GDP.

Can we discuss each of these categories?

Let's begin with personal expenditure on consumer goods and services.

Personal Expenditure on Consumer Goods and Services By far, the largest component of total expenditure is *personal expenditure on consumer goods and services.* In the national income accounts, this item includes only spending by households on consumer goods and services. Consumer goods and services include durable consumer goods (such as cars, washing machines, household furniture, stereo systems, home computers, and refrigerators); semi-durable consumer goods (such as clothing and automobile tires); non-durable goods (such as hamburgers, orange juice, milk, chicken, soap, and cheese); and services (such as taxis, legal services, dental services, and plumbing).

Consumer expenditure constitutes the largest component of expenditure-based GDP.

You should note that the purchase of a house by a household is not included in the category of personal expenditure on consumer goods and services. Instead, Statistics Canada treats this expenditure as an investment expenditure (discussed below). Note also that government purchases of consumer goods and services are likewise excluded from this category, since the emphasis is on personal expenditure. This expenditure category does not therefore represent *total* expenditure on consumer goods and services but only *households'* expenditures on consumer goods and services. In 2010, personal expenditure on consumer goods and services amounted to $941.4 billion, or about 58.0% of total expenditures. We will use the letter *C* to represent this economic aggregate.

Government Current Expenditure on Goods and Services The expenditure category of *government current expenditure on goods and services* includes purchases of currently produced goods and services by the various levels of government. Purchases of uniforms, police services, educational services, and health and defence services are all included in this category. Remember, however, that government transfer payments are not included in this category because they do not represent expenditures for current production. As Table 5.4 shows, government current expenditure on goods and services amounted to $352.7 billion in 2010, accounting for about 21.7% of total spending. We will use *G* to symbolize government current expenditure on goods and services.

Government Gross Fixed Capital Formation and Government Inventories We can combine *government gross fixed capital formation* and *government inventories* into one category and refer to it as *government investment.* An example of fixed capital formation (real investment) by the government is the construction of a dam or the construction of a bridge. Inventories are stocks of finished and semi-finished goods. They are, of course, unsold, but they are treated as if the government buys them. Government investment was almost $67.3 billion in 2010—just about 4.2% of total spending.

Business Gross Fixed Capital Formation Three items constitute *business gross fixed capital formation*: residential structures, non-residential structures, and machinery and equipment. Residential structures include dwellings. Some types of dwellings are bought and rented out to earn a return, so it is relatively easy to see why these are categorized as investment. But even if the owner occupies the dwelling, it is still considered an investment and not consumption, because the owner could rent it out and earn a return.

Non-residential structures include the construction of such items as warehouses, office buildings, and commercial and industrial spaces. Machinery and equipment include tools and the various types of machines that are purchased by businesses. In 2010, the three items in the business gross fixed capital formation category amounted to approximately $289.4 billion or 17.8% of total spending.

It is still not clear why the purchase of a home is considered investment instead of consumption. After all, the purchase of a family car is considered to be consumption.

Perhaps it is easier to see the investment aspect of residential structures if viewed from the perspective of a developer. Developers construct new homes strictly as an investment. These new homes are accounted for as investment in national income accounting. To count them again as consumption when they are sold would constitute double counting.

Great! It's clear now.

Business Investment in Inventories Business inventories are treated similarly to government inventories—we assume that the firms that own them bought them. It is important to note that it is the value of the physical change in inventories that is recorded in the national accounts under this category. If firms start the year with an inventory of 500 metric tons of flour and end the year with 575 metric tons, then this difference of 75 metric tons must have been produced during the year and must therefore be added to the year's production. By similar reasoning, a decrease in inventories means that total expenditures during the year exceeded that year's total production. Thus, increases in inventories are added to business total expenditures, whereas decreases are subtracted. Let us use the symbol I_g to represent gross investment. The figure for business investment in inventories in 2010 was $2048 billion.

Total investment or gross investment consists of government and business gross fixed capital formation and government and business investment in inventories. We will see later how firms respond to changes in their inventories, and how such responses affect total production of goods and services.

Exports of Goods and Services A significant portion of our domestic production is bought by foreigners. Expenditures by foreigners on goods and services produced in Canada are referred to as *exports of goods and services.* Most of our exports (over 73%) are sold to the United States. Other important markets for our exports are the United Kingdom, other countries of the European Union, and Japan. Clearly, the value of exports must be included in our GDP. In 2010, Canada exported a total of $476.5 billion in goods and services. To put this figure in proper perspective, foreign countries purchased about 29% of our total output. We will use X to designate exports of goods and services.

Imports of Goods and Services Just as foreign countries purchase a significant portion of our total output, Canada buys a considerable amount of goods and services from foreign countries. Purchases of goods and services from foreign countries constitute imports. The major countries from which Canada buys its imports include the United States, which accounts for over 63% of Canada's imports, the United Kingdom, other countries of the European Union, and Japan. Canada's GDP is a measure of the value of the goods and services produced in Canada. Because expenditures on imports do not represent expenditures on domestic production, they must be deducted from GDP calculations. To include them would overstate the value of our total output. In 2010, Canada's *imports of goods and services* amounted to $507.3 billion. We will use the letter M to denote imports of goods and services.

net exports the difference between a country's sale of exports and its purchase of imports

Note: National income statisticians usually deduct imports from exports and refer to the result as **net exports** $(X - M)$. Net exports represent the difference between a country's sale of exports and its purchase of imports.

Statistical Discrepancy Statistical discrepancy is a balancing item in the national income and expenditure accounts. Statistics Canada compares the figures obtained from the income approach with those obtained from the expenditure approach. The difference between the two amounts is then divided by two. This amount (half of the difference) is then added to the smaller GDP figure and subtracted from the larger GDP figure, thus ensuring that GDP income-based and GDP expenditure-based are identical.

What is that item "Final domestic demand"?

Final domestic demand is the sum of four of the major items in this list: personal expenditure on consumer goods and services, government current expenditure on goods and services, government gross fixed capital formation, and business gross fixed capital formation. Final domestic demand in 2010 amounted to $1650.79 billion.

Can we summarize GDP expenditure-based?

Sure. Using the symbols introduced during the discussion, and using GDP_E to denote expenditure-based GDP, we can summarize the GDP expenditure-based as follows:

$$GDP_E = C + I_g + G + (X - M)$$

GDP income-based and GDP expenditure-based are just different methods of measuring the value of all goods and services produced in the economy. Therefore, the following identity must hold:

$$GDP_Y \equiv GDP_E$$

We have talked about gross investment. Is there such a concept as net investment?

In fact, there is. Let us take a closer look at the investment component in the GDP equation above. Gross investment (I_g) is the value of capital produced during the year. If from this value we subtract the depreciation suffered by the capital stock (i.e., capital consumption), we obtain net investment.

If we let I represent net investment and D depreciation (or capital consumption allowances) as before, then the following equation shows the relationship between gross investment and net investment:

$$I_g - I_n = D$$

Reading Comprehension

The answers to these questions can be found on MyEconLab at www.myeconlab.com. MyEconLab

1. What are the main items included in the expenditure approach to measuring GDP?
2. Why are imports entered with a negative sign in the expenditure approach to calculating GDP?
3. What is the role of the *statistical discrepancy* item in the national accounts?

LO 5.6 Discuss the shares of income and expenditure in the gross domestic product

Income and Expenditure Shares in the GDP

Can we show the income and expenditure shares in the GDP graphically?

Yes. Let's use pie charts to do so. Diagram A of Figure 5.2 shows the income components of GDP, while Diagram B shows the expenditure components of GDP. The percentage share of each is indicated in the graph.

Figure 5.2 Income and Expenditure Shares

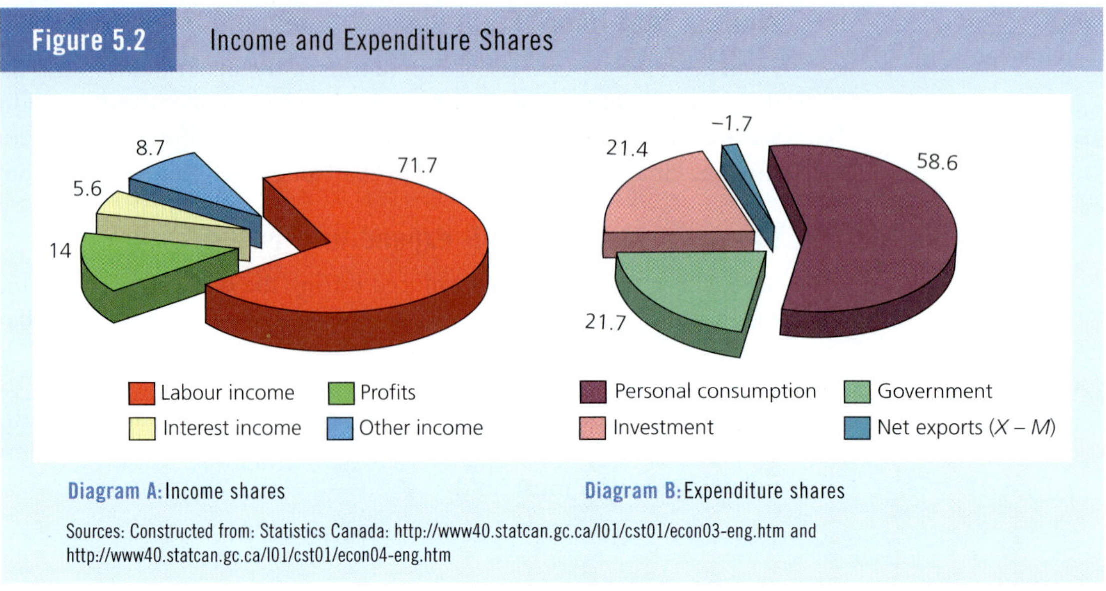

Sources: Constructed from: Statistics Canada: http://www40.statcan.gc.ca/l01/cst01/econ03-eng.htm and http://www40.statcan.gc.ca/l01/cst01/econ04-eng.htm

In the income shares, the profit component includes corporate profits and government enterprise profits. Other income includes accrued net income of farm operators from farm production and net income of non-farm unincorporated business, including rent. In the expenditure shares, the investment component includes both business and government investment.

Reading Comprehension

The answers to these questions can be found on MyEconLab at www.myeconlab.com. MyEconLab

1. Which component of income-based GDP accounts for the largest share of GDP?
2. Which component of expenditure-based GDP accounts for the largest share of GDP?

LO 5.7 Discuss the provincial and territorial gross domestic product

The Provincial Accounts

Do we have any information about the GDP of the provinces and territories?

Yes, we do. And we should look at the relevant data. So far, we have been discussing the income and product accounts for Canada. But we must remember that Canada is a country that is made up of 13 provinces and territories. The perception that we get when we look at the income and product accounts of Canada may be quite different from the situation in individual provinces or territories. Table 5.5 contains the GDP figures for the provinces and territories. The national (Canada) GDP is included for comparison.

You will notice from Table 5.5 that Ontario accounts for almost 40% of the total output of goods and services produced in Canada. Clearly, Ontario is the economic giant of Canada. The four Atlantic Provinces account for about 6% of Canadian output,

Table 5.5 Provincial and Territorial Gross Domestic Product, 2009

Canada: Provinces and Territories	GDP ($ mil)	% of Total
Newfoundland & Labrador	24 970	1.63
Prince Edward Island	4 750	0.31
Nova Scotia	34 283	2.24
New Brunswick	27 490	1.80
Quebec	303 747	19.90
Ontario	578 183	37.87
Manitoba	50 973	3.34
Saskatchewan	56 553	3.70
Alberta	247 184	16.20
British Columbia	191 006	12.51
Yukon	2 026	0.13
Northwest Territories	4 124	0.27
Nunavut	1 506	0.13
Canada	1 527 258	100.00

Source: Calculated from Statistics Canada:**http://www40.statcan.gc.ca/l01/cst01/econ04-eng.htm**

while Quebec and Ontario together produce almost 60% of the country's GDP. The Western Provinces (Manitoba, Saskatchewan, Alberta, and British Columbia) account for about 35% of the total output, while the Territories produce less than half of 1%.

Reading Comprehension

The answers to these questions can be found on MyEconLab at www.myeconlab.com. MyEconLab

1. In what way does a knowledge of the provincial and territorial accounts aid our understanding of the Canadian economy?
2. Which province or territory accounts for the largest share of Canada's GDP?

LO 5.8 Discuss concepts related to the national income accounts

Some Related Concepts

Is there a difference between gross domestic product and gross national product?

Gross domestic product (GDP) and gross national product (GNP) are very closely related, but they are not identical concepts. Before 1986, Statistics Canada used GNP as the basic measure of the economy's output of goods and services. In 1986, Canada joined the majority of Western nations by adopting GDP as the major national income accounting aggregate, leaving the United States, at that time, as the only major exception. In 1991, the United States switched to GDP as well.

That's good information, but it does not address the difference between GDP and GNP.

The difference between the two concepts can be seen by the following definitions:

> *Gross domestic product (GDP)* is the market value of all final goods and services produced within the borders of Canada, regardless of who owns the resources used to produce the output.

> *Gross national product (GNP)* is the market value of all final goods and services produced by the country's resources, regardless of where the resources are located.

Foreigners own some factors of production located in Canada. For example, American businesses own some of the buildings, machinery, and other productive assets located in Canada. Payments for those factors do not accrue to Canadians as income. They are included in GDP (because the production takes place in Canada) but not in GNP (because the resources are not owned by Canadian nationals). Also Canadians own factors of production located abroad. For example, Canadians own banks and other businesses in other countries. Payments to the owners of these factors of production accrue to Canadians as income. They are included in Canada's GNP but not in Canada's GDP. Thus, to obtain GNP from GDP, we must add the investment income that Canadians receive from investing abroad and deduct the investment income paid to foreigners for their investment in Canada. That is, we must add net investment income received from non-residents:

$$\text{GDP} + \text{Net investment income from non-residents} = \text{GNP}$$

Comparing GDP and GNP, which is usually bigger?

Usually, there is more foreign investment in Canada than Canadian investment abroad. Consequently, GDP is usually greater than GNP for Canada.

What is personal income?

personal income the total income of individuals from all sources before personal income taxes are paid

Personal Income There is a difference between the total income earned by individuals and total income received by individuals. **Personal income** is the total income of individuals from all sources before personal income taxes are paid. Personal income includes wages, salaries, rental income, interest and dividend income, and certain transfer payments from government and business. It is equal to the total of all factor incomes and transfer payments to that person (before taxes).

The discrepancy between income earned and income received occurs because factor owners do not receive all of the income they earn. Reductions include undistributed corporation profits or retained earnings and corporate income tax. Also, some households receive income that is not currently earned by them. This income comprises transfer payments, such as welfare payments, old age security benefits, employment insurance benefits, and Canada and Quebec Pension Plan benefits. Personal income in 2009 was estimated to be about $1228.4 billion.

Is personal income the same as disposable income? If not, what is disposable income?

Disposable Income Many people would be happy if personal income and disposable income were identical. Unfortunately, individuals have to pay taxes and make other con-

disposable income after-tax income that an individual can spend or save

personal saving the part of disposable income not spent on consumer goods and services

tributions to the government. Taxes include personal income taxes and personal property taxes. Personal transfers to the government include Canada and Quebec Pension Plans, workers' compensation, and employment insurance. These deductions from personal income result in a figure called **disposable income**—after-tax income that an individual can spend or save.

Disposable income = Personal income − Personal taxes − Personal transfers to government

You can think of disposable income as take-home pay that you can use to spend or save.

Consumers spend a part of their disposable income on consumer goods and services. The remainder is **personal saving**, the part of disposable income not spent on consumer goods and services—or the difference between an individual's disposable income and his or her consumption. Therefore,

Disposable income = Consumption + Saving

In 2009, disposable income in Canada totalled $965.6 billion, of which about $44 billion was allotted to personal saving.

Can a circular flow diagram illustrate the relationships between the major macroeconomic aggregates that we have studied so far?

We can construct a circular flow model that focuses on the relationship between the income and expenditure flows discussed so far in this chapter. Such a model is presented as Figure 5.3.

The diagram might look somewhat intimidating but it is really easy to understand. The cast of characters in this play includes firms, households, government, and the rest of the world. We have greatly simplified the interaction between the characters; otherwise, the model would resemble a network of blood vessels!

Let us begin with the bottom half, which shows the income half of the circular flow, and let us pick up the flow at the firms. The firms produce the economy's output of goods and services (GDP), which generates aggregate income. Out of the aggregate income, government collects taxes, so taxes flow from aggregate income to the government. The government also makes transfer payments, so these transfer payments flow from the government back into the income stream. We can calculate the disposable income by subtracting taxes and adding transfer payments. These relationships are illustrated in the bottom half of the diagram.

Let us now turn our attention to the top half of the diagram. This, of course, is the expenditure half. Let us start with the households. They have only two options for allocating their disposable income: they can spend it on consumer goods and services, or they can save it. Thus, consumption and saving flow out from households. Consumption continues in the expenditure stream, while saving flows into the financial sector, which includes banks and other financial institutions that collect funds from savers and lend them to borrowers.

For simplicity, we will assume that only households save. Firms invest by borrowing the savings of households, which are now in the hands of the financial sector. Thus, we see investment (I_g) flowing from the financial sector into the expenditure stream, joining consumption (C) to become $C + I_g$. This flow of $C + I_g$ is then joined by the flow of government purchases (G) to form $C + I_g + G$.

Now, some of this expenditure is siphoned off into imports (M), because households, firms, and government buy goods and services from the rest of the world. But at the same time, the rest of the world buys goods and services from Canada. These

Figure 5.3 The Circular Flow of the Relationship between Aggregate Income and Aggregate Expenditure

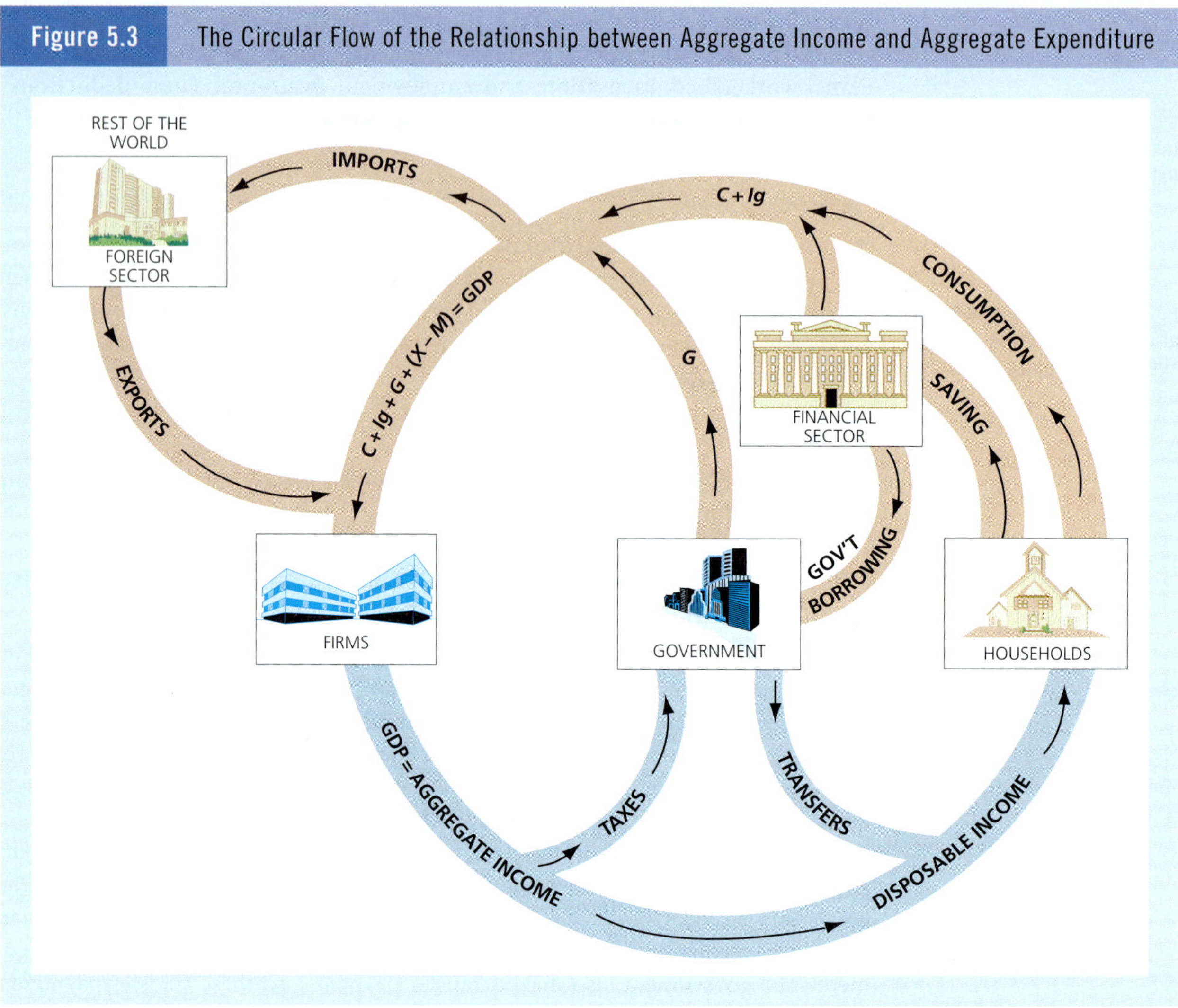

exports (X) enter the expenditure stream as shown in the diagram. So now, our expenditure stream becomes the familiar $C + I_g + G + (X - M)$, which of course, is GDP expenditure-based. The circular flow shows graphically that

$$\text{GDP} = \text{aggregate expenditure} = C + I_g + G + (X - M)$$

Reading Comprehension

The answers to these questions can be found on MyEconLab at **www.myeconlab.com**. MyEconLab

1. What is the difference between GDP and GNP? Which of these economic aggregates is likely to be larger in Canada and why?
2. What are the components of personal income? Which of these components do not constitute income *earned* by the owners of the factors of production?
3. What is personal income? What is the relationship between personal income and disposable income?
4. Refer to the circular flow diagram shown as Figure 5.3. What is the role of the financial sector?

LO 5.9 Explain how to use price indexes to deflate and inflate the gross domestic product

Inflating and Deflating the Gross Domestic Product

Do changes in prices affect the GDP?

Yes. Because GDP is expressed in monetary terms, price changes can affect our measure of the total value of the economy's output of goods and services. The following example illustrates the effect of price changes on GDP.

Suppose an economy produces only one product: potatoes. Let us assume that in Year 1, the output of potatoes was 500 000 kg. If potatoes were sold at \$0.50 per kg, the gross domestic product of our hypothetical economy would be

$$500\,000 \times \$0.50 = \$250\,000$$

In Year 2, if the output of potatoes was 520 000 kg of potatoes and the price of potatoes had risen to \$0.75 per kg, the gross domestic in Year 2 would be

$$520\,000 \times \$0.75 = \$390\,000$$

The GDP would therefore show an increase of 56%, but the output of potatoes would show an increase of only 4%. This is the effect of valuing the output at market prices. In making comparisons, we must adjust the GDP for price changes.

How can we adjust the GDP of this hypothetical economy in Year 2 to account for price changes?

base year or base period a year chosen as a reference point against which other years are measured

price indexes numbers that measure changes in prices over time

Let us use Year 1 as our reference point or **base year** or **base period**. The base year is a year chosen as a reference point against which other years are measured. The base year always has an index of 100. This means that we are going to use the price prevailing in Year 1 to evaluate the GDP in Year 1 and Year 2.

We then construct **price indexes** (numbers that measure changes in prices) for each year, based on the percentage change in prices. In our example, in Year 1, the price of potatoes was \$0.50. In Year 2, the price rose to \$0.75—an increase of 50%. We always give the base period a value or an index of 100. We must then give Year 2 an index of 150 to indicate the 50% price increase.

To calculate the *real* increase in output, we deflate the GDP by dividing it by the price index (P) and multiplying by 100. Thus, we can calculate the real gross domestic product (real GDP) for Year 2 as follows:

$$\frac{390\,000 \times 100}{150} = \$260\,000$$

In general, the formula for converting GDP to real GDP is

$$\text{Real GDP} = \frac{\text{GDP}}{P} \times 100$$

where P is the price index.

GDP that is not adjusted for price changes is referred to as nominal GDP.

> We can calculate the price index for a hypothetical one-product economy quite easily. However, for a modern economy with a vast number of different goods and services, the calculation of price indexes is more difficult. We will return to price indexes in a later chapter. Once we have calculated the price indexes, we can easily deflate the GDP. That is, we can easily express the gross domestic product in real terms.

Of course, if we know real GDP and nominal GDP, we can easily calculate the price index by using the following formula:

$$\text{Price index} = \frac{\text{Nominal GDP}}{\text{Real GDP}} \times 100$$

Example: If nominal GDP in a given year was $1374 billion, and the real GDP in the same was $1248 billion, then the price index can be calculated as:

$$\text{Price index} = \frac{1374 \times 100}{1248} = 110$$

Can we illustrate further how price indexes can be used to express the GDP in real terms?

nominal GDP GDP expressed in current dollars

real GDP GDP expressed in constant dollars

Let's study Table 5.6. All the figures for the years before 2002 (the base year) have been inflated, and the figures for the years after 2002 have been deflated. We can now compare the figures in column 4, because they are all expressed in the same unit—namely, 2002 dollars. The figures for GDP in column 2 are expressed in current dollars. We call these figures **nominal GDP**—GDP expressed in current dollars. The figures for gross domestic product in column 4 are expressed in constant (2002) dollars. We call these figures **real GDP**—GDP expressed in constant dollars.

Table 5.6 Deflating GDP for Price Level Changes (hypothetical data)

Year (1)	Nominal GDP ($ mil) Current prices (2)	Price Indexes (2002 = 100) (3)	Calculation of Real GDP in 2002 dollars ($ mil) Constant prices (4)
2000	1315	86	$\frac{1315}{86} \times 100 = 1529$
2001	1470	95	$\frac{1470}{95} \times 100 = 1547$
2002	1595	100	$\frac{1595}{100} \times 100 = 1595$
2003	1700	105	$\frac{1700}{105} \times 100 = 1619$
2004	1810	109	$\frac{1810}{109} \times 100 = 1661$
2005	2040	113	$\frac{2040}{113} \times 100 = 1805$
2006	2169	118	$\frac{2169}{118} \times 100 = 1838$
2007	2319	122	$\frac{2319}{122} \times 100 = 1901$
2008	2510	127	$\frac{2510}{127} \times 100 = 1976$
2009	2695	133	$\frac{2695}{133} \times 100 = 2026$

Table 5.7 Canada's GDP in Constant 2002 Dollars, 2010

Item	Value (2002 $ mil)
Personal expenditure on consumer goods and services	841 868
Government current expenditure on goods and services	281 575
Government gross fixed capital formation	56 085
Government inventories	–26
Business gross fixed capital formation	246 275
Business investment in inventories	8 834
Exports of goods and services	444 381
Imports of goods and services	566 472
Statistical discrepancy	–381
Real GDP at market prices	1 325 085

Source: Statistics Canada:**http://www40.statcan.gc.ca/l01/cst01/econ05-eng.htm**.

How do we interpret the figures in columns 2 and 4?

We can interpret the figures in columns 2 and 4 as follows: $1315 million in 2000 was equivalent to $1529 million in 2002, and $2695 million in 2009 was worth only $2026 million in 2002.

Are statistics available for real GDP for Canada?

In Table 5.7 we show real GDP for Canada. Statistics Canada used 2002 as the base year for this table.

Reading Comprehension

The answers to these questions can be found on MyEconLab at **www.myeconlab.com**. MyEconLab

1. Explain why a change in prices will affect a country's GDP.
2. What is the difference between nominal GDP and real GDP?
3. How are price indexes used to deflate a country's GDP?

LO 5.10 Discuss gross domestic product as a measure of economic well-being

Gross Domestic Product as a Measure of Economic Well-Being

How good is GDP as a measure of a nation's standard of living?

Earlier in this chapter, we noted that the value of the goods and services produced by an economy could give some indication of the standard of living in that economy. In this context, the relevant concept is *real* GDP.

However, for a number of reasons that we will discuss below, the real GDP of a country may not adequately indicate how well off the people in that economy are. The size of the population, the distribution of output, non-marketed goods and services, the underground economy, leisure, the quality of life, and the health of a nation's environment are all important factors in determining the well-being of a society.

Can we discuss each of these factors?

Let us begin with the size of the population.

The Size of the Population The GDP does not tell us anything about the number of people who must share in the total output of goods and services. The real GDP of a country may increase from one year to another, but if the population increases at a faster

real per capita output real GDP divided by the population

rate than the output does, then the people will be worse off on average. A more meaningful measure of economic well-being is **real per capita output**. Real per capita output is GDP divided by the population.

$$\text{Real GDP per capita} = \frac{\text{Real GDP}}{\text{Population}}$$

Real per capita output, or output per person, is a measure of how much each individual in the country would receive if the total output were divided equally among the population.

Can this idea be illustrated, perhaps by an arithmetic example?

Let's look at Table 5.8, which presents hypothetical GDP data for a very small region.

The table shows a steady increase in real GDP from Year 1 to Year 5. During the same period, however, population increased at the same rate. Real GDP per capita (or real per capita output), therefore, did not change.

The Distribution of Output Another shortcoming of GDP is that it does not measure who receives the wealth of a country. Although the real GDP per capita is a more meaningful measure of economic well-being than real GDP, we should remember that per capita output is just an average; it tells us nothing about the distribution of total output among households. For example, let's compare two societies. In the first society, an output of $50 million is fairly evenly distributed among all the households. In the second society, the same volume of output is divided so that 10% of the population receives 90% of the total output, while the majority of households barely manage to survive. Which of these two societies is better off? Most people would agree, correctly, that the first society would enjoy a better living standard than the second. Many societies experience these sharp differences in the distribution of wealth.

underground economy all economic activities that are not reported to government and on which no taxes are paid

Non-marketed Goods and Services Because the GDP is the *market value* of all goods and services produced, it includes, for the most part, only those goods and services that are sold in regular, recognized markets. Thus, many goods and services produced do not get counted in the GDP, because they are not sold. These include housework, home garden cultivation, garage chores, meal preparation, child care, and volunteer work. To the extent that these productive services are omitted from GDP, the recorded GDP figures underestimate the true GDP. This suggests that the society might be better off than is indicated by the GDP figures.

Table 5.8 Real GDP, Population, and Real GDP Per Capita (hypothetical data)

Year	Real GDP ($)	Population	Real GDP per Capita ($)
1	10 000	200	50
2	12 000	240	50
3	13 000	260	50
4	15 000	300	50
5	16 000	320	50

The Underground Economy The **underground economy** refers to all economic activities that are not reported to government and on which no taxes are paid; thus, they are not reported by national income statisticians. Such transactions include illegal activities, such as prostitution and illicit drug trading, and so-called under-the-table transactions, such as the payment of cash to a roofer without receiving any receipt.

How big is this underground economy?

Statistics Canada has estimated that the size of the underground economy is about 5.2% of GDP, or approximately

$84.3 billion. To put the size of the underground economy in perspective, it is about 90% of the size of the combined GDP of Newfoundland and Labrador, Nova Scotia, and New Brunswick.

Wow! That's massive. Does illegal activity increase well-being?

The answer to that question is probably more subjective than objective. It is debatable whether illegal activities increase well-being. The individuals who willingly engage in such activities must feel that they do derive some net benefits. From the viewpoint of the society as a whole, however, these activities may be considered as discommodities (i.e., bads rather than goods).

The case of under-the-table transactions is different. Each year, babysitters, dentists, private tutors, carpenters, accountants, and so on, provide a wide variety of services. Such services do increase the total amount of goods and services produced during the year and therefore add to our economic well-being. They are, however, not reflected in the national accounts if they are paid for under the table.

Leisure GDP also does not adequately account for leisure. The number of hours spent to produce a given volume of GDP has decreased considerably over the years, because of productivity improvement. This means that there has been an increase in leisure time, which obviously represents a gain in well-being. This gain in well-being, however, is not reflected in GDP, because leisure is not explicitly traded in the formal market. We could produce a greater GDP by working 50 hours a week instead of 40. If we choose to work only 40 hours a week, it is because we feel that we are better off working 40 hours instead of 50 hours a week. So although leisure is part of a high standard of living, it is not part of GDP.

Quality of Life and Environmental Issues In discussing how well off we are, we are, in fact, discussing the quality of life. That's why we can say that an increase in the amount of leisure available results in an improvement in the quality of life. Other things being equal, the more we produce, the better will be the quality of life for us. But our production and consumption of goods and services cause a certain amount of environmental damage. Polluted rivers and lakes, destroyed vegetation and animal life, noise, foul air, and smog are just some of the environmental problems that plague us. These things obviously reduce the quality of life, but they are not reflected in GDP.

Is there a better measure of economic well-being than the GDP?

The discussion so far has pointed to a number of flaws or limitations in using GDP as a measure of economic and societal welfare or well-being. A better measure of economic well-being (BMEW) would require some adjustments to the GDP. By adding certain items to GDP and by subtracting some other items, we can arrive at a better measure of economic well-being:

$$\text{GDP} + \text{Non-marketed goods and services} + \text{Under-the-table transactions} - \text{Environmental damage} = \text{BMEW}$$

Is there any official index of human well-being?

Human Development Index (HDI) a composite index designed to measure human well-being in a country

In 1990, a Pakistani economist named Mahbub ul Haq developed the **Human Development Index (HDI)**, which is a composite index designed to measure human well-being in a country. Since 1993, the United Nations Development Programme (UNDP) has used the HDI to rank countries according to well-being. The Human Development Report 2010 ranked countries into four categories: very high human development, high human development, medium human development, and low human development. Canada ranked eighth in the very high human development category behind Norway, Australia, New Zealand, United States, Ireland, Liechtenstein, and Netherlands.

According to the United Nations, "human development is about much more than the rise or fall of national incomes. It is about creating an environment in which people can develop their full potential and lead productive, creative lives in accord with their needs and interests" (http://hdr.undp.org/hd/). In addition to the GDP per capita, the component elements of the HDI include life expectancy at birth, adult literacy rate, and combined primary, secondary, and tertiary gross enrolment ratio. Thus, a country with a high GDP per person could have a relatively low HDI if it were severely deficient in the other components of HDI.

Reading Comprehension

The answers to these questions can be found on MyEconLab at www.myeconlab.com. MyEconLab

1. Discuss the advantage of real GDP over real GDP per capita as a measure of the standard of living.
2. Does GDP adequately measure the standard of living of a country? Explain why or why not. If GDP does not adequately measure the well-being of a country, what adjustments can be made to obtain a better measure of economic well-being?
3. Give four examples of non-marketed goods and services. How do these affect GDP as a measure of economic well-being?
4. What do you understand by the term "underground economy"? Give some indication of the magnitude of Canada's underground economy.
5. Describe the composition of the Human Development Index (HDI). For what is this index used?

Review

1. Review the learning objectives listed at the beginning of the chapter.
2. Have you accomplished all the objectives? One way to determine this is to answer the Reading Comprehension Questions at the end of each section. This will help you assess the extent to which you have accomplished the learning objectives.
3. If you have not accomplished an objective, review the relevant material before proceeding.

Key Points to Remember

1. LO 5.1 National income accounting is the process of collecting and recording data on the economy's output of goods and services. The statistics collected are extremely important for public and private decision making.
2. LO 5.2 Gross domestic product, or GDP, is the market value of all final goods and services produced in an economy during a specific period.
3. LO 5.3 We can measure the value of the total output of goods and services produced in the economy (the GDP) by adding the incomes earned in the process of production (the income approach) or by adding all expenditures on the economy's output (the expenditure approach).
4. LO 5.4, 5.5 The main items included in the income approach are wages and salaries, rental income, investment income, and profit income. The main items included in the expenditure approach are personal expenditure on consumer goods and services, investment expenditure, government purchases of goods and services, and net exports.

5 LO 5.6 Wages and salaries constitute the largest income share in the gross domestic product. Personal expenditure on consumer goods and services constitutes the largest expenditure share in the gross domestic product.

6. LO 5.7 The gross domestic product of the provinces and territories helps to give us a clearer understanding of Canada's GDP. By looking at the parts we get a better picture of the whole.

7. LO 5.8 Other aggregates related to national income accounting include gross national product, personal income, disposable income, and personal saving. A circular flow diagram can be used to show the relationship between the income and expenditure flows.

8. LO 5.9 To compare one year's GDP with that of another year, we must express the figure for GDP in constant (real) dollars. To do this, we deflate each year's GDP by the appropriate price index.

9. LO 5.10 GDP does not adequately measure well-being because (1) it ignores the size of the population, (2) it ignores the distribution of output among citizens, (3) it omits non-marketed goods and services and the underground economy, (4) it does not account for leisure, and (5) it does not measure the quality of life or the health of the environment.

10. LO 5.10 The Human Development Index (HDI) is a summary index that is used by the United Nations Development Programme (UNDP) to measure the well-being of countries. The index comprises GDP per capita, life expectancy at birth, and adult literacy.

Economic Word Power

Base year or base period (p. 145)
Capital consumption allowance (p. 135)
Disposable income (p. 143)
Double counting (p. 128)
Expenditure approach (p. 131)
Final product (p. 128)
Government transfer payments (p. 129)
Gross domestic product (GDP) (p. 127)
Human Development Index (HDI) (p. 149)
Income approach (p. 131)
Intermediate products (p. 128)
National income accounting (p. 126)
Net exports (p. 138)
Nominal GDP (p. 146)
Personal income (p. 142)
Personal saving (p. 143)
Price indexes (p. 145)
Private transfer payments (p. 129)
Real GDP (p. 146)
Real per capita output (p. 148)
Statistics Canada (p. 126)
Underground economy (p. 148)
Value added (p. 128)

Problems and Exercises

Basic

1. LO 5.2 Which of the following should be included in Canada's GDP for 2010?
   a. Allowances totalling $2000 from a father to his teenage daughter in 2010
   b. Payments amounting to $4000 from a business person to a gardener for gardening services provided in 2010
   c. Cars produced in 2010 but sold only in January 2011
   d. A 2009 automobile sold in 2010
   e. A sum of $5000 received in 2010 for the sale of an antique chair at least 100 years old

2. LO 5.2 Suppose that sheep ranchers produce $60 million worth of wool, which they sell to wool processors. The wool processors process the wool, which they sell to suit manufacturers for $85 million. The suit manufacturers produce suits, which they sell to wholesalers for $105 million, who in turn, sell the suits for $180 million. Complete Table 5.9, showing sales and values added at each stage of production.

Table 5.9 Value Added

	Sales ($ mil)	Value Added ($ mil)
Sheep ranchers	______	______
Wool processors	______	______
Suit manufacturers	______	______
Wholesalers	______	______
Retailers	______	______

3. LO 5.4, 5.5 Under which category of the national income accounts for Canada would you include each of the following? Use the following symbols:
   C = consumption
   I = investment
   G = government purchases
   X = exports of goods and services

M = imports of goods and services
W = wages and salaries
R = rental income
i = interest and dividends
π = profits

a. The purchase of an airline ticket to Jamaica
b. The payment made to a garage for car repairs
c. The amount of money earned on Laura's savings account
d. The purchase of a new home
e. The government builds a new hospital
f. Canadian firms purchase merchandise from China
g. Canadian families spend $1500 on hotel accommodation and transportation in Antigua
h. Canadian corporations pay out a part of their earnings to shareholders
i. A government school board purchases paper and other office supplies
j. The net income earned by a Canadian business

4. LO 5.4, 5.5 For the same list in Question 3, indicate whether each of the categories would be recorded in GDP income-based (GDP_Y) or GDP expenditure-based (GDP_E).
5. LO 5.4, 5.5 Assume that there are no taxes and no depreciation. Use a simple circular flow diagram with only households and firms to show the income and expenditure approaches to measuring an economy's GDP.

Questions in the Intermediate and Challenging Sections cover several different concepts, and have not been organized by learning objectives.

Intermediate

1. Table 5.10 contains data for an economy. On the basis of the data provided, calculate

Table 5.10 Data for Calculating GDP, Expenditure- and Income-Based

Item	($ mil)
Rent	30
Personal consumption expenditure	1 500
Corporate income taxes	80
Undistributed profits	20
Net exports	10
Dividends	40
Capital consumption allowance (Depreciation)	200
Interest	90
Indirect business taxes	180
Compensation for employees	1 420
Government purchases of goods & services	400
Proprietors' income	100

a. GDP expenditure-based
b. GDP income-based
c. Net investment

2. Table 5.11 contains data for an economy. On the basis of the data provided, calculate

Table 5.11 Data for Calculating Demand, GDP, and Net Investment

Item	Value ($ mil)
Wages and salaries	2 000
Personal expenditure on consumer goods and services	1 200
Capital consumption allowance (Depreciation)	50
Gross investment	200
Exports	60
Rent	100
Government purchases	250
Imports	50
Corporation income	600
Interest and dividends	10
Net income from farm production	300

a. Final domestic demand
b. GDP expenditure based
c. Net investment

3. Given the national income data in Table 5.12, calculate

Table 5.12 Data for Calculating GDP, Demand, and Net Domestic Product

Item	Value ($ mil)
Wages and salaries	200
Exports of goods and services	12
Capital consumption allowance (Depreciation)	12
Government purchases of goods and services	60
Taxes on factors of production	20
Net investment	50
Taxes on products	40
Personal expenditure on consumer goods and services	240
Imports of goods and services	10

a. GDP
b. Final domestic demand
c. Net domestic product at basic prices

4. The data in Table 5.13 are available for an economy. Calculate
   a. Personal income
   b. Disposable income
   c. Personal saving

Table 5.13 Data for Hypothetical Economy

Item	Value ($ mil)
Wages and salaries	500
Rental income	60
Interest and dividend income	40
Transfer payments	100
Consumption	550
Personal taxes	40
Personal transfers to government	50

5. Under what circumstances would the GDP and GNP of a country be identical?

Challenging

1. The information in Table 5.14 is available for an economy.

   Your friend, a mathematics student who has not taken economics, calculates that GDP in this economy has grown by 57.8% from 2000 to 2007. On the basis of this result, the student calculates that the economy has performed really well during this period.

Table 5.14 Calculating Real GDP

Year	GDP ($ bil)	Price Index	Real GDP ($ bil)
2000	90	75	
2001	95	85	
2002	105	95	
2003	109	100	
2004	120	110	
2005	126	122	
2006	135	130	
2007	142	142	

   a. Calculate the real GDP and complete the right-hand column.
   b. Use your data to explain the true performance of the economy to your math friend.

2. In an attempt to support her position that the economy has performed exceptionally well under her watch, a provincial premier quotes the data in Table 5.15. She emphasizes that the GDP has doubled from 2001 to 2004 and has more than doubled from 2002 to 2006.

   Explain why the premier's assertions, though mathematically correct, are misleading. Illustrate by constructing hypothetical price indexes and then using them to calculate real GDP.

Table 5.15 A Province's GDP

Year	GDP ($ bil)
2001	30
2002	38
2003	48
2004	60
2005	71
2006	80
2007	91

3. Table 5.16 contains data for two economies, Lower Land and Higher Land, from 2000 to 2004.
   Which of these two economies has performed better during the 2000–2004 period, other things being equal?

Table 5.16 Hypothetical Data for Two Economies

Data for Lower Land

Year	Nominal GDP ($ bil)	Price Level
2000	1000	92
2001	1106	96
2002	1157	100
2003	1280	108
2004	1350	112

Data for Higher Land

Year	Nominal GDP ($ bil)	Price Level
2000	1250	81
2001	1375	90
2002	1480	100
2003	1595	110
2004	1700	122

MyEconLab Visit the MyEconLab website at **www.myeconlab.com**. This online homework and tutorial system puts you in control of your own learning with study and practice tools directly correlated to this chapter's content.

Study Guide

Self-Assessment

What's your score?

Circle the letter that corresponds with the correct answer.

1. National income accounting for Canada involves
   a. Counting the money distributed by banks
   b. Accounting for the number of hours worked by illegal immigrants
   c. Keeping records of the number of trips Canadians make abroad
   d. Accounting for all the goods and services produced in Canada

2. The federal government agency responsible for national income accounting in Canada is
   a. Canada Revenue Agency
   b. Statistics Canada
   c. The Bank of Canada
   d. All of the above

3. National income statistics serve only to
   a. Provide employment for statisticians
   b. Provide jobs for government economists
   c. Show the rest of the world how great a country Canada is
   d. None of the above

4. Gross domestic product (GDP) is
   a. The total value of all goods and services sold domestically during a specific period
   b. The total amount of goods and services existing in a country at a particular time
   c. Another name for the amount of money in a country
   d. The total value of all final goods and services produced domestically during a specific period

5. In national income accounting, double counting is
   a. Counting an item exactly twice, no more, no less
   b. Counting an item more than once
   c. Counting final goods twice and twice only
   d. None of the above

6. To avoid double counting, we should
   a. Subtract the value of the final products from the value of the intermediate products
   b. Add the intermediate products and the final products
   c. Calculate only the values added at each stage of production
   d. None of the above

Use the following information to answer Questions 7 and 8.

A wheat farm sells wheat to a mill for 10 cents. The mill sells the flour to a bakery for 30 cents. The bakery makes bread and sells the bread to a poor economics student for 75 cents.

7. How much did this set of transactions add to GDP?
   a. 20 cents
   b. 65 cents
   c. 95 cents
   d. 75 cents

8. The value added by the bakery was
   a. 20 cents
   b. 45 cents
   c. 25 cents
   d. 55 cents

9. An intermediate product is
   a. The same as a final product, but it is worth more
   b. One that is expected to last from three to five years
   c. A product that is intended for resale or further processing
   d. None of the above

10. Transfer payments include
   a. Wages and salaries
   b. Interest and investment income
   c. Government purchases of goods and services
   d. Government grants and employment insurance payments

11. GDP income-based is calculated by adding
   a. All expenditures during the year
   b. Wages and other factor incomes, and subtracting taxes on factors of production

c. Exports to total domestic expenditure
d. None of the above

12. GDP expenditure-based is calculated by adding
a. All personal expenditures on consumer goods and services
b. All the expenditures of the economy's customers on domestically produced goods and services
c. All the incomes generated in the process of production and making adjustments for capital consumption allowances and certain taxes and subsidies
d. Exports to total domestic expenditure

13. Which of the following is the largest single component of GDP expenditure-based?
a. Wages and salaries
b. Personal expenditure on consumer goods and services
c. Corporation profits before taxes
d. Government purchases of goods and services

14. Which Canadian province produces the largest amount of goods and services?
a. Alberta
b. Quebec
c. British Columbia
d. Ontario

15. The output of a Canadian-owned firm operating in the Caribbean is
a. Part of Canada's GDP but not part of its GNP
b. Part of Canada's GNP but not part of its GDP
c. Part of Canada's GDP as well as part of its GNP
d. None of the above

16. Usually for Canada
a. GDP = GNP
b. GDP < GNP
c. GDP > GNP
d. GDP rises while GNP falls

17. If all prices have doubled in the last 10 years, and all quantities have fallen to half their former levels, then
a. Real GDP is unchanged but nominal GDP has grown
b. Nominal GDP is unchanged but real GDP has fallen
c. Nominal GDP is unchanged but real GDP has grown
d. Real GDP is unchanged but nominal GDP has fallen

18. Which of the following is a non-marketed good or service?
a. Housework
b. Volunteer work
c. Garage chores
d. All of the above

19. Which of the following reduces the accuracy of GDP as a measure of well-being?
a. The underground economy
b. Non-marketed goods and services
c. Environmental damage
d. All of the above

20. The Human Development Index (HDI) includes
a. GDP per capita
b. Life expectancy at birth
c. Adult literacy
d. All of the above

Problems and Exercises (Use Quad Paper for Graphs)

Answers to these questions can be found on MyEconLab at www.myeconlab.com. MyEconLab

1. Table 5.17 gives data for the Canadian economy in 2003. There is no statistical discrepancy.

Table 5.17 National Income Data for Canada, 2003

Item	Value ($ mil)
Personal expenditure on consumer goods and services	687 791
Government current expenditure on goods and services	236 631
Taxes less subsidies on products	85 048
Wages and salaries	617 753
Accrued net income of farm operators	1 280
Exports of goods and services	461 266
Capital consumption allowances	163 602
Gross capital formation and inventories	244 873
Corporation profits before taxes	147 592
Taxes less subsidies on factors of production	56 376
Interest and miscellaneous investment income	50 223
Imports of goods and services	414 370
Net income of non-farm unincorporated business, including rent	77 158
Government enterprise profits	11 630
All other income	5 302

Source: Statistics Canada, *Canadian Economic Observer*, November 2005, p. 3.

Calculate each of the following:
a. Net domestic product at basic prices
b. GDP, income-based
c. GDP, expenditure-based
d. Net investment

2. In February 2009, you sold your 2002 Ford car to one of your buddies for $3500. A few days later, you bought a new (2009) GM car for $18 000, which you sold in September 2009 because you decided to leave the country. Which of these transactions would be included in the GDP for 2009? Why?

3. Under which component of the national income accounts would you include each of the following? (For example, payment to a company clerk would be recorded as wages and salaries.)
   a. The purchase of a brand-new family car
   b. Money paid to a gardener for his or her services
   c. The purchase of a new photocopy machine by a company
   d. The purchase of microcomputers by a public school board in your province or territory from a local computer manufacturer
   e. The income earned by a corporation after deducting expenses
   f. The purchase of new television sets from Japan
   g. The sale of a shipment of softwood lumber to the United States
   h. The payment of interest to Canadians by Canadian banks
4. You are given the following data about a country's economy:
   Consumption = $5.4 million
   Personal saving = $1.2 million
   Personal taxes = $2.0 million

   Calculate
   a. Personal income
   b. Disposable income
5. The data in Table 5.18 are available for a hypothetical economy.

Table 5.18 National Income Data for a Hypothetical Economy

Item	Value ($ mil)
Rent	120
Personal consumption expenditure	5 400
Taxes less subsidies on products	600
Net exports	35
Corporate income taxes	325
Undistributed profits	90
Interest and dividends	585
Wages and salaries	5 140
Income from unincorporated business	485
Taxes less subsidies on factors of production	215
Gross investment	1 200
Capital consumption allowances	900
Government purchases of goods and services	1 825

   Calculate each of the following:
   a. GDP expenditure-based
   b. GDP income-based
   c. Total factor income
   d. Net domestic product at basic prices
   e. Net investment
6. Indicate whether each of the following would be recorded in GDP income-based (GDP_Y), GDP expenditure-based (GDP_E), or both (B) for the Canadian economy.
   a. The purchase of wine from France
   b. The wages earned by a mechanic
   c. Automobiles produced by Chrysler but not sold in the year in which they were produced
   d. Statistical discrepancy
   e. The sale of Canadian wheat to France
7. In a small country's economy, GDP expenditure-based is $500 million. There is no statistical discrepancy. Net domestic product (NDP) at basic prices is $450 million. Taxes less subsidies on products amount to $20 million. How much is capital consumption allowance?
8. Table 5.19 gives data for the state of Simpleville.

Table 5.19 Output and Price Level Data for Simpleville

Year	Average Level of Prices ($)	Quantity of Output
1980	15	650
1990	20	1 000
2000	25	1 500

   a. Calculate the GDP for 1980, 1990, and 2000.
   b. By using 1990 as the base year, give price indexes for 1980 and 2000.
   c. By using the price indexes calculated in (b), express GDP in Simpleville for 1980, 1990, and 2000.
9. Table 5.20 gives data for a hypothetical economy. Fill in the blanks.

Table 5.20 Hypothetical Economic Data

Year	Real GDP (1990 $)	GDP (current $)	Price Index (1990 = 100)
1960	300	____	25
1980	____	750	85
1990	1 500	____	____
2000	____	3 000	200

Chapter 6

Unemployment and Inflation

Learning Objectives

After studying this chapter, you should be able to

- **6.1** Understand the meaning and the types of unemployment
- **6.2** Explain how unemployment is measured
- **6.3** Understand the incidence and costs of unemployment
- **6.4** Explain the classical and Keynesian theories of unemployment
- **6.5** Understand inflation, its measurement, and its effects
- **6.6** Compare the rates of unemployment and inflation among the provinces and between Canada and other countries

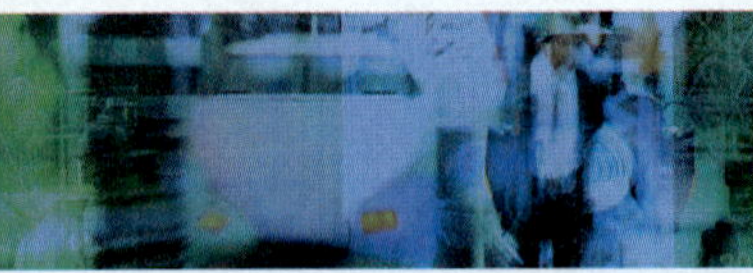

Assess Your Knowledge

MyEconLab

Answers to these questions can be found on MyEconLab at **www.myeconlab.com.**

1. Is someone necessarily unemployed if he or she does not have a job?
2. Can technological advance cause unemployment?
3. Which of the following demographic groups is likely to have the highest unemployment rate?
   a. University graduates
   b. High school dropouts
   c. Men 25 years and older
   d. Highly skilled workers
4. How does inflation affect your savings?
5. Inflation is a situation of severe unemployment over a long period. True or false?

LO 6.1 Understand the meaning and the types of unemployment

The Meaning of Unemployment and Types of Unemployment

What is unemployment?

unemployment an economic condition that exists when workers are without jobs even though they are willing and able to work

Unemployment is a state of joblessness. It is an economic condition that exists when workers are without jobs even though they are willing and able to work. Statistics Canada defines the unemployed as those individuals 15 years and older who are without jobs and who are actively looking for work and available for work.

What are the different types of unemployment, and why does the type of unemployment matter?

Let's answer the second part of the question first. Individuals who are unemployed are not concerned about which type of unemployment has disrupted their lives. However, the type of unemployment is important to economists and policymakers, because different types of unemployment require different remedies. Let us now deal with the first part of the question—the types of unemployment. It is a common practice among economists to group unemployment into the following four broad categories:

- Frictional unemployment
- Seasonal unemployment
- Structural unemployment
- Cyclical unemployment

Can we briefly discuss each of these types of unemployment?

Let us begin with frictional unemployment.

frictional unemployment unemployment that results from people moving between jobs or entering or re-entering the labour force

Frictional Unemployment In any economic system in which people are free to change their jobs and in which employers can dismiss employees, a certain level of unemployment, knows as **frictional unemployment**, is inescapable, and it may even be desirable.

Frictional unemployment is unemployment that results from people moving between jobs or entering or re-entering the labour force. It results from people leaving jobs, in the hope of finding a better job, before they have lined up another job (job leavers); people entering the labour force for the first time (new entrants); and people being laid off by their employers because of unsatisfactory performance (layoffs). After you graduate from college or university, it may take you a little while to find a job. Until you do, you will be considered to be frictionally unemployed.

This type of unemployment can be reduced to some extent by providing better information about job opportunities to workers and about available workers to employers. However, we cannot completely eliminate frictional unemployment. Because a certain amount of unemployment is inevitable, allowance is made for this fact when we use the term **full employment**. Full employment is a condition that prevails when the only unemployment is frictional and *structural* (defined below) unemployment.If we assume frictional and structural unemployment is 3%, then we define full employment as the employment of 97% of the labour force.

full employment a condition that prevails when the only unemployment is frictional and structural unemployment

Seasonal Unemployment It is reasonable to expect unemployment to vary with the seasons in a country such as Canada, where the seasons are pronounced. **Seasonal unemployment** is unemployment that is caused by seasonal variations. In Canada, agricultural activities slow down during the winter, and as a result unemployment in the agricultural sector increases. Construction activities also decrease significantly during the winter; unemployment therefore increases in that sector also. During the summer, unemployment increases among workers whose jobs are related to winter activities, such as ice skating and skiing.

seasonal unemployment unemployment caused by seasonal variations

But even in economies in which seasonal variations are slight, workers may still experience seasonal unemployment. For example, in the winter many tropical countries depend heavily on the tourist trade from North America and Western Europe. Such countries often experience an increase in their rate of unemployment during the summer months when the flow of tourists from North America and Western Europe declines. Obviously, the scope of policies to reduce seasonal unemployment in these countries is severely limited.

Do the official figures of unemployment take into account seasonal changes?

Yes, Statistics Canada adjusts the unemployment rate to reflect differences in economic activities caused by seasonal variations. In the winter, although certain economic activities increase and others decrease, the overall level of economic activities decreases. Thus, the rate of unemployment is normally higher in the winter than it is in other seasons. Since Statistics Canada has been keeping monthly records of unemployment for a long time, it is able to estimate the long-run average rate of unemployment for each month. Based on this long-run average rate of unemployment, it adjusts the rate of unemployment in a month, depending on whether the actual rate of unemployment is above or below the long-run rate. Suppose the long-run average rate of unemployment for February is 2 percentage points higher than the annual rate of unemployment and the unadjusted (actual) rate in February of a particular year is 3 percentage points higher than the average, Statistics Canada raises the seasonally adjusted official rate of unemployment by only 1 percentage point. Statistics Canada makes similar adjustments in the summer season.

structural unemployment unemployment that is caused by a mismatch between the types of skills that unemployed workers possess and the types of workers that employers would like to hire

technological unemployment a type of structural unemployment caused by the introduction of labour-saving equipment or methods of production

cyclical unemployment unemployment that arises because of declines in aggregate expenditure and aggregate output, such as during recessions

Structural Unemployment A growing economy is constantly undergoing structural changes. Domestic demand patterns change. Methods of production improve as technology advances. Trade patterns between Canada and the rest of the world evolve. **Structural unemployment** is unemployment that is caused by a mismatch between the types of skills that unemployed workers possess and the types of workers that employers would like to hire. In other words, it occurs because of the mismatch between the supply of labour and the demand for labour. This mismatch can occur regionally or nationally.

For example, structural unemployment can be caused by a permanent decline in the demand for textiles by Canadian and foreigner consumers or by technological advancement in the production of textiles; the textile industry would employ fewer workers, and unemployment in the textile sector would increase, which could raise the national rate of unemployment.

The introduction of labour-saving technology in the economy has created a special kind of structural unemployment: **technological unemployment**.

Consider the number of people whose jobs have become obsolete because of computers. Do not lose sight, however, of the fact that the introduction of computers has created employment for some people, such as programmers, computer technicians, and computer course instructors.

There is a misconception that only the less educated, unskilled, or untrained workers are subject to technological unemployment. In fact, even highly trained individuals can become redundant in the wake of rapid technological progress. Structural unemployment can be reduced by providing retraining for workers whose skills are no longer in demand and by facilitating the flow of workers from regions where an industry is declining to regions where new industries are expanding. This may prove to be a difficult task, however, especially in the case of older workers.

Cyclical Unemployment A reduction in total spending may cause firms to reduce the sale of their goods and services. This deficiency in aggregate expenditure leads to an increase in the firms' inventories. The increase in unplanned inventories results in a decrease in production and an increase in unemployment. A market economy goes through periods of ups and downs known as business cycles. When the economy is on the upswing, unemployment decreases, and when it is on the downswing, unemployment increases. **Cyclical unemployment** is unemployment that arises because of declines in aggregate expenditure and total output, such as during recessions.

Reading Comprehension

The answers to these questions can be found on MyEconLab at www.myeconlab.com. MyEconLab

1. What is the difference between frictional and structural unemployment?
2. How is full employment defined?
3. How do economic fluctuations affect the rate of unemployment?

LO 6.2 Explain how unemployment is measured

The Measurement of Unemployment

How is unemployment in an economy measured?

unemployment rate the number of people unemployed expressed as a percentage of the labour force

The state of unemployment in an economy is generally measured by the rate of unemployment or the **unemployment rate**. You have no doubt heard statistics on the unemployment rate.

But what exactly is it and how is it determined?

Let us first define the unemployment rate, and then we will see how Statistics Canada estimates it. The unemployment rate expresses the number of people unemployed as a percentage of the labour force.

But that definition is meaningful only if we know what is meant by the labour force. So what is the labour force?

labour force the sum of all employed and all unemployed people who are willing and able to work

The **labour force** is the sum of the number of employed and unemployed people 15 years and older who are willing and able to work.

Let us use *LF* to denote the labour force, *Un* to denote the number unemployed, and *Em* to denote the number employed. We can then express the labour force as

$$LF = Un + Em$$

Symbolically, we can express the unemployment rate (*UR*) as follows:

$$UR = \frac{Un}{LF} \times 100$$

For example, if the labour force has 100 000 people, 10 000 of whom are unemployed, then the unemployment rate is calculated as follows:

$$UR = \frac{Un}{LF} \times 100 = \frac{10\ 000}{10\ 000} \times 100 = 10\%$$

The unemployment rate, in this case, is 10%. It is worth noting our reference to unemployment relates to only one factor of production: labour. An unemployment rate of 10% does not tell us anything directly about the employment of land or capital. We would, of course, expect that a high unemployment rate would result in a low level of the utilization of capital and other inputs.

Is there an indicator that shows the extent to which a nation uses its factories and machinery?

capacity utilization rate shows the degree to which firms use their factories and machinery

Yes, the indicator is known as the **capacity utilization rate**. It shows the degree to which firms use their factories and machinery. It indicates the percentage of factory space and machinery that firms use at a given time. When firms use all of their factory space and all of their machinery, it is said that they are operating at full capacity. When they don't use all of their factory space and machinery, it is said that they are operating at less than full capacity. Firms rarely operate at full capacity, but in general the capacity utilization rate varies inversely with the unemployment rate.

Should we be familiar with any other labour force statistics?

labour force participation rate the labour force expressed as a percentage of the adult population

Yes, two more. You should be familiar with the **labour force participation rate**, also known as the *participation rate*. It is the percentage of the population 15 years and older that is in the labour force. As can be seen from Figure 6.1, the participation rate has been increasing in Canada over the last 50 years or so mostly because of the increase in the participation of women in the labour force. The increase in the participation of women is due to sociological and economic factors. Sociologically, more and more women are entering the labour market as certain jobs and professions, which were once dominated by men, for example the medical and legal professions, have become accessible to women. In fact, in the medical and legal professions, women today constitute the majority. Economically, the number of two-income households has increased as couples attempt to raise or to maintain their standards of living. At the same time, the Canadian economy has experienced significant transformation over the last 50 years. The service sector, which usually employs more women than men, has been expanding over the years, raising the participation of women in the labour force. On the other hand, the manufacturing sector, which employs mostly men, has been declining because of technological change and because of foreign competition, reducing the participation of men in the labour force.

In the United States, a historic milestone took place in the summer of 2010, when women overtook men in the labour market. For the first time in American history, women now constitute the majority of the employed labour force. And given the trend in the participation rates of men and women in Canada, women will account for most of the employed labour force in Canada as well within a few years.

employment rate indicates the percentage of the labour force that is employed

Second, there is another rate that you have to be familiar with: **the employment rate**. We define it as the percentage of the labour force that is employed. From the equation above, recall that the labour force is composed of the number of people employed and the number of people unemployed. If you divide both sides of the equation by the

Figure 6.1 The Participation Rate by Gender

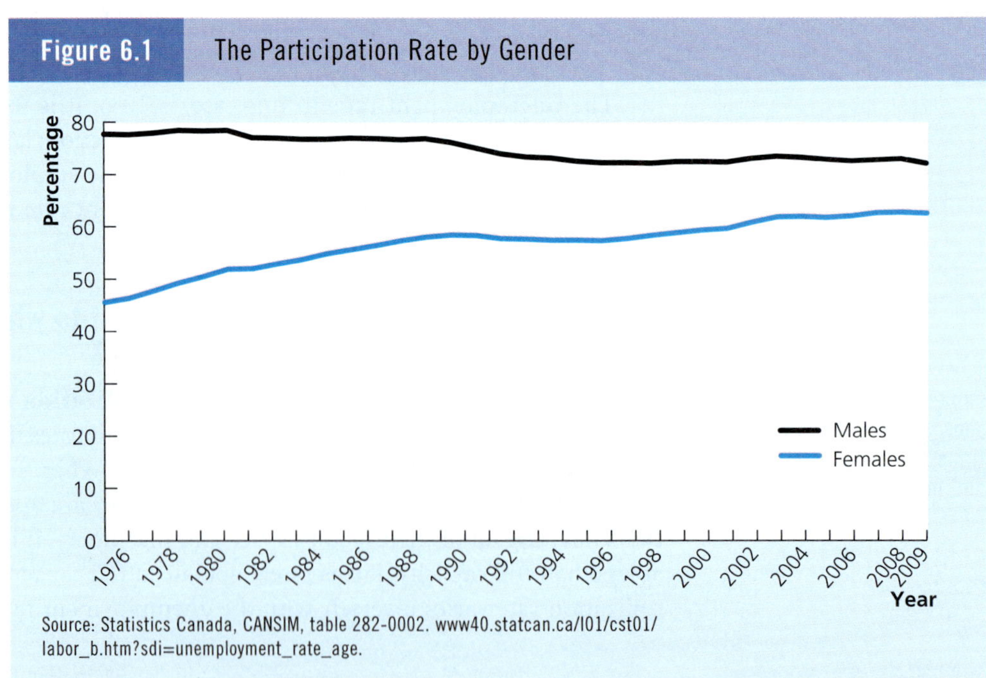

Source: Statistics Canada, CANSIM, table 282-0002. www40.statcan.ca/l01/cst01/labor_b.htm?sdi=unemployment_rate_age.

Table 6.1 Labour Force Characteristics, 2009

Characteristics	Value
Adult population	27,309.20
Labour force	18,368.70
Employed	16,848.90
Unemployed	1,519.80
Not in labour force	8,940.50
Characteristics	**Percent**
Participation rate	67.3
Unemployment rate	8.3

Source: Statistics Canada, CANSIM, tables 282-0002 and 282-0022 and Catalogue no. 71F0004XCB. www40.statcan.ca/l01/cst01/econ10.htm. Extracted March 23, 2011.

labour force and multiply it by 100, you will easily see that the employment rate and the unemployment rate add up to 100%.

$$(LF/LF)^{*}100 = (Un/LF)^{*}100 + (Em/LF)^{*}100$$

$$100\% = \text{unemployment rate} + \text{employment rate}$$

This means if you know the rate of unemployment, you will easily calculate the rate of employment. For example, if the rate of unemployment is 10%, then the rate of employment will be 90%.

Are these labour force statistics available for the Canadian economy?

Let's look at the data for Canada in 2009 in Table 6.1. The table shows the number of Canadians in each category of the labour force, but we can understand better the changes taking place in the labour force if we examine the stocks (at a given time) and flows (per unit of time) of the working population in four categories: new entrants, employed, unemployed, and discouraged workers. Figure 6.2 below shows the stocks and flows of these four categories. The rectangular boxes represent the number of people in a category at a given time (the stocks), while the arrows represent the movement of people (flows) among the categories. The net flow from one category to another determines the size of a category at a given time, for example, at the end of a month.

Figure 6.2 starts with the stock of new entrants into the labour market. The new entrants could be graduates from high schools, colleges and universities, or people who were previously outside the labour force. Depending on their ability to find jobs, some of the new entrants will find jobs and become employed, others may not find jobs and become unemployed, and some may even give up looking for work and become discouraged workers. This movement represents a flow of people in one direction, from new entrants to the employed, the unemployed, and the discouraged workers. But there is a two-way flow of people among the employed, the unemployed, and the discouraged workers, as shown in Figure 6.2.

Figure 6.2 Stocks and Flows in the Labour Force

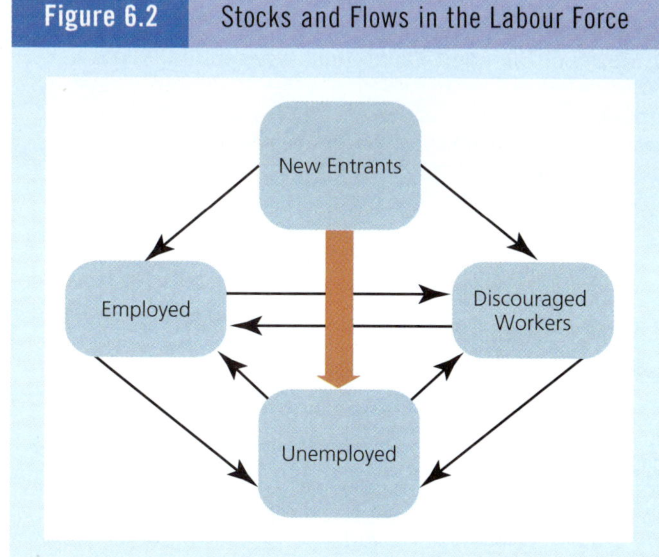

The number of people in each category of the labour force—the employed, unemployed, and the discouraged workers—varies with the net flow of people among the categories. For example, the number of unemployed people in a given month depends on the number of new entrants who could not find a job, and the net flow of people between the employed and the unemployed, and between the discouraged workers and the unemployed. The net flow of people among the categories of course depends on the conditions in the labour market. If the demand for labour is high, as is the case in an economic boom, employment increases, unemployment decreases, and previously discouraged workers may want to try their luck once more and start looking for work. On the other hand, if the demand for labour is low, as is the case in a recession, the number of people employed decreases, the number of people unemployed increases, and the number of discouraged workers increases.

Can the relationship between these major labour force statistics be represented in a diagram for further emphasis?

Let's look at Figure 6.3. The diagram shows that, in 2009, 16.9 million people were employed (the green rectangle) and 1.5 million were unemployed (the yellow rectangle). Thus, the labour force consisted of the green rectangle plus the yellow rectangle, which represents 18.4 million people. The diagram also shows that there were 8.9 million people who were not in the labour force (the blue rectangle). When these are added to the 1.5 million people who were unemployed, we arrive at 10.4 million people who were not working (the blue rectangle plus the yellow rectangle). The sum of the employed (the green area), the unemployed (the yellow area), and the number not in the labour force (the blue area) equals the adult population of 27.3 million in 2009. The size of the working population depends on the population of a country.

How does Statistics Canada go about measuring unemployment, and what are some of the issues involved in the statistics?

The Measurement of Unemployment Each month, Statistics Canada conducts a survey of Canadian households, interviewing about 56 000 of them (about 110 000 individuals) to determine their employment status. Based on the results of the survey, Statistics Canada estimates the unemployment rate. Although most people regard the estimate as fairly reliable, it has several limitations. To understand these limitations, you must understand the definitions of the key terms used in the survey.

First, Statistics Canada defines a person as *employed* if that person had a job at the time of the interview or was away from work for such reasons as illness, vacation, strikes or lockouts, familial obligations, and so on. Second, Statistics Canada defines a person as *unemployed* if that person was actively looking for work and was actually available for work during the past month, or who was laid off for more than 26 weeks, even if he

Figure 6.3 Employment Status of the Adult Population, 2009 (000 000s)

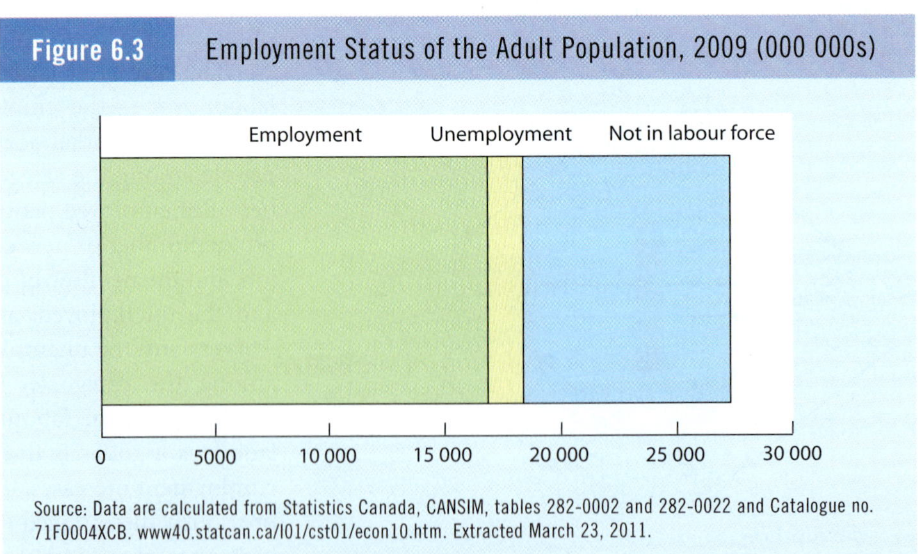

Source: Data are calculated from Statistics Canada, CANSIM, tables 282-0002 and 282-0022 and Catalogue no. 71F0004XCB. www40.statcan.ca/l01/cst01/econ10.htm. Extracted March 23, 2011.

or she was not looking for another job. Third, the survey defines the adult working population as persons 15 years of age and older, excluding people in the armed forces, inmates of institutions, and Native people on reserves.

Let us now address some of the issues arising from these definitions. Just how *actively* must people look for work in order to be counted as unemployed? Consider the following situation. Jin is a young man from a well-to-do family. He reads the classified advertisements, hoping to find a well-paying job of his liking just to have something to do. Jin would be classified as unemployed if he told the interviewer that he has been trying to find a job during the reference week.

underemployment a situation in which workers accept low-paying jobs or part-time jobs because they cannot find a full-time job consistent with their qualifications

Some people accept part-time jobs or jobs that are well below their education, training, and skills. A case in point would be an MBA graduate who could find employment only as a teller in a bank. This is an example of **underemployment**. Underemployment is a situation in which workers accept low-paying jobs or part-time jobs because they cannot find a full-time job consistent with their qualifications.

This means the survey does not account for underemployment and classifies underemployed people simply as employed. In such cases, the unemployment statistics do not adequately reflect the extent of unemployment.

discouraged workers workers who have abandoned the search for jobs because they are unable to find work

To be officially unemployed, a person must be in the labour force. Hence, if Lydia has looked for work for several weeks without success and then gives up looking for work actively because she is convinced that nothing is available, the survey would list her as not being in the labour force and therefore not among the unemployed, even though she would be happy to accept employment if she were offered a job. Economists classify a worker like Lydia as a discouraged worker. **Discouraged workers** are workers who have abandoned the search for jobs because they are unable to find work. They are not counted as unemployed.

If underemployed and discouraged workers were counted as unemployed, the unemployment rate would be higher than the officially reported figure. To take account of discouraged workers, Statistics Canada conducts a special survey every six months to determine the number of workers who are not in the labour force.

The unemployment rate does not tell us anything about how long the unemployed worker is out of work. It only measures the rate of unemployment at a particular time. However, for the unemployed person, there is certainly a big difference between bouts of unemployment lasting for four weeks and those lasting for six months or longer. The average duration of unemployment has important implications for the economy as well. When the duration is long, when workers cannot find jobs for a long time, unemployment is not only a loss of income for the unemployed workers during the extended period, but also results in a loss of output for the economy. That's why some economists use the average duration of unemployment during a recession as an indicator of the severity of a recession; if the average duration is short, the recession is considered mild, and if the average duration is long, the recession is considered serious. For example, in the United States in the summer of 2009, the median duration of unemployment reached its highest level since 1948, indicating that the 2007–2009 recession was severe. The high duration of unemployment is one of the reasons why some economists have labelled this recession in the United States as the Great Recession.

It is also important to note that national unemployment figures do not tell us anything about how the rate of unemployment is distributed among the various regions. When we say that the unemployment rate in Canada is 8%, we must realize that it may be 5% in some regions and 11% in others.

The foregoing discussion suggests that care should be taken when looking at official unemployment statistics. Yet despite these limitations, the consistency with which the monthly labour force statistics are measured makes the unemployment rate a fairly reliable indicator of movements in the labour force.

Reading Comprehension

The answers to these questions can be found on MyEconLab at **www.myeconlab.com**. MyEconLab

1. Identify the important rates in the labour force.
2. How has the rate of participation changed in Canada over the last 50 years?
3. How does underemployment affect the reported official rate of unemployment?

LO 6.3 Understand the incidence and costs of unemployment

The Incidence and Costs of Unemployment

Are all workers equally likely to be unemployed?

Not all demographic groups are equally susceptible to being unemployed. In general, a more educated and a better skilled worker is more likely to find a job and less likely to be laid off than a less educated and an unskilled worker. A skilled and younger worker is also more likely to find a job than an unskilled and older worker. But a younger unskilled worker is more likely to be unemployed than an older skilled worker. This is due partly to the fact that unskilled high-school dropouts experience considerable difficulty in finding jobs and partly due to the fact that it often takes a while for unskilled young workers to find employment after they enter the labour force.

Youth unemployment is frictional unemployment, right?

Some of the youth unemployment could be frictional. Since young workers have fewer obligations, such as raising children or paying for the mortgage, than older workers do, they are more likely to change jobs more frequently than older workers. If young workers are dissatisfied with their employment, they are likely to quit their current employment in search of a better job with another company or even move to a different region.

In the past, the unemployment rate for women used to be higher than it was for men, but today men have a higher rate of unemployment. The change in the incidence of unemployment for men and women is mostly due to structural changes that have taken place in the economy. As mentioned earlier, employment in the manufacturing sector, where traditionally the majority of the employed are men, has diminished because of technological change and competition from abroad. On the other hand, employment in the service sector, where most of the employed are women, has expanded, providing women with more employment opportunities than in the past. In the past, the higher rate of unemployment among women was due, in large part, to discrimination against women in the labour market. Efforts to end discrimination against women in the labour market seem to have contributed to the reduction in the incidence of unemployment among women. Figure 6.4 shows the unemployment rate according to age and sex.

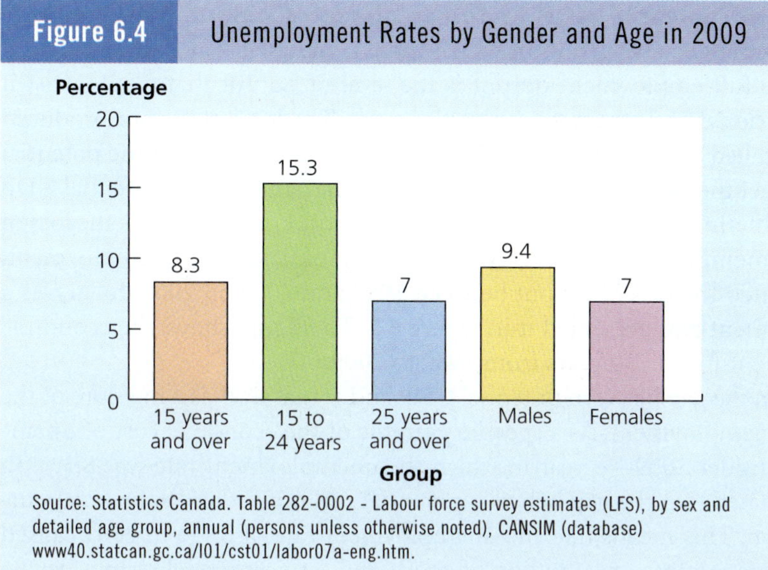

Figure 6.4 Unemployment Rates by Gender and Age in 2009

Source: Statistics Canada. Table 282-0002 - Labour force survey estimates (LFS), by sex and detailed age group, annual (persons unless otherwise noted), CANSIM (database) www40.statcan.gc.ca/l01/cst01/labor07a-eng.htm.

Note that among the groups of unemployed people, people between the ages of 15 and 24 have the highest rate of unemployment, most probably because of their low level of education, low experience, and low skills. The unemployment rate is lowest among people aged 25 years and over, probably because of their superior education, better skills, and long experience compared to younger workers.

What are some of the costs of unemployment?

The costs of unemployment derive from the adverse effects that unemployment has on the economy, on the unemployed and their families, and on the society as a whole. For the purpose of this discussion, let us divide the costs of unemployment into economic costs and non-economic costs.

What are the *economic* costs of unemployment?

Unemployment imposes costs on the unemployed individual and on the society as a whole. Unemployment hurts individuals economically because it reduces their incomes. Individuals and their families may be forced to curtail their consumption drastically. The loss of income may also force individuals to liquidate some of their assets—often at a loss—in order to meet their financial obligations.

Not only do unemployed workers suffer financial losses, but when they find jobs, many have to accept jobs outside their field of experience and training, often at lower wages. For those who are unlucky to enter the labour force during periods of high unemployment, they start at lower salaries than they would have in good economic conditions. Studies have shown that, even after a person has been employed for 10 years, the income gap remains high between those who started when unemployment was high and those who started when unemployment was low.

Unemployment results in a loss of output of goods and services that could have been produced by the unemployed. An economy with a high unemployment rate is producing at a level of output substantially below its potential. The total production of goods and services is less than it could have been at full employment.

Second, unemployment costs society financially as well. The government provides employment insurance benefits to unemployed individuals, amounting to billions of dollars each year. If these individuals had been employed, the government could have spent this money on providing better health care services or education, on improving Canada's infrastructure, or on other services. Consequently, because of unemployment, everyone loses.

How can one measure the economic cost of unemployment?

The economic cost of unemployment to society can be measured by the resulting loss in total output or total income. The level of output that the economy could produce at full

potential GDP or full-employment output the economy's output at full employment

actual output the level of output produced by the economy

output gap or income gap the difference between the potential output and the actual output of an economy

employment is called **potential GDP** or **full-employment output**. Since we have defined full employment as a situation in which there is only frictional and structural unemployment, the full-employment output is the level of output that would exist if there were only frictional and structural unemployment. The level of output produced by the economy is called the **actual output**. If we subtract the actual from the potential level of output, we get the **output gap**.The output gap is the gap between potential GDP and actual GDP. Sometimes called the **income gap**, the output gap represents the loss of output because of unemployment—a measure of the economic cost of unemployment.

We have estimated the loss of output between 1980 and 2009, in 2002 dollars, as a result of unemployment and presented it in Figure 6.5. The figure shows the economic cost of unemployment for the 30 years from 1980 to 2009.

As stated earlier, the gap between potential GDP and actual GDP is a measure of the economic cost of unemployment. As a specific example of the economic cost of unemployment, let us consider 2009—a year in which the unemployment rate was 8.3%. In 2009, we have estimated that the gap between potential real output and actual real output was $84.4 billion. This means that the unemployment rate of 8.3% in 2009 caused the Canadian economy to lose $84.4 billion of goods and services in real terms. Exactly how large was this loss? To get a clearer perspective of the magnitude of this loss of output, consider the following. If the $84.4 billion were divided equally among every household in Canada in 2009, each household would have received more than $5200. Or to look at it another way, $84.4 billion is significantly larger than the combined GDP of Prince Edward, Nova Scotia, and New Brunswick in 2009.

Is there an economic theory that indicates the economic cost of unemployment?

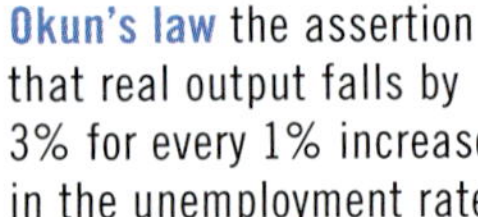

Okun's law the assertion that real output falls by 3% for every 1% increase in the unemployment rate

There is an economic law known as **Okun's law**, named after a famous American economist Arthur Okun (1928–1980); it describes a linear relationship between percentage changes in unemployment and percentage changes in GDP. It states that if the unemployment rate rises by 1%, real output falls by 3%. Okun proposed this relationship in 1962. Later, economists have estimated the relationship between unemployment and potential GDP to be a percentage ratio of 1:2. Some economists believe that an Okun percentage ratio of 1:2 is applicable to Canada.

Figure 6.5 An Estimate of Loss of Potential Output Resulting from Unemployment, 1980–2009

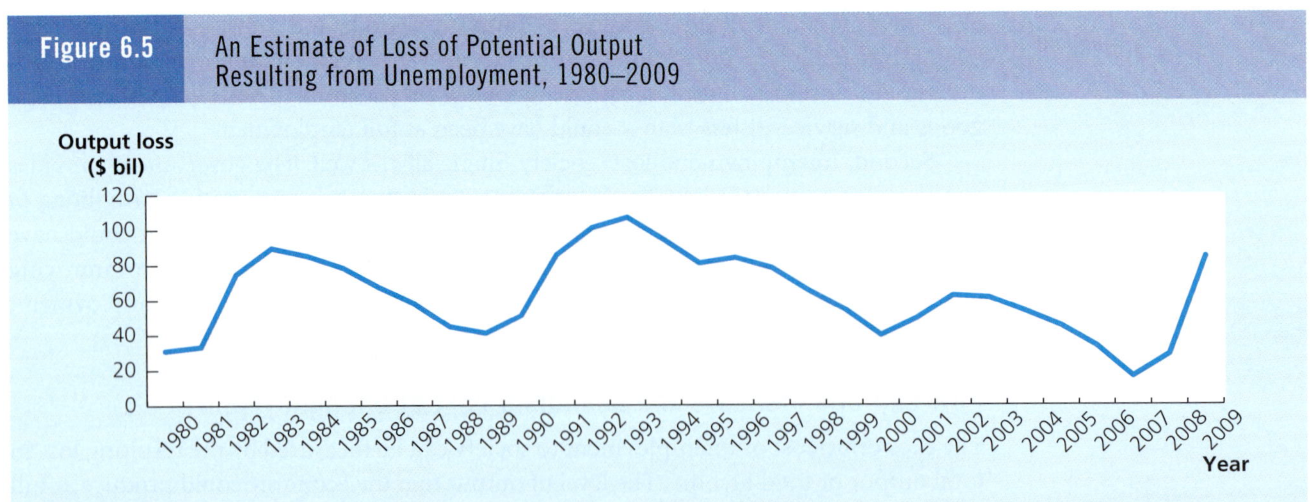

Let us use this ratio to calculate the loss in output in the Canadian economy in 2009. Real output in 2009 was $1297.4 billion and the unemployment rate was 8.3%. Applying Okun's law and using a ratio of 1:2, (and assuming that full employment was at 5%) we can conclude that the economy produced 3.3% × 2 = 6.6% less than its potential for that year. The potential output was therefore $1363.8 billion (that is, 6.6% more than $1279.4 billion).

What are the non-economic costs of unemployment?

Unemployed individuals can become discouraged and frustrated because of their inability to find jobs. These frustrations may manifest themselves in different forms of anti-social behaviours. Family relationships may be permanently ruined. The self-esteem of the unemployed person may be adversely affected. Evidence suggests that unemployment is linked to heart disease, mental illness, stress, emotional instability, and even suicide. The children of the unemployed may bear a tremendous cost in the form of loss of education and good health, which may affect them adversely for many years in the future. The unemployment statistics do not adequately measure the misery, suffering, and indignity that the unemployed must endure. But the costs are real and significant.

Reading Comprehension

The answers to these questions can be found on MyEconLab at **www.myeconlab.com**. MyEconLab

1. Why do younger workers have a higher rate of unemployment than older ones?
2. Why is the rate of unemployment higher for men than it is for women?
3. What do you understand by the term *potential GDP*?

BUSINESS SITUATION 6.1

You have just become a member of a powerful group of business owners, most of whom are chief executive officers. This influential group of business executives has consistently opposed policies to reduce unemployment, claiming that unemployment reduces wages, which in turn reduces production costs. Lower production costs mean increased profits for businesses.

Comment on this view from a business perspective.

The answer to this Business Situation can be found in Appendix A.

LO 6.4 Explain the classical and Keynesian theories of unemployment

The Classical and Keynesian Theories of Unemployment

Are there economic theories that explain unemployment?

Yes, and we will briefly present two theories of unemployment: classical and Keynesian.

Let's begin with the classical theory.

classical economists eighteenth-, nineteenth-, and early twentieth-century economists who argued that the economy would automatically achieve full employment if wages and prices were flexible

The Classical Theory of Unemployment The economists of the eighteenth, nineteenth, and early twentieth centuries are generally referred to as **classical economists**. Their views on the workings of the economy dominated economic thinking until the 1930s. They argued that an economy would automatically achieve full employment because prices, the rate of interest, and wages are flexible. If spending by households and firms was insufficient to produce full employment, firms would end up with a surplus of consumer and investment goods. This surplus would exert a downward pressure on prices which, in turn, would stimulate spending on consumer and investment goods.

Classical economists maintained that a decrease in spending by consumers means that consumers increase their savings. The increase in savings means that the supply of funds available for lending will increase. The increase in the supply of funds exerts downward pressure on the rate of interest. Also, a decrease in spending by firms represents a fall in the demand for loans for investment purposes. The decrease in demand for loans causes the rate of interest to fall. Because of the decrease in the interest rate, consumer and investment spending increase.

The classical economists claimed that, if there is unemployment in the economy, competition among workers for the available jobs will cause wages to fall. Lower wages will act as an incentive for firms to hire more workers and thus restore full employment. Thus, as far as the classical economists were concerned, deviations from full employment last only for a short time, since market forces will automatically eliminate them.

Classical theory suggests that, when the wage rates are set above the equilibrium wage rate, the high wage rate creates unemployment. Their position is illustrated by the familiar diagram shown in Figure 6.6.

Say's law the assertion that the production of goods and services creates a market for those goods and services: supply creates its own demand

The diagram represents the labour market. The demand for labour is line *DD* and the supply is line *SS*. The demand curve is downward sloping because smaller quantities of labour services will be demanded at higher wage rates; and the supply curve is upward sloping because more labour services will be offered at higher wage rates. The equilibrium wage rate is *W*, where the demand and supply curves intersect. If the wage rate is fixed at W_1, then the quantity of labour supplied will be L_1, and the quantity demanded will be L_0. The quantity of labour supplied will exceed the quantity demanded. This excess of labour services in the labour market, represented by $L_1 - L_0$, is unemployment. This surplus of labour services would force the wage rate to decrease until the market clears. In summary, the classical economists maintained that the economy operates at full employment provided that output prices and wages are flexible. Because of their belief in automatic full employment, the classical economists emphasized inflation more than unemployment.

Figure 6.6 Unemployment in Classical Theory

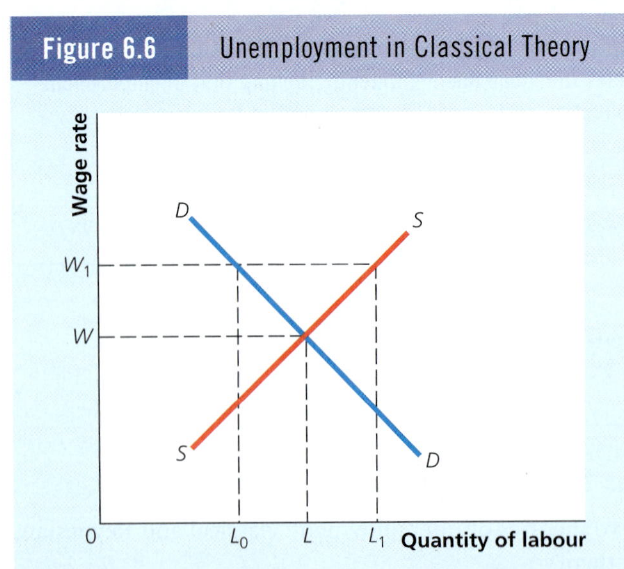

How did the classical economists arrive at their conclusion of automatic full employment?

The basis of the classical theory of employment is **Say's law**, named after the French economist, Jean-Baptiste Say (1767–1832). Say's law is usually summarized by the phrase *supply creates its own demand*—or that the production of goods and services creates a market for the goods and services. The law can be explained as follows.

People engage in the production of goods and services, not so much for the sake of work, but to be able to earn income and to purchase goods and services to satisfy their needs and wants. In other words, production constitutes demand for goods and services. That being the case, a situation in which the total production of goods and services exceeds the total amount of output that customers want to buy is most unlikely, if not impossible; production represents an equal amount of corresponding demand for goods and services.

Is the Keynesian theory of unemployment much different from the classical theory?

Keynesian theory this theory of unemployment states that unemployment can be caused by low aggregate expenditure

The **Keynesian theory** of unemployment takes a radically different approach from that taken by the classical economists. The Great Depression (1929–1939)—a period of high and prolonged unemployment—caused economists to seriously re-examine the classical conclusion of automatic full employment. A British economist by the name of John Maynard Keynes (1883–1946) was foremost among those who questioned the classical framework. In 1936, before the industrial world had recovered from the Great Depression, Keynes published his book *The General Theory of Employment, Interest, and Money*—one of the most influential economics books written.

In *The General Theory*, Keynes shows that unemployment can result from a deficiency of aggregate expenditure. Simply stated, Keynes's theory of unemployment says that if total spending is insufficient for firms to sell their output of goods and services, they will reduce their production, lay off workers, causing the economy to settle down at a less-than-full employment equilibrium. This situation requires government intervention, in the form of an increase in government spending or a decrease in taxes or a combination of both, to restore full employment. The Keynesian theory will occupy our attention in subsequent chapters.

Reading Comprehension

The answers to these questions can be found on MyEconLab at www.myeconlab.com. MyEconLab

1. Discuss the classical theory of unemployment.
2. What did the classical economists suggest that government do to reduce unemployment?
3. What does Keynesian theory suggest that the government do to reduce unemployment?

LO 6.5 Understand inflation, its measurement, and its effects

Inflation: Definition, Measurement, and Effects

What exactly is inflation?

inflation a sustained increase in the average level of prices over time; a persistent increase in the cost of living

It is unlikely that you have heard a great deal about inflation around the breakfast table, on television, or on the radio. Why? Because the Canadian economy has been experiencing relative price stability over the past several years. But this has not always been the case, and no one can state categorically that inflation will never be a major economic problem in Canada. Before we discuss the effects of inflation, let us define inflation. **Inflation** is a sustained increase in the average level of prices over time or a persistent increase in the cost of living.

Figure 6.7 Inflation versus a Once-Only Rise in the Price Level

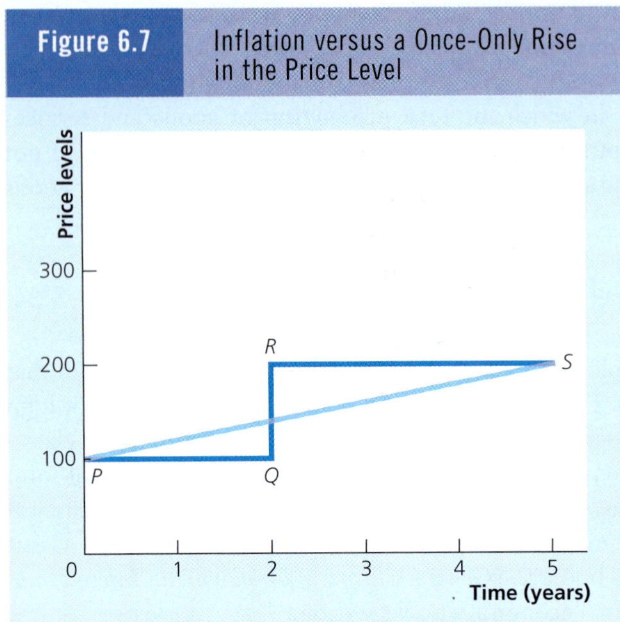

We should distinguish between an increase in the price of a product resulting from changes in demand and supply in particular markets and an increase in the average level of prices. If the demand for textbooks increases, perhaps because of a substantial increase in enrolment in schools, other things being equal, the price of textbooks will rise. The increase in the price of textbooks, however, is a change in relative prices. It may not indicate the presence of inflationary forces, because other prices may be falling in other markets. For inflation to exist, most prices must be rising.

It is also important to distinguish between a persistent rise in the average level of prices and a once-and-for-all increase in the price level. The difference between the two concepts is illustrated in Figure 6.7.

Figure 6.7 shows the relationship between the average price level, as measured by a price index, and time, measured in years. The steadily rising line *PS* shows a persistent rise in the price index from 100 in Year 0 to 200 in Year 5. The slope of the line *PS* represents changes in the average level of prices over time and could be used to calculate inflation. By contrast, line *PQ* shows the price level remaining constant at 100 from Year 0 to Year 2. Then at Year 2, the price level suddenly increases from 100 to 200, as shown by the vertical line *QR*, and then remains constant at 200 for the remaining three years. This situation is described as a once-and-for-all increase in the price level in Year 2. We cannot describe this situation as inflationary because the price rise is not sustained.

In an inflationary situation, the purchasing power of money falls. When there is inflation, $100 will buy less today than it did last year and more today than it will next year.

What is meant by the *rate* of inflation?

rate of inflation is the rate of change of the average level of prices

The **rate of inflation** is the rate of change in the average level of prices. It tells how fast inflation is increasing. The rate of inflation is usually expressed as a monthly or an annual rate. If the rate of inflation is 5% per year, then a box of paper clips that costs $1 now will cost $1.05 a year later.

How is inflation measured?

consumer price index an index that measures changes in the prices of consumer goods and services

producer price index an index that measures changes in the prices of producer goods

implicit price deflator or GDP deflator an index that measures changes in the average level of prices of all final goods and services

We can measure changes in the price level by using price indexes. Let us recall that, in Chapter 5, we discussed that price indexes could be used to deflate the GDP. There are many price indexes, but the three popular ones are the *consumer price index (CPI)*, the *producer price index (PPI)* or the *wholesale price index*, and the *GDP deflator* or the *implicit GDP price index*. Of the three price indexes, the CPI is used most often. The **consumer price index** is an index that measures changes in the prices of consumer goods and services. In constructing the CPI, Statistics Canada collects information on the prices of a fixed basket of goods and services and calculates the average change over time. The **producer price index** is an index that measures changes in the prices of producer goods (goods bought by manufacturers). The **implicit price deflator** (also called the **GDP deflator**) is an index that measures changes in the average level of prices of all final goods and services. The *implicit price deflator* is therefore the most comprehensive of the three price indexes.

Can you explain how Statistics Canada constructs the CPI?

Statistics Canada more or less follows the following steps in constructing the CPI. First, it determines the composition of a fixed basket of goods and services that the typical individuals and families living in urban and rural areas—what it calls the target population—buy each month in a selected year. The selected year is used for reference purposes. The current reference year is 2005. Within the basket, it assigns different weights (importance) to each item, depending on the proportion of total expenditures spent on each time. Then it surveys retail outlets regularly to find out the cost of buying the fixed basket of goods and services. But to make the comparison consistent across the years, it chooses the cost of buying the basket in a base year (currently, 2002). To obtain the CPI, it divides the cost of buying the basket in a particular year by the cost of buying the basket in the base year and multiplies the result by 100.

Can you give us an example of how the CPI is constructed?

It can be demonstrated easily. Let us assume that the typical household buys only two items, apples and bus tickets (the data on the quantities and prices are fictitious). Table 6.2 shows hypothetical quantities and prices of apples and bus tickets that the typical household bought per month in 2010 and 2011, and demonstrates the construction of the CPI. Let us assume that in 2010 the price of an apple was $1.00 and that typical household bought 20 apples, costing the household a total of $20.00. If we assume that in 2010 a bus ride cost $3.00 and the typical family took 10 bus rides, it cost the family $30.00. The total cost of apples and bus rides in 2010 was $50.00 per month. If the price of apples increased by 5 cents and the bus fare rose by 10 cents in 2011, then the total cost of buying apples and taking bus rides would be $52.00 per month. With these numbers, we can show the construction of the CPI. Notice that we have held the quantities of both apples and bus tickets unchanged as we have increased their prices.

If we take 2010 as the base year, then to construct the CPI, we must divide the cost of buying the basket of goods and services in 2011 and other years by that of 2010, and multiply the result by 100. This gives us the CPI. Notice that the CPI has no unit since it is a ratio of two monetary values. The CPI for each year is then calculated as follows.

The CPI in 2010 = ($50/$50)*100 = 100

The CPI in 2011 = ($52/$50)*100 = 104

Table 6.2 An Example of the Construction of the CPI

Purchases in 2010

Item	Quantity	Price	Cost	CPI
Apples	20	$1	$20	
Bus rides	10	$3	$30	100
Total Cost			$50	

Purchases in 2011

Item	Quantity	Price	Cost	CPI
Apples	20	$1.05	$21	
Bus rides	10	$3.10	$31	104
Total Cost			$52	

How do we then calculate the rate of inflation?

The rate of inflation between two periods is calculated by taking the percentage change in the CPI between the two periods. The formula to calculate the rate of inflation is a general formula used to calculate percentage changes in any variable that we introduced in Chapter 1.

So, the rate of inflation between two years is:

$$\text{Rate of Inflation} = \left(\frac{\text{CPI}_{\text{current year}} - \text{CPI}_{\text{previous year}}}{\text{CPI}_{\text{previous year}}}\right) \times 100$$

Therefore, applying this formula, the rate of inflation between 2010 and 2011 will be:

$$\{(104 - 100)/100\}*100 = 4\%$$

Should volatile prices be included in the CPI?

core rate of inflation or core CPI excludes volatile prices such as prices of gasoline and some food items

Some economists assert that, because the CPI includes certain products whose prices tend to be volatile, the CPI tends to overstate increases in the cost of living. To obtain an unbiased estimation of inflation, they suggest that these volatile prices, such as the price of gasoline and food, be excluded from the calculation of the rate of inflation. This calculation is known as the **core rate of inflation**. Since 2006 Statistics Canada has been publishing monthly data on the **core CPI**, which excludes eight of the most volatile prices, including the price of fuels, vegetables, cigarettes; the interest payment on mortgages; and indirect taxes.

Are there any problems in using the CPI to estimate the rate of inflation?

Yes, the CPI has certain limitations. First, the composition of the basket is fixed and only changes infrequently. During the period that Statistics Canada keeps the composition of the basket fixed, consumers may have changed the combination of the goods and services they buy. If the relative price of a product increases, it is likely that consumers may purchase a relatively inexpensive substitute. Second, it is also possible that consumers may buy new products that may have been introduced into the market while Statistics Canada was keeping the basket fixed. Third, it is possible that the quality of a product may have improved as its price increased, but while the increase in the price of the product is reflected in the CPI, the improvement in the quality of the product is not. Because of these limitations, the changes in the CPI may not reflect the actual changes in the cost of consumer goods and services.

Is there any way of reducing these limitations of the CPI?

Chained Price Index for Consumption (CPIC) is an index based on the consumption expenditures reported in the national income accounts

As an alternative, some economists suggest the use of a different index, known as the **Chained Price Index for Consumption (CPIC)**. The index is based on the consumption expenditures reported in the national income accounts, and is constructed by dividing current consumption expenditures by real consumption expenditures and multiplying the result by 100. The index reflects the purchases of consumers in a given year, but it may not indicate the actual changes in the cost of buying consumer goods and services since it is based on the GDP deflator, which includes the price of non-consumer goods and services.

Can we calculate how long it will take the price level to double if we know the rate of inflation?

rule of 70 a formula for determining the number of years required for a number to double for a given rate of change

In fact, there is a rule or formula that we can use. The so-called **rule of 70** is a formula for determining the number of years required for a number (in this case, the average price level) to double for a given rate of change (in this case, the rate of inflation). According to this rule, the number of years required for a doubling of the price level is determined by dividing 70 by the annual rate of inflation. That is,

$$N = \frac{70}{\text{Rate of inflation}}$$

where N is the number of years necessary for the price level to double.

Obviously, the higher the rate of inflation, the shorter the time required for the average price level to double. If the rate of inflation is 5% per year, then the average price level will double in $(70 \div 5) = 14$ years. If the rate of inflation of 4.8% in 2000 had continued indefinitely, then the consumer price index would have doubled in $(70 \div 4.8) = 14.4$ years or by approximately 2014.

How do we analyze the effects of inflation?

The effects of inflation depend on whether inflation is anticipated or unanticipated, and whether individuals have the capacity to adjust their nominal income. Therefore, to examine properly the consequences of inflation, we must distinguish between anticipated and unanticipated inflation. If everyone expects a rate of inflation of 3% next year and that rate materializes, then we say inflation is fully *anticipated.* Conversely, if everyone expects an inflation rate of 4% next year and the actual rate turns out to be 6%, then we say inflation is *unanticipated.* Thus, inflation is fully anticipated if the expected rate turns out to be the actual rate. It is unanticipated if the expected rate turns out to be less than the actual rate.

Because different rates of inflation have quite different effects, it is also important to distinguish between different rates of inflation and to be familiar with the terminology used to describe these different rates. Some people have classified inflation into three categories: *creeping inflation*, *galloping inflation*, and *hyperinflation* or *runaway inflation.* These classifications are arbitrary, and there is no specific line or demarcation between them.

hyperinflation or runaway inflation an excessively high rate of inflation, usually 100% or more annually

Hyperinflation **Hyperinflation** is an excessively high rate of inflation, also called **runaway inflation**. A good example of hyperinflation is Germany in the early 1920s, when the annual inflation rate was well over 1 million percent.

This rate of inflation is difficult to conceive. To add some perspective to such a staggering rate of inflation, just imagine what the situation would be if the amount of money required to purchase a huge mansion in one year was not enough to purchase a box of matches one year later. Some countries, such as Angola, Democratic Republic of Congo, Zimbabwe, Bulgaria, Romania, Brazil, Nicaragua, and Peru, have all experienced what many would describe as hyperinflation or runaway inflation.

Why is inflation considered to be a problem?

Inflation distorts the capacity of prices to act as signals for the allocation of resources by households and firms. It makes it difficult for consumers and firms to make the right allocative decisions, to use their resources efficiently. Further, some individuals have to pay increasingly higher prices for goods and services with a fixed sum of money. But although it is true that inflation reduces people's purchasing power, we must not lose sight of the fact that not all individuals are equally affected by inflation.

Are you saying that there are winners and losers in inflation?

real income nominal income adjusted for the rate of inflation

Yes. But before we identify the winners and losers, we need to distinguish the difference between nominal income and **real income**. Nominal income is the income that individuals earn in a month or a year; it does not take into account the rate of inflation. Real income is nominal income adjusted for the rate of inflation. It represents the purchasing power of income. The change in real income depends on the difference between the percentage change in nominal income and the rate of inflation. An example will illustrate how inflation affects real income. Let's take two individuals, Rebecca and Julian, in 2010. Suppose Rebecca's salary increased by 5% while Julian's remained unchanged, and suppose the rate of inflation was 2% in 2010. Rebecca's real income increased by 3% but Julian's decreased by 2%.

Can the winners and losers be identified?

Let's begin with the winners.

The Winners Those who benefit during an inflation include debtors (borrowers) and producers (sellers). Debtors (borrowers) gain from inflation because they repay their debts with money whose value has fallen. Producers of goods and services benefit from inflation because during a period of inflation, the prices of goods and services tend to rise faster than the increase in the prices of inputs, especially nominal wages. This means that profits increase during inflationary periods.

The Losers Those who lose as a result of inflation include creditors (lenders), people on fixed incomes, and people whose nominal income lags behind inflation. Creditors (lenders) lose because, when they are repaid, the money they receive will have lost some purchasing power. People on fixed incomes and salaries lose because, as the price level increases, they have to spend a larger sum of money for the same quantity of goods and services while their incomes remain unchanged. In other words, their real income or purchasing power declines.

> You should realize that the adverse effects of inflation on various groups apply mainly in the case of unanticipated inflation and their inability to adjust nominal income. For example, creditors who anticipate an inflation rate of 4% may protect themselves from loss by adding 4% to the rate of interest that they would have charged had there been no inflation. People on contractual income may protect their purchasing power by negotiating to have their income indexed to the inflation rate. This means that if the price level rises by 3%, incomes will automatically rise by 3%. Such cost of living adjustment (COLA) clauses are common in many employment contracts.

We have seen that inflation affects certain individuals and groups, but how does it affect the economy as a whole?

The previous section showed that inflation affects individuals by redistributing income among various groups. The redistributive effect of inflation is only a part of the story. Inflation also affects the entire economy through its effect on resource allocation. In an inflationary period, some people may try to protect the purchasing power of their income by buying durable goods and other assets. Thus, inflation may result in a misallocation of the economy's resources.

Moreover, some economists argue that inflation reduces the incentive to work. As stated earlier, since nominal wages lag behind the rate of inflation or real wages decline in a period of inflation, people may consider it pointless to work harder. This could have adverse economic consequences. Inflation also affects the amount of taxes individuals and firms pay. Inflation tends to push people into higher income brackets. If the tax system is progressive, the proportion of taxes paid out of income will increase. To avoid paying higher taxes because of moving into a higher income bracket, some people may reduce their work effort (for example, refuse to work overtime or take time off from work without pay). Although some economists claim that a mild inflation may stimulate profits, investment, and economic growth, the fear is that even a mild inflation may eventually turn into a hyperinflation.

Because money loses its value so fast during hyperinflation, people try to spend it as fast as they get it. This situation can degenerate to the point where people refuse to accept money as payment for goods and services, and revert to an inefficient barter system in which goods and services are exchanged without the use of money. Hyperinflation may require monetary reform; otherwise, the entire economy could suffer.

Is there any relationship between inflation and unemployment?

The relationship between unemployment and inflation is important in macroeconomics and will be examined in considerable depth in Chapter 16. In this section, we merely introduce some key points of that important and sometimes controversial relationship. Figure 6.8 will help us understand the relationship.

The level of aggregate spending in an economy affects both the rate of inflation and the rate of unemployment. If total spending falls to very low levels, firms will find themselves with a large volume of unsold goods and services (unplanned inventories). They will lay off workers, and they will not raise their prices. This will increase the rate of unemployment. The economy will be operating in section *A* of Figure 6.8, where output (and employment) is well below its full employment level denoted by *F*. The unemployment rate will be high.

If total spending rises, unplanned inventories increase and firms will notice an increase in demand for their goods and services. Their inventories may even fall below desired levels, and so they hire more workers to increase production; the unemployment rate falls. As this continues, resources become relatively scarcer, and as a result, resource prices rise. Labour demands wage increases. As a result, the price level begins to rise. The economy will be operating in section *B* of Figure 6.8, which shows the price level, output, and hence employment rising; the unemployment rate is falling.

If total spending continues to rise, the economy will eventually reach the full employment level (point *F* in Figure 6.8). Output and employment cannot rise beyond this level—that is, the unemployment rate cannot fall any lower. The pressure of spending on the now fixed total output results in higher prices, as shown by section C of Figure 6.8.

The analysis above suggests an inverse relationship between inflation and unemployment, in the upward sloping segment of the curve in Figure 6.8. On the basis of this relationship, some economists argue that it may be necessary to tolerate a certain amount of inflation in order to reduce the rate of unemployment. Other economists argue that this type of trade-off is possible only in the short run; in the long run, increases in inflation produce few gains in reducing the unemployment rate.

Figure 6.8 Relationship between Unemployment and Inflation

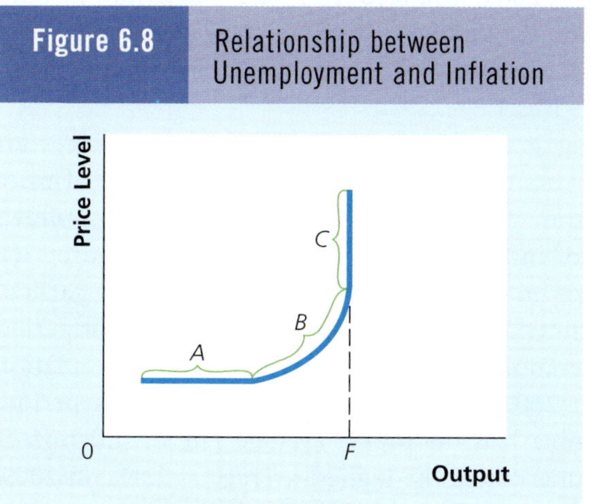

Will we be studying this controversial issue?

We will return to this issue in Chapter 16.

Reading Comprehension

The answers to these questions can be found on MyEconLab at www.myeconlab.com. MyEconLab

1. How does inflation affect the purchasing power of money?
2. How do we calculate the rate of inflation?
3. What is the difference between nominal income and real income?
4. How are inflation and unemployment related?

LO 6.6 Compare the rates of unemployment and inflation among the provinces and between Canada and other countries

The Rates of Unemployment and Inflation in Canada and Other Countries

How are the unemployment and inflation rates different among the provinces?

When we hear or read economic statistics about Canada, we sometimes forget that those statistics will not accurately reflect the condition in every province and territory. For example, the overall unemployment rate may be falling in Canada but rising in a particular province. Table 6.3 contains the relevant data. In 2009, the rate of unemployment in Newfoundland and Labrador was almost twice the national average and more than three times the rates in Saskatchewan and Manitoba. Newfoundland and Labrador and Prince Edward Island had double-digit unemployment rates in 2009, while Manitoba, Saskatchewan, Alberta, and British Columbia had rates below 8%. In 2009, Saskatchewan had the lowest unemployment rate of 4.8%. The differences in the rates of unemployment in the provinces reflect the differences in the economic structures of the provinces.

Table 6.3 The Rate of Unemployment by Province, 2009

Province	Unemployment Rate (%)
Newfoundland and Labrador	15.5
Prince Edward Island	12
Nova Scotia	9.2
New Brunswick	8.9
Quebec	8.5
Ontario	9
Manitoba	5.2
Saskatchewan	4.8
Alberta	6.6
British Columbia	7.6
Canada	8.3

Source: Statistics Canada. CANSIM, Table 282-0002 - www40.statcan.ca/l01/cst01/labor07a.htm, www40.statcan.ca/ l01/cst01/labor07b.htm, and www40.statcan.ca/l01/cst01/labor07c.htm.

In general, provincial inflation was relatively low from 2005 to 2009. In 2009, it ranged from -0.2% in Prince Edward Island and Nova Scotia to 1% in Saskatchewan as can be seen from Table 6.4. The national average rate of inflation between 2005 and 2009 was 1.8%.

By looking at the rates of inflation in the provinces for the past five years (2005–2009), we get a fair picture of price movements from year to year. For example, Table 6.4 shows that the rate of inflation in Nova Scotia, as measured by the consumer price index, was 2.8% in 2005, increased to 3.0% in 2008, and declined to -0.2% in 2009. Over the five-year period under consideration, in most provinces, the rate of inflation was lowest in 2009 and highest in 2008. Over this period, British Columbia had the lowest average rate of inflation at 1.5%, while Alberta had the highest average at 2.8%. In 2009, all provinces, with the exception of Saskatchewan, were enjoying

Table 6.4 The Rate of Inflation by Province 2005–2009

Province	2005	2006	2007	2008	2009	Average
Newfoundland and Labrador	2.7%	1.8%	1.5%	2.9%	0.3%	1.8%
Prince Edward Island	3.1%	2.3%	1.8%	3.4%	−0.2%	2.1%
Nova Scotia	2.8%	2.0%	1.9%	3.0%	−0.2%	1.9%
New Brunswick	2.4%	1.7%	1.9%	1.7%	0.3%	1.6%
Quebec	2.3%	1.7%	1.6%	2.1%	0.6%	1.6%
Ontario	2.2%	1.8%	1.8%	2.3%	0.4%	1.7%
Manitoba	2.7%	2.0%	2.0%	2.3%	0.6%	1.9%
Saskatchewan	2.2%	2.1%	2.8%	3.3%	1.0%	2.3%
Alberta	2.1%	3.9%	5.0%	3.1%	−0.1%	2.8%
British Columbia	2.0%	1.7%	1.8%	2.1%	0.0%	1.5%
Canada	**2.2%**	**2.0%**	**2.2%**	**2.3%**	**0.3%**	**1.8%**

(Year columns: 2005–2009)

Source: Statistics Canada, CANSIM, Table 326-0021 and Catalogue nos. 62-001-X and 62-010-X. www40.statcan.ca/l01/cst01/econ09a.htm. Extracted March 23, 2011.

very low inflation rates of less than 1%, with Saskatchewan experiencing the highest rate at 1%, because of the recession in Canada. In 2009, three provinces, Nova Scotia, New Brunswick, and Alberta, experienced deflation—a decrease in the average price level.

How do Canada's rates of unemployment and inflation compare with those of the other industrialized countries?

Figure 6.9 shows unemployment and inflation rates for 20 industrialized countries, including Canada, over the period 2001–2011.

The rates of unemployment and inflation in a country depend on its economic structure, resource endowment, and past and current economics policies. As the chart shows, of the 20 countries selected, Switzerland had the lowest unemployment rate—an average of only 3.4% over the 2001–2011 period. Spain had the highest average annual rate of unemployment at 12.8%. Canada had the eleventh-lowest (or ninth-highest) unemployment rate among the selected countries. Turning to the rate of inflation for the same period, we observe that 9 of the 20 selected countries had lower

Figure 6.9 Unemployment and Inflation Rates for 20 Industrialized Countries, Averages, 2001–2011

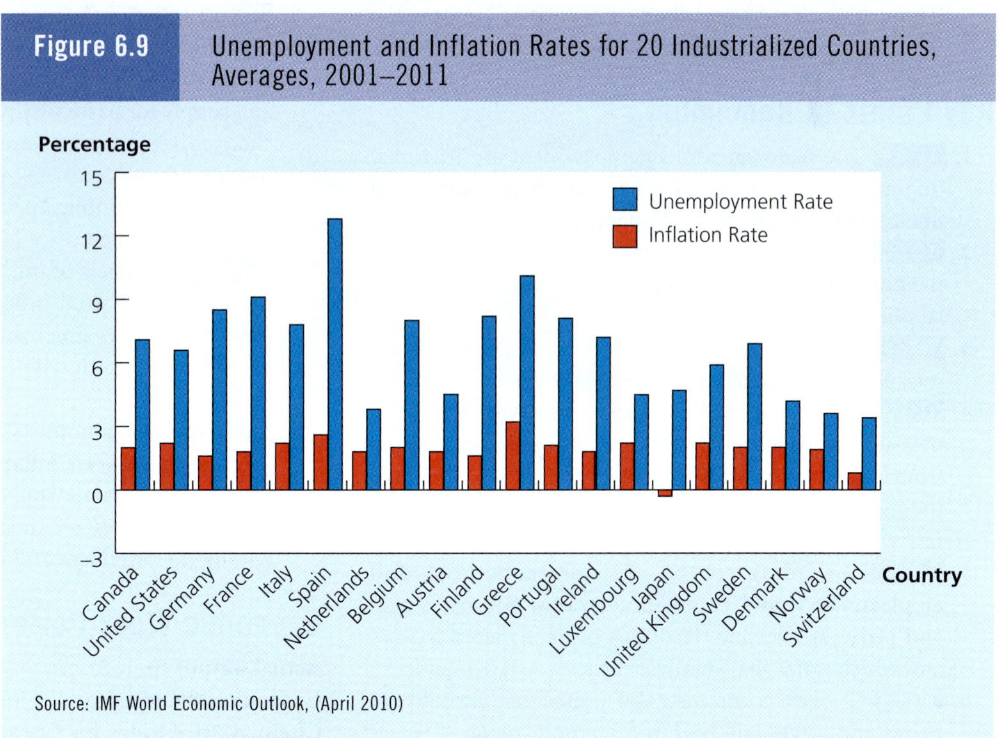

Source: IMF World Economic Outlook, (April 2010)

average annual rates of inflation than Canada. Norway had the highest rate of inflation (3.2%), while Japan had the lowest. In fact, Japan actually had deflation, with the price level falling by 0.3%.

Reading Comprehension

The answers to these questions can be found on MyEconLab at www.myeconlab.com. MyEconLab

1. Why does the rate of unemployment vary across the provinces?
2. How does Canada's rate of inflation compare with that of the other developed countries?
3. How does Canada's rate of unemployment compare with that of the other developed countries?

Review

1. Review the learning objectives listed at the beginning of the chapter.
2. Have you accomplished all the objectives? One way to determine this is to answer the Reading Comprehension Questions at the end of each section. This will help you assess the extent to which you have accomplished the learning objectives.
3. If you haven't accomplished an objective, review the relevant material before proceeding.

Key Points to Remember

1. LO 6.1 The main types of unemployment are frictional unemployment, seasonal unemployment, structural unemployment, and cyclical unemployment.
2. LO 6.2 The unemployment rate is obtained by expressing the number of people unemployed as a percentage of the labour force.
3. LO 6.3 The groups most likely to be unemployed are unskilled workers and those between the ages of 15 and 24.
4. LO 6.3 The economic cost of unemployment can be measured in terms of the lost output or income resulting from unemployment. The non-economic costs include the mental anguish, the frustration, and the loss of dignity and self-worth that the unemployed suffer.
5. LO 6.4 According to the classical economists, full employment would automatically occur because wages and prices are flexible. The basis of their theory is Say's law, which states that supply creates its own demand.
6. LO 6.4 Classical economists also argued that flexibility in prices and wages will lead to full employment. If wages don't decrease, they suggested, it is mostly because of government policy.
7. LO 6.4 The Keynesian theory of unemployment states that a deficiency of total spending could cause the economy to achieve a less-than-full employment equilibrium, and that government intervention in the economy may be necessary to push it toward full employment.
8. LO 6.5 Inflation is a sustained increase in the average level of prices over time and should not be confused with increases in relative prices caused by changes in demand and supply for particular products. Price indexes measure changes in the average level of prices. The three common indexes are the consumer price index, the producer price index, and the implicit price index (GDP deflator). There is also the chained price index for consumption.
9. LO 6.5 The effects of inflation depend on the severity of the inflation. A mild inflation does not seem to disrupt the economy very much, but a high inflation redistributes income and wealth. Hyperinflation can cause economic collapse.
10. LO 6.5 Some economists claim that an inverse relationship exists between inflation and unemployment. This view, however, is not supported by all economists.
11. LO 6.6 The rates of unemployment and inflation vary among the provinces and across countries.

Economic Word Power

Actual output (p. 168)
Capacity utilization rate (p. 161)
Chained Price Index for Consumption (CPIC) (p. 174)

Problems and Exercises

Basic

1. LO 6.1 Consider each of the following situations and determine whether the person is employed, unemployed, or not in the labour force. Indicate the employment status in each case:
   a. A 14-year-old girl delivers newspapers early in the morning.
   b. A 22-year-old university graduate is out of work but has given up searching for a job because she believes that none is currently available.
   c. A factory worker is temporarily laid off but will be recalled within two or three days.
   d. The closure of a store causes the manager to lose her job. She is now looking for work.
   e. A man takes night classes at college but works during the day.
2. LO 6.2 You are given the following information about an economy:
   Labour force 200 000
   Number employed 180 000
   Adult population 250 000
   Calculate:
   a. The unemployment rate
   b. The labour force participation rate
   c. The number of people unemployed
3. LO 6.1 Identify the type of unemployment in each of the following cases:
   a. Elizabeth has just graduated from university and is still looking for her first job.
   b. A long-term decline in the demand for cotton has resulted in unemployment in the cotton industry.
   c. During the summer months, unemployment in winter resort towns increases.
   d. Harry and four other workers were laid off because of a general downturn in economic activity.
   e. Accounting clerks lose their jobs because of the computerization of accounting.
4. LO 6.5 Indicate whether these groups are winners or losers from unanticipated inflation:
   a. Banks that lend money
   b. Retirees on fixed incomes
   c. People who lend money
   d. Firms engaged in production
   e. People who have savings accounts

Questions in the Intermediate and Challenging Sections cover several different concepts, and have not been organized by learning objectives.

Intermediate

1. The following data are available for an economy:

Adult population	350 000
Not in the labour force	140 000
Number employed	175 000

   Calculate
   a. The labour force
   b. The number unemployed
   c. The unemployment rate
   d. The labour force participation rate

2. Use a demand/supply graph for labour services to illustrate that inflexible wage rates can result in unemployment.
3. In 2009, the price level in a certain economy was 120. If the rate of inflation in that economy remains steady at 3.5%, when will the price level double? (Use the rule of 70.)
4. During a period of inflation, there are winners and losers. What can the losers do to protect themselves from anticipated inflation?

Challenging

1. Consider the situations regarding inflation shown in Table 6.5. The average annual rate of inflation is 4% in each situation. Explain why inflation is likely to be less harmful in situation B than in situation A.

Table 6.5 Two Inflation Situations

Situation A

Year	2000	2001	2002	2003	2004
Inflation (%)	4	2	4	6	4

Situation A

Year	2000	2001	2002	2003	2004
Inflation (%)	4	4	4	4	4

2. How might each of the following affect the unemployment rate?
   a. An increase in minimum wage
   b. A better match between employees and jobs
   c. An increase in the belief that women should stay home and raise their children

Study Guide

Self-Assessment

What's your score?

Circle the letter that corresponds with the correct answer.

1. According to Statistics Canada, people are unemployed
   a. As long as they are not working
   b. If they are without jobs and are actively looking and available for work
   c. If they are on more than a two-week sick leave
   d. All of the above
2. Unemployment resulting from a deficiency of aggregate spending is called
   a. Deficiency unemployment
   b. Aggregate unemployment
   c. Frictional unemployment
   d. Cyclical unemployment
3. Unemployment resulting from changes in demand patterns is called
   a. Frictional unemployment
   b. Cyclical unemployment
   c. Structural unemployment
   d. None of the above
4. Full employment exists only when
   a. The unemployment rate is zero
   b. One hundred percent of the labour force is employed
   c. There is only frictional and structural unemployment
   d. The unemployed consists only of discouraged workers
5. Which of the following statements is true of seasonal unemployment?
   a. It affects only countries with marked seasonal variations

b. It results in unemployment only during one season of the year
c. It affects only young workers who are not yet seasoned in their jobs
d. It affects even countries where seasonal variations are slight

6. Which of the following could result in structural unemployment?
a. The introduction of labour-saving machines
b. Permanent decline in the demand for the products of a particular industry
c. A decision by a country to switch from oil to solar energy as its main source of power
d. All of the above

7. Cyclical unemployment is unemployment that results from
a. People who are moving between jobs
b. A deficiency in aggregate spending
c. A secular decline in demand for the products of particular industries
d. Seasonal variations

8. The labour force participation rate is
a. The percentage of the labour force actually employed
b. The percentage of the population actually looking for work
c. The labour force expressed as a percentage of the adult population
d. None of the above

9. Which of the following groups is most likely to be unemployed?
a. Children under the age of 12
b. People between the ages of 15 and 24
c. Men over the age of 25
d. None of the above

10. Which of the following groups is most likely to be underemployed?
a. Educated workers for whose qualification there is little demand
b. Skilled and highly educated workers
c. Workers who are close to retirement
d. All of the above

11. Discouraged workers are workers who
a. Hold on to their jobs even though they are dissatisfied with conditions at work
b. Have abandoned the search for jobs because, after a long search, they are convinced that their search will be unsuccessful
c. Get discouraged easily as soon as problems arise at work
d. All of the above

12. The total economic cost of unemployment is measured by
a. The amount paid out in employment insurance
b. The loss in income tax caused by unemployment
c. The difference between potential output and actual output
d. All of the above

13. Okun's law expresses a linear relationship between
a. Unemployment and the percentage change in GDP
b. Inflation and unemployment
c. Inflation and the percentage change in GDP
d. None of the above

14. According to Keynes, unemployment results from
a. Wage and price flexibility
b. The unwillingness of people to work
c. A deficiency in total spending
d. All of the above

15. Inflation is
a. Any increase in the average level of prices
b. A sustained increase in the money supply
c. A sustained increase in the average level of prices
d. All of the above

16. Which of the following is the most comprehensive price index?
a. The consumer price index
b. The producer price index
c. The GDP deflator
d. None of the above

17. Inflation may cause
a. A misallocation of resources
b. A redistribution of income
c. A reduction in work incentive
d. All of the above

18. For which of the following demographic groups has the participation rate increased significantly?
a. Men
b. The youth
c. Women
d. Older workers

19. Winners from inflation may include
a. Debtors
b. Producers (sellers)
c. Owners of durable goods
d. All of the above

20. International comparisons of unemployment and inflation
a. Help us to put Canada's unemployment and inflation in perspective
b. Are not meaningful because all countries have different problems
c. Distort Canada's unemployment and inflation data
d. None of the above

Problems and Exercises (Use Quad Paper for Graphs)

Answers to these questions can be found on MyEconLab at www.myeconlab.com. MyEconLab

1. Table 6.6 contains data for a hypothetical economy.

Table 6.6 Data for a Hypothetical Economy

Item	Number
Adult population (15 and over)	16 000 500
Employed	9 200 000
Unemployed	900 000

Use the data to calculate
   a. The labour force
   b. The participation rate
   c. The unemployment rate

2. The data contained in Table 6.7 are for the economy of Grandstand. Complete the table by filling in the blank spaces.

Table 6.7 Economy of Grandstand

Item	Number or Percentage
Labour force	10.5 million
Unemployment rate (%)	10.5
Employment rate (%)	______
Number employed	______
Number unemployed	______

3. A labour force survey contains the data shown in Table 6.8 for a hypothetical economy. Complete the table by filling in the blanks.

Table 6.8 Data for a Hypothetical Economy

Characteristics	Jan.	Feb.	Mar.	Apr.
Adult population	200	200	220	220
Not in labour force	80	___	90	90
Labour force	___	110	___	___
Employed	100	___	___	___
Unemployed	___	10	30	20
Unemployment rate (%)	___	___	___	___
Participation rate (%)	___	___	___	___

4. In 2009, the unemployment rate in Botillia (a fictitious country) was 15%, and the total output in that year was $200 billion. If an employment rate of 95% is considered full employment, use Okun's law (with a ratio of 1:2) to calculate the loss of output attributable to unemployment.

5. Classify each of the following as employed, unemployed, underemployed, or not in the labour force:
   a. A spouse who stays at home and takes care of the children
   b. A 13-year-old student who does odd jobs for the neighbours for pocket money
   c. An economics professor who has a job but is actively looking for another job as a consultant
   d. An adult who has a part-time job but would like to work full time
   e. A painter who has been laid off but expects to be called back to work within three days
   f. A 19-year-old college graduate looking for a job for the first time
   g. A university graduate with a Ph.D. in history who is currently working as a tour guide but hopes to find a job that is more in line with her qualifications
   h. A radio announcer who has looked for work for several months, would like to work, but has now given up hope of ever finding a job
   i. The spouse of a wealthy person who stays at home and reads the want adsoccasionally to find an interesting job
   j. An administrative assistant who left the workforce two years ago but is now actively looking for work

6. Classify each of the following into one of the main categories of unemployment:
   a. College graduates looking for their first jobs
   b. Coal miners who have been dismissed because of a permanent decline in the demand for coal
   c. Construction workers who have been laid off for the winter
   d. Workers who have been dismissed because of a general decrease in the total demand for goods and services
   e. Workers who have lost their jobs because of automation

7. A country has an annual rate of inflation of 6.8%. Use the rule of 70 to calculate the number of years it would take for this country's price level to double.

8. Some economists have defined the sum of the unemployment rate and the inflation rate as the *misery index*. On this basis, use the data in Tables 6.3 (p. 178) and 6.4 (p. 179) to determine which Canadian province had the highest misery index in 2009 and which had the lowest.

Chapter 7

The Aggregate Demand (*AD*)–Aggregate Supply (*AS*) Model: Short-Run Analysis

Learning Objectives

After studying this chapter, you should be able to

7.1 Differentiate between the demand for a particular product and aggregate demand

7.2 Discuss the rationale for the shape of the aggregate demand curve

7.3 Examine the factors that shift the *AD* curve

7.4 Explain the meaning of aggregate supply

7.5 Describe each of the three ranges that constitute the short-run aggregate supply curve

7.6 Examine the factors that shift the *SRAS* curve

7.7 Explain the determination of real output and the price level in a short-run equilibrium

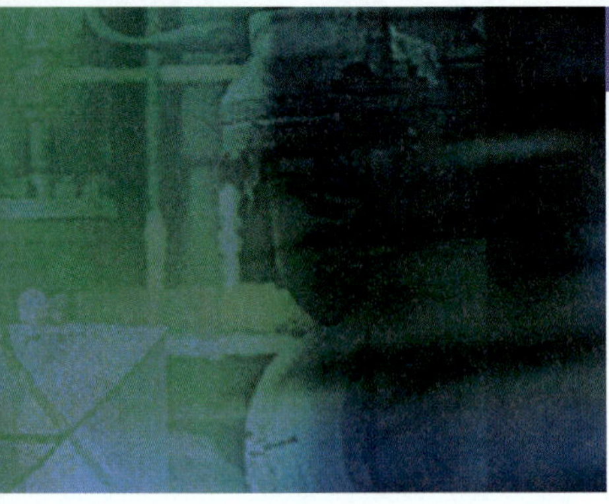

7.8 Analyze the effects of changes in aggregate demand on equilibrium real GDP and price

7.9 Discuss the implications of the *AD–AS* model for demand-side policies

7.10 Analyze the effects of changes in aggregate supply on equilibrium real GDP and price

7.11 Discuss the implications of the *AD–AS* model for supply-side policies

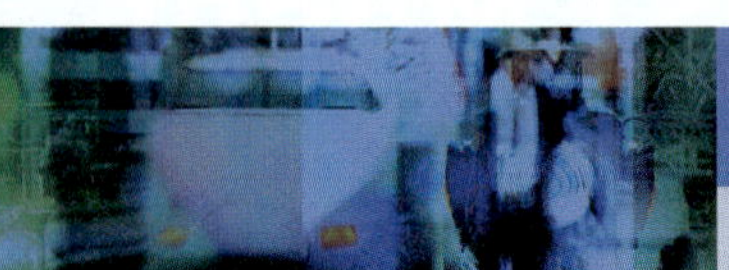

Assess Your Knowledge

MyEconLab

Answers to these questions can be found on MyEconLab at **www.myeconlab.com.**

1. If interest rates fall, other things being equal, what will happen to consumer spending? What will happen to spending by firms?
2. Describe three important factors that affect consumer spending.
3. What relationship would you expect to find between interest rates and investment?
4. Explain how changes in technology affect a country's aggregate supply.
5. What will happen to the price level if aggregate supply increases?

LO 7.1 Differentiate between the demand for a particular product and aggregate demand

Aggregate Demand

What is aggregate demand?

aggregate demand the total demand for all goods and services in the economy during a specific period; the various levels of real output that will be demanded at various price levels

We know that *aggregate* means "total," and we know that *demand* refers to the quantity of an item that an individual is both willing and able to buy, from our lesson in Chapter 3. When we consider the term **aggregate demand**, we are referring to the total demand for all goods and services in the economy during a specific period. More specifically, aggregate demand refers to the various levels of real output, including all goods and services, that will be demanded at various price levels.

Aggregate demand describes the relationship between real output and the price level. You may have noticed the analogy between the definition of aggregate demand and the definition of the demand for a single product given in Chapter 3.

Is there a relationship between the quantity of real output demanded and the average level of prices?

The relationship between the quantity of real GDP demanded and the average level of prices can be expressed in a statement similar to the law of demand discussed in Chapter 3.

> As the price level falls, other things being equal, the quantity of real GDP demanded increases; and as the price level increases, other things being equal, the quantity of real GDP demanded decreases.

Figure 7.1 The Aggregate Demand Curve

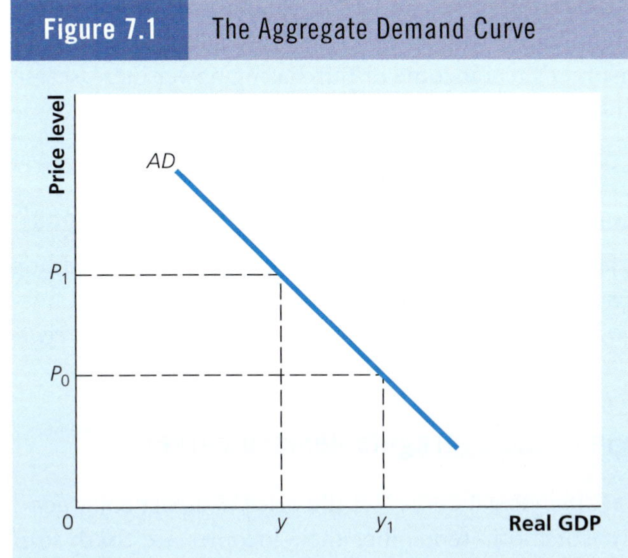

In other words, an inverse relationship exists between the quantity of real GDP demanded and the price level.

We studied the demand curve for a particular product. Is there also an aggregate demand curve?

The Aggregate Demand Curve In the same way that we use a demand curve to portray consumer preferences for an individual good or service, we can use an aggregate demand curve to depict the total demand for all final goods and services. The **aggregate demand curve** is a graph that shows the relationship between the total amount of all goods and services that will be demanded at various price levels.

aggregate demand curve a graph that shows the relationship between the total amount of all goods and services that will be demanded at various price levels

You will probably expect the aggregate demand curve to slope downward because the demand curve for a particular product slopes downward from left to right. And that is exactly the case, as is illustrated in Figure 7.1.

At a price level of P_0, the total quantity of real output (real GDP) demanded is y_1. At a price level of P_1, the total quantity of real GDP demanded is y. As the price level rises, the total quantity of real GDP that will be demanded falls, other things being equal; and as the price level falls, the total quantity of real GDP that will be demanded rises. Remember the law of demand presented in Chapter 3? That same inverse relationship (albeit for different reasons), this time between real GDP and the price level, applies here as well.

Reading Comprehension

The answers to these questions can be found on MyEconLab at www.myeconlab.com. MyEconLab

1. What is meant by aggregate demand?
2. Sketch the aggregate demand (*AD*) curve, carefully labelling the diagram.

LO 7.2 Discuss the rationale for the shape of the aggregate demand curve

Understanding the Aggregate Demand Curve

Does the aggregate demand curve slope downward for the same reasons that the demand curve for an individual good or service slopes downward?

Let's briefly review the fundamental reasons for the negative slope of the demand curve for an individual good or service. First, as the price of a good or service falls, consumers tend to purchase a greater quantity of it, because it becomes less expensive relative to other goods and services—the substitution effect studied in Chapter 3. Second, as the price of a good or service falls, an individual's income can purchase a larger quantity of this item. In other words, the consumer's real income or purchasing power increases, so it is likely that a greater quantity of this good or service will be demanded—the income effect, also studied in Chapter 3.

So does the aggregate demand curve slope downward for these reasons?

It is tempting to think that the aggregate demand curve can be obtained by adding together the market demand curves for individual goods and services but this is a misconception. An analysis of the *market* demand curve does not explain why the *aggregate* demand curve slopes downward.

How can we explain the shape of the aggregate demand curve?

Reasons for the Shape of the Aggregate Demand Curve If the price of a particular good rises, consumers will be relatively worse off (remember their incomes are fixed, so if prices rise they can now buy less); therefore, they will purchase a smaller quantity of the item. Such is not the case with aggregate demand. If we were to add the individual demand curves in an attempt to arrive at the aggregate demand curve, we would be guilty of what is called the **fallacy of composition**—the assumption that what is true of the parts must also be true of the whole.

fallacy of composition the assumption that what is true of the parts must also be true of the whole

Instead, when the price *level* increases, the prices of resources, including labour, also increase, and so incomes increase too. With larger incomes, more goods and services can be purchased.

Can you provide a simple example to illustrate the fallacy of composition?

Suppose, for simplicity, that there are only two products, A and B. If the price of A rises, other things being equal, consumers are worse off because a given sum of money now buys less than it previously afforded. This is a case of market demand. But if the price of A, the price of B, and income all rise by, say, 5%, then consumers on the whole are not worse off. Relatively speaking, nothing has changed. This is a case of aggregate demand. It is possible for the price of product A to rise; however, before we draw any conclusions, we must consider what is happening to the price of product B and consumer incomes. We would be guilty of the fallacy of composition in the aggregate model if we drew conclusions based solely on changes in the price of product A, without considering product B or resource prices.

Let's return to the shape of the aggregate demand (AD) curve. Why does it slope downward to the right? The price level, you recall, is an average price of all goods and services. What effect does a rise in the price level have on the total amount of goods and services that will be demanded? Remember that total expenditure or aggregate expenditure (AE) on the economy's output of final goods and services is the sum of consumer spending (C), investment (I), government purchases (G), and net exports ($X - M$)—that is,

$$AE = C + I + G + (X - M)$$

To see the effect of changes in the price level on the total output of goods and services that will be demanded, we can examine the effects of changes in the price level on the components of aggregate expenditure. These effects can be summarized as the *interest rate effect*, the *foreign trade effect*, and the *real wealth effect*. Let us begin with the interest rate effect.

The Interest Rate Effect An increase in the price level means that, on average, most goods and services that households and firms buy are now more expensive. Hence, households and firms need more money to make these purchases. This increase in the demand for money, other things being equal, raises the price of money (rate of interest). When interest rates rise, it becomes more costly to borrow money, so firms that borrow funds to invest in capital goods reduce their spending. Thus, investment falls. Also, consumers who borrow money to purchase such items as automobiles, furniture, household appliances, and vacations reduce their purchases of these items. From this analysis, we can conclude that as the price level rises, the consumption (*C*) and investment (*I*) components of aggregate expenditure (*AE*) fall. This fall in *AE* implies that less of the total output will be demanded. The effect of changes in interest rates on *C* and *I* is often referred to as the **interest rate effect**. The interest rate effect is the impact of changes in interest rates on consumption and investment and thus on total spending.

interest rate effect the impact of changes in interest rates on consumption and investment and thus on total spending

The Foreign Trade Effect An increase in the price level in Canada means that, on average, Canadian goods are now more expensive in foreign countries than before the price level increase, and foreign goods are now relatively less expensive to Canadians. Other things being equal, Canadians will buy more foreign goods (an increase in *M*), and foreign countries will buy fewer Canadian goods (a decrease in *X*). Thus, as the price level rises, the (*X* – *M*) component of aggregate expenditure falls. This fall in *AE* implies that less of the total output of goods and services will be demanded. The effect of changes in the price level on exports and imports is referred to as the **foreign trade effect**. The foreign trade effect is the impact of changes in the price level on exports and imports and thus on the quantity of real GDP demanded.

foreign trade effect the impact of changes in the price level on exports and imports and thus on the quantity of real GDP demanded

The Real Wealth Effect If the price level rises, holders of financial assets, such as savings accounts and bonds, lose purchasing power. Their real wealth decreases. This decrease in real wealth results in a fall in expenditures on consumer goods and services. In other words, as the price level rises, the *C* component of *AE* falls; and this fall implies that less of the total real output will be demanded. This effect of changes in the price level on real wealth, and thus on the quantity of real GDP demanded, is called the **real wealth effect**.

real wealth effect the impact of changes in the price level on real wealth and thus on the quantity of real GDP demanded

BUSINESS SITUATION 7.1

The interest rate effect explains how, when prices are rising in the economy, there is a greater demand for money. This greater demand for money causes the price of money, or the interest rate, to rise.

As a business owner who is thinking of investing in capital equipment, and using the level of aggregate demand as a guide, when might be a good time to make such investments?

The answer to this Business Situation can be found in Appendix A.

Reading Comprehension

The answers to these questions can be found on MyEconLab at www.myeconlab.com. MyEconLab

1. What is the fallacy of composition? Provide an example to illustrate the fallacy.
2. Explain why the aggregate demand curve cannot be derived by adding all the demand curves for individual goods and services.
3. Why does the aggregate demand curve slope downward?

LO 7.3 Examine the factors that shift the *AD* curve

Shifting the Aggregate Demand Curve

What factors can cause the aggregate demand curve to shift?

Changes in the price level will not cause the *AD* curve to shift; instead, they will cause movements *along* the curve. An increase in aggregate demand means that at any given price level, a greater quantity of real GDP is demanded. The *AD* curve will shift if there is a change in aggregate expenditure (*AE*). Thus, if any component of *AE* changes, then the *AD* curve will shift. For example, an increase in government spending, a decrease in imports, or an increase in investment will raise *AE* and cause the *AD* curve to shift to the right, as shown in Diagram A of Figure 7.2. Alternately, a decrease in government spending, an increase in imports, or a fall in investment will cause the *AD* curve to shift to the left, as shown in Diagram B of Figure 7.2.

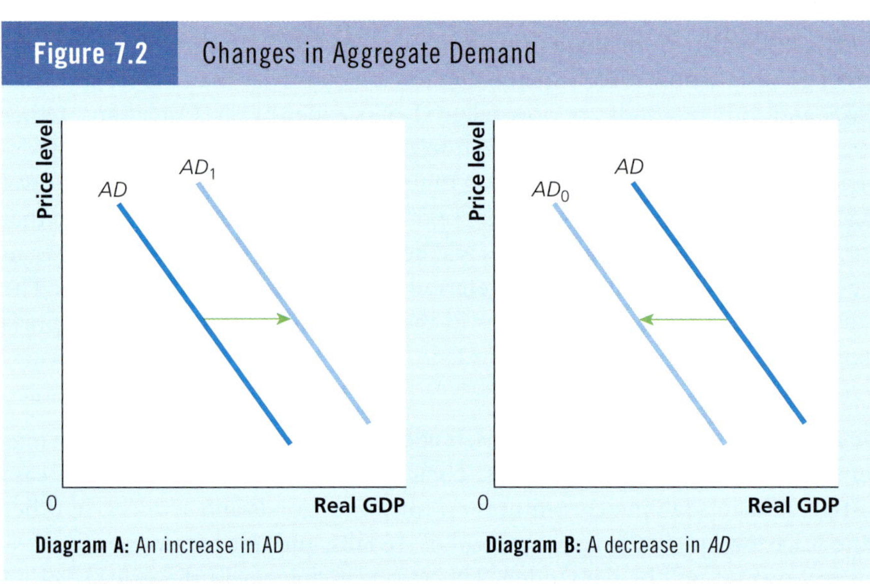

Diagram A: An increase in AD

Diagram B: A decrease in *AD*

BUSINESS SITUATION 7.2

You are the sales manager of a company that produces a wide variety of products for sale across the country. You have observed an increase in the aggregate quantity of goods and services purchased, including an increase in purchases from your company. You interpret this change to mean that there is an increase in aggregate demand, so you instruct your production department to increase output, and you hire additional salespeople to satisfy the assumed increase in demand. At the same time, you increase the prices of your products.

What mistake might you have made?

The answer to this Business Situation can be found in Appendix A.

Can we do an analysis of the factors that shift the *AD* curve?

Analysis of *AD* Shifters To better appreciate the factors that can shift the AD curve, let us return to the components of aggregate expenditure (AE):

$$AE = C + I + G + (X - M)$$

Anything, apart from price level changes, that affects any of these components will cause the *AD* curve to shift. Factors that cause the aggregate demand curve to shift are known as ***AD* shifters** (or **demand-side shocks**).

***AD* shifters or demand-side shocks** factors that cause the aggregate demand curve to shift

> The factors that can shift the aggregate demand curve are called *AD shifters* and are components of aggregate expenditure: consumption, investment, government spending, and net exports.

We can now identify some major *AD* shifters and briefly analyze their effects on *AD*. Let us begin with consumption.

What are some of the non-price-level determinants of consumer spending?

Consumer wealth, taxes, expectations, and interest rates are all non-price-level determinants of consumer spending. Each can cause the aggregate demand curve to shift.

Consumer Wealth If the price level remains constant and consumer wealth increases, perhaps because of an increase in property values, then consumers will tend to increase spending, thereby increasing *AE* and shifting the *AD* curve to the right. Conversely, a fall in property values will reduce consumer wealth and consumption, and shift the *AD* curve to the left.

Taxes A fall in personal income taxes increases disposable income. At each price level, consumers are able to purchase more goods and services, so *AE* increases and the *AD* curve shifts to the right. Conversely, tax hikes will reduce disposable income, reduce consumer spending, lower *AE*, and shift the *AD* curve to the left.

Expectations If consumers have good reasons to be optimistic about their future economic circumstances, they will increase their current consumption, thereby increasing *AE* and shifting the *AD* curve to the right. If they expect their real incomes to fall, they will reduce their current consumption and cause the *AD* curve to shift to the left.

Interest Rates Certain types of consumer spending (automobiles, furniture and appliances, entertainment devices, and vacation packages) are sensitive to changes in interest rates. If the price level remains constant and interest rates fall, consumer loans become more affordable and consumers will tend to purchase these items. Thus, falling interest rates increase consumer spending and shift the *AD* curve to the right. Similarly, rising interest rates tend to reduce consumer spending and shift the *AD* curve to the left.

What effect does investment spending have on the *AD* curve?

Investment refers to the purchase of capital goods and is an important component of *AE*. If investment changes, other things being equal, then *AE* will change and the *AD* curve will shift. Important non-price determinants of investment spending include interest rates, changes in income, perceived profitability of investment projects, and technological advance. Let's discuss each of these, beginning with interest rates.

Interest Rates Declining interest rates, given the price level, reduce the cost of acquiring investment funds and thus increase investment spending. More investment means greater *AE*, which shifts the *AD* curve to the right. Rising interest rates, conversely, will reduce investment spending and shift the *AD* curve to the left.

Changes in Income With a constant price level, an increase in income causes consumers to purchase more goods and services. This increase in demand for goods and services will likely lead firms to invest more in production and technology. The *AD* curve will shift to the right. By similar reasoning, a fall in income will reduce demand, lower the investment spending of firms, and reduce aggregate demand, shifting the *AD* curve to the left.

Perceived Profitability of Investment Projects If businesses perceive investment projects as lucrative they will likely invest in those projects, raising *AE* and shifting the *AE* curve to the right. However, if the prospects for profitable investment opportunities appear to be gloomy, investment spending will fall, and the *AD* curve will shift to the left.

Technological Advance Advancements in technology present new investment opportunities. Just consider the vast investment expenditures that have been made as a direct result of increases in computer technology. Such technological advances increase investment and cause the *AD* curve to shift to the right.

Does government spending shift the *AD* curve as well?

An increase in government purchases of goods and services at each price level will increase *AE* and shift the *AD* curve to the right, other things being equal. For example, if the federal government purchases a new fleet of helicopters to replace an aging fleet, or a few new submarines to augment our military equipment, *AE* will rise, and the *AD* curve will shift to the right. Similarly, reductions in government spending in the areas of health and education will reduce *AE* and cause the *AD* curve to shift to the left. The answer to the question posed above is yes, government spending certainly will affect the *AD* curve, causing it to shift up or down (right or left), depending on the magnitude of the government spending (or cutbacks).

What about net exports?

Net exports can shift the *AD* curve too. Any non-price-level factor that affects exports (X) or imports (M) will affect net exports ($X - M$) and shift the *AD* curve. If, for example, income in the United States increases, Americans will purchase more Canadian goods, so Canada's exports to the United States will increase. Other things being equal, this increase in Canada's exports will increase *AE* and shift the *AD* curve to the right. If the value of the Canadian dollar falls relative to the U.S. dollar, thus making the price of Canadian goods more attractive to Americans, then Canadian exports to the U.S. will rise. At the same time, U.S. goods will be relatively more expensive to Canadians, so Canadian imports from the United States will fall. This means that ($X - M$) will rise, *AE* will increase, and the *AD* curve will shift to the right. Take, for example, the fairly recent appreciation of the Canadian dollar that occurred over the period of 2003–2008. In

2003, the Canadian dollar was valued at approximately 62.5¢ U.S. At that time, Canada had a trade surplus close to $55 billion dollars. Exports to the United States were the chief contributor to that large surplus. Once the Canadian dollar began to appreciate and approach (and eventually surpass) par, Canadian exports to the United States began to quickly dissipate, resulting in the first trade deficit in over 30 years! In terms of net exports and the impact on the *AD* curve, this example shows that the appreciation of the Canadian dollar contributed to the decline in net exports ($X - M$), causing *AE* to decrease and *AD* to shift to the left.

Reading Comprehension

The answers to these questions can be found on MyEconLab at www.myeconlab.com. MyEconLab

1. What are demand-side shocks?
2. Identify some of the factors that will cause the *AD* curve to shift.
3. Describe the effect on the *AD* curve of (i) an increase in government spending; (ii) a decrease in exports.

LO 7.4 Explain the meaning of aggregate supply

Aggregate Supply

What is aggregate supply?

aggregate supply the total supply of all goods and services in the economy during a specific period; the various quantities of output that will be supplied at various price levels

Aggregate supply refers to the total supply of all goods and services in the economy during a particular period. More specifically, aggregate supply refers to the various levels of real GDP that will be supplied (that the economy's producers will be willing and able to provide) at various price levels.

This definition makes it clear that aggregate supply describes the relationship between real GDP and the price level. Note once again that the definition of aggregate supply is analogous to the definition of the supply of an individual good or service.

Is there an obvious relationship between the quantity of real output supplied and the average level of prices?

The relationship between the quantity of real GDP supplied and the average level of prices can be expressed in a statement similar to the law of supply discussed in Chapter 3.

> As the price level falls, other things being equal, the quantity of real GDP supplied falls; and as the price level increases, other things being equal, the quantity of real GDP supplied increases.

In other words, a direct relationship exists between the quantity of real GDP supplied and the price level.

Can we derive the aggregate supply curve by adding together the supply curves of all the individual commodities?

Just as it would be erroneous to try to derive the aggregate demand curve by adding together the individual demand curves, so too would we be in error if we attempted to derive the aggregate supply curve by adding together the supply curves of individual goods and services. In constructing the supply curve of an individual commodity, only the price of the commodity being studied is allowed to vary. But in constructing the aggregate supply curve, the average level of prices is allowed to vary.

Does the time frame become important in the derivation of the aggregate supply curve?

On the supply side it has become fairly standard practice in macroeconomics to distinguish between the long run and the short run when analyzing the aggregate supply curve. In this chapter, we focus on the short run and leave the discussion of the long run for Chapter 8.

What is the short run in the context of aggregate supply?

short run a situation in which firms cannot vary all their inputs or productive resources; thus, they operate with some fixed costs

The **short run** is a situation in which firms cannot vary all their inputs or productive resources; thus, they operate with some fixed costs. In discussing the short-run aggregate supply curve, we assume that input prices are constant while output prices are allowed to vary in response to market forces. This means that in the short run, firms face some fixed production costs.

In the short run, because some resource costs are fixed, changes in the average level of prices influence firms' decisions regarding real output. For example, if the price level rises, while some costs remain fixed, firms have an incentive to increase output in order to make more profits. Rising output prices coupled with fixed production costs signal greater profits.

What is the short-run aggregate supply curve?

short-run aggregate supply curve a graph that shows the various levels of real GDP that will be supplied at various price levels in the short run

The **short-run aggregate supply curve** can be used to illustrate the total supply of all goods and services in much the same way that a supply curve can be used to depict the supply of an individual good or service. The short-run aggregate supply curve is a graph that shows the various levels of real GDP that will be supplied at various price levels in the short run.

Can you make a prediction about the shape of the short-run aggregate supply curve?

You might expect it to be upward sloping, like the supply curve of an individual good or service. In fact, the short-run aggregate supply curve *may* be upward sloping. But as we will see shortly, certain sections of the short-run aggregate supply curve may have different shapes.

Reading Comprehension

The answers to these questions can be found on MyEconLab at www.myeconlab.com. MyEconLab

1. What is aggregate supply?
2. What is the short run as it applies to aggregate supply?
3. What is the short-run aggregate supply curve?

LO 7.5 Describe each of the three ranges that constitute the short-run aggregate supply curve

Understanding the Aggregate Supply Curve

Certain sections of the short-run aggregate supply curve may have different shapes? That sounds rather interesting. Can we discuss it now?

The short-run aggregate supply curve can be divided into three sections or ranges, as shown in Figure 7.3.

For a level of real output (GDP) from 0 to y, the short-run aggregate supply curve is horizontal. For real output levels from y to y_1, it is upward sloping, and when real output reaches y_1, the short-run aggregate supply curve becomes vertical.

Why are these three sections of the short-run *AS* curve different?

Let us address this issue by examining each section in turn.

Keynesian range the horizontal section of the *AS* curve that represents high unemployment and low real GDP

intermediate range the upward-sloping section of the *AS* curve that represents high price levels

The Horizontal Section If the economy is operating at low levels of real output and low levels of employment, then increasing real GDP is possible even without any appreciable increase in the price level. This horizontal section of the short-run *AS* curve is called the **Keynesian range**, because it represents substantial unemployment and low real GDP—a topic of great concern to John Maynard Keynes during the Great Depression of the 1930s. Because at this stage there are significant quantities of unemployed workers and other resources that can be used to increase real output, average cost will tend to be constant as output increases. And because average cost is constant, firms do not need to receive higher prices for their output in order to induce them to increase production. During the recession of 2008–2009, the unemployment rate reached 8.3% in Canada and GDP fell significantly below potential. During this period it can be said that the Canadian economy was operating in the Keynesian range of the aggregate supply curve. Statistics also reveal that the initial increases in GDP that were experienced during the recovery in 2009 were accompanied by only negligible price level increases.

Figure 7.3 The Short-Run Aggregate Supply Curve

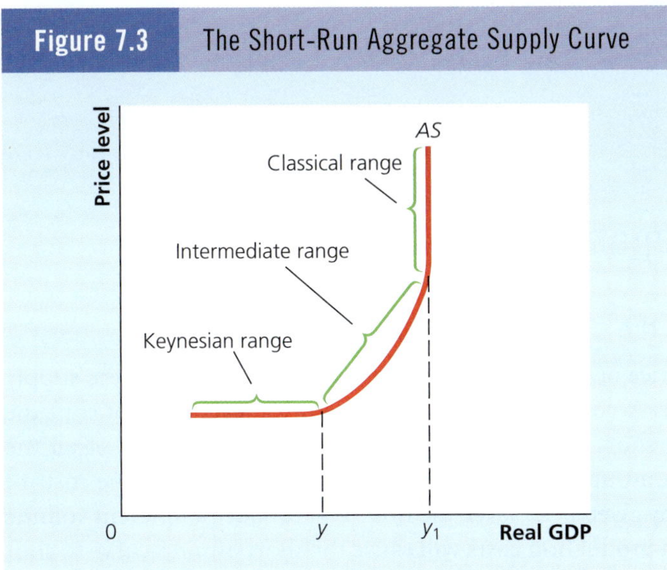

The Intermediate Section As real output continues to increase beyond y, factor inputs will become relatively scarce. Throughout this range, some of the unemployed resources that existed in the horizontal section have become employed. Competition among firms for these less abundant inputs will cause both input prices and hence production costs to increase. Firms will have to compensate by increasing output prices to induce them to expand production. Also, as output expands, an increasing number of industries will approach their capacity limits, making it increasingly difficult and costly to continue to increase output. Thus, in the **intermediate range**, a *direct* relationship exists between real GDP and the price level. The short-run *AS* curve is upward sloping in this section. As real output rises, the *AS* curve becomes steeper.

The Vertical Section Once the full-employment level of real output (i.e., potential real GDP) is reached, y_1, increasing output beyond that level is virtually impossible, *regardless of the increase in the price level.* Hence, the short-run *AS* curve becomes vertical. This vertical section of the short-run *AS* curve is called the **classical range**, because it relates to the unique situation with which so many classical economists were concerned. Recall that, in Chapter 4, you learned that classical economists believed that the economy would tend to operate at full employment. Thus, the classical range is the vertical section of the aggregate supply curve that represents output at its maximum; expansion in the short-run is virtually impossible because the economy is already operating at its full potential or capacity output level.

classical range the vertical section of the *AS* curve that represents output at its maximum

The horizontal (Keynesian) range and the vertical (classical) range are generally regarded as extreme cases, rather than as exact descriptions of economic reality with respect to the behaviour of output and prices. Nevertheless, there are times when the economy is operating well below its potential and it may then be possible to increase real GDP without exerting much upward pressure on prices. There are also times when the economy is operating at high levels of real output and employment. Of course, it will always be possible to squeeze a little more output out of existing resources by running the machines a little harder and by employing labour resources more intensively (for example, by offering overtime and paying lucrative "holiday" wages where possible). But in general, at such times further output expansion may be extremely difficult in the short run and will exert upward pressure on prices. The Keynesian and classical ranges of the short-run *AS* curve are intended as approximations of these situations.

Reading Comprehension

The answers to these questions can be found on MyEconLab at www.myeconlab.com. MyEconLab

1. What is another name for the horizontal section of the *AS* curve?
2. Discuss the level of real output consistent with the classical range of the *AS* curve.
3. Is expansion in the short run possible if the economy is operating in the vertical range of the *AS* curve?
4. Why are the horizontal and vertical sections of the *AS* curve described as "extreme cases"?

LO 7.6 Examine the factors that shift the *SRAS* curve

Shifting the Aggregate Supply Curve

What factors can cause the short-run *AS* curve to shift?

Recall that a change in the price of a particular good or service will not shift the supply curve of that good or service. Accordingly, a change in the price level will not shift the aggregate supply curve. The short-run *AS* curve is based on the behaviour of all the firms that produce the total output of goods and services in an economy. If the costs of production change, then at any given price level, the firms will produce a different volume of real output. A reduction in production costs will cause the short-run *AS* curve to shift to the right, as shown in Diagram A of Figure 7.4, whereas an increase in costs will cause

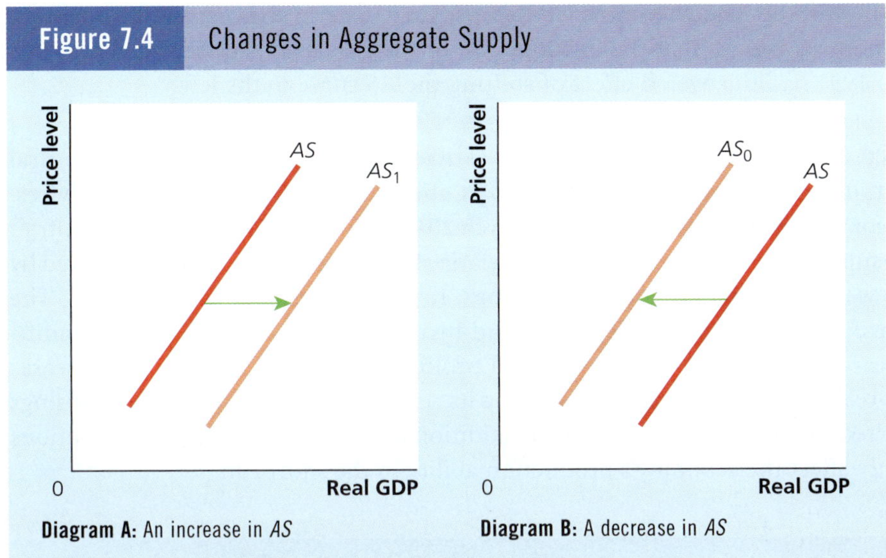

Diagram A: An increase in *AS*

Diagram B: A decrease in *AS*

it to shift upward to the left, as shown in Diagram B of Figure 7.4. A national disaster, such as an earthquake, can also cause the short-run *AS* curve to shift.

Can we analyze the factors that shift the short-run *AS* curve?

We can, and should, look closely at the determinants of aggregate supply. Each of these factors will affect the position of the short-run aggregate supply curve.

Analysis of *AS* Shifters The economy's total output of goods and services is produced by many firms operating under different conditions. Non-price-level factors that affect the firms' decisions will affect the short-run *AS* curve. These ***AS* shifters (supply-side shocks)**—factors that cause the aggregate supply curve to shift—include production costs, changes in resources, changes in technology, tax policies, and natural disasters.

***AS* shifters or supply-side shocks** factors that cause the aggregate supply curve to shift

Production Costs As noted earlier, changes in the costs of production will cause the short-run aggregate supply (*AS*) curve to shift. For example, if labour costs increase because of a shortage of labour, firms will experience a significant increase in their production costs. If the price of an important input, such as oil, increases, production costs will rise. Such increases in costs will shift the short-run *AS* curve to the left. Conversely, cost reductions will shift the *AS* curve to the right.

Changes in the Quantity or Quality of Resources If a country acquires more resources (land, labour, capital), then the short-run *AS* curve will be affected by a rightward shift. If, through training, the economy's labour force becomes more skilled and hence more productive, then its short-run *AS* curve will shift to the right. If resources are destroyed, perhaps because of fires or floods, then the short-run *AS* curve will shift to the left. If Canada adopts a more liberal immigration stance and allows more immigrants to take up residence in Canada, other things being equal, Canada's *AS* curve will shift to the right because of an increased supply of labour. Conversely, the destruction of fish stock through overfishing or pollution will shift the short-run *AS* curve to the left.

Changes in Technology Advances in technology enhance a country's ability to produce goods and services. If Canada develops technologies that allow firms to use their resources more productively, then the economy will be able to obtain a greater volume of real output from given resources, and the short-run *AS* curve will shift to the right.

Tax Policies Tax policies that are favourable to business will shift the short-run *AS* curve to the right as they lower a firm's costs, while unfavourable or hostile tax policies will shift the *AS* curve to the left because they increase the costs of the business. Some economists believe that the introduction of the goods and services tax (GST) in Canada in 1991 had the overall effect of shifting the *AS* curve to the left.

Natural and Other Disasters Earthquakes, tornadoes, hurricanes, and other natural disasters can seriously hamper the economy's ability to produce goods and services. Consider for a moment the effects of the March 2011 tsunami in Japan on that country's aggregate supply curve. That earthquake, the largest in the country's history, followed by a massive water assault, destroyed fields, crops, roads, bridges, and entire villages. The nuclear facilities of Japan were destroyed and further damage resulted, posing significant nuclear threats. Forest fires, severe and prolonged droughts, insects, and diseases can also wreak havoc on an economy, shifting its *AS* curve to the left. The civil uprisings that occurred in Egypt and Libya provide additional examples of disastrous situations that directly affect the economy's production ability in the short run.

BUSINESS SITUATION 7.3

The government has just announced an overall reduction in business taxes.

What changes should firms expect in the overall level of prices resulting from the proposed reduction in taxes?

The answer to this Business Situation can be found in Appendix A.

It would be convenient to have a summary of all of the *AD–AS* shifters.

A summary of all of the *AD–AS* shifters is presented in Table 7.1.

Table 7.1 Summary of Aggregate Demand and Aggregate Supply Shifters

AD Shifters	AS Shifters
1. Consumption	**1. Production Costs**
a. Consumer wealth	a. Labour costs
b. Taxes	b. Changes in other input prices
c. Expectations	**2. Changes in Quantity and/or Quality of Resources**
d. Interest rates	a. Land
2. Investment	b. Labour
a. Interest rates	c. Capital
b. Changes in income	d. Entrepreneurial ability
c. Perceived profitability of investment projects	**3. Changes in Technology**
d. Technological advance	**4. Tax Policies**
3. Government Spending	**5. Natural and Other Disasters**
4. Net Exports	
a. Increases in income abroad	
b. Changes in exchange rates]	

Reading Comprehension

The answers to these questions can be found on MyEconLab at www.myeconlab.com. MyEconLab

1. What are supply-side shocks?
2. What are the main factors that will cause the short-run *AS* curve to shift?
3. How will increases in production costs affect the short-run *AS* curve?

LO 7.7 Explain the determination of real output and the price level in a short-run equilibrium

Short-Run Equilibrium of Real Output and the Price Level

equilibrium price level the price at which quantity demanded equals quantity supplied

equilibrium level of real GDP the level of real GDP at which the *AD* and *AS* curves intersect

What do short-run aggregate demand and short-run aggregate supply have to do with short-run equilibrium level of real GDP and the price level?

We can bring short-run aggregate demand and short-run aggregate supply together to help determine short-run equilibrium level of real GDP and the equilibrium price level. Figure 7.5 will help with the analysis.

The analysis here parallels that presented in Chapter 3, where we discussed the equilibrium price and quantity in the market for a single product. Any price level above *P* (such as P_1) results in the production of an output level that exceeds the total amount that will be demanded at that price level. Consequently, the price level and real GDP will tend to fall. Any price level below *P* (such as P_0) will result in a lower level of production than customers are willing to purchase at that price level. Consequently, the price level and real GDP will tend to rise. Only at a price level of *P* will the total amount of all goods and services that are demanded exactly equal the total amount of all goods and services that are supplied. Hence, *P* is the **equilibrium price level** and *Y* is the **equilibrium level of real GDP**. Equilibrium price level is the price level at which quantity demanded equals quantity supplied; thus, there is no tendency for this price level to change. The equilibrium level of real GDP is the level of real GDP at which the *AD* and *AS* curves intersect.

Figure 7.5 Determination of Equilibrium Real GDP and the Price Level in the Short Run

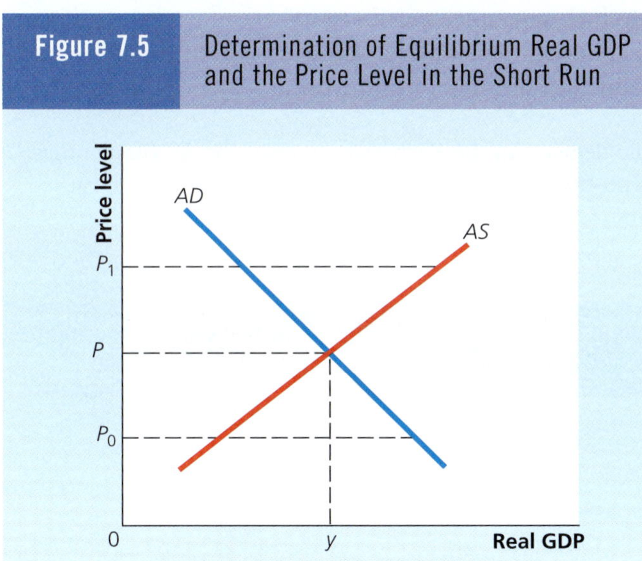

Reading Comprehension

The answers to these questions can be found on MyEconLab at www.myeconlab.com. MyEconLab

1. Explain the determination of the short-run equilibrium real GDP and the equilibrium price level.
2. How do we determine the equilibrium price level?

LO 7.8 Analyze the effects of changes in aggregate demand on equilibrium real GDP and price

Effects of Changes in Aggregate Demand

How do changes in aggregate demand affect real GDP and the price level?

The answer to this question depends upon at what point the *AD* curve intersects the *AS* curve. Depending on the section of the *AS* curve that is intersected (horizontal, intermediate, or vertical) the effect of a change in *AD* will be different. Let's examine this further. If the *AS* curve is upward sloping (i.e., in the intermediate range), as shown in Figure 7.6, then an increase in aggregate demand will cause the price level and real GDP to rise, other things being equal.

An increase in aggregate demand is shown by an upward (or rightward) shift of the *AD* curve from *AD* to AD_1. This results in an increase in the price level from *P* to P_1, and an increase in real GDP from *y* to y_1.

> An increase in aggregate demand in the intermediate range of the *AS* curve, other things being equal, results in an increase in the equilibrium price level and an increase in equilibrium real GDP.

What happens if the *AD* curve intersects the *AS* curve in the Keynesian (horizontal) range?

To answer this question, let's look at Figure 7.7, which shows *AD* and *AS* intersecting in the horizontal (Keynesian) range of the *AS* curve.

An increase in aggregate demand from *AD* to AD_1 results in an increase in real GDP from y_0 to y_1, while the price level remains unchanged at *P*. This is due to the existence of a considerable amount of idle human and capital resources, and likely high unemployment, which allows the production of more output without any increase in prices.

> An increase in aggregate demand in the Keynesian range of the AS curve, other things being equal, has no effect on the equilibrium price level; however, it causes an increase in equilibrium real GDP.

Figure 7.6 The Effect of an Increase in Aggregate Demand in the Intermediate Range

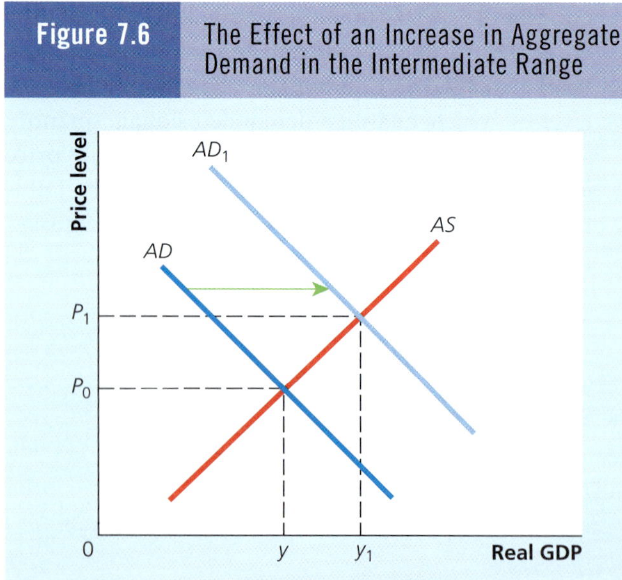

Figure 7.7 The Effect of an Increase in Aggregate Demand in the Keynesian Range

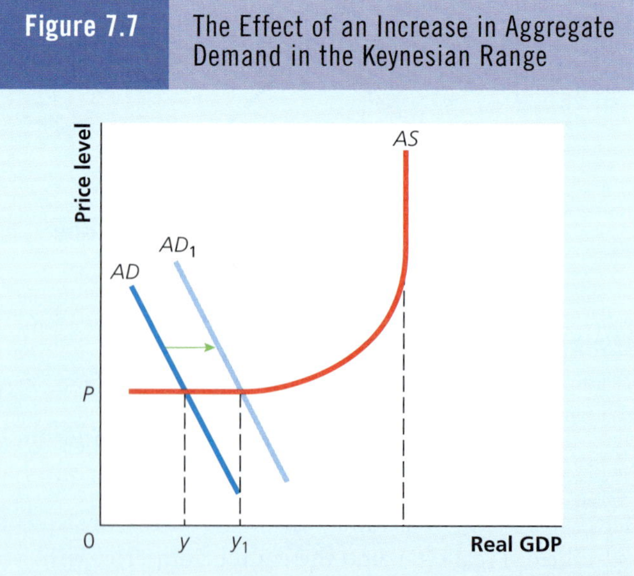

Figure 7.8 The Effects of an Increase in Aggregate Demands in the Classical Range

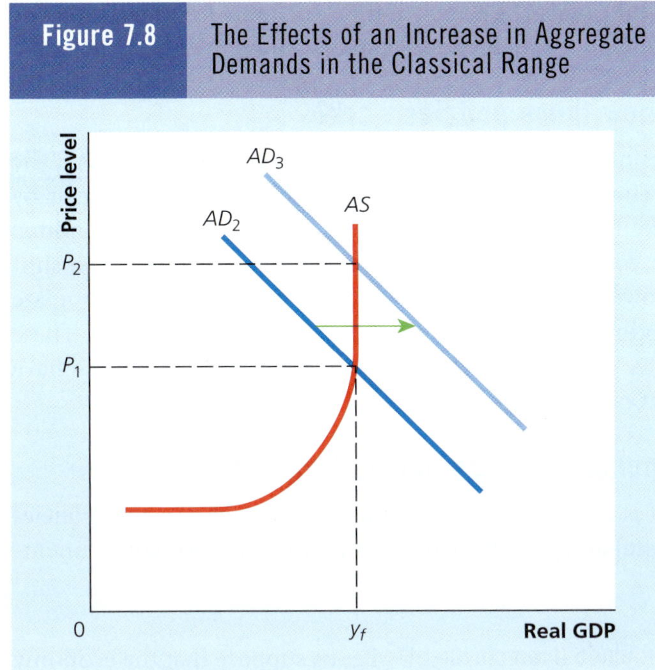

What happens if the *AD* curve intersects the *AS* curve in the classical (vertical) range?

Figure 7.8 illustrates the answer. If the short-run *AS* curve is vertical (that is, in the classical range), as shown in Figure 7.8, an increase in aggregate demand from AD_2 to AD_3 results in an increase in the price level from P_1 to P_2. You might have already noticed there is no increase in real output. This is because when the *AS* curve is vertical the economy is operating at the full-employment level of real GDP (recall that y_f represents full-employment or potential real GDP).

An increase in aggregate demand in the classical range of the *AS* curve, other things being equal, results in an increase in the equilibrium price level, but no change in equilibrium real GDP.

You can easily work out the effects of a decrease in aggregate demand in each of the three sections of the short-run *AS* curve.

Reading Comprehension

The answers to these questions can be found on MyEconLab at www.myeconlab.com. MyEconLab

1. Sketch the effects of an increase in *AD* if the intersection occurs in the Keynesian range of the *AS* curve.
2. In what range of the *AS* curve will a shift in *AD* have *no effect* on equilibrium price?
3. In what range of the *AS* curve will a shift in *AD* have *no effect* on equilibrium real GDP?
4. Repeat the analysis of a change in aggregate demand given above, this time illustrating a decrease in *AD* (a leftward shift) for all three ranges of the *AS* curve. Summarize the effects on equilibrium real GDP and the price level.

LO 7.9 Discuss the implications of the *AD–AS* model for demand-side policies

Demand-Side Policies

What are demand-side policies?

fiscal policy the deliberate use of government spending and taxation in order to influence aggregate demand

monetary policy involves the manipulation of the money supply and interest rates by the central bank to influence aggregate demand

Demand-side policies are actions aimed at shifting the aggregate demand curve. We have seen that changes in aggregate demand can affect real GDP and the price level, depending on the shape of the short-run *AS* curve. The government can affect aggregate expenditure (*AE*) and can therefore shift the *AD* curve to the right or to the left. The government and the monetary authorities who control the money supply have two main policies that they can use to affect the *AD* curve. The government can use **fiscal policy**, which is the deliberate use of government spending and taxation in order to influence aggregate demand, while the monetary authorities can use **monetary policy**, which involves the manipulation of the money supply and interest rates by the central bank to influence aggregate demand.

Because monetary and fiscal policies are such important tools for stabilizing the economy, we will spend a great deal of time in later chapters studying these policies.

Can we get some idea of how these policies work?

Because government purchases of goods and services (*G*) are a component of *AE*, the government can shift the *AD* curve to the right by increasing its own spending or by using its taxing powers to encourage consumers and firms to increase their spending. Also, the monetary authorities, mainly the central bank (the Bank of Canada) can shift the *AD* curve to the right by lowering interest rates. Lower interest rates will stimulate investment and consumer spending and thus increase *AE* and shift the *AD* curve. These policies work because the primary variables through which they are accomplished have a direct and appreciable impact on aggregate expenditure.

Can fiscal and monetary policies reduce unemployment?

A reduction in unemployment is one of the primary purposes for which these policies are designed. Let us see how fiscal and monetary policies may be used to reduce unemployment.

Fiscal and Monetary Policies to Reduce Unemployment Let us suppose that the economy is experiencing substantial unemployment (for example, 20%), similar to that experienced during the Great Depression. The economy would be operating at a level of real output that is well below its potential or full-employment output level. In other words, it is far away from the vertical position of the short-run aggregate supply curve. This situation is illustrated in Figure 7.9, where the economy is operating at a real GDP level of output, *y*, within the Keynesian (horizontal) section of the short-run *AS* curve.

The aggregate demand curve is AD_0. To move the economy out of the current recession and toward full employment, the government can shift the *AD* curve from AD_0 to AD_1 through the use of fiscal policy. (This will be discussed in more detail in Chapter 11.) The Bank of Canada can achieve the same effect by using monetary policy. Note that because the economy is operating substantially below capacity (recall that it is in the Keynesian or horizontal range), the rightward shift of the *AD* curve will not exert any significant upward pressure on the price level.

Figure 7.9 Fiscal and Monetary Policies to Reduce Unemployment

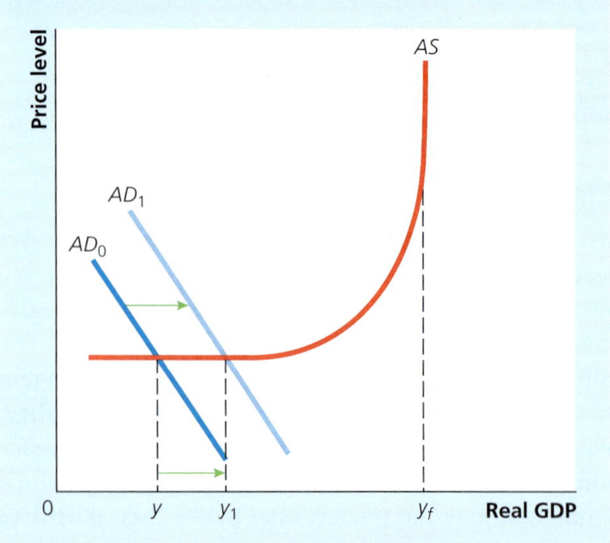

Can fiscal and monetary policies also work against inflation?

Fiscal and Monetary Policies to Reduce Inflation In the same way that monetary and fiscal policies can be used to shift the *AD* curve to the right, they can be used to shift the *AD* curve to the left. Suppose that the economy is experiencing severe inflation, such as that which occurred in Canada during the 1970s (in 1974, the rate of inflation as measured by the consumer price index was almost 11%). The situation can be illustrated by Figure 7.10, where the economy is operating in the vertical (classical) range of the *AS* curve.

Figure 7.10 Fiscal and Monetary Policies to Reduce Inflation

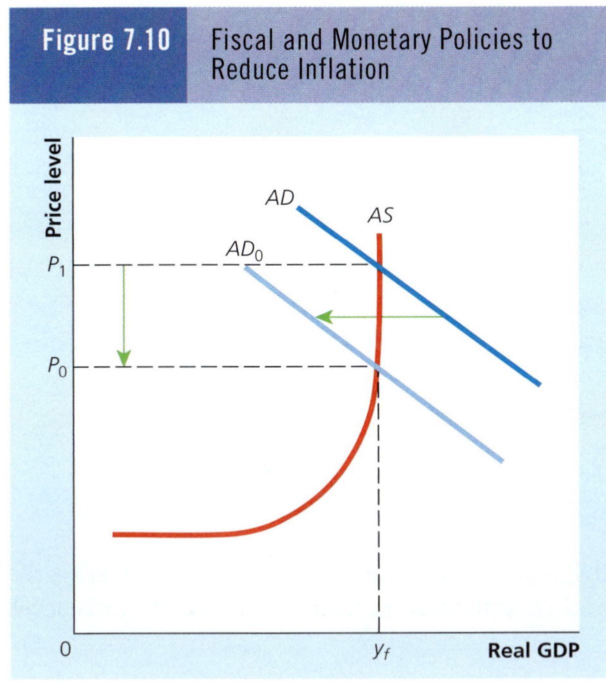

In this figure, the initial equilibrium occurs where *AD* intersects *AS*. The price level is P_1 and output is y_f. To lower the price level and relieve the inflationary pressure, the government can shift the *AD* curve from *AD* to AD_0 by using fiscal policy. Perhaps it cuts government spending, increases taxes, or does some combination of the two. The Bank of Canada can achieve the same effect by using monetary policy. Specifically, it can raise interest rates. Higher interest rates will tend to reduce the investment and consumption components of *AE*. Such policies will reduce *AE* and thus shift the aggregate demand curve to the left from *AD* to AD_0. The result is a fall in the price level from P_1 to P_0, while output remains the same at y_f.

Monetary and fiscal policies designed to combat unemployment and inflation are more complicated than presented here. Subsequent chapters will present more detailed accounts of monetary and fiscal policies and how they can be used to improve the performance of the economy.

Reading Comprehension

The answers to these questions can be found on MyEconLab at www.myeconlab.com. MyEconLab

1. What are demand-side policies?
2. Explain how the government and the Bank of Canada can use fiscal and monetary policies to combat (i) inflation and (ii) unemployment.

LO 7.10 Analyze the effects of changes in aggregate supply on equilibrium real GDP and price

Effects of Changes in Aggregate Supply

How do changes in aggregate supply affect real GDP and the price level?

The price of an individual good or service and the quantity demanded and supplied of that good or service can change if the supply curve for that good or service shifts. Similarly, the price level and real GDP will change if the *AS* curve shifts.

Let us examine the effects of changes in aggregate supply on real output (GDP) and the price level. Aggregate supply changes as a result of supply-side shocks. These may include things like crop failure, natural disaster, or changes in production costs. An increase in aggregate supply causes the *AS* curve to shift to the right, while a decrease in aggregate supply causes the *AS* curve to shift to the left. An improvement in technology or an increase in productivity, for example, will cause the aggregate supply curve to shift to the right, signifying that a greater quantity of real GDP than before will be supplied at each price level.

Let us assume that the economy is in equilibrium in the intermediate range, as shown in Figure 7.11.

Figure 7.11 The Effect of an Increase in Aggregate Supply

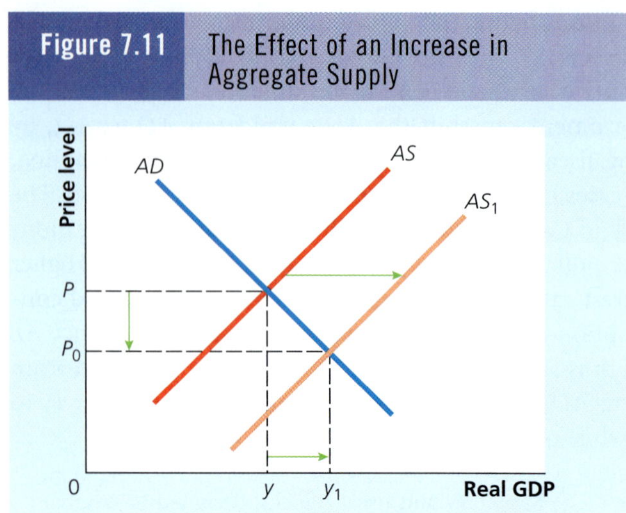

Figure 7.12 The Effect of a Decrease in Aggregate Supply

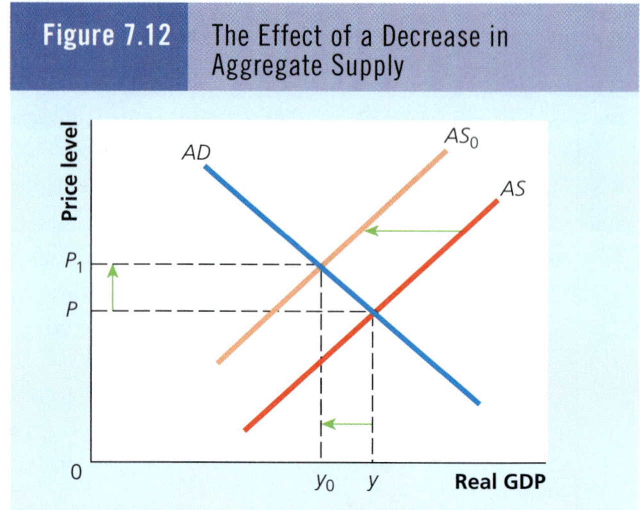

The equilibrium level of real GDP is *y* and the price level is *P*. An increase in aggregate supply from *AS* to AS_1 causes real GDP to increase from *y* to y_1 and the price level to fall from *P* to P_0.

An increase in aggregate supply results in an increase in real GDP and a fall in the price level.

Suppose that the aggregate supply curve shifts to the left because of a global shortage of an important resource, such as oil, which pushes production costs up. The effect of such a shift is illustrated in Figure 7.12.

The initial aggregate demand and aggregate supply curves are *AD* and *AS*, respectively. A decrease in aggregate supply shifts the curve from *AS* to AS_0; this results in an increase in the price level from *P* to P_1, and a fall in real GDP from *y* to y_0.

A decrease in aggregate supply results in a decrease in real GDP and an increase in the price level.

Reading Comprehension

The answers to these questions can be found on MyEconLab at www.myeconlab.com. MyEconLab

1. Discuss the effect of an increase in aggregate supply on real output (GDP) and the price level.
2. With the help of a graph, sketch the effects of a decrease in aggregate supply on real output (GDP) and the price level.

LO 7.11 Discuss the implications of the *AD–AS* model for supply-side policies

Supply-Side Policies

What are supply-side policies?

Supply-side policies are policies designed to influence real GDP and the price level by shifting the *AS* curve. Keynesian economics emphasizes the management of *aggregate*

supply-side policies policies designed to influence real GDP and the price level by shifting the *AS* curve

demand by controlling the components of aggregate expenditure. Supply-side economics, conversely, is concerned mainly with policies to influence the supply side, that is, the *AS* curve, by affecting incentives to work, save, and invest.

Our previous analysis of monetary and fiscal policy to combat inflation can illustrate the differences between demand-side and supply-side policies. In order to fight inflation, we saw that policies designed to reduce aggregate demand may result in a simultaneous increase in unemployment and reduction in real GDP. While these demand-side policies might be effective in fighting inflation, there is an obvious trade-off—to achieve lower prices, we must give up some employment and some output. So, instead of shifting aggregate demand to reduce prices, supply-side economists prefer to stimulate aggregate supply. The rationale is that unemployment and inflation can be solved by greater productivity and growth in real output.

The concept of the *marginal tax rate* (*MTR*) is important for an understanding of supply-side policies. The marginal tax rate is the change in tax receipts resulting from a change in income. That is,

$$MTR = \frac{\Delta T}{\Delta Y}$$

where T represents taxes and Y represents income.

The marginal tax rate is the ratio of the change in taxes to the change in income.

A marginal tax rate of 0.3 means that an increase in income of \$100 million will result in an increase in taxes of (\$100 × 0.3) = \$30 million.

How do supply-side policies shift the *AS* curve?

Laffer curve a curve showing the relationship between tax revenues and tax rates

Supporters of supply-side economics favour changing taxes, reducing government deficit spending (i.e., government spending in excess of taxes), and deregulating industries to stimulate the supply side of the economy. Tax cuts designed to encourage consumer saving provide funds for business investment. Lower marginal tax rates provide an incentive for workers to do extra work because the extra income earned is not as heavily taxed as before the tax cut. Greater investment tax credits and lower business taxes encourage capital investment. Relieving business enterprises of many of the burdens of government regulation and reducing the level of government deficit spending provide greater scope for business activity. According to supply-siders, all these measures increase productivity and therefore shift the *AS* curve to the right.

Figure 7.13 The Laffer Curve

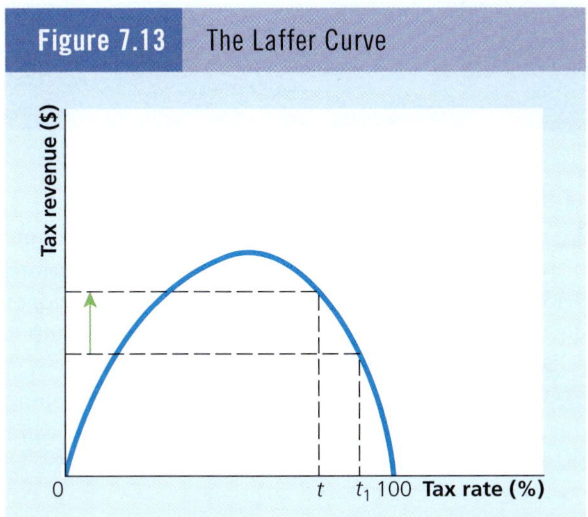

Can you explain how tax cuts work in supply-side policies?

The relationship between tax rates and tax revenues helps to explain the supply-side philosophy. We can plot this relationship on a **Laffer curve**, named after Arthur Laffer (1940–), who reportedly first drew the curve on a napkin in the Two Continents Restaurant in Washington, D.C. The Laffer curve is a curve showing the relationship between tax revenues and tax rates as illustrated in Figure 7.13. It shows that as tax rates increase, so do tax revenues—but only up to a point. Further tax rate increases cause tax revenues to fall.

In Figure 7.13, the tax rate of t_1 is so high that it discourages work effort. What is the point of working if almost all of the resulting income is taxed away? A reduction in the tax rate from t_1 to t will provide incentives for people to work harder and thereby increase total output. This increase in total output (income) will result in greater tax revenues. Many supply-siders would argue that today's combination of tax rate and tax revenues lies on the falling portion of the Laffer curve; that is, tax rates are so high that they discourage work.

How effective are supply-side policies?

That seems to depend on whether or not you are a supporter of supply-side economics. Supply-side economists contend that supply-side measures to increase work incentives have significant effects on growth and productivity. Critics of supply-side economics claim that the effects of supply-side policies on labour supply, saving, and investment are quite small but that the benefits for business owners are high. Nobel laureate (1970) Paul Samuelson (1915–), who has had a long association with the Massachusetts Institute of Technology (MIT), is particularly critical of supply-side economics. He claims that the 1982 recession in the United States was attributable to the failure of supply-side policies. The effectiveness of supply-side policies continues to be a controversial issue among economists of different persuasions.

Reading Comprehension

The answers to these questions can be found on MyEconLab at www.myeconlab.com. MyEconLab

1. Discuss the basic argument of supply-side economists.
2. How are supply-side policies fundamentally different than demand-side policies?
3. Explain the concept of the *marginal tax rate* (*MTR*).
4. What criticisms have been leveled against supply-side economics?

Review

1. Review the learning objectives listed at the beginning of the chapter.
2. Have you accomplished all the objectives? One way to determine this is to answer the Reading Comprehension questions at the end of each section. These will help you assess your understanding of the learning objectives.
3. If you have not accomplished an objective, review the relevant material before proceeding.

Key Points to Remember

1. **LO 7.1** Aggregate demand refers to the various amounts of real output (GDP) that will be demanded at various price levels. The aggregate demand (*AD*) curve slopes downward, indicating that a smaller quantity of output (GDP) will be demanded as the price level rises.
2. **LO 7.2** The shape of the *AD* curve is downward sloping due to the interest rate effect, the foreign trade effect, and the real wealth effect.

3. LO 7.3 The *AD* curve will *shift* if any component of aggregate expenditure changes. Price level changes will cause a movement *along* the *AD* curve. The four components of aggregate expenditure (*AE*) are consumption, investment, government spending, and net exports.
4. LO 7.4 Aggregate supply refers to the various quantities of real GDP that will be supplied at various price levels.
5. LO 7.5 The short-run aggregate supply (*AS*) curve can be defined in terms of three ranges: a horizontal (Keynesian) section, an upward sloping (intermediate section), and a vertical (classical) section.
6. LO 7.6 The short-run aggregate supply curve will shift in response to supply-side shocks, such as changes in production costs (factor prices), technology, and Mother Nature. The *AS* curve will not shift as a result of changes in the price level.
7. LO 7.7 The short-run equilibrium level of real GDP and the average level of prices are simultaneously determined by the intersection of the aggregate demand and aggregate supply curves.
8. LO 7.8 Governments and central banks can use fiscal and monetary policies to shift the *AD* curve in an attempt to reduce unemployment and inflation. The effects of a shift in *AD* will depend on what range of the *AS* curve it intersects.
9. LO 7.9 Demand-side policies are complex but they can be effective in combating inflation and unemployment.
10. LO 7.10 Aggregate supply shocks, such as a shortage of an important input, can cause the short-run aggregate supply curve to shift to the left. Improvements in production technology or improvements in productivity can cause the *AS* curve to shift to the right.
11. LO 7.11 An increase in short-run aggregate supply can reduce the equilibrium price level and increase equilibrium real GDP. A reduction in short-run aggregate supply can increase the equilibrium price level and reduce equilibrium real GDP. Supply-side economics emphasizes changes in supply as a means of solving inflation and unemployment problems. They encourage tax measures and other means of affecting incentives to work, save, and invest.

Economic Word Power

***AD* shifters or demand-side shocks** (p. 191)
Aggregate demand (p. 186)
Aggregate demand curve (p. 187)
Aggregate supply (p. 193)
***AS* shifters or supply-side shocks** (p. 197)
Classical range (p. 196)
Equilibrium level of real GDP (p. 199)
Equilibrium price level (p. 199)
Fallacy of composition (p. 188)
Fiscal policy (p. 201)
Foreign trade effect (p. 189)
Interest rate effect (p. 189)
Intermediate range (p. 195)
Keynesian range (p. 196)
Laffer curve (p. 205)
Monetary policy (p. 201)
Real wealth effect (p. 189)
Short run ((p. 104)
Short-run aggregate supply curve (p. 194)
Supply-side policies (p. 205)

Problems and Exercises

Basic

1. Table 7.2 contains data on the price level, aggregate quantity demanded, and aggregate quantity supplied for a hypothetical economy.
   a. LO 7.2, 7.7 With the price level on the vertical axis and real GDP on the horizontal axis, draw the aggregate demand (*AD*) and the aggregate supply (*AS*) curves.
   b. LO 7.7 Determine the equilibrium price level and the equilibrium real GDP.
   c. LO 7.7 At a price level of 85, what can be said about the quantity of real GDP demanded compared to the quantity of real GDP supplied? What effect will this have on the price level?

Table 7.2 Hypothetical Economy

Price Level	Quantity of Real GDP Demanded ($ mil)	Quantity of Real GDP Supplied ($ mil)
75	90	30
80	80	40
85	70	50
90	60	60
95	50	70
100	40	80
105	30	90
110	20	100

d. LO 7.7 At a price level of 105, what can be said about the quantity of real GDP demanded compared to the quantity of real GDP supplied? What effect will this have on the price level?

2. LO 7.8 Referring to the hypothetical economy presented in Question 1, suppose that the quantity of real GDP demanded increases by $20 million at each price level while the quantity of real GDP supplied remains unchanged.
   a. Determine the new equilibrium price level and the new equilibrium real GDP.
   b. Explain why the initial equilibrium price level is no longer the equilibrium price level.
3. LO 7.10 Referring again to the hypothetical economy presented in Question 1, suppose now that the quantity of real GDP supplied increases by $20 million while the quantity of real GDP demanded remains unchanged from the original table.
   a. Determine the new equilibrium price level and the new equilibrium real GDP.
   b. Explain why the initial price level is no longer the equilibrium price level.
4. Consider the data in Table 7.3 for an economy.

Table 7.3 Hypothetical Economy

Price Level	Aggregate Quantity Demanded ($ mil)	Aggregate Quantity Supplied ($ mil)
60	140	50
70	120	60
80	110	70
90	100	80
100	90	90
110	80	100
120	70	110

   a. LO 7.2, 7.5 On a diagram with the price level on the vertical axis and real GDP on the horizontal axis, graph the *AD* and *AS* curves.
   b. LO 7.7 Determine the equilibrium price level and the equilibrium real GDP.
   c. LO 7.10 If the quantity of real GDP supplied increases by $20 million at each price level, graph the new *AS* curve on your diagram and determine the new equilibrium price level and the new equilibrium real GDP.

Questions in the Intermediate and Challenging Sections cover several different concepts, and have not been organized by learning objectives.

Intermediate

1. Use *AD–AS* diagrams to show the effect of each of the following on the equilibrium price level and the equilibrium real GDP. Assume that the economy is operating in the intermediate section of the *AS* curve and that other things are equal (ceteris paribus):
   a. An increase in income that results in an increase in imports
   b. A significant increase in the price of oil
   c. Workers are trained and thus become more productive
   d. Economic optimism that results in an increase in consumption
   e. Developers build several new houses
2. Use the *AD–AS* model to show the effects of each of the following events on the equilibrium price level and the equilibrium real GDP, other things being equal:
   a. The economy is operating in the intermediate range, and there is an increase in exports.
   b. The short-run *AS* curve is vertical when it intersects the *AD* curve, and a wave of new technology increases overall productivity.
   c. The short-run *AS* and *AD* curves intersect when the *AS* curve is horizontal and there is a reduction in government purchases.
   d. *AD* and *AS* are intersecting in the intermediate range of the *AS* curve, and government purchases are increasing, when a national catastrophe suddenly and adversely affects the country's productivity.
3. A personal income tax cut can affect either the demand side or the supply side of the economy. Carefully explain how this is possible.

Challenging

1. Assume that the economy is in short-run equilibrium with significant unemployment. The policymakers do not want interest rates to fall, and there is no current threat of inflation. What course of action can policymakers follow to move the economy toward full employment? (Should they use fiscal policy or monetary policy?)
2. Use the concept of the Laffer curve to demonstrate that a personal tax cut might actually increase government revenue.

MyEconLab Visit the MyEconLab website at **www.myeconlab.com**. This online homework and tutorial system puts you in control of your own learning with study and practice tools directly correlated to this chapter's content.

Study Guide

Self-Assessment

What's your score?

Circle the letter that corresponds with the correct answer.

1. Aggregate demand is
   a. Total consumer purchases at a constant price level
   b. The sum of consumption and investment
   c. The total output bought by domestic and foreign consumers
   d. The various amounts of real GDP that will be purchased at various price levels

2. Aggregate demand is a relation between
   a. Income and real output
   b. Real GDP and the rate of interest
   c. The price level and net exports
   d. None of the above

3. The mistaken view that what is true of the parts is always true of the whole is called
   a. The fallacy of composition
   b. The invalid hypothesis
   c. The parts-and-whole mistaken assumption
   d. None of the above

4. Which of the following is a reason for the shape of the *AD* curve?
   a. The interest rate effect
   b. The foreign trade effect
   c. The real wealth effect
   d. All of the above

5. An increase in the price level causes
   a. Consumption to rise and investment to fall
   b. Both consumption and investment to rise
   c. Both consumption and investment to fall
   d. Consumption to fall and investment to rise

6. As the price level falls, other things being equal,
   a. Holders of financial assets lose purchasing power
   b. Holders of financial assets may increase their purchases of consumer goods because of the increase in wealth
   c. The aggregate demand curve shifts to the left
   d. None of the above

7. Other things being equal, the *AD* curve will shift to the right if
   a. Government spending increases
   b. Investment increases
   c. Imports fall
   d. All of the above

8. Which of the following will not cause the *AD* curve to shift?
   a. A change in consumption
   b. A change in the price level
   c. A change in government spending
   d. A change in exports

9. The short-run aggregate supply curve assumes that
   a. The price level varies
   b. At low levels of real output, it is relatively difficult to increase real output
   c. An inverse relationship exists between the price level and real GDP
   d. As real output rises, it becomes relatively easy to increase real output even further

10. The short-run *AS* curve shows a relation between
   a. Real GDP and the price level
   b. Real GDP and income levels
   c. Total production and unemployment
   d. None of the above

11. A fall in the average level of prices will
   a. Shift the short-run *AS* curve to the right
   b. Shift the short-run *AS* curve to the left
   c. Have no effect on the short-run *AS* curve
   d. Cause the *AD* and *AS* curves to intersect

12. The vertical section of the short-run aggregate supply curve is called
   a. The Keynesian range
   b. The classical range
   c. The intermediate range
   d. None of the above

13. The Keynesian range of the short-run *AS* curve is
    a. Upward sloping
    b. Vertical
    c. Horizontal
    d. Downward sloping
14. If an increase in *AD* occurs when the *AD* curve is cutting the short-run *AS* curve on the vertical section, then
    a. Real output and the price level will both increase
    b. Real output and the price level will both decrease
    c. Real output will increase, but the price level will fall
    d. Real output will not change, but the price level will rise
15. If the short-run *AS* curve is upward sloping, then, other things being equal, an increase in *AD* will
    a. Increase real GDP and the price level
    b. Decrease real GDP and the price level
    c. Increase real GDP and reduce the price level
    d. Reduce real GDP and increase the price level
16. Which of the following will cause aggregate supply to decrease?
    a. An increase in the price level
    b. A fall in the price level
    c. A widespread disaster that disrupts production
    d. A reduction in production costs
17. A fall in aggregate supply, other things being equal, will result in
    a. A fall in real GDP and an increase in the price level
    b. A fall in real GDP and a decrease in the price level
    c. An increase in real GDP and a fall in the price level
    d. An increase in real GDP and a rise in the price level
18. An increase in government spending and a lowering of taxes to control economic activity constitute
    a. Monetary policy
    b. Fiscal policy
    c. Dictatorial policy
    d. None of the above
19. According to supply-side economists
    a. An increase in the marginal tax rate will stimulate economic activity
    b. Tax cuts will encourage saving and free up funds for investment
    c. Deregulation of industries will simply slow down the pace of economic activity
    d. Supply-side policies should be used only after demand-side policies have failed
20. If the economy is operating on the downward-sloping section of the Laffer curve, then
    a. Tax cuts will increase work incentive
    b. Tax increases will cause people to work harder
    c. Deregulation of industries is the only means of stimulating economic activity
    d. None of the above

Problems and Exercises (Use Quad Paper for Graphs)

Answers to these questions can be found on MyEconLab at www.myeconlab.com. MyEconLab

1. Table 7.4 contains data for a hypothetical economy.

Table 7.4 Hypothetical Economy

Price Level (index)	Quantity of Real GDP Demanded ($ mil)	Quantity of Real GDP Supplied ($ mil)
92	80	20
96	70	30
100	60	40
104	50	50
108	40	60
112	30	70
116	20	80
120	10	90

   a. Plot and graph the aggregate demand curve.
   b. On the same graph, plot and draw the aggregate supply curve.
   c. Use your graph to determine the equilibrium price level and the equilibrium real GDP.
2. Referring to the data in Table 7.4, suppose the quantity of real GDP demanded increases by $20 million at each price level while the aggregate supply remains unchanged.
   a. Graph the original and the new aggregate demand curves.
   b. On the same diagram, graph the original aggregate supply curve.
   c. From your diagram, determine the new equilibrium level of real GDP and the corresponding price level after the increase in aggregate demand.
3. Table 7.5 contains data on aggregate demand and aggregate supply for a hypothetical economy.

Table 7.5 Aggregate Demand and Aggregate Supply Data for a Hypothetical Economy

Price Level ($ mil)	Real GDP Demanded ($ mil)	Real GDP Supplied ($ mil)
140	40	220
130	80	200
120	120	180
110	160	160
100	200	140
90	240	120
80	280	100

a. On graph paper, draw the *AD* curve.
b. On the same graph, draw the *AS* curve.
c. What is the equilibrium price level?
d. What is the equilibrium real output?

4. Referring to the data in Table 7.5, suppose aggregate supply increases by $60 million at each price level.
a. Complete the new *AS* schedule below, in Table 7.6.
b. Draw the new *AS* curve on your graph and label it AS_1.
c. Assuming no change in aggregate demand, what is the new price level?
d. What is the value of real GDP?

Table 7.6 Price Level and Real GDP

Price Level	Real Output ($ mil)
140	
130	
20	
110	
100	
90	
80	

5. Assume that an economy is operating in the intermediate range of the short-run aggregate supply curve. Use diagrams to show the effect of each of the following on the economy's equilibrium real GDP and the price level.
a. Firms become optimistic and increase their investment spending.
b. A tax cut increases disposable income.
c. The discovery of an important productive input reduces production costs.
d. Active research results in an overall improvement in technology.
e. Labour becomes more productive, and workers are successfully induced to work harder.

6. Use the *AD–AS* model to show the effects of each of the following events on the price level and real GDP. (Assume that other things are equal.)
a. The short-run aggregate supply curve (*AS*) is upward sloping and there is an increase in consumption and investment.
b. The short-run *AS* curve is horizontal, and there is an increase in government purchases.
c. The aggregate supply curve is vertical, and net exports fall.
d. The short-run *AS* curve is upward sloping, and a national catastrophe reduces the economy's productive capacity.

7. Assume that an economy is operating in the intermediate range of the short-run *AS* curve. Use diagrams to show the effect of each of the following on the economy's equilibrium real GDP and price level:
a. Government increases its purchases of goods and services.
b. Firms increase their investment spending because of the prospects of greater profits.
c. A new technology increases labour productivity.
d. Americans increase their purchases of Canadian goods.

8. Use the *AD–AS* model to show that fiscal and monetary policies designed to increase real output and employment need not be inflationary. Under what circumstances will such demand-side policies most likely be inflationary?

9. Supply-side economists support tax cuts as a means of providing incentive to work. Draw a Laffer curve and indicate on the curve the situation assumed by supply-side economists.

Chapter 8

The Aggregate Demand (*AD*)–Aggregate Supply (*AS*) Model: Long-Run Analysis and Economic Growth

Learning Objectives

After studying this chapter, you should be able to

- **8.1** Derive the long-run aggregate supply curve and provide a rationale for its vertical shape
- **8.2** Identify the factors that shift the long-run aggregate supply curve
- **8.3** Determine a position of long-run macroeconomic equilibrium
- **8.4** Analyze the effects that a shift of the *LRAS* curve has on equilibrium real GDP and the price level

8.5 Analyze the effects of a change in aggregate demand under conditions of long-run equilibrium

8.6 Discuss the possibility of equilibrium at, above, or below the full-employment level of real GDP

8.7 Understand the meaning of economic growth and how to calculate it

8.8 Discuss the desirability of economic growth and the issue of sustainability

8.9 Identify the determinants of economic growth and the measures to promote it

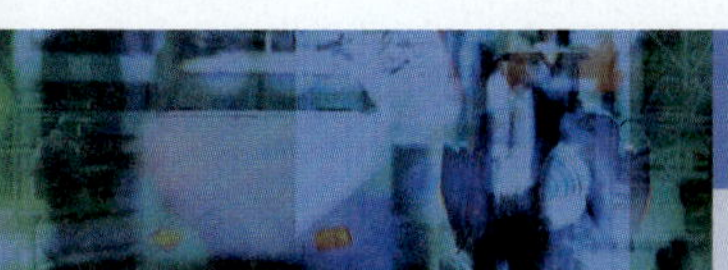

Assess Your Knowledge

MyEconLab

Answers to these questions can be found on MyEconLab at **www.myeconlab.com.**

1. What are the factors that determine an economy's productive capacity?
2. What does *labour productivity* mean?
3. What effect will a long-term, consistent improvement in labour productivity have on the average level of prices?

LO 8.1 Derive the long-run aggregate supply curve and provide a rationale for its vertical shape

Long-Run Aggregate Supply

What is the meaning of the long run in the context of aggregate supply?

long run a situation in which firms are unconstrained by fixed factors and therefore can vary all their inputs and adjust fully to market conditions

The **long run** is a situation in which firms are unconstrained by fixed factors, have the ability to vary all their inputs, and adjust fully to market conditions. Also, in the long run, firms and resource owners have adequate information on which to base their decisions. In the long run, aggregate supply will be an amount of real GDP that the economy can produce under conditions of full employment.

What is the long-run aggregate supply curve?

long-run aggregate supply (*LRAS*) curve a vertical line representing the economy's potential real GDP in the long run at full employment

The **long-run aggregate supply** (*LRAS*) **curve** is a graph that shows the amount of real GDP that will be supplied after the economy has adjusted fully; it is a vertical line representing the economy's capacity real GDP in the long run at full employment. Finance Canada, the OECD, and other organizations estimate Canada's potential real GDP. The Parliamentary Budget Office (PBO) estimated that potential real GDP for Canada in 2011 was $1420 billion. PBO's estimates also indicate that growth in potential real GDP will average 1.9% over the 2009–2014 period. Given these estimates, it is likely that the full-employment level of real output in Canada will reach $1496 billion in 2014.

What is the shape of the long-run aggregate supply curve?

Recall the production possibilities curve from Chapter 2 to assist in the discussion of the shape of the long-run aggregate supply curve (*LRAS*). A production possibility curve (p-p curve) is illustrated in Figure 8.1.

Along the horizontal axis are capital goods; all other goods are measured along the vertical axis. At any point *inside* the p-p curve (such as point *A* in Figure 8.1), the economy is operating below full employment and there exist unemployed resources (unemployment). At any point *on* the curve (such as point *B* or *C*), the economy is operating at full employment. Production on the curve represents potential real output. Now we will translate this analysis to the long-run aggregate supply curve.

We stated earlier that the long-run aggregate supply curve represents the economy's real output at full employment. Therefore, the long-run aggregate supply will be the economy's output at *B* or *C*, or any other point along the curve in Figure 8.1. This amount is the maximum output possible, given the economy's resources and its technology. Figure 8.2 represents such a full-employment real output.

> The long-run aggregate supply curve is a vertical line demonstrating the economy's potential real output of goods and services.

Figure 8.1 Production Possibility Curve

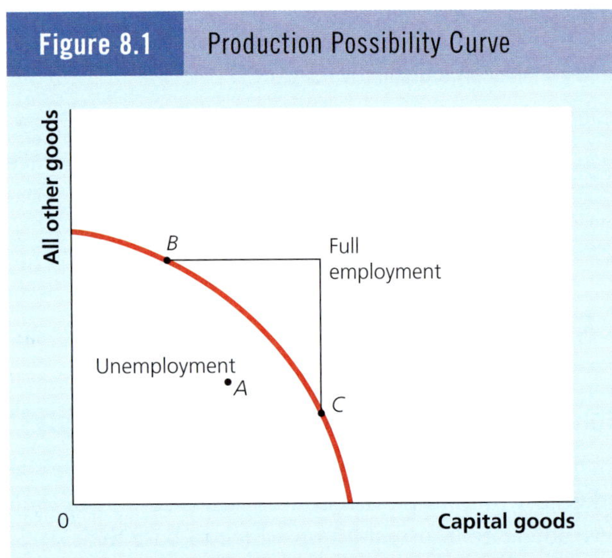

Figure 8.2 Long-Run Aggregate Supply Curve

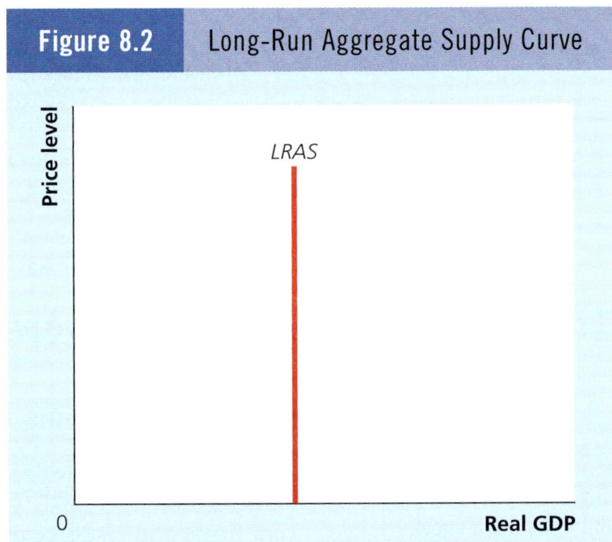

Reading Comprehension

The answers to these questions can be found on MyEconLab at www.myeconlab.com. MyEconLab

1. What do economists mean by the long run?
2. What is the long-run aggregate supply (*LRAS*) curve? What is its shape?
3. Is there any relation between an economy's production-possibility (p-p) curve and its long-run aggregate supply curve? Explain.

LO 8.2 Identify the factors that shift the long-run aggregate supply curve

LRAS Shifters: Factors Affecting the Long-Run Aggregate Supply Curve

What factors can cause the *LRAS* curve to shift?

Again, we can rely on the production possibilities model to help us answer this question. You may recall the factors that can cause the p-p curve to shift: the quantity or quality of the country's economic resources or changes in technology. Each of these factors will affect the economy's productive capacity or potential and, therefore, the position of the p-p curve. These same factors will cause the *LRAS* curve to shift. Specifically, changes in labour productivity, natural or human resource endowment, capital stock, and technology will affect the position of the *LRAS* curve. In Figure 8.3, Diagram A shows the initial p-p curve as *PPC*, and Diagram B shows the initial long-run aggregate supply curve as *LRAS*.

Let's assume that the economy acquires more resources in the form of labour or capital. This acquisition will shift the economy's p-p curve to the right from *PPC* to PPC_1, as shown in Diagram A of Figure 8.3. The long-run aggregate supply curve will shift from *LRAS* to $LRAS_1$, as shown in Diagram B of Figure 8.3.

What happens to the position of the *LRAS* curve in the event that a catastrophe or natural disaster cripples the economy by destroying many of its resources?

Mother Nature can be a powerful force. Hurricanes, tornados, or other natural disasters can wreak havoc on a country's economic resources. Take, for instance, the earthquake that destroyed much of Haiti in January, 2010. The labour force, natural resources, and infrastructure of that country all suffered a monumental setback as a direct result of Mother Nature. The situation in Haiti is a real-life example of how the *LRAS* curve of a country can shift to the left. As another example, consider the country of China. Natural disasters occur frequently in China, affecting more than 200 million people every year.

Figure 8.3 An Increase in Long-Run Aggregate Supply

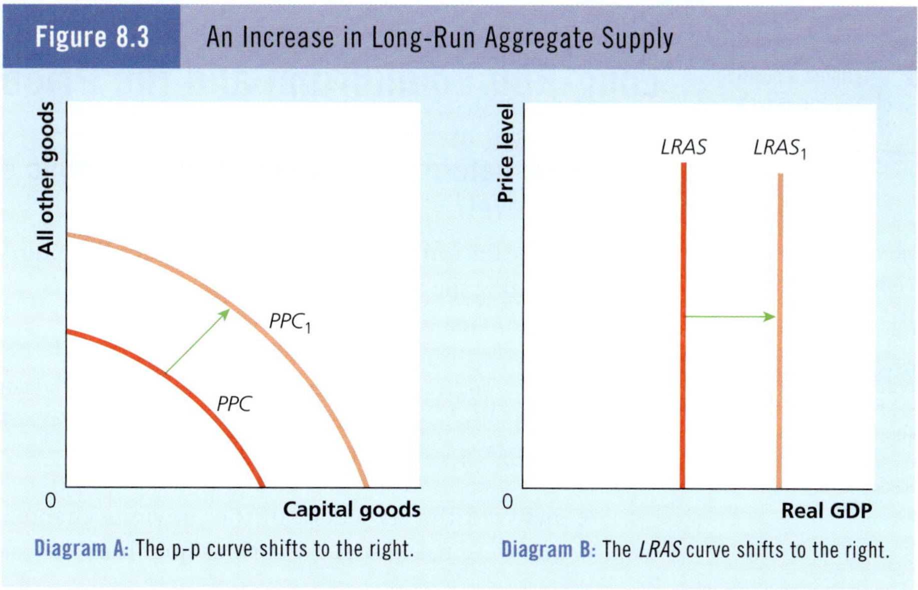

Diagram A: The p-p curve shifts to the right.

Diagram B: The *LRAS* curve shifts to the right.

They are definitively a restricting factor for economic and social progress. The Great Chinese Famine which occurred between 1958 and 1961 is said to be responsible for taking the lives of over 30 million people (close to the entire population of Canada). Mother Nature is not alone as a determinant of a decline in a country's productive capacity. Plague, famine, war, and insurrection can also create a situation where a country's productive capacity is seriously compromised.

BUSINESS SITUATION 8.1

The uprising and political unrest that occurred in Egypt in early 2011 crippled the economy and had ripple effects around the world. In particular, many worried that the supply of oil was threatened as the Suez canal is a critical mode of oil transportation.

Would a small business owner in Calgary, Alberta, be affected in any way by this crisis? Discuss.

The answer to this Business Situation can be found in Appendix A.

Reading Comprehension

The answers to these questions can be found on MyEconLab at www.myeconlab.com. MyEconLab

1. What are the main factors that can cause the economy's p-p curve to shift? Do these same factors cause the *LRAS* curve to shift?
2. What effect (if any) will a sustained increase in the number of immigrants to Canada have on Canada's *LRAS* curve?
3. What effect, if any, will the development of new productive technology have on the p-p curve? Will this affect the position of the *LRAS* curve?
4. Can you imagine the effect on the *LRAS* curve of the 2011 tsunami in Japan? What about the 2008 Sichuan earthquake? Sketch the effects of these natural disasters on the *LRAS* curve for these economies.

LO 8.3 Determine a position of long-run macroeconomic equilibrium

Long-Run Equilibrium and the Price Level

How do we determine long-run macroeconomic equilibrium and the price level?

long-run macroeconomic equilibrium the condition that exists when the economy's *AD* curve and its *LRAS* curve intersect, which occurs at the full-employment level of real GDP

We determine the **long-run macroeconomic equilibrium** and the price level simultaneously by locating the intersection of the aggregate demand (*AD*) and long-run aggregate supply (*LRAS*) curves.

> The long-run macroeconomic equilibrium is the condition that exists when the economy's *AD* curve and its *LRAS* curve intersect, which occurs at the full-employment level of real GDP.

We analyzed the *AD* curve in the previous chapter, but a quick review will be helpful. The *AD* curve shows the various quantities of real GDP that will be demanded

Figure 8.4 Long-Run Macroeconomic Equilibrium

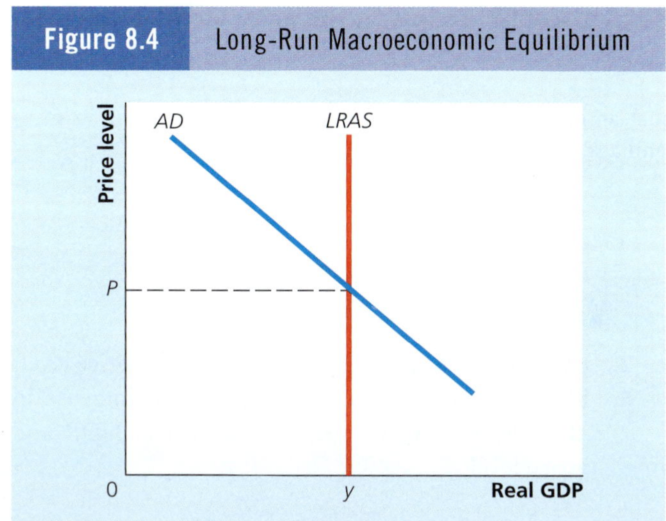

at various price levels. It is downward sloping, indicating that smaller quantities of real GDP will be demanded at higher price levels, other things being equal. Figure 8.4 shows the aggregate demand curve as *AD*.

The long-run aggregate supply curve is also shown in Figure 8.4 as the vertical line labeled *LRAS*. The intersection of the aggregate demand curve (*AD*) with the long-run aggregate supply curve (*LRAS*) determines the long-run equilibrium level of real GDP of *y* and the equilibrium price level of *P*.

Reading Comprehension

The answers to these questions can be found on MyEconLab at www.myeconlab.com. MyEconLab

1. Carefully explain how an economy's long-run equilibrium real output and price level are determined.

2. What is another name for the level of real output under conditions of long-run macroeconomic equilibrium?

LO 8.4 Analyze the effects that a shift of the *LRAS* curve has on equilibrium real GDP and the price level

Effects of a Shift in *LRAS* on Equilibrium Real GDP and the Price Level

What will happen to long-run macroeconomic equilibrium if the long-run aggregate supply curve shifts to the right?

The model of long-run macroeconomic equilibrium that we have just presented can help answer that question.

In Figure 8.5, the initial long-run equilibrium condition occurs where *AD* and *LRAS* intersect, giving the economy-wide equilibrium real output of *y* and a price level of *P*. Now suppose that the long-run aggregate supply curve shifts to the right, perhaps because of a steady improvement in labour productivity over the years or an improvement in technology. The long-run aggregate supply curve shifts from *LRAS* to $LRAS_1$. Assuming other things are equal (the *AD* curve does not shift), real GDP increases from y to y_1, and the price level falls from P to P_0. This sustained decline in the price level resulting from an increase in long-run

Figure 8.5 The Effect of an Increase in the Long-Run Aggregate Supply

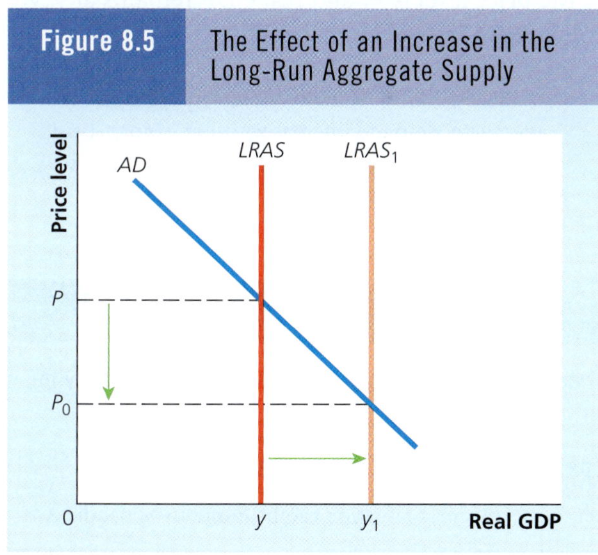

secular decline in the price level a persistent decline in the average level of prices over time

aggregate supply is referred to as a **secular decline in the price level**—a persistent decline in the average level of prices over time.

Other things being equal, an increase in long-run aggregate supply will result in an increase in real GDP and a secular decline in the price level.

Reading Comprehension

The answers to these questions can be found on MyEconLab at www.myeconlab.com. MyEconLab

1. Explain the effect, if any, of a decrease in *LRAS* on an economy's real GDP and price level.
2. What is meant by a secular decline in the price level?
3. Illustrate graphically the effects of an increase in the *LRAS* curve on an economy's real GDP and price level.

LO 8.5 Analyze the effects of a change in aggregate demand under conditions of long-run equilibrium

Effects of a Change in Aggregate Demand on Equilibrium Real GDP and the Price Level

Figure 8.6 Effect of an Increase in Aggregate Demand When the Economy is in Long-Run Equilibrium

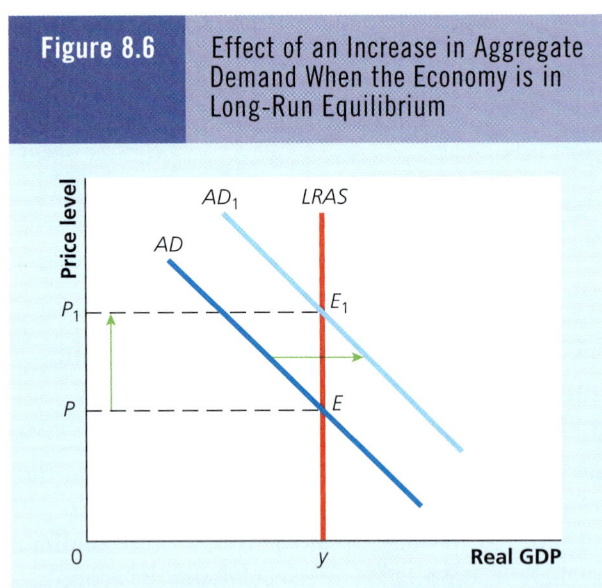

What happens to equilibrium real output and the price level if aggregate demand increases when the economy is in long-run equilibrium?

Let's assume that the initial long-run equilibrium condition of the economy is as shown in Figure 8.6. The *AD* and *LRAS* curves intersect at *E*, where the level of real output is *y* and the price level is *P*.

An increase in aggregate demand shifts the *AD* curve from *AD* to AD_1. The economy moves up the *LRAS* curve to E_1 and settles at a new equilibrium position, where the price level is P_1 and real GDP remains at *y*. We can conclude the following:

If the economy is in long-run equilibrium and aggregate demand increases, other things being equal, the price level will rise, but real GDP will remain unchanged.

BUSINESS SITUATION 8.2

Assume that the economy is in long-run equilibrium. The government surprisingly announces that it will use fiscal policy to force an increase in real GDP.

As a business manager, what action would you take in anticipation of the effect of such a policy?

The answer to this Business Situation can be found in Appendix A.

Reading Comprehension

The answers to these questions can be found on MyEconLab at www.myeconlab.com. MyEconLab

1. Assume that the economy is in long-run equilibrium. What effect will a fall in aggregate demand (*AD*) have on the price level?
2. Sketch the effect of an increase in *AD* on the equilibrium level of real output.

LO 8.6 Discuss the possibility of equilibrium at, above, or below the full-employment level of real GDP

Equilibrium at, above, or below the Full-Employment Level of Real GDP

Will equilibrium always occur at full-employment real GDP?

Figure 8.7 shows an economy initially in long-run and short-run equilibrium with the price level at *P* and real GDP at *y*. Short-run equilibrium prevails at *E*, because the aggregate demand (*AD*) and short-run aggregate supply (*SRAS*) curves intersect at *E*. Long-run equilibrium also prevails because the aggregate demand (*AD*) and long-run aggregate supply (*LRAS*) curves intersect at *E*. In this situation, equilibrium occurs at the full-employment level of real GDP.

Now that we have established what the long-run equilibrium position looks like (Figure 8.7), let's use Figure 8.8 to analyze some changes. Suppose aggregate demand increases from *AD* to AD_1, other things being equal. In response, the economy's production levels can be represented graphically by a movement upwards and along its short-run aggregate supply (*SRAS*) curve from point *E* to point E_1, where the economy will be in short-run equilibrium with a price level of P_1 and a real GDP level of y_1. However, at E_1 the economy is also in long-run disequilibrium. While the *AD* curve does intersect the *SRAS* curve at E_1 it does not intersect the *LRAS* curve at all at a price of P_1. The economy is in short-run equilibrium but it is also *above* the full-employment level of real GDP. (Check Figure 8.8 to satisfy yourself that $y_1 > y$.)

Figure 8.7 The *SRAS*, *AD*, and *LRAS* Curves Intersect at a Common Point *E*

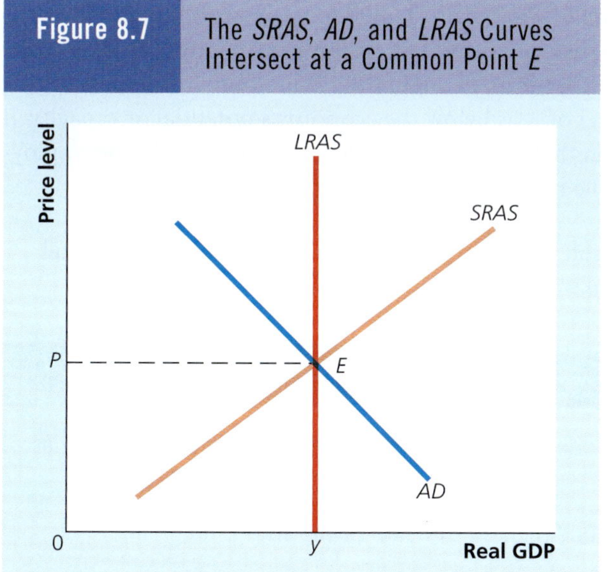

Let us return to the initial *AD* curve in Figure 8.8. Suppose aggregate demand falls from *AD* to AD_0. The economy's production responds with a movement down its short-run aggregate supply (*SRAS*) curve from point *E* to point E_0, where the economy will be in short-run equilibrium. As you might have already guessed, the economy will be in long-run disequilibrium at E_0. Again, it is off the *LRAS* curve (check Figure 8.8 to satisfy yourself that $y_0 < y$). From this analysis, we can conclude that the economy will not always achieve equilibrium at full employment. Long-run equilibrium, however, will always be at the full-employment level of real GDP.

Figure 8.8 Changes in Aggregate Demand and Equilibrium at Different Levels of Real GDP

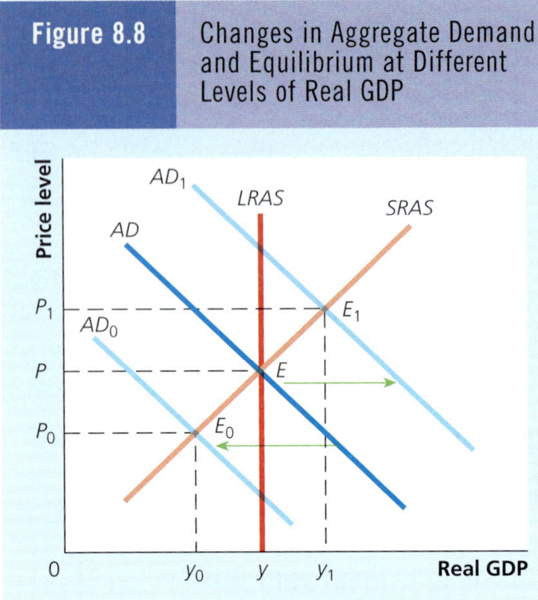

Figure 8.9 Changes in Aggregate Supply and Equilibrium at Different Levels of Real GDP

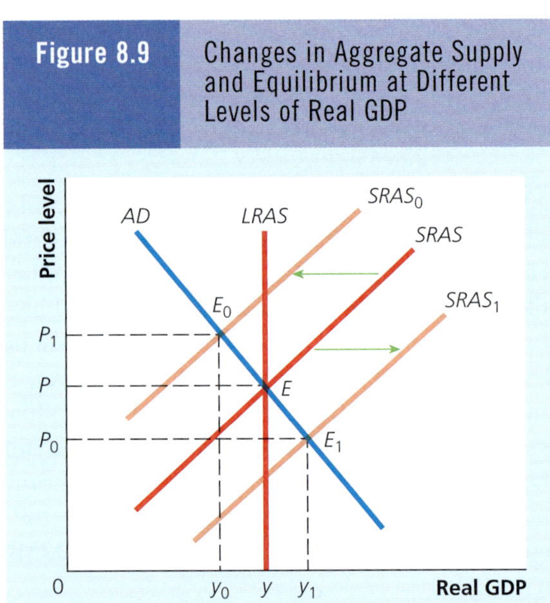

The economy can be in short-run equilibrium at, above, or below the full-employment level of real GDP. But long-run equilibrium can only occur at the full-employment level of real output.

Can shifts in the short-run aggregate supply curve also result in equilibrium above or below the potential or full-employment level of GDP?

This is correct; however, let's do the analysis with the help of the *AD-AS* model. Figure 8.9 shows an economy initially in short-run equilibrium at a price level of *P* and a real GDP of *y*, where *AD* and *SRAS* intersect at *E*. The economy is also in long-run equilibrium at a price level of *P* and a real GDP of *y*, where *AD* and *LRAS* intersect at *E*.

Let us begin by assuming that the short-run aggregate supply curve shifts to the right, perhaps because of changes in government tax policies favouring producers. The short-run aggregate supply curve will shift from *SRAS* to $SRAS_1$. Other things being equal, the economy moves down along its *AD* curve from *E* to E_1. The price level falls from *P* to P_0,and real GDP increases from *y* to y_1. Here, the economy is in short-run equilibrium but in long-run disequilibrium. You can easily see that the output level y_1 associated with E_1 is in excess of the full employment output level. This economy is actually over-producing.

Let us return to the initial equilibrium condition in Figure 8.9, with the equilibrium price and quantity at *P* and *y*, respectively. Now, suppose the price of an important input increases. This will cause the aggregate supply curve to shift upward (or leftward) from *SRAS* to $SRAS_0$. The economy moves up along its *AD* curve from *E* to E_0. At E_0, the economy is in short-run equilibrium with a price level of P_1 and a real GDP of y_0. However, long-run equilibrium is disturbed, and the economy is in long-run disequilibrium. Another look at Figure 8.9 will confirm that, at E_0, the output level of y_0 is below the economy's potential or capacity. It can be seen that y_0 is an output level consistent with unemployment or idle resources. We can conclude the following:

Supply-side shocks can result in short-run equilibrium above or below the full-employment level of real GDP.

BUSINESS SITUATION 8.3

As the owner of a large chicken farm in rural Nova Scotia, you are anticipating a new set of extensive agricultural subsidies which will impact the entire poultry industry.

What effect do you expect these subsidies to have on your business in the short run? In the long run?

The answer to this Business Situation can be found in Appendix A.

Reading Comprehension

The answers to these questions can be found on MyEconLab at www.myeconlab.com. MyEconLab

1. Is it true or false that equilibrium will always occur at the full-employment level of real GDP? Discuss.
2. Explain the difference between short-run macroeconomic equilibrium and long-run macroeconomic equilibrium.

LO 8.7 Understand the meaning of economic growth and how to calculate it

The Meaning of Economic Growth

What is economic growth?

There's a pervasive understanding that economic growth is a good thing. In fact, for most countries, economic growth, together with full employment and price level stability, rank among the most important macroeconomic goals. News of the prospects of rapid economic growth in an economy inspires a feeling that good times are ahead. Optimistic news is particularly welcome during periods of recession and high unemployment. Prospects of economic growth bring hope of jobs for the unemployed, and a feeling of security, and often anticipation of higher wages, for those who are employed. News of no growth or of very little growth is received with much less enthusiasm and is viewed as an omen of difficult times ahead. Let me turn to the question "What is economic growth?" One notion of **economic growth** is an increase in a country's real gross domestic product. If the real gross domestic product of a country were $40 billion in 2005, and it increased steadily to $50 billion in 2010, we might say that the country experienced economic growth between 2005 and 2010.

economic growth an increase in a country's real GDP

Economic growth can be defined as an increase in a country's real gross domestic product.

Is this the only meaning of economic growth?

If a country experiences economic growth, we expect its citizens to be better off on the average. Economic growth increases the amount of goods and services that are available. However, if the population grows just as fast as real gross domestic product, then the citizens will be no better off than before the growth period, despite the increase in real gross domestic product. Because of this fact, it is often necessary to modify the above definition of economic growth to take changes in population into account. Economic growth therefore focuses on changes in **real GDP per capita** and is often defined as follows:

real GDP per capita a measure of GDP that accounts for changes in the population

Real GDP per capita = real GDP / population

Economic growth refers to a sustained increase in a country's real gross domestic product per capita over time.

Figure 8.10 An Outward Shift of the p-p Curve Illustrating Economic Growth

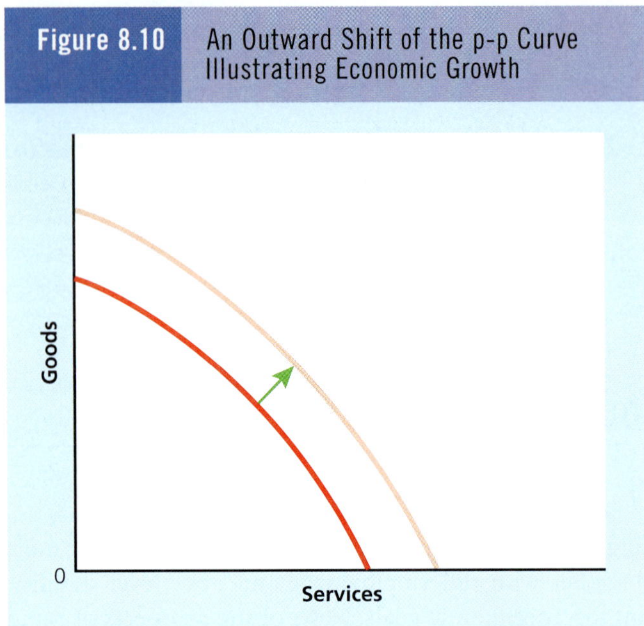

Are there any other concepts of economic growth?

Yes, there is one other concept. The term economic growth can also describe an increase in a country's *productive capacity*. This concept of economic growth is usually illustrated by an outward shift of the production possibility curve. Figure 8.10 shows this shift. The outward shift of the curve illustrates an increasing capacity to produce goods and services.

> Economic growth can describe an increase in a country's productive capacity.

What is the growth rate?

The term **growth rate**—frequently used in discussions relating to a country's economic progress—refers to the rate of growth of a country's real gross domestic product per capita.

growth rate the percentage change in a country's real GDP per capita

> The growth rate of real gross domestic product is the percentage change in a country's real gross domestic product per capita.

For example, if the real GDP per capita of an economy increased by 2.5% from 2009 to 2010, we say that the growth rate for that period was 2.5%.

How is the growth rate calculated?

The definition of the growth rate makes it clear that the growth rate is a percentage change. You will recall that in Appendix 1A, we looked at a formula that can be used to calculate percentage change. The same concept can be applied here.

$$\text{Economic Growth} = \frac{\text{Real GDP/capita}_{\text{current}} - \text{Real GDP/capita}_{\text{previous}}}{\text{Real GDP/capita}_{\text{previous}}} \times 100$$

Can you give an example of how to use this formula?

Using the information about real GDP and the population in the Table 8.1, we can easily calculate real GDP per capita. Once we have this information, we can determine the change in real GDP per capita, or the growth rate.

The rate of growth in 2010 is 2.2%. To calculate this rate, use the formula given above for economic growth:

$$\text{Economic Growth}_{2010} = \frac{\text{Real GDP /capita}_{2010} - \text{Real GDP /capita}_{2009}}{\text{Real GDP/capita}_{2009}} \times 100$$

$$= \frac{36\,041 - 35\,257 \times 100}{35\,257}$$

$$= 2.2\%$$

Now that you understand how to use the formula to compute economic growth, it is worthwhile mentioning the negative growth rates experienced in 2008 and 2009. You

Table 8.1 Real GDP and Canadian Population Figures for 2006–2010

Year	Real GDP (billion)	Population (million)	Real GDP/capita	Growth rate
2006	$1191	32.723	36 396	
2007	$1219	33.115	36 811	1.14 %
2008	$1227	33.506	36 620	−0.52 %
2009	$1195	33.894	35 257	−3.7 %
2010	$1234	34.238	36 041	2.2 %

Source: Data from Statscan CANSIM Database, http://cansim2.statcan.ca.

are no doubt aware at this point that this is a direct result of the most recent recession of 2008/2009. GDP fell significantly during this period as unemployment increased. At the same time, however, the population continued to expand. Together, these contributed to the negative growth in real GDP per capita during this period. The various agencies responsible for economic forecasting are predicting rates of growth for the Canadian economy to be in the 1.9%–2.5% range through to 2014.

Reading Comprehension

The answers to these questions can be found on MyEconLab at www.myeconlab.com. MyEconLab

1. What is economic growth?
2. Define the growth rate of real GDP.
3. Explain how the growth rate of real GDP can be calculated.

LO 8.8 Discuss the desirability of economic growth and the issue of sustainability

The Desirability of Economic Growth: The Issue of Sustainability

Is economic growth desirable?

It would seem obvious that economic growth is desirable, but it is a controversial issue. In 1956, the population of Canada was 16 081 000. By 2009, it was almost 34 million. This means that the population of Canada more than doubled in 53 years. Between 2001 and 2009, Canada's population increased by about 13%. During the same time, Canada's real GDP increased by about 48%. If the rate of growth of real domestic product had fallen behind the rate of growth of the population over this period, the standard of living of Canadians would have fallen. But because the economy experienced a rate of growth of real GDP that exceeded the rate of growth of the population, the standard of living has improved substantially over these years. Thus, in order to maintain our current living standards, our productive capacity must increase over time. And in order to improve our current living standards, our productive capacity must grow at a faster rate than the rate of increase in the population.

When an economy is growing, current industries are expanding and new industries are being established. These new and expanding industries create new jobs. Hence, economic growth reduces unemployment. It can also be argued that economic growth makes it easier for the government to redistribute income in order to reduce economic inequality among persons. Economic growth facilitates an increase in government revenues. With increased revenues, the government can provide more social services and more opportunities for the less fortunate.

Economic growth, in addition to the improvement in living standards that higher output and income will bring, is also positively correlated to longer life expectancy, better physical health which arises from health-care spending, nutrition, high sanitation standards, and a high quality, literate labour force. Is economic growth desirable? Indeed it is!

Is there any opposition to economic growth? The term "sustainability" is often used in conjunction with the goal of economic growth. What does this mean?

The benefits of economic growth are truly impressive. This fact explains why the objective of economic growth is vigorously pursued by so many countries. The advantages of economic growth, however, should not obscure the reality that economic growth has costs as well as benefits. Critics argue that economic growth causes social problems such as traffic congestion, the destruction of the countryside, and overcrowding in our cities. Rapid expansion of GDP creates pollution, smog, and excess waste. Additional opposition to economic growth comes from those who argue that a greater output of goods and services will, in fact, not help us to achieve the good life. On the contrary, a greater real gross domestic product, they feel, can be achieved only by lowering current consumption.

Recognition of the costs associated with economic growth has led to several attacks on the objective of rapid economic growth. The opposition is not to economic growth per se, but rather an opposition to *rapid* growth, which occurs at the expense of *sustainable* growth.

Environmental regulation is not only a result of those actions by individuals and groups who oppose rapid economic growth, but also an attempt by government officials and agencies to protect non-renewable or finite quantity resources—clean air, lakes, streams, fisheries, and mines—which many Canadians value dearly. Because these things are intangible, it makes it difficult to place a value on them—it does not, however, make them less important. Many argue that environmental regulation impedes economic growth; however, it should be recognized that such regulations are designed to prevent the depletion of our precious natural resources which are a *stock* variable. On the one hand the exploitation of these resources will increase our *current* gross domestic product. On the other hand, it will forever reduce our stock of certain non-renewable natural resources. Clearly there is a trade-off.

sustainable development development that meets the needs of the present without compromising the ability of future generations to meet their own needs

Sustainable development is intended to achieve the benefits of economic growth, while at the same time balancing this growth with our ability to *sustain* it into the future. Sustainable development, in terms of Canada's goal of economic growth, refers to our country's desire to achieve stated goals of economic growth (and all of the benefits that it bestows on its citizens) while, at the same time, being cautious about the exploitation of its non-renewable resources and the fragile state of the environment. It is an approach that aims to achieve economic growth without excessive depletion of precious resources, thus allowing time for natural resources to replenish or renew. This approach is one which attempts to address the current needs of Canadians (growth of GDP, higher incomes, employment opportunities, improved living standards), without compromising the ability of future generations of Canadians to do the same.

The World Commission on Environment and Development (WCED) published a report in *Our Common Future*, also known as the Brundtland Report, which provides the most frequently quoted definition of sustainable development. According to this report,

> Sustainable development is development that meets the needs of the present without compromising the ability of future generations to meet their own needs. It contains within it two key concepts:
>
> - the concept of **needs**, in particular the essential needs of the world's poor, to which overriding priority should be given; and
> - the idea of **limitations** imposed by the state of technology and social organization on the environment's ability to meet present and future needs.

In Canada, the National Round Table on the Environment and the Economy (NRTEE) provides leadership in the area of sustainable development. NRTEE has worked to address the need to reconcile economic and environmental challenges for over two decades:

> "concerns about climate change, air quality, and water availability have made Canadians and their governments increasingly aware of the need to reconcile economic and environmental challenges as they have become increasingly interlinked. They are the flip sides of the same coin. That need for reconciliation—and the process of working towards it—is the National Round Table on the Environment and the Economy's raison d'être."

BUSINESS SITUATION 8.4

Dupont has a clear mission of sustainable growth. Go to:
www2.dupont.com/Our_Company/en_US/glance/sus_growth/sus_growth.html
to read about their commitment to sustainable growth.

What are some of the things that a small business owner operating in Canada can do to reduce its environmental footprint?

The answer to this Business Situation can be found in Appendix A.

Reading Comprehension

The answers to these questions can be found on MyEconLab at www.myeconlab.com. MyEconLab

1. Why is economic growth such a high priority for so many countries?
2. What are some objections to economic growth?
3. What is meant by sustainable growth?

LO 8.9 Identify the determinants of economic growth and the measures to promote it

Determinants of Economic Growth

What are some of the important determinants of economic growth?

Economists still search actively for the factors that explain most fully how economies grow. Although no general agreement exists on the relative importance of these growth factors, the following are generally cited as determinants or sources of a country's long-term economic growth:

1. The size of the labour force
2. The quality of the labour force
3. Natural resources
4. Capital formation
5. Technological change

The Size of the Labour Force The size of a country's labour force determines, to a large extent, its rate of economic growth. *Other things being equal*, the larger the labour force, the greater the economy's real output of goods and services.

Labour must be combined with other productive factors to produce the economy's output. If the labour force increases while the other factors of production and technology remain constant, after a while diminishing returns will set in. Thus, a given labour force may be too large or too small. The label we give to it depends on its effect on real output per worker. The size of the labour force that leads to the maximum real output per worker is the **optimal labour force**, given the other factors of production.

optimal labour force the labour force that is consistent with maximum real GDP per worker

The optimal labour force is that which is consistent with maximum real output per worker.

In Figure 8.11, a labour force greater than line segment OL is too large to maximize real output per worker.

We should remember, though, that the optimal labour force is not constant. It changes continuously as the other factors of production and technology change.

Figure 8.11 The Optimal Labour Force

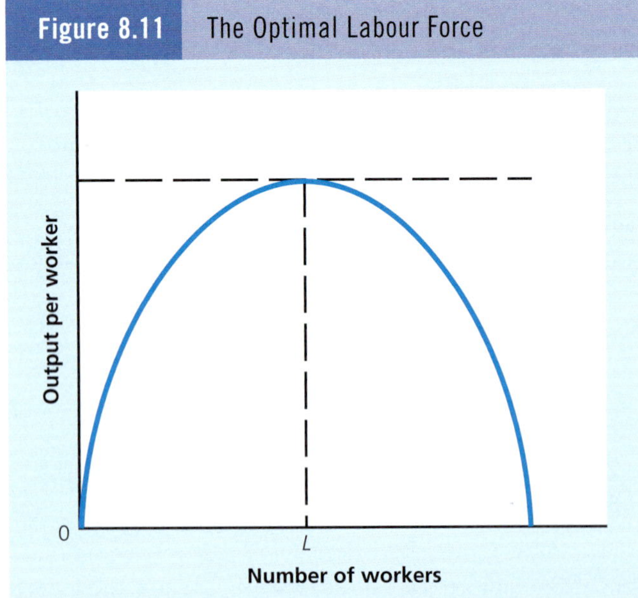

The Quality of the Labour Force To a large extent, the quality of the labour force determines economic growth. A highly skilled and well-trained labour force will doubtlessly contribute greatly to the amount of goods and services that an economy will be able to produce. The same is true of a healthy, energetic, and imaginative labour force. The educational level of the population 15 years and older is a good approximation of the quality of the labour force.

The other aspect of the duo that constitutes human capital is the state of health of the population. Human capital includes the education, skills, and health of the labour force. We can get some idea of the state of health of the labour force by looking at the medical facilities and health-care professions available to the population.

Natural Resources The role of natural resources in economic growth is a controversial issue. The case of Japan is often used to support the argument that a country can achieve rapid economic growth without possessing an abundance of natural resources. But most experts would probably agree that a bountiful supply of natural resources helps enormously to achieve a high growth rate. Mineral and energy resources, as well as fertile land, contribute to economic growth. Canada is relatively well-endowed with a variety of natural resources; the natural resources sector has played and will continue to play a vital role in the country's economic growth.

Capital Accumulation Most theories of economic growth have given a central role to capital formation. The greater the economy's stock of plants, equipment, and machinery, the greater its capacity to produce goods and services. Since investment increases an economy's stock of capital, we can expect the rate of investment to influence the rate of economic growth. But we must be careful not to conclude that increases in investment alone ensure rapid economic growth. Other factors must also be taken into consideration.

Technological Change An increase in technology occurs when a given level of output can be produced with fewer inputs or when the same level of output can be produced with fewer inputs. The way in which the economy's resources combine to produce the output of goods and services obviously determines to a large extent the economy's productive capacity. A method of production (technology) that requires fewer inputs to produce a given level of output will be chosen over one that requires more inputs to produce the same level of output, other things being equal.

Measures to Promote Economic Growth

What can a government do to promote economic growth?

Our discussion of the factors likely to generate economic growth suggests some measures that may be taken to promote long-term economic growth. First, the government can encourage investment in human capital by providing scholarships, educational grants, and loans to students on easy terms. By making education more easily accessible, more people will be able to develop their human capital and thus promote economic growth. Financial support to colleges and universities and other institutions of learning will also help to improve the quality of human capital and thus propel economic growth. Canada, in fact, has a program of financial assistance to students in the form of loans and grants. Several government scholarships are also available, and the colleges and universities are heavily subsidized. Many of these initiatives are undertaken by both federal and provincial governments.

Second, the government can promote technological change by encouraging research and development (R&D). A number of private firms already undertake research and development. The government can provide incentives to these and other firms to increase their R&D activities. Tax dollars used to support research and development can often be justified by the fact that economic growth benefits society. The government can also finance some research and development projects of its own. In Canada, the federal government supports R&D through the National Research Council (NRC), the Natural

Sciences and Engineering Research Council (NSERC), the Social Science and Humanities Research Council (SSHRC), and the Medical Research Council of Canada (MRC).

Third, the government can foster economic growth by encouraging investment. This can be achieved partly through interest rate policies (low interest rates tend to stimulate real investment), and partly through tax incentives for investment in plant and equipment.

Reading Comprehension

The answers to these questions can be found on MyEconLab at www.myeconlab.com. MyEconLab

1. What are the main factors that contribute to economic growth?
2. Define the optimal labour force.
3. Discuss the role of capital in promoting economic growth.
4. What measures can a government take to promote long-term economic growth?
5. What have governments in Canada done to promote long-term economic growth?

Review

1. Review the learning objectives listed at the beginning of the chapter.
2. Have you accomplished all the objectives? One way to determine this is to answer the Reading Comprehension questions at the end of each section. These will help you assess your understanding of the learning objectives.
3. If you have not accomplished an objective, review the relevant material before proceeding.

Key Points to Remember

1. **LO 8.1** The long-run aggregate supply (*LRAS*) curve shows the amount of real GDP that the economy can produce at full employment. The *LRAS* curve is a vertical line at the potential or capacity level of real GDP.
2. **LO 8.2** The *LRAS* curve will shift if the economy's productive capacity changes. Such factors as changes in the labour force, technology, capital stock, and resource endowment will affect the economy's productive potential and will therefore shift the *LRAS* curve.
3. **LO 8.3** Long-run, economy-wide equilibrium occurs when the aggregate demand (*AD*) curve and the *LRAS* curve intersect. Long-run macroeconomic equilibrium always occurs at the full-employment level of real GDP.
4. **LO 8.4** Changes in long-run aggregate supply affect the equilibrium price level and the equilibrium level of real GDP. When the *LRAS* curve shifts both the equilibrium price and output levels will be affected.
5. **LO 8.5** Increases in aggregate demand, when the economy is in long-run equilibrium, will cause increases in the price level, but will have no effect on long-run equilibrium real GDP.
6. **LO 8.6** Short-run macroeconomic equilibrium can occur at, above, or below full-employment real output.
7. **LO 8.7** Economic growth refers to the situation in which real GDP per capita is increasing. It is measured by the increase in real GDP per capita between two time periods, as a proportion of the original period's real GDP per capita, times one hundred.
8. **LO 8.8** Economic growth is desirable, but somewhat controversial. Economic growth brings with it several benefits, including lower unemployment and a higher standard of living. The negative effects of economic growth include

traffic congestion, pollution, and the potentially serious side effects from the overuse or depletion of scarce resources. Sustainable development refers to development that meets the needs of the present (an increase in productive capacity) without compromising the ability of future generations to meet their own needs (excessive depletion of natural resources).

9. LO 8.9 The sources or determinants of economic growth are the quantity and quality of the labour force, natural resources, capital formation, and technological change.

Economic Word Power

Problems and Exercises

Basic

1. Table 8.2 shows the various price levels and the quantity of real GDP demanded at each price level. Potential real GDP is $70 billion.

Table 8.2 Price Levels and Real GDP

Price Level	Quantity of Real GDP Demanded ($ bil)	Long-Run Aggregate Supply ($ bil)
90	100	
95	90	
100	80	
105	70	
110	60	
115	50	
120	40	

   a. LO 8.1 Complete the long-run aggregate supply (*LRAS*) column.
   b. LO 8.3 Determine the equilibrium price level and the equilibrium real GDP.
   c. LO 8.5 If aggregate demand increases by $10 billion, other things being equal, determine the new equilibrium price level and the equilibrium level of real GDP.
   d. LO 8.5 Explain why the equilibrium real GDP remains unchanged when aggregate demand increases.

2. LO 8.2 Which of the following will cause the long-run aggregate supply curve (*LRAS*) to shift?
   a. Technological advance
   b. An increase in resources
   c. An increase in total income
   d. A rise in the average level of prices
   e. A more liberal or open immigration policy
   f. Advancements in technology or greater use of new equipment to enhance labour productivity

3. LO 8.3, 8.5 By using the data in Table 8.2, graph the aggregate demand (*AD*) and *LRAS* curves. On your graph, indicate the equilibrium price level and the equilibrium real GDP. Suppose that the quantity of real GDP increases by $10 billion at each price level. On your graph, draw the new *AD* curve. How has the increase in *AD* affected the price level and real GDP?

4. Referring to Table 8.2, suppose potential GDP increases by $10 billion while *AD* remains unchanged.
   a. LO 8.5 Draw the *AD* curve on a graph.
   b. LO 8.1 Draw the original *LRAS* curve on your graph.
   c. LO 8.3 Indicate the equilibrium price level and the equilibrium real GDP.
   d. LO 8.2 On your graph, draw the new *LRAS* curve.
   e. LO 8.6 What has happened to the equilibrium price level and the equilibrium real GDP?

5. LO 8.7 Suppose a new technology increases the efficiency with which snowboards can be made. How would this affect the p-p curve between snowboards and butter tarts? Now suppose that there were increases in the efficiency of tart production, but no change in the efficiency of snowboards. How would the p-p curve change? Finally, assume that technologies were invented which increased the efficiency of production of both goods. How would the p-p curve be affected in this case?

6. LO 8.8 What are the benefits of economic growth? What arguments do critics present for their beliefs that rapid economic growth is harmful?

7. LO 8.9 What effect does government subsidized post-secondary education and government-funded health care have on the quality of the labour force? How might the removal of such programs affect the long-run aggregate supply curve?

Questions in the Intermediate and Challenging Sections cover several different concepts, and have not been organized by learning objectives.

Intermediate

1. Use the *AD-AS* model to show the effect of each of the following events on the equilibrium price level and real GDP. Assume that the economy is initially in short-run and long-run equilibrium.
   a. A heavy snowfall cripples economic activity for a week
   b. A sustained erosion of the economy's natural resources
   c. An increased emphasis on education and training
   d. A substantial increase in government purchases of goods and services
   e. Firms drastically reduce their expenditures on plant and facilities on a long-term basis
2. Use the *AD-AS* model to show that an economy can be in equilibrium with real GDP above potential GDP. Is this equilibrium long-run or short-run?
3. Figure 8.12 shows an economy in long-run equilibrium.

Figure 8.12 An Economy in Long-Run Equilibrium

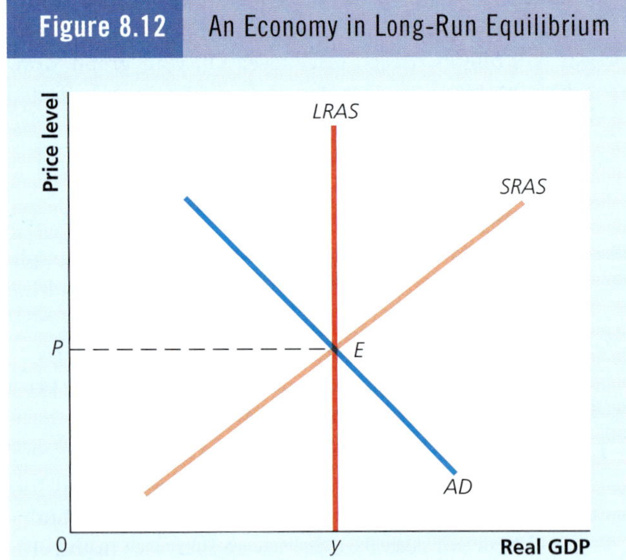

   a. Show how an increase in consumer spending will affect the price level and real GDP in the short run.
   b. Show how the price level and real GDP will be affected in the long run.
4. Using the information for a hypothetical economy in Table 8.3, find the following:
   a. Real GDP/capita in 2008
   b. Real GDP/capita in 2009
   c. Economic growth in 2008
   d. Economic growth in 2009

Table 8.3 Data for a Hypothetical Economy

	Real GDP (billions)	Population (millions)
2007	1234.5	45.786
2008	1298.6	46.143
2009	1312.4	46.998

Challenging

1. An economy is in short-run equilibrium at less than full-employment real GDP.
   a. Use the *AD-AS* model to show that either demand-side or supply-side policies can move the economy to long-run equilibrium.
   b. What is the effect on the price level of using either demand-side or supply-side policies?
2. An economy is in equilibrium at less than full employment, and the price level is substantially higher than the desired level. Use the *AD-AS* model to decide whether a demand-side or a supply-side policy would be preferable to move the economy to full-employment equilibrium.
3. It has been argued that, in today's affluent and technically advanced society, there is no longer any need to fear the extinction of our valuable natural resources. Provide a rationale for someone who believes this.

MyEconLab Visit the MyEconLab website at **www.myeconlab.com**. This online homework and tutorial system puts you in control of your own learning with study and practice tools directly correlated to this chapter's content.

Study Guide

Self-Assessment

What's your score?

Circle the letter that corresponds with the correct answer.

1. In economics, the long run is defined as
   a. A period longer than five years
   b. A period long enough for firms to vary some, but not all, of their inputs
   c. A situation in which firms can vary all their inputs and adjust fully to market conditions
   d. A situation in which firms can adjust to changes in input prices but not to changes in output prices

2. The long-run aggregate supply is
   a. The real GDP actually produced during a specific period
   b. The real GDP that the economy can produce at full employment
   c. The sum of the various amounts produced in the short run
   d. None of the above

3. The long-run aggregate supply (*LRAS*) curve is
   a. Vertical
   b. Upward sloping
   c. Horizontal
   d. Downward sloping

4. If an economy's production possibility (p-p) curve shifts to the right, then its *LRAS* curve will
   a. Become steeper
   b. Shift to the right
   c. Become flatter
   d. Shift to the left

5. Which of the following will cause the *LRAS* curve to shift to the right?
   a. An increase in the price level
   b. A decrease in the price level
   c. A sustained increase in labour productivity
   b. Both b and c

6. Which of the following is true?
   a. An economy will be in long-run equilibrium as long as it is in short-run equilibrium
   b. An economy will be in short-run equilibrium as long as it is in long-run equilibrium
   c. An economy can be in long-run equilibrium and short-run equilibrium at the same time
   d. An economy cannot be in long-run equilibrium and short-run equilibrium at the same time

7. In the long run
   a. The *AD* curve is vertical, but the *LRAS* curve is horizontal
   b. The *AD* curve is downward sloping, but the *LRAS* curve is vertical
   c. The *LRAS* curve is upward sloping, but the *AD* curve is downward sloping
   d. The *AD* and *LRAS* curves are both downward sloping

8. When the *AD* and *LRAS* curves intersect
   a. The economy is in long-run equilibrium
   b. The equilibrium price level is determined but the equilibrium real GDP is unknown
   c. The equilibrium real GDP is determined but the equilibrium price level is unknown
   d. None of the above

9. If the *LRAS* curve shifts to the left, other things being equal, we can predict that
   a. The price level will rise but real GDP will not change
   b. The price level will fall but real GDP will not change
   c. Real GDP will fall but the price level will not change
   d. None of the above

10. A secular decline in the price level can be caused by
   a. Increases in *LRAS*
   b. A decrease in *LRAS*
   c. An increase in *AD*
   d. None of the above

11. If the economy is in long-run equilibrium and *AD* increases, other things being equal,
   a. The price level will fall, but real GDP will not change
   b. The price level will rise, but real GDP will not change
   c. The price level and real GDP will both fall
   d. The price level and real GDP will both rise

12. Long-run macroeconomic equilibrium
   a. May occur above the full-employment level of real GDP
   b. May occur below the full-employment level of real GDP
   c. Will occur at the full-employment level of real GDP
   d. None of the above

13. The economy can be in short-run equilibrium
   a. At the full-employment level of real GDP
   b. Above the full-employment level of real GDP
   c. Below the full-employment level of real output
   d. All of the above

14. The economy is in long-run disequilibrium if
    a. It is in short-run equilibrium above its full-employment level of real GDP
    b. It is in short-run equilibrium below its potential real GDP
    c. The quantity of real GDP demanded is greater or less than the economy's potential real GDP
    d. All of the above
15. Short-run supply-side shocks have
    a. No effect on real GDP
    b. No effect on the price level
    c. No effect on long-run equilibrium
    d. None of the above
16. Economic growth is calculated using
    a. Two consecutive periods of nominal GDP
    b. Two consecutive periods of real GDP
    c. The ratio of nominal GDP to real GDP times 100
    d. The change in real GDP per capita expressed as a proportion of the previous period's real GDP per capital, times 100
17. All of the following are sources of economic growth except
    a. Technological change
    b. Capital formation
    c. Natural resources
    d. Interest rates
18. Economic growth which occurs at a rate such that the needs of future generations are not compromised to meet the needs of today's citizens for current consumption is called
    a. Real growth
    b. Nominal growth
    c. Exploited growth
    d. Sustainable growth
19. The optimal labour force refers to
    a. The size of the labour force that leads to the maximum real output per worker
    b. The size of the labour force that minimizes the transfer payments through the unemployment insurance program
    c. The size of the labour force that allows for the minimum amount of unemployment, given minimum wage legislation
    d. A situation where the optimal number of labour force participants have completed post-secondary education
20. If real GDP per capita in year 1 is 10 000 and real GDP per capita in year 2 is 10 500, then the rate of growth is
    a. 2.5%
    b. 5%
    c. 1.05%
    d. cannot be determined

Problems and Exercises (Use Quad Paper for Graphs)

Answers to these questions can be found on MyEconLab at www.myeconlab.com. MyEconLab

1. Table 8.4 contains data for a hypothetical economy. Potential real GDP is $50 million.

Table 8.4 Data for a Hypothetical Economy

Price Level (index)	Quantity of Real GDP Demanded ($ mil)	Long-Run Aggregate Supply ($ mil)
92	80	50
96	70	
100	60	
104	50	
108	40	
112	30	
116	20	
120	10	

   a. Plot and graph the aggregate demand (*AD*) curve.
   b. On the same graph, plot and draw the long-run aggregate supply (*LRAS*) curve.
   c. Use your graph to determine the equilibrium price level and the long-run equilibrium real GDP.
2. Referring to the data in Table 8.4, suppose *LRAS* increases by $10 million at every price level, while the aggregate demand (*AD*) remains unchanged.
   a. Graph the original and the new *LRAS* curves.
   b. On the same diagram, graph the original *AD* curve.
   c. From your diagram, determine the new long-run equilibrium level of real GDP and the corresponding price level after the increase in *LRAS*.
3. An economy is initially in long-run equilibrium.
   a. Draw the aggregate demand (*AD*), short-run aggregate supply (*SRAS*), and long-run aggregate supply (*LRAS*) curves. Indicate the equilibrium real GDP, *y*, and the equilibrium price level, *P*.
   b. On your diagram, show the effect of a fall in consumption resulting from an increase in personal income taxes.
   c. On another diagram, show the effect of a sudden increase in the price of oil, an important production input.
4. Assume that the economy is initially in short-run and long-run equilibrium. Show the effect of each of the following on equilibrium real GDP and the price level:
   a. A persistent increase in labour productivity over time
   b. A sustained flow of immigrants into the country
   c. The destruction of a significant amount of the economy's natural resources

5. The *AD* and *LRAS* curves for an economy are shown in Figure 8.13.

Figure 8.13 *AD* and *LRAS* Curves for an Economy

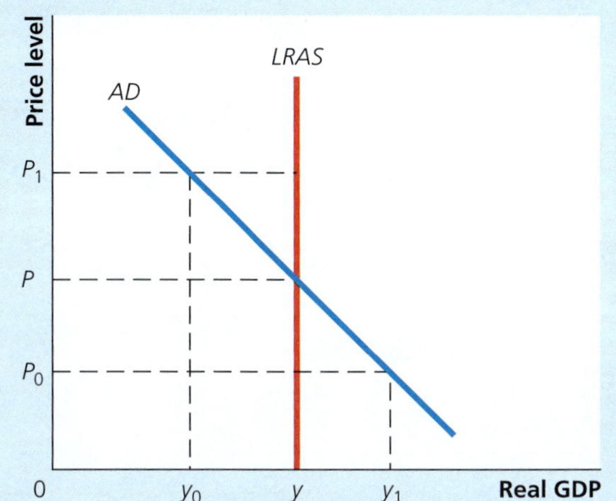

a. What is the equilibrium price level?
b. What is the equilibrium real GDP?
c. Explain what would happen if the price level were at P_1.
d. Explain what would happen if the price level were at P_0.

6. Given the following information in Table 8.5, for the hypothetical economy of Sardina, calculate:

Table 8.5 Data for the Hypothetical Economy of Sardina

	Real GDP (billions)	Population (millions)
2008	1678.55	34.75
2009	1692.25	35.15
2010	1721.45	35.95

a. real GDP per capita in 2009
b. real GDP per capita in 2010
c. economic growth for 2009
d. economic growth for 2010

7. Sketch a p-p curve with a consumer good on the vertical axis and a capital good on the horizontal axis. How would this curve be affected by the following:
   a. technological advancements in the consumer good producing sector only
   b. technological advancements in the capital goods producing sector only
   c. a natural disaster such as a hurricane or earthquake
   d. new productive technology that increases efficiency in both consumer goods and capital goods
8. What arguments support the opinion that economic growth ought to be constrained by government agencies through the use of environmental regulation policies?
9. Identify the benefits associated with increases in a country's productive capacity.

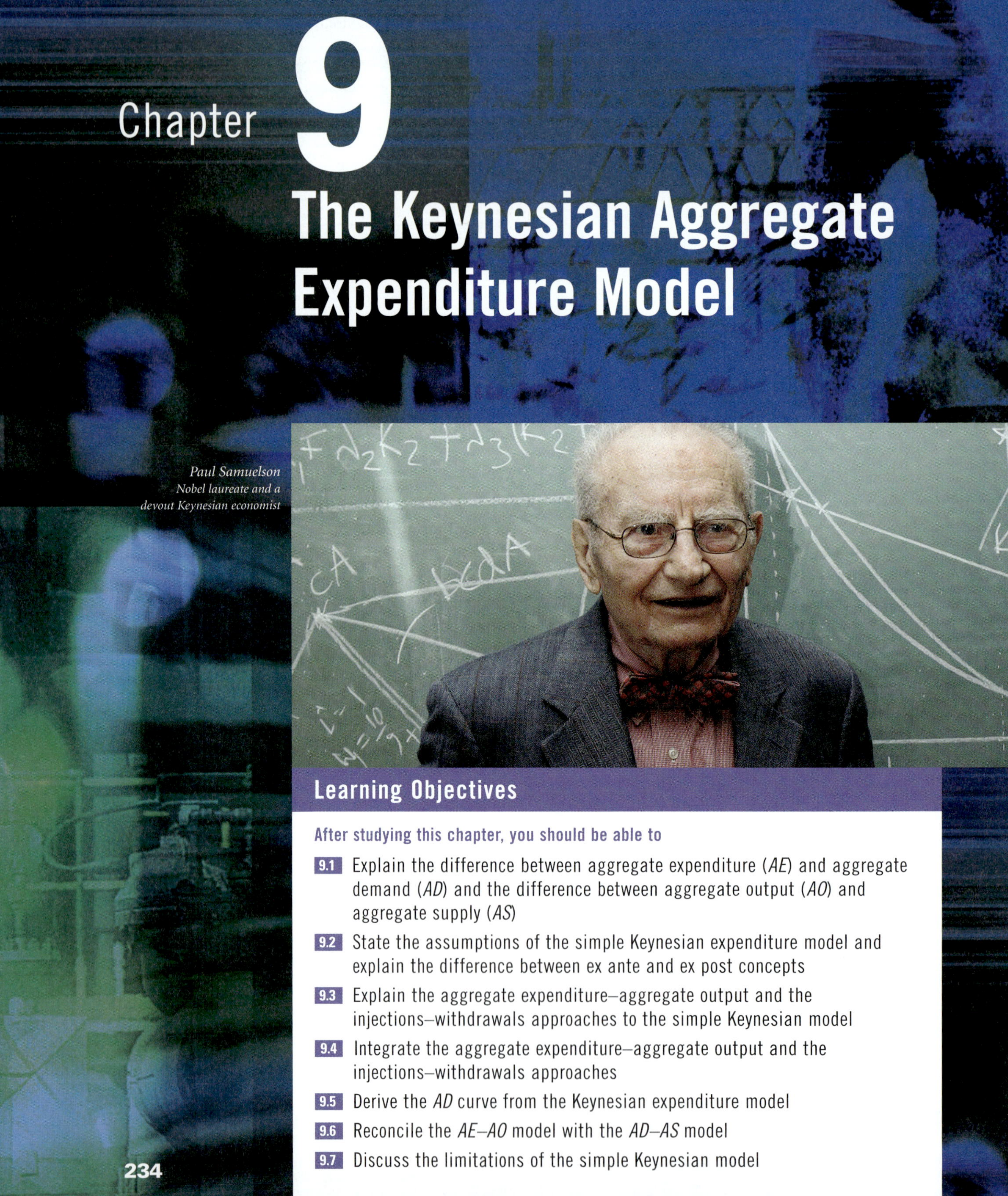

Chapter 9

The Keynesian Aggregate Expenditure Model

Paul Samuelson
Nobel laureate and a devout Keynesian economist

Learning Objectives

After studying this chapter, you should be able to

9.1 Explain the difference between aggregate expenditure (*AE*) and aggregate demand (*AD*) and the difference between aggregate output (*AO*) and aggregate supply (*AS*)

9.2 State the assumptions of the simple Keynesian expenditure model and explain the difference between ex ante and ex post concepts

9.3 Explain the aggregate expenditure–aggregate output and the injections–withdrawals approaches to the simple Keynesian model

9.4 Integrate the aggregate expenditure–aggregate output and the injections–withdrawals approaches

9.5 Derive the *AD* curve from the Keynesian expenditure model

9.6 Reconcile the *AE*–*AO* model with the *AD*–*AS* model

9.7 Discuss the limitations of the simple Keynesian model

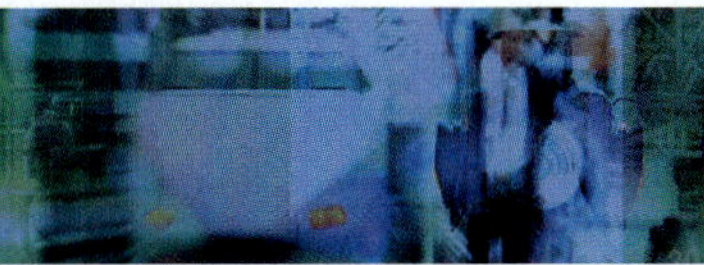

Assess Your Knowledge

MyEconLab

Answers to these questions can be found on MyEconLab at **www.myeconlab.com.**

Indicate whether each of the following is true (T) or false (F).

1. In a closed economy without government, aggregate expenditure is the sum of consumer spending and investment spending.
2. If total income increases, we expect total consumption to increase also.
3. Given a certain level of income, if consumption increases, saving must also increase.
4. If income increases, saving will likely decrease.

LO 9.1 Explain the difference between aggregate expenditure (*AE*) and aggregate demand (*AD*), and the difference between aggregate output (*AO*) and aggregate supply (*AS*)

Aggregate Expenditure (*AE*) and Aggregate Output (*AO*)

What is the difference between aggregate expenditure and aggregate demand?

aggregate expenditure the total expenditure on the economy's output of goods and services

Many authors use the terms aggregate demand and aggregate expenditure interchangeably. In this text, however, we do make a distinction. You will recall that aggregate demand (*AD*) refers to the various levels of real GDP that will be demanded at various price levels. **Aggregate expenditure** (*AE*), on the other hand, is simply the total expenditure on the economy's output of goods and services.

Is aggregate output also different from aggregate supply?

aggregate output the total amount of goods and services produced in an economy

Yes, they are different. Although aggregate output (AO) and aggregate supply (AS) are related, they are not identical. Aggregate supply, you will recall, refers to the various amounts of real GDP that will be supplied at various price levels. **Aggregate output** (*AO*), on the other hand, is the total amount of goods and services produced in an economy or the economy's GDP.

Reading Comprehension

The answers to these questions can be found on MyEconLab at www.myeconlab.com. MyEconLab

1. What is aggregate expenditure? How does it differ from aggregate demand?
2. What is aggregate output? How does it differ from aggregate demand?
3. Is there any relationship between aggregate output and GDP?

LO 9.2 State the assumptions of the simple Keynesian expenditure model and explain the difference between ex ante and ex post concepts

Assumptions of the Simple Keynesian Expenditure Model

When constructing an economic model, we always make assumptions. What are the assumptions of this model?

In this model, we make several simplifying assumptions. These assumptions will help us to explain the determination of the equilibrium level of income in the product market. We will relax these assumptions as we extend the model in subsequent chapters. For the moment, however, we make the following assumptions:

closed economy an economy that does not engage in foreign trade

1. We are dealing with a **closed economy** (i.e., an economy that does not engage in foreign trade).
2. There are no government expenditures, and there are no taxes and government transfer payments.
3. The spending and saving decisions of households depend only on their incomes.
4. Firms decide to spend a fixed amount for new investment (net investment) each period, and the amount does not depend on the level of income. In other words, investment is autonomous(**autonomous investment** is investment that does not vary with income).
5. The economy is operating with unemployed labour and other resources.
6. The price level is constant. Relative prices may change in response to changes in demand and supply in individual markets, but the average level of prices remains unchanged.

autonomous investment investment that does not vary with income

Because assumptions 5 and 6 resemble the situation in which the economy is operating in the Keynesian (i.e., horizontal) range of the aggregate supply (*AS*) curve, we refer to this model as the **Keynesian expenditure model**. The Keynesian aggregate expenditure model is a macroeconomic model that emphasizes aggregate expenditure, with the assumptions of a constant price level and unemployed resources.

Keynesian expenditure model a macroeconomic model that emphasizes aggregate expenditure, with the assumptions of a constant price level and unemployed resources

Is it not true from national income accounting that aggregate expenditure (*AO*) equals the value of total output? Does this not mean that *AE* and *AO* are always equal?

In discussing the forces that lead to macroeconomic equilibrium, we must distinguish between planned and actual outcomes. Let's discuss the difference by using the concepts of ex ante and ex post.

ex ante before the fact; planned or intended

ex post after the fact; actual or realized

Ex Ante and Ex Post Concepts

The Latin phrase **ex ante** means before the fact or planned or intended; the phrase **ex post** means after the fact or actual or realized. Ex ante concepts relate to plans or intentions; ex post concepts relate to realized or actual (historical) facts.

Now, in an ex post sense, the assertion about the identity between aggregate expenditure and aggregate output is correct. Total expenditure on the economy's output of goods and services must be equal to the value of that output. Thus, we have the identity to which you referred:

$$\text{Total expenditure} \equiv \text{Value of total output}$$

or

$$AE \equiv AO$$

This identity holds for any level of income or output. Although the above expression is a tautology (that is, true by definition) in an ex post sense, that is not the case in an ex ante sense. Households and firms may plan to spend more or less than the total output of the economy; hence, total planned or desired expenditure need not be equal to total output. You will see also that the plans of households and firms are not always realized. When we discuss equilibrium income (output), it is ex ante concepts that are relevant.

Reading Comprehension

The answers to these questions can be found on MyEconLab at www.myeconlab.com. MyEconLab

1. What is meant by a closed economy?
2. Explain why planned investment might be different from realized investment.
3. What is the difference between ex ante and ex post concepts, such as saving and investment?

LO 9.3 Explain the aggregate expenditure-aggregate output and the injections–withdrawals approaches to the simple Keynesian model

Approaches to the Simple Keynesian Expenditure Model

Is there a single approach to the simple Keynesian expenditure model of income determination?

No. In fact, we are going to look at two alternative approaches: the aggregate expenditure–aggregate output (*AE–AO*) approach and the injections–withdrawals approach. To facilitate your understanding of the process of equilibrium income determination in the simple Keynesian framework, we will present the analysis in arithmetical, tabular, and graphical forms.

Shall we begin with the aggregate expenditure–aggregate output (*AE–AO*) approach?

Because we have assumed that we are modelling an economy in which there is no foreign trade and in which government neither spends nor taxes, aggregate expenditure is the sum of consumption (C) and investment (I). That is,

$$AE = C + I$$

The other components of AE are all zero by assumption.

Arithmetical Analysis Suppose that, at a current output of \$70 million, consumers plan to spend \$65 million on consumer goods and services, while firms plan to purchase \$10 million worth of investment goods. Desired aggregate expenditure will exceed current output of goods and services. This excess expenditure may result in a reduction of inventories of goods previously produced or in queues of unsatisfied buyers. In either case, there is a clear signal that a greater quantity of output could be sold if it could be produced. Because we have assumed that there are unemployed resources in this economy, the firms can be expected to respond to this signal by increasing production. This, of course, translates into an increase in income. Thus we conclude the following:

> If desired aggregate expenditure exceeds aggregate output ($AE > AO$), inventories will fall below desired levels. Firms will then tend to increase their production levels, and the level of income will tend to rise.

Let us now consider the situation in which desired aggregate expenditure falls short of aggregate output. Suppose that, at an output of $90 million, consumers plan to spend $75 million on consumer goods and services, while firms plan to invest $10 million. Total desired expenditure is $75 million + 10 million = $85 million. This total desired expenditure of $85 million is not enough to allow the firms to sell their entire output. There will therefore be an accumulation of unplanned inventories of unsold goods. The firms will reduce their levels of output, thus causing income to fall. We can conclude the following:

> If desired aggregate expenditure falls short of aggregate output ($AE < AO$), there will be an unintended increase in inventories; firms will tend to reduce their production levels, and income will tend to fall.

Suppose now that total output of goods and services in the economy is $80 million. At this output level, if desired consumption expenditures amount to $70 million and investment expenditures amount to $10 million, then desired aggregate expenditure is $80 million—exactly equal to aggregate output. No unintentional stockpiling of unsold goods and no unintentional reduction of inventories will occur. Therefore, firms will have no incentive to alter their volume of output. Income (output) will be at its equilibrium level. Hence, we can draw the following conclusion:

> Income will be at its equilibrium level when desired aggregate expenditure equals aggregate output ($AE = AO$).

Can we derive the same result from a tabular analysis?

Tabular Analysis Table 9.1 presents possible levels of output with associated consumption and investment expenditures.

At any level of output below $80 million, desired aggregate expenditure is greater than aggregate output. Output and income will therefore tend to rise. Consider a level of output of $50 million. At this level of output, desired aggregate expenditure is $65 million, consisting of $55 million of consumption and $10 million of investment. Firms will attempt to increase their output to meet this level of expenditure; thus output and income will tend to rise. At any level of output above $80 million, desired aggregate expenditure is less than aggregate output. Income and output will tend to fall.

Consider a level of output of $100 million. At this level of output, desired aggregate expenditure is $90 million, consisting of $80 million of consumption and $10 million of investment. Firms will tend to reduce their output levels as they notice an increase in unplanned inventories; thus output and income will tend to fall. At an output level of $80 million, desired aggregate expenditure equals aggregate output. Output (income) will therefore be at its equilibrium level.

Table 9.1 Consumption, Investment, and Aggregate Expenditure (hypothetical data)

Value of Output ($ mil)	Desired Consumption ($ mil)	Desired Investment ($ mil)	Desired AE ($ mil)	Pressure on Income
0	30	10	40	upward ↓
40	50	10	60	upward ↓
50	55	10	65	upward ↓
60	60	10	70	upward ↓
70	65	10	75	upward ↓
80	70	10	80	none —
90	75	10	85	downward ↑
100	80	10	90	downward ↑
110	85	10	95	downward ↑
120	90	10	100	downward ↑

Are we going to proceed to a graphical analysis now?

Graphical Analysis Before we can proceed to a graphical analysis, we need to equip our tool kit with some new analytical tools. The first is the consumption–income relation.

consumption schedule a table showing the relationship between total consumption and total income

The Consumption–Income Relation Look at the first two columns of Table 9.1. They give us a **consumption schedule**, which shows the relationship between total income and total consumption. Because, by assumption, there are no taxes and no government transfer payments, total income is the same as disposable income.

We will introduce other analytical tools at the appropriate time as we continue our analysis. But right now, we need to introduce a few new concepts: the average propensity to consume, the average propensity to save, the marginal propensity to consume, and the marginal propensity to save.

Are these terms difficult to understand?

Let's take the time now to clearly explain each of these terms. Remember that *propensity* means *tendency*, which is a less daunting term.

average propensity to consume the fraction of total income that goes into consumption

The **average propensity to consume** (*APC*) is defined as the fraction of total income allocated to consumption. That is,

$$APC = \frac{C}{Y}$$

where C is consumption and Y is income. The average propensity to consume is the ratio of total consumption to total income. If, out of an income of $100 million, total consumption is $80 million, then

$$Y = \frac{80}{100} = 0.8$$

average propensity to save the fraction of total income that is saved

The **average propensity to save** (*APS*) is defined as the fraction of total income that is saved. That is,

$$APS = \frac{S}{Y}$$

where S is saving and Y is income. The average propensity to save is the ratio of total saving to total income. If, out of an income of $100 million, total saving is $20 million, then

$$APS = \frac{20}{100} = 0.2$$

This seems to suggest that the average propensity to consume and the average propensity to save make up 100% of total income. Is this correct?

That is correct. If your friend consumes three-fifths of his or her disposable income, it follows that he or she saves two-fifths. If you consume two-thirds of your disposable income, it means that you save one-third of your disposable income. Clearly then, $APC + APS = 1$.

This fact can be shown by simple algebra. Disposable income is either consumed or saved. Hence,

$$Y = C + S$$

By dividing each term by Y, we obtain

$$\frac{Y}{Y} = \frac{C}{Y} + \frac{S}{Y}$$

That is,

$$1 = APC + APS$$

marginal propensity to consume the fraction of extra income allocated to consumption

The **marginal propensity to consume** (MPC) is defined as the fraction of extra income allocated to consumption. That is,

$$MPC = \frac{\Delta C}{\Delta Y}$$

where ΔC is the change in consumption and ΔY is the change in income. The marginal propensity to consume is the ratio of the change in consumption to the change in income. If an increase in income of $10 million causes consumption to increase by $7 million, then

$$MPC = \frac{7}{10} = 0.7$$

marginal propensity to save the fraction of extra income allocated to saving

The **marginal propensity to save** (MPS) is defined as the fraction of extra income allocated to saving. That is,

$$MPS = \frac{\Delta S}{\Delta Y}$$

where ΔS is the change in saving and ΔY is the change in income. The marginal propensity to save is the ratio of the change in saving to the change in income. If an increase in income of $10 million results in an increase in total saving of $3 million, then

$$MPS = \frac{3}{10} = 0.3$$

The sum of *MPC* and *MPS* equals 1, just as with *APC* and *APS*. Right?

Right! And again, this result can be derived algebraically as follows:

$$Y = C + S$$
$$\Delta Y = \Delta C + \Delta S$$

Dividing by ΔY, we obtain

$$\frac{\Delta Y}{\Delta Y} = \frac{\Delta C}{\Delta Y} + \frac{\Delta S}{\Delta Y}$$

That is,

$$1 = MPC + MPS$$

Is it possible to show these concepts in a table for illustrative purposes?

Table 9.2 shows marginal propensity to consume, marginal propensity to save, average propensity to consume, and average propensity to save for a hypothetical economy. Income and consumption data are also provided in the first two columns. At an income level of \$60 million, households spend exactly \$60 million on consumer goods and services. This means, of course, that saving is zero. This level of income is called the **break-even level of income**. The break-even level of income is that level at which consumption equals income or saving is zero.

break-even level of income the level of income at which consumption equals income or saving is zero

Note that at the break-even level of income, the *APC* equals 1 because consumption and income are equal. Below the break-even level, $APC > 1$ because consumption is greater than income; above the break-even level, $APC < 1$ because consumption is less than income. Note also that even at a current level of income of \$0, consumers still spend \$30 million purchasing consumer goods and services. The amount of consumption that takes place when income is zero is called **autonomous consumption**. In the present case, autonomous consumption is \$30 million. Autonomous consumption is consumption that does not depend on income.

autonomous consumption consumption that does not depend on income

Table 9.2 Consumption Schedule with *MPC, MPS, APC,* and *APS*

Income (\$ mil)	Consumption (\$ mil)	MPC	MPS	APC	APS
0	30			—	—
		0.50	0.50		
40	50			1.25	–0.25
		0.50	0.50		
50	55			1.10	–0.10
		0.50	0.50		
60	60			1.00	0.00
		0.50	0.50		
70	65			0.93	0.07
		0.50	0.50		
80	70			0.88	0.12
		0.50	0.50		
90	75			0.83	0.17
		0.50	0.50		
100	80			0.80	0.20
		0.50	0.50		
110	85			0.77	0.23
		0.50	0.50		
120	90			0.75	0.25

How is this possible? How can consumers purchase anything when their income is zero?

dissaving a situation in which current consumption exceeds current income, so that saving is negative

induced consumption the portion of consumption that depends on the level of income

This is possible if consumers borrow or if they finance a part of their consumption out of past saving—a concept referred to as dissaving. **Dissaving** is a situation in which current consumption exceeds current income, so that saving is negative. It occurs when consumers spend more than their current income on current consumption.

Although one portion of consumption is autonomous, the rest depends on the level of income. The portion that depends on the level of income is called **induced consumption**. Induced consumption is the portion of consumption that is influenced by income.

Can the consumption–income relation in Table 9.2 be represented by a graph?

consumption curve a curve that shows the relation between consumption and income

The data in the first two columns of Table 9.2 are plotted in Figure 9.1, which is a graphical representation of the consumption–income relation. Note that as income increases, consumption also increases. The curve that shows the relation between consumption and income is referred to as the **consumption curve**.

ΔC and ΔY are specifically indicated on Figure 9.1. Is this significant?

The slope of the consumption curve in Figure 9.1 is $\Delta C/\Delta Y$. Does this ratio remind you of anything?

Yes, it is the marginal propensity to consume.

That's right! You have just made the following discovery:

> The marginal propensity to consume is the slope of the consumption curve. Note that the consumption curve shown in Figure 9.1 is linear. This is only a simplifying assumption, and it should not be interpreted to mean that consumption curves are always linear.

Do we now have all the tools and pieces to complete the *AE–AO* model?

Figure 9.1 The Consumption Curve

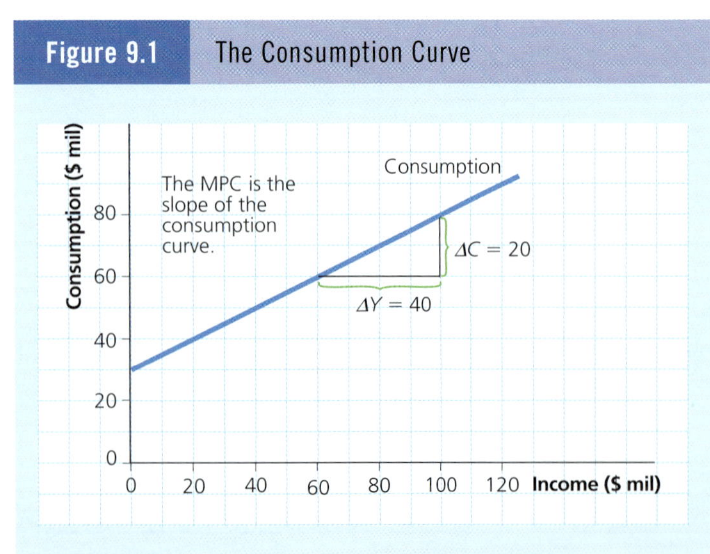

Before we can use the *AE–AO* approach to determine the equilibrium level of income graphically, we need to introduce one more piece of analytical equipment. That is the 45-degree line. This line will prove to be quite convenient in future analysis. Figure 9.2 shows a 45-degree line.

Note that if aggregate expenditure and income are on the axes (as in Figure 9.2), any point on the 45-degree line represents the equality of aggregate expenditure and aggregate output or income. Thus, at point *E*, aggregate expenditure ($70 million) equals income ($70 million). Note also that an income of $70 million can be measured vertically upward from the horizontal axis at $70 million to the 45-degree line. For this reason, the 45-degree line can be labelled *AO* for aggregate output.

Figure 9.2 The 45-Degree Line

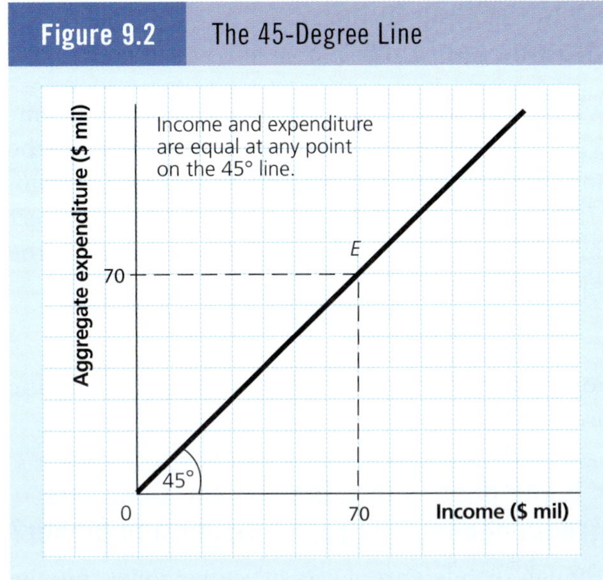

Let us bring the pieces together now. We know that for equilibrium to exist, *AE* and *AO* must be equal. But *AE* and *AO* are equal only along the 45-degree line. Hence equilibrium must occur along the 45-degree line. The graph of the equilibrium level of income that uses the 45-degree line, illustrated in Figure 9.3, is often referred to as the **Keynesian cross**. The Keynesian cross diagram is the 45-degree diagram showing aggregate expenditure and aggregate output.

The consumption curve, *C*, and the line $C + I$, representing the sum of consumption and investment (*AE* in this case), are derived from Table 9.1. The $C + I$ line is parallel to the consumption curve because fixed investment has been added to consumption. The equilibrium level of income is \$80 million, where total intended expenditure $(C + I)$ just equals total output (income). At any other level of income, there would be an imbalance between desired aggregate expenditure and aggregate output. For reasons already discussed, such a level of income would not be maintained.

Keynesian cross the 45-degree diagram showing aggregate expenditure and aggregate output

Figure 9.3 The Equilibrium Level of Income by the *AE*–*AO* Approach

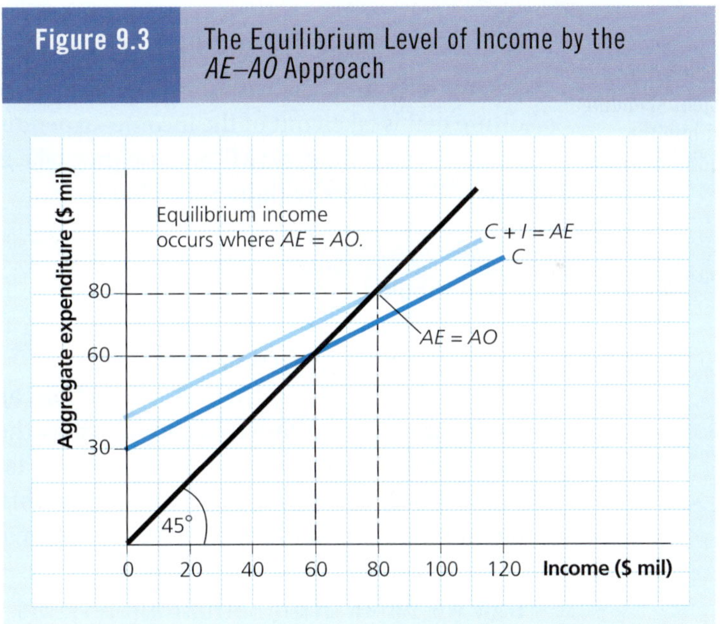

BUSINESS SITUATION 9.1

Select Printers is a manufacturer of a specific brand of electronic printers that are sold mainly to retailers.

What signs can Select Printers look for to determine when an increase in production is warranted?

The answer to this Business Situation can be found in Appendix A.

The aggregate expenditure–aggregate output approach owes much to the work of J.M. Keynes (1883–1946).

Are we now going to proceed to the injections–withdrawals approach?

The Injections–Withdrawals Approach Let us begin with some definitions. An **injection** is any income or expenditure that is pushed into the flow of income and expenditure—the income–expenditure stream. Since investment (I), government spending (G), and exports (X) inject money into the economy, we classify them as injections. Let us use the letter J to denote injections. That is:

$$J = I + G + X$$

Clearly, injections will tend to increase the level of income in the income–expenditure stream.

Money is always being pushed into the stream. Does this mean that the stream necessarily grows bigger and bigger?

Not necessarily. Although spenders are always injecting money into the stream through investment, government spending, and exports, people are always withdrawing or pulling some of it out. For example, savers take some of the money out of the stream.

injection any income or expenditure such as investment, government spending that is pushed into the income–expenditure stream

Is there a name for the money that is pulled out of the income stream?

Yes, we refer to it as a withdrawal or leakage, and it is defined as any income or expenditure that is taken out of the income–expenditure flow. Withdrawals include saving (S), taxes (T), and imports (M) because they take money out of the economy. Let us use the letter W to denote withdrawals. That is:

$$W = S + T + M$$

It should be obvious that withdrawals will tend to reduce the level of income in the income–expenditure flow. Actually, you can think of the withdrawals as offsetting or counteracting the effects of injections.

Since we are using J to denote injections and W to denote withdrawals, we can refer to the injections–withdrawals approach as the J–W approach. In this model, we have assumed that government spending (G) and taxes (T) are zero and that exports (X) and imports (M) are also zero. Therefore, in this particular model, the only injection is investment (I), and the only withdrawal is saving (S).

Can we do an arithmetical analysis as we did with the *AE–AO* approach?

Arithmetical Analysis Suppose that the economy produces a total output of \$70 million. Suppose also that at that level of output, households decide to save (withdraw) \$5 million, while firms plan to invest (inject) \$10 million. Clearly, if households save \$5 million out of a total disposable income of \$70 million, they must be consuming \$65 million. The current level of output is not enough to allow both households and firms to realize their plans to spend \$75 million (\$65 million for consumption plus \$10 million for investment). Firms will therefore tend to increase their output, which will cause income to rise. We can therefore draw the following conclusion:

> In a closed economy in which the government neither spends nor taxes, if planned investment exceeds planned saving, the level of income will tend to rise.

Let us now suppose than at an output of $100 million, consumers desire to save $20 million while firms plan to invest $10 million. This implies that consumers want to spend $80 million on consumer goods and services. The volume of output produced ($100 million) is thus greater than that required for the plans of households and firms to be realized. They plan to spend only $90 million ($80 million for consumption plus $10 million for investment). Firms will tend to reduce their production levels, and in so doing, income will fall. Hence:

> In a closed economy in which there is neither government spending nor taxes, if intended investment is less than intended saving, the level of income will tend to fall.

If, however, the level of output is $80 million, and households plan to save $10 million while firms plan to invest $10 million, then both households and firms will be able to realize their plans, and there will be no incentive for firms to produce a different level of output. The equilibrium level of income will be $80 million. This leads to the following conclusion:

> A closed economy, in which there is neither government spending nor taxes, will be in equilibrium when intended saving equals intended investment.

Using Y to denote the level of income, we can summarize the discussion above as follows:

If $I > S$, then $Y\uparrow$.
If $I < S$, then $Y\downarrow$.
If $I = S$, then Y will be at equilibrium.
The arrows indicate the direction of the change in income.

Tabular and graphical analyses were presented when we studied the *AE–AO* approach. Can we do the same for the *J–W* approach?

Tabular and Graphical Analyses Let's deal with the tabular analysis first. Table 9.3 shows various possible levels of income and the amounts that consumers desire to save at each level of income.

saving schedule a table that shows the relationship between saving and income

Columns 1 and 3 give the relationship between income and saving, which is the **saving schedule**. The saving schedule is drawn on the assumption that as income increases, saving also increases. At an income level of $40 million, consumers will be dissaving (consumption is greater than income or saving is negative). At an income level of $60 million, saving will be zero; hence, the break-even level of income is $60 million.

At any level of income below $80 million, the amount that firms want to invest exceeds the amount that households want to save. For example, at an income level of $70 million, the amount that firms want to invest is $10 million. The amount the households want to save, however, is only $5 million. This injection by firms is greater than the withdrawal by households. Income will therefore tend to rise.

Conversely, if income is at a level of $90 million, the withdrawal by households ($15 million) will exceed the injection by firms ($10 million). Income will therefore tend

Table 9.3 Saving and Investment Schedules (hypothetical data)

Income ($ mil) (1)	Consumption ($ mil) (2)	Saving ($ mil) (3)	Investment ($ mil) (4)	Pressure on Income (5)
0	30	–30	10	upward ↓
40	50	–10	10	upward ↓
50	55	–5	10	upward ↓
60	60	0	10	upward ↓
70	65	5	10	upward ↓
80	70	10	10	none —
90	75	15	10	downward ↑
100	80	20	10	downward ↑
110	85	25	10	downward ↑
120	90	30	10	downward ↑

to fall. Only at an income level of $80 million will the saving decisions of households coincide with the investment decisions of firms. Hence, the equilibrium level of income is $80 million.

Is there a saving curve? If so, what does it look like?

The Saving–Income Relation Columns (1) and (3) of Table 9.3 give us a saving schedule. If we plot this information on a graph, we obtain the saving curve shown in Diagram A of Figure 9.4. The **saving curve** is a graph that shows the relationship between saving and income. Note that the slope of the of the saving curve is

saving curve a graph that shows the relationship between saving and income

$$\frac{\Delta S}{\Delta Y}$$

which is the marginal propensity to save.

Figure 9.4 The Saving and Investment Curves

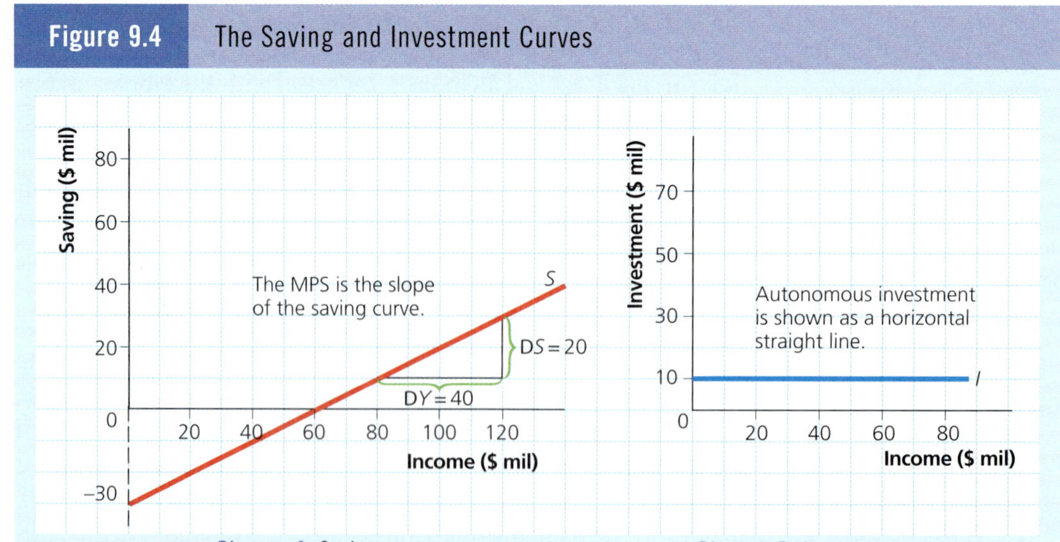

Diagram A: Saving curve

Diagram B: Investment curve

The marginal propensity to save is the slope of the saving curve.

You should note that the linear saving curve results from our simplifying assumption that the *MPS* is constant. It should not be inferred that the actual relation between saving and disposable income is linear.

Investment is assumed to be constant. Does this mean that the investment line is horizontal?

That's exactly what it means. Diagram B of Figure 9.4 shows autonomous investment as a horizontal line.

Now will we put the saving and investment lines together on the same diagram to see how the equilibrium level of income is determined?

Figure 9.5 helps to tell the story.

Saving and investment are measured along the vertical axis and income is measured along the horizontal axis. The equilibrium level of income is determined by the intersection of the saving curve and the investment line. This occurs at an output level of $80 million.

In a closed economy without government, equilibrium income occurs at the intersection of the saving curve and the investment line.

Figure 9.5 Determination of the Equilibrium Level of Income

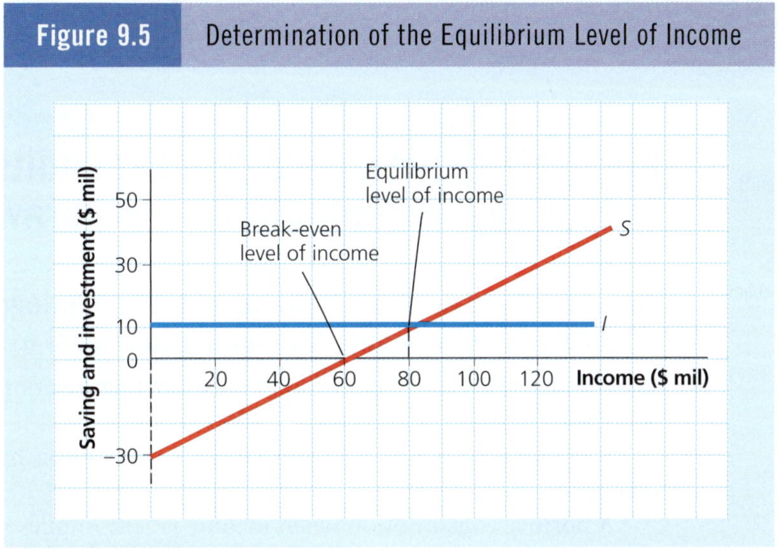

BUSINESS SITUATION 9.2

Your uncle, who has had no training in business or economics, operates a small convenience store. One morning, while listening to the radio, he hears a report from Statistics Canada that the saving rate in Canada will rise considerably over the next two years. Knowing that you are taking a course in economics, your uncle calls on you to explain the implications of the report for his business.

What would you tell him?

The answer to this Business Situation can be found in Appendix A.

Reading Comprehension

The answers to these questions can be found on MyEconLab at www.myeconlab.com. MyEconLab

1. How is it possible for current consumption to exceed current income? What is this phenomenon called?
2. Define aggregate expenditure and aggregate output. Are they always equal? Can they ever be equal?
3. What is the difference between the aggregate expenditure (*AE*) curve and the aggregate demand (*AD*) curve?
4. What is the relation between (a) the marginal propensity to consume (*MPC*) and the marginal propensity to save (*MPS*)? (b) the average propensity to consume (*APC*) and the average propensity to save (*APS*)?
5. In the *AE–AO* approach to income determination, equilibrium income will always occur along the 45-degree line. Is this true or false? Explain.
6. Explain the relationship between saving and consumption.
7. In the income–expenditure stream, what is an injection? Give an example of an injection. What is a withdrawal? Give an example.
8. How do injections and withdrawals affect the level of income in the income–expenditure stream?
9. If saving is on the vertical axis and income is on the horizontal axis, what is the shape of the saving curve?
10. What is the meaning of autonomous investment? What is the shape of the autonomous investment line if investment is on the vertical axis and income is on the horizontal axis?
11. What is meant by the break-even level of income?
12. "In a closed economy without government spending and taxes, the equilibrium level of income occurs where saving and investment are equal." Explain why.

LO 9.4 Integrate the aggregate expenditure–aggregate output and the injections–withdrawals approaches

Integrating the Aggregate Expenditure–Aggregate Output and the Injections–Withdrawals Approaches

Can the *AE–AO* and the *J–W* approaches be integrated to show the similarity in determining the equilibrium level of income?

The two diagrams can be lined up to illustrate their relationship to the determination of equilibrium income.

Diagram A of Figure 9.6 shows the *AE–AO* approach, while Diagram B shows the *J–W* approach.

A positive consumption when income is zero implies negative saving when income is zero. When income is zero, Diagram A shows that consumption is \$30 million. Diagram B shows that saving is –\$30 million when income is zero. The break-even level of income (\$60 million) is shown in Diagram A, where consumption and income are equal, and in Diagram B, where saving is zero. Finally, note that the aggregate expenditure line intersects the 45-degree line at the same level of income at which the saving and investment lines intersect.

Figure 9.6 Integration of the *AE–AO* and the *J–W* Approaches

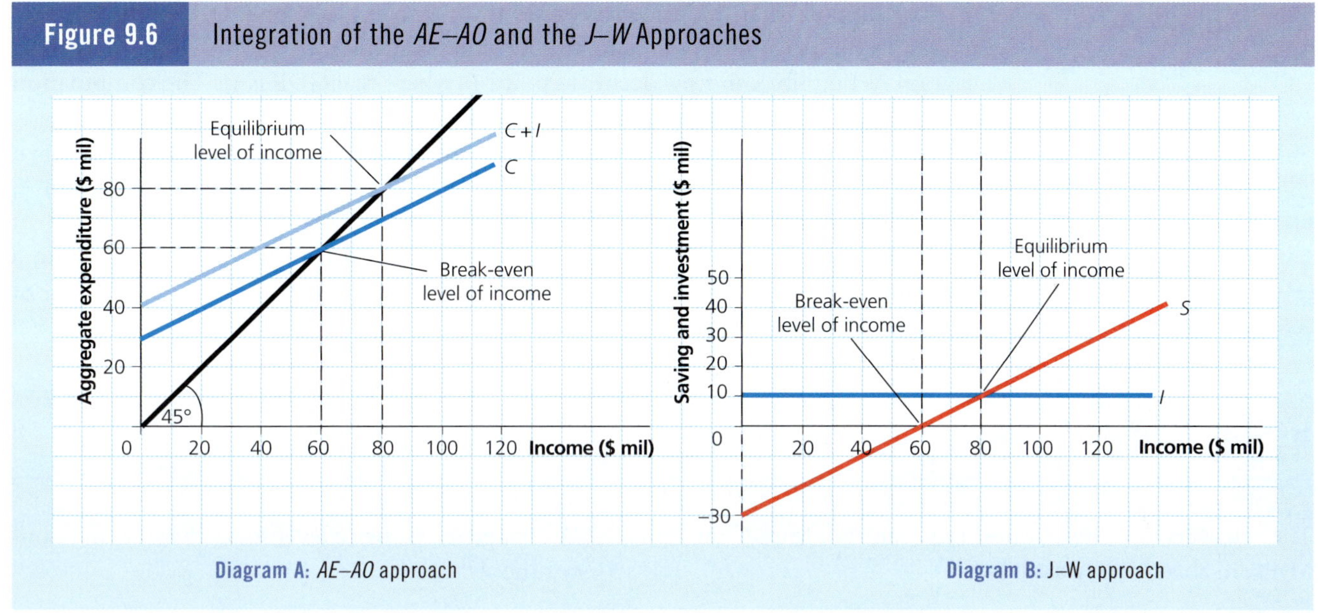

Diagram A: *AE–AO* approach

Diagram B: J–W approach

Reading Comprehension

The answers to these questions can be found on MyEconLab at www.myeconlab.com. MyEconLab

1. In what sense are the *AE–AO* approach and the *J–W* approach just different ways of looking at the same thing?
2. What is the significance of the fact that the aggregate expenditure line intersects the 45-degree line at the same level of income at which the saving and investment lines intersect?

LO 9.5 Derive the *AD* curve from the Keynesian expenditure model

Derivation of the *AD* Curve

We learned that the *AD* curve will shift if any of the components of *AE* change. Clearly then, *AE* and *AD* are closely related. Can the *AD* curve be derived from the *AE–AO* model?

The *AD* curve can be derived from the Keynesian *AE–AO* model of income determination. In deriving the *AD* curve, we will assume that *AE* and *AO* are in real terms. (Earlier we discussed the *AE–AO* model in nominal terms, and the *AD–AS* model in real terms.) Let us consider Figure 9.7.

In Diagram A of Figure 9.7, *AE* and *AO* (the 45-degree line) intersect at point A to determine the equilibrium level of real GDP, *y*. This equilibrium occurs at some price level, say, *P*. This price level of *P*, and the equilibrium level of real GDP of *y*, are illustrated in Diagram B by point *A*. (Diagrams A and B are lined up for convenience.)

Now suppose that the price level rises from P to P_1, as shown in Diagram B. This increase in the price level will shift the *AE* curve down from *AE* to AE_0, as shown in Diagram A. Equilibrium now occurs at point *B*, where real GDP is y_0. The combination of P_1 and y_0 is shown in Diagram B as point *B*.

Let's return to the initial price level of *P*. If the price level falls from *P* to P_0, as shown in Diagram B, aggregate expenditure will rise from *AE* to AE_1, as shown in Diagram A. The equilibrium real GDP will rise from *y* to y_1. This combination of P_0 and y_1 is shown as point *C* in Diagram B. By connecting points *B*, *A*, and *C* in Diagram B we obtain a curve that expresses the relationship between the price level and real GDP. This, of course, is the *AD* curve.

Reading Comprehension

The answers to these questions can be found on MyEconLab at www.myeconlab.com. MyEconLab

1. Indicate whether the following statement is true or false:

"A change in the price level shifts the *AD* curve but not the *AE* curve."

LO 9.6 Reconcile the *AE–AO* model with the *AD–AS* model

Reconciliation of *AE–AO* with *AD–AS* Analysis

We have seen that the *AE–AO* and the *J–W* approaches to equilibrium income determination can be integrated, and we have seen that the *AD* curve can be derived from the *AE–AO* model. Can the *AE–AO* approach be reconciled with the *AD–AS* model?

Your question suggests that you believe, at least intuitively, that there is a close relationship between the *AE–AO* analysis and the *AD–AS* analysis. The answer to the question is yes, and we will formally reconcile the *AE–AO* and *AD–AS* analyses. The Keynesian cross diagram presented in Diagram A of Figure 9.8 shows the equilibrium level of income occurring at the point where the *AE* line crosses the 45-degree line. The equilibrium level of real GDP is *y*. According to this analysis, firms adjust their output levels to suit aggregate expenditure at the existing price level. Recall our assumption that the price level is constant. If *AE* exceeds *AO*, real GDP expands. If *AE* is less than *AO*, real GDP contracts.

The fact that firms are able to increase their production levels without any increase in the price level suggests that the economy is operating in the Keynesian (horizontal) section of the *AS* curve. Diagram B of Figure 9.8 shows the *AD* curve intersecting the *AS* curve in the horizontal range. The two diagrams are lined up to emphasize the relation between the two approaches.

In Diagram A, we assume that the price level is *P*. The equilibrium level of real GDP is *y*, where desired aggregate expenditure equals aggregate output. This is the same level of real GDP shown in Diagram B, where aggregate demand equals aggregate supply at a price level of *P*.

Now suppose planned aggregate expenditure increases from *AE* to AE_1 in Diagram A. The equilibrium level of real GDP rises from *y* to y_1. The increase in *AE* shifts the *AD*

Figure 9.7 Derivation of the *AD* Curve

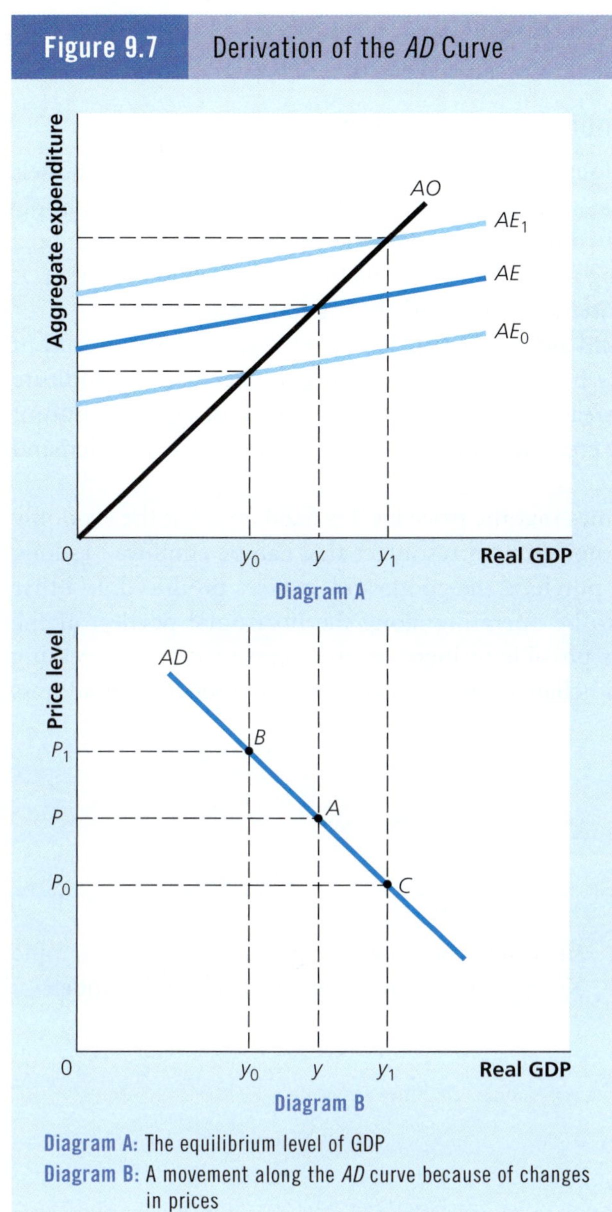

Diagram A: The equilibrium level of GDP
Diagram B: A movement along the *AD* curve because of changes in prices

Figure 9.8 Reconciliation of *AE–AO* with *AD–AS*

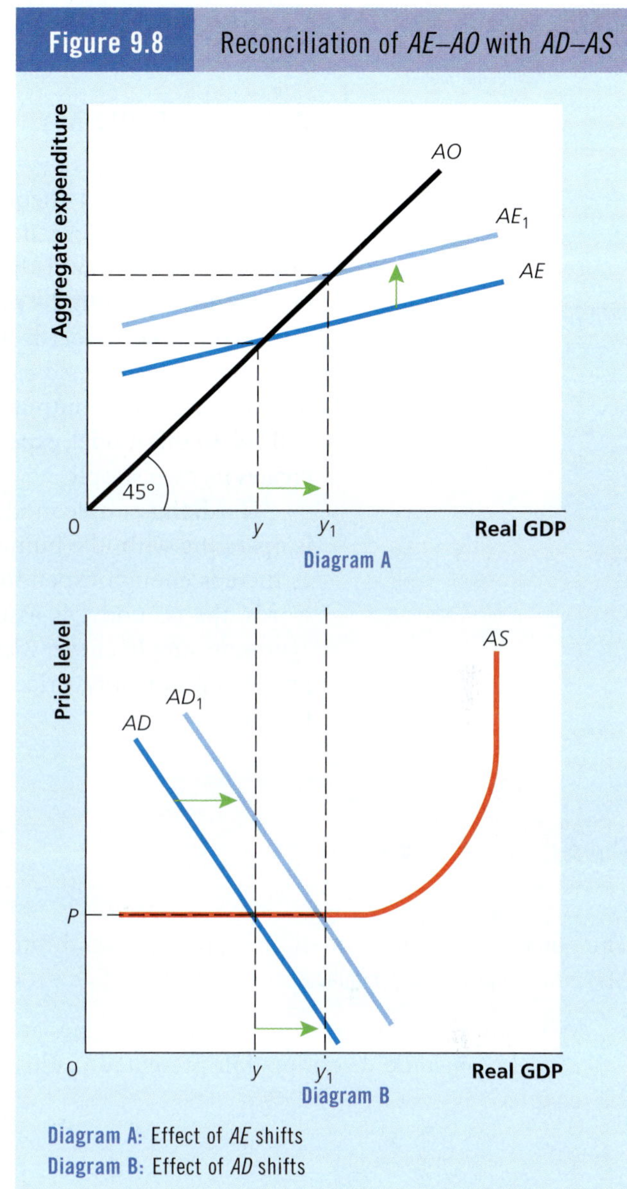

Diagram A: Effect of *AE* shifts
Diagram B: Effect of *AD* shifts

curve from *AD* to AD_1, as shown in Diagram B. The level of real output increases from y to y_1 but the price level remains at P because the economy is in the Keynesian range.

Reading Comprehension

The answers to these questions can be found on MyEconLab at **www.myeconlab.com**. MyEconLab

1. What is the effect of an increase in aggregate expenditure on aggregate demand, other things being equal? (If the *AE* curve shifts up, what happens to the *AD* curve?)
2. If an increase in *AD*, other things being equal, has no effect on the price level, what can you conclude about the state of the economy?

LO 9.7 Discuss the limitations of the simple Keynesian model

Limitations of the Simple Keynesian Model

Does this simple Keynesian model have any limitations?

All economic models have limitations in the sense that the assumptions of the models place limitations on them. We can identify three specific limitations of the simple Keynesian model. First, it is not a complete model of the macroeconomy. The model does not analyze what is happening in the money market and in the labour market. It deals exclusively with the product market—the market for goods and services.

Second, the model is a demand-side model in the sense that the level of output (income) is determined exclusively by aggregate expenditure. If aggregate expenditure increases, aggregate output will increase. If aggregate expenditure falls, aggregate output will fall. In this model, expenditure creates output. Alternatively, we can say that demand creates its own supply.

Third, this simple model assumes that the price level is fixed and that the economy is operating with idle human and non-human resources that can be employed as long as there is enough expenditure to purchase the goods and services produced. In other words, the economy is assumed to be operating along the horizontal portion of the aggregate supply curve, where it is possible to increase production without increasing prices. But in reality, price levels do change, and a more complete model must address this fact.

Reading Comprehension

The answers to these questions can be found on MyEconLab at www.myeconlab.com. MyEconLab

1. What are the limitations of the simple Keynesian model of income determination presented in this chapter?
2. In what sense can it be said that the simple Keynesian model is a demand-side-only model?

Review

1. Review the learning objectives listed at the beginning of the chapter.
2. Have you accomplished all the objectives? One way to determine this is to answer the Reading Comprehension Questions at the end of each section. This will help you assess the extent to which you have accomplished the learning objectives.
3. If you have not accomplished an objective, review the relevant material before proceeding.

Key Points to Remember

1. LO 9.1 Aggregate expenditure and aggregate demand are not identical, and aggregate output and aggregate supply are not identical.
2. LO 9.3 The consumption curve shows the direct relationship between current consumption and current disposable income. A portion of consumption is autonomous while a portion is induced.
3. LO 9.3 The average propensity to consume is the ratio of consumption to income. The average propensity to save is the ratio of saving to income.
4. LO 9.3 The marginal propensity to consume is the ratio of the change in consumption to the change in income. The marginal propensity to save is the ratio of the change in saving to the change in income.
5. LO 9.3 In a closed economy in which government neither spends nor taxes, equilibrium income (output) occurs when desired aggregate expenditure equals aggregate output.
6. LO 9.3 In the injections–withdrawals approach, when government neither spends nor taxes, and when there is no foreign trade, equilibrium income occurs where the saving curve and the investment line intersect.
7. LO 9.5 The *AD* curve can be derived from the *AE–AO* model.
8. LO 9.7 The limitations of the simple Keynesian model of income determination include the fact that the model concentrates only on the product market, it focuses only on the demand side, and it does not allow for changes in the price level.

Economic Word Power

Aggregate expenditure (p. 235)
Aggregate output (p. 235)
Autonomous consumption (p. 241)
Autonomous investment (p. 236)
Average propensity to consume (p. 239)
Average propensity to save (p. 239)
Break-even level of income (p. 241)
Closed economy (p. 236)
Consumption curve (p. 242)
Consumption schedule (p. 239)
Dissaving (p. 242)
Ex ante (p. 236)
Ex post (p. 236)
Induced consumption (p. 242)
Injection (p. 244)
Keynesian cross (p. 243)
Keynesian expenditure model (p. 236)
Marginal propensity to consume (p. 240)
Marginal propensity to save (p. 240)
Saving curve (p. 246)
Saving schedule (p. 245)

Problems and Exercises

Basic

1. LO 9.1 Indicate which of the following is a component of aggregate expenditure:
   a. Wages and salaries
   b. Consumption
   c. Interest
   d. Investment
   e. Corporation profits
   f. Net exports
   g. Government purchases
   h. Rent
2. LO 9.3 Data in Table 9.4 are available for a closed economy without government.

Table 9.4 Sample Data for a Closed Economy

Income/ Output ($ bil)	Desired Consumption ($ bil)	Desired Investment ($ bil)	Desired *AE* ($ bil)
0	20	20	
20	30	20	
40	40	20	
60	50	20	
80	60	20	
100	70	20	
120	80	20	
140	90	20	

   a. Fill in the Desired *AE* column.
   b. Determine the equilibrium level of income.
   c. Explain what would happen to income if it were at $60 billion and why.
3. LO 9.3 The income and consumption data are given for an economy in Table 9.5.
   a. Complete the *MPC*, *MPS*, *APC*, and *APS* columns.
   b. With income on the horizontal axis and consumption on the vertical axis, graph the consumption curve.
   c. Calculate the slope of the consumption line.
   d. On your graph, indicate the break-even level of income.
   e. What is the value of autonomous consumption?

Table 9.5 Income and Consumption Data

Income	*C*	*MPC*	*MPS*	*APC*	*APS*
0	10				
20	16				
40	32				
60	48				
80	64				
100	80				
120	96				
140	112				

4. LO 9.3 Consider Figure 9.9, which is a diagram of an economy.

Figure 9.9 Diagram of an Economy

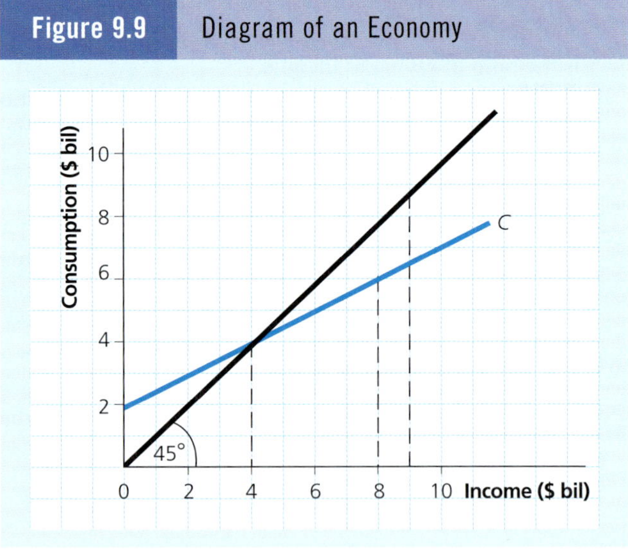

   a. What is the level of consumption if income is $8 billion?
   b What is the level of consumption when income is $2 billion?
   c. How much will have to be borrowed if income is $2 billion?
   d. What is the break-even level of income?
5. LO 9.3 Table 9.6 contains saving and investment data for a closed economy without government.

Table 9.6 Saving and Investment Data

Income	Saving	Investment
40	–5	10
60	0	10
80	5	10
100	10	10
120	15	10
140	20	10
160	25	10

a. Graph the saving and investment lines.
b. Indicate the break-even level of income.
c. Indicate the equilibrium level of income.
d. Calculate the MPS.
e. Calculate the MPC.

Questions in the Intermediate and Challenging sections cover several different concepts, and have not been organized by learning objectives.

Intermediate

1. Figure 9.10 is for a closed economy without government. Investment is autonomous and is 40.

Figure 9.10 Diagram of a Closed Economy

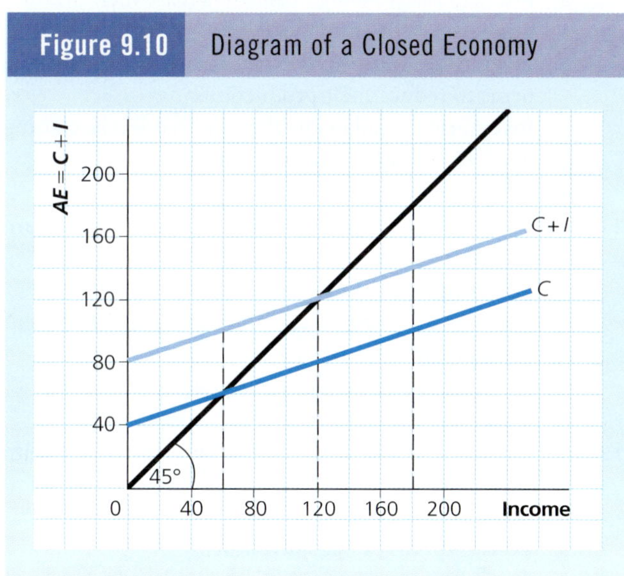

a. What is the break-even level of income?
b. At a level of income of 60, what is *AE*?
c. At a level of income of 120, what is consumption?
d. At a level of income of 180, by how much does *AO* exceed *AE*?
e. Indicate the equilibrium level of income.

2. Table 9.7 contains data for a hypothetical closed economy without government. (Y = income, C = consumption, S = saving, I = investment, *AE* = aggregate expenditure.)

Table 9.7 Data for a Closed Economy

Y	*C*	*S*	*I*	*AE*
40	50			
60	60			
80	70			
100	80			
120	90			
140	100			

a. Complete the saving column.
b. If autonomous investment is 20, complete the investment and *AE* columns.
c. On the basis of the data contained in the table, draw an *AE–AO* diagram lined up with the saving–investment diagram to show that both approaches lead to the same conclusion about the determination of equilibrium income.

3. Suppose that the *MPC* in a certain economy is constant at 0.8 and the break-even level of income is \$10 billion. If income is \$15 billion, how much will be consumed and how much will be saved?

Challenging

1. Consider a closed economy without government. Use the *AE–AO* model to explain the adjustment that will take place if income is above or below the equilibrium level. Be sure to include the role of inventories in your explanation.
2. Illustrate with the help of the *AE–AO* model that when *AE* > *AO*, the effect is an increase in employment.
3. Suppose that consumption equals \$100 billion when income is \$0, and each increase of \$100 billion in income causes consumption to increase by \$70 billion. By using this information, graph the saving line.

Study Guide

Self-Assessment

What's your score?

Circle the letter that corresponds with the correct answer.

1. Aggregate expenditure is
   a. Total injections plus total withdrawals
   b. Total spending on the economy's output of goods and services
   c. The sum of the expenditures of all households
   d. All of the above

2. Aggregate expenditure and aggregate demand are
   a. One and the same thing
   b. Totally unrelated
   c. Both dependent on the price level
   d. None of the above

3. Aggregate output is
   a. Always identical to aggregate expenditure
   b. Identical to aggregate supply
   c. The total output of goods and services produced
   d. None of the above

4. In an ex ante sense,
   a. Total expenditure must equal the value of total output
   b. Total expenditure and the value of total output have no significance
   c. Total expenditure and the value of total output may not be equal
   d. None of the above

5. The decision-making process is such that
   a. The plans of households and firms are always realized
   b. The plans of households and firms are based on identical objectives
   c. The realization of the plans of firms depends, in part, on decisions made by households
   d. Households and firms must hold frequent meetings to ensure that their plans will be realized

6. Which of the following is correct?
   a. Aggregate expenditure and aggregate demand are synonymous
   b. Aggregate expenditure and aggregate demand are different but related concepts
   c. Aggregate expenditure relates spending to the price level
   d. None of the above

7. In a closed economy without government
   a. Planned *AE* and *AO* must be equal
   b. Planned *AE* must exceed *AO* because there are more consumers than producers
   c. Planned *AO* must exceed *AE* because firms are in charge of production
   d. None of the above

8. In a closed economy without government, aggregate expenditure is
   a. The sum of income and consumption
   b. The sum of consumption and investment
   c. Income plus investment
   d. None of the above

9. If desired aggregate expenditure exceeds current output, we expect
   a. Inventories of finished goods to increase
   b. Inventories to fall below desired levels, causing firms to increase production
   c. Prices to fall to encourage more sales
   d. Firms to reduce their production levels and lay off workers

10. If desired aggregate expenditure is less than current output, we expect
   a. Prices to rise, causing firms to increase their production levels
   b. Inventories to rise above their desired levels, causing firms to reduce their production
   c. Inventories to fall below their desired levels, causing firms to increase their production
   d. None of the above

11. In a closed economy without government, equilibrium income occurs when
   a. Consumption and income are equal
   b. The sum of planned consumption and investment equals total output
   c. Investment and income are equal
   d. Consumption and investment are equal

12. In a closed economy without government, equilibrium income will rise if
   a. Income exceeds consumption
   b. Consumption exceeds investment
   c. Output exceeds the sum of consumption and investment
   d. None of the above

13. If total income increases from $250 billion to $275 billion, and total consumption increases from $200 billion to $220 billion, then the *MPC* is
   a. 0.80
   c. 0.90
   b. 1.25
   d. 1.10

14. If income is below the break-even level, then
  a. $APC > 1$ c. $APC < 1$
  b. $APC = MPC$ d. $APC = 0$

15. When total income rises from $500 million to $600 million, total consumption increases from $400 million to $480 million. From this we know that the *MPS* is
  a. 0.80 c. 0.20
  b. 1.25 d. 0.75

16. Referring to the data in Question 15, indicate which of the following is incorrect:
  a. When income is $500, the *APC* is 0.80
  b. When income is $600, the *APC* is 0.80
  c. When income is $500, the *APS* is 0.80
  d. None of the above

17. The equilibrium level of income is that level that
  a. Produces the maximum output
  b. Indicates where consumers and producers are most happy
  c. Will be maintained unless it is disturbed
  d. Occurs when consumption is at its highest level

18. The break-even level of income occurs where
  a. The *APC* is 1
  b. Saving is zero
  c. The saving line cuts the horizontal (income) axis
  d. All of the above

19. In a closed economy without government, equilibrium income occurs where
  a. The sum of saving and investment equals output
  b. The sum of saving and investment equals consumption
  c. Saving equals investment
  d. All of the above

20. Which of the following is a limitation of the simple Keynesian expenditure model?
  a. It's a demand-side-only model
  b. It deals only with the product market
  c. It assumes that the price level is fixed and that the economy is operating with significant unemployed resources
  d. All of the above

Problems and Exercises (Use Quad Paper for Graphs)

Answers to these questions can be found on MyEconLab at www.myeconlab.com. MyEconLab

1. Table 9.8 shows income and saving data for a simple economy. There is no government spending and there are no taxes. Also, the economy is closed.
  a. Fill in the consumption column.
  b. Graph the saving curve and the consumption curve on the same diagram.
  c. On your graph, indicate the break-even level of income.

Table 9.8 Income and Saving Data

Income ($ mil)	Saving ($ mil)	Consumption ($ mil)
350	–4	
360	0	
370	4	
380	8	
390	12	
400	16	
410	20	

2. Table 9.9 gives data on disposable income and consumption.

Table 9.9 Income and Consumption Data

Income	Consumption	*APC*	*APS*	*MPC*	*MPS*
400	320				
500	400				
600	480				
700	560				
800	640				
900	720				
1 000	800				

  a. Complete the table.
  b. Plot and draw the consumption curve.
  c. alculate the slope of the consumption curve and compare your answer with the MPC.

3. Table 9.10 contains data on disposable income and consumption for a closed economy without government. Autonomous investment is 15.

Table 9.10 Income and Consumption Data

Disposable Income	Consumption	Investment	*AE = C + I*
60	70		
80	85		
100	100		
120	115		
140	130		
160	145		
180	160		
200	175		

a. Complete the table.
b. On graph paper, draw a 45-degree line.
c. On your diagram, draw the consumption curve and the *AE* line, and indicate the equilibrium level of income.

4. The data shown in Table 9.11 are for a closed economy without government.

Table 9.11 Consumption and Income Data

Income	Consumption	Saving	*AE*
400	420		
500	500		
600	580		
700	660		
800	740		
900	820		
1 000	900		

a. Complete the saving column.
b. If investment is fixed at 40 for every level of income, what is the equilibrium level of income?
c. With investment constant at 40, complete the *AE* column.
d. At what level of income does aggregate expenditure equal aggregate output? Compare this with your answer for part (b).

5. Table 9.12 gives data for a hypothetical economy without government and without foreign trade.

Table 9.12 Saving and Investment Data for a Hypothetical Economy

Income	Saving	Investment
60	–10	15
80	–5	15
100	0	15
120	5	15
140	10	15
160	15	15
180	20	15
200	25	15

a. On a graph, draw the saving curve and the investment line.
b. On your graph, indicate the break-even level of income.
c. On your graph, indicate the equilibrium level of income.
d. Calculate the slope of the saving curve.

6. The data in Table 9.13 are for a hypothetical economy without government and without foreign trade. (Y = income, C = consumption, S = saving, I = investment, and AE = aggregate expenditure)

Table 9.13 Data for a Hypothetical Economy

Y	*C*	*S*	*I*	*AE*
60	70			
80	80			
100	90			
120	100			
140	110			
160	120			
180	130			
200	140			

a. Complete the saving column.
b. If autonomous investment is 30, complete the investment column and the *AE* column.
c. On the basis of the data contained in Table 9.13, draw an *AE–AO* (Keynesian cross) diagram lined up with *J–W* diagram (saving and investment) to show both approaches to equilibrium income determination.

7. Figure 9.11 shows consumer and investment spending in a closed economy without government spending.

Figure 9.11 Consumer and Investment Spending

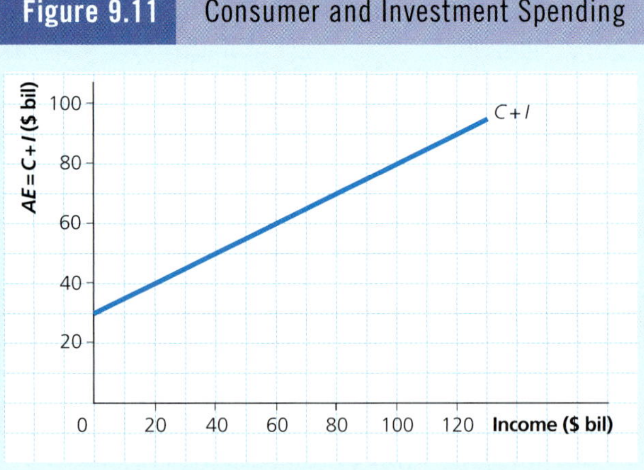

a. What is planned aggregate expenditure when income is $120 billion?
b. What is intended aggregate expenditure when income is $40 billion?
c. Indicate the equilibrium level of income.
d. If income is $120 billion, explain the process by which equilibrium is achieved.
e. What is autonomous spending?

Appendix

9A Income Determination

A Simple Mathematical Model of Income Determination

So far in this text, we have not had to rely on any advanced mathematics in studying economics. Does this appendix require any mathematics beyond elementary algebra?

This mathematical appendix does not require any mathematics beyond elementary algebra. Our intention is to show how simple mathematical tools can be used to explain the Keynesian model. This appendix should familiarize you with the simple mathematics of income determination within the simple Keynesian framework.

Is this a different theory of income determination from the simple Keynesian model?

This presentation is not a different theory of income determination. It is the same theory presented earlier in the chapter, but the analytical tools are different. Here, we also assume that we are dealing with a closed economy and that government neither spends nor taxes.

Can we arrive at the equilibrium level of income without using tables or graphs?

That is precisely what we are going to do in this appendix. Let us begin with the consumption function.

The Consumption Function If we assume that disposable income is the only determinant of consumption, then, using the functional notation, we can express the consumption function as

$$C = C(Y_d) \qquad (1)$$

where C is consumption and Y_d is disposable income.

> The consumption function is an equation that expresses the direct relationship between consumption and disposable income.

Let us assume that the relationship between consumption and disposable income is linear. The consumption-income relation can then be expressed as:

$$C = a + bY_d,\ a > 0,\ b > 0 \tag{2}$$

Here, the value of a represents the amount of consumption that will take place when income is zero. In other words, a is autonomous consumption, and b is the slope of the consumption curve or the marginal propensity to consume. Because we assume a linear relation between C and Y_d, b is constant.

Autonomous consumption is consumption that is independent of current income.

The consumption function, for example, could be expressed by the following equation:

$$C = 30 + 0.5Y_d \tag{3}$$

Here, 30 is autonomous consumption and $0.5Y_d$ is induced consumption.

The Investment Function We assume that investment is a fixed amount each period and does not vary with the level of income.

How can autonomous investment be represented by a function when it does not depend on the level on income?

Because investment is assumed to be autonomous, we can express the investment function as

$$I = I_a \tag{4}$$

where I_a is a fixed amount. For example, investment could be expressed as

$$I = 20 \tag{5}$$

On a graph, equation (5) would be represented as a horizontal straight line.

Determination of the Equilibrium Level of Income

How do we determine the equilibrium level of income from these equations and functions?

We know that the equilibrium level of income occurs where desired aggregate expenditure equals aggregate output. This equilibrium condition can be expressed as

$$Y_d = C + I \tag{6}$$

We can now collect all the equations to show the complete model:

$$C = a + bY_d \tag{7}$$

$$I = I_a \tag{8}$$

$$Y_d = C + I \tag{9}$$

By solving these equations for Y_d, we can obtain the equilibrium value of Y_d. Thus,

$$Y_d = C + I \tag{10}$$

But

$$C = a + bY_d \tag{11}$$

By substituting $a + bY_d$ for C in equation (10), we obtain

$$Y_d = a + bY_d + I \tag{12}$$

By transposing, we obtain

$$Y_d - bY_d = a + I \tag{13}$$

By factoring, we obtain

$$Y_d(1 - b) = a + I \tag{14}$$

$$Y_d = \frac{a + I}{1 - b} \tag{15}$$

But $a + I$ is autonomous expenditure
consisting of autonomous consumption and autonomous investment. If we use A to denote autonomous expenditure, we can rewrite equation (15) as

$$Y_d = \frac{A}{1 - b} = \frac{1}{1 - b} \times A \tag{16}$$

For example, consider the following set of equations.

$$C = 30 + 0.5Y_d$$

$$I = 20$$

The equilibrium condition is given by

$$Y_d = C + I$$

Here, $A = 50$ (autonomous consumption of 30 + autonomous investment of 20) and $b = 0.5$. Therefore,

The equilibrium level of income is therefore 100.

$$Y_d = \frac{A}{1 - b} = \frac{50}{1 - 0.5} = 100$$

Problems and Exercises

1. You are given the following consumption equation: $C = 16 + 0.7Y_d$.
   a. What is autonomous consumption?
   b. What is the *MPC*?
   c. If autonomous investment is 15, what is autonomous expenditure?
2. Suppose the consumption function is given by the equation $C = 8 + 0.8Y_d$.
   a. What is the *MPS*?
   b. What is autonomous consumption?
3. If the *MPC* in an economy is 0.9 and autonomous expenditure is 25, what is the equilibrium level of income?

4. If consumption in a certain economy is given by $C = 12 + 0.8Y_d$, what is consumption when disposable income is the following?
   a. 80
   b. 100
   c. 120
5. If consumption is $C = 15 + 0.9Y_d$, what is the break-even level of disposable income?
6. Use each of the following sets of equations to determine the equilibrium level of income.
   a. $C = 10 + 0.5Y_d$
      $I = 30$
   b. $C = 8 + 0.8Y_d$
      $I = 10$
   c. $C = 4 + 0.9Y_d$
      $I = 10$
7. You are given the following consumption equation: $C = 20 + 0.8Y_d$. Autonomous investment is 8.
   a. Complete the consumption (C) and AE schedules in Table 9A.1.
   b. Use your schedules to determine the equilibrium level of income.
   c. Prove your answer mathematically.

Table 9.A1 Consumption and *AE* Schedules

Y_d	C	I	$AE = C + I$
0			
20			
40			
60			
80			
100			
120			
140			
160			

Chapter 10

Changes in Income and the Multiplier

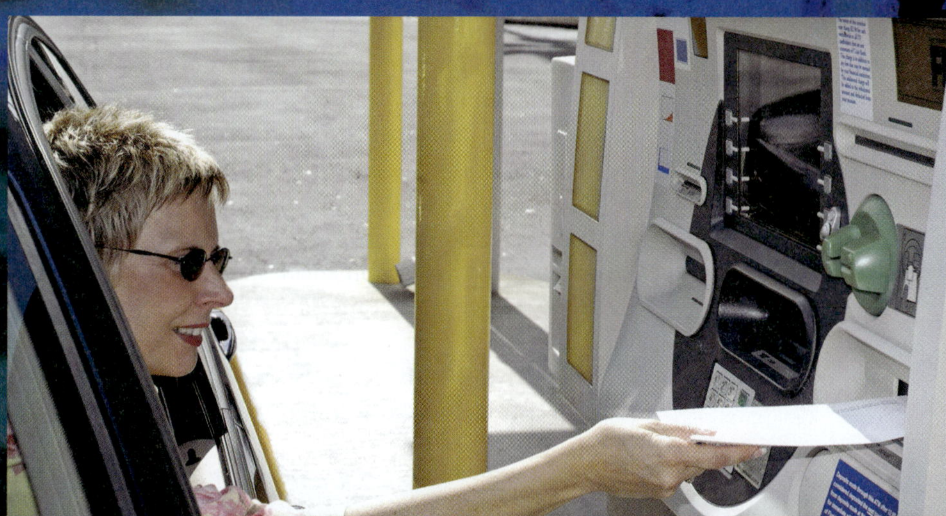

Learning Objectives

After studying this chapter, you should be able to

10.1 Discuss the effects of changes in investment on the equilibrium level of income

10.2 Understand the effects of changes in saving on the equilibrium level of income

10.3 Understand the concept of the multiplier and its relationship with the *MPC* and the *MPS*

10.4 Explain the inflationary and deflationary gaps and understand the need for active economic policy to close them

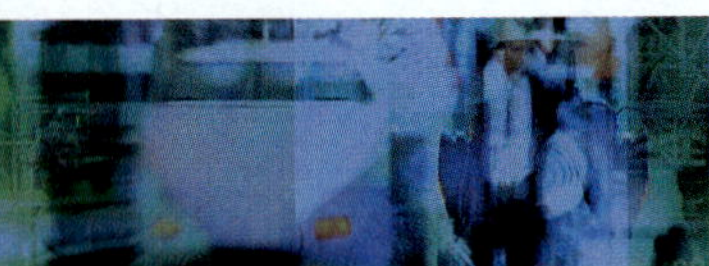

Assess Your Knowledge

MyEconLab

Answers to these questions can be found on MyEconLab at **www.myeconlab.com.**

1. What effect will an increase in investment have on the equilibrium level of income?
2. Is it possible for an initial increase in spending of $5 million to result in an increase in income of more than $5 million?
3. Can an increase in planned aggregate saving ultimately result in a fall in actual saving?

LO 10.1 Discuss the effects of changes in investment on the equilibrium level of income

The Income Effects of Changes in Investment

We already know that an increase in investment will increase the equilibrium level of income. Does an increase in investment do more than that?

The fact that an increase in investment, other things being equal, will increase the equilibrium level of income is only a part of the story. Consider the saving and investment schedules in Table 10.1.

At a level of investment of $10 million, the equilibrium level of income is $80 million. Now, suppose that firms decide to invest $20 million instead of the original $10 million. The decision to increase investment spending could be influenced by factors such as optimistic business outlook, lower costs of borrowing money for investment purposes, tax concessions given to businesses, etc. Note that investment is still autonomous, not affected by changes in income. How will this increase in investment affect the equilibrium level of income?

When investment increases to $20 million, the level of income at which saving equals investment is $100 million—an increase of $20 million over the initial level. Thus, an increase in investment of $10 million has generated an even greater increase in income—$20 million. (The mechanism through which this occurs will be discussed below.) Note that if investment had fallen to only $5 million, total income would have fallen from its initial level of $80 million to $70 million. Thus, a given reduction in investment generates an even greater reduction in the equilibrium level of income.

Table 10.1 Saving and Investment Schedules (hypothetical data, $ mil)

Income	Consumption	Saving	Original Level of Investment	New Level of Investment
40	50	–10	10	20
50	55	–5	10	20
60	60	0	10	20
70	65	5	10	20
80	70	10	10	20
90	75	15	10	20
100	**80**	**20**	**10**	**20**
110	85	25	10	20
120	90	30	10	20

A change in investment, other things being equal, will result in an even greater change in equilibrium income.

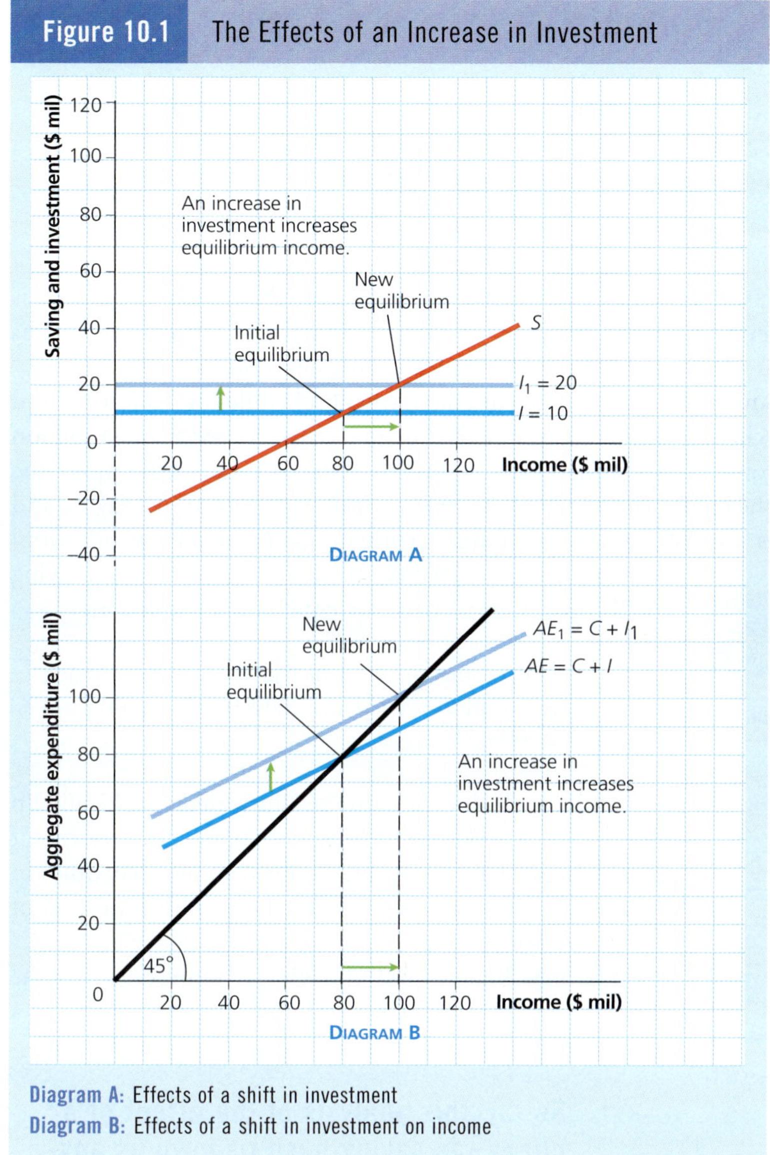

Diagram A: Effects of a shift in investment
Diagram B: Effects of a shift in investment on income

Can the effect of a change in investment on the equilibrium level of income be illustrated graphically?

Look at Figure 10.1.

In Diagram A of Figure 10.1, *S* and *I* are the initial saving and investment lines respectively. The initial equilibrium level of income is $80 million—where the *S* and *I* lines intersect. The new level of investment is represented by I_1. The new investment line intersects the saving line at a level of income of $100 million.

The effects of changes in investment on the equilibrium level of income can also be illustrated by the *AE–AO* diagram. In Diagram B of Figure 10.1, the initial equilibrium level of income is shown to be $80 million—where *AE* and the 45-degree line intersect. The increase in autonomous investment causes the *AE* line to shift to AE_1. The new equilibrium level of income is now $100 million.

You should now work through the same exercise to demonstrate the effect on income of a reduction in investment.

Note that throughout the analysis, we assume that the saving–income relationship remains unchanged; thus, the saving line does not shift.

Reading Comprehension

The answers to these questions can be found on MyEconLab at www.myeconlab.com. MyEconLab

1. What effect will an increase in investment have on the equilibrium level of income?
2. Why might firms decide to increase their investment spending?
3. How is an increase in investment shown on (a) a savings–investment graph? (b) an aggregate expenditure–aggregate output graph?

LO 10.2 Understand the effects of changes in saving on the equilibrium level of income

The Income Effects of Changes in Saving

We have learned that an increase in saving results in a reduction in equilibrium income, other things being equal. Why? Saving is a withdrawal. Is there more to saving than that?

In this analysis, we are considering changes in saving resulting from changes in non-income determinants. Hence, an increase in saving means that at any given level of income, a greater amount is saved. A decrease in saving means that a smaller amount is saved out of any given level of income. Thus, a change in saving in this context means that the entire saving schedule changes—or that the saving curve shifts.

paradox of thrift or paradox of saving the apparent contradiction in the fact that an increase in intended aggregate saving results in a decrease in actual saving

Table 10.2 reproduces the initial saving and investment schedules of Table 10.1, and shows a new saving schedule, which has resulted from an increase in saving of $5 million at each level of income. We assume that investment remains fixed throughout the analysis. Recall that the equilibrium level of income generated by the original saving and investment schedules was $80 million. With the increase in saving, the new equilibrium level of income is $70 million (where the new level of saving equals investment). Thus, we conclude the following:

Table 10.2 Saving and Investment Schedules (hypothetical data, $ mil)

Income	Initial Saving	New Saving	Investment
40	−10	−5	10
50	−5	0	10
60	0	5	10
70	**5**	**10**	**10**
80	10	15	10
90	15	20	10
100	20	25	10
110	25	30	10
120	30	35	10

> Other things being equal, a given increase in saving results in an even greater reduction in equilibrium income.

This conclusion can also be illustrated graphically. In Figure 10.2, S and I are the original saving and investment lines derived from the saving and investment schedules in Table 10.2. They intersect to give the equilibrium level of income of $80 million.

The new higher level of saving is represented by the saving curve S_1, which intersects the investment line at a level of income of $70 million.

Figure 10.2 The Effect of an Increase in Saving

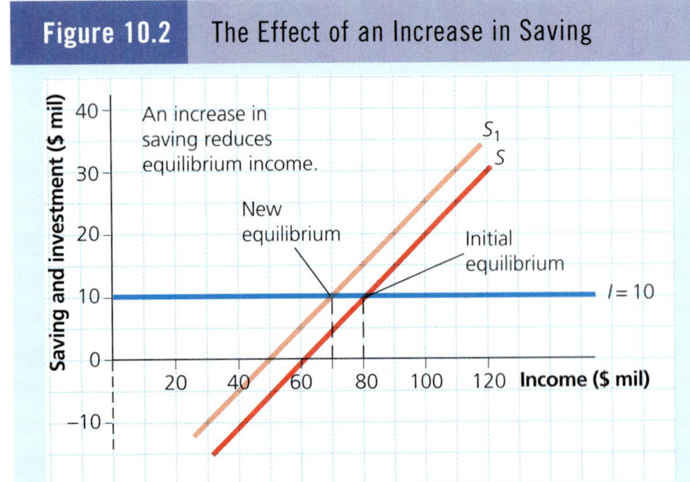

So far, this analysis of the effect of a change in saving hasn't shown us anything new.

But now let's look at something new—a paradox—a statement that is apparently or intuitively contradictory on the surface, but that on closer examination is true. In this case, the paradox is about thrift or saving.

The Paradox of Thrift You have seen that an increase in saving, other things being equal, results in a fall in income. You know also that when income falls, saving also falls. This rather interesting result has been termed the **paradox of thrift** or the **paradox of saving**. The paradox of thrift states that an increase in intended aggregate saving, other things being equal, will lead to a fall in total income and hence to a fall in actual aggregate saving. The paradox of thrift can be defined as the apparent contradiction in the fact that an increase in intended aggregate saving results in a decrease in actual saving. Note that the statement appears to be totally contradictory if the words "intended aggregate" and "actual" are omitted.

The paradox of thrift has another dimension. Saving by individuals makes them better off in the future (provided that inflation does not severely reduce the value of their saving) and is therefore considered a virtue. But from an economy-wide point of view, thrift may be considered a social vice, because it makes the entire economy worse off in the future.

Can the paradox of thrift be illustrated graphically?

induced investment investment that varies with the level of income

To do this, we relax our assumption that investment is independent of income and assume instead that investment is induced by changes in income. Thus, investment increases as income increases. Investment that varies with income is called **induced investment**. Induced investment is investment that varies with the level of income.

In Figure 10.3, the investment curve I is upward sloping, indicating that as income increases, investment also increases. The saving curve has the usual shape.

The saving curve S and the investment curve I intersect at E, where the equilibrium level of income is $0Y$. The saving curve S_1 represents the higher level of saving. As a result of the increase in saving, the equilibrium level of income falls from $0Y$ to $0Y_0$. Note that the new level of saving, Y_0A, is less than the initial level, YE. Now you can try to demonstrate graphically the effect of a reduction in aggregate saving on the equilibrium level of income.

Figure 10.3 Illustration of the Paradox of Thrift

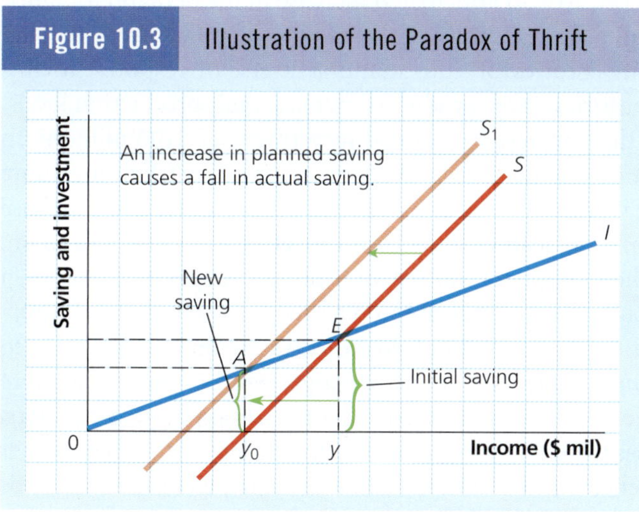

Before we leave the paradox of thrift, we should draw your attention to the following observations. First, the paradox of thrift applies to a situation in which aggregate saving increases with no offsetting changes in investment. Other things were assumed to be constant. Second, we have examined only the effects of changes in investment and saving on the equilibrium level of income. But, in fact, our analysis can be extended to include any injection and any withdrawal. An increase in total injections will tend to increase income. An increase in total withdrawals will tend to reduce total income. Stated somewhat differently, anything that causes the AE curve to shift upward will increase the equilibrium level of income; anything that causes it to shift downward will reduce the equilibrium level of income.

BUSINESS SITUATION 10.1

Statistics Canada has just announced that, over the past two years, saving by consumers has increased and that this increase in saving is likely to continue for at least another two years.

Why might businesspeople see this as good news?

The answer to this Business Situation can be found in Appendix A.

Reading Comprehension

The answers to these questions can be found on MyEconLab at www.myeconlab.com. MyEconLab

1. What would happen to the equilibrium level of income in Canada if Canadians increased their saving?
2. Carefully explain the paradox of thrift.
3. Explain why saving might be good on an individual level but not necessarily good on an economy-wide level.

LO 10.3 Understand the concept of the multiplier and its relationship with the *MPC* and the *MPS*

The Multiplier

What is the process by which a change in spending generates a change in income that is greater than the change in spending?

multiplier effect the ultimate change in equilibrium income is greater than the change in spending that caused it

In discussing the effect of an increase in investment on the equilibrium level of income, we noted that in the particular case examined, an increase in investment of $10 million led to an increase in income of $20 million. Let us now examine, in some detail, the curious result known as the **multiplier effect**. The multiplier effect is the result that the ultimate change in equilibrium income is greater than the change in spending that caused it.

Suppose that there is an increase in expenditure of $100 million on investment goods. This may come about because of an anticipated increase in the demand for automobiles. Automobile dealers will purchase more cars from auto manufacturers, causing an unplanned decline in the inventories of auto manufacturers. In response to this unplanned decline in their inventories, these producers increase their production levels.

Now, what is the effect of this increase in planned investment of $100 million? To manufacture additional automobiles, the automobile producers must employ more workers or require the existing workers to put in more hours. They must also purchase more steel, more tires, more tin, more leather or fabric, more electrical parts, and so on. The auto manufacturers and their suppliers will pay out more in wages and salaries, a part of which will be spent, resulting in an increase in planned aggregate expenditure.

What happens then is that extra production leads to extra income, which leads to additional spending on consumer goods and services. People will buy more furniture and household appliances, more television and stereo sets, more shoes, more computers, more clothes, and more suitcases to go on more vacation trips. Sellers of these consumer goods and services will experience an unplanned decline in their inventories, and this will cause them to place new orders. This will result in a further increase in production and further increases in income in the manner explained earlier.

Very interesting! We would hardly have thought of it that way.

What should be clear from our analysis so far is that an increase in planned investment results in an increase in output and expenditure that is greater than the initial investment. But by how much greater is the increase in income? This depends on the amount of additional spending that occurs out of additional income. In other words, it depends on the marginal propensity to consume.

Table 10.3 The Multiplier Process

Expenditure ($ mil)			Income Generated ($ mil)
Initial increase in spending	=	100.00	100.00
2nd round spending = (0.8 × 100)	=	80.00	80.00
3rd round spending = (0.8 × 80)	=	64.00	64.00
4th round spending = (0.8 × 64)	=	51.20	51.20
5th round spending = (0.8 × 51.20)	=	40.96	40.96
6th round spending = (0.8 × 40.96)	=	32.77	32.77
etc.			
TOTAL (all rounds)	=		500.00

Can this process be demonstrated arithmetically?

Let us suppose that the economy's marginal propensity to consume (*MPC*) is constant at 0.8. If firms initially spend $100 million, then under this assumption, this initial spending will stimulate a second round of spending of $80 million (0.8 of $100 million). This additional spending will result in another increase in income, which will again lead to additional expenditure, and so on. The process is demonstrated in Table 10.3.

Because the initial increase in investment of $100 million leads to an increase in total income of $500 million, we say that the multiplier is 5. A formula for finding the total income generated will be presented shortly.

Can the multiplier effect be illustrated graphically?

Graphical Illustration of the Multiplier Effect In Figure 10.4, S and I are the initial saving and investment lines. The equilibrium level of income associated with these levels of saving and investment is Y. The diagram shows that an increase in investment from I to I_1 causes income to increase from Y to Y_1.

Note that the change in income is greater than the change in investment that generated it. The number by which the change in spending is multiplied to get the change in income is called the **multiplier**. If an initial investment of $10 causes income to increase by $30, then the multiplier is 3.

multiplier the number by which a change in spending is multiplied to arrive at the change in income

The multiplier can be calculated from the following formula:

$$\text{Multiplier} = \frac{\Delta Y}{\Delta I} = \frac{Y_1 - Y}{}$$

The arithmetic demonstration of the multiplier process suggests a relationship between the multiplier and the *MPC*.

Figure 10.4 Illustration of the Multiplier Effect

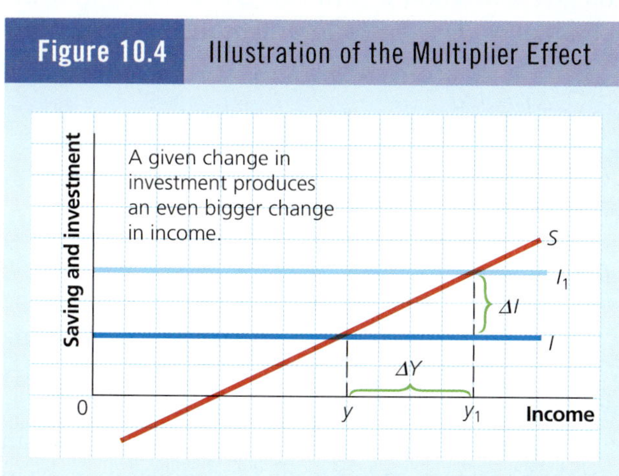

Relation among the Multiplier, the *MPC*, and the *MPS* It is evident that if the marginal propensity to consume in Table 10.3 were greater than 0.8, the increase in income would be greater than $500 million. In other words, the value of the multiplier would be greater than 5. We have just defined the multiplier as the change in income divided by the change in investment. That is, the multiplier is

$$\frac{\Delta Y}{\Delta I}$$

If we use k to represent the multiplier, then $k = \Delta Y/\Delta I$, from which we obtain

$$\Delta Y = k\Delta I$$

Refer to Figure 10.4 and you will observe that the slope of the saving line, which is the *MPS*, is

$$\frac{\Delta I}{\Delta Y}$$

Hence, the multiplier is the inverse of the marginal propensity to save:

$$\text{Multiplier} = \frac{1}{MPS}$$

The multiplier is the reciprocal of the *MPS*.

Because $MPC + MPS = 1$, it follows that $MPS = 1 - MPC$. Hence, the formula for the multiplier can be expressed as follows:

$$\text{Multiplier} = \frac{1}{1 - MPS}$$

For example, given a marginal propensity to consume of 7/9, the marginal propensity to save would be

$$1 - \frac{7}{9} = \frac{2}{9}$$

And the multiplier would be $9/2 = 4.5$.

Example 1: In a certain economy, the *MPC* is 5/8. What effect will an increase in investment expenditure of $54 million have on the equilibrium level of income?

Solution: Because the *MPC* is 5/8, the *MPS* is 3/8. The multiplier (k) is then 8/3. We need to find the change in income (ΔY). The change in income (ΔY) is given by:

$$\begin{aligned}\Delta Y &= k\Delta I \\ &= 8/3 \times \$54 = \$144 \text{ million}\end{aligned}$$

Therefore, income will increase by $144 million.

Example 2: You are told that consumers spend 4/7 of every extra dollar they receive. How will an investment expenditure of $105 million affect the level of income in that economy?

Solution: From the information given, we know that the *MPC* is 4/7. Therefore the *MPS* is $1–4/7 = 3/7$. Since the multiplier (k) is the reciprocal of the *MPS*, we know that $k = 7/3$.

$$\Delta Y = k\Delta I$$

But $\Delta I = \$105$ million, therefore

$$\Delta Y = 7/3 \times \$105 = \$245 \text{ million}$$

Income will increase by $245 million.

It is easy to see that the smaller the marginal propensity to save, the larger the multiplier will be. Mathematically, the *MPS* measures the slope (steepness) of the saving curve. The steeper the saving curve (that is, the higher the *MPS*), the less the multiplier effect will be. Figure 10.5 shows two saving curves, S and S_1, with different slopes.

With the less steep saving curve S, an increase in investment from I to I_1 causes an increase in income from Y_3 to Y_4. With the steeper saving curve S_1, a similar increase in investment causes a much lower increase in income—from Y_1 to Y_2.

Figure 10.5 The Effect of an Increase in Investment with Saving Lines of Different Slopes

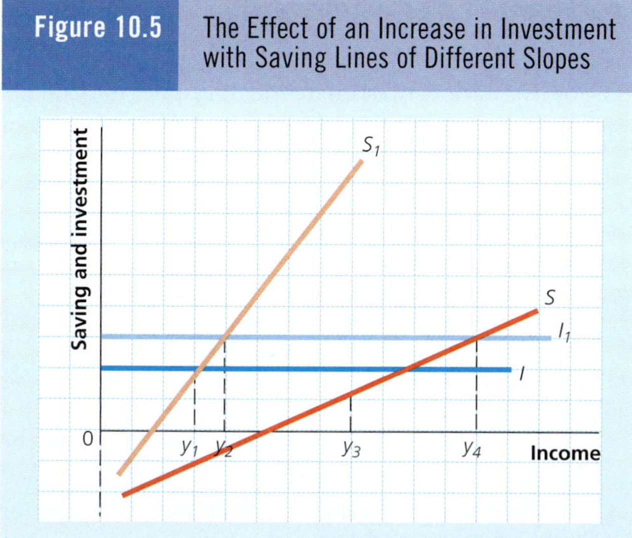

The flatter the saving curve, the greater the multiplier effect.

How realistic is this multiplier?

The discussion of the multiplier so far assumes that saving is the only withdrawal from the income–expenditure stream. But, in fact, as you learned earlier, taxes and imports are also withdrawals from the flow of income and expenditure. We need to consider a more realistic multiplier.

A More Realistic Multiplier When we consider all the withdrawals in an economy, we have to modify the formula for the simple multiplier. The simple multiplier (1/*MPS*) will no longer be valid. The fraction of extra income allocated to saving, taxes, and imports can be termed the **marginal propensity to withdraw** (*MPW*), which can be expressed as

marginal propensity to withdraw the fraction of extra income allocated to saving, taxes, and imports

$$MPW = \frac{\Delta W}{\Delta Y}$$

The marginal propensity to withdraw is the fraction of extra income allocated to savings, taxes, and imports (withdrawals).

This formula for the more realistic multiplier, sometimes called the **generalized multiplier**, is

generalized multiplier the multiplier that results from considering all withdrawals; the reciprocal of the marginal propensity to withdraw

$$\frac{1}{MPW}$$

The generalized multiplier is the multiplier that results from considering all withdrawals. It is the reciprocal of the marginal propensity to withdraw. The generalized multiplier is smaller than the simple multiplier because some portion of income is allocated to taxes and imports.

Table 10.4 Estimating the Multiplier for Canada, 2003–2004

Item	Value ($ bil)
Change in GDP (ΔY)	74.0
Change in withdrawals (ΔW)	36.3

Calculation:

$$\text{MPW} = \frac{\Delta W}{\Delta Y} = \frac{36.3}{74.0} = 0.4905$$

$$\text{Multiplier} = \frac{1}{0.4905} = 2.04$$

Is it possible to estimate the multiplier for Canada?

If we can determine the change in total withdrawals and the change in income during a specific period, we can estimate the multiplier for Canada.

Estimating the Multiplier for Canada Between 2003 and 2004, the GDP of Canada increased by $74 billion. In the same period, total withdrawals changed by $36.3 billion. Details are presented in Table 10.4.

The marginal propensity to withdraw, as shown in Table 10.4, is 0.4905. Because the multiplier is the reciprocal of the marginal propensity to withdraw, then an estimate of the multiplier for Canada (2003–2004) is 2.04.

How does this estimate compare with other estimates of the multiplier for Canada?

The Bank of Canada and other economists variously estimate the multiplier for Canada in a range from 1.2 to 3.0. Therefore, our estimate is consistent with other estimates of the multiplier for Canada.

Reading Comprehension

The answers to these questions can be found on MyEconLab at www.myeconlab.com. MyEconLab

1. What is the multiplier? Briefly explain how it works.
2. What is the relationship between the *MPC*, the *MPS*, and the multiplier in a simple closed economy in which government neither spends nor imposes taxes?
3. Explain why the reciprocal of the *MPS* would not be an accurate measure of the multiplier for Canada.
4. Explain how you would estimate the multiplier for Canada.

LO 10.4 Explain the inflationary and deflationary gaps and understand the need for active economic policy to close them

The Full-Employment Gaps

In our study of the AD–AS model, we learned that an economy can be in short-run equilibrium at the full-employment level of GDP, above the full-employment level of GDP, or below the full-employment level of GDP. Are we going to pursue this issue?

We know that if desired total spending exceeds total output, firms will expand production. Total income will then increase. Conversely, if intended aggregate expenditure falls short of aggregate output, firms will reduce production. Total income will then fall. When equilibrium is reached, as your comment correctly observes, it may not necessarily be at the full-employment level of output. These conclusions were based on the assumption that the economy's resources were not fully employed and that output could expand without any appreciable increase in the price level. In other words, we assumed that the economy was operating in the horizontal section of the *AS* curve.

We will now examine situations in which aggregate expenditure exceeds or falls short of the full-employment level of output. To do so, we relax the restrictions that the economy operates with a constant price level and that output is below the full-employment level. Our analysis applies to the short run.

Is there a term that describes the situation in which aggregate expenditure exceeds aggregate output at full employment?

The term used is *inflationary gap*. Let us examine that situation.

The Inflationary Gap Consider a situation in which the economy's resources are fully employed and aggregate expenditure exceeds that full-employment level of output. In such a situation, real output tends to be stable because it can expand only slightly

Table 10.5 Aggregate Expenditure and Aggregate Output (hypothetical data, $ mil)

Output	Consumption	Aggregate Investment	Expenditure
40	50	10	60
50	55	10	65
60	60	10	70
70	65	10	75
80	70	10	80
90	75	10	85
100	80	10	90
110	85	10	95
120	90	10	100

beyond the full-employment level. Prices, however, will tend to move upward. Let us analyze the situation with the help of Table 10.5, which shows desired aggregate expenditure and aggregate output for a simple closed economy with no government spending or taxation.

The equilibrium level of income is $80 million where intended aggregate expenditure equals aggregate output. Now, let us suppose that the full-employment level of output is $60 million. At that level of output, desired aggregate expenditure is $70 million. Desired consumption and investment spending together exceed the full-employment output. There is a gap of $10 million between aggregate expenditure and the full-employment level of output, which exerts upward pressure on prices. Prices then tend to rise. This gap is referred to as an inflationary gap. The **inflationary gap** is the amount by which desired aggregate expenditure exceeds aggregate output at full employment.

inflationary gap the amount by which desired aggregate expenditure exceeds aggregate output at full employment

output gap the difference between the potential output and the actual output of an economy

income gap the difference between the equilibrium level of income and the full-employment level of income

In our example, intended aggregate expenditure would have to fall by $10 million to reach the full-employment level of output. Note that the inflationary gap of $10 million with a multiplier of 2 will cause income to increase by $20 million (from $60 million to $80 million). Of course, this increase is not in real terms but in nominal terms. It is due to inflation of prices.

Can the inflationary gap be illustrated by the Keynesian cross diagram?

Look at Figure 10.6.

At the full-employment level of output (Y_f = $60 million), intended aggregate expenditure exceeds full-employment aggregate output by GH; hence, GH is the inflationary gap. The gap between the full-employment level of output, Y_f, and the equilibrium level of output, Y, is the **output gap**. You can also measure this same gap in terms of income: the difference between the equilibrium level of income and the full-employment level of income. This is known as the **income gap**.

Figure 10.6 Graphical Illustration of the Inflationary Gap

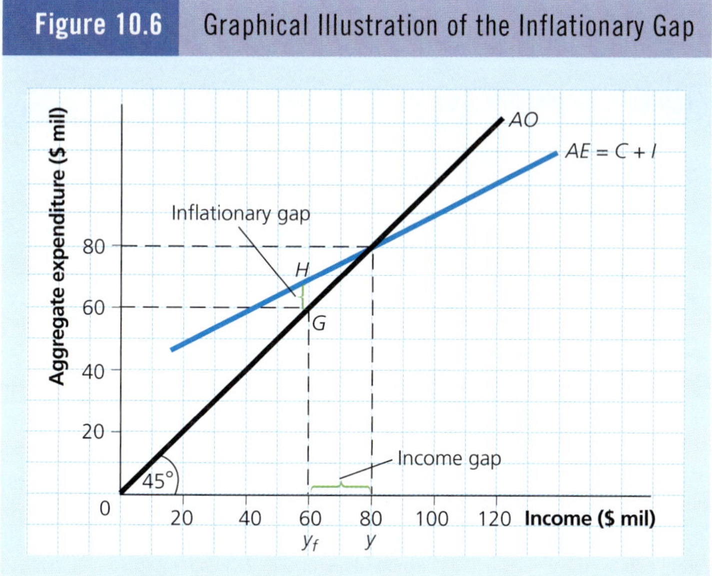

What term is used to describe the situation where aggregate expenditure is less than aggregate output at full employment?

We refer to this situation as either a *deflationary gap* or a *recessionary gap*. Let's examine the situation.

In a deflationary gap situation, an economy's resources will not be fully employed, and prices may even fall. This describes a deflationary situation—a situation of falling prices. But we are likely to witness a reduction in production levels and an increase in unemployment much sooner than a fall in prices. For this reason, the term *recessionary gap* is preferred, and we will use it in this text.

Figure 10.7 Graphical Illustration of the Recessionary Gap

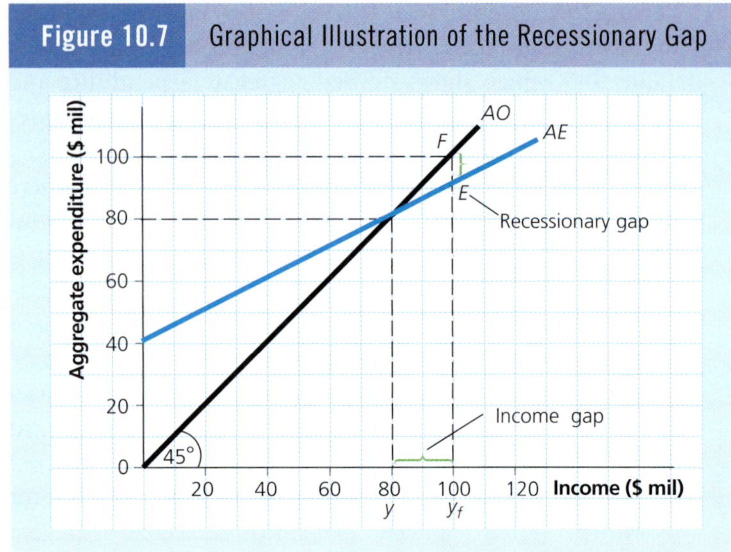

Let us return for a moment to Table 10.5. Suppose that the full-employment level of output is $100 million. At that level of output, desired aggregate expenditure is $90 million. Because total intended spending falls short of the full-employment output, the economy cannot attain its full-employment level of output, so some resources are unemployed. There is a **deflationary gap** or a **recessionary gap**. The recessionary gap is the amount by which aggregate expenditure falls short of aggregate output at full employment.

In our example, aggregate expenditure would have to increase by $10 million to reach the full-employment level of output; hence, the size of the recessionary gap is $10 million. Note that a recessionary gap of $10 million with a multiplier of 2 gives a $20 million difference between the full-employment output of $100 million and the equilibrium level of income of $80 million.

deflationary gap or recessionary gap the amount by which aggregate expenditure falls short of aggregate output at full employment

Can the recessionary gap be illustrated graphically?

Let's consider Figure 10.7.

At the full-employment level of output (Y_f = $100 million), desired aggregate expenditure falls short of the full-employment output by *EF*. Thus, *EF* is the recessionary gap.

How can these gaps be closed or narrowed?

The Need for Macroeconomic Policy Closing or reducing inflationary and recessionary gaps is a matter for macroeconomic policy. Let's see how policy can be used to move the economy from an undesirable state to a more desirable state. Figure 10.8 will help with the analysis.

Figure 10.8 Closing the Full-Employment Gaps

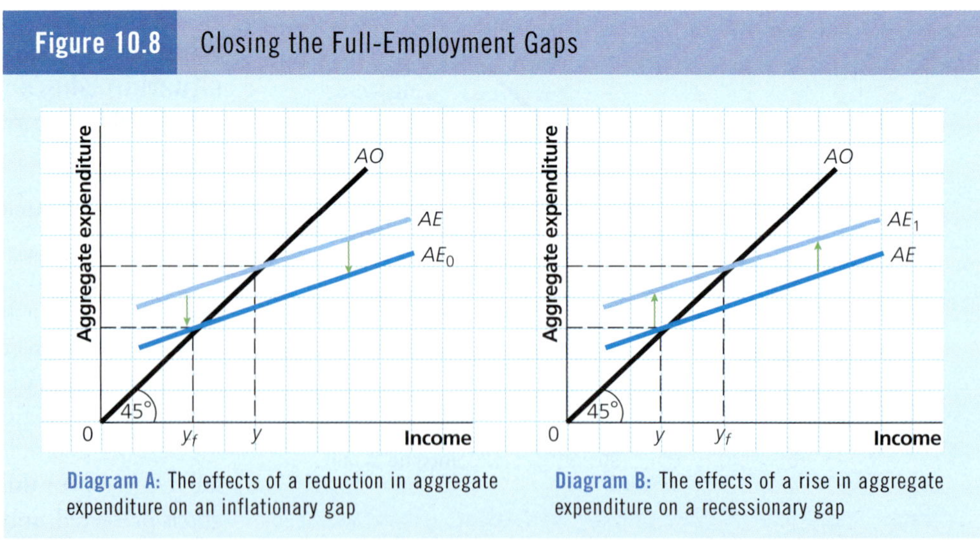

Diagram A: The effects of a reduction in aggregate expenditure on an inflationary gap

Diagram B: The effects of a rise in aggregate expenditure on a recessionary gap

In the inflationary gap situation shown in Diagram A of Figure 10.8, there is a need for macroeconomic policy that will reduce desired aggregate expenditure from AE to AE_0 and thus eliminate the gap. Desired aggregate expenditure will then exactly equal the full-employment output. Equilibrium will occur at full employment without inflation.

In the recessionary gap situation shown in Diagram B of Figure 10.8, there is a need for macroeconomic policy that will raise the desired aggregate expenditure curve from AE to AE_1. Equilibrium will then occur at the full-employment level, and there will be no inflation.

During the recent global recession, the recessionary gap for Canada was relatively wide. That is, the difference between full-employment output and aggregate expenditure was unusually large. The government implemented programs that resulted in increases in spending in an attempt to narrow the gap between full-employment output and aggregate expenditure. Details of appropriate macroeconomic policies designed to change desired aggregate expenditure will be discussed in subsequent chapters.

Reading Comprehension

The answers to these questions can be found on MyEconLab at **www.myeconlab.com**. MyEconLab

1. Explain how full-employment gaps (inflationary gaps and recessionary gaps) can originate.
2. What is the difference between the inflationary gap and the recessionary gap?
3. What is the difference between the recessionary gap and the output or income gap?
4. What is the implication of the full-employment gaps for macroeconomic policy?

Review

1. Review the learning objectives listed at the beginning of the chapter.
2. Have you accomplished all the objectives? One way to determine this is to answer the Reading Comprehension Questions at the end of each section. This will help you assess the extent to which you have accomplished the learning objectives.
3. If you have not accomplished an objective, review the relevant material before proceeding.

Key Points to Remember

1. **LO 10.1** A given change in investment will generate an even greater change in the equilibrium level of income.
2. **LO 10.2** The paradox of thrift refers to the fact that an increase in desired aggregate saving, other things being equal, leads to a fall in total income and hence to a fall in actual aggregate saving.
3. **LO 10.3** The multiplier effect refers to the fact that an increase in spending generates an even greater increase in equilibrium income. For a simple closed economy with neither government spending nor taxation, the multiplier is the reciprocal of the *MPS*. More generally, the multiplier is the reciprocal of the marginal propensity to withdraw (*MPW*). The marginal propensity to withdraw in Canada in 2003–2004 was approximately 0.49. This allows us to estimate the multiplier for Canada to be 2.04.

4. LO 10.4 The inflationary gap is the amount by which aggregate expenditure exceeds aggregate output at full employment. When an inflationary gap exists, prices will tend to rise.The recessionary gap is the amount by which aggregate expenditure falls short of aggregate output at full employment. When a recessionary gap exists, output and employment will tend to fall. Depending on the size of the gap, prices may also fall.
5. LO 10.5 Macroeconomic policy can be used to shift the aggregate expenditure curve and thus close inflationary and recessionary gaps.

Economic Word Power

Deflationary gap or recessionary gap (p. 274)
Generalized multiplier (p. 271)
Income gap (p. 273)
Induced investment (p. 267)
Inflationary gap (p. 273)
Marginal propensity to withdraw (p. 271)
Multiplier (p. 269)
Multiplier effect (p. 268)
Output gap (p. 273)
Paradox of thrift or paradox of saving (p. 266)

Problems and Exercises

Basic

1. LO 10.1 Table 10.6 contains data on income, saving, and investment.

Table 10.6 Income, Saving, and Investment Data

Income ($ bil)	Saving ($ bil)	Investment ($ bil)
40	–10	20
60	0	20
80	10	20
100	20	20
120	30	20
140	40	20
160	50	20

a. On a diagram, draw the saving and investment lines based on the data in the table.
b. Indicate the equilibrium level of income.
c. Suppose the level of income investment increases by $10 billion. Draw the new investment line.
d. What is the new level of equilibrium income? Compare the change in investment with the resulting change in income.

2. LO 10.2 Table 10.7 contains data on saving and investment for a hypothetical economy.
a. Graph the saving and investment lines.
b. On your graph, indicate the equilibrium level of income.
c. Saving increases by $10 billion at each level of income. Draw the new saving line.

Table 10.7 Saving and Investment in a Hypothetical Economy

Income ($ bil)	Saving ($ bil)	Investment ($ bil)
20	–10	20
40	0	20
60	10	20
80	20	20
100	30	20
120	40	20

d. What is the new equilibrium level of income? Compare the change in saving with the change in income.

3. LO 10.3 Table 10.8 gives the following data for a closed economy without government.

Table 10.8 Data for a Closed Economy without Government

Income ($ mil)	Consumption ($ mil)
0	15
20	30
40	45
60	60
80	75
100	90
120	105
140	120

a. Calculate the *MPC* and the *MPS*.
b. If autonomous investment is $10 million, what is the equilibrium level of income?
c. If autonomous investment increases to $15 million, what will be the new equilibrium level of income?
d. Calculate the multiplier.
e. Given the multiplier calculated in (d), what effect will an increase in spending of $5 million have on the equilibrium level of income?

4. LO 10.3, 10.4 Table 10.9 provides income and consumption data for a closed economy without government.

Table 10.9 Income and Consumption Data for a Closed Economy without Government

Income ($ mil)	Consumption ($ mil)
300	200
400	280
500	360
600	440
700	520
800	600
900	680

a. Calculate the *MPS*.
b. Calculate the multiplier.
c. If investment is fixed at $160 million and the full-employment level of income is $700 million, is there an inflationary gap or a recessionary gap? What is the numerical value of the gap (if any)?
d. If the full-employment level of income is $400 million and autonomous investment is $160 million, is there an inflationary gap or a recessionary gap? What is the numerical value of the gap (if any)?

Questions in the Intermediate and Challenging Sections cover several different concepts, and have not been organized by learning objectives.

Intermediate

1. In a certain economy, the marginal propensity to withdraw is 7/12. What effect will an increase in expenditure of $84 million have on the equilibrium level of income in that economy?
2. Total investment in an economy increased from $80 billion to $120 billion; consequently, the equilibrium level of income rose from $400 billion to $520 billion. Calculate the *MPC* in that economy.
3. Figure 10.9 represents a closed economy without government.

Figure 10.9 A Closed Economy without Government

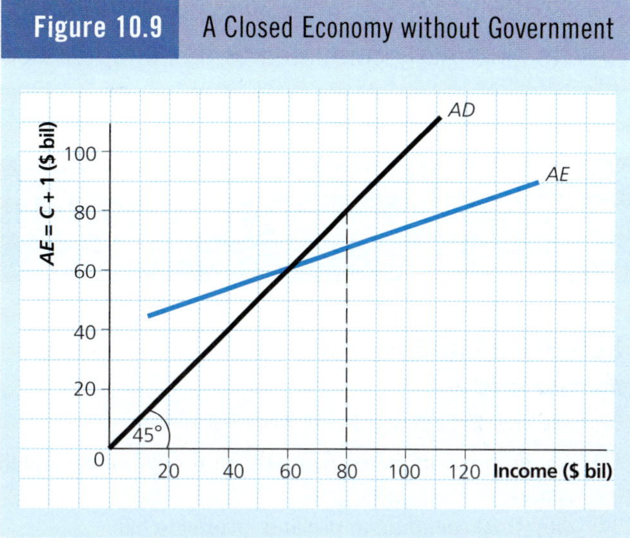

a. If the full-employment level of income is $80 billion, by how much will aggregate expenditure (*AE*) have to rise in order to achieve equilibrium at full employment?
b. Draw the *AE* curve that will lead to equilibrium at full employment.
c. Calculate the multiplier.

4. The *MPC* for a hypothetical economy is 0.75, and the equilibrium level of income is $500 billion.
   a. What effect will an increase in investment of $10 billion have on the equilibrium level of income?
   b. What would happen to equilibrium income if, instead of an increase in investment, there was a $10 billion drop in investment?

Challenging

1. A closed economy without government is in equilibrium at $400 billion. The full-employment level of income is $480 billion. If the *MPC* is 0.8, by how much must *AE* increase for the economy to be in equilibrium at full employment? Illustrate the situation on a graph.
2. With the help of an appropriate diagram, show that an increase in saving is not necessarily good or bad for an economy but depends on what happens to the savings.
3. Use a saving-investment diagram to show that the impact of an increase in investment on equilibrium income is greater if investment increases with income than if investment is autonomous.

Study Guide

Self-Assessment

What's your score?

Circle the letter that corresponds with the correct answer.

1. An increase in investment, other things being equal, causes
   a. Total spending to rise and income to fall
   b. Total spending and income to rise
   c. Total spending to fall and income to rise
   d. Total spending and income to fall
2. A change in investment can be correctly viewed as
   a. A change in injections
   b. A change in withdrawals
   c. Neither (a) nor (b)
   d. Both (a) and (b)
3. An increase in investment, other things being equal, results in
   a. A fall in income as resources are diverted away from consumption
   b. An increase in income as aggregate expenditure rises
   c. Adepletion of savings and hence a fall in income
   d. None of the above
4. A change in saving can be correctly viewed as
   a. A change in injections
   b. A change in withdrawals
   c. Neither (a) nor (b)
   d. Both (a) and (b)
5. An increase in saving, other things being equal, will cause
   a. Income and consumption to rise
   b. The price level to rise
   c. The equilibrium level of income to fall
   d. None of the above
6. Other things being equal, an increase in saving implies
   a. A fall in consumption
   b. An increase in consumption
   c. A reduction in withdrawals
   d. None of the above
7. Other things being equal, an increase in total desired saving will result in
   a. An increase in income
   b. A fall in income
   c. An increase in actual saving
   d. No change in income
8. The paradox of thrift refers to the effect of
   a. An increase in actual saving
   b. An increase in investment
   c. A fall in planned consumption
   d. Rising price levels on aggregate saving
9. Induced investment is investment that
   a. Depends on the price level
   b. Is independent of income
   c. Changes as income changes
   d. None of the above
10. According to the paradox of thrift
    a. Thrifty consumers always come out ahead
    b. Thrifty consumers end up consuming more
    c. An increase in saving always increases income
    d. None of the above
11. In a closed economy without government, the formula for the multiplier is
    a. $1 - MPC$
    b. $MPC + MPS$
    c. $1/MPS$
    d. $1 - MPS$
12. Other things being equal, an increase in investment of $30 million will cause equilibrium income to
    a. Increase by $30 million
    b. Increase by more than $30 million
    c. Increase by less than $30 million
    d. Fall by $30 million
13. In a closed economy without government, if the *MPC* is 7/9, then the multiplier is
    a. 2/9
    b. 9/7
    c. 7/9
    d. 9/2

14. In a closed economy without government, the *MPS* is 0.25. If investment increases from $20 million to $30 million, income will increase by
   a. $40 million
   b. $10 million
   c. $30 million
   d. $50 million

15. An inflationary gap exists when
   a. Output is far below the equilibrium level
   b. Aggregate expenditure is far below the equilibrium level of income
   c. Aggregate expenditure exceeds aggregate output at full employment
   d. None of the above

Questions 16, 17, and 18 refer to Figure 10.10.

Figure 10.10 Full-Employment Gaps

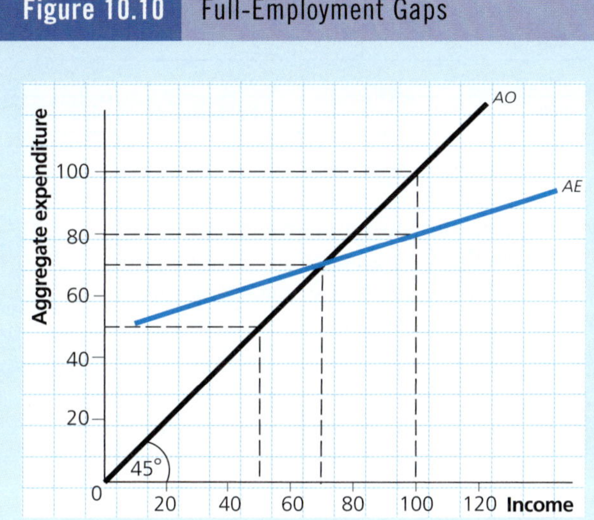

16. If the full-employment level of output is 100, there is
   a. An inflationary gap of 20
   b. An inflationary gap of 30
   c. A recessionary gap of 20
   d. A recessionary gap of 30

17. To eliminate this gap, aggregate expenditure must
   a. Fall by 20
   b. Fall by 40
   c. Rise by 20
   d. Rise by 30

18. In this case, the multiplier is
   a. 4
   b. 1.5
   c. 2
   d. 2/3

19. The greater the slope of the saving line,
   a. The greater the multiplier
   b. The smaller the multiplier
   c. The greater the slope of the consumption line
   d. The flatter will be the saving line

20. If the *AE* and *AO* lines intersect at the full-employment level of output, then macroeconomic policy is required to
   a. Raise *AE*
   b. Lower *AE*
   c. Eliminate the gap
   d. None of the above

Problems and Exercises (Use Quad Paper for Graphs)

Answers to these questions can be found on MyEconLab at www.myeconlab.com. MyEconLab

1. Use a saving-investment diagram similar to Figure 10.1 (Diagram A, p. 265) to show the effect of a reduction in investment on the equilibrium level of income. Compare the change in investment with the resulting change in income.
2. Demonstrate graphically the effect of a reduction in saving, given the level of income, on the equilibrium level of income.
3. An expenditure of $15 million is made to repair a part of the Trans-Canada Highway. If the marginal propensity to withdraw in Canada is 5/9, what effect will such expenditure have on total income in Canada?
4. In a simple closed economy without government, an increase in investment from $60 million to $90 million results in an increase in income from $400 million to $520 million. What is the *MPC* in this economy?
5. Table 10.10 gives data for a hypothetical economy without government and without foreign trade.

Table 10.10 Hypothetical Economy without Government or Foreign Trade

Income	Consumption
6000	5000
6100	5075
6200	5150
6300	5225
6400	5300
6500	5375
6600	5450
6700	5525
6800	5600
6900	5675

a. Calculate the marginal propensity to consume at an income level of $6400 million.
b. Calculate the marginal propensity to save at an income level of $6400 million.
c. If the full-employment output is $6700 million and investment is fixed at $1200 million, is there an inflationary gap or a recessionary gap? What is the numerical value of the gap (if any)?
d. If the full-employment output is $6900 million and investment is fixed at $1200 million, is there an inflationary gap or a recessionary gap? What is the numerical value of the gap (if any)?

6. Table 10.11 gives data for a simple closed economy in which government neither spends nor taxes.

Table 10.11 Consumption and Investment Data

Y	*C*	*I*	*AE*
30	45	10	55
40	50	10	60
50	55	10	65
60	60	10	70
70	65	10	75
80	70	10	80
90	75	10	85
100	80	10	90
110	85	10	95
120	90	10	100

a. If the full-employment output is 120, calculate the amount by which this full-employment output exceeds the equilibrium level of income.
b. Calculate the gap between the full-employment output and aggregate expenditure. Is this an inflationary gap or a recessionary gap?
c. Calculate the multiplier.
d. Multiply your answer for part (b) by your answer for part (c). The result now should be the same as your answer for part (a).

7. Table 10.12 contains data on income and consumption for a closed economy with no government spending and no taxes.

Table 10.12 Consumption Schedule

Income	Consumption
100	80
200	160
300	240
400	320
500	400
600	480
700	560

a. Draw the consumption curve.
b. On the same graph, draw the saving curve.
c. Calculate the slope of the saving curve
d. Calculate the multiplier.

Chapter 11

Government Spending, Taxes, and Fiscal Policy

Jim Flaherty, Canada's Finance Minister in 2011

Learning Objectives

After studying this chapter, you should be able to

- **11.1** Discuss the importance of government spending in an economy
- **11.2** Explain how government spending affects the equilibrium level of income
- **11.3** Explain how taxes affect the equilibrium level of income
- **11.4** Discuss equilibrium income with government spending and taxes
- **11.5** Identify a budget deficit, a budget surplus, and a balanced budget
- **11.6** Explain the effect of a balanced budget change in spending on equilibrium income
- **11.7** Describe the automatic stabilizers and how they work

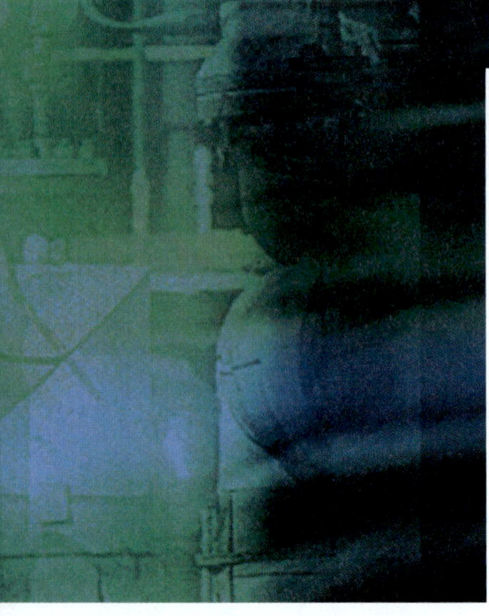

- 11.8 Explain how discretionary fiscal policy can be used to close full-employment gaps
- 11.9 Discuss the pros and cons of using government spending and taxes to control macroeconomic activity
- 11.10 Discuss the significance of the full-employment budget
- 11.11 Explain the supply-side considerations of fiscal policy
- 11.12 Discuss the total effects of fiscal policy
- 11.13 Discuss the limitations of fiscal policy
- 11.14 Discuss Canada's response to the 2008–2009 recession

Assess Your Knowledge

MyEconLab

Answers to these questions can be found on MyEconLab at **www.myeconlab.com.**

1. What is fiscal policy?
2. Who conducts fiscal policy?
3. What effect does an increase in government spending have on the equilibrium level of income?
4. What effect does an increase in taxes have on the equilibrium level of income?
5. What is a budget deficit?

LO 11.1 Discuss the importance of government spending in an economy

The Importance of Government Spending

Now we are discussing the government purchases component (G) of the aggregate expenditure equation $AE = C + I + G + (X - M)$. Is government spending related to fiscal policy?

fiscal policy the use of government spending and taxes to regulate economic activity

Perhaps we should begin our discussion by providing a formal definition of **fiscal policy**. You will then see why we relate fiscal policy to government spending. The government, through its spending and taxing powers, can influence economic activity. When it does this, it is said to conduct fiscal policy.

> Fiscal policy is the use of government spending and taxes to influence economic behaviour.

The government's budget is the main vehicle through which fiscal policy is conducted; hence, some people refer to fiscal policy as *budgetary policy*.

Although we speak of *the* government in connection with fiscal policy, we must note that all levels of government conduct fiscal policy.

Table 11.1 Government Spending as a Percentage of Aggregate Expenditure, 2006–2010

Year	GDP ($ bil)	Government Purchases ($ bil)	Government Purchases as % of GDP
2006	1450.4	277.6	19.1
2007	1529.6	293.6	19.2
2008	1599.6	314.3	19.6
2009	1527.3	333.9	22.3
2010	1621.5	352.7	21.8

Source: Statistics Canada: **www40.statcan.gc.ca/101/cst01/econ04-eng.htm.** Accessed March 23, 2011.

How important is government spending in aggregate expenditure?

If we limit government spending (just for now) to government current expenditure on goods and services, and if we consider the multitude of goods and services that all levels of government buy—services of health-care workers, services of educators, military goods, services of civil servants, soldiers' uniforms, and so on, the magnitude of government spending will quickly become evident.

Without government involvement in the economy, it is certain that many aspects of the economy would function quite differently. There are those who claim that government interference in the economy makes the economy less efficient. As can be seen in Table 11.1, government current purchases of goods and services account for about 19% of aggregate expenditure in Canada.

Reading Comprehension

The answers to these questions can be found on MyEconLab at **www.myeconlab.com**. MyEconLab

1. Formulate a definition of fiscal policy.
2. Why do some people refer to fiscal policy as budgetary policy?
3. "In Canada, only the federal government conducts fiscal policy." Is this true or false? Why?

LO 11.2 Explain how government spending affects the equilibrium level of income

Government Spending and Equilibrium Income

What is the condition for equilibrium income to be achieved in a closed economy with government spending?

We assume that the expenditures of all levels of government (federal, provincial or territorial, and local) are autonomous, that is, independent of income. Thus, changes in income will not affect the level of government spending. Under the assumption that there are neither exports nor imports, aggregate expenditure (*AE*) consists of consumer spending, investment spending, and government spending. If intended *AE* $(C + I + G)$ exceeds aggregate output (*AO* or *Y*), there will be either lines of unsatisfied customers or an unplanned reduction of the inventories of goods previously produced. Either of these situations will signal firms to increase their production; and increased production will result in increased income. Conversely, if desired *AE* $(C + I + G)$ is less than aggregate output, then the inventories of firms will accumulate beyond their planned levels. This situation will result in a reduction in total production and income. The equilibrium level of income, therefore, will be that level at which desired *AE* $(C + I + G)$ equals aggregate output. At that level of income, there will be no incentive to change production

Table 11.2 Government Spending and Equilibrium Income ($ mil)

Income	*C*	*I*	*G*	*AE*
50	55	20	20	95
60	60	20	20	100
70	65	20	20	105
80	70	20	20	110
90	75	20	20	115
100	80	20	20	120
110	85	20	20	125
120	90	20	20	130
130	95	20	20	135
140	100	20	20	140

levels, because the spending plans of households, firms, and government will coincide with the production plans of firms.

> In a closed economy with government spending, equilibrium income is achieved when $Y = C + I + G$.

Can we do a tabular analysis to show the effect of government spending on the equilibrium level of income?

Let's look at Table 11.2.

The table illustrates the effect of government spending on the equilibrium level of income. Government spending is assumed to be $20 million at each level of income. Without government spending, the equilibrium level of income is $100 million where $Y = C + I$. With government spending of $20 million, desired aggregate expenditure is now $120 million. Because desired $AE > AO$ at an income level of $100, firms will increase their production and income rises. Income will reach its equilibrium level at $140 million, where intended aggregate expenditure equals aggregate output. The addition of government spending to intended consumer and investment spending causes the equilibrium level of income to increase.

Can we show graphically how government spending affects equilibrium income?

Yes. This is done in Figure 11.1.

The consumption curve and the $C + I$ line are plotted from the data in Table 11.2. Desired aggregate expenditure is represented by the $C + I + G$ line. At an income level of $100 million, for example, the aggregate expenditure line is above the 45-degree line. This excess of desired aggregate expenditure over aggregate output causes firms to expand their production levels; as a result, income will rise. At an output level of $160 million, desired aggregate expenditure is below aggregate output. Firms will therefore reduce their production levels and, consequently, income will fall. But at a level of income of $140 million, the $C + I + G$ line crosses the 45-degree line. As you already know, the $C + I + G$ line represents desired aggregate expenditure, and the 45-degree line represents aggregate output. When the two lines intersect, intended aggregate expenditure equals aggregate output—the condition required for equilibrium. The equilibrium level of income is $140 million.

Figure 11.1 The Effect of Government Spending on Equilibrium Income

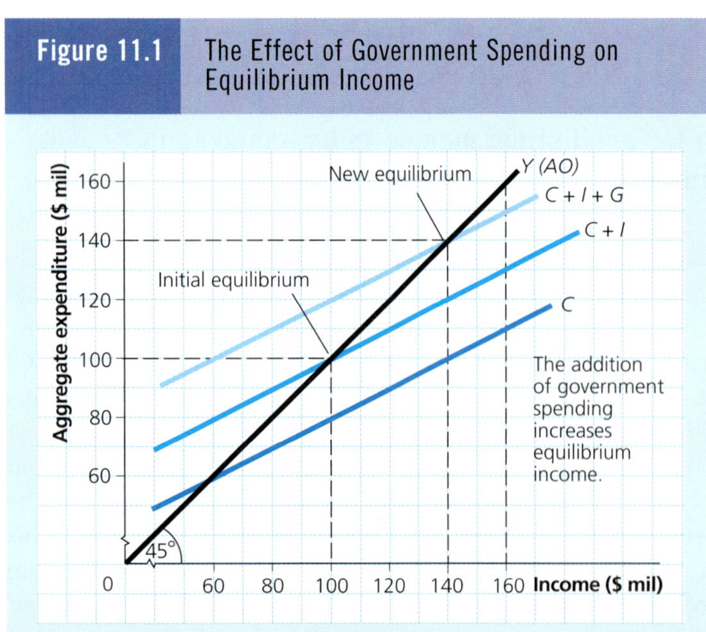

> In a closed economy with government spending, the equilibrium level of income occurs where the $C + I + G$ line intersects the 45-degree line.

Figure 11.2 Effect of an Increase in Government Spending

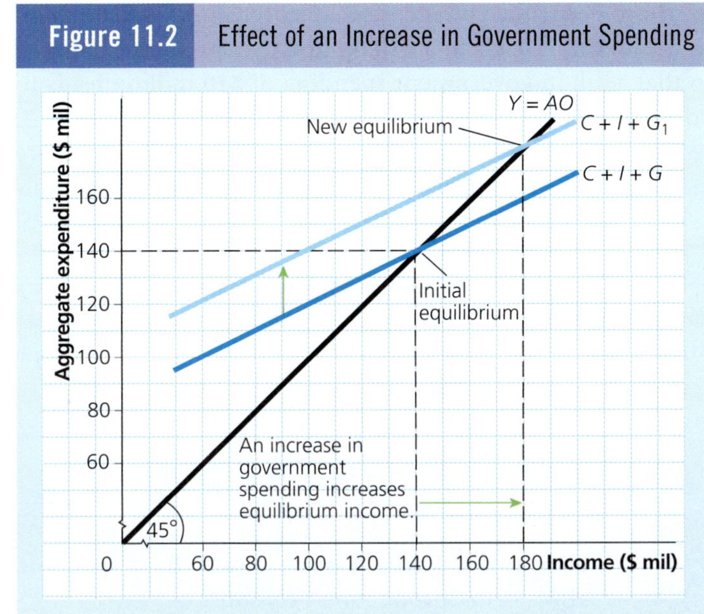

What effect does an increase in government spending have on the equilibrium level of income?

Well, we can figure this out logically. Because government spending (G) is an injection, an increase in G will raise the level of income, other things being equal. We can also show the effect graphically, by using the aggregate expenditure–aggregate output diagram.

Effect of an Increase in Government Spending Suppose the economy is in equilibrium at \$140 million with government spending at \$20 million and consumption and investment as shown in Table 11.2. This equilibrium condition is illustrated in Figure 11.2.

Now suppose government spending increases from \$20 million to \$40 million. This \$20 million increase in government spending will shift the $C + I + G$ line up to $C + I + G_1$, as shown in Figure 11.2. The effect is an increase in the equilibrium level of income from \$140 million to \$180 million.

> An increase in government spending, other things being equal, increases equilibrium income.

Does this imply that a decrease in government spending will shift the *AE* line down and reduce equilibrium income?

Exactly! And, of course, we can show this on a graph as well. Consider Figure 11.3.

Effect of a Decrease in Government Spending The initial equilibrium level of income is \$140 million where the $C + I + G$ line intersects the 45-degree line. Now, suppose that government spending falls from its initial level of \$20 million to \$10 million. The aggregate expenditure curve will shift downward from $C + I + G$ to $C + I + G_0$. The \$10 million reduction in government spending causes a decrease in the equilibrium level of income from \$140 million to \$120 million.

Figure 11.3 Effect of a Decrease in Government Spending

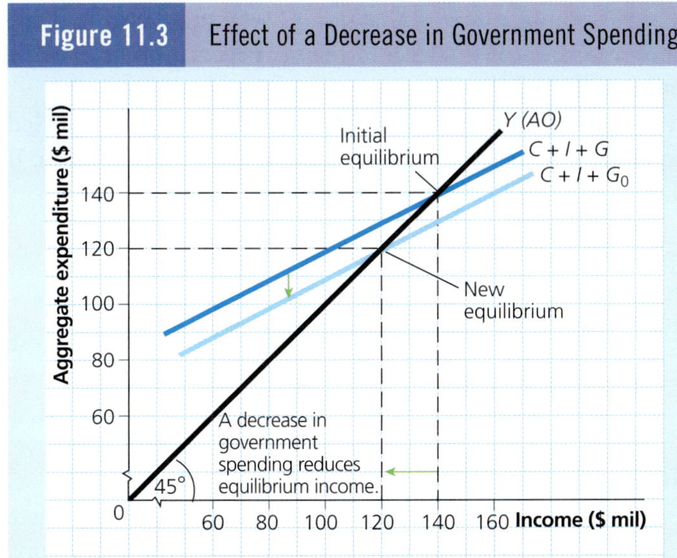

> A reduction in government spending reduces the equilibrium level of income.

The change in the equilibrium level of income resulting from the change in government spending is greater than the change in government spending. Why is this?

This is because of the multiplier effect that we studied earlier. You will recall that the simple multiplier for a change in investment spending is the reciprocal of the *MPS*. You have seen that an increase in government spending of $20 million, given the data in Table 11.2, leads to a $40 million increase in equilibrium income. You have seen also that a fall in government spending of $10 million leads to a decrease in equilibrium of $20 million. The government multiplier in this case is 2. A quick look back at Table 11.2 will reveal that the *MPC* is 0.5. The *MPS* is therefore 1 – 0.5 = 0.5. This gives an investment multiplier of 2. The government spending multiplier is exactly the same as the investment multiplier. Each is the reciprocal of the *MPS*.

The government spending multiplier is the number by which a change in government spending is multiplied to arrive at the change in equilibrium income. It is the reciprocal of the *MPS*.

Reading Comprehension

The answers to these questions can be found on MyEconLab at www.myeconlab.com. MyEconLab

1. Briefly explain why an increase in government spending, other things being equal, will increase the equilibrium level of income.
2. How might an increase in government spending affect firms' production decisions?
3. If the government spending multiplier is 2.5, what effect will an increase in government spending of $450 million have on the equilibrium level of income, other things being equal?

LO 11.3 Explain how taxes affect the equilibrium level of income

Taxation and the Equilibrium Level of Income

How does the imposition of a tax affect the equilibrium level of income?

Up to this point, we have assumed that the government does not impose any taxes. We must now remove that restriction to examine the effect of taxation on the equilibrium level of income. To focus on the effect of taxation, let us assume that government spending is zero. To avoid unnecessary complications at this point, we assume also that the government collects a fixed tax regardless of the level of the tax payers' income. Such a tax is referred to as a **lump-sum tax**.

lump-sum tax a fixed tax that is independent of the level of income

Let us assume now that the amount of the tax is $20 million and that it is levied on personal income. If personal income is $150 million, the tax will be $20 million. If personal income is $250 million, the tax will still be $20 million.

That means that disposable income is now $20 million less than what it was before. Right?

Exactly! The immediate effect of such a tax is to reduce disposable income. And because consumer spending depends on disposable income, the imposition of the tax will reduce consumer spending.

We are now in a position to examine the effect of taxation on the equilibrium level of income. Table 11.3 contains the relevant data.

In Table 11.3, the equilibrium level of income occurs at $60 million where aggregate output (*AO*) equals intended aggregate expenditure (*AE*). In the absence of the tax,

Table 11.3 Taxation and Equilibrium Income ($ mil)

Income (*AO*)	Taxes	Disposable Income	*C*	*I*	*AE*
50	20	30	45	10	55
60	20	40	50	10	60
70	20	50	55	10	65
80	20	60	60	10	70
90	20	70	65	10	75
100	20	80	70	10	80
110	20	90	75	10	85
120	20	100	80	10	90
130	20	110	85	10	95
140	20	120	90	10	100

Table 11.4 Equilibrium Income without Taxation ($ mil)

Income	*C*	*I*	*AE*
50	55	10	65
60	60	10	70
70	65	10	75
80	70	10	80
90	75	10	85
100	80	10	90
110	85	10	95
120	90	10	100
130	95	10	110
140	100	10	120

disposable income would be identical to income (*AO*); and because the *MPC* is 0.5, consumption would increase by $10 million at each level of income. The equilibrium level of income would be $80 million, as shown in Table 11.4.

Thus, we see that the effect of the tax is to reduce the equilibrium level of income.

A tax reduces the equilibrium level of income.

Can we arrive at the same conclusion with a graphical analysis?

Let's carry out a graphical analysis by using the data in Tables 11.3 and 11.4. Figure 11.4 shows the equilibrium levels of income with and without taxation. Without the tax, the equilibrium level of income is $80 million, where the $C + I$ line intersects the 45-degree line. With the tax, the relevant desired aggregate expenditure line is $C_0 + I$. The tax reduces consumption and thus reduces aggregate expenditure. The equilibrium level of income is $60 million, where the $C_0 + I$ line intersects the 45-degree line $Y(AO)$.

Figure 11.4 Equilibrium Income with and without Taxation

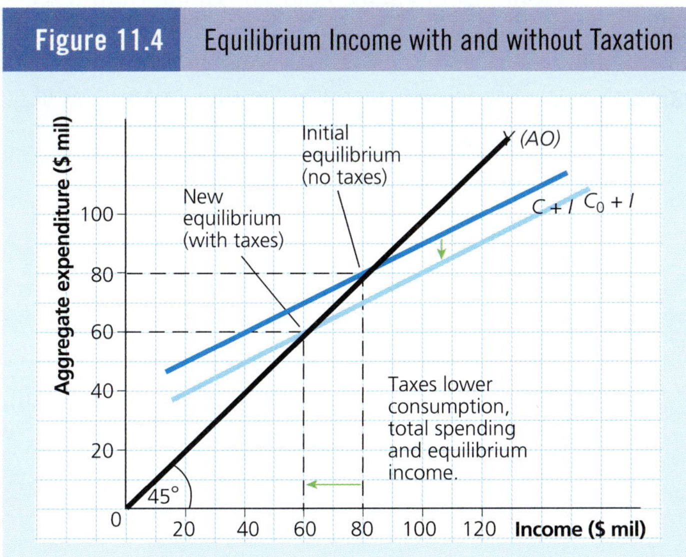

How will an increase in taxes affect the equilibrium level of income?

The Effect of an Increase in Taxes Let's investigate. Given the data in Table 11.3, the equilibrium level of income is $60 million. Now, suppose that taxes increase by $10 million (from $20 million to $30 million). The $10 million increase in taxes causes disposable income to fall by $10 million. Because the *MPC* in our example is 0.5, this fall in disposable income causes consumption to fall by $5 million and saving to fall by $5 million. The $5 million fall in consumption causes the $C + I$ line in Figure 11.5 to shift downward to $C_0 + I$.

Figure 11.5 Effect of an Increase in Taxes

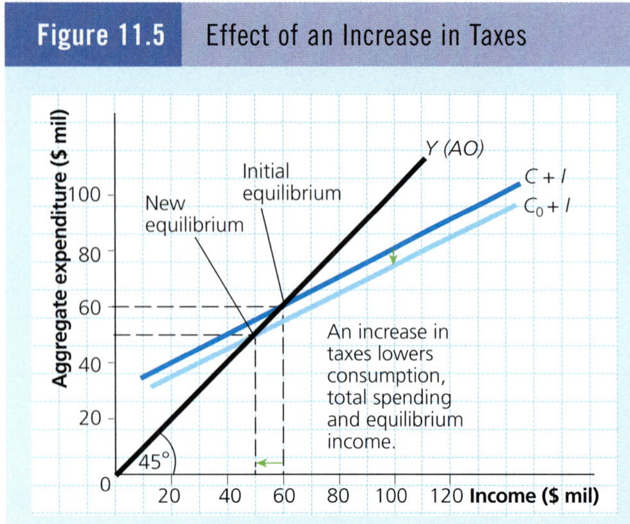

Figure 11.6 Effect of a Decrease in Taxes

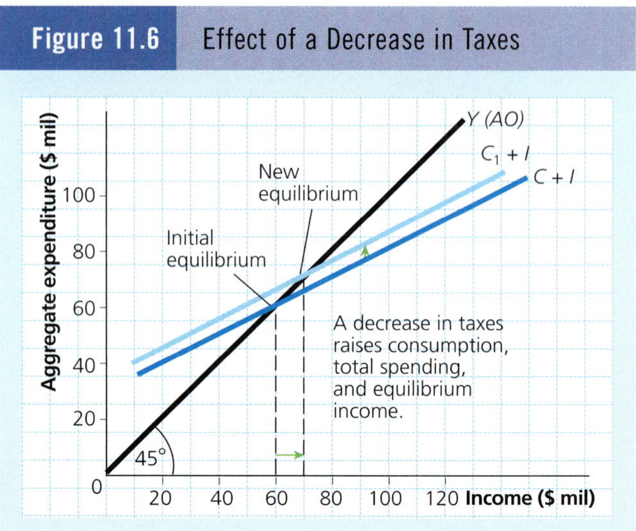

The equilibrium level of income falls from \$60 million to \$50 million. The conclusion is as follows:

> An increase in taxes, other things being equal, reduces the equilibrium level of income.

So a decrease in taxes will raise the equilibrium level of income. Correct?

Correct. Let's do a graphical analysis.

Effect of a Decrease in Taxes We assume that the initial situation is as shown in Figure 11.6, where the aggregate expenditure line is $C + I$ and the equilibrium level of income is \$60 million. Suppose now that there is a reduction in taxes of \$10 million. This reduction in taxes will result in an increase of \$10 million in disposable income. Consumption will consequently increase by \$5 million (the *MPC* is 0.5), causing the $C + I$ line to shift upward to $C_1 + I$,as shown in Figure 11.6. The equilibrium level of income rises from \$60 million to \$70 million.

> Other things being equal, a decrease in taxes increases the equilibrium level of income.

Reading Comprehension

The answers to these questions can be found on MyEconLab at **www.myeconlab.com**. MyEconLab

1. "A tax increase is contractionary." Explain.
2. How does the imposition of a lump-sum tax affect consumption and equilibrium income?
3. What is the effect of an income tax cut on consumption? aggregate expenditure? equilibrium level of income?

LO 11.4 Discuss equilibrium income with government spending and taxes

Equilibrium Income with Government Spending and Taxes

So far, we have studied the effects of government spending and taxes in isolation. Can we develop a model that studies these effects together?

Let's assume that the government spends \$20 million and collects \$20 million in taxes. We continue to assume that the tax is a lump-sum tax, independent of the level of income and that government spending is autonomous. Consumption and investment remain as before. The relevant data are contained in Table 11.5.

At a level of income of \$100 million, desired aggregate expenditure (*AE*) is just equal to aggregate output. At any other level of income, desired aggregate expenditure will be either greater or less than aggregate output, and firms will tend to increase or reduce their production levels accordingly. Hence, the equilibrium level of income is \$100 million.

Can we use the injections–withdrawals approach to arrive at the equilibrium level of income with government spending and taxes?

The Injections–Withdrawals Approach Recall that equilibrium occurs when the sum of the desired injections equals the sum of desired withdrawals. Government spending injects money into the income–expenditure stream. For example, if the government spends money to extend a highway, the incomes of firms building the highway, and of firms supplying the materials as well as the incomes of people hired to do the work, will increase. Taxes levied on the incomes of households reduce the amount that they can spend on the output of firms. Taxes therefore represent a withdrawal or leakage from the income–expenditure stream.

Under our present assumption, the withdrawals are savings and taxes. The injections are investment and government spending. The equilibrium level of income occurs when the sum of the desired withdrawals equals the sum of desired injections. That is, when

$$S + T = I + G$$

Table 11.5 Equilibrium Income with Government Spending and Taxes (\$ mil)

Total Income	Taxes	Disposable Income	*C*	*S*	*I*	*G*	*AE*
50	20	30	45	–15	10	20	75
60	20	40	50	–10	10	20	80
70	20	50	55	–5	10	20	85
80	20	60	60	0	10	20	90
90	20	70	65	5	10	20	95
100	20	80	70	10	10	20	100
110	20	90	75	15	10	20	105
120	20	100	80	20	10	20	110
130	20	110	85	25	10	20	115
140	20	120	90	30	10	20	120

From Table 11.5, we can see that the only level of income at which desired withdrawals ($S + T$) = desired injections ($I + G$) is \$100 million. At a level of income of \$120 million, for example, desired $S + T =$ \$40 million while desired $I + G =$ \$30 million. Because desired withdrawals exceed desired injections, the level of income will tend to fall. Conversely, at a level of income of \$90 million, desired injections ($I + G$) = \$30 million, while desired withdrawals ($S + T$) = \$25 million. Because desired injections exceed desired withdrawals, the level of income will tend to rise. The equilibrium level of income is \$100 million.

Figure 11.7 The Equilibrium Level of Income

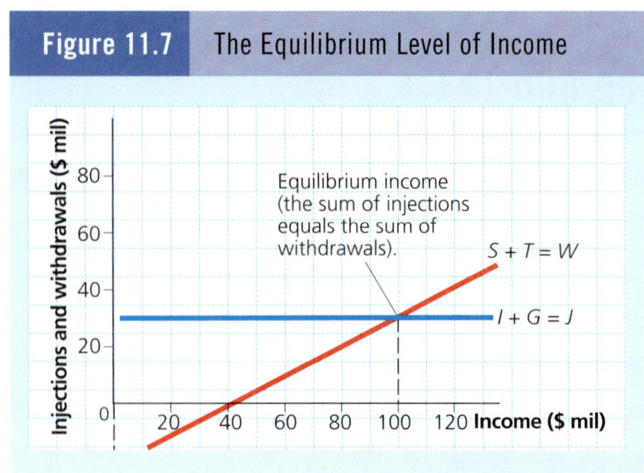

In a closed economy with government spending and taxation, the equilibrium level of income occurs when the sum of investment and government spending equals the sum of saving and taxes.

Can we show all this on a graph?

We can illustrate the injections–withdrawals (*J–W*) approach graphically. Figure 11.7 shows the $I + G$ and $S + T$ lines derived from the data in Table 11.5.

The injections ($I + G$) line intersects the withdrawals ($S + T$) line at a level of income of $100 million—the equilibrium level of income.

The intersection of the injections line and the withdrawals line determines the equilibrium level of income.

Our analysis of the effects of taxes so far is based on the assumption of a lump-sum tax. How would a tax based on income affect our analysis?

Effect of a Proportional Tax We assumed that the tax was a lump-sum tax for simplicity only. Let us move closer to reality by assuming that taxes are set at 20% of total income, as shown in Table 11.6. Such a tax is called a *proportional tax.*

Pre-tax consumption is shown so that the proportional tax can be easily discerned. Column 1 shows that before the tax is imposed, total income (Y), personal income (PI), and disposable income (DI) are all equal. Column 2 shows desired consumption before the imposition of the tax. The consumption–income relation is similar to that assumed in earlier tables. The proportional tax of 20% of total income is shown in column 3. The tax reduces disposable income, as shown in column 4; and because consumption varies with disposable income, the after-tax consumption is less than the pre-tax consumption, as can be seen by comparing columns 2 and 5.

Table 11.6 The Effect of a Proportional Tax ($ mil)

Total Income (Y) = PI = DI (1)	Desired Pre-Tax Consumption (2)	Taxes (3)	After-Tax Disposable Income (4)	Desired After-Tax Consumption (5)
50	55	10	40	50
60	60	12	48	54
70	65	14	56	58
80	70	16	64	62
90	75	18	72	66
100	80	20	80	70
110	85	22	88	74
120	90	24	96	78
130	95	26	104	82
140	100	28	112	86

Figure 11.8 The Effect of a Proportional Tax on Income

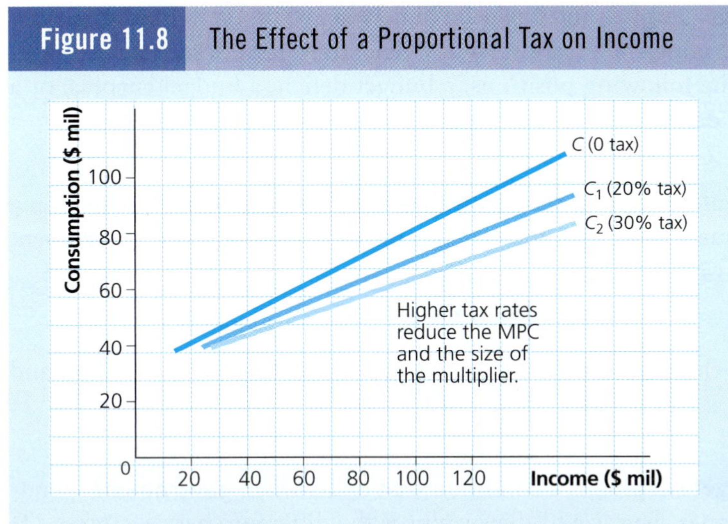

In Figure 11.8, the pre-tax consumption is shown by the *C* line and the after-tax consumption by the C_1 line.

Note that the consumption curve with the proportional tax is flatter than the consumption curve without the tax.

Suppose that the tax were 30% of total income instead of 20%. How would the consumption curve be affected?

Let's investigate. As Figure 11.8 shows, an increase in the tax rate from 20% to 30% lowers the consumption curve to the C_2 line. Does this also affect the desired aggregate expenditure? The answer is yes. Because the tax rate affects the consumption curve, it also affects aggregate expenditure. An increase in the tax rate also reduces the slope of the consumption curve (the *MPC*) and, therefore, increases the *MPS*. Thus, it reduces the multiplier. We have reached the following conclusion:

An increase in the tax rate reduces desired consumer spending and hence desired aggregate expenditure. An increase in the tax rate also reduces the slope of the consumption curve and hence reduces the size of the multiplier.

Reading Comprehension

The answers to these questions can be found on MyEconLab at www.myeconlab.com. MyEconLab

1. What is a proportional tax? How does a proportional tax affect income?
2. What effect does a change in the tax rate have on the consumption curve?
3. In a closed economy with government spending and taxation, explain what will happen to income if $(I + G) < (S + T)$

LO 11.5 Identify a budget deficit, a budget surplus, and a balanced budget

Budget Positions

What do the terms *budget deficit*, *budget surplus*, and *balanced budget* mean?

Before we answer that question, it's a good idea to first define the government budget.

The government budget is a plan of the intended revenues and expenditures of the government for the ensuing fiscal year. It is the main instrument used by the government to execute its economic policies.

Budget deficit, budget surplus, and balanced budget are terms often used in discussions of government spending and taxation. At any given time, the government's budget can be in only one of the following positions: a budget deficit, a budget surplus, or a balanced budget. Let us define each of these terms.

budget deficit the condition in which government spending is greater than tax revenues

Budget Deficit A **budget deficit** is a condition that exists when government spending is greater than tax revenues. The size of the deficit is the difference between government spending (G) and taxes (T):

$$\text{Budget deficit} = G - T$$

For example, if in 2010 the government collected taxes amounting to $600 billion and spent $630 billion, then it had a budget deficit of $30 billion in 2010.

budget surplus the condition in which government spending is less than tax revenues

Budget Surplus A **budget surplus** is a condition that exists when government spending is less than tax revenues. The size of the surplus is the difference between taxes (T) and government spending (G):

$$\text{Budget surplus} = T - G$$

For instance, if in 2009 the government collected $580 billion in taxes and spent $570 billion, then it had a budget surplus of $10 billion in 2009.

balanced budget a condition in which government spending equals tax revenues

Balanced Budget A **balanced budget** is the situation that exists when the government currently spends exactly as much as it collects in taxes; government spending is equal to tax revenues:

$$\text{Balanced budget: } G = T$$

For example, a government would have a balanced budget if it collected $600 billion in tax revenues in a given year and spent $600 billion in the same year.

functional finance the intentional use of deficits and surpluses to achieve desired economic objectives

Can these budget positions be illustrated graphically?

Let's look at Figure 11.9. In this diagram, we assume that government spending is a fixed amount, independent of the level of income, and that taxes are proportional to income.

At a level of income of Y, $G = T$. The budget, therefore, is balanced. At any income level below Y, the budget is in deficit. And at any income level above Y, the budget is in surplus. The classical economists firmly believed that sound government finance consisted of balancing the budget. We will see shortly that, following Keynesian economics, **functional finance** (that is, the intentional use of budget deficits and surpluses to achieve desired economic objectives) can be used as an effective weapon against recessionary and inflationary situations.

Figure 11.9 Budget Positions

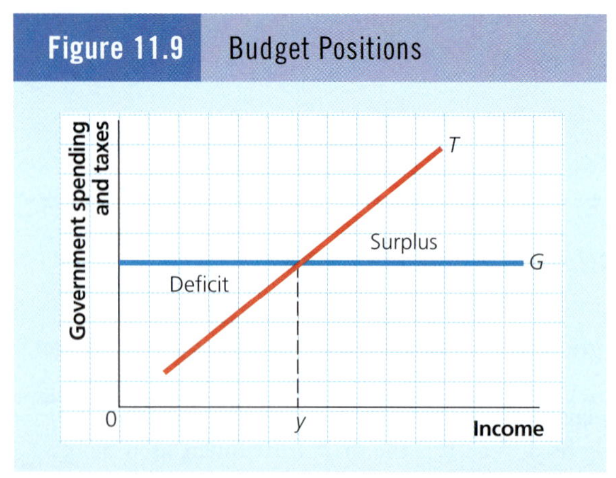

Reading Comprehension

The answers to these questions can be found on MyEconLab at www.myeconlab.com. MyEconLab

1. Define each of the following terms:
   a. Budget deficit
   b. Budget surplus
   c. Balanced budget
2. What is the key instrument used by the government to implement its economic policy?

LO 11.6 Explain the effect of a balanced budget change in spending on equilibrium income

The Balanced Budget Multiplier

If the government increases its spending and raises taxes by the same amount, would the effect on equilibrium income be neutral?

This is an excellent question and one that is worth careful study. Our analysis so far has shown that an increase in government spending tends to increase desired aggregate expenditure and hence the equilibrium level of income, whereas an increase in taxes tends to reduce intended aggregate expenditure and hence the equilibrium level of income. But what happens to equilibrium income if the increase in government spending equals the increase in taxes? When this occurs, we say that there is a **balanced budget change in spending**. A balanced budget change in spending is the condition in which a change in government spending equals the change in taxes.

balanced budget change in spending the condition in which a change in government spending equals the change in taxes

$$\text{Balanced budget change in spending: } \Delta G = \Delta T$$

For example, if in 2010 the government increased its spending by $40 billion and at the same time it increased taxes by $40 billion, then it undertook a balanced budget increase in spending. Similarly, if it reduced its spending by $50 billion and at the same time reduced taxes by the same amount, then it undertook a balanced budget decrease in spending.

It is tempting to conclude that a balanced budget change in spending would leave equilibrium income unchanged. But before we come to that conclusion, recall that, in an example earlier in this chapter, we showed that an increase in government spending of $10 million resulted in an increase in equilibrium income of $20 million, whereas an increase in taxes of $10 million caused equilibrium income to fall not by $20 million, but by $10 million. Thus, a given change in government spending seems to exert a more powerful effect on the equilibrium level of income than does an equivalent change in taxes.

Can we examine why this is so?

Let us assume that the multiplier is 2 throughout the economy. An increase in government spending of $10 million will generate an increase in income of $20 million. A government spending multiplier of 2 implies a marginal propensity to save of 0.5 and a marginal propensity to consume of 0.5. An increase in taxes of $10 million will therefore cause domestic spending to fall initially not by $10 million, but by $5 million (one half of $10 million). With a multiplier of 2, the total decrease in income will be $10 million.

balanced budget theorem the theory that states that if government spending and taxes increase by the same amount, the resulting increase in income will equal the increase in government spending

Thus, we see that a balanced budget change in spending is not neutral. In fact, the result we have derived is called the **balanced budget theorem**, which states that if government spending and taxes increase by the same amount, the resulting increase in income will equal the increase in government spending.

Looked at another way, we can say that the balanced budget multiplier is 1. An increase in government spending of $50 million followed by an increase in taxes of $50 million will increase equilibrium income by $50 million.

Reading Comprehension

The answers to these questions can be found on MyEconLab at www.myeconlab.com. MyEconLab

1. Is a balanced budget change in spending the same as a balanced budget? Explain.
2. An increase in government spending of $500 billion has exactly the same impact on the economy as a tax cut of $500 billion. Is this true or false? Explain.
3. Can the government stimulate the economy without changing the size of its deficit? Explain.

LO 11.7 Describe the automatic stabilizers and how they work

Automatic Stabilizers

Are there any fiscal measures built into the economy that operate without deliberate government action?

automatic fiscal policy or automatic (built-in) stabilizers the fiscal policy measures that are built into the economy

discretionary fiscal policy deliberate changes in government spending and taxes to achieve desired economic objectives

In fact, there are. Fiscal policy (i.e., changes in government spending and taxes) is one of the main policy tools available to the government. It is analytically useful to distinguish between **automatic fiscal policy** and **discretionary fiscal policy**.

Automatic fiscal policy measures are those that have been built into the economic system. They operate automatically to increase the budget surplus in inflationary periods and increase the budget deficit in periods of recession. Because they tend to stabilize the economy, they are called **automatic (built-in) stabilizers**.

Conversely, some fiscal policy measures are not built into the system and therefore have to be formulated and implemented deliberately. These are the discretionary fiscal policy measures, which are deliberate changes in government spending and taxes designed to achieve desired economic objectives. During the 2008–2009 recession, the Canadian government significantly increased its spending, allotting almost $30 billion to economic stimulus—programs designed to stimulate economic activity.

Can you provide some examples of automatic stabilizers?

Examples of automatic stabilizers are progressive taxes, government assistance to agriculture, and employment insurance. Let us examine each of these briefly.

progressive tax system a system in which the tax rateincreases as income increases

Progressive Taxes As income increases in a **progressive tax system**, the proportion paid in taxes increases. A progressive tax system is a system in which the tax rate increases as income increases. In other words, the more income you earn, the greater the percentage of that income you must pay in taxes.

Government assistance to agriculture helps to stabilize the economy.

Because taxes are withdrawals from the income–expenditure stream, they tend to have a contractionary effect on income. Progressive taxes prevent the economy from expanding as fast as it would in the absence of progressive taxes. Conversely, when the economy is in a recession, income tends to fall. And in a progressive tax system, taxes fall even faster. This decrease in taxes prevents the economy from falling as deeply into the recession as would be the case in the absence of progressive taxes.

Government Assistance to Agriculture If the economy is in a recession, then income and aggregate expenditure will both fall. The demand for goods and services (including the demand for agricultural products) will fall. Other things being equal, the prices of agricultural products will fall, resulting in a fall in farmers' incomes. This fall in incomes in the agricultural sector will result in an increase in government spending to support the agricultural sector. This increase in government spending will tend to lessen the severity of the recession. In a period of rapid economic expansion, farmers will require less subsidizing; hence, government spending in this area declines. The decline in government spending slows down the rapid expansion in expenditure, which might otherwise be inflationary.

Employment Insurance Benefits In a period of economic slowdown and increasing unemployment, the number of people eligible for employment insurance benefits increases. Consequently, there is an increase in government spending, which tends to promote economic activity. Conversely, if the economy is expanding rapidly and heading for an inflationary period, unemployment will fall, employment insurance benefits will decrease, and, consequently, government spending will fall, resulting in a contraction of aggregate expenditure.

Do these automatic stabilizers always work as desired?

The Fiscal Drag Unfortunately, no! You have seen that built-in stabilizers help to prevent the economy from accelerating into inflation and decelerating into a recession. This type of stability is desirable. But built-in stability is not always desirable. Let us consider a situation in which the economy is recovering from a state of severe unemployment and low level of economic activity. As income increases, under a progressive tax system, taxes increase at a faster rate. The increase in taxes will exert a downward pressure on the economy and will thus hamper economic recovery. This built-in stabilization is called **fiscal drag**, defined as a phenomenon in which automatic stabilizers prolong the time it takes the economy to recover from a recession. It is caused by an undesirable built-in stabilizer that prevents the economy from recovering from a state of high unemployment and low economic activity.

fiscal drag the phenomenon in which automatic stabilizers prevent the economy from recovering from a recession

Discretionary fiscal policy, deliberate changes in government spending and taxes, can be required to counteract the fiscal drag. Although the automatic stabilizers help to reduce instability in the economy, they do not do the job completely; discretionary fiscal policy is often required.

Reading Comprehension

The answers to these questions can be found on MyEconLab at www.myeconlab.com. MyEconLab

1. What is the difference between automatic fiscal policy and discretionary fiscal policy?
2. Identify two automatic stabilizers and explain how they work.
3. What are the limitations of automatic stabilizers?
4. What is fiscal drag?

LO 11.8 Explain how discretionary fiscal policy can be used to close full-employment gaps

Discretionary Fiscal Policy: Closing the Gaps

How can fiscal policy be used to combat inflation?

Our analysis of the effect of changes in government spending and taxes on aggregate expenditure and equilibrium income suggests that fiscal policy can be used to reduce inflation and unemployment. The objective of fiscal policy is to move the economy toward its full-employment level of income without inflation. In other words, the objective is to achieve equilibrium at full employment.

The Use of Fiscal Policy to Combat Inflation Figure 11.10 illustrates an inflationary situation. Current aggregate demand is represented by AD_1. It intersects the *AS* curve at a higher price level of P_1 instead of at the desired full-employment price level of *P*. Aggregate demand must be reduced from AD_1 to *AD* to eliminate the inflationary pressure.

contractionary fiscal policy decreases in government spending and increases in taxes that result in a reduction in aggregate expenditure

The appropriate fiscal policy in this situation is a reduction in government spending or an increase in taxes, or some combination of both. In other words, a reduction of the deficit or an increase in the surplus is required.

A reduction in government spending reduces desired aggregate expenditure and hence income. The reduction in income causes a reduction in planned consumption and investment. Figure 11.10 shows decreased intended aggregate expenditure as a shift in the *AD* curve from AD_1 to *AD*. The inflationary pressure is eliminated as equilibrium occurs at the full-employment level of output (y_f). A similar result can be obtained by increasing taxes. An increase in taxes reduces disposable income, which in turn decreases planned consumption and investment spending. As before, the *AD* curve shifts downward from AD_1 to *AD*, reducing or eliminating the inflationary pressure. Any policy that results in a decrease in aggregate expenditure is said to be a *contractionary policy*. Decreases in government spending and increases in taxes that result in a reduction in aggregate expenditure are therefore **contractionary fiscal policies** because they result in a contraction in the economy.

Figure 11.10 Removing an Inflationary Gap

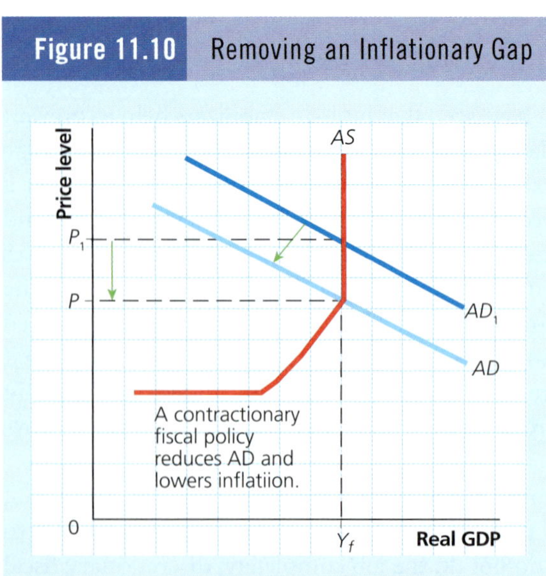

If the economy is experiencing inflation without unemployment, the appropriate fiscal policy to eliminate the inflationary pressure is a contractionary fiscal policy.

Figure 11.11 Removing an Output Gap

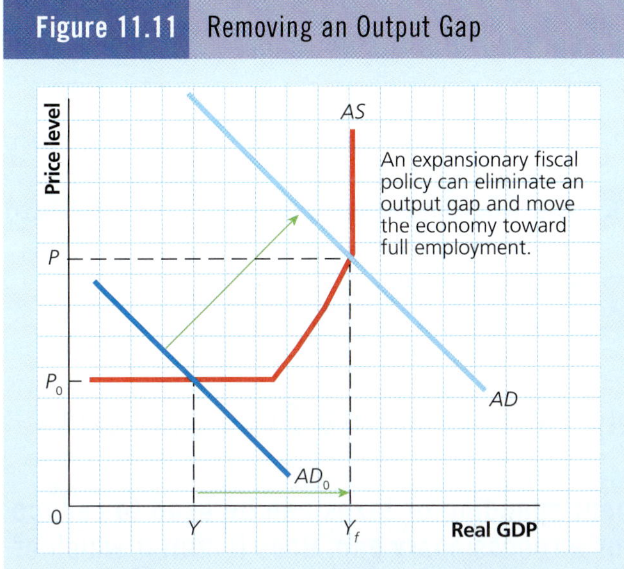

Can fiscal policy be used to combat unemployment?

Let's analyze the situation.

The Use of Fiscal Policy to Combat Unemployment

Assume that the economy is experiencing unemployment and a low level of income and output. There is an output gap as shown in Figure 11.11 by the difference between the full-employment output (y_f) and the equilibrium level of output (y). The aggregate demand curve (AD_0) and the aggregate supply curve (AS) intersect at a price level of P_0 and an equilibrium real GDP of y. The desired equilibrium is a price level of P and a real GDP of y_f. An increase in government spending or a reduction in taxes or a combination of both will stimulate the economy toward full employment. That is, an increase in the deficit or a reduction in the surplus is required. For the economy to achieve full employment, desired aggregate expenditure must increase. An increase in government spending will result in an increase in desired aggregate expenditure and, hence, an increase in income. The increase in income will cause planned consumption and investment to increase. The aggregate demand curve will shift from AD_0 to AD as shown in Figure 11.11. The output gap is thus eliminated.

A reduction in taxes will produce a similar result. A fall in taxes increases disposable income, which in turn increases consumption and investment spending. As before, the aggregate demand curve shifts upward, eliminating the output gap. Any policy that results in an increase in aggregate expenditure is said to be an *expansionary policy*. Increases in government spending and reductions in taxes are therefore **expansionary fiscal policies**, because they result in an expansion of aggregate expenditure, income, and employment.

expansionary fiscal policy increases in government spending and increases in taxes that result in an increase in aggregate expenditure

> If the economy is experiencing a recession, with high unemployment and no inflation, the appropriate fiscal policy to move the economy toward full employment is an expansionary fiscal policy.

BUSINESS SITUATION 11.1

The economy is experiencing a period of severe unemployment. The government has announced that it will undertake an expansionary fiscal policy, increasing government spending and reducing taxes. A business manager was contemplating hiring additional workers to better serve her clients.

Should the manager hire the workers before the implementation of the government policy or should she wait until after the policy has been implemented?

The answer to this Business Situation can be found in Appendix A.

Reading Comprehension

The answers to these questions can be found on MyEconLab at www.myeconlab.com. MyEconLab

1. What is the appropriate fiscal policy during a period of high inflation?
2. What is the appropriate fiscal policy during a deep recession?
3. Is it wise for a government to pursue a balanced budget policy during periods of high unemployment or high inflation? Explain.

 Discuss the pros and cons of using government spending and taxes to control macroeconomic activity

Government Spending or Taxes? The Pros and Cons

We have seen that government spending or taxes can be used to reduce or eliminate an inflationary or a recessionary gap. Does it matter which of these two fiscal policy tools the government uses to control the economy?

Yes, it does matter. We can examine the arguments for and against each of the tools of fiscal policy.

Government Spending: The Pros One of the advantages of using government spending to control macroeconomic activity is that it is a more powerful tool than tax changes. A $20 million increase in government spending will have a greater impact on the economy than a tax cut of the same amount. (Recall our discussion of the balanced budget theorem.)

Another advantage of changes in government spending over tax changes is that changes in government spending can be focused on certain regions. For example, if there is widespread unemployment in certain regions but not in others, a tax cut designed to reduce unemployment in those regions may cause inflation in other regions. In such a case, government spending programs can be designed to increase aggregate expenditure in regions suffering from high unemployment.

Government Spending: The Cons A major disadvantage of government spending programs is that they take a long time to get under way. Highway construction and other public works programs require a considerable amount of planning time. Some of the reasons for the delays in government spending will be discussed in a later chapter.

Another disadvantage of government spending as a fiscal policy tool is the difficulty of reversing certain government spending programs. Indeed, it may be political suicide to try to eliminate certain programs. Moreover, certain projects, once in progress, cannot be abandoned without immense waste of resources. What good is an incomplete highway from a city to an airport?

Changes in Taxes: The Pros A tax cut designed to stimulate the economy is likely to be more favourably received by the public than an increase in government spending. The tax cut will likely benefit more people directly as it increases their disposable income. Furthermore, people who believe that the government is already too big will resist increases in government spending.

Another advantage of using changes in taxes is that it may be easier and less wasteful to change taxes when economic conditions change. For example, if a tax cut is instituted to combat high unemployment, it may be easier to re-impose taxes when the situation improves than to cut certain government programs. This, however, is not to suggest that tax changes are easy.

Yet another advantage of tax changes over changes in government spending is the relative speed with which tax changes can be implemented. In cases where a quick change is desired, tax changes may be preferable to changes in government spending.

Changes in Taxes: The Cons One big disadvantage of using tax changes as a fiscal policy tool is that its effect is national rather than local or regional. And, as you saw earlier, regional considerations can be an important element in macroeconomic policy decisions.

Another disadvantage of tax changes is that they are less effective, dollar for dollar, than changes in government spending. Thus, during periods of severe unemployment and undesirably low aggregate expenditure, the choice of fiscal policy tools may favour an increase in government spending over tax cuts.

Reading Comprehension

The answers to these questions can be found on MyEconLab at www.myeconlab.com. MyEconLab

1. What are the pros and cons of using government spending to control the economy?
2. What are the pros and cons of using taxes to control the economy?

LO 11.10 Discuss the significance of the full-employment budget

The Full Employment Budget

Can we conclude that the existence of a budget deficit indicates an expansionary fiscal policy, whereas the existence of a budget surplus indicates a contractionary fiscal policy?

Let us examine this issue. In times of economic prosperity, with rising incomes, government tax revenues increase. Because people find themselves generally in better economic circumstances, government transfer payments tend to fall automatically. The budget may change passively, therefore, from a deficit position to a surplus position. Likewise, in recessionary times, government tax revenues fall. Government spending on such items as employment insurance benefits, welfare payments, subsidies, and government transfer payments in general then increase automatically as more and more people find themselves in straitened circumstances. As a result, the budget may change passively from a surplus position to a deficit position.

Is there any way to differentiate between budget changes that are automatic and budget changes that indicate changes in discretionary fiscal policy?

full-employment budget the position of the budget if the economy were at full employment

Yes. To distinguish between policy-induced (intentional) changes in the budget and automatic (passive) changes, we use the concept of the **full-employment budget** or

Figure 11.12 The Full-Employment Budget

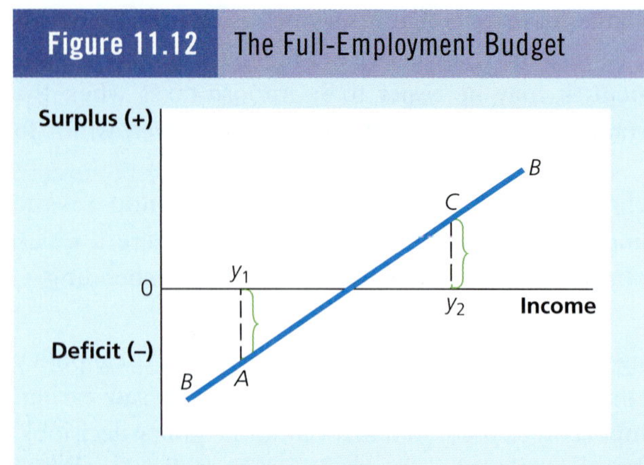

Figure 11.13 Fiscal Policy and the Full-Employment Budget

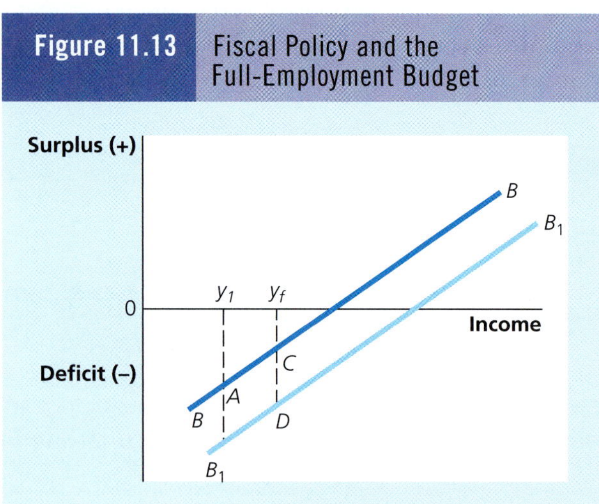

high-employment budget, defined as the position of the budget if the economy were at full employment, given the level of government spending and taxes.

Figure 11.12 illustrates the concept of the full-employment budget.

If the full-employment level of income is Y_2, then the full-employment surplus is Y_2C. If the full-employment level of income is Y_1, then the full-employment deficit is Y_1A.

Now, consider Figure 11.13. Y_1 is the current level of income. If income increases from Y_1 to the full-employment level of income (Y_f), without any policy-induced changes in government spending and taxes, the actual budget deficit will decrease from Y_1A to Y_fC. The full-employment deficit would remain unchanged, however, at Y_fC.

If the government intentionally increased the deficit in order to move the economy from Y_1 to Y_f, then the budget line would shift from BB to B_1B_1. As a result, the full-employment deficit would increase from Y_fC to Y_fD. Thus, we can draw the following conclusion:

> Changes in the budget do not necessarily indicate changes in fiscal policy. Changes in the full-employment budget, however, do indicate changes in fiscal policy.

Reading Comprehension

The answers to these questions can be found on MyEconLab at www.myeconlab.com. MyEconLab

1. What is your understanding of the full-employment budget?
2. What is the significance of the full-employment budget?

LO 11.11 Explain the supply-side considerations of fiscal policy

Supply-Side Consideration of Fiscal Policy

So far, the effects of changes in government spending and taxes have been on the demand side, as only *AE* is affected. Does fiscal policy affect the supply side also?

Fiscal policy affects both the demand and supply sides of the economy. Anything that increases the productive capacity of the economy is a supply-side factor. If the government spends money on education and health, then the spending increases the economy's productive capacity. Government spending on capital goods, such as infrastructure (roads, rail systems, water systems, etc.), increases the economy's overall productivity. Such expenditures increase aggregate supply. A decrease in government spending can have a negative effect on the economy's production possibilities and hence can therefore reduce aggregate supply.

> An increase in government spending that increases the economy's productive capacity increases aggregate supply. A decrease in government spending can reduce aggregate supply.

Let us now consider the supply-side effects of taxes. An increase in taxes reduces work incentives and causes people to save less. A reduction in saving reduces the funds available for productive investment purposes. Therefore, an increase in taxes reduces aggregate supply. A reduction in taxes, however, encourages work effort and increases saving. A reduction in taxes therefore increases aggregate supply.

> An increase in taxes reduces aggregate supply. A reduction in taxes increases aggregate supply.

Figure 11.14 Effects of Fiscal Policy

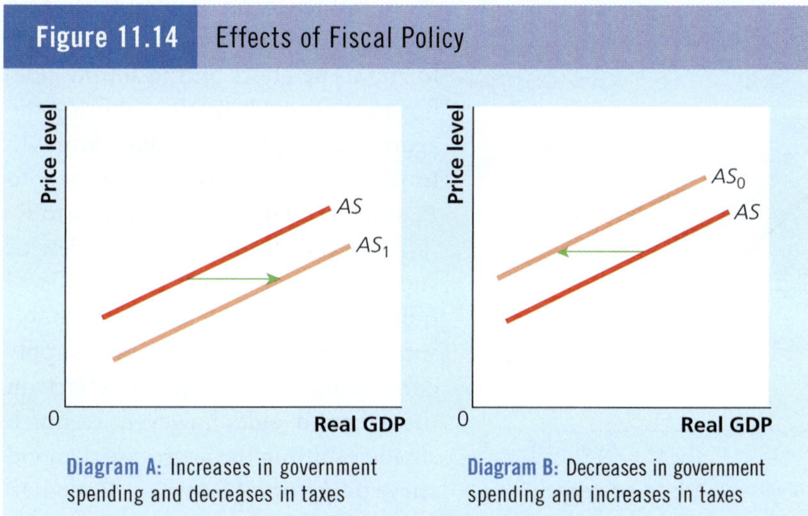

Diagram A: Increases in government spending and decreases in taxes

Diagram B: Decreases in government spending and increases in taxes

Can we use graphs to illustrate the effects of fiscal policy on aggregate supply?

Figure 11.14 illustrates the effects of fiscal policy on aggregate supply. In Diagram A, the initial aggregate supply curve is *AS*. An increase in government spending that increases the economy's productive capacity or a reduction in taxes shifts the aggregate supply curve from *AS* to AS_1.

In Diagram B, the initial aggregate supply curve is *AS*, as in Diagram A. A decrease in government spending that reduces the economy's productive capacity or an increase in taxes shifts the aggregate supply curve from *AS* to AS_0.

BUSINESS SITUATION 11.2

You own and operate a small business and have very little control over the price that you charge. The market determines your price. The government has embarked on a massive program of investing in infrastructure, incentives for education and training, and research leading to improvements in technology. As a business owner, you are interested in the long-term effects of the government's program on your business.

How might this program affect your business?

The answer to this Business Situation can be found in Appendix A.

Reading Comprehension

The answers to these questions can be found on MyEconLab at www.myeconlab.com. MyEconLab

1. Changes in government spending and taxes are clearly demand-side-only policies because they affect only the demand side of the economy. Discuss briefly.
2. Distinguish between the demand side and the supply side of the economy.

LO 11.12 Discuss the total effects of fiscal policy

The Combined Effects of Fiscal Policy

What conclusions can we draw from the effect of fiscal policy when we combine the demand-side and supply-side effects?

Let's perform a graphical analysis of the total effects of fiscal policy in the *AD–AS* framework. Many economists argue that an expansionary fiscal policy exerts a greater influence on aggregate demand than it does on aggregate supply. Diagram A of Figure 11.15 illustrates this view.

Figure 11.15 Two Views of the Combined Effects of Fiscal Policy

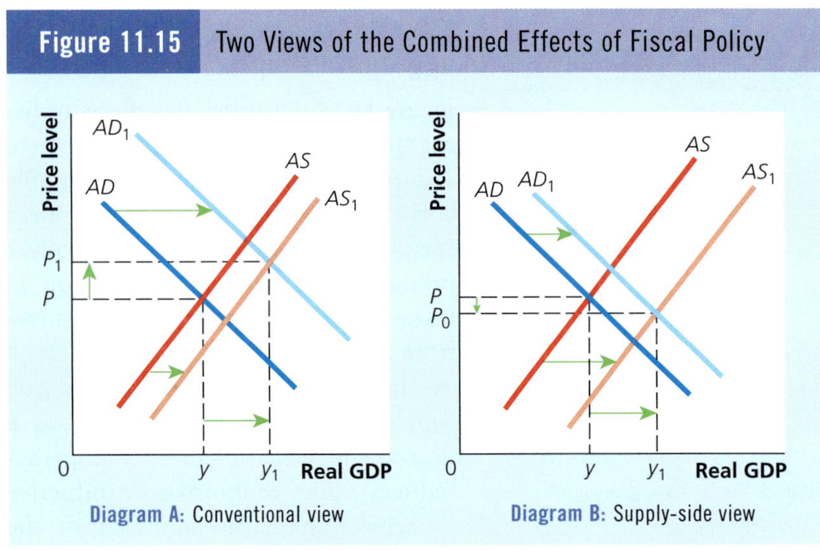

Expansionary fiscal policy exerts a great influence on demand, shifting the aggregate demand curve from *AD* to AD_1. The effect on the supply side, however, is much smaller, shifting the aggregate supply curve only from *AS* to AS_1. The price level rises from *P* to P_1 and real GDP increases from *y* to y_1.

Diagram B illustrates the view of supply-siders. Expansionary fiscal policy exerts a great influence on supply, shifting the aggregate supply curve from *AS* to AS_1. The effect on the demand side however, is much smaller, shifting the aggregate demand curve only from *AD* to AD_1. Real GDP increases from *y* to y_1, but the price level falls from *P* to P_0.

Reading Comprehension

The answers to these questions can be found on MyEconLab at www.myeconlab.com. MyEconLab

1. Show that an expansionary fiscal policy can result in an increase in the price level.
2. Show that an expansionary fiscal policy can result in a decrease in the price level.

LO 11.13 Discuss the limitations of fiscal policy

Limitations of Fiscal Policy

What are the main limitations of fiscal policy?

recognition lag the time that elapses before a problem is fully recognized

decision lag the time that elapses between the recognition of a problem and the decision to act

implementation lag the time that elapses between the decision to act and the implementation of the decision

impact lag or effect lag the time that elapses between the implementation of a decision and its effects on the economy

Four main problems are associated with fiscal policy. Let us consider the problem of time lags. First, there is a **recognition lag**. A problem (inflation or unemployment) may begin and be in progress for some time before it is recognized. The economy could well be in a mild recession before the statistics tell the tale.A recognition lag is the time that elapses before a problem is fully recognized.

Second, there is a **decision lag**. Once the problem is recognized, the decision makers need time to decide what action to take. They must decide whether to change government spending or taxes and choose the specific forms that these changes will take. A decision lag is the time that elapses between the recognition of a problem and the decision to act.

Third, there is an **implementation lag**. An implementation lag is the time that elapses between the decision to act and the implementation of the decision. After the decision is made as to the type of fiscal policy that will be used, there will be some time before the policy is actually implemented. A tax change, for example, may not take effect immediately; a program of government expenditure may require a considerable time before it is actually launched. Plans have to be drawn up, tenders invited and considered, and contracts awarded. The actual construction period can be quite long, depending on the nature of the project.

Finally, there is the **impact lag**or the **effect lag**. After the decision is implemented, it might take a while for the effects of the policy to be felt. An impact lag is the time that elapses between the implementation of the decision and its effects on the economy.

Figure 11.16 illustrates the time lags associated with fiscal policy.

The implication is that the entire process can take so long that the effects of the policy may be felt only after the need for the policy has passed.

A second limitation of fiscal policy is the difficulty of varying government spending and taxes as the need arises. Many expenditure items cannot be varied to any appreciable extent. For example, the salaries of civil servants cannot be varied as a means of stabilizing the economy. Similarly, the amounts spent on defence and as interest payments on the public debt cannot be varied in response to fluctuations in economic activity. To see just how difficult it can be to vary government spending, try to write down on paper some areas where you think cuts in government spending can be made—and consider

Figure 11.16 Time Lags Associated with Fiscal Policy

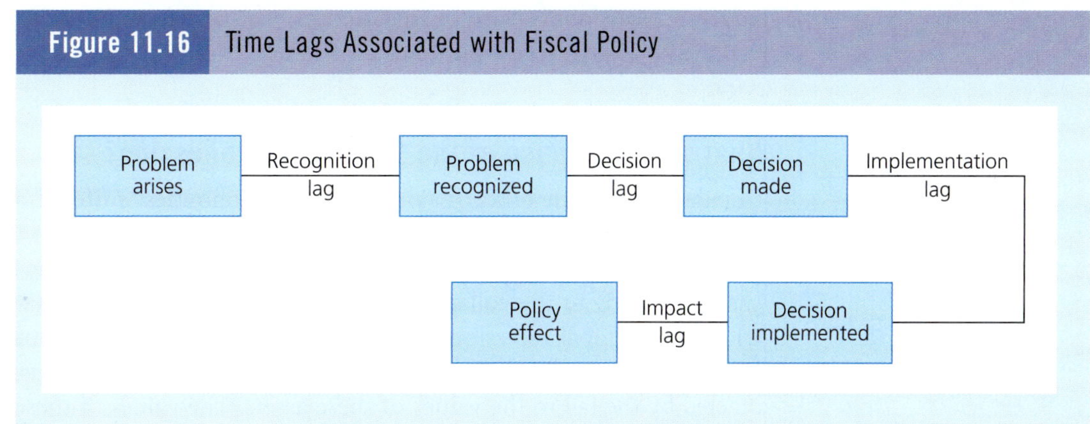

the social and political repercussions. And how about tax changes? To the government, tax cuts are attractive because voters like them. Tax increases are considerably less popular. So although it may be relatively easy to reduce taxes, it can be considerably more difficult to increase them when the economic situation so dictates.

A third problem associated with fiscal policy relates to our governmental structure. During a recession, an expansionary fiscal policy is appropriate, but the revenues of governments decline during a recession. Government spending, then, also tends to decline. Thus, the actions of provincial, territorial, and municipal governments can reduce the effectiveness of the fiscal policy being pursued by the federal government. Greater cooperation among the various levels of government will make fiscal policy a more effective stabilization tool.

A fourth problem with the use of fiscal policy is that during periods of heavy national debt when the government is committed to reducing the deficit and to arresting the growth of the national debt, it may be difficult for the government to use expansionary fiscal policy to stimulate the economy. We will return to this issue when we discuss the deficit and the public debt in a later chapter.

Reading Comprehension

The answers to these questions can be found on MyEconLab at www.myeconlab.com. MyEconLab

1. Mention three problems that are associated with the use of fiscal policy.
2. Define each of the following:
   a. Decision lag
   b. Implementation lag
   c. Impact lag
3. Explain why there is a need for cooperation and policy coordination between the various levels of government for fiscal policy to be effective.

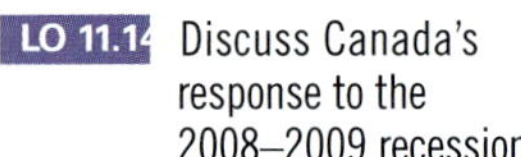
LO 11.14 Discuss Canada's response to the 2008–2009 recession

Fiscal Policy in Action: The 2008–2009 Recession and Canada's Response

Earlier in this chapter, we demonstrated that fiscal policy can be used to eliminate or reduce a recessionary gap. In this section, we show how Canada used fiscal policy to respond to a great recession that had a stranglehold on the economy during 2008 and 2009.

What was the cause of the 2008–2009 recession?

Canada, along with other major industrial economies, suffered a major recession in 2008–2009. It is generally agreed that this recession was the worst that was experienced since the Great Depression of 1929–1939. Experts concede that the 2008–2009 recession was due mainly to the collapse of the U.S. housing prices that started about two years prior to the global recession. Banks and other financial institutions around the world that had purchased U.S. home mortgages and related financial assets were negatively affected by the fall in the values of these assets. The values of these financial assets had fallen to such an extent that they were referred to as "toxic assets." A financial crisis ensued. Banks failed and credit became tight. The tight credit situation meant that businesses had difficulty obtaining credit. This had a negative impact on productivity and employment globally.

How was Canada affected by this recession?

The U.S and Canadian economies are very closely linked. The Americans buy most of our exports, and most of our imports come from the United States. The United States of America is by far Canada's most important trading partner. Between 2008 and 2009, Canada's real GDP fell from $1 321 360 million to $1 286 431 million—a decline of 2.6% over the period. At the same time, the unemployment rate rose from 6.1% in 2008 to 8.3% in 2009.

Looking at our foreign sector, we observe that our total exports fell from $489 856.8 million in 2008 to $369 708.2 million in 2009—a decline of 24.5%. Declines in our exports of natural gas, forestry products, and automotive products were particularly noticeable. Our exports of these items declined by 52%, 24%, and 28% respectively.

What fiscal policy measures were adopted to deal with this situation?

The government's fiscal policy measures are typically reflected in its budget. Acknowledging that the Canadian economy was in a recession, the federal government embarked on an Economic Action Plan in 2009 to deal with the recession. We have learned that the appropriate fiscal response to a recession is an expansionary fiscal policy. The government adopted such a policy in its 2009 budget when it allotted almost $30 billion (1.9% of GDP) in economic stimulus. These expenditures included action to help Canadians and stimulate spending, action to build infrastructure, and action to support businesses and communities.

Was the Economic Action Plan a one-year phenomenon?

No. The government realized that although the economy had started to recover from the recession, it was fragile and needed continued support. Thus, in its budget of March 4, 2010, the government promised that its Economic Action Plan would continue to strengthen the economy and help Canadian families and workers. The specific measures included:

- Income tax relief ($3.2 billion)
- Actions to create jobs ($4 billion)
- Infrastructure stimulus ($7.7 billion)
- Support for industries and communities ($1.9 billion)

Thus, the federal government committed $19 billion in new federal stimulus for 2010.

Was the Economic Action Plan successful?

Whether or not the government's economic stimulus program was successful is an issue that is being debated. Some analysts believe that the Economic Action Plan was a success. In December 2009, the economy recorded growth of 0.6 per cent in real GDP, and the unemployment rate was 8.2 per cent in February 2010. One must be careful not to attribute these results entirely to the government's fiscal policy response since other factors could have played a role. Others claim that the government's program had little or no effect of the performance of the economy, but that private investment should be credited with the improved economic condition. A question well worth asking is whether the recession would have been more severe and longer lasting had the government not adopted its Economic Action Plan.

Reading Comprehension

The answers to these questions can be found on MyEconLab at www.myeconlab.com. MyEconLab

1. Briefly explain the cause of the 2008–2009 recession.
2. To what extent did the recession affect Canada? (What happened to real GDP and employment?)
3. What kind of fiscal policy did the federal government adopt as a response to the recession? Why do you generally agree or disagree with that policy?
4. Do you think that the government's Economic Action Plan played any role in the economic recovery? Explain.

Review

1. Review the learning objectives listed at the beginning of the chapter.
2. Have you accomplished all the objectives? One way to determine this is toanswer the Reading Comprehension Questions at the end of each section. This will help you assess the extent to which you have accomplished the learning objectives.
3. If you have not accomplished an objective, review the relevant material before proceeding.

Key Points to Remember

1. LO 11.1, 11.2 Government spending constitutes over 19% of total spending. An increase in government spending, other things being equal, will cause an increase in the equilibrium level of income. A decrease in government spending, other things being equal, will cause a reduction in the equilibrium level of income.
2. LO 11.2 The government spending multiplier is the reciprocal of the *MPS*, which is the same as the investment multiplier.
3. LO 11.3 An increase in taxes, other things being equal, results in a fall in the equilibrium level of income. A reduction in taxes, other things being equal, results in an increase in the equilibrium level of income.
4. LO 11.4 In a closed economy with government spending and taxes, the equilibrium level of income occurs where the sum of investment and government spending equals the sum of saving and taxes.
5. LO 11.5 A budget deficit exists when government spending exceeds tax revenues. A budget surplus exists when tax revenues exceed government spending. A balanced budget exists when government spending equals tax revenues.
6. LO 11.6 The balanced budget theorem states that if government spending and taxes increase by the same amount, then income will increase by an amount equal to the increase in government spending. That is, the balanced budget multiplier is 1.
7. LO 11.7 Automatic stabilizers are built-in fiscal policy measures that operate automatically to produce economic stability. They include progressive taxes, assistance to agriculture, and employment insurance benefits. The fiscal drag is the phenomenon in which automatic stabilizers prevent the economy from recovering from a recession.
8. LO 11.8 In an inflationary situation, the appropriate fiscal policy is to reduce government spending and increase taxes. In a recessionary situation, the appropriate fiscal policy is to increase government spending and reduce taxes.

9. LO 11.9 Advantages of government spending are that they are more powerful than taxes, and they can be specifically focused. Disadvantages are that they have a lengthy implementation period, and they are difficult to reverse. The advantages of taxes are more favourable public acceptance, ease of change, and quick implementation. The disadvantages of taxes are that they are national in scope and they are less effective than government spending.
10. LO 11.10 Changes in the budget do not necessarily indicate changes in fiscal policy. Changes in the full-employment budget, however, do indicate changes in fiscal policy. The full-employment budget allows us to differentiate between automatic budget changes and discretionary fiscal policy.
11. LO 11.11, 11.12 Fiscal policy affects both the demand and supply sides of the economy. The effect of fiscal policy on the economy requires consideration of both demand-side and supply-side effects.
12. LO 11.13 The major limitations of fiscal policy are the difficulties imposed by time lags, varying government spending in response to business fluctuations, coordinating expenditures among the various levels of government, and the restriction imposed by a huge deficit and the public debt.
13. LO 11.14 Canada responded to the 2008–2009 recession by quickly putting into action an Economic Action Plan that involved increased government spending and tax cuts. These fiscal policy measures prevented the economy from slipping into a Great Depression.

Economic Word Power

Automatic fiscal policy or automatic (built-in) stabilizers (p. 294)
Balanced budget (p. 292)
Balanced budget change in spending (p. 293)
Balanced budget theorem (p. 294)
Budget deficit (p. 292)
Budget surplus (p. 292)
Contractionary fiscal policy (p. 296)
Decision lag (p. 303)
Discretionary fiscal policy (p. 294)
Expansionary fiscal policy (p. 297)
Fiscal drag (p. 295)
Fiscal policy (p. 282)
Full-employment budget (p. 299)
Functional finance (p. 292)
Impact lag or effect lag (p. 303)
Implementation lag (p. 303)
Lump-sum tax (p. 286)
Progressive tax system (p. 294)
Recognition lag (p. 303)

Problems and Exercises

Basic

1. LO 11.2 Table 11.7 shows data for a hypothetical closed economy with government spending. Investment (I) is fixed at 10 and government spending (G) is fixed at 5.
   a. Complete the remaining columns.
   b. Determine the equilibrium level of income *without* government spending.
   c. Determine the equilibrium level of income *with* government spending.
   d. What effect did government spending of $5 billion have on the equilibrium level of income?

Table 11.7 A Closed Economy with Government Spending

Income	Consumption	*I*	*G*	*AE*
40	50			
60	65			
80	80			
100	95			
120	110			
140	125			
160	140			
180	155			

2. LO 11.2 Referring to the data in Question 1, explain what would happen to income if it were $180 billion. Explain what would happen if income were $80 billion.
3. LO 11.2 On the basis of the data in Question 1:
   a. Draw a Keynesian cross diagram without government spending.
   b. Determine the equilibrium level of income and indicate it on your graph.
   c. On your graph, show how government spending of $5 billion will affect your *AE* line.
   d. Indicate the new equilibrium income that results from the $5 billion government expenditure.
   e. Explain why the $5 billion government spending causes income to increase by more than $5 billion.
4. LO 11.3 Table 11.8 contains data for a closed economy with government. (Y = income, T = taxes, Y_d = disposable income, C = consumption, $C(-t)$ = consumption after taxes, I = investment)

Table 11.8 A Closed Economy with Government

Y	*T*	*Yd*	*C*	*C(– t)*	*I*
40	20		40		20
60	20		50		20
80	20		60		20
100	20		70		20
120	20		80		20
140	20		90		20
160	20		100		20
180	20		110		20

   a. Complete the Y_d column.
   b. What is the equilibrium level of income?
   c. What is the *MPC*?
   d. If the tax were removed, how would consumption be affected?
   e. Complete the $C(-t)$ column.
   f. What would be the equilibrium level of income?
5. LO 11.3 Use the *AE–AO* model to show how a lump-sum tax will affect the equilibrium level of income.
6. LO 11.8 Figure 11.17 represents a closed economy with government spending and taxes. The equilibrium level of income is Y and the full-employment level is Y_f. Show how fiscal policy can be used to move the economy toward full employment. Consider changes in both government spending and taxes.

Figure 11.17 Diagram of a Closed Economy with Government

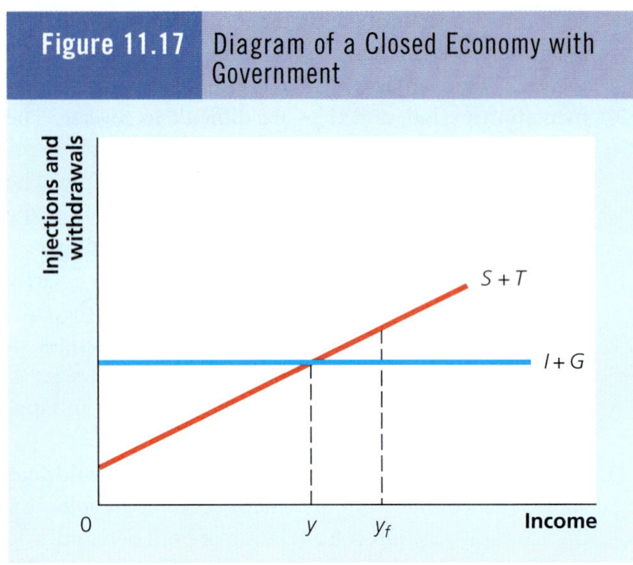

Questions in the Intermediate and Challenging sections cover several different concepts, and have not been organized by learning objectives.

Intermediate

1. Consider the data in Table 11.9 for a hypothetical closed economy. (Y = income, C = consumption, I = investment, G = government spending, and AE = aggregate expenditure)

Table 11.9 Hypothetical Closed Economy

Y	*C*	*I*	*G*	*AE*
100	200	60	40	
200	250	60	40	
300	300	60	40	
400	350	60	40	
500	400	60	40	
600	450	60	40	
700	500	60	40	
800	550	60	40	

   a. Complete the *AE* column.
   b. On quad paper, draw the 45-degree line and the *AE* line.
   c. On your graph, indicate the equilibrium level of income by *Y*.
   d. If the full-employment level of income is 700, what is the income/output gap?
   e. By how much should the government increase its spending to close the gap?

2. Table 11.10 contains income and consumption data for a hypothetical economy.

Table 11.10 Income and Consumption Data

Disposable Income ($ mil)	Consumption ($ mil)
0	500
500	900
1000	1300
1500	1700

a. If taxes are equal to $200 million regardless of the level of income, graph consumption against income (as opposed to disposable income).
b. How would an increase in taxes to $300 million affect your consumption curve?

3. LO 11.8 The *MPC* in a certain economy is 0.6. The full-employment level of income is $750 million and the economy is in equilibrium at $600 million.
a. How much is the income/output gap?
b. By how much should government spending increase to eliminate this gap?
c. By how much should the government cut taxes to eliminate the gap?
d. What balanced budget change in government spending would eliminate the gap?

Challenging

1. An income gap of $500 billion exists in an economy. The *MPC* in that economy is 0.9, autonomous expenditure is $400 billion, and all taxes are autonomous.
a. Calculate the level of full-employment income.
b. What change in government spending would eliminate the income gap?
c. What change in lump-sum tax would eliminate the gap?
d. What balanced budget change in government spending would eliminate the gap?

2. The *AD–AS* diagram in Figure 11.18 is for a hypothetical economy. At the equilibrium level of income of y, there is significant unemployment. The full-employment level of income is y_f. At the equilibrium price level of p, the rate of inflation is very high. How can fiscal policy be used to reduce the economy's current economic problems? Explain with the help of the graph.

Figure 11.18 *AD–AS* Diagram

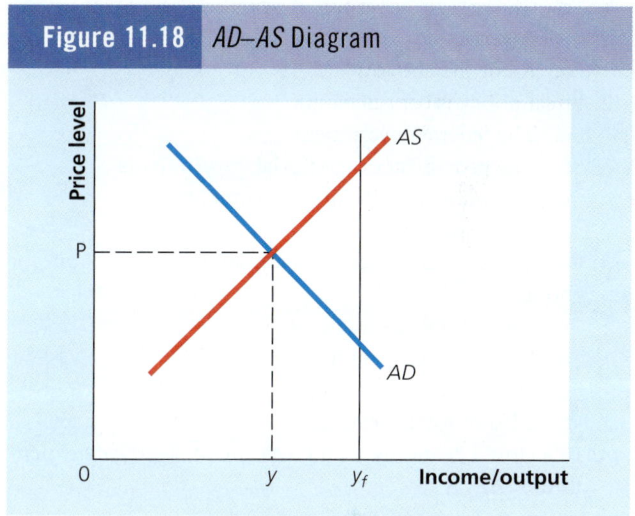

MyEconLab Visit the MyEconLab website at **www.myeconlab.com**. This online homework and tutorial system puts you in control of your own learning with study and practice tools directly correlated to this chapter's content.

Study Guide

Self-Assessment

What's your score?

Circle the letter that corresponds with the correct answer.

1. Fiscal policy refers to
   a. Changes in government spending and taxes by the central bank
   b. Changes in the money supply and interest rates by the government
   c. Changes in government spending and taxes by the government
   d. All of the above
2. Fiscal policy is conducted by
   a. The federal government
   b. The provincial or territorial governments
   c. The municipal (local) governments
   d. All of the above
3. Government purchases of goods and services account for about
   a. 5% of total spending
   b. 53% of total spending
   c. 19% of total spending
   d. 34% of total spending
4. In a closed economy with government, aggregate expenditure (*AE*) is
   a. $C + I + G$
   c. $C + I$
   b. $I + G$
   d. $I + G - C$
5. If a closed economy with government spending and taxation is in equilibrium, then
   a. $G = T$
   c. $AE > AO$
   b. $C + I + G = AO$
   d. None of the above
6. In a closed economy with government spending and taxes, the equilibrium level of income occurs where
   a. $Y = C + I + G$
   b. The $C + I + G$ line cuts the 45-degree line
   c. $I + G = S + T$
   d. All of the above
7. Other things being equal, an increase in government spending necessarily results in
   a. A decrease in the equilibrium level of income
   b. An increase in the equilibrium level of income
   c. A movement of the economy toward the full-employment level of income
   d. An imbalance in the budget
8. The government spending multiplier is
   a. The reciprocal of the *MPC*
   b. 1 – *MPC*
   c. Greater than 0 but less than 1
   d. None of the above
9. A lump-sum tax is
   a. The sum of all taxes levied during a specific period
   b. Consumption taxes less income taxes
   c. A fixed dollar amount that does not vary with income
   d. A tax that is proportional to income
10. Other things being equal, an increase in taxes
    a. Increases the equilibrium level of income
    b. Reduces the equilibrium level of income
    c. Will not affect the equilibrium level of income
    d. Will reduce government spending
11. A proportional tax is
    a. A fixed dollar amount regardless of the level of income
    b. One that produces a constant dollar revenue
    c. Expressed as a fixed percentage of income
    d. One that increases as income falls
12. An increase in the proportional tax rate
    a. Reduces desired consumer spending
    b. Increases desired *AE*
    c. Increases the size of the multiplier
    d. Increases the slope of the consumption curve

Questions 13, 14, and 15 refer to Figure 11.19. The full-employment level of income is $90 billion.

Figure 11.19 Government Spending and Taxes

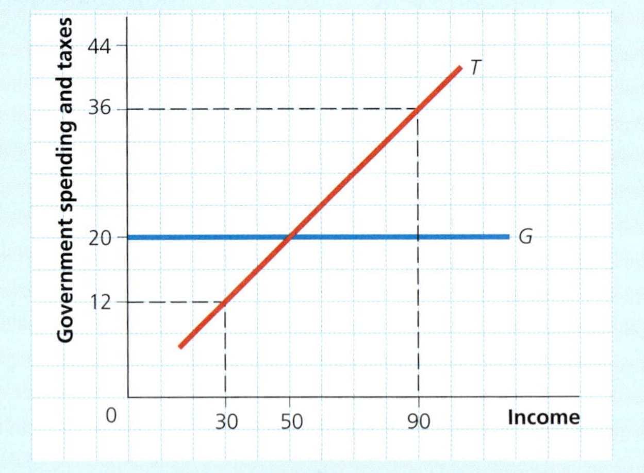

13. The full-employment budget
    a. Has a deficit of $16 billion
    b. Has a deficit of $8 billion

c. Is in balance
d. Has a surplus of $16 billion

14. At what level of income is the budget balanced?
a. $30 billion
b. $20 billion
c. $50 billion
d. $90 billion

15. Suppose that at $Y = \$90$ billion, desired consumption is $50 billion, and desired investment is $10 billion. If full employment is achieved by changing *G*, leaving the tax system unchanged, which of the following should result?
a. A reduced full-employment surplus
b. A full-employment deficit
c. A balanced full-employment budget
d. None of the above

16. If government spending and taxes both increase by $50 million, other things being equal, the equilibrium level of income will
a. Increase by $50 million
b. Remain constant
c. Increase by less than $50 million
d. None of the above

17. To combat an inflationary situation, the government could
a. Increase its spending and reduce taxes
b. Increase its spending and increase taxes
c. Reduce its spending and increase taxes
d. None of the above

18. In general, the advantages of using government spending rather than taxes to regulate economic activity include
a. Government spending is more powerful
b. Government spending can be focused on specific regions
c. Neither (a) nor (b)
d. Both (a) and (b)

19. Which of the following is correct?
a. Fiscal policy affects only the demand side of the economy
b. Fiscal policy affects only the supply side of the economy
c. The effects of fiscal policy on real GDP cannot be determined
d. Fiscal policy affects both the demand and the supply sides of the economy

20. Which of the following is a limitation of fiscal policy?
a. The presence of time lags
b. The inflexibility of government spending and tax measures
c. Poor coordination among various levels of government
d. All of the above

Problems and Exercises (Use Quad Paper for Graphs)

Answers to these questions can be found on MyEconLab at www.myeconlab.com. MyEconLab

1. Table 11.11 contains data for a hypothetical closed economy in which government does not levy any taxes.

Table 11.11 Data for a Hypothetical Economy

Income	Consumption
400	420
500	500
600	580
700	660
800	740
900	820
1000	900

a. If planned investment is 40, and government spending is 0, what is the equilibrium level of income?
b. Assume now that government spending is 20 at each level of income. What is the new equilibrium level of income?
c. Illustrate graphically the equilibrium level of income with government spending at 20.

2. Refer to Table 11.11. Assume that government spending increases from 20 to 40.
a. What will be the new equilibrium level of income?
b. What is the government spending multiplier?

3. Table 11.12 contains data for a closed economy with a government sector.

Table 11.12 Data for a Closed Economy with a Government Sector

Income	*C*	*I*	*G*	*AE*
40	30	10	20	
60	45	10	20	
80	60	10	20	
100	75	10	20	
120	90	10	20	
140	105	10	20	
160	120	10	20	
180	135	10	20	
200	150	10	20	

a. Complete the aggregate expenditure (*AE*) column.
b. On graph paper, draw the 45-degree line and graph the *AE* line.
c. On your graph, indicate the equilibrium level of income by *Y* on the horizontal axis.
d. Now suppose government spending increases by 20 at each level of income. Graph the new *AE* line and indicate the new equilibrium level of income by Y_1.
e. What are the numerical values of *Y* and Y_1?

4. Table 11.13 contains data for a hypothetical economy. Intended investment is fixed at 15, and government spending at each level of income is 10.

Table 11.13 Data for a Hypothetical Economy

Income	*C*	*I*	*G*	*AE*	*T*
100	100				
120	115				
140	130				
160	145				
180	160				
200	175				
220	190				
240	205				

a. Complete the table (except for the tax column) and determine the equilibrium level of income.
b. Suppose now that the government imposes a lump-sum tax of 20. Make a new table showing disposable income and consumption.
c. What will be the new equilibrium level of income?

5. Refer to Table 11.13. If government spending increases by 20 (from 10 to 30) and at the same time taxes rise by 20 (from 20 to 40), what will be the new equilibrium level of income?

6. The data in Table 11.14 are for a hypothetical closed economy.

Table 11.14 Data for a Hypothetical Closed Economy

Income	*C*	*I*	*G*	*AE*
60	50	15	15	
70	55	15	15	
80	60	15	15	
90	65	15	15	
100	70	15	15	
110	75	15	15	
120	80	15	15	
130	85	15	15	
140	90	15	15	

a. Complete the aggregate expenditure (*AE*) column.
b. On a graph, draw the 45-degree line and graph the *AE* line.
c. On your graph, indicate the equilibrium level of income by *Y* (on the horizontal axis).
d. If the full-employment income is 120, by how much should government spending increase to move the economy to its full-employment level of income?

7. Use the *AE–AO* diagram to show the effect of each of the following on the equilibrium level of income:
a. The imposition of a lump-sum tax on income
b. An increase in the tax rate

Chapter 12 Economic Fluctuations

Learning Objectives

After studying this chapter, you should be able to

12.1 Explain the phenomenon of business cycles

12.2 Understand and describe the phases of the business cycle

12.3 Explain how a business cycle affects different sectors of the economy

12.4 Understand economic theories of business fluctuations

12.5 Explain the role of politics in economic fluctuations

12.6 Discuss the real business cycle

12.7 Discuss policymakers' ability to control the business cycle

12.8 Understand how economists forecast business cycles

Assess Your Knowledge

MyEconLab

Answers to these questions can be found on MyEconLab at **www.myeconlab.com.**

1. What are business cycles?
2. What is a recession?
3. What would you expect to happen to investment if income increases?
4. Mention two factors that could cause economic fluctuations.

LO 12.1 Explain the phenomenon of business cycles

The Meaning of Business Cycles

What exactly are business cycles?

Over time, periods of expansions and contractions can be observed in the economy. These ups and downs in economic activity seem to occur in most sectors of the economy at the same time. These alternating periods of economic expansions and contractions have come to be known as **business cycles**. In a sense, this is a misnomer, because the term "cycles" suggests a recurrence at regular time intervals or in some circular manner. This, however, is not the case with business cycles. For this reason, some economists prefer to use the term **economic fluctuations** or **business fluctuations**.

business cycles, economic fluctuations, or business fluctuations alternating periods of economic expansions and contractions

For one reason or another, income may increase. This increase in income results in an increase in spending. This increase in spending reduces inventories below their desired levels and triggers production, which increases GDP. But this period of economic expansion (called a **boom**) does not continue forever. The cycle will reach a point at which total production catches up to aggregate demand. Businesses have restored their inventories to their desired levels. They then reduce their demand for inventories, and their suppliers reduce production, possibly closing plants and laying off workers. A period of economic contraction (called a **bust**) ensues. These periods of boom and bust are what we just defined as business cycles.

boom a period of economic expansion

bust a period of economic contraction

Reading Comprehension

The answers to these questions can be found on MyEconLab at www.myeconlab.com. MyEconLab

1. What are business cycles?
2. How appropriate is the term "cycles" as applied to economic fluctuations?

LO 12.2 Understand and describe the phases of the business cycle

Phases of the Cycle

What are the phases of a business cycle?

Business cycles do not occur with any striking regularity. Nevertheless, each one, whether mild or severe, whether short or long, goes through the same four phases:

trough, expansion, peak, and recession. These four phases are illustrated in Figure 12.1, which shows that real GDP tends to fluctuate around a long-term upward trend.

Can we discuss each phase briefly?

Let's begin with the trough. As we discuss each phase, it's a good idea to look at Figure 12.1.

trough the lowest point in the business cycle

Trough The **trough** is the lowest point (or bottom) of the business cycle. Here, actual output might be significantly less than potential output. Unemployment is likely to be high, businesspeople's expectations about the future will be pessimistic, and, as a result, investment will be low. Total demand for consumer goods and services will also be low. Moreover, banks will experience an increase in the amount of money available for loans because of an inability to find good and willing borrowers. If the fall in real output and the increase in unemployment are severe, the economy will be described as being in a **depression**. A depression is an economic period characterized by low economic activity and severe unemployment. You are, by now, quite familiar with the Great Depression of the 1930s.

depression an economic period characterized by low economic activity and severe unemployment

expansion or recovery the phase of the business cycle characterized by an increase in employment, income, and economic activity in general

peak the phase of the business cycle in which economic activity has reached its highest point

Expansion As Figure 12.1 shows, **expansion** is the phase that follows the trough and refers to the phase of the business cycle characterized by an increase in employment, income, and economic activity in general. In this phase of the cycle, output begins to expand, and income increases. Consumption expenditures and employment also increase. Businesspeople become optimistic about the future and increase their investment spending. People are confident and feel quite good about the economy. The prime minister and the government are usually popular. This is a good time to call an election. Because the economy appears to be recovering from a state of low growth or stagnation, we say that it has entered a period of **recovery**.

Figure 12.1 Phases of a Business Cycle

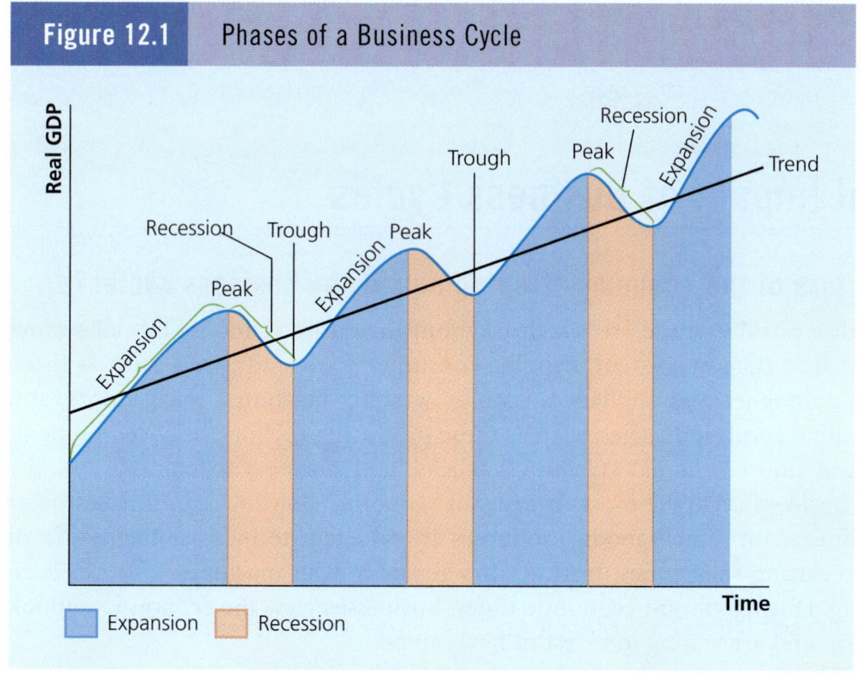

Peak Everyone likes a recovery, but good things must come to an end, and an expansion or a recovery is no exception. The end of the recovery comes when the use of the economy's resources has reached capacity. When this occurs, we say that the economy has entered the phase called the **peak**. During a peak, economic activity has reached its highest level. (See Figure 12.1.) Because the economy's resources are fully employed, increases in demand lead not to increases in real output but to increases in prices. In fact, prices will tend to begin to rise even before the economy has peaked.

recession a phase of the business cycle characterized by a general downswing in economic activity

Recession The phase that follows the peak is called a **recession**. This is a period of economic contraction, characterized by a general downswing in economic activity. In this phase of the cycle, consumption and investment spending decline. Many business ventures that were profitable during the expansion phase now become unprofitable. Business failures occur with increasing frequency and may even become widespread, depending on the severity of the recession. Real output decreases and unemployment increases. This is no time to call an election, unless the ruling party believes that the economic situation will get even worse. The 2008–2009 recession may still be fresh in your mind. A recession is typically defined, to the chagrin of many economists, as a decline in GDP for two or more consecutive quarters. The dissatisfaction with this definition stems from the fact that, as noted above, a recession involves changes in variables other than just GDP.

Do we know how long and how intense each phase of the cycle usually is?

A direct answer is no. A recession, for example, can be quite mild and short, such as the 1970 recession; or it can be long and severe with widespread unemployment, such as the 10-year Great Depression of the 1930s, or more recently, the 2008–2009 recession. Similarly, the expansion phase can extend over several years, such as the expansion of the 1960s; or it can be so short that the effects of the previous trough may still be evident in many sectors of the economy. The 1976 expansion is an example of a short expansionary period.

Reading Comprehension

The answers to these questions can be found on MyEconLab at www.myeconlab.com. MyEconLab

1. What are the phases of a business cycle? Mention the characteristics of each phase.

2. A popular definition of a recession is a decline in GDP for two or more consecutive quarters. Why is this definition unpopular among many economists?

LO 12.3 Explain how a business cycle affects different sectors of the economy

Sectoral Impact of Business Cycles

Are all sectors of the economy affected equally by business cycles?

The effects of a business cycle are felt throughout the entire economy but all sectors are not affected to the same extent. Durable consumer goods industries, such as those producing automobiles and appliances such as washing machines, refrigerators, and stoves and capital goods industries, such as those producing tractors, heavy equipment, residential and non-residential structures, trucks, and business machinery, feel the impact of a business cycle the most. During an economic slowdown, businesses postpone expenditures on capital goods. Producers are reluctant to increase their stock of capital goods during such times. Instead, they repair broken machines to try to keep them running. During vibrant economic times, businesses view the economic outlook with optimism and are willing to invest in new capital.

Expenditures on durable consumer goods follow a similar pattern. In an economic downturn, consumers are reluctant to replace automobiles and appliances with new ones, preferring instead to call in the repair person and to pay the mechanic to repair the old car. They may defer plans to purchase new furniture for a year or so. These decisions have negative impacts on the manufacturers of these consumer durables. During periods of economic expansion, manufacturers of capital goods and durable consumer goods receive the greatest benefits.

How about producers of non-durable consumer goods? How do they fare?

Whereas it may be relatively easy to keep the suite of furniture for another year or two, and to hold on to the old automobile for a while longer, it may not be so easy to postpone the purchase of food, school supplies, and medical and dental services. These service industries and producers of non-durable consumer goods are somewhat shielded from an economic downturn. In fact, some service businesses such as repair technicians, mechanics, and upholsterers may even prosper during a recession.

Reading Comprehension

The answers to these questions can be found on MyEconLab at www.myeconlab.com. MyEconLab

1. Why do business cycles severely affect manufacturers of capital goods and durable consumer goods?
2. In what way are service industries and producers of non-durable consumer goods insulated from the effects of business cycles?

LO 12.4 Understand economic theories of business fluctuations

Economic Theories of Business Fluctuations

Have economists formulated any theories to explain business cycles?

Yes. In fact, economists have formulated an impressive array of theories to explain economic fluctuations. Let us examine some of these theories.

The Underconsumption Theory According to the underconsumption theory of the business cycle, economic fluctuations are caused by variations in consumer spending. National income accounting figures show that personal expenditure on consumer goods and services is the largest component of aggregate expenditure. If consumption changes (other things being equal), then aggregate expenditure also changes. Output then changes as well. The underconsumption theory states that as income increases, people spend less of the increase on consumption and put more into saving. This situation may cause planned saving to exceed planned investment, resulting in a fall in income. When income falls, people spend a larger proportion of their income on consumer goods and services and a smaller proportion on savings. At this level of income, intended investment may exceed intended saving, resulting in an increase in output and income. To summarize, then, the underconsumption theory states that fluctuations in consumer spending result in an imbalance between intended saving and investment, which, in turn, causes ups and downs in income and employment.

> According to the underconsumption theory of the business cycle, economic fluctuations are caused by variations in consumer spending.

The Volatile Investment Theory According to the volatile investment theory, increases and decreases in inventory investment cause economic fluctuations. Of all the components of aggregate expenditure, investment is the most volatile. Because investment fluctuates substantially from one period to the next, many economists consider it to be the prime cause of fluctuations in economic activity. Inventory investment is relatively small but highly unstable. Its instability is the major cause of fluctuations in total investment. Proponents of this theory use the term **inventory cycles** to refer to the volatile investment theory of the business cycle. Inventory cycles are economic fluctuations caused by changes in inventory investment. During a period of low economic activity, businesspeople run down their production levels in response to reductions in their orders, and unemployment results. When the economy recovers, they restore their inventory levels. This investment in inventories increases employment and income.

inventory cycles economic fluctuations caused by changes in inventory investment

> Increases and decreases in inventory investment cause fluctuations in economic activity.

Government Spending Theory According to the government spending theory, variations in government spending contribute to economic instability. This theory states that during wars, national disasters, or other emergency situations, government spending rises sharply. Such rapid increases in government spending cause increases in income and employment, which may exert upward pressure on the price level. But when the emergency passes, government spending is reduced, and this reduction in government spending can result in a significant reduction in output and employment. In this way, government spending can be a destabilizing force.

> Changes in government spending may account for fluctuations in economic activity.

The Expectations Theory The expectations theory states that businesspeople's expectations play a key role in business fluctuations. In a recession, businesspeople become pessimistic about the future economic outlook. This pessimism results in postponement of investment spending and possibly leads to cutbacks in certain business ventures. Certain investment projects remain on the drawing board, and others are shelved. Output and employment decrease as a result. When economic activity revives, businesspeople become optimistic about the future. Projects that were shelved are now reactivated and investment spending increases. Consequently, employment, income, and output also increase.

> Changes in expectations may result in fluctuations in economic activity.

The Innovations Theory The innovations theory of the business cycle owes its origin to the work of Joseph Schumpeter (1883–1950), an Austrian-born economist who worked at Harvard University. According to this theory, innovations are the main cause of business cycles. Those who subscribe to this view argue that innovations are introduced when economic activity is on the upswing. The introduction of these innovations is accompanied by a flood of economic activity that sooner or later subsides. After a period of low economic activity, another set of innovations is introduced, and this leads to another round of increased business activity.

> Innovations are a prime cause of business cycles.

The Monetary Theory The monetary theory states that the availability of money and the rise and fall of interest rates cause business fluctuations. You will not fully understand the effect of money on economic activity until we have studied monetary theory and policy. That should not, however, prevent you from getting an idea of the role of money in economic fluctuations. Monetary theory maintains that when the economy is in the expansion phase, business ventures are profitable. Banks are therefore willing to extend business loans. Eventually, the amount of money available for loans diminishes. The demand for loans then causes banks to increase their interest rates. Businesspeople also have a harder time securing loans. This tight credit situation results in a reduction in economic activity. Many experts maintain that the recent (2008–2009) recession was due to tight credit conditions caused by the financial crisis that originated in the United States. When banks acquire more lending money, credit becomes easier, and the economy then re-enters an expansion phase.

> Changes in the availability of money and fluctuating interest rates cause business fluctuations.

Does the multiplier theory that we studied in Chapter 10 have anything to do with the business cycle?

In fact, there is a multiplier–accelerator theory of the business cycle.

The Multiplier–Accelerator Theory According to the multiplier–accelerator theory, a change in income induces an even bigger change in investment. To understand this theory, you must first understand the acceleration principle. The acceleration principle, or simply the **accelerator**, is closely associated with the concept of induced investment, which you have already learned. The **acceleration principle** states that an increase in income leads to an accelerated increase in investment.

acceleration principle or accelerator the theory that an increase in income leads to an accelerated increase in investment

> According to the acceleration principle, a change in income induces an amplified change in investment.

Table 12.1 illustrates the operation of this principle.

We assume that there is no depreciation of capital. There is therefore no difference between gross and net investment. We assume also that it takes $4 worth of capital to produce $1 of output per year. In other words, the **capital–output ratio** (that is, the ratio of the value of capital stock to the value of annual output) is assumed to be 4:1.

capital–output ratio the ratio of the value of capital stock to the value of annual output

Why would anyone spend $4 on capital to produce only $1 of output?

That is a legitimate question. Is there any wisdom in spending $4 on capital to produce $1 of output? The idea is not at all ludicrous when we consider that the $4 expenditure

Table 12.1 The Acceleration Principle

Year	Total Output ($000)	Required Capital Stock ($000)	Investment ($000)
1	50	200	0
2	52	208	8
3	52	208	0
4	54	216	8
5	56	224	8
6	58	232	8
7	59	236	4
8	62	248	12
9	66	264	16
10	70	280	16

on capital will yield a stream of output of $1 in each successive year. The investment can therefore be profitable.

Let us focus on Table 12.1. It shows that an annual output of $50 000 requires a capital stock of $200 000. An increase in output of $2000 in Year 2 (from 50 000 to $52 000) requires an increase in capital stock from $200 000 to $208 000—that is, an investment of $8000. The table shows that if total output increases at a constant rate (as in Years 4 to 6), investment will remain at a constant level. If the rate of increase in output falls off (as from Year 6 to Year 7), investment will fall. Investment will increase when total output increases at an increasing rate, as in Years 7 to 9. It is important to note also that investment is proportional to the change in total output. Given the change in total output, the amount of investment required can be calculated by multiplying the change in output by the capital–output ratio—or the *accelerator*, as it is often called.

The formula for the required investment can be developed by using simple algebra. We will have K = required capital stock and Y = total output/income.

$$\text{Let } K/Y = \upsilon, \text{ where } \upsilon \text{ is constant}$$

$$\text{Then } K = \upsilon Y$$

$$\Delta K = \upsilon \Delta Y$$

That is,

$$I = \upsilon \Delta Y$$

where I is the required investment.

Can you give an example to illustrate how the formula can be used?

The following is an illustrative example:

Example: Given a capital–output ratio of 4, how much investment is required to increase output from $56 000 to $58 000?

Solution:

$$K/Y = \upsilon = 4; \Delta Y = 2000$$

$$I = \upsilon \Delta Y$$

$$I = 4 \times 2000 = 8000$$

The required investment is $8000.

How realistic is the accelerator theory?

You must not forget that the accelerator theory is a model; as such, it incorporates assumptions. For example, it assumes that an increase in demand for consumer goods and services translates into demand for the capital goods that produce these consumer goods and services. This implies that there is no excess capacity in the industries producing consumer goods. You should keep in mind, however, that in reality firms sometimes do have excess capacity. In cases where they do, it is unlikely that they will purchase new equipment as soon as there is an increase in demand. Firms are more likely to use up any excess capacity before undertaking new investment.

The simple acceleration principle also assumes that excess capacity exists in the industries producing capital goods. However, keep in mind that, in certain circumstances, the capital goods industries may not be able to respond immediately to increases in demand for capital goods. Thus they must delay investment.

We have not yet explained the multiplier–accelerator theory of the business cycle.

Professor Paul Samuelson (1915–2009) demonstrated that the interaction of the multiplier and the accelerator can produce wide fluctuations in economic activity. If the economy is expanding, the increase in income accelerates investment. The increased investment generates an even greater increase in income. But as the economy's resources become fully employed, the acceleration of output slows down. And, as we have already seen, a deceleration in output hinders investment. The decreased investment, other things being equal, causes an even greater reduction in output via the multiplier. Hence, the interaction of the multiplier and the accelerator acts to intensify fluctuations in economic activity.

The multiplier–accelerator interaction magnifies the business cycle.

Figure 12.2 Possible Causes of Economic Fluctuations

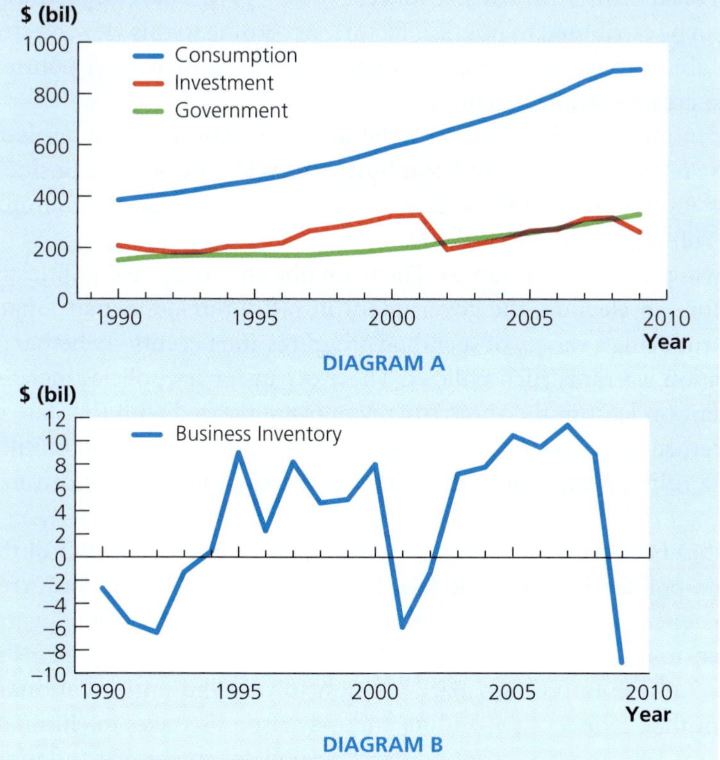

Diagram A: Consumption, investment, and government spending in Canada, 1990–2009

Diagram B: Inventory component of investment

Source: Statistics Canada, *Canadian Economic Observer*, various years, and Statistics Canada website at: http://www40.statcan.gc.ca l01/cst01/econ04-eng.htm

We have considered several plausible causes of business cycles. Which one is the most important?

Good question! Is the biggest culprit consumption, investment, government spending, or some other factor?

Let's look at Figure 12.2. Diagram A shows the behaviour of consumption, private investment, and government spending in Canada from 1990 to 2009. Diagram B shows the inventory component of investment in order to emphasize its relative volatility. Clearly, the annual fluctuations in investment spending and government spending have been greater than the fluctuations in consumer spending. But the greatest fluctuations are seen in inventory investment.

Diagram B seems to lend strong support to the volatile investment theory and especially to the notion of inventory cycles. It is likely that it is combinations of these and other factors (including monetary factors), rather than any single dominant factor, that drive fluctuations in economic activity.

Reading Comprehension

The answers to these questions can be found on MyEconLab at www.myeconlab.com. MyEconLab

1. Briefly explain each of the following theories of the business cycle:
   a. The volatile investment theory
   b. The innovations theory
   c. The monetary theory
2. Explain how each of the following can be destabilizing:
   a. Consumer spending
   b. Government spending
   c. Multiplier–accelerator interaction
3. Briefly explain the principle of acceleration.
4. What relation, if any, exists between the accelerator and the capital–output ratio?

LO 12.5 Explain the role of politics in economic fluctuations

Politics and the Business Cycle

What role does politics play in the business cycle?

Several prominent economists, including the German political economist Karl Marx (1818–1883) and the Polish economist Michal Kalecki (1899–1970), have argued that many business cycles can be attributed to political factors. According to this view, elected politicians can use or abuse tools of economic policy to advance their own political objectives, instead of to create economic stability.

political business cycle a business cycle that is caused by changes in government spending and taxes to achieve political rather than economic ends

Fluctuations in economic activity caused by the use of economic policy tools to further political ends are referred to as the **political business cycle**. The political business cycle describes business cycles believed to be due to the use of government economic policies to achieve the ruling parties' political end.

Consider the following set of circumstances. The main objective of elected politicians is to be re-elected. Before an election, the government in office pursues expansionary economic policies—introducing a variety of spending programs and tax cuts—whether or not the economic situation warrants such policies. These expansionary policies increase income and employment (at least in the short run). Voters are pleased with the state of the economy, so they return the government to power. To express the situation bluntly, the government (or the ruling party) "buys" the election through politically motivated fiscal policies.

Once the election has been won (or bought), however, the long-term impact of the expansionary economic policies begins to be felt. If the economic stimulus occurred when the economy was operating close to full employment, then the increase in aggregate expenditure is likely to result in inflation after the election. The electorate begins to complain and protest, and the opposition parties begin to demand anti-inflationary action. The government then reduces its spending and may also raise taxes to eliminate the inflationary pressures and appease those demanding policies to combat inflation. These contractionary policies plunge the economy into a recession. The recession succeeds in eliminating the inflationary pressures. By the time this process is completed, it is again close to another election, and the government is again ready to engage in another round of pre-election spending that will simply start the whole process again.

Actual events seem to lend some credence to the political business cycle. During election periods, the economy tends to expand more frequently than it contracts. This correlation, however, may be due to the fact that governments are much more likely to call elections during periods of prosperity than during periods of high unemployment and low economic growth.

Reading Comprehension

The answers to these questions can be found on MyEconLab at www.myeconlab.com. MyEconLab

1. Explain the political business cycle.

2. Is it rational for a government to increase its spending even though it knows that such action may be inflationary?

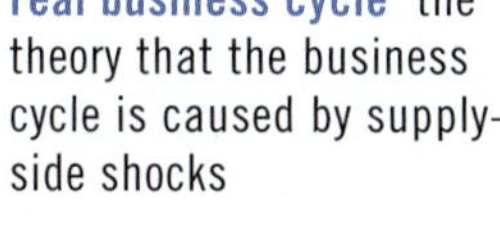

The Real Business Cycle

Can supply-side factors also contribute to economic fluctuations?

real business cycle the theory that the business cycle is caused by supply-side shocks

Some economists believe so. According to the **real business cycle** theory, economic fluctuations are caused primarily by shifts in aggregate supply. Real business cycle theorists claim that nominal shocks do not affect real output and employment, because the economy will quickly adjust to its natural levels of output and employment.

Supporters of the real business cycle believe that a business cycle can be initiated by any severe supply-side shock, such as a prolonged drought that adversely affects agricultural production on a large scale. Other supply-side changes, such as changes in technology or changes in the supply of labour that occur constantly or simultaneously in several industries, can also generate business cycles.

The real business cycle theory can be explained with the help of the *AD–AS* model developed earlier in this text. In Figure 12.3, we assume that the *AS* curve is vertical. The economy is initially in equilibrium at a real output of *y* and a price level of *P*.

Figure 12.3 Illustration of the Real Business Cycle

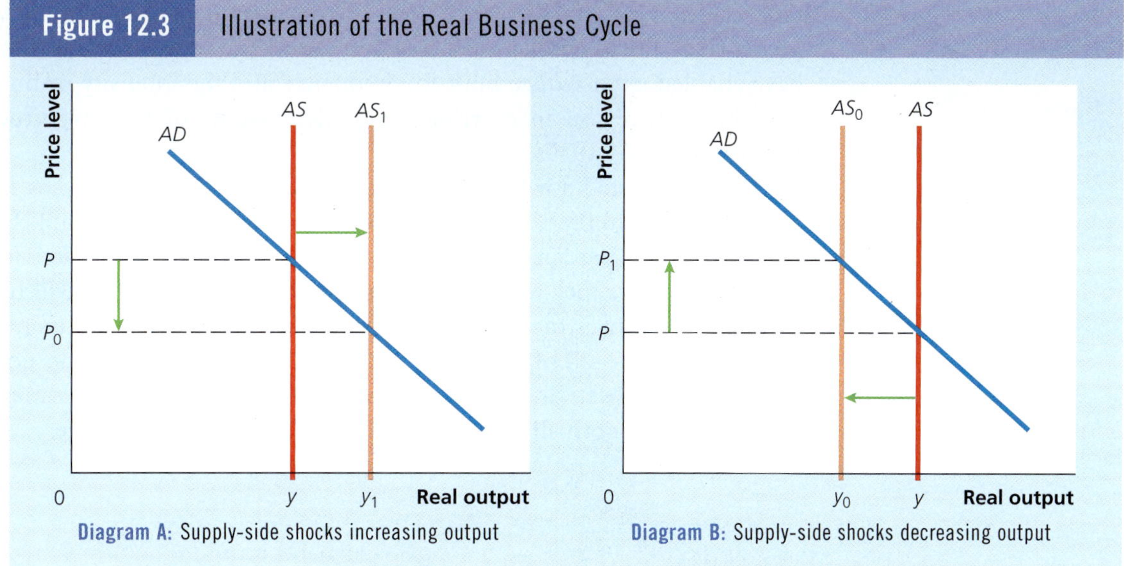

Diagram A: Supply-side shocks increasing output

Diagram B: Supply-side shocks decreasing output

Let us assume that a supply-side shock shifts the aggregate supply curve to the right from *AS* to AS_1, as shown in Diagram A. Consequently, real output increases from *y* to y_1, while the price level falls from *P* to P_0. An aggregate supply-side shock, such as a tremendous shortage of energy resources, would shift the aggregate supply curve to the left from *AS* to AS_0, as shown in Diagram B. Consequently, real output falls from *y* to y_0, while the price level rises from *P* to P_1. Such changes in aggregate supply result in fluctuations in real output and employment.

Reading Comprehension

The answers to these questions can be found on MyEconLab at www.myeconlab.com. MyEconLab

1. Briefly explain the real business cycle theory.
2. Suppose it were possible to control supply-side shocks. Would that guarantee full control over economic fluctuations? Explain.

LO 12.7 Discuss policymakers' ability to control the business cycle

Controlling the Business Cycle

Can it be said that we have conquered the business cycle?

One of the main reasons for developing theories about economic phenomena is to be able to understand them and, hopefully, to control them. Following the publication of *The General Theory* and the understanding of the general message of Keynesian economics, many economists and policymakers believed that with the judicious use of macroeconomic policies, business cycles could be reduced.

The Canadian economy enjoyed a period of about 16 years (from 1992 to 2008) without a recession; and perhaps some people had just begun to consider business cycles as a thing of the past. Whether or not this view was overly optimistic was answered by the recession of 2008–2009. There is considerable agreement, however, that our increased ability to predict business fluctuations and to use macroeconomic policy tools have enabled us to reduce both the frequency and the intensity of business cycles. We have been successful in averting major depressions of the magnitude of the Great Depression of the 1930s.

Although our knowledge of the operation of the economy has improved greatly since the 1930s, to the point where another Great Depression is unlikely, our knowledge is still imperfect. We can expect mild ups and downs in economic activity, resulting from any of the causes that we have discussed in this chapter. There will be fluctuations in private-sector investment (including inventories) and government spending, and changes in taxes—all of which are potentially destabilizing. We do not yet possess the knowledge of how to fine-tune the system to the state at which we can iron out all of the wrinkles and smooth all the ripples. This is a continuing challenge.

Reading Comprehension

The answers to these questions can be found on MyEconLab at www.myeconlab.com. MyEconLab

1. To what extent can policymakers control the business cycle?
2. Discuss the view that macroeconomic policies are useless against the business cycle.

LO 12.8 Understand how economists forecast business cycles

Forecasting Business Cycles

To what extent are economists able to forecast business cycles?

The ability to forecast business cycles would greatly enhance our ability to control them. Economists have made some progress in forecasting economic fluctuations. You must remember, however, that economics is not an exact science, and forecasts, though quite useful, are not exact. A very simple method of forecasting business cycles is to use *leading indicators.*

leading indicators economic variables that turn downward before the cycle peak and upward before the trough

coincidental indicators variables that coincide exactly with the business cycle

lagging indicators variables that turn downward after the peak and upward after the trough

Indicators of economic activity fall into three main categories: leading indicators, coincidental indicators, and lagging indicators. **Leading indicators** are economic variables that typically turn downward *before* the cycle peak and upward *before* the trough. Examples of leading indicators are stock prices, orders for durable goods, and the rate of change of the money supply. **Coincidental indicators** are variables that coincide exactly with the business cycle. Their peaks and troughs coincide with the peaks and troughs of the business cycle. Examples of coincidental indicators are GDP, employment, and business profits. **Lagging indicators** are variables that turn downward *after* the peak and upward *after* the trough. Examples of lagging indicators are inventories and personal income.

Table 12.2 contains a list of economic indicators.

Economists rely on leading indicators to forecast peaks and troughs in the business cycle. For example, if the leading indicators turn upward, economists suspect that a trough is imminent. If they turn downward, economists suspect that the economy is about to peak. Unfortunately, economic forecasting is a more difficult exercise than just looking at leading indicators. Moreover, these leading indicators sometimes send false messages. For these reasons, economists combine the use of leading indicators with other forecasting techniques, and a great deal of effort is expended in improving the existing tools and in developing new and more reliable methods.

Table 12.2 List of Economic Indicators

Leading Indicators	Coincident Indicators	Lagging Indicators
Stock prices	GDP	Inventories
Durable goods orders	Employment	Personal income
Growth of money supply	Business profits	Labour costs
Net business formation	Industrial production index	
New building permits		

Can we discuss one of the other approaches used to forecast business activity?

Favourable and Unfavourable Factors Another approach used to forecast general business activity is to consider favourable and unfavourable factors. To use this approach, the forecaster must be familiar with the factors that contribute to economic expansion and those that lead to economic slowdowns. Favourable factors are those that are likely to contribute to economic expansion or recovery. Unfavourable factors are those that contribute to recessions. Among the favourable factors are the following:

- A fall in the unemployment rate
- Falling interest rates
- An increase in purchasing intentions
- A fall in the saving rate
- An increase in construction
- An increase in the purchases of consumer durables
- An increase in marriages and new families

The unfavourable factors include the following:

- Rising inflation
- Contractionary monetary and fiscal policies
- Falling foreign demand
- Rapid increases in the world price of oil and other forms of energy
- Instability in the foreign exchange market
- A huge and mounting public debt

On the basis of macroeconomic theory, the forecaster must analyze the situation to determine the probable impact that these factors will have on the economy. If the impact of the favourable factors outweighs the impact of the unfavourable factors, then the forecaster will forecast an increase in economic activity. If the unfavourable factors are likely to have a more powerful impact than the favourable factors, then the prognosis will be a recession.

BUSINESS SITUATION 12.1

You are a business analyst, and you have been asked to forecast the probable course of GDP for the near future. You examine the leading indicators and observe that they indicate an upward tendency.

What would you conclude about the probable future course of GDP?

The answer to this Business Situation can be found in Appendix A.

Can we learn any important lessons from the 2008–2009 recession?

History teaches us lessons if we are willing to learn, and the 2008–2009 recession has its own lessons. Some of these lessons are new while others merely reinforce what we already knew. Let us list the major lessons that can be learned from the 2008–2009 recession.

1. We have a great deal more to learn about business cycles.
2. A financial crisis can spill over into the real sector of the economy with adverse effects. The two sectors are closely related.
3. Proactive monetary and fiscal policies can dull the edge of a recession.
4. A credit crunch can cripple an economy.
5. We have not yet conquered the business cycle.
6. Both big and small businesses are susceptible to a recession.
7. It is still difficult to forecast business cycles.

Reading Comprehension

The answers to these questions can be found on MyEconLab at www.myeconlab.com. MyEconLab

1. What are leading indicators? How can they be used to forecast business cycles?
2. List four important lessons that can be learned from the 2008–2009 recession.

Review

1. Review the learning objectives listed at the beginning of the chapter.
2. Have you accomplished all the objectives? One way to determine this is to answer the Reading Comprehension Questions at the end of each section. This will help you assess the extent to which you have accomplished the learning objectives.
3. If you have not accomplished an objective, review the relevant material before proceeding.

Key Points to Remember

1. LO 12.1, 12.2 The economy is subject to periods of economic fluctuations or business cycles. Each cycle has its own peculiarities, but we can identify four phases common to all cycles: trough, expansion, peak, and recession or contraction.
2. LO 12.3 Business cycles affect the entire economy, but they affect different sectors differently.
3. LO 12.4 Among the theories advanced to explain business cycles are the underconsumption theory, the volatile investment theory, the government spending theory, the expectations theory, the innovations theory, the monetary theory, and the multiplier–accelerator theory.
4. LO 12.4 The acceleration principle states that investment depends on the rate of change of income. As income increases, the demand for consumer goods increases. A larger capital stock is required to produce a larger volume of consumer goods. Investment will then increase.
5. LO 12.5 The political business cycle is the result of changes in government spending and taxes by elected government officials in an attempt to secure their political positions rather than to stabilize the economy.
6. LO 12.6 The real business cycle theory states that business fluctuations are due mainly to aggregate supply shocks.
7. LO 12.7 Although business cycles are not a thing of the past, economists have made progress in understanding them and in formulating policies to reduce their frequency and severity.
8. LO 12.8 Leading indicators tend to turn downward before the peak and upward before the trough. Economists use leading indicators to help them forecast business cycles. They also use favourable and unfavourable factors.

Economic Word Power

Acceleration principle or accelerator (p. 319)
Boom (p. 314)
Business cycles or economic fluctuations or business fluctuations (p. 314)
Bust (p. 314)
Capital–output ratio (p. 319)
Coincidental indicators (p. 325)
Depression (p. 315)
Expansion or recovery (p. 315)
Inventory cycles (p. 318)
Lagging indicators (p. 325)
Leading indicators (p. 325)
Peak (p. 315)
Political business cycle (p. 322)
Real business cycle (p. 323)
Recession (p. 316)
Trough (p. 315)

Problems and Exercises

Basic

1. LO 12.2 Draw a diagram showing the four phases of the business cycle, beginning with the peak.
2. LO 12.4 Each item below implies a particular theory of the business cycle. Identify the theory implied by each item.
   a. Fluctuations in the relation between saving and investment cause economic cycles.
   b. Fluctuating interest rates and credit conditions result in business fluctuations.
   c. Inventory volatility causes fluctuations in economic activity.
   d. Alternating pessimistic and optimistic economic outlooks result in ups and downs in output and employment.
   e. Fluctuations in government spending cause changes in output and employment.
   f. Research and development lead to new ways of doing things that produce temporary upswings in economic activity.
   g. A change in income causes a change in investment, which causes a change in income, and so on.
3. LO 12.4 Assume that it requires $3 worth of capital to produce $1 of output per year. How much investment would be required to increase output from $650 000 to $680 000?
4. LO 12.4 An increase in capital from $100 million to $110 million results in an increase in output from $60 million to $65 million. Calculate the accelerator.
5. LO 12.6 Indicate which of the following are associated with the real business cycle:
   a. Diseased crops cripple the agricultural sector from time to time.
   b. Increases in the money supply raise demand and the price level.
   c. Changes in taxes produce changes in employee and employer motivation.
   d. Changes in government spending affect aggregate expenditure.
   e. Technological changes affect labour productivity.
6. LO 12.8 Arrange the following indicators as leading, coincident, or lagging indicators:
   a. GDP
   b. New building permits
   c. Money supply growth
   d. Employment
   e. Personal income
   f. Labour costs
   g. Net business formation
7. LO 12.8 Group the following into favourable or unfavourable factors with regard to business cycles:
   a. Falling interest rates
   b. Falling saving rates
   c. An increase in consumer and producer optimism
   d. Increasing demand for new homes
   e. Rapid and prolonged increases in the world price of crude oil
   f. An increase in construction
   g. A reduction in exports
   h. Falling unemployment
   i. Unstable foreign exchange rates
   j. Rising inflation

Questions in the Intermediate and Challenging sections cover several different concepts, and have not been organized by learning objectives.

Intermediate

1. Economists have determined that the economy has peaked. From your knowledge of business cycle theory, explain the fiscal policy measures that should be taken to prevent fluctuations in economic activity. Assume that the economy responds quickly to economic policy stimulus.
2. Referring to Question 1 above, how would your prescription change if the economy were in the expansionary phase of the cycle?

Challenging

1. Assume that you believe in the validity of the political business cycle. Suggest how such cycles might be prevented. Is there any downside to your suggestions?
2. "Clearly, economic fluctuations are due to changes in aggregate demand. Therefore, if policymakers can effectively control aggregate demand, then business cycles will be a thing of the past." Challenge this argument.
3. "There is not a shred of evidence to support the view that economists have not conquered the business cycle." Challenge this argument.

MyEconLab Visit the MyEconLab website at **www.myeconlab.com**. This online homework and tutorial system puts you in control of your own learning with study and practice tools directly correlated to this chapter's content.

Study Guide

Self-Assessment

What's your score?

Circle the letter that corresponds with the correct answer.

1. Business cycles are
 a. Celebrated economic events that occur at regular intervals over a 10-year period
 b. Periods when the economy fails to respond to economic stimuli
 c. Alternating periods of expansion and contraction in economic activity
 d. All of the above

2. Business cycles refer to
 a. Periods of rapid inflation
 b. Situations of severe unemployment, such as that experienced in the 1930s
 c. Fluctuations in economic activity
 d. None of the above

3. A boom is
 a. Another name for a recession
 b. Equivalent to a trough
 c. Also called a bust
 d. Another name for an expansionary period

4. A period of economic contraction is called a
 a. Cycle
 b. Boom
 c. Bust
 d. None of the above

5. Which of the following is not a phase of the business cycle?
 a. Recession
 b. Recovery
 c. Inflation
 d. Trough

6. The number of distinct phases of a business cycle is
 a. 3
 b. 4
 c. 5
 d. 6

7. The phase of the business cycle that follows the peak is the
 a. Trough
 b. Recovery
 c. Recession
 d. Inflation

8. Which of the following is a phase of the business cycle?
 a. Peak
 b. Trough
 c. Recovery
 d. All of the above

9. The phase of the business cycle that precedes the peak is
 a. Expansion
 b. Recession
 c. Trough
 d. Depression

10. If investment, consumption, real output, and employment are increasing, the economy is most likely
 a. In its recessionary phase
 b. In a depression
 c. At its peak
 d. In the expansion phase

11. A trough is characterized by
 a. Rapid inflation and expanding real GDP
 b. High unemployment and no economic growth
 c. A rapid increase in employment and investment
 d. None of the above

12. Which of the following is a theory of the business cycle?
 a. The expansion theory
 b. The cycle theory
 c. The innovations theory
 d. All of the above

13. Which of the following is not a theory of business cycles?
 a. The cyclical theory
 b. The innovations theory
 c. The inventory cycles theory
 d. The monetary theory

14. Which theory claims that business cycles are caused by changes in the availability of money and fluctuating interest rates?
    a. The underconsumption theory
    b. The acceleration theory
    c. The interest–multiplier theory
    d. None of the above
15. If the capital–output ratio is 2.4, and there is no excess capacity in consumer goods industries, then to increase output by $24 million requires an increase in investment of
    a. $10 million
    b. $21.6 million
    c. $26.4 million
    d. $57.6 million
16. The notion that business cycles may be caused by government manipulation of spending and taxes is called the
    a. Political business cycle
    b. Electioneering business cycle
    c. Government-induced business cycle
    d. None of the above
17. The real business cycle theory states that business cycles are caused by
    a. Changes in real spending
    b. Demand-side changes
    c. Changes in aggregate supply
    d. None of the above
18. Business cycles that originate from the supply side of the economy are called
    a. Economy-wide cycles
    b. Secular cycles
    c. Real business cycles
    d. Real inventory cycles
19. Leading indicators turn
    a. Downward before the peak and upward before the trough
    b. Downward after the peak and upward after the trough
    c. Downward before the peak and upward after the trough
    d. None of the above
20. Which of the following is an example of a leading indicator?
    a. Orders for durable goods
    b. Gross domestic product (GDP)
    c. Inventories
    d. None of the above

Problems and Exercises (Use Quad Paper for Graphs)

Answers to these questions can be found on MyEconLab at www.myeconlab.com. MyEconLab

1. Table 12.3 contains data for a hypothetical economy.

Table 12.3 Data for a Hypothetical Economy

Period	Real GDP ($ mil)
1	40.7
2	43.6
3	47.8
4	53.6
5	50.2
6	46.0
7	42.9
8	44.3
9	48.7
10	55.6
11	61.2
12	56.0

Plot the information from Table 12.3 on a graph and indicate each of the following:
    a. Peak
    b. Recession
    c. Trough
    d. Recovery
2. The total demand for goods and services in an economy increases from $205 billion to $215 billion. Given a capital–output ratio of 3, compute the amount of investment required to meet this increase in total demand.
3. In a hypothetical economy, it requires a capital expenditure of $2.50 to increase output by $1.00. If the demand for goods and services increases by $20 million, calculate the amount of investment required to meet this increase in total demand.
4. Assume that you are one of the Canadian finance minister's economic advisers. All the leading indicators have just turned downward. What advice would you give to the minister in terms of fiscal policy measures?

Chapter 13

Money: Its Nature and Functions

Learning Objectives

After studying this chapter, you should be able to

13.1 Explain what money is and describe its characteristics and functions

13.2 Distinguish between money and money substitutes

13.3 Understand how the money supply is defined and measured in Canada

13.4 Describe the Canadian payments system

13.5 Understand the meaning of the value of money

13.6 Discuss the relationship between the money supply, inflation, and unemployment

Assess Your Knowledge

MyEconLab

Answers to these questions can be found on MyEconLab at **www.myeconlab.com.**

1. Are debit (Interac) cards money?
2. What is barter?
3. What is currency?
4. Is the Canadian dollar backed by gold? Is it backed by anything?
5. Are credit cards, such as Visa and MasterCard, money?
6. What happens to the value of money if the price level rises?

LO 13.1 Explain what money is and describe its characteristics and functions

The Meaning of Money

What exactly is money?

You'll soon find out that the answer to this question is far from obvious. There are differing views as to what constitutes money. Most Canadians recognize the items we use as money: quarters, dimes, two-dollar coins, ten-dollar bills, and so on. But because these items are money in Canada now does not mean that these same items have been money all through the ages and throughout the world. What constitutes money at one time may not be considered money at some other time; and what is money in one society may not be viewed as such in some other society.

money anything that is generally accepted as final payment for goods and services

For this reason, economists prefer to define money in terms of its functions, rather than in terms of some particular medium. We define **money** as anything that is generally accepted as final payment for goods and services or as settlement of a debt. This abstract definition of money avoids identifying money with any particular object that may, at one time or another, be used as money.

What kinds of things have served as money? All sorts of things have been accepted as money throughout the ages: beads, salt, stones, gold, silver, paper, cattle, trinkets, animal skins. When the word *money* is mentioned, most people's first thought is of the notes (bills) and coins that they carry around in their pockets, wallets, and purses. Some will think also of their chequing and savings accounts at banks and other financial institutions. In other words, people tend to think of money as the items they exchange for goods and services.

The Characteristics and Functions of Money

What are the characteristics of money in a modern economy?

As noted earlier, many items have provided the functionality of money over time throughout the world: shells, beads, gold, silver, and furs are just a few. However, the notes and coins with which we are familiar today have formed the basis for our monetary economy dating back to 1817. From Confederation until 1935, when the Bank of

Canada was given exclusive power as the sole issuer of the currency, our currency consisted of government issued notes or "Dominion notes."

Since that time, the Bank of Canada has replaced the original series of 1935 with high-quality notes which have been re-designed to maintain certain characteristics which have made these notes viable. Table 13.1 gives a brief account of the evolution of the Canadian currency from Confederation forward.

Table 13.1 The History of the Canadian Currency: From Confederation Forward

1867:	The Dominion of Canada was formed. The central government assumed responsibility for money and banking, becoming the sole issuer of the currency. A new series of coins in 5-, 10-, 25-, and 50-cent denominations were issued. These coins were recognized as legal tender in four confederation provinces: Ontario, Quebec, New Brunswick, and Nova Scotia. Remaining U.S. coins were exported.
1887:	Ottawa issued $1, $2, $50, $500 and $1000 notes and took over all the paper money under the control of private banks.
1908:	The first domestically produced coin was introduced at the opening of the Royal Mint. It was a silver 50-cent coin bearing the image of King Edward VII.
1922:	Silver was replaced with nickel, a cheaper substitute, as the basis metal for Canadian coins. Canada is the world's leading nickel producer.
1931:	The Ottawa branch of the Royal Mint became the Canadian Royal Mint, a wholly Canadian institution. In 1935 the silver dollar was coined
1937:	New Canadian coinage is introduced bearing the image of the new King, George VI. Well-known Canadian emblems including the beaver, the maple leaf, the Bluenose fishing schooner, the Coat of Arms, and the caribou appear on the reverse.
1943:	War time armament made nickel scarce during the early 1940s. At this time the Mint began to substitute "tombac," a type of brass, for the five-cent coin. It was a unique coin, formed with 12 sides to distinguish it from the bronze penny. The popular image of the beaver was replaced with the symbol "V" (the roman numeral for five and for Victory) and a burning torch. The rim of the coin revealed a message in Morse code which says, "We win when we work willingly".
1953:	The first image of a young Queen, Elizabeth II, wearing a floral wreath on her head, appeared on Canada's coins
1959:	The new simplified Canadian Coat of Arms appeared on a 50-cent coin.
1965:	The image of a maturing monarch, donning a jewelled tiara, replaced the effigy of the young sovereign.
1967:	Six new images were minted to celebrate the 100th anniversary of the Confederation. The coins contained images of popular Canadian wildlife.
1969:	The Royal Canadian Mint began operating under a new mandate. As a Crown Corporation they were charged with operating as a profitable business.
1976:	A modernized, high-speed, high-tech coin pressing facility was opened in Winnipeg. All of Canada's circulation coins, as well as coins for foreign governments, were made at the Winnipeg plant. To celebrate the 21st Olympics in Montreal, $5 and $10 silver coins were introduced. The first modern Olympic gold coin, with a face value of $100, was created, as were the medals awarded to the Olympic champions.
1980:	On July 1st, 1980 Canada officially adopted the National Anthem "O Canada." A $100 gold coin was pressed to celebrate!
1987:	One-dollar bank notes were replaced by a less expensive $1 coin called the "Loonie." The image on this eleven-sided bronze-plated, pure nickel coin is that of a graceful Canadian Loon, designed by R. R. Carmichael.
1996:	After the success of the Loonie as a cost-saving measure, the $2 note was replaced by the "Toonie" in early 1996. This bi-metallic coin has a unique locking system engineered by the Royal Canadian Mint. The outer ring of the coin is composed of pure nickel, while the inner core is aluminum bronze (copper and aluminum). Within a single year, the Winnipeg plant created an impressive 375 million of these unique coins.
1997:	The penny, which had been made of copper, was replaced by a cheaper substitute in the inner core—zinc—and then copper-plated.
2000:	The first coloured coin, a 25-cent piece featuring a red and white Canadian flag, was issued.
2001:	Another cost-saving production technique was introduced: the 5-, 10-, 25- and 50-cent coins are now made of nickel-plated steel blanks. Instead of using zinc as the core of the penny, a steel blank plated with copper was designed.
2006:	Recent activity at the Royal Mint included a variety of marketing initiatives, including a $1 "lucky Loonie" featuring the Olympic logo, unveiled four years after a loonie was secretly hidden at centre ice during the 2002 Olympics, a 25-cent coin to promote breast cancer awareness, a 10th anniversary $2 coin featuring a "name the bear" contest, and a new Mint mark bearing the image of Queen Elizabeth II added to the side on all circulation coins.

The world's largest gold bar was made by the Mitsubishi Materials Corporation (a subsidiary of the automaker Mitsubishi). It weighs just over 550 pounds and is on display at the Toi Gold Mine. It is valued at USD $3.7 M.

So what makes a country's currency viable?

Let's examine six features or characteristics that make a currency work effectively for a long period of time.

Accepted and Secure People have to be willing to use a particular form of money—that is, it must be generally and widely accepted by the people who use it. Also, it has to be easily recognized and difficult to replicate. The Bank of Canada encountered some problems with counterfeiting, which was reported to have reached a peak in 2004, at which point they began to recall the currency and replace it with enhanced security features including fluorescent visibility, transparent icons, ghost images, a holographic stripe, and a security thread. As a result of a request from the RCMP and the Solicitor General in 2000, $1000 bills were withdrawn altogether because they were, it was feared, being used for organized crime and money laundering. However rare, the $1000 bill is still a form of legal tender.

Portable and Divisible One of the problems encountered during the period when gold prevailed as money was that it was heavy and difficult to transport—it lacked portability. Further, prior to the introduction of gold coins, gold bars were not easy to divide, making it impossible to give change. Consider a society that uses livestock as a form of money—obvious problems of divisibility arise! These examples illustrate two characteristics that a practical form of money should possess: portability and divisibility. The Canadian currency consists of five different bills, $5, $10, $20, $50 and $100, each measuring 6 × 2.75 inches and weighing less than a gram, no matter which denomination. It also consists of seven coins, 1-cent, 5-cent, 10-cent, 25-cent, $1.00 and $2.00.

Durable A practical choice for a currency is something which has longevity. A government does not want to replace the currency with great frequency because it is expensive to do so. People would be reluctant to accept a currency that might erode, rot, or break to the point where it was no longer useful or accepted. When the Royal Canadian Mint coins a new issue of "tokens" they anticipate that this new issue will remain in circulation for over 20 years. These coins will be used repeatedly and touch billions of hands at a cost of around 12 cents each.

Controlled Whatever the choice to serve as a country's currency, suffice it to say that it cannot grow in one's backyard. Could you imagine what would happen if English Oak leaves formed the basis of the Canadian currency? Everyone would plant oak trees in the yard. People would surely fill their property with such plantings, while others would begin to purchase land on which to grow these trees. Where would it stop? While this sort of behaviour would be great for the environment, it would quickly lead to serious inflation—there would surely be too much money in the economy, chasing too few goods. An effective currency is one for which the quantity can be controlled by a monetary authority and be relatively scarce in order to maintain value.

To summarize, the features or characteristics of an effective, practical form of money are:

1. Acceptability
2. Security
3. Portability
4. Divisibility
5. Durability
6. Controllability

What are the economic functions of money?

Money performs the following three basic economic functions:

1. Medium of exchange
2. Unit of account
3. Store of value

medium of exchange any item that is used to effect a purchase or a sale

barter the direct exchange of goods and services for other goods and services, without the use of money

double coincidence of wants a situation in which a buyer finds a seller who has what the buyer wants and who wants what the buyer has

Medium of Exchange The main function of money is to serve as a **medium of exchange**. A medium of exchange is any item that is used to effect a purchase or a sale. Without money, exchange would take place by means of **barter**, which is the direct exchange of goods and services for other goods and services, without the use of money. In a very simple economy with very limited specialization, barter exchange might be adequate. With few choices, it is easier to satisfy a double coincidence of wants. Obviously, barter is quite cumbersome—far less efficient than exchange with the use of money. Under a barter system of exchange, a double coincidence of wants is necessary for any exchange to occur. By **double coincidence of wants** we mean a situation in which a buyer finds a seller who has what the buyer wants and who, in return, wants what the buyer has to sell. A person who has wheat and wants to exchange it for shoes must find someone who has shoes and wants wheat in exchange. This may be easy to do in a society where there are only a few goods—wheat, shoes, milk, and lumber. The chances that the buyer will find a seller who is ready and willing to trade can be relatively high. However, in a complex economic system, with far more choices and many buyers and sellers, you can see that achieving a double coincidence of wants will be far more difficult to accomplish.

With the use of money, a double coincidence of wants is not necessary for exchange to take place. The person who has wheat can sell it to anybody who wants to buy wheat. With the money obtained from the sale of wheat, the person can buy shoes from a different seller. Money serves as a medium of exchange when we use it for such purposes as buying movie tickets, paying utility bills, and, perhaps to your chagrin, paying for an economics textbook!

unit of account or measure of value the common unit for expressing the value of goods and services

Unit of Account A second important economic function of money is to serve as a **unit of account**. In other words, money is the common unit for expressing the value of all goods and services. The gross domestic product of the Canadian economy consists of a wide variety of goods and services. Yet we can express the economy's annual output as a single value. When we say that the GDP of Canada is more than $1600 billion, we are using money as a unit of account or as a **measure of value**, as it is also called. Distance is measured in kilometres or miles, and weight is measured in kilograms or pounds. So too, value is measured in terms of money, and in our case, dollars and cents. When we see a pair of shoes with a price tag of $149.99 in a store window, we are witnessing an example of money serving as a measure of value.

store of value or store of wealth money or other assets put away for future use

Store of Value A third important economic function of money is to serve as a **store of value** or **store of wealth**—money or other assets put away for future use.We do not always spend all of our current income on consumer goods and services. We put some of it away, called savings, for future use. The money we deposit in a savings account serves as a store of value: it represents stored-up purchasing power. Money is not the only thing that is used to perform the store-of-value function; real estate, paintings, and other non-monetary assets also serve the function of storing value. If the value of an item deteriorates substantially with the passage of time, then it will not qualify as a good store of wealth.

liquidity the ease with which an asset can be converted into cash with minimal loss

It may be desirable to convert the store of value quickly into the medium of exchange. The ease with which an asset can be converted into cash is called **liquidity**. Money is, of course, the most liquid of all assets.

Reading Comprehension

The answers to these questions can be found on MyEconLab at www.myeconlab.com. MyEconLab

1. Discuss the characteristics of an effective form of money.
2. Explain what characteristics ivory beads would lack in forming an effective medium of exchange.
3. Briefly describe the main functions of money. Which do you think is most important?

LO 13.2 Distinguish between money and money substitutes

Kinds of Money, Near Money, and Money Substitutes

Are there different kinds of money in Canada?

In Canada, we commonly use three kinds of money to conduct business transactions:

1. Coins
2. Notes
3. Chequing accounts

currency or hand-to-hand money the notes and coins that serve as a country's medium of exchange

Coins and Notes The notes and coins that serve as a country's medium of exchange are often called **currency** or **hand-to-hand money**. You are quite familiar with the nickels, dimes, quarters, loonies, etc. that make up our supply of metallic currency—our "change." You are likewise familiar with the various bills ($5, $10, $20, $50, etc.) that make up our supply of paper currency (notes).

A point worth noting, however, is that our coins and paper currency are worth much less as a commodity than as money. There is an old saying that "money has no value, except in parting." A toonie in your pocket does very little for you. It is only when you hand it over to the cashier at the local Tim Hortons and take a sip of a steaming hot cup of coffee that it provides you with any utility at all. The value of the $2 coin only arises when you give it away in exchange for something you desire. Also, we understand that a $2 coin purchases $2 worth of goods and services. However, consider the value of the metal used to make it. The $2 bi-metallic coin contains an amount of metal worth much less on the market. In fact, it costs only 16 cents to mint a $2 coin and it is expected to remain in circulation for 20 years. Money whose face value exceeds its commodity value is called **token money**. What if that $2 coin were composed of gold instead? The toonie weighs nearly 7.5 grams. Can you imagine how much that would fetch on the market? It would be just over $700!

token money money whose face value exceeds its commodity value

Why would a rational person give up valuable goods and services in exchange for metallic and paper money with little or no intrinsic value?

That's an interesting question. Many would answer by saying that our paper money is backed by gold. But this is just one of the many misconceptions that people have about the Canadian currency. In fact, the Canadian dollar is **fiat money**. Fiat money is money that circulates as money by government decree. Fiat money is legal tender money that is not backed by gold or any other precious metal, and thus it cannot be converted into gold as a matter of right.

fiat money legal tender money that is not backed by gold or any other precious metal

Before 1940, Canadian paper currency was backed by gold. This meant that the holder of a $20 bill could present it for payment of $20 in gold. The government abandoned the gold backing in 1940. Ironically, Canadian paper currency continued to carry the statement "will pay to the bearer on demand" for 14 years after the gold backing was removed. Of course, paper currency can be used to buy gold, just as it can be used to buy anything else. Although the price of gold does fluctuate, in August 2011 the price of one ounce of gold was just over $1855 USD.

Interesting! But why do people accept paper money?

People are willing to accept paper money in exchange for valuable goods and services because other people are willing to do the same thing! The declaration in law that our currency is **legal tender** has helped to increase its general acceptability. This is so because declaring money to be legal tender means that if it is offered in payment of a debt, it must be accepted; otherwise, the debt is considered to be legally discharged. Fiat money is legal tender.

legal tender money that must legally be accepted if offered as payment to settle debt

Note that the legal tender declaration does not guarantee the general acceptability of fiat money. Business establishments often post signs that certain bills ($100 bills for example) will not be accepted because of concerns that those bills might be counterfeit.

Has money always been "token money"?

No. There was a time when the face value of metallic money equalled the value of the commodity from which it was made. That type of money was referred to as **good money**. If the face value were greater than the value of the material from which it was made, it was called **bad money**.Therefore, token money is bad money.

good money money whose face value equals its commodity value

bad money money whose face value exceeds its commodity value

Gresham's law the hypothesis that bad money will drive good money out of circulation

If good money and bad money were in circulation at the same time, people would tend to hold on to the good money for its intrinsic value and spend the bad money instead. In the case of gold *toonies*, they would quickly disappear. Ultimately, only the "bad" money would remain in circulation. This tendency to hoard the good money and spend the bad money is known as **Gresham's law**, named after Sir Thomas Gresham (1519–1579), a financial adviser to Queen Elizabeth I.

What are chequing accounts?

chequing accounts bank deposits that are transferable by cheques

demand deposits bank deposits that can be withdrawn without prior notice

Chequing accounts are bank deposits where money is transferable by paper orders or cheques. Because the depositor can withdraw these bank deposits without prior notice, economists call these accounts **demand deposits**.

We should note that it is the chequing *accounts* (that is, the deposits), and not the cheques themselves, that are considered money. The cheque is just an order to the bank to transfer funds from the account on which the cheque is drawn to another account or to convert funds from a chequing account into cash.

What is near money?

Money, as a medium of exchange in the form of currency and chequing accounts, is not the only instrument that can be used to obtain goods and services. There is considerable debate as to whether the medium-of-exchange concept of money should be extended to include other highly liquid assets. This leads us into a discussion of near money.

notice deposits interest-earning deposits subject to notice before withdrawal

near money highly liquid assets that can be easily converted into currency or demand deposits without any appreciable loss of value

There are some assets, other than currency and demand deposits, which can be readily converted into currency and demand deposits. Examples of such assets are **notice deposits** (savings accounts, for example) in commercial banks; deposits in other financial institutions, such as credit unions and caisses populaires, and trust companies; and Canada Savings Bonds (CSBs). Notice deposits are defined as interest-earning deposits subject to notice before withdrawal. These assets serve as temporary stores of value, but they do not directly perform the medium-of-exchange function. They can, however, be readily converted into cash or demand deposits. Because these assets are so closely related to money, economists call them **near money**. Near money refers to highly liquid assets that can be easily converted into currency or demand deposits without any appreciable loss of value.

Why do people not hold all their liquid assets entirely in the form of near money?

That's a highly relevant question. As you know, when you hold your assets in the form of currency and chequing accounts, you earn little or no interest. When you hold assets in the form of near money (such as CSBs) you do earn interest. Why indeed do people not hold their liquid assets entirely in the form of near money?

The answer is convenience. If people did not hold some currency and demand deposits, they would have to make frequent trips to the bank—every time they wanted to purchase something. The convenience of being able to make payments by writing cheques or paying by debit card clearly outweighs the interest earning potential if the money were deposited in a non-chequable interest-earning account.

Are credit cards money?

The common use of major credit cards (Visa, MasterCard, and American Express) and their fairly wide acceptance as a means of obtaining goods and services in recent times have caused some people to confuse credit cards with money. In fact, credit cards have even been called "plastic money." But are they really money? Let us answer this question by looking at two scenarios: one in which a transaction is carried out with the use of currency or demand deposits, the other in which a transaction is carried out with the use of a credit card.

Lucas and Gabriella were at Sporting Life to purchase some new ski equipment. Gabriella purchased her new Rossignol skis with a cheque drawn on her account at the

Be careful not to confuse these items with money. Credit cards are temporary substitutes for money, while debit cards are means of accessing money quickly.

Town Bank. Lucas used his credit card to buy some new Oakley goggles. Several days after, Lucas received a bill from the credit card company demanding that payment be made at a specific date. Gabriella received no such bill from anyone. Why? Gabriella's debt was discharged when she paid for her skis—she used money. Lucas' debt was not discharged—he did not use money. Lucas must now pay his bill with currency or demand deposits. He cannot discharge this debt by using a credit card. Thus, it is quite clear that credit cards are not money. They are temporary substitutes for money, because they enable us to obtain goods and services without immediately using money. We can summarize the difference between money and credit as follows:

> The use of money in transactions discharges debts, but the use of credit cards establishes debts that must ultimately be discharged by using money at a later time. The use of a credit card simply postpones the discharge of a debt.

BUSINESS SITUATION 13.1

Credit card companies charge merchants a fee, over and above the cost of the transaction, for accepting credit cards at their places of business. The merchant is usually charged a commission of 1%–3% of the value of each transaction paid for by credit card.

Given the existence of this charge, why might the owner of a small business, such as a snowboarding equipment and apparel store like Skiis & Biikes, accept credit cards?

The answer to this Business Situation can be found in Appendix A.

Reading Comprehension

The answers to these questions can be found on MyEconLab at www.myeconlab.com. MyEconLab

1. What are the main types of money in common use in Canada?
2. State Gresham's law and briefly explain why it might be expected to hold.
3. What is the difference between the following sets of terms: (a) good money and bad money (b) demand deposits and notice deposits.
4. Explain why credit cards are not considered money.

LO 13.3 Understand how the money supply is defined and measured in Canada

The Money Supply in Canada

monetary aggregates different measures of the money supply

What is meant by the money supply?

We can define the money supply in various ways. These different ways of defining the money supply are referred to as **monetary aggregates**, or simply as different measures of the total money supply.

Narrowly defined, the money supply includes currency *outside banks* (i.e., bank notes and coins *in circulation*) plus personal chequing accounts and current accounts at banks. This narrow definition of the money supply focuses on the medium-of-exchange function of money and is usually referred to as M1.

Many economists questioned the usefulness of the M1 concept of the money supply. It was too narrow and, given the removal of reserve requirements, there is very little distinction between demand deposits and notice deposits insofar as financial institutions allocate their deposits. In February 2007, the Bank of Canada abandoned the calculation of M1 statistics altogether. The last published figure for M1 (February 2007) was $189 billion (currency in circulation was $49 billion and demand deposits were $140 billion). A broader measure of the money supply adds all deposits in personal savings accounts, term deposits, and non-personal deposits (collectively called "notice deposits") to the composite known as M1. This broader measure of the money supply is referred to as M2. The Bank of Canada continues to publish statistics on the M2 concept of money.

Because banks are not the only providers of deposit facilities, an even broader measure of the money supply is provided. This broader measure, referred to as M2+, includes all deposits at non-chartered deposit accepting, loan-granting institutions. These institutions are sometimes called "near banks" and include trust and mortgage companies, caisses populaires, and credit unions. A still broader measure of the money supply, referred to as M2++, includes all types of mutual funds and Canada Savings Bonds. There is even another monetary aggregate referred to as M3, which is M2 plus chartered bank non-personal term deposits plus foreign currency deposits of residents.

M1 = currency in circulation plus personal chequing accounts and current accounts at chartered banks

M2 = M1 plus personal savings accounts and other chequing accounts, term deposits, and non-personal notice deposits

M2+ = M2 plus deposits at non-bank deposit-taking institutions

M2++ = M2+ along with mutual funds and Canada Savings Bonds

M3 = M2 plus chartered bank non-personal term deposits plus foreign currency deposits of residents

Table 13.2 shows various measures of the money supply in Canada.

Canadian coins are issued by the Royal Canadian Mint. Although coins represent only a small proportion of our money supply, they are, nevertheless, quite important. They enable us to make purchases of low-priced items. Coins also make our currency highly divisible, and allow for the dispersing of *change* when the amount offered as payment exceeds the monetary value of the transaction.

Table 13.2 Monetary Aggregates, June 2010

Monetary Aggregate	Amount ($ mil)
M2	994 100
M2+ (May 2010)	1 327 473
M2 ++ (May 2010)	1 901 484
M3	1 374 496

Source: CANSIM Table 176-0025 **http://cansim2.statcan.gc.ca/cgi-win/cnsmcgi.pgm**

Notes, or bills, are now issued only by the Bank of Canada, Canada's central bank or monetary authority. Quantitatively, notes are about 10 times as prevalent as coins. Notes and coins together constitute about 23% of the money supply (narrowly defined as M1) and about 7% of the money supply (defined broadly as M2). Some notes previously in circulation have now been retired. These include chartered banks' notes, Dominion of Canada notes, notes issued by the provinces, and defunct banks' notes.

Demand deposits are now the most important type of money (narrowly defined) in Canada. Quantitatively, they are substantially more important than notes and coins combined. Demand deposits constitute about 78% of narrow money. Payment by cheque and debit card represents a very high proportion (upwards near 90%) of the total dollar volumes of all transactions.

Demand deposits are the most important type of money in Canada.

Reading Comprehension

The answers to these questions can be found on MyEconLab at www.myeconlab.com. MyEconLab

1. Why does the Bank of Canada no longer compute M1 statistics?
2. What is the most liquid measure of the money supply?
3. What is the difference between M2, M2+, and M2++?
4. Do you think that Canada Savings Bonds should be included in the money supply?

LO 13.4 Describe the Canadian payments system

The Canadian Payments System

What is meant by a payments system?

payments system a set of arrangements that facilitate the exchange of goods and services

In any exchange economy, there must be some arrangements for exchanging purchasing power among individuals. The **payments system** is the set of arrangements that facilitates the exchange of goods and services. What mechanism do people use to acquire the goods and services they want? The answer depends on the payments system.

The Canadian payments system is constantly evolving—from the *wampum* (shell beads) of the pre-colonial period, to *furs* during the fur trade period, then to *card money* (ordinary playing cards) in New France in the mid-1680s, then to *gold* and *silver coins* and *paper money* in British North America, and finally to *fiat* and *deposit money* today.

What is the payments system like today?

The Payments System Today Currently, Canadian coins and Bank of Canada notes are used extensively to effect payment. But in terms of the dollar value of transactions, chequing accounts are the most widely used medium of exchange. Generally, smaller purchases (coffee, newspapers, lunch) are made with currency. On the other hand, big ticket items, such as a new car, new furniture, an expensive stereo system, or a Caribbean cruise are normally accomplished by using one's chequing account. Of course, credit cards are used in many of these transactions as well. We have shown, however, that in such circumstances, final settlement of the debt incurred must be ultimately settled with currency or deposit money.

A relatively recent development in the Canadian payments system was the establishment of the Canadian Payments Association in 1980.

What is this Canadian Payments Association?

The Canadian Payments Association (CPA) is the body that is responsible for clearing and settling accounts among depository institutions, that is, financial institutions that accept deposits from the public. All chartered banks in Canada must be members of the CPA. Trust and mortgage loan companies, caisses populaires, and credit unions (i.e., near banks) have the option to join. Member banks hold deposit accounts with the Bank of Canada.

Let us consider the following scenario. Mr. Alexander, who has an account at Bank A, writes a cheque for $500 to Mr. Barnes, who has an account at Bank B. At the same time, Ms. Browne, who has an account at Bank B, writes a cheque for $800 to Mr. Aoki, who has his account at Bank A. The outcome of all these transactions is that Bank A owes Bank B $500, while Bank B owes Bank A $800. The net indebtedness between Bank A and Bank B, then, is that Bank B owes Bank A $300. The debt is settled by increasing Bank A's account at the Bank of Canada by $300 and reducing Bank B's account by $300. Since 1984, this clearing system has been automated through the use of computers.

Have there been any other recent changes to the payments system?

Yes—changes that you are no doubt familiar with. We are deep in the electronic age. It is not at all surprising therefore that electronic technology is used in the payments system. Corporations now send payment instructions to financial institutions by using electronically coded records. The institutions then make the appropriate entries in their accounts. Thus, an employee is more likely to receive an automatic deposit than a cheque on payday. Canada also has a nation-wide system known as Interac Direct Payment that was launched in 1994. At that time it was established that about half of all Canadian retailers offered Interac services. Today, 99 percent of retailers have adopted the Interac payment system.

automated teller machines (ATMs) banking machines that facilitate transactions electronically

Another development worthy of note is **automated teller machines (ATMs)**.These machines have been in use in Canada since the early 1980s, but it wasn't until the mid-1990s that skepticism waned and people began to trust their security. In fact, bank machines are so popular today, it is estimated that there are over 2 million of these machines worldwide, although they are used most frequently in the United States, Canada, Europe, and Japan. These banking machines facilitate transactions electronically but, above all, offer unprecedented convenience to businesses and consumers alike. Financial institutions install these machines at convenient locations so that their clients have easy access to them at any time. These machines allow clients to perform a wide variety of banking transactions, including withdrawing and depositing, transferring funds from one account to another, paying bills, and checking account balances.

What can we predict about the direction of future payments systems?

The payments system of the future depends to a great extent on technological developments and on our ability and willingness to use the technology to transfer purchasing power from individual to individual. It is therefore very difficult, if not impossible, to predict with any degree of accuracy what kind of payments system will emerge in the distant future. We can, however, say something about the payments system of the immediate future—it will be increasingly electronic.

electronic funds transfer system (EFTS) a system whereby funds can be transferred instantly between accounts

A comprehensive system of transferring funds electronically—the **electronic funds transfer system (EFTS)**—is already being used nationwide. It allows for the instantaneous transfer of funds between accounts by electronic computers.

debit card cards that electronically transfer funds from the customer's account to the merchant's account

Note that the use of **debit cards**, unlike the use of credit cards, requires the necessary funds to be currently in the customer's accounts. Some people have predicted that moving in this direction will lead to a cashless society. Only time will tell.

Reading Comprehension

The answers to these questions can be found on MyEconLab at www.myeconlab.com. MyEconLab

1. What is the electronic funds transfer system (EFTS)?
2. What are debit cards? How do they differ from credit cards?
3. What is Interac? Who uses it?

LO 13.5 Understand the meaning of the value of money

The Value of Money

What makes money valuable?

Previously, you learned that money in Canada consists of coins, Bank of Canada notes, and deposits in banks. You also know that our currency is fiat money, with no gold backing and with little or no intrinsic value. A bank account is merely a figure in the bank's electronic records. Yet you know that money is valuable. You want money because you can buy things with it. If you were trying to sell your old iPod in order to purchase an updated model, you would not accept pieces of paper with numbers on them unless you were confident that the seller of the new iPod would also accept those same pieces of paper as payment. We can conclude, then, that money is valuable because people will accept it as payment for goods and services.

What is the relationship between the value of money and the price level?

It is important to note that when we talk about the value of money, we are not talking about the value of the Canadian dollar in terms of the U.S. dollar, the British pound, or the euro. That is a different matter—the exchange rate—which we will study in a later chapter. When we talk about the value of money, we are talking about what money will buy. If a dollar can buy more goods and services today than it could have bought a year ago, then prices have fallen and the value of the dollar has risen. Conversely, if a dollar can buy fewer goods and services today than it could have bought a year ago, then prices have risen and the value of the dollar has fallen. Thus, the value of the dollar depends on the price level. During periods of high inflation, a given amount of money buys less this year than it did last year and more this year than it will next year. The value of money is inversely related to the price level.

Note that it is possible for the Canadian dollar to rise against the American dollar and yet still purchase more or less the same amount within Canada. That is, the exchange rate does not determine the value of money within an economy.

How stable has the value of the Canadian dollar been in recent decades?

Although we have not had runaway inflation in Canada, we have had years of fairly rapid increases in the price level. The value of the Canadian dollar has fallen over the years.

For example, in 1992, it would have cost $121.90 to buy what could have been bought for $24.10 in 1960. Most of this loss of value occurred during the inflation period of the 1970s. By the 1980s, the fall in value was already slowing down: $1 in 1992 could buy what $0.52 could buy in 1980. This decline in value slowed even more after 1992. In 2005, $127.20 was equivalent to $100 in 1992. In effect, over the past 20 years, the Canadian dollar has remained relatively stable. This stability reflects the effectiveness of monetary policy in recent years, a topic to be considered in detail in Chapter 15.

Reading Comprehension

The answers to these questions can be found on MyEconLab at www.myeconlab.com. MyEconLab

1. What are we talking about when we refer to the "value" of money?
2. How is the value of money related to the price level?
3. Discuss the stability in the value of the Canadian dollar over the past few decades.

LO 13.6 Discuss the relationship between the money supply, inflation, and unemployment

The Money Supply, Inflation, and Unemployment

Is there any relationship between the money supply and inflation?

In Chapter 4, you studied the record of inflation in Canada, and you saw that although we have not had hyperinflation here, we have had some periods of rapid price increases, which caused some anxiety for consumers and policymakers. To answer the question posed above, severe inflations have resulted from excessive increases in the money supply. When the quantity of money increases, people find themselves with more money. Desired aggregate expenditure will therefore increase. As the economy reaches full employment, further increases in the quantity of money result in further increases in desired aggregate expenditure and inflation. Further increases in the money supply at this point simply add fuel to the inflation.

When money loses its value fast, people tend to spend it quickly. In extreme cases, they may even refuse to accept it as payment for goods and services and may resort to barter exchange instead. In this situation, money will cease to perform its most important function—that is, to serve as a medium of exchange.

Is there any relationship between the money supply and unemployment?

You will suspect that if rapid increases in the money supply result in inflation, then drastic reductions in the money supply can cause unemployment. This section will confirm your suspicion. In our study of business cycles in Chapter 12, we noted that recessions could be caused by inadequate growth of the money supply. We also learned that recessions are characterized by high levels of idle resources, specifically, high unemployment rates.

Consider the following scenario. The Bank of Canada reduces the rate of growth of the money supply in order to curb inflationary pressures. Consequently, there is a slowdown in desired aggregate expenditure as people adjust their spending under the tighter monetary conditions. This reduction in desired aggregate expenditure leads to a reduction in total income and output. The now-lower levels of aggregate expenditure trickle throughout the economy; businesses respond to the lower level of *AE*, quite often decreasing production and laying off workers. The result is higher levels of unemployment.

BUSINESS SITUATION 13.2

Suppose that the Bank of Canada has just announced that it is loosening monetary policy in response to recessionary pressures.

As a business owner, can you anticipate how this policy action may affect your decisions regarding production and employment levels?

The answer to this Business Situation can be found in Appendix A.

Reading Comprehension

The answers to these questions can be found on MyEconLab at www.myeconlab.com. MyEconLab

1. Describe the relationship between the money supply and inflation.
2. Explain how a reduction in the money supply might cause unemployment.

Review

1. Review the learning objectives listed at the beginning of the chapter.
2. Have you accomplished all the objectives? One way to determine this is to answer the Reading Comprehension questions at the end of each section. These will help you assess your understanding of the learning objectives.
3. If you have not accomplished an objective, review the relevant material before proceeding.

Key Points to Remember

1. LO 13.1 Money is anything that is generally accepted by the members of a society as final payment for goods and services or as settlement of a debt. The most important function of money is to serve as a medium of exchange. Other important functions of money are the unit of account and the store of value functions. An effective form of money is acceptable, secure, portable, durable, divisible, and controlled.
2. LO 13.2 Near money refers to assets, such as notice deposits and Canada Savings Bonds, that can readily be converted into cash or demand deposits without much loss. Credit cards are temporary substitutes for money, because they enable us to obtain goods and services without immediately using money.
3. LO 13.3 The money supply, narrowly defined as M1, consists of currency outside banks and demand deposits. The M2 definition of money consists of currency outside banks, demand deposits, and notice and personal term deposits. Demand deposits are the most important type of money in Canada.
4. LO 13.4 The Canadian payments system has evolved from a simple system of exchange that used useful commodities as money to a very advanced system whereby funds are transferred electronically. A cashless society may not be too far away.
5. LO 13.5 The value of money refers to what money can buy. The value of money is inversely related to the price level. The Canadian dollar has lost value gradually over the years as the price level has slowly risen.
6. LO 13.6 Rapid increases in the money supply are likely to cause inflation. Inadequate increases or reductions in the money supply may lead to unemployment.

Economic Word Power

Automated teller machines (ATMs) (p. 342)
Bad money (p. 337)
Barter (p. 335)
Chequing accounts (p. 338)
Currency or hand-to-hand money (p. 336)
Debit cards (p. 343)
Demand deposits (p. 338)
Double coincidence of wants (p. 335)
Electronic funds transfer system (EFTS) (p. 342)
Fiat money (p. 337)
Good money (p. 337)
Gresham's law (p. 337)
Legal tender (p. 337)
Liquidity (p. 336)
Medium of exchange (p. 335)
Monetary aggregates (p. 339)
Money (p. 332)
Near money (p. 338)
Notice deposits (p. 338)
Payments system (p. 341)
Store of value or store of wealth (p. 336)
Token money (p. 337)
Unit of account or measure of value (p. 335)

Problems and Exercises

Basic

1. LO 13.1 Listed below are the basic economic functions of money. Provide an example of each function.
   a. Unit of account
   b. Store of value
   c. Medium of exchange
2. LO 13.1 Listed below are the basic characteristics of money. Using gold bars as the form of money, explain how gold may or may not be a viable form of money given each of these characteristics.
   a. Acceptable
   b. Secure
   c. Portable
   d. Divisible
   e. Durable
   f. Controlled
3. LO 13.1 Listed below are ways in which money is used. Identify the particular function for which money is used in each case.
   a. A total of $375 is used to purchase groceries for a week
   b. The price of a book is indicated as $69.95
   c. You go shopping and spend $110.00
   d. You have $1150 in a savings account
   e. Your assets are evaluated at $15 000
   f. Your brand-new coat is worth $99.00
   g. A country's GDP is estimated to be $205 billion
   h. Your parents give you $7000 toward the purchase of a car
   i. You use $7000 to purchase a car
4. LO 13.2 Explain the difference between a cheque and a chequing account. Which of them is money?
5. LO 13.2 Which of the following items are currently money in Canada?
   a. Gold
   b. Paper currency
   c. German mark
   d. Canada Savings Bonds
   e. Chequing accounts at Canadian chartered banks
   f. Major credit cards, such as Visa and MasterCard
   g. Coins issued by the Royal Canadian Mint
   h. Debit cards (Interac)
6. Table 13.2 provides data about a hypothetical economy.

Table 13.3 An Economy's Money

Item	Amount ($ mil)
Currency in circulation	40 000
Personal chequing accounts	70 000
Current accounts at chartered banks	60 000
Personal savings accounts	105 000
Other chequing accounts	25 000
Term and non-personal notice deposits	80 000
Chartered bank non-personal term deposits	30 000
Foreign currency deposits of residents	10 000

   LO 13.3 On the basis of the data contained in the table, calculate:
   a. M1
   b. M2
   c. M3

Questions in the Intermediate and Challenging sections cover several different concepts, and have not been organized by learning objectives.

Intermediate

1. "Increases in the money supply enable people to purchase more goods and services. It follows logically, then, that rapid and prolonged increases in the money supply will be beneficial to the economy." Evaluate this statement.
2. Detect the error (if any) in the following statement: "Economists define money as anything that is generally accepted as final payment for goods and services. Debit cards (Interac) are generally accepted as final payment; therefore, by definition, they are money."

Challenging

1. Recent developments in the payments system, including electronic funds transfer, debit cards, and so on, are certainly leading to a moneyless society. Discuss.
2. The distinction between money and near money is useless because the items identified as near money perform exactly the same functions as money. Discuss.

MyEconLab Visit the MyEconLab website at **www.myeconlab.com**. This online homework and tutorial system puts you in control of your own learning with study and practice tools directly correlated to this chapter's content.

Study Guide

Self-Assessment

What's your score?

Circle the letter that corresponds with the correct answer.

1. Money is defined as
   a. Gold and other assets that represent wealth
   b. Major credit cards, such as Visa and MasterCard, used to obtain goods and services
   c. Anything that is generally accepted as final payment for goods and services
   d. All of the above
2. Which of the following is money in Canada?
   a. Gold
   b. Credit cards
   c. Bank of Canada notes
   d. All of the above
3. Which of the following economic functions does money perform?
   a. It acts as a medium of exchange
   b. It acts as a store of value
   c. It serves as a unit of account
   d. All of the above
4. Exchange with the use of money is more efficient than barter because
   a. Money makes everyone happy
   b. Exchange with the use of money does not require a double coincidence of wants
   c. Barter exchange does not require a double coincidence of wants
   d. None of the above
5. A price tag of $95.00 on an item in a store is an example of money functioning as
   a. A medium of exchange
   b. A store of value
   c. A measure of value
   d. None of the above
6. Suppose that the price of copper on the world market were to increase such that the value of the copper contained in the penny was worth far more than the value of the coin. Which would occur?
   a. The penny would no longer be considered "token currency"
   b. People would hoard the pennies until they were all removed from circulation
   c. People would not be willing to trade the penny for a penny's worth of goods.
   d. All of the above
7. Which of the following is the most liquid asset?
   a. Gold bars
   b. A $50 bill
   c. Crude oil
   d. A credit card
8. One reason why gold was abandoned as currency was because
   a. It was not widely accepted
   b. It lacked divisibility
   c. It lacked portability
   d. It lacked durability

9. Which of the following is true of the Canadian dollar?
   a. It is not backed by gold
   b. It is fiat money
   c. It is legal tender
   d. All of the above
10. According to Gresham's law
    a. Bad money will drive good money out of circulation
    b. Good money will drive bad money out of circulation
    c. Legal tender money can be used to make payments only up to certain limits
    d. Money is the root of all evil
11. The Canadian dollar is
    a. Fiat money
    b. Backed by gold
    c. Backed by Canada's vast resources
    d. None of the above
12. Demand deposits are
    a. Deposits that the provinces must make to the Bank of Canada
    b. Compulsory savings that the federal government must deposit on accounts at the Bank of Canada
    c. Chequing accounts at chartered banks
    d. None of the above
13. Near money refers to
    a. Money substitutes, such as credit cards
    b. Money items that are backed by gold
    c. Assets, such as savings deposits in banks, that serve as stores of value but not as media of exchange
    d. Assets that can be converted into precious metals
14. Which of the following is an example of near money?
    a. A debit card
    b. A credit card
    c. A savings account
    d. All of the above
15. The single largest component of the Canadian money supply is
    a. Coins
    b. Currency
    c. Gold bars
    d. Demand deposits
16. The M1 definition of money includes
    a. Coins
    b. Demand deposits
    c. Paper currency
    d. All of the above
17. Which of the following items has served as money in Canada?
    a. Wampum
    b. Gold
    c. Furs
    d. All of the above
18. The value of money is
    a. Inversely related to the price level
    b. Directly related to the price level
    c. Independent of the price level
    d. Constantly rising because of inflation
19. Rapid increases in the money supply may result in
    a. Inflation
    b. An increase in the value of money
    c. Unemployment
    d. None of the above
20. Continuous reductions in the money supply may result in
    a. Inflation
    b. An increase in the value of money
    c. Unemployment
    d. None of the above

Problems and Exercises (Use Quad Paper for Graphs)

Answers to these questions can be found on MyEconLab at www.myeconlab.com. MyEconLab

1. You are given the information shown in Table 13.4.

Table 13.4 Money Items

Item	Amount ($ mil)
Notes	1 169
Demand deposits	11 258
Coins	268
Notice and personal term deposits	25 268

   Calculate
   a. The amount of currency
   b. M1
   c. M2
2. Which function of money is evident in each of the following?
   a. You purchase a set of books from the bookstore and pay $289
   b. You deposit $1500 in a savings account
   c. You are told that the price of a CD player is $245
   d. You use $45 to purchase a gift
   e. You are told that an estate is worth $950 000
3. Which of the following items are money in Canada?
   a. Shares in Air Canada
   b. Bank of Canada notes
   c. Canadian Tire coupons
   d. Bell stocks
   e. A chequing account at a chartered bank
   f. Gold bars
   g. Canada Savings Bonds
   h. American Express credit cards
   i. HBC store credit cards
   j. Coins issued by the Royal Canadian Mint that have no intrinsic value

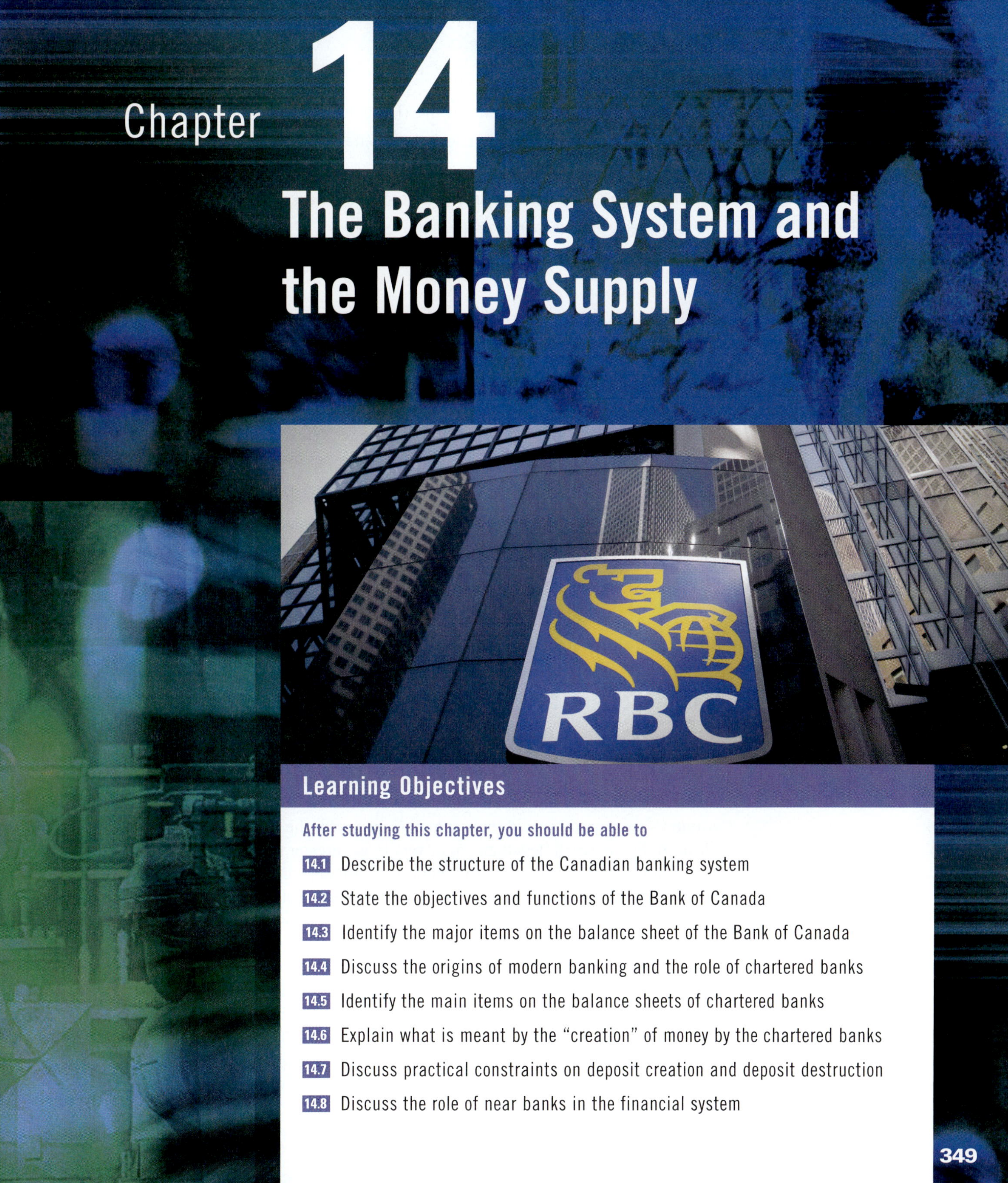

Chapter 14

The Banking System and the Money Supply

Learning Objectives

After studying this chapter, you should be able to

- 14.1 Describe the structure of the Canadian banking system
- 14.2 State the objectives and functions of the Bank of Canada
- 14.3 Identify the major items on the balance sheet of the Bank of Canada
- 14.4 Discuss the origins of modern banking and the role of chartered banks
- 14.5 Identify the main items on the balance sheets of chartered banks
- 14.6 Explain what is meant by the "creation" of money by the chartered banks
- 14.7 Discuss practical constraints on deposit creation and deposit destruction
- 14.8 Discuss the role of near banks in the financial system

Assess Your Knowledge

MyEconLab

Answers to these questions can be found on MyEconLab at **www.myeconlab.com.**

Indicate whether each of the following is true (T) or false (F).

1. In Canada, the central bank is a network of chartered banks.
2. The Bank of Canada is the largest commercial bank in Canada.
3. Credit unions and caisses populaires are commercial banks.
4. Chartered banks create money.

LO 14.1 Describe the structure of the Canadian banking system

The Canadian Banking System

banking system the association of the central bank and the chartered banks as part of a larger financial network

What exactly is the banking system?

The **banking system** describes the association between the central bank and the chartered banks, which interact to provide banking services to customers. The Canadian banking system is a subset of a larger network —the financial system—which consists of the following institutions:

1. The Bank of Canada
2. Chartered banks
3. Near banks
4. Other financial institutions

> The financial system consists of banks and other financial institutions that provide a variety of financial services to their customers.

What is a central bank?

The Bank of Canada is Canada's central bank. Central banks are a country's *monetary authority* and they are a characteristic feature of modern economies. Before the establishment of the Bank of Canada, the Department of Finance conducted central banking operations for the country. It might be hard to believe that some time ago, each of the country's large banks issued their own currency, with the finance department responsible for only very small (less than $5) or very large (greater than $500) notes. At that time, the largest operating bank was the Bank of Montreal, which acted as the government's banker. Suggestions were made as early as 1914 to establish a central bank, but no action to that effect was taken at that time. Regulation of the banking system rested with the Canadian Bankers Association.

During the Great Depression, many felt that the policies of the nation's banks worsened the situation and made the economic circumstances far harder to bear. It was felt that the economy would perform better if there were better management of the country's monetary system. Consequently, in 1933, the Royal Commission on Banking and Finance, chaired by Lord Macmillan, was appointed. The mandate of the Macmillan Commission was to inquire into the desirability of establishing a central bank in Canada.

Incumbent governor of the Bank of Canada Mark Carney (2008–present)

In the fall of 1933, the Macmillan Commission submitted its report in favour of establishing a central bank. It is interesting to note that the chartered banks were *not* in favour of the Commission's recommendation. However, the *Bank of Canada Act* establishing the central bank was passed in 1934, and the Bank of Canada thus became a reality. The Bank of Canada began to operate in 1935 as a privately owned bank. However, in 1938 it became a crown corporation, fully owned by the government (in effect by the Canadian taxpayers) with the governor appointed by the Cabinet. Among other things, the responsibility for creating small bills was transferred from the finance department, and the private banks were required to remove their currency from circulation by 1949. The Bank of Canada had become the sole issuer of Canadian currency.

In short, the Bank of Canada was established in response to calls for better monetary management.

Who manages the Bank of Canada?

The Bank of Canada is under the management of a board of directors. This board comprises the governor of the Bank, the deputy governor, and 12 directors. The governor and deputy governor are appointed by the directors (with the approval of the Cabinet) for terms of seven years. The directors are appointed by the Minister of Finance for terms of three years each. Directors must be under 75 years of age and must be Canadian citizens. Moreover, they must not be full-time employees of any federal, provincial, or territorial government and must not be directors, partners, or employees of an institution that deals directly with the Bank of Canada. The executive committee, which acts on behalf of the board of directors, consists of the governor, the deputy governor, and from two to four directors. The executive committee meets at least once a week. The deputy minister of finance is a member of the board but has no voting rights.

chartered banks or commercial banks financial institutions operating under federal charter; they accept deposits and make loans and investments

So if the Bank of Canada is the country's central bank, what about all those other financial institutions? How do they fit in?

You will recall that the Canadian banking system is a subset of a larger network, called the financial system. In addition to the Bank of Canada, we have chartered banks, near banks, and "other" financial institutions. **Chartered banks**, also called **commercial banks**, are financial institutions offering a variety of services, not the least of which are accepting deposits and granting loans. According to the Department of Finance, Canada's chartered banks have over 8200 branches and almost 18 000 automated banking machines (ABMs) across the country. Further, Canada has the highest number of ABMs per capita in the world and has the highest access levels within electronic channels including debit cards and online and telephone banking.

Table 14.1 Schedule I Banks—2010 Revenues

Rank	Bank	Revenue ($ bil)
1	Royal Bank of Canada	28.3
2	Toronto Dominion	19.6
3	The Bank of Nova Scotia	15.5
4	Bank of Montreal	12.2
5	CIBC	12.1

Source: Data from RBC annual report www.rbc.com/investorrelations/pdf/ar_2010_e.pdf; Toronto Dominion annual report www.td.com/ar2010/pdfs/ar2010.pdf; The Bank of Nova Scotia annual report www.scotiabank.com/images/en/filesaboutscotia/25448.pdf; The Bank of Montreal annual report www.bmo.com/ar2010/downloads/bmo_ar2010.pdf; CIBC annual report www.cibc.com/ca/pdf/about/ar10-en.pdf.

Banks are named under three schedules of the *Bank Act*. Schedule I banks (top-tier) are banks that are authorized to accept deposits and are not subsidiaries of foreign banks. They include the "big five": Royal Bank of Canada (RBC), TD Canada Trust (TD), Bank of Nova Scotia (Scotiabank), Bank of Montreal (BMO), and Canadian Imperial Bank of Commerce (CIBC), along with National Bank of Canada. In accordance with the *Bank Act*, these banks are widely held, meaning that no single individual or company may control more than a tenth of the voting stock and foreign ownership is strictly limited to 25%.

In contrast, Schedule II banks are closely held, meaning that ownership in these banks is more concentrated. Schedule II banks are foreign bank subsidiaries that are authorized to accept deposits. They include Amex Bank of Canada, Bank of China (Canada), Citibank Canada, and ING Bank of Canada. These second tier organizations are largely Canadian domestic banking organizations. Finally, Schedule III banks include foreign banks which are permitted to provide banking services in Canada. They include Barclays Bank PLC, Canada Branch; Capital One Bank (Canada Branch); First Commercial Bank, The Royal Bank of Scotland N.V.; and JPMorgan Chase Bank N.A. Unlike Schedule II banks, these banks are NOT incorporated under the *Bank Act* and they operate in Canada, usually within the country's largest cities, including Toronto, Montreal, and Vancouver, under specific restrictions outlined in the Act.

near banks financial institutions other than banks that accept deposits from the public

Table 14.2 Schedule II & III Banks—2010 Revenues

Institution	Revenue ($ bil)
ING Bank of Canada	54.9
Manulife Financial Corp.	37.6
Power Financial Corp.	27.9
CMHC	15.3
Desjardins Group	11.6
Fairfax Financial Holdings Ltd.	6.2
National Bank of Canada	4.3

Source: Data from ING Annual Report www.ing.com/Our-Company/Investor-relations/Annual-Reports.htm; Manulife www.manulife.com/public/files/202/1/mfc_annualreport2010.pdf; Power Financial Corporation www.powerfinancial.com/index.php?lang=eng&comp=powerfinancial&page=annrep; CMHC www.cmhc.ca/en/corp/about/anrecopl/upload/CMHC_AR2009_MDA-2005-2010- Highlights.pdf; Desjardins Group www.desjardins.com/en/a_propos/societes_filiales/reseau_caisses/caisse_centrale/ rapport_annuel/rapport-annuel-caisse-centrale-2010.pdf; Fairfax Financial Holdings www.fairfax.ca/Theme/Fairfax/files/doc_financials/AR2010.pdf; National Bank of Canada www.nbc.ca/bnc/files/bncpdf/en/2/e_ri_ar2010.pdf.

Near banks are financial institutions, other than chartered banks, that accept deposits from the public. They include caisses populaires and credit unions, trust companies, and mortgage loan companies.

The last group of financial institutions—the group we referred to as "other" financial institutions—does not accept deposits from the public. This group includes financial institutions such as mutual funds, sales finance companies, consumer loan companies, and insurance companies. The banking system, which is our main concern in this chapter, consists of the central bank (the Bank of Canada) and the chartered banks. Because the near banks provide services that are similar to the services provided by chartered banks, we will pay some attention to their activities. The activities and influence of non-depository financial institutions, though important in the financial system, lie outside the scope of our present study. Table 14.1 shows the 2010 revenue levels for the "big five" banks. Table 14.2 presents the 2010 revenue levels for some of the Schedule II and Schedule III banks operating in Canada.

Reading Comprehension

The answers to these questions can be found on MyEconLab at www.myeconlab.com. MyEconLab

1. What constitutes the Canadian banking system?
2. Distinguish between the banking system and the financial system.
3. What circumstances led to the establishment of the Bank of Canada?

LO 14.2 State the objectives and functions of the Bank of Canada

The Objectives and Functions of the Bank of Canada

What are the objectives of the Bank of Canada?

Bank of Canada Act federal legislation that established the Bank of Canada in 1934

The main objectives of the Bank of Canada are set out in the preamble to the ***Bank of Canada Act*** as follows:

> *"... to regulate credit in the best interest of the economic life of the nation, to control and protect the external value of the national monetary unit and to mitigate by influence fluctuations in the general level of production, trade, prices and employment so far as may be possible within the scope of monetary action, and generally to promote the economic and financial welfare of the Dominion."*

Restated, the Bank of Canada is charged with the responsibility of executing monetary policy to achieve economic stability, economic growth, and a viable balance of payments. The achievement of these objectives is no easy matter! And because measures taken to achieve one objective often push us further away from achieving other objectives (sometimes called a "double-edged" sword), the task can become very difficult indeed.

The objectives of the Bank of Canada are clear. What are its functions?

The Bank of Canada, like other central banks, performs five basic functions:

1. Controller of the money supply
2. Banker to the commercial banks
3. Fiscal agent and financial adviser to the government
4. Manager of the country's monetary policy
5. Supporter of the financial system

Let us look at each of these functions in turn.

Controller of the Money Supply You have already learned that the quantity of money has an important effect on the levels of output and prices in the economy. Recall the model of *AD–AS* from Chapter 7. If the money supply increases too rapidly, the *AD* curve shifts up and to the right, resulting in price level increases—inflation results. This is the situation described as "too much money chasing too few goods." Conversely, an inadequate money supply may result in unemployment. Again, recall the *AD–AS* model from Chapter 7—the *AD* curve shifts down and to the left, resulting in lost output and unemployment. Controlling the money supply is considered the most important function of any central bank. In Canada, the only institution empowered to issue bank notes is the Bank of Canada. An important distinction should be made between the right to "issue money" (which is the sole responsibility of the Bank of Canada), and the ability to "create money," which is largely done by commercial banks through taking deposits and issuing loans. It is interesting to note, however, that the Bank of Canada "issues" less than 5% of Canada's money supply; more than 95% of Canada's money is "created" by commercial banks, through the process of multiple deposit expansion to be discussed shortly.

Banker to the Commercial Banks Another important function of the Bank of Canada is to serve as banker to the commercial banks. All Canadian chartered banks have an account at the Bank of Canada where they keep a fraction of their deposits as desired cash reserves. Cash reserves of chartered banks become liabilities of the Bank of Canada. The Bank of Canada stands ready to provide loans to the chartered banks if ever they find themselves facing liquidity problems. In this capacity, the Bank of Canada is referred to as the "lender of last resort"—a role designed to heighten the level of consumer confidence in the banking system. Another aspect of the Bank of Canada's relationship with the chartered banks is to monitor and regulate their activities so they do not get into financial distress. The Bank of Canada, together with other federal regulatory bodies including the **Canada Deposit Insurance Corporation (CDIC)**, the Department of Finance, and the **Office of the Superintendent of Financial Institutions (OSFI)**, conduct periodic risk assessments. Their general purpose is to create a stable, secure, safe financial system in Canada. According to a recent World Economic Forum report, the Canadian banking system is widely considered the most efficient and safest banking system in the world. In terms of the international arena, the Canadian system is ranked number one for financial soundness. In the 2010–2011 report, Canada is ranked first in the "soundness of banks" indicator.

Canada Deposit Insurance Corporation a federal crown corporation established in 1967 that insures bank deposits up to $100 000, in the case of bankruptcy at a participating bank

Office of the Superintendent of Financial Institutions the principal regulatory body that supervises financial institutions

Fiscal Agent and Financial Adviser to the Government The Bank of Canada also serves as fiscal agent and financial adviser to the federal government. Mark Carney, the incumbent governor of the Bank of Canada, as well as the directors of the Bank, are appointed by the federal Cabinet. These appointments are based on experience and expertise, not political affiliation. The term of the position for governor of the Bank of Canada is seven years, extending beyond the term of a particular government in office. The intention is that the Bank of Canada will advise the government on banking in Canada, rather than comply with short-term political aspirations of the incumbent party. The governor of the Bank of Canada works closely with the Finance Minister to achieve the stated mandate of coordinated monetary and fiscal policies. In addition to an advisory role, the Government of Canada keeps a chequing account with the Bank of Canada, on which it draws to make payments. The Government of Canada also borrows money from the Bank of Canada. The Bank of Canada grants these loans to various government agencies by buying securities from the government and paying for them by crediting the government's account with a deposit for the value of the securities. For example, if the government wants to borrow $100 million from the Bank of Canada, it prints $100 million worth of bonds and sells them to the Bank of Canada. The Bank of Canada then credits the government's account with a deposit of $100 million. Thus the Bank of Canada acts as the government's bank. Over the years, the Bank of Canada has played many important roles as fiscal agent, in accordance with government mandates including: financing the war effort during WWII, buying the government's debt, establishing the Industrial Development Bank (now called the Business Development Bank of Canada) to stimulate investment, and encouraging economic growth. The Bank of Canada's current mission statement is:

> *To focus on the goals of low and stable inflation, a safe and secure currency, financial stability, and the efficient management of government funds and public debt.*

Monetary Policy In consultation with the federal government, the Bank of Canada executes the country's monetary policy. Although the Bank of Canada enjoys a considerable degree of independence in establishing and implementing monetary policy, the federal government reserves the right—and the responsibility—to instruct the Bank of the country's monetary policy. When Louis Rasminsky assumed governorship of the Bank in 1961, he formalized this principle as follows:

> *in the ordinary course of events, the Bank has the responsibility for monetary policy, and if the government disapproves of the monetary policy being carried out by the Bank, it has the right and responsibility to direct the bank as to the policy which the Bank is to carry out.*

These sentiments have now been clearly expressed in the amended *Bank of Canada Act* in 1967. The *Bank of Canada Act* now specifies that (1) there must be ongoing consultation between the federal government and the Bank of Canada; (2) if the government and the Bank disagree over monetary policy, the minister of finance may, with the approval of the Cabinet, and after consulting with the governor of the Bank, give a written directive to the governor stating the monetary policy that should be followed; and (3) if such a directive is given, it must be for a specified period, and the Bank must comply.

Designing monetary policy which promotes economic and financial welfare in Canada is no easy task. It used to be that such policy was intended to accomplish two things: assist the economy in achieving a full-employment level of output and assist the economy in achieving a non-inflationary level of output. Two significant macroeconomic variables, unemployment and inflation, are mentioned explicitly in this statement. A shift in focus began to appear in 2006, when the Bank's stated goal was to achieve stability in the value of money. The practice of monetary policy, however, is narrow and specific: the Bank aims to keep inflation at a 2% target, midway between the 1% and 3% inflation-control target range. This is called the Bank's target for inflation. The target is expressed in terms of total CPI inflation. Recall from our discussion of inflation in Chapters 4 and 6 that the CPI provides a measure of price movements, produced by Statistics Canada. It is obtained by comparing the retail prices of a representative "shopping basket" of goods and services. The Bank of Canada uses the concept of core inflation as a guide for monetary policy. **Core CPI** refers to an adjusted version of total CPI that excludes the most volatile components including seasonal produce like fruit and vegetables, gasoline, fuel oil, natural gas, mortgage interest, and tobacco products. **Core inflation**, a measure of inflation using the core CPI, provides a better measure of the underlying trend of inflation and tends to be a better predictor of future changes in the price level.

core CPI refers to an adjusted version of total CPI excluding the most volatile components including seasonal produce like fruit and vegetables, gasoline, oil, natural gas, mortgage interest, and tobacco products

core inflation a measure of inflation using the core CPI

Table 14.3 shows inflation rates using both total CPI and core CPI, for the period from 2006–2010.

Supporter of the Financial System The Canadian monetary system is based on trust and confidence—that is, it is a **fiduciary monetary system**. We accept paper currency from other people in exchange for valuable goods and services because we are confident that others will, in turn, accept it from us. Likewise, we accept entries in banks' books (deposit accounts) as money because others accept them as money. If we lose confidence in the monetary system and rush to the banks to cash in all our deposit accounts, there will be utter chaos.

fiduciary monetary system monetary system based on trust or confidence

> A fiduciary monetary system is one that is based on trust. People accept currency in a fiduciary system because they are confident that others will accept it from them.

Table 14.3 Inflation Rates, 2006–2010

	2006		2007		2008		2009		2010	
	Total CPI	Core CPI	Total CPI	Core CPI	Total CPI	Core CPI	Total CPI	Core CPI	Total CPI	Core CPI
January	2.8	1.6	1.1	2.3	2.2	1.4	1.1	1.9	1.9	2.0
February	2.2	1.7	2.0	2.3	1.8	1.5	1.4	1.9	1.6	2.1
March	2.2	1.7	2.3	2.3	1.4	1.3	1.2	2.0	1.4	1.7
April	2.4	1.6	2.2	2.5	1.7	1.5	0.4	1.8	1.8	1.9
May	2.8	2.0	2.2	2.2	2.2	1.5	0.1	2.0	1.4	1.8
June	2.4	1.7	2.2	2.5	3.1	1.5	-0.3	1.9	1.0	1.7
July	2.3	2.0	2.2	2.3	3.4	1.5	-0.9	1.8	1.8	1.6
August	2.1	2.0	1.7	2.2	3.5	1.7	-0.8	1.6	1.7	1.6
September	0.7	2.3	2.5	2.0	3.4	1.7	-0.9	1.5	1.9	1.5
October	1.0	2.4	2.4	1.8	2.6	1.7	0.1	1.8	2.4	1.8
November	1.4	2.2	2.5	1.6	2.0	2.4	1.0	1.5	2.0	1.4
December	1.7	2.1	2.4	1.5	1.2	2.4	1.3	1.5	2.4	1.5

Source: Bank of Canada. **www.bankofcanada.ca/rates/price-indexes/cpi/.**

The Bank of Canada supports the financial system and prevents the loss of confidence that might cause panic and ensuing bank failures.

Reading Comprehension

The answers to these questions can be found on MyEconLab at **www.myeconlab.com**. MyEconLab

1. What are the main objectives and functions of the Bank of Canada?
2. Give a brief account of the organization and management of the Bank of Canada.
3. Distinguish between the *Bank Act* and the *Bank of Canada Act.*
4. Distinguish between the following sets of terms: (a) inflation and core inflation (b) total CPI and core CPI.

LO 14.3 Identify the major items on the balance sheet of the Bank of Canada

The Balance Sheet of the Bank of Canada

What is a balance sheet?

balance sheet a statement of assets, liabilities, and owner's equity or capital

A **balance sheet** is a statement of the assets and liabilities of an economic unit. An *asset* is anything that is owned by the unit. A *liability* is anything owed by the unit. A liability is a debt. The difference between the total assets and the total liabilities is called *capital* or *owner's equity.* Thus, a balance sheet can be defined as a statement of assets, liabilities, and owner's equity or capital.

Familiarity with the concept of a balance sheet will enhance your comprehension of much of the material presented in later sections of this chapter. The composition of the balance sheet of the Bank of Canada reflects its functions and responsibilities.

What are the main assets of the Bank of Canada?

To answer that question let us look at the balance sheet obtained from the *Bank of Canada Annual Report, 2010* (shown in Table 14.4). Assets of the Bank of Canada include cash and foreign deposits, securities purchased under resale agreements, advances to members of the Canadian Payments Association, investments in government securities, and other investments. Let us look briefly at each of these asset items.

Table 14.4 Balance Sheet of the Bank of Canada, December 31, 2010

BALANCE SHEET
As at 31 December 2010
(Millions of dollars)

Assets	**Amount ($ mil)**	**Percentage**
Cash and foreign deposits	9.7	0.0
Loans and Receivables		
Securities purchased under resale agreements	2 062.4	3.4
Advances to members of the Canadian Payments Association	22.5	
Other receivables	2.1	0.00
	2 087	
Investments		
Treasury bills of Canada	24 906.1	40.9
Government of Canada bonds	33 550.6	55.1
Other Investments	38.0	0.06
	58 494.7	
Property and Equipment	149.3	0.25
Other investments	149.1	0.25
Total Assets	60 884.8	100.0
Liabilities And Capital		
Bank notes in circulation	57 874.2	95.0
Deposits		
Government of Canada	1 869.4	3.1
Members of the Canadian Payments Association	47.5	0.08
Other deposits	639.9	1.05
	2 556.8	
Other liabilities	323.8	0.53
	60 754.8	
Capital	130	0.2
Total Liabilities	60 884.8	100.0

Source: *Bank of Canada Annual Report,* 2010. **http://www.bankofcanada.ca/wp-content/uploads/2011/06/annualreport2010.pdf**

Cash and Foreign Deposits This item represents liquid demand deposits that the Bank of Canada keeps with other central banks. These deposits are a part of our country's foreign exchange reserves. As can be seen in Table 14.4, in December 2010, cash and foreign currency deposits amounted to $9.7 million.

Securities Purchased Under Resale Agreements These agreements occur where the Bank of Canada agrees to buy government securities with the intention of selling them back at a predetermined price. These actions are conducted to reinforce the target overnight interest rate. Most transactions occur with the agreement of settling the next day and are accomplished through buyback transactions with security dealers in the Government of Canada. Some agreements have terms longer than one business day, acquired through an auction process, with the intention of providing liquidity to support efficiency in the banking system.

Advances to Members of the Canadian Payments Association The function of the Bank of Canada as lender of last resort is reflected in this item in the Bank's asset portfolio. Prior to October 2009, advances to banks were made under the Bank's Standing Liquidity Facility, with interest rates on overnight advances computed at the Bank Rate. In 2009, these advances included term advances made through the Bank's Term Loan Facility. This facility ended in October 2009. In 2010 advances to members of the Canadian Payments Association was $22.5 million.

Investments in Government Securities As can be seen from Table 14.4, the most important asset item for the Bank of Canada is Government of Canada securities, accounting for 96% of the total assets of the Bank of Canada. In December 2010, Government of Canada bonds accounted for just over 55% and Treasury Bills accounted for just under 41% of the total assets of the Bank of Canada. This shows that the Bank of Canada makes substantial loans to the Government of Canada and functions as the government's bank.

Other Investments The Bank of Canada engages in investment activities. These investments amounted to almost $150 million at the end of December 2010.

What are the main liabilities of the Bank of Canada?

The main liabilities of the Bank of Canada are notes in circulation and Canadian dollar deposits. Let us discuss each of these items in turn.

Bank of Canada Notes As you already know, the Bank of Canada has a monopoly on note issuance. The Bank of Canada issues all Canadian paper currency. Notes in circulation at the end of December 2010 amounted to $57.9 billion, accounting for 95% of the total liabilities of the central bank.

Canadian Dollar Deposits The items under this heading reveal that the Government of Canada, the chartered banks, other members of the Canadian Payments Association, and foreign central banks all have deposits at the Bank of Canada. Recall that the chartered banks hold desired cash reserves on deposit at the Bank of Canada. Deposits of chartered banks and other members of the Canadian Payments Association totalled only \$47.5 million at the end of December 2010. This number is down from the nearly \$3 billion that was held by the Bank of Canada in 2009. The dramatic drop in this category reflects the tight monetary environment that prevailed during this time.

Reading Comprehension

The answers to these questions can be found on MyEconLab at www.myeconlab.com. MyEconLab

1. What are the major components on the asset side of the balance sheet for the Bank of Canada?
2. On the asset side, which component is the most significant?
3. What are the main liabilities on the balance sheet for the Bank of Canada?

LO 14.4 Discuss the origins of modern banking and the role of chartered banks

The Origins of Modern Banking and the Role of the Chartered Banks

What is the origin of modern banking?

We can trace the origin of modern banking to seventeenth-century England, where goldsmiths accepted gold deposits for safekeeping in their secure safes. Depositors of gold received receipts from the goldsmiths certifying that the deposits were made. On presentation of the receipts to the goldsmiths, they were obliged to deliver the stipulated amount of gold to the owner of the receipt. Because the gold was redeemable on demand, the goldsmiths had to ensure that the gold was always available whenever a receipt was presented.

If a depositor (let's call her Alexandra) wanted to purchase an item from Bonita, she went to her neighbourhood goldsmith, withdrew some of her gold, and used it to pay Bonita for the item. Bonita then took the gold to the goldsmith for safekeeping. As time progressed, people realized that they could save the time of going back and forth to their goldsmiths if a purchaser simply handed the goldsmith's receipt to the seller. Provided that the goldsmith who issued the receipt was reputable, the seller would normally be willing to accept the receipt because it could be presented to the goldsmith at any time for gold.

For convenience, depositors began to ask for receipts to be given in smaller denominations. For example, instead of having one receipt for 10 pounds of gold, depositors were choosing to have 10 receipts, each for 1 pound of gold. The goldsmiths became issuers of paper money. This function was later performed by the first commercial banks but now is performed exclusively by central banks.

Once these paper receipts began to circulate and became widely accepted, the goldsmiths observed that they had gold in their possession for long periods. They began to make loans. But instead of lending gold, they simply lent notes (receipts). Thus, the total value of all receipts exceeded the value of gold deposited with the goldsmiths, because both the original depositors and the borrowers had notes to the same quantity of gold. You will see shortly that this situation bears a striking resemblance to our present fractional reserve banking system.

What is the role of chartered (commercial) banks?

When banks were first established, their main function was to cater to the needs of commerce by extending commercial loans, hence the term *commercial banks.* Commercial loans were typically short-term loans (not exceeding one year) granted to merchants and traders for such purposes as acquiring inventories and paying for raw materials. Such loans were considered to be appropriate because the goods would be sold within a short time and the loan could be repaid from the proceeds of the sale. Thus, the risk of default was low. Although commercial bank lending is not presently limited to commercial loans, the term *commercial bank* persists. In Canada, commercial banks are also called *chartered banks* because, before 1980, a bank could be established in Canada only by a special charter by the federal Parliament.

How is the Canadian banking system structured?

branch banking system a banking system based on relatively few banks with many branches

Bank Act federal legislation that governs the operations of chartered banks

Canada's banking structure has changed from one of more than 50 banks in the years following Confederation—a period of rapid bank expansion—to a structure with only a few Canadian-owned banks. The major Canadian banks have many branches all over the country. The Canadian banking structure can therefore be described as a **branch banking system**—a banking system based on relatively few banks with many branches. This is in sharp contrast to the banking system typical of the United States, where there are several thousand independent banks without branches.

The federal legislation that governs the operations of chartered banks in Canada is the ***Bank Act***. This act is subject to review every 10 years, the most recent major review having just been completed in 2011.

What specifically does the "art of banking" refer to?

Commercial banks are privately owned; as a result, they seek to earn a return for their shareholders. At the same time, commercial banks must keep sufficient funds to meet the monetary needs of their depositors. The problem that confronts the banker is the fact that assets that yield high earnings tend to be non-liquid; and liquid assets tend to yield little or no earnings. For example, if a bank keeps all its assets in cash, it will be 100% liquid, but it will earn nothing on these cash assets for its shareholders. If it keeps all of its assets in loans and long-term securities, which have high interest earnings, it will have a major liquidity problem. It will not long survive.

Banks therefore face conflicting needs for profitability on the one hand and liquidity on the other. Good banking consists of being able to use bank funds profitably while at the same time having due regard for liquidity needs. That, in a nutshell, is the art of banking.

What services do commercial banks offer and how do they make money?

Commercial banks perform a variety of services, including, but not limited to, the granting of loans; the establishing of chequing and savings accounts; the safekeeping of valuables; and the provision of foreign exchange services, automatic teller machine (ATM) services, funds transfer between accounts, telephone and internet banking, bill payment services, and credit card and debit services. Commercial banks obtain some of their earnings by charging a fee for some of the services they provide. Their largest earnings, however, are derived from the loans that they make to borrowers.

Here is how it works. Let's assume that a customer makes a deposit at a bank. The bank may pay 3% interest on that deposit. The bank then lends out the money and charges 9% interest. The difference between the rate of interest that banks charge for loans and the interest rate that they pay their depositors is called the **interest spread**. This spread is earnings for the bank. Like other businesses, banks too have expenses. For example, they pay rent for their facilities, communications and utility bills, and salaries. The difference between a bank's revenues from all sources and its expenses is its profits.

interest spread the difference between the interest rate that banks charge for loans and the interest rate they pay their depositors

Reading Comprehension

The answers to these questions can be found on MyEconLab at www.myeconlab.com. MyEconLab

1. Why is the Canadian banking system called a fractional reserve banking system?
2. "The banker must walk a tightrope between profitability and safety." Discuss.
3. What is a chartered (commercial) bank? What services do chartered banks provide?
4. How can you calculate interest spread?

LO 14.5 Identify the main items on the balance sheets of chartered banks

The Balance Sheets of Chartered Banks

What are the main assets of chartered banks?

The assets of chartered banks include notes and deposits with the Bank of Canada, foreign currency deposits with other banks, cheques and other items in transit, Government of Canada Treasury bills, loans, and mortgages.

Because a liability is a debt, it is clear that customers' deposits are liabilities of the banks. What are some of the other liabilities of chartered banks?

The liabilities of a bank represent claims on its assets. The liabilities of commercial banks include deposits, advances from the Bank of Canada, acceptances, guarantees, letters of credit, and shareholders' equity.

What are the main sources and uses of funds for commercial banks?

We can glean a great deal of information about banks' sources and uses of funds by examining their balance sheets. Let us first consider the main source of commercial banks' funds.

Main Sources of Funds The banks' liabilities tell us about their sources of funds. Table 14.5 shows a specimen balance sheet of commercial banks.

As the liability items show, the most important source of funds for commercial banks is the deposits of their customers. These deposits typically account for more than 30% of the banks' total liabilities. In addition, Canadian chartered banks obtain a substantial amount of deposits in foreign currencies.

Table 14.5 Specimen Assets and Liabilities of Commercial Banks in Percentage Terms

Item	Percentage
ASSETS	
Canadian dollar liquid assets:	
Bank of Canada deposits, notes and coins	0.30
Treasury bills	1.60
Government of Canada securities	3.46
Less liquid Canadian dollar assets:	
Loans in Canadian dollars	50.00
Canadian securities	4.45
Foreign currency assets	40.95
TOTAL ASSETS	
LIABILITIES	
Canadian dollar deposits:	
Personal savings deposits	22.05
Non-personal and term deposits	10.39
Government of Canada	0.12
Subordinated debt	1.17
Shareholders' equity	4.39
TOTAL LIABILITY	

Personal Savings Deposits Most of these deposits are personal savings deposits of Canadians, which typically represent about 20% of total commercial bank liabilities.

Non-personal Term and Notice Deposits Non-personal term and notice deposits also provide funds for commercial banks. These deposits typically account for about 10% of total liabilities of the banks.

Government of Canada Deposits Another source of funds for chartered banks is the federal government. The Government of Canada holds deposits at the chartered banks. As you will see later, these deposits exist to help control the money supply. Quantitatively, however, they represent only about 0.1% of the banks' total liabilities.

debentures bonds secured by the creditworthiness of the borrower rather than by specific assets

Capital and Subordinated Debt The banks' capital (shareholders' equity) and subordinated debt (debentures) also provide funds for the banks' operations. **Debentures** are bonds that are secured by the creditworthiness of the issuer (borrower) rather than by specific assets. In addition to providing funds for their operations, banks' capital funds also provide a margin of safety for the banks' depositors. Banks' subordinated debt typically amounts to just more than 1% of their total liabilities, while shareholders' equity accounts for about 4% of total liabilities.

We will now examine the main uses of banks' funds.

Main Uses of Funds By looking at the asset side of the banks' balance sheet, we can get a clearer understanding of the ways that banks use their funds and make loans.

Cash Reserves and Highly Liquid Assets Commercial banks keep in cash only a fraction of the total amount deposited with them; thus, the system is referred to as a **fractional reserve banking system**. Up until fairly recently, the Bank of Canada required that chartered banks keep a secondary reserve requirement. The central bank once dictated that the chartered banks keep secondary reserves equal to 20% of their demand deposits. In 1991, because of the obvious soundness of the Canadian branch banking system, governance under the *Bank Act*, and the deposit insurance provided by the CDIC, the Bank of Canada dropped the secondary reserve requirement. However, for issues of security banks continue to hold cash reserves either in their vaults or on deposit at the Bank of Canada. The fraction of their demand deposits that banks hold as cash reserves is called the **target reserve ratio**. Today, most chartered banks set a target reserve ratio equal to 10%. This means that banks desire to keep cash reserves equal to 10% of their demand deposits. The minimum amount of reserves that banks desire to hold is called **desired reserves**.

fractional reserve banking system a banking system in which banks keep only a fraction of their deposits in cash reserves

target reserve ratio the fraction of demand deposits that chartered banks hold as cash reserves

desired reserves the minimum amount of reserves that banks desire to hold

primary reserves bank reserves held in cash

secondary reserves liquid assets, such as currency, day-to-day loans, treasury bills, and call and short loans, held as reserves

Recall that a large proportion of the banks' deposit liabilities is payable on demand or on short notice. Therefore, chartered banks keep a certain amount of their assets in the form of cash. These bank reserves held in cash are known as **primary reserves**. Banks also hold **secondary reserves**—liquid assets, such as currency, day-to-day loans, treasury bills, and call and short loans, held as reserves.

Government of Canada Bonds Government of Canada bonds are liquid assets that earn interest income for their holders. The chartered banks use some of their funds to acquire these bonds. Chartered banks hold about 3% of their assets in Government of Canada bonds.

Loans in Canadian Dollars Most of the funds collected by chartered banks are used to extend general loans to businesses and individuals. In addition, chartered banks extend loans to the provinces and the municipalities. Also, chartered banks are substantially involved in mortgage lending. Loans of various types in Canadian dollars account for about 50% of the total assets of commercial banks.

Canadian Securities Chartered banks also use some of their funds to purchase Canadian securities issued by provincial and municipal governments and by corporations. These securities typically account for about 4% of commercial banks' total assets, with corporate securities accounting for about 80% of these.

Foreign Operations Canadian chartered banks are active on the international banking scene. Canadian banks have more than 300 branches and offices in more than 25 countries around the world. They extend loans for a variety of purposes, including the financing of dams, airports, office buildings, and public utilities. Foreign currency assets represent about 40% of commercial banks' total assets.

BUSINESS SITUATION 14.1

Suppose that you are the owner of a medium-sized production company making cardboard boxes. You are interested in expanding your operations but realize that in order to do so you will require some steep loans provided by your local chartered bank branch. You have just read in the paper that your branch is over-reserved.

How might this affect the likelihood that you will get a loan?

The answer to this Business Situation can be found in Appendix A.

Reading Comprehension

The answers to these questions can be found on MyEconLab at www.myeconlab.com. MyEconLab

1. What is the most important asset of a chartered bank? What is its most important liability?
2. What are the main sources of funds for chartered banks? What are the main uses of funds?

LO 14.6 Explain what is meant by the "creation" of money by the chartered banks

The Creation of Money by Chartered Banks: Fundamentals of Deposit Creation

Can we show the mechanics of deposit creation in a simple way?

We can construct a simple model of deposit creation to illustrate the way in which chartered banks "create" money.

A Simple Model of Deposit Creation in a Multi-bank System Let's make the following simplifying assumptions: (1) chartered banks desire to keep a cash reserve of 10%; (2) all deposits are demand deposits; (3) banks invest only in loans; and (4) banks extend as many loans as they can.

Assume that a customer, Mr. Deslauriers, deposits $1000 cash into his chequing account at Atlantic Bank. This deposit is called an **initial deposit** or a **primary deposit**. Initial deposits or primary deposits are deposits that deposit-taking institutions sell for cash.

initial deposit or primary deposit a deposit that a deposit-taking institution sells for cash

T-accounts show changes in the balance sheet resulting from transactions. The $1000 deposit will cause changes in the balance sheet of Atlantic Bank. Table 14.6 shows these changes.

Atlantic Bank wants to keep as desired cash reserves only 10% of the $1000 deposited. The bank therefore has **excess reserves** of $900. Excess reserves are cash reserves held in excess of the desired cash reserves. As a profit-seeking institution, the bank will not allow $900 to lie idly in its vault. Thus, we have the following equation:

excess reserves cash reserves held in excess of the desired cash reserves

Excess reserves = Actual reserves − Desired reserves

Table 14.6 Balance Sheet Changes at Atlantic Bank

Atlantic Bank			
Assets		**Liabilities**	
Desired reserves	+$ 100	Demand deposits:	
Excess reserves	+ 900	Mr. Deslauriers	+$1000
TOTAL	+$ 1000	TOTAL	+$1000

Let's assume that another customer, Mr. Ephraim, goes to the bank to borrow $900 to purchase a new laptop. The bank grants the loan by adding $900 to Mr. Ephraim's chequing account. Note that the bank does not give the customer its excess reserves of $900. Instead, it has created a new deposit by granting the loan to the customer. The new deposit, however, is an amount equal to the bank's excess reserves. Note also that the new deposit of $900 is different from the primary deposit. This new deposit was created by the bank when it extended the loan and is known as a **derivative deposit** or **secondary deposit**. The bank is essentially passive as far as the initial deposit is concerned but plays an active role in creating or producing the derivative deposit.

derivative deposit or secondary deposit a deposit that is created by a bank when it extends a loan

How will the loan transaction affect Atlantic Bank's balance sheet?

Table 14.7 shows how the loan transaction will affect the bank's balance sheet.

Has the money supply been affected?

Mr. Deslauriers's deposit of $1000 did not affect the money supply. It was just a matter of converting one type of money (cash) into another type (demand deposits). The loan granted to Mr. Ephraim, however, has increased the money supply by $900. Mr. Ephraim now has $900 in his account that did not previously exist.

Banks increase the money supply by creating deposits.

Table 14.7 Balance Sheet Changes after the Loan Transaction

Atlantic Bank			
Assets		**Liabilities**	
Cash:		Demand deposits:	
Desired reserves	+$190	Mr. Deslauriers	+$1000
Excess reserves	+ 810	Mr. Ephraim	+ 900
Loans	+ 900		
TOTAL	+1900	TOTAL	+ 1900

What happens when Mr. Ephraim spends the $900?

Mr. Ephraim has learned of a sale on laptops at Best Byte Home Electronics. He rushes to this store and buys a laptop, paying for it by writing a cheque for $900. Best Byte deposits the cheque in its account at Bartlet Bank. Bartlet Bank now has a cheque written on Mr. Ephraim's account at Atlantic Bank. It is quite likely that Atlantic Bank will have cheques written on accounts at Bartlet Bank also. Through a clearing system, the net indebtedness of each bank is determined. If Atlantic Bank has to make a net payment to the Bartlet Bank, then Atlantic Bank's account at the central bank will be reduced by the amount of the payment, and Bartlet Bank's account will be increased by a similar amount. Note that the settlement is accomplished by bookkeeping entries at the central bank rather than by physical transfers of funds.

Let's resume our discussion. The transaction between Mr. Ephraim and Best Byte Electronics will change Atlantic Bank's balance sheet, as shown in Table 14.8. But note the changes in the balance sheet of Bartlet Bank shown in Table 14.9.

Table 14.8 Balance Sheet Changes at Atlantic Bank

Atlantic Bank			
Assets		**Liabilities**	
Desired reserves	+$ 100	Demand deposits:	
Loan	+ 900	Mr. Deslauriers	+$1000
TOTAL	+$1000	TOTAL	+$1000

Table 14.9 Balance Sheet Changes at Bartlet Bank

Bartlet Bank			
Assets		**Liabilities**	
Desired reserves	+$ 90	Demand deposits:	
Excess reserves	+$ 810	Low Price Appliances	+$900
TOTAL	+$ 900	TOTAL	+$900

Table 14.10 Balance Sheet Changes at Bartlet Bank

Bartlet Bank			
Assets		**Liabilities**	
Desired reserves	+$ 171	Demand deposits:	
Excess reserves	+ 729	Low Price Appliances	+$ 900
Loans	+ 810	Ms. Abram	+$ 810
TOTAL	+$ 1710	TOTAL	+$ 1710

Table 14.11 Balance Sheet Changes at Bartlet Bank

Bartlet Bank			
Assets		**Liabilities**	
Desired reserves	+$ 90	Demand deposits:	
Loans	+ 810	Low Price Appliances	+$900
TOTAL	+ $900	TOTAL	+$900

Table 14.12 Balance Sheet Changes at Country Bank

Country Bank			
Assets		**Liabilities**	
Desired reserves	+$ 81	Demand deposits:	
Excess reserves	+ 729	No Frills Airlines	+$810
TOTAL	+$ 810	TOTAL	+$810

The purchase of the computer has not resulted in any change in the money supply. Atlantic Bank has lost $900 in reserves. But Bartlet Bank has gained $900 in new demand deposits.

What happens if another customer borrows money from Bartlet Bank?

Let's investigate. Suppose Ms. Abram borrows $810 from Bartlet Bank. The bank grants the loan by adding $810 to Ms. Abram's chequing account. Table 14.10 shows how this loan transaction will affect Bartlet Bank's balance sheet.

By granting this loan of $810, Bartlet Bank has increased the money supply by $810. The initial deposit of $1000 on Atlantic Bank has resulted so far in an increase in the money supply of $1710 ($900 + $810) in the form of deposit liabilities of commercial banks.

Now what happens when Ms. Abram writes a cheque for the amount she has just borrowed?

Ms. Abram writes a cheque for $810 to No Frills Airlines for a ticket. No Frills Airlines deposits the cheque into its account at the Country Bank. Table 14.11 shows Bartlet Bank's position after the cheque is cleared, and Table 14.12 shows Country Bank's position.

When will this process of deposit expansion end?

Notice that Country Bank has excess reserves; the process of money (deposit) creation could go on and on. Money creation would come to an end when the entire initial deposit of $1000 becomes desired reserves. Because the ratio of desired reserves to deposits is assumed to be 10%, then total reserves of $1000 could support total deposits of $10 000.

The amount of deposits can be obtained by multiplying the initial deposit by the reciprocal of the reserve ratio. The reciprocal of the reserve ratio is called the **deposit expansion multiplier**, or simply the **money multiplier**. The deposit multiplier is the number (or a factor) by which an initial bank deposit is multiplied to arrive at the resulting total deposits.

deposit expansion multiplier or money multiplier the number by which an initial bank deposit is multiplied to arrive at the resulting total deposits

The following formula expresses the money multiplier:

$$MM = 1/rr$$

where MM is the money multiplier and rr is the reserve ratio. Thus, if the reserve ratio is 10%, then the money multiplier is 1/10% = 10. This can be interpreted as a "factor of ten."

Table 14.13 The Deposit Expansion Process

Steps	Deposits ($)	Desired Reserves ($)	Loans = Excess Reserves ($)
1	1000.00	100.00	900.00
2	900.00	90.00	810.00
3	810.00	81.00	729.00
4	729.00	72.90	656.10
5	656.10	65.61	590.49
6	590.49	59.05	531.44
.	.	.	.
.	.	.	.
.	.	.	.
Sum (all steps)	10 000.00	1000.00	9 000.00

We use this factor to determine the amount by which the money supply can increase, given the size of the initial deposit. In this case, the initial or primary deposit of $1000 is multiplied by 10, the money multiplier, to support $10 000 in total new deposits. If the reserve ratio is 20%, then the money multiplier is 1/20% = 5. Table 14.13 summarizes the step-by-step approach that we have taken.

We used a multi-bank system to illustrate the process of money creation (deposit expansion). The result would have been the same if we had assumed a monopoly bank situation.

Reading Comprehension

The answers to these questions can be found on MyEconLab at www.myeconlab.com. MyEconLab

1. "Only the central bank can create money. Chartered banks merely lend out funds deposited with them and earn a return by charging interest on their loans." Discuss.
2. Briefly explain the process of money (deposit) expansion by commercial banks.
3. Describe the relationship between the reserve ratio and the size of the money multiplier.

BUSINESS SITUATION 14.2

You are the manager of a bank. Your bank has excess reserves. The economy is in a depressed state.

How would you utilize your bank's excess reserves?

The answer to this Business Situation can be found in Appendix A.

LO 14.7 Discuss practical constraints on deposit creation and deposit destruction

Practical Constraints on Deposit Creation and Deposit Destruction

Will banks always be able to expand deposits to the theoretical limit?

The direct answer to this question is no. The conditions under which we have discussed the process of deposit creation are simplistic and artificial. We followed this approach deliberately to help you learn the fundamentals of deposit creation. We must now relax some of our assumptions so that we can focus on the practical limits to deposit creation. Excess reserves, limited demand for loans, and currency drain are practical constraints on deposit creation. Let us examine each in turn.

Excess Reserves In our analysis so far, we have assumed that banks do not desire to keep any excess reserves. However, it is reasonable to expect banks to keep some cash beyond the minimum desired cash reserve. Banks cannot predict with certainty their depositors' demand for cash; hence, they will want to keep some excess reserves for precautionary purposes. Banks will try to avoid undue exposure to what is called *bankers' risk*—the risk of not being able to convert their depositors' demand deposits into currency on demand. Clearly, keeping excess cash reserves limits the amount of funds that can be used for loans, and hence it limits banks' power to create deposits through loans.

Limited Demand for Loans We have assumed that, at any given time, there are so many creditworthy borrowers seeking loans that banks have absolutely no trouble making profitable loans. Clearly, this condition will not always exist in practice. An economic situation may be such that the public may be reluctant to borrow even if banks are willing to lend. The unwillingness of customers to borrow affects banks' ability to create deposits through loans.

Currency Drain Finally, we have assumed that any cheques received by the public were promptly deposited as demand deposits at banks. This assumption ignores the reality that people also use currency as a medium of exchange. If you receive a cheque for $1000, it is likely that you will deposit a part of it in your account at a bank and take a part of it in cash. The amount of money in currency represents potential cash reserves for banks—reserves that could be used to support further deposit creation. Whenever there is a *currency drain* (a withdrawal of currency from the bank), the total money supply will fall by more than the amount of the currency drain.

Is it possible for the expansion process to work in reverse? If so, what are the main factors that lead to the destruction of deposits by banks?

Let us examine two factors that lead to the destruction of deposits and the reduction of the money supply. These are the repayment of a loan and a currency drain.

Loan Repayment To study the effect of a loan repayment on bank deposits, let us assume that the bank's current position is as shown in Table 14.14.

Suppose now that some of the bank's creditors repay a total of $150 000 of their loans. The creditors do this by writing cheques for a total of $150 000 drawn on their accounts at the bank. The bank's loan assets will fall by $150 000, and its deposit liability will fall by an equivalent amount. Other things being equal, this implies a reduction of $150 000 in the money supply. Table 14.15 illustrates the situation.

Note that the repayment of the loan has caused the bank to end up with excess reserves of $15 000.

Currency Drain Let us return to the situation shown in Table 14.14. The bank has desired cash reserves of $300 000 and no excess reserves. Suppose that some depositors withdraw a total of $50 000 cash from their accounts. On the surface, it may seem as if

Table 14.14 Balance Sheet of a Bank

Assets		Liabilities	
Desired cash reserves	$ 300 000	Demand deposits:	
Excess reserves	0	Previous	$ 885 000
Government securities	100 000	Additional	2 115 000
Loans:		Capital stock	500 000
Previous	485 000		
Additional	2 115 000		
Property	500 000		
Total	$ 3 500 000	Total	$ 3 500 000

Table 14.15 Bank's Balance Sheet after Loan Repayment

Assets		Liabilities	
Desired cash reserves	$ 285 000	Demand deposits:	
Excess reserves	15 000	Previous	$ 3 000 000
Government securities	100 000	Current	2 850 000
Loans:		Capital stock	500 000
Previous	2 600 000		
Current	2 450 000		
Property	500 000		
Total	$ 3 350 000	Total	$ 3 350 000

the customers of the bank have merely exchanged demand deposits for cash and that the money stock would not change. However we should study this situation more closely. The bank makes cash payments totalling $50 000 by reducing its cash holdings by that amount. The bank's cash reserves will now total $250 000, but its deposit liabilities total $3 million. The bank must reduce its deposit liabilities to $2.5 million. In practice, a bank can reduce its deposits by calling in matured loans and by not making new loans. As we have seen, the effect of the cash withdrawal of $50 000 is to reduce the money supply by several times the amount of cash withdrawal.

Reading Comprehension

The answers to these questions can be found on MyEconLab at www.myeconlab.com. MyEconLab

1. Is it possible that banks keep excess reserves? Under what conditions is this likely? What effect will this have on their ability to create money?
2. What are the factors that limit the amount of deposits that commercial banks can create?
3. Describe how a loan repayment can lead to deposit destruction.

LO 14.8 Discuss the role of near banks in the financial system

The Role of Near Banks

Can you provide a description of a near bank?

Near banks are financial institutions whose main liabilities are very close substitutes for the deposit liabilities of commercial banks. These institutions include caisses populaires, credit unions, trust companies, and mortgage loan companies.

What are caisses populaires and credit unions?

Caisses populaires and credit unions are important elements in the financial sector of the Canadian economy. The credit union movement is of particular interest to Quebec because it originated there and was organized by native Quebecers. In 1900, the caisses populaires were founded in Lévis, Quebec, by Alphonse Desjardins. It should not be surprising then that the credit union movement is more popular in Quebec than in any other province of Canada.

Unlike chartered banks, caisses populaires and credit unions operate under provincial legislation. The local credit unions and caisses populaires in each province belong to a central credit union operating in the province.

What are the main sources and uses of funds for caisses populaires and credit unions?

The sources and uses of funds for caisses populaires and credit unions are revealed in their balance sheets (see Table 14.16). The list of their liabilities reveals that their major sources of funds are deposits and members' equity. You will notice the similarity between the deposit liabilities of credit unions and caisses populaires and those of the chartered banks. Deposit liabilities of caisses populaires and credit unions represent about 85% of their total liabilities, while members' equity accounts for about 7%.

Caisses populaires and credit unions obtain most of their funds from customers' deposits.

Table 14.16 Major Assets and Liabilities of Caisses Populaires and Credit Unions

Item	Percentage (%)
ASSETS	
Cash and demand and notice deposits	6.5
Term deposits	7.2
Personal and other loans	25.4
Mortgages	55.5
LIABILITIES	
Loans payable	6.1
Deposits	84.9
Members' equity	6.6

Caisses populaires and credit unions use their funds mainly for mortgage lending. Personal cash loans and other cash loans are also important uses. Mortgage loans account for approximately 55% of the assets of caisses populaires and credit unions, while personal and other loans account for about 25% of total assets.

Caisses populaires and credit unions use their funds mainly for mortgage lending and cash loans.

What are trust and mortgage loan companies?

Trust and mortgage loan companies are similar in many ways in terms of their operations. In fact, trust companies and mortgage loan companies sometimes

Table 14.17 Major Assets and Liabilities of Trust and Mortgage Loan Companies

Item	Percentage (%)
ASSETS	
Government of Canada treasury bills	4
Short-term paper and bankers' acceptances	6
Government of Canada bonds	4
Mortgages	45
Personal loans	25
LIABILITIES	
Savings deposits	20
Term deposits, guaranteed investment certificates, and debentures	67
Shareholders' equity	5

operate their businesses as one unit. As would be expected, mortgage loan companies have a greater proportion of their assets as mortgage loans than trust companies do.

What are the main sources and uses of funds for trust and mortgage loan companies?

As the liabilities section in Table 14.17 shows, trust and mortgage loan companies obtain a great deal of their funds from term deposits. They also obtain funds from chequable and non-chequable deposits.

Term deposits, guaranteed investment certificates, and debentures account for about 67% of total liabilities. Savings deposits account for about 20%.

Term deposits constitute the main source of funds for trust and mortgage loan companies.

As for the uses of funds, the asset section of Table 14.17 provides the answer. Because trust and mortgage loan companies offer chequing accounts, we can expect them to keep a certain portion of their assets in very liquid form. Most of their funds, however, are used to extend mortgage loans. Mortgage loans amount to about 45% of the total assets of trust and mortgage loan companies.

Most of the funds of trust and mortgage loan companies are used for mortgage lending.

Reading Comprehension

The answers to these questions can be found on MyEconLab at **www.myeconlab.com**. MyEconLab

1. Why is the credit union movement of particular significance to Quebec?
2. What are the main sources and uses of funds for caisses populaires and credit unions?
3. What are the main sources and uses of funds for trust and mortgage loan companies?

Review

1. Review the learning objectives listed at the beginning of the chapter.
2. Have you accomplished all the objectives? One way to determine this is to answer the Reading Comprehension questions at the end of each section. These will help you assess your understanding of the learning objectives.
3. If you have not accomplished an objective, review the relevant material before proceeding.

Key Points to Remember

1. LO 14.1 The Bank of Canada and a number of chartered banks make up the Canadian banking system.
2. LO 14.2 The main functions of the Bank of Canada are to issue currency in adequate quantities, to act as banker to the chartered banks, to act as fiscal agent and financial adviser to the government, to conduct the country's monetary policy, and to support the financial system.
3. LO 14.3 The main asset of the Bank of Canada is Government of Canada securities. The main liability of the Bank of Canada is Bank of Canada notes in circulation.
4. LO 14.4 Origins of modern banking can be traced back to the seventeenth century when the role of goldsmiths was prominent. The banking system has evolved greatly since that time. Today our banking system is described as a branch banking system. The operations of chartered banks in Canada are governed by the provisions of the *Bank Act*. Banks must try to strike a balance between profitability on the one hand and liquidity and safety on the other. They make a profit by charging a higher rate of interest on money they lend out than the rate they pay their depositors.
5. LO 14.5 The assets of the chartered banks include deposits at the central bank, foreign currency deposits, cheques in transit, government T-bills, loans, and mortgages. Liabilities include deposits, advances from the Bank of Canada, acceptances, guarantees, and letters of credit.
6. LO 14.6 Chartered banks increase the money supply by extending loans to borrowers and by crediting the amount of the loan to their deposit accounts. Borrowers are not given cash. The reciprocal of the desired reserve ratio gives the maximum money expansion multiplier.
7. LO 14.7 A variety of circumstances can prevent a bank from realizing its maximum deposit expansion. There are practical constraints on deposit creation which include excess reserves, limited demand for loans, and currency drain. In the same way that banks can create deposits and thus increase the money supply, they can also destroy deposits and thus reduce the money supply. Two factors that lead to the destruction of deposits are the repayment of a loan and a currency drain.
8. LO 14.8 The main sources of funds for credit unions and caisses populaires are deposits and members' equity. Fund share is allocated mainly to mortgage lending and cash loans to members. Term deposits constitute the major source of funds for trust companies and mortgage loan companies. The main use of their funds is mortgage lending.

Economic Word Power

Balance sheet (p. 356)
Bank Act (p. 360)
Bank of Canada Act (p. 353)
Banking system (p. 350)
Branch banking system (p. 360)
Canada Deposit Insurance Corporation (p. 354)
Chartered banks or commercial banks (p. 351)
Core CPI (p. 355)
Core inflation (p. 355)
Debentures (p. 362)
Deposit expansion multiplier or money multiplier (p. 366)
Derivative deposit or secondary deposit (p. 365)
Desired reserves (p. 363)
Excess reserves (p. 364)
Fiduciary monetary system (p. 355)
Fractional reserve banking system (p. 363)
Initial deposit or primary deposit (p. 364)
Interest spread (p. 361)
Near banks ((p. 352)
Office of the Superintendent of Financial Institutions (p. 354)
Primary reserves (p. 363)
Secondary reserves ((p. 363)
Target reserve ratio (p. 363)

Problems and Exercises

Basic

1. LO 14.1 Which of the following are part of the Canadian banking system?
   a. RBC (Royal Bank of Canada)
   b. Caisses populaires
   c. Royal Trust
   d. TD (Toronto Dominion Bank)
   e. BMO (Bank of Montreal)
   f. Niagara Finance Company
   g. Bank of Canada
   h. Canada Mortgage and Trust
   i. GMAC (General Motors Acceptance Corporation)
   j. Scotiabank
   k. Manulife Financial
   l. National Bank of Canada
   m. Canada Trust
   n. Laurentian Bank

2. Indicate whether each of the following is true (T) or false (F):
   a. LO 14.4 The Royal Bank of Canada (RBC) is Canada's central bank.
   b. LO 14.5 The chartered banks are in full control of the country's money supply.
   c. LO 14.2 The Bank of Canada and the chartered banks perform identical functions.
   d. LO 14.2 Many individuals and businesses hold chequing accounts at the Bank of Canada.
   e. LO 14.2 The Bank of Canada is the only institution empowered to issue bank notes (paper currency).
   f. LO 14.4 Canadian chartered banks keep deposits at the Bank of Canada.
3. LO 14.3 List the Bank of Canada's major assets and liabilities.
4. LO 14.3 Indicate whether each of the following is an asset or liability of the Bank of Canada:
   a. Bank of Canada deposits in the Bank of England (England's central bank)
   b. Paper currency issued by the Bank of Canada
   c. Loans by the Bank of Canada to a Canadian financial institution
   d. Government of Canada securities held by the Bank of Canada
   e. Deposits of financial institutions with the Bank of Canada
   f. Foreign central banks' deposits with the Bank of Canada
5. LO 14.4 Which of the following services do commercial banks perform?
   a. Granting loans
   b. Offering official financial advice to the government as a primary function
   c. Providing foreign exchange services
   d. Conducting the country's monetary policy
   e. Conducting the country's fiscal policy
   f. Serving as banker of last resort
   g. Providing bill-payment services
   h. Furnishing automatic teller machine (ATM) services
6. LO 14.5 List the major assets and liabilities of chartered banks.

Questions in the Intermediate and Challenging Sections cover several different concepts, and have not been organized by learning objectives.

Intermediate

1. Use T-accounts to illustrate how each of the following transactions will affect a bank's balance sheet:
   a. A customer deposits $1000 in her savings account
   b. A customer writes a cheque for $500 drawn on his account and the cheque is cashed
   c. The bank buys $10 million Government of Canada bonds
   d. A borrower makes a loan payment of $300
   e. A customer withdraws $400 from her savings account
2. Suppose a group of businesspeople decides to open a bank and issues $100 000 of capital stock to set it up. Some $80 000 of this is used to purchase the building. The other $20 000 is kept as cash. What will the original balance sheet be and how will it change with each of the following transactions?
   a. Customers deposit $30 000 in demand deposit accounts in the bank
   b. The bank decides to buy $20 000 of government bonds.
3. Assume the desired reserve ratio is 20%, and a bank receives a deposit of $10 000.
   a. What is the maximum deposit expansion multiplier?
   b. What is the maximum amount of money the bank can create?
   c. What is the total deposit?
4. Table 14.15 illustrates multiple deposit expansion in a multi-bank system. In Table 14.18 below, assume that the required reserve ratio is 20% and the initial deposit is $10 000. Complete the table.

Table 14.18 Multiple-Deposit Expansion

Bank	Desired Deposits ($)	Excess Reserve (20%) ($)	Reserves ($)	Loans ($)
1	10 000			
2				
3				
4				
5				
6				
Total (all banks)				

Challenging

1. Present an argument to convince your friend that chartered banks can actually create more money than the deposits they receive.
2. Banks create money by lending out their excess reserves. Discuss.

MyEconLab Visit the MyEconLab website at **www.myeconlab.com**. This online homework and tutorial system puts you in control of your own learning with study and practice tools directly correlated to this chapter's content.

Study Guide

Self-Assessment

What's your score?

Circle the letter that corresponds with the correct answer.

1. The Canadian banking system consists only of
   a. The Bank of Canada and the chartered banks
   b. The chartered banks and the near banks
   c. The Bank of Canada, the chartered banks, and the near banks
   d. None of the above
2. Which of the following is correct?
   a. Banks accept deposits from the public while near banks don't
   b. Near banks accept deposits from the public while banks don't
   c. Both banks and near banks accept deposits from the public
   d. Neither banks nor near banks accept deposits from the public
3. Canada's central bank is
   a. The Royal Bank of Canada (RBC)
   b. The Federal Reserve System
   c. The Bank of Canada
   d. The Canadian Imperial Bank of Commerce (CIBC)
4. Which of the following is a function of Canada's central bank?
   a. To control the money supply
   b. To support the financial system
   c. To act as fiscal agent for the government
   d. All of the above
5. The central bank serves as banker to the commercial banks when it
   a. Keeps the government's accounts
   b. Conducts the country's monetary policy
   c. Administers the country's fiscal policy
   d. Keeps their cash reserves
6. The most important asset item for the Bank of Canada is
   a. Currency and demand deposits
   b. Government of Canada securities
   c. Deposits on commercial banks
   d. Customers' deposits
7. The main liability item of the Bank of Canada is
   a. Deposits on commercial banks
   b. Chartered banks' reserves
   c. Bank of Canada notes in circulation
   d. Treasury bills
8. The structure of Canada's banking system can be described as
   a. A unit banking system
   b. A mixed banking system
   c. An integrated system
   d. A branch banking system
9. Services provided by commercial banks include
   a. The granting of loans
   b. The establishment of savings accounts
   c. The provision of foreign exchange services
   d. All of the above
10. The main assets of chartered banks include
    a. Loans
    b. Foreign currency assets
    c. Government of Canada securities
    d. All of the above
11. The most important liability of commercial banks is
    a. Notes and coins in circulation
    b. Shareholders' equity
    c. Customers' deposits
    d. Subordinated debt
12. When a bank grants a loan
    a. Its assets increase
    b. Its liabilities decrease
    c. Its assets and liabilities remain the same
    d. Its assets decrease
13. The maximum deposit expansion multiplier is
    a. Always 1
    b. The same as the reserve ratio
    c. The inverse of the desired reserve ratio
    d. $1 - rr$ where rr is the desired reserve ratio

14. If the desired reserve ratio is 10%, then
   a. The maximum deposit expansion multiplier is 10
   b. Desired reserves equal 10% of total reserves
   c. The maximum deposit expansion multiplier is 1
   d. None of the above

15. The simple deposit (money) expansion multiplier can be defined as
   a. The cash reserve ratio
   b. The ratio of the change in the money supply to the change in actual cash reserves that brought it about
   c. The reciprocal of the desired cash reserve ratio
   d. Both (b) and (c)

16. Chartered banks are able to affect the money supply because of
   a. The fractional reserve banking system
   b. Their ability to create new deposit accounts as a by-product of their profit-seeking activities
   c. Their ability to make profits for their shareholders
   d. Both (a) and (b)

17. Which of the following is a near bank in Canada?
   a. Bank of Montreal
   b. Bank of Nova Scotia
   c. Bank of Canada
   d. None of the above

18. Caisses populaires and credit unions are
   a. Near banks
   b. Commercial banks
   c. Central banks
   d. None of the above

19. The major liability of caisses populaires and credit unions is
   a. Loans payable
   b. Customers' deposits
   c. Mortgage loans
   d. None of the above

20. The main source of funds for trust and mortgage loan companies is
   a. Treasury bills
   b. Mortgages
   c. Term deposits
   d. Shareholders' equity

Problems and Exercises (Use Quad Paper for Graphs)

Answers to these questions can be found on MyEconLab at www.myeconlab.com. MyEconLab

1. Draw up a hypothetical partial balance sheet for a central bank, listing major assets and liabilities.

2. State whether each of the following statements is true or false, and briefly explain your reason:
   a. The Bank of Canada is owned and operated by the major Canadian chartered banks.
   b. The Bank of Canada is completely independent of the government and is therefore free to pursue any monetary policy it pleases.
   c. The paper currency we use is recorded on the asset side of the balance sheet of the Bank of Canada.

3. Draw a hypothetical partial balance sheet for a chartered bank showing only the major assets and liabilities.

4. Draw a table showing the main sources and uses of funds for a chartered bank.

5. Use T-accounts to illustrate the effects of each of the following transactions on a bank's balance sheet:
   a. Customer Peter May deposits $500 in his chequing account.
   b. Customer Ruth Wilson withdraws $100 cash from her savings account.
   c. Customer Cora Hunt makes a cash payment of $250 on her loan account.
   d. Customer Nikisha Williams writes a cheque for $75 and the cheque is cashed.

6. Assume the following:
   a. All banks decide to keep 10% of their deposit liabilities as cash reserves.
   b. They keep no excess reserves.
   c. They can lend out as much money as they want.

   How much money will the banking system be able to create from a deposit of $500?

7. Referring to Question 6, if banks keep 5% of their deposit liabilities as cash reserves instead of 10%, how much money will they be able to create from a deposit of $500?

8. Draw a table showing the main sources and uses of funds for credit unions or caisses populaires.

9. Draw a table showing the main sources and uses of funds for a commercial bank.

Chapter 15

Monetary Theory and Monetary Policy

Irving Fisher (1867–1947) made significant contributions to monetary theory and monetary policy.

Learning Objectives

After studying this chapter, you should be able to

- **15.1** Understand the quantity theory of money
- **15.2** Discuss the Keynesian theory of money
- **15.3** Explain the liquidity preference theory of interest rate determination
- **15.4** Explain how changes in the demand for and supply of money affect the equilibrium rate of interest
- **15.5** Understand the relationship between the quantity of money and the level of gross domestic product
- **15.6** Discuss the meaning and objectives of monetary policy
- **15.7** Discuss the tools of monetary policy and explain how monetary policy works
- **15.8** Discuss the role of monetary policy in dealing with the 2008–2009 recession
- **15.9** Discuss the effectiveness and limitations of monetary policy

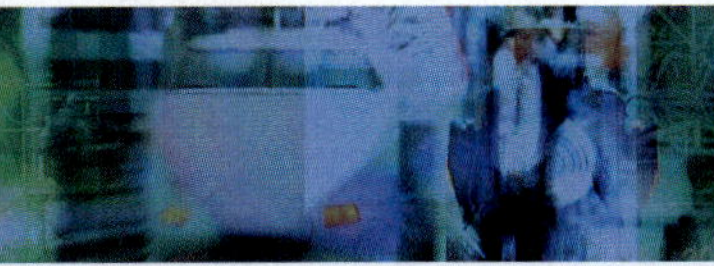

Assess Your Knowledge

MyEconLab

Answers to these questions can be found on MyEconLab at **www.myeconlab.com.**

1. Is there any relationship between the quantity of money and the value of money?
2. Is there any relationship between the level of income and the quantity of money that will be demanded?
3. Indicate whether each of the following is true (T) or false (F):
   a. The higher the rate of interest, the greater the amount of money that will be deposited in savings accounts.
   b. Monetary policy is conducted by the Department of Finance.
   c. The actions of the Bank of Canada have no effect on the rate of interest.
   d. The commercial banks can borrow from the Bank of Canada.
   e. Monetary policy can be used to combat unemployment but not inflation.

LO 15.1 Understand the quantity theory of money

The Quantity Theory of Money

What is monetary theory?

Monetary theory deals with the effects of the demand for and supply of money on income, output, and the price level. Is there a relationship between the quantity of money and the price level? How is the rate of interest determined? How does an increase in the demand for money affect interest rates and output? All these questions relate to monetary theory.

Is there any economic theory linking the quantity of money and the price level?

quantity theory of money the theory that states that changes in the price level are due to changes in the quantity of money

An important strand of classical economics was the **quantity theory of money**, which, in its crudest form, states that changes in the price level are due to changes in the quantity of money. This theory had its heyday in the nineteenth and early twentieth centuries.

The quantity theory and much of classical economics fell in popularity in the 1930s and were supplanted, though not usurped, by Keynesian theory, which apparently did a better job of explaining the Great Depression. Since then, largely because of the work of Milton Friedman and the apparent failure of Keynesian economics to explain the coexistence of inflation and unemployment in the 1970s, the quantity theory has reappeared under the name of monetarism.

Let us now look at the crude quantity theory of money.

The Crude Quantity Theory of Money Classical economists established a relationship between the quantity of money and the price level. This crude quantity theory of money states that the price level is proportional to the quantity of money. Doubling the quantity of money would result in a doubling of the price level.

> The crude quantity theory of money states that the quantity of money is directly proportional to the price level.

To see how the classical economists arrived at this conclusion, we need to introduce two new concepts: the velocity of circulation and the equation of exchange. Let's begin with the velocity of circulation.

velocity of circulation the number of times, on average, that a unit of money is spent per year

The Velocity of Circulation of Money **Velocity of circulation** refers to the number of times, on average, that a unit of money (such as a dollar) is spent per year in purchasing final goods and services. For example, if the gross domestic product is $500 billion, and the quantity of money is $50 billion, then it means that, on average, each dollar buys $10 worth of the economy's output of goods and services; that is, each dollar is spent 10 times a year, on average—the velocity of circulation is 10.

The velocity of circulation can be expressed symbolically as

$$V = \text{GDP}/M$$

where V is the velocity of circulation, GDP is gross domestic product, and M is the quantity of money.

When the concept of the velocity of circulation of money was first developed, there was no measure for gross domestic product. How then could the velocity of circulation be expressed? You will recall that real GDP is nominal GDP divided by the price level. That is,

$$\text{Real GDP} = \text{GDP}/P$$

$$\text{or GDP} = P \times \text{Real GDP}$$

where P is the price level. If Q denotes real GDP, we have

$$\text{GDP} = P \times Q$$

We can now express the velocity of circulation as

$$V = \text{GDP}/M = (P \times Q)/M$$

> The velocity of circulation of money can be computed by multiplying real GDP by the price level and dividing the result by the quantity of money.

equation of exchange an expression that equates the product of the quantity of money and the velocity of circulation (*MV*) with the product of the price level and real output (*PQ*)

The Equation of Exchange The next major concept in the quantity theory of money is the **equation of exchange** developed by Irving Fisher (1867–1947) in the 1900s. (His picture is on page 376.) The equation of exchange can be expressed as the following identity:

$$MV = PQ$$

where M, V, and Q have the same meanings as in the velocity equation in the previous section.

The equation of exchange seems to be closely related to the velocity equation.

As a matter of fact, we can obtain the equation of exchange simply by multiplying the velocity equation by M.

Let us examine the equation of exchange a little more closely. The left side of the equation (MV) is simply the amount spent in purchasing goods and services. If the quantity of money is $50 billion, and each dollar is spent 10 times a year on average, then total spending must be $500 billion. As you saw earlier, the right side of the equation (PQ)

is the gross domestic product in nominal terms. Because the total amount spent on the economy's output of goods and services must equal the value of that output, the equation of exchange is a truism or tautology (meaning that it is true by definition).

> The equation of exchange expresses the idea that the amount of money spent in purchasing goods and services equals the value of the goods and services purchased.

We have discussed the velocity of circulation and the equation of exchange. How do these concepts help us to develop the quantity theory of money?

As it stands, the equation of exchange is not a theory at all, because it tells us nothing about how anything is determined. The classical economists, however, made certain assumptions about the variables in the equation of exchange, which enabled them to arrive at a theory of money and the price level. These assumptions are as follows:

1. The quantity of money is exogenously determined by the monetary authorities. Hence, M is given.
2. V, the velocity of circulation, is determined by institutional factors, such as payment practices of individuals and firms and the frequency of receipt of income, and is independent of M, P, and Q. Therefore, V is a constant.
3. Real GDP, Q, is fixed at the full-employment level, at least in the short run.

Thus, P, the average level of prices, is the only passive variable in the equation. This means that the price level does not affect the other variables, but it can be affected by them. The effect of these assumptions can be seen readily if we divide the equation of exchange by V to obtain

$$\mathrm{M} = \frac{Q}{V} \times P$$

Clearly, with Q/V being constant, M is directly proportional to P. The conclusion of the quantity theorists is as follows:

> The price level is determined by the quantity of money. Changes in the quantity of money cause proportional changes in the price level.

What exactly is the logic behind the quantity theory of money?

The logic behind the quantity theory of money is that any increase in the quantity of money will cause households and firms to end up with more money than they want to hold for transactions. According to the classical economists, money is held for transaction purposes only. Households and firms tend to keep some portion of their wealth in the form of currency and demand deposits so that they can pay for the goods and services they want. The classical economists saw no reason for holding more money than was required for this purpose. They based their argument on the fact that assets held in the form of currency and demand deposits earn little or no interest. Because of the assumption of full employment, output cannot increase in response to the increase in total spending. The quantity of money therefore forces prices up.

Are there any weaknesses in this theory?

Yes. The quantity theory of money just presented has some limitations. Let us discuss them.

Figure 15.1 The Velocity of Circulation, 1990–2009

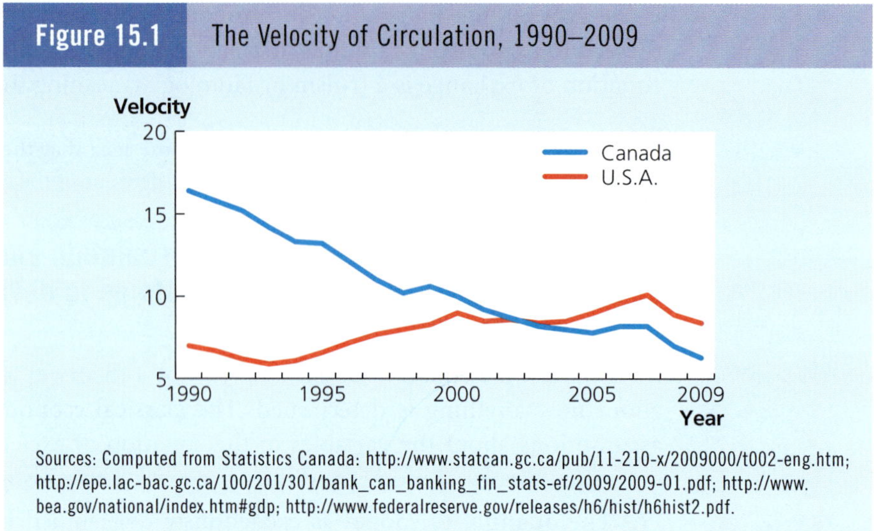

Sources: Computed from Statistics Canada: http://www.statcan.gc.ca/pub/11-210-x/2009000/t002-eng.htm; http://epe.lac-bac.gc.ca/100/201/301/bank_can_banking_fin_stats-ef/2009/2009-01.pdf; http://www.bea.gov/national/index.htm#gdp; http://www.federalreserve.gov/releases/h6/hist/h6hist2.pdf.

Limitations of the Crude Quantity Theory The quantity theory of money we just presented has been called the crude or naive quantity theory. The assumption that output remains constant at the full-employment level is one of the weaknesses of the theory. The economy is quite often operating at less than full employment, as you have seen in previous chapters. Consequently, the output of goods and services is subject to some degree of variation. With *Q* varying, the possibility arises that an increase in *M* may lead to an increase in *Q*, rather than to an increase in *P*. Or an increase in *M* may affect both *P* and *Q*. But the increase in *P* may not be proportional to the increase in *M*.

A second limitation of the crude quantity theory is that it assumes the velocity of circulation to be constant. The velocity of circulation may be fairly constant under certain circumstances. However, in times of rapid inflation, households and firms will be unwilling to hold money because its value will decrease. Thus, the velocity of circulation tends to increase sharply during periods of inflation as people try to spend money whose value is falling. Figure 15.1 shows the velocity of circulation of money in Canada and the United States from 1990 to 2009.

In Canada, the velocity of circulation has followed a generally downward trend, from 16.4 in 1990 to as low as 6.3 in 2009. In the United States, the velocity of circulation reached a low of 5.9 in 1993 and peaked at 10.1 in 2007. In light of these statistics, we can hardly claim that the velocity of circulation has been constant in Canada or the United States over the years.

Has the crude quantity theory been modified in any way?

The limitations of the crude quantity theory—the assumptions that (1) output remains constant at the full-employment level and (2) the velocity of circulation of money is constant—have led to the development of a new and more sophisticated version of the quantity theory of money. Let us look at this new, refined version of the quantity theory.

The New Quantity Theory (Monetarism) Monetarism is basically a new version of the quantity theory. It maintains that output is variable because the economy may be operating at less than full employment. The velocity of circulation is assumed to vary only slightly over time, and such variations are considered to be predictable. Whereas the

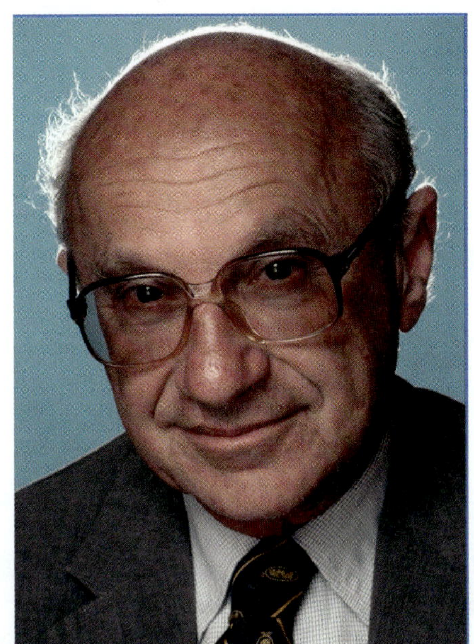

The new quantity theory of money owes much to the work of Nobel laureate Milton Friedman (1912–2006).

crude quantity theory stressed the relationship between the quantity of money and the price level, the modified version emphasizes the relationship between the quantity of money and nominal (money) income. This relation is expressed in the following form:

$$M = (1/V)P \times Q$$

If V were assumed to be constant, $1/V$ (which we can denote by k) would also be a constant. The product of P and Q is simply total income, which we denote by Y. We can rewrite the above equation as

$$M = kY$$

It is clear that if k is a constant, the quantity of money will be proportional to total income. But because V is assumed to vary slightly over time, k is not a constant. The new quantity theory predicts, therefore, that increases in the quantity of money will increase nominal income, while reductions in the quantity of money will decrease nominal income.

> The new quantity theory of money links the quantity of money to nominal income.

The revival of interest in the quantity theory is due largely to the work of Milton Friedman (1912–2006), a very prominent economist who proposed a restatement of the quantity theory. According to Friedman, the quantity theory is a theory about the demand for money. Specifically, it assumes that the demand for money is a stable function of income and the rate of interest. Without going through the details of Friedman's restatement of the quantity theory, we can state the main conclusions:

monetarism the school of thought that claims that changes in the money supply are the major cause of economic fluctuations and that macroeconomic stability can be achieved by a steady increase in the money supply

1. The demand for money varies directly with the price level.
2. Real income is an important determinant of the demand for money.
3. There is a consistent direct relation between the quantity of money and the growth rate of nominal income.

Because of its emphasis on money, the new quantity theory is often referred to as the monetarist model or **monetarism**. Monetarism is the school of thought that claims that changes in the quantity of money are the major cause of economic fluctuations and that macroeconomic stability can be achieved by a steady increase in the quantity of money.

Reading Comprehension

The answers to these questions can be found on MyEconLab at www.myeconlab.com. MyEconLab

1. According to the crude quantity theory of money, what is the relationship between the quantity of money and the price level?
2. Define the velocity of circulation of money. How can the velocity of circulation of money be measured?
3. Explain the equation of exchange. Is this equation a theory of money?
4. What are the assumptions of the crude quantity theory of money?
5. Does the Canadian or U.S. experience in recent years support the assumption of a constant velocity of circulation of money? Explain.
6. How does the new quantity theory differ from the crude quantity theory?
7. What are the main conclusions of the new quantity theory of money?

LO 15.2 Discuss the Keynesian theory of money

The Keynesian Theory of Money

Is the Keynesian theory an extension of the classical quantity theory?

The Keynesian theory of money is an *alternative* to the quantity theory. You will soon see that Keynes placed a great deal of emphasis on the demand for money. The demand for money in this context is the amount of money households and firms wish to hold. The question is, why do households and firms hold money?

Yes! Why do people hold money?

Keynes noted three reasons for holding money: for transaction purposes, for precautionary purposes, and for speculative purposes. Let us discuss each of these motives for holding money.

The Transactions Demand for Money In our study of the classical theory of money, we saw that households and firms will hold a part of their wealth in the form of currency and demand deposits so that they can carry out certain transactions. This is the **transactions demand for money**—the desire to hold money for transaction purposes.

transactions demand for money the desire to hold money for transaction purposes

What determines the amount of money that will be held for transaction purposes?

The amount of money that will be demanded (i.e., held) for transaction purposes will depend on the number of anticipated transactions, which, in turn, depends on the level of income. If the annual income of a family increases from $50 000 to $60 000, we can expect the family to keep more money for transaction purposes. In the same way, then, if total income in the economy increases, we expect the demand for money for transaction purposes to increase.

> The transactions demand for money varies directly with the level of income.

The Precautionary Demand for Money In addition to holding money for regular transactions, such as paying rent, buying food, and purchasing gasoline, people will tend to hold some money to meet unexpected contingencies, such as a broken furnace, a blown muffler, or a really big sale at a major department store. This motive for holding money is called the **precautionary demand for money**—the desire to hold money for unexpected contingencies. Clearly, the precautionary demand for money is closely related to the transactions demand. In times of uncertainly, a greater amount of money is held for precautionary purposes.

precautionary demand for money the desire to hold money for unexpected contingencies

What determines the amount of money that will be held for precautionary purposes?

We can expect the level of income to influence the precautionary demand for money. Like the transactions demand for money, the precautionary demand for money varies directly with the level of income. Clearly, the availability and wide use of credit cards reduce the need to hold much money for precautionary purposes.

> The precautionary demand for money varies directly with the level of income.

The Speculative Demand for Money Finally, Keynes claimed that people hold money for speculative purposes. When the purchasing power of money is rising (prices are falling), people will tend to hold more money. By so doing, they hope to gain by purchasing goods at lower prices in the future. When money is losing its value (prices are rising), people will tend to convert their money into goods to avoid incurring a loss. People also hold money in anticipation of a decrease in the price of financial assets. If they expect the price of financial assets to decrease in the future, or the rate of interest to increase, they will hold more money balances. The desire to hold money in the hope of gaining financially from price changes or in anticipation of movements in the prices of financial assets is called the **speculative demand for money**.

speculative demand for money the desire to hold money in anticipation of movements in the prices of financial assets

To illustrate the concept of the speculative demand for money, let us assume that the public can hold its wealth in two forms only: (1) money that earns no interest and (2) bonds that do earn interest. The price of a bond, like the price of any other commodity for which the price is not controlled, will vary with changes in demand and supply. If a long-term bond worth \$100 is issued at a 10% rate of interest per year, the purchaser of the bond will receive \$10 annually. If the owner of the bond sells it for \$200, the new owner will still receive \$10 annually. As far as the new owner is concerned, 5% will be earned annually on the bond purchase. Thus, to say that bond prices rise is equivalent to saying that interest rates fall.

What determines the amount of money that will be held for speculative purposes?

If interest rates are high (bond prices are low) and people expect them to fall (bond prices to rise), they will buy bonds now, hoping to sell them for future profit. This implies that the higher the rate of interest, the smaller the amount of money that will be held. If interest rates are expected to rise (bond prices are expected to fall), people will convert their bonds into cash before prices actually fall. The lower the rate of interest, the greater the amount of money that people will want to hold. The quantity of money demanded for speculative purposes is inversely related to the rate of interest.

The speculative demand for money is inversely related to the rate of interest.

Is there any other reason for holding money?

You will recall that money functions as a store of value or liquid asset. People can choose to hold their wealth in various ways, including real estate, government bonds, stocks issued by corporations, and savings accounts. Because money is the most liquid of all assets, people find it convenient to hold a part of their financial assets in the form of money. The desire to hold money as an asset is referred to as the asset demand for money.

There are advantages and disadvantages to holding money as an asset. Money has the advantage that it can be used to purchase other assets as the occasion arises. There's no issue of lack of liquidity. One disadvantage of holding money as an asset is that it earns little or no interest. Another disadvantage is that money loses purchasing power during inflationary times.

The amount of money that people will hold as a liquid asset depends on the rate of interest. The opportunity cost of holding money as an asset is the interest that is foregone by not putting the money in interest-earning assets. Thus, the higher the rate of interest, the less money people will want to hold as an asset, and vice versa.

The asset demand for money is inversely related to the interest rate.

Does this mean that the total demand for money comprises the transaction, precautionary, speculative, and asset demands?

That's exactly what it means. Let's examine the total demand for money.

The Total Demand for Money The various demands for money discussed above can be combined to give the total demand for money. The desire to hold wealth in the form of money, rather than in the form of less liquid interest-earning assets, is called the **liquidity preference**.

liquidity preference the desire to hold money rather than less liquid interest-earning assets

There is a cost for holding money, because instead of holding money, people have the option of buying interest-earning assets, such as bonds or savings accounts. The rate of interest can therefore be viewed as the opportunity cost of holding money. Given the level of income, when interest rates are high, interest-earning assets are more attractive than money; thus, people hold less money. When interest rates are low, people will hold more money since the cost of holding money (in terms of lost interest earnings) will be low.

This inverse relation between the rate of interest and the quantity of money that people are willing to hold is shown graphically in Figure 15.2. The demand curve for money shown in the diagram is often called the **liquidity preference curve**. The liquidity preference curve (or the total demand for money curve) shows the inverse relationship between the quantity of money demanded and the rate of interest.

liquidity preference curve the curve showing the inverse relationship between the quantity of money demanded and the rate of interest

At a rate of interest of 14%, the quantity of money demanded is \$70 billion. When the rate of interest falls to 8%, the quantity of money demanded increases to \$110 billion.

How do changes in income affect the demand for money?

Before we answer that question, we should note that changes in the rate of interest do not affect the demand for money; instead they affect the quantity of money demanded. Stated differently, changes in the rate of interest cause a movement along the demand curve for money, but these changes do not cause the curve to shift. Let's now examine how changes in income affect the demand for money.

Figure 15.2 The Liquidity Preference or the Demand for Money Curve

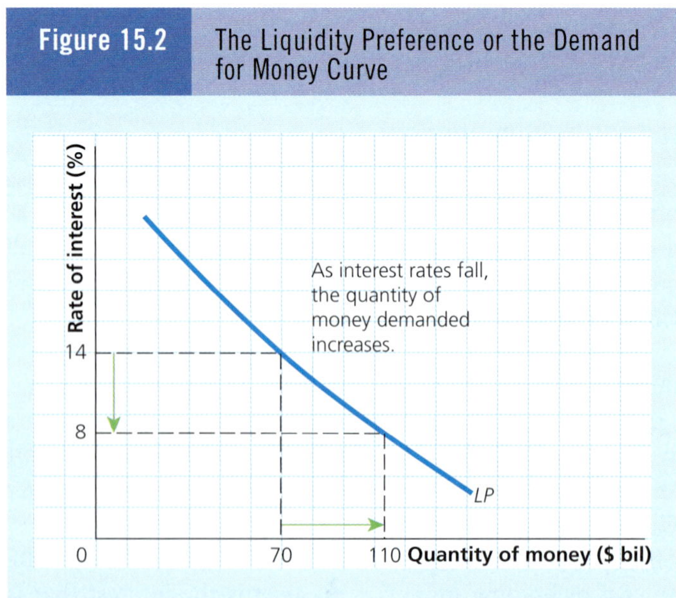

Effect of Changes in Income on the Demand for Money Consider the demand for money curve, *LP* (liquidity preference), shown in Diagram A of Figure 15.3. This demand for money curve assumes that income is held constant. If the level of income increases, households and firms will want to hold more money at each rate of interest. The demand curve will shift to the right, from *LP* to LP_1, as shown in Diagram A.

Figure 15.3 Effect of a Change in Income on the Demand for Money

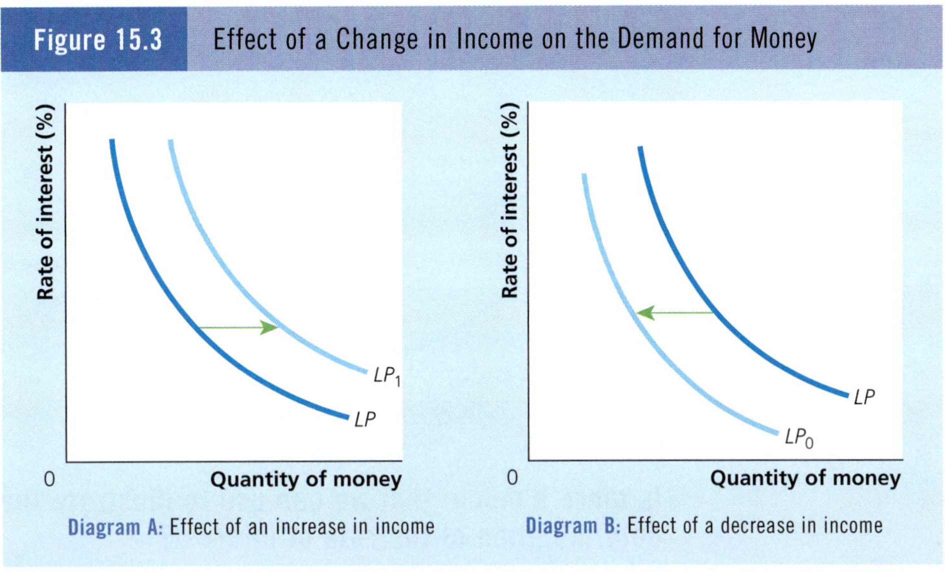

Diagram A: Effect of an increase in income

Diagram B: Effect of a decrease in income

But if the level of income falls, the demand curve for money will shift to the left, from *LP* to LP_0, as shown in Diagram B.

> Other things being equal, an increase in income causes the demand curve for money to shift to the right; a decrease in income causes the curve to shift to the left.

Reading Comprehension

The answers to these questions can be found on MyEconLab at www.myeconlab.com. MyEconLab

1. According to the classical economists, people hold money for transaction purposes only. What additional reasons (motives) do people have for holding money?
2. Explain the asset demand for money. How do changes in interest rates affect the quantity of money held as an asset?
3. What is liquidity preference?

LO 15.3 Explain the liquidity preference theory of interest rate determination

Interest Rate Determination (Liquidity Preference Theory)

How is the rate of interest determined?

The rate of interest can be thought of as the price of money. In the same way that the price of DVDs is determined in the market by demand and supply, so too is the price of money (the rate of interest) determined in the money market by demand and supply.

Figure 15.4 Demand for Money Curve

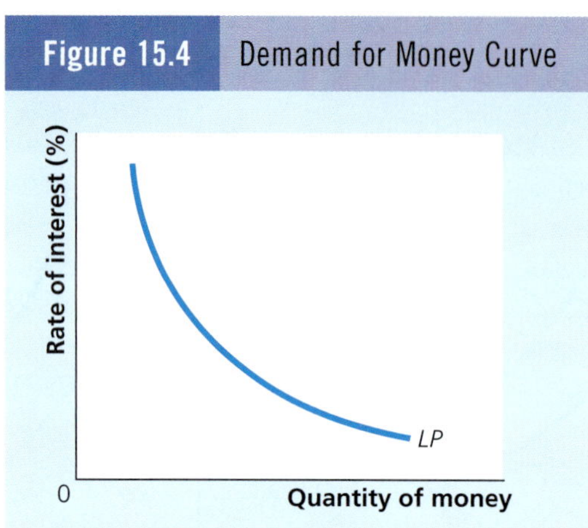

Figure 15.5 Money Supply Curve

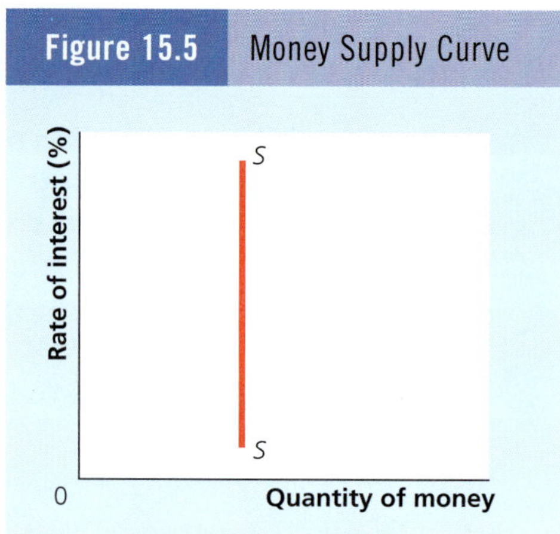

Is there a model that we can use to illustrate the determination of the rate of interest?

In fact, there is more than one model of interest rate determination, but we will use the liquidity preference theory here. Let us first consider the total demand for money. We have seen in the previous section that the demand curve for money (the liquidity preference curve) is downward sloping when plotted against the rate of interest, as shown in Figure 15.4.

At higher interest rates, people will hold a smaller quantity of money. We need to determine the rate of interest at which the amount of money that people want to hold equals the quantity supplied by the monetary authorities (i.e., the Bank of Canada). Therefore, we need to know the money supply.

money supply the total quantity of money supplied at various rates of interest

The Money Supply The **money supply** refers to the total quantity of money supplied at various rates of interest. To simplify our analysis, we assume that the money supply is fixed by the monetary authorities. In other words, the quantity of money is exogenously determined.

Figure 15.6 Determination of the Equilibrium Rate of Interest

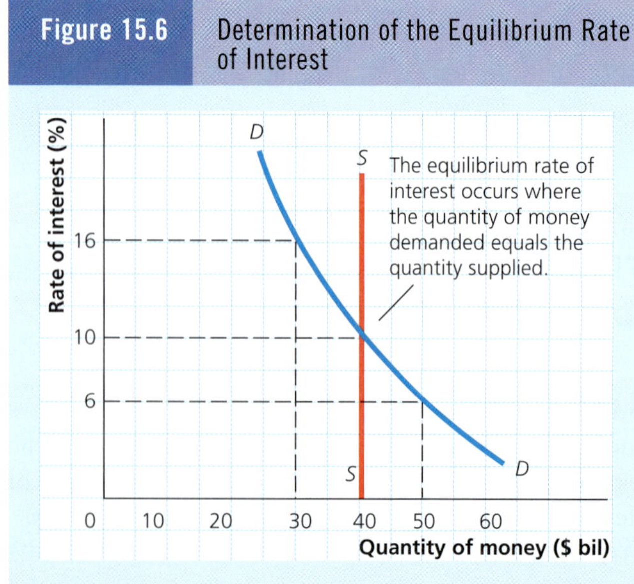

Under these conditions, what will be the shape of the money supply curve?

Because, by assumption, changes in the rate of interest will not affect the quantity of money supplied, we draw the money supply curve as the vertical line *SS* shown in Figure 15.5.

How do the demand for money and the supply of money affect the interest rate?

Interest Rate Determination By bringing the demand for money and the supply of money together, we can illustrate the equilibrium rate of interest. This is done in Figure 15.6. *DD* is the demand curve for money, and *SS* is the supply curve of money.

At an interest rate of 16%, the quantity of money demanded is $30 billion, but the quantity of money supplied is $40 billion. Clearly, the interest rate is too high for the quantity of money demanded to equal the quantity supplied. There is a surplus of money on the money market; therefore, the rate of interest must fall. At a rate of interest of 6%, the quantity of money demanded is $50 billion, but the quantity supplied is only $40 billion. The excess quantity demanded (shortage) will exert an upward pressure on the rate of interest. Now, consider a rate of interest of 10%. At this rate of interest, the amount of money that the public wants to hold (the quantity of money demanded) is $40 billion, which exactly equals the quantity supplied by the monetary authorities. Therefore, the equilibrium rate of interest for this particular graph is 10%.

Reading Comprehension

The answers to these questions can be found on MyEconLab at www.myeconlab.com. MyEconLab

1. Briefly explain the liquidity preference theory of interest rate determination.
2. If the quantity of money demanded exceeds the quantity supplied, explain the process by which the equilibrium rate of interest is achieved.
3. If the quantity of money demanded is less than the quantity supplied, explain the process by which the equilibrium rate of interest is achieved.

LO 15.4 Explain how changes in the demand for and supply of money affect the equilibrium rate of interest

Money Supply and Demand and Interest Rates

Is it correct that an increase in the demand for money, other things being equal, will raise the rate of interest and a decrease in demand will lower it?

Yes. That's correct. Let's demonstrate the idea graphically, beginning with the effect of an increase in the demand for money.

Figure 15.7 Effect of an Increase in the Demand for Money on the Rate of Interest

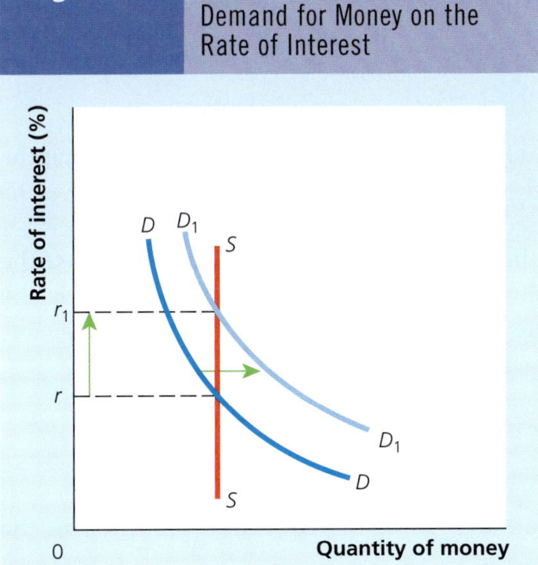

Effect of an Increase in the Demand for Money on the Rate of Interest Let us assume that the rate of interest is at its equilibrium level of r, where the demand for money curve DD and the supply of money curve SS intersect, as shown in Figure 15.7. Suppose the demand for money increases as a result of an increase in income. The demand curve will shift to the right from DD to D_1D_1, as shown in the diagram.

As a result of this increase in demand, the equilibrium rate of interest rises from r to r_1.

> Other things being equal, an increase in the demand for money will result in an increase in the rate of interest.

Let us now analyze the effect of a decrease in the demand for money.

Figure 15.8 Effect of a Decrease in the Demand for Money on the Rate of Interest

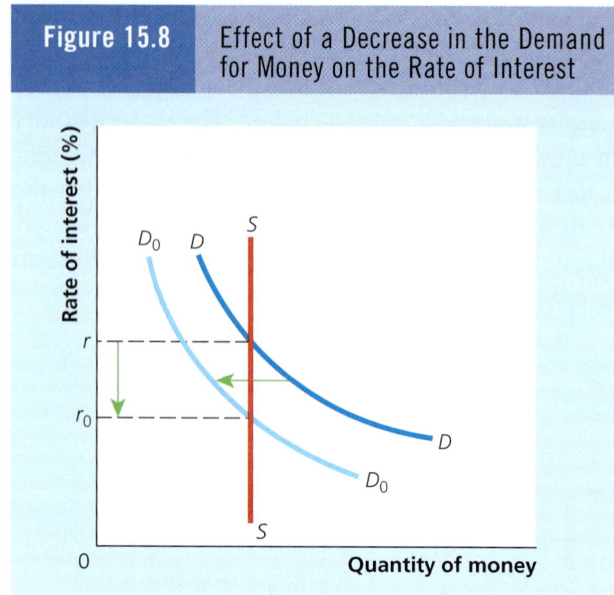

Figure 15.9 Effect of an Increase in the Money Supply on the Rate of Interest

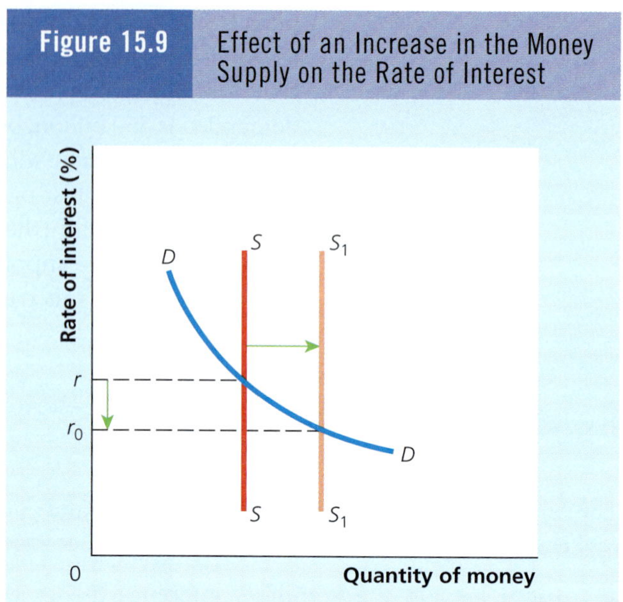

Effect of a Decrease in the Demand for Money on the Rate of Interest In Figure 15.8, *DD* and *SS* are the initial demand and supply of money, respectively. The equilibrium rate of interest is *r*. A decrease in demand is shown by shifting the demand curve to the left from *DD* to D_0D_0, as shown in the diagram.

As a result of the decrease in the demand for money, the equilibrium rate of interest falls from *r* to r_0.

> Other things being equal, a decrease in the demand for money will result in a fall in the rate of interest.

Is it correct that an increase in the supply of money, other things being equal, will lower the rate of interest and a decrease in supply will raise it?

Yes. Let's illustrate the idea graphically, beginning with the effect of an increase in the money supply.

Effect of an Increase in the Money Supply on the Rate of Interest Let us assume that the rate of interest is at its equilibrium level of *r*, where the demand for money curve *DD* and the supply of money curve *SS* intersect, as shown in Figure 15.9.

Suppose that, for whatever reason, the monetary authorities decide to increase the money supply. The supply curve will shift to the right from *SS* to S_1S_1, as shown in the diagram. As a result, the equilibrium rate of interest will fall from *r* to r_0. We can conclude the following:

> Other things being equal, an increase in the money supply will result in a fall in the rate of interest.

Let us now turn our attention to an analysis of the effect of a reduction in the money supply on the rate of interest.

BUSINESS SITUATION 15.1

The Bank of Canada announces that it will pursue a policy of monetary expansion.

How will this policy affect the decisions of businesses that are planning to borrow money for investment purposes?

The answer to this Business Situation can be found in Appendix A.

Figure 15.10 Effect of a Reduction in the Money Supply on the Rate of Interest

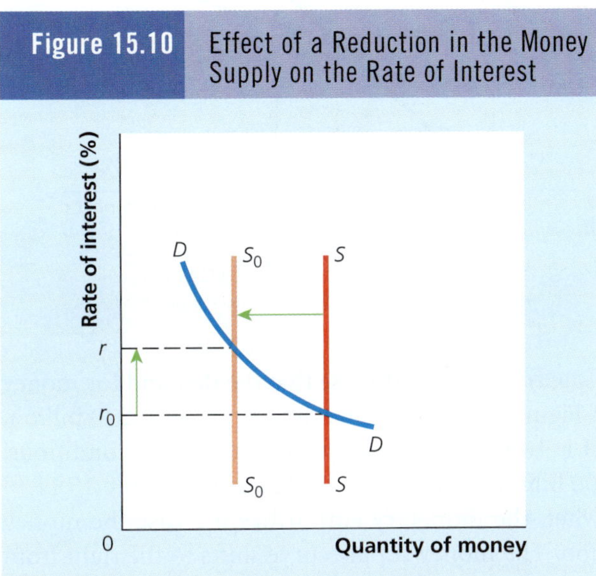

Effect of a Reduction of the Money Supply on the Rate of Interest Let us assume that *DD* and *SS* are the initial demand and supply curves for money. The equilibrium rate of interest is *r*, as determined by the intersection of the *DD* and *SS* curves in Figure 15.10.

Suppose the monetary authorities decide to reduce the money supply. The supply curve will shift to the left from *SS* to S_0S_0, as shown in Figure 15.10. As a result of the reduction in the money supply, the rate of interest rises from *r* to r_1. We can therefore conclude the following:

> Other things being equal, a reduction in the supply of money will result in an increase in the rate of interest.

Reading Comprehension

The answers to these questions can be found on MyEconLab at www.myeconlab.com. MyEconLab

1. Explain the process by which an increase in the demand for money, other things being equal, results in an increase in the equilibrium rate of interest.
2. Explain the process by which a decrease in the demand for money, other things being equal, results in a fall in the equilibrium rate of interest.
3. Other things being equal, how will an increase in income affect the equilibrium rate of interest?
4. Explain the process by which an increase in the supply of money, other things being equal, results in a decrease in the equilibrium rate of interest.
5. Explain the process by which a decrease in the supply of money, other things being equal, results in an increase in the equilibrium rate of interest.

LO 15.5 Understand the relationship between the quantity of money and the level of gross domestic product

Changes in the Money Supply and Total Income

The quantity theory of money predicts that increases in the quantity of money will increase total income, whereas decreases in the quantity of money will reduce income. Does the Keynesian model also lead to these conclusions?

Let's begin with the effects of an increase in the money supply.

Figure 15.11 Effect of an Increase in the Money Supply on GDP

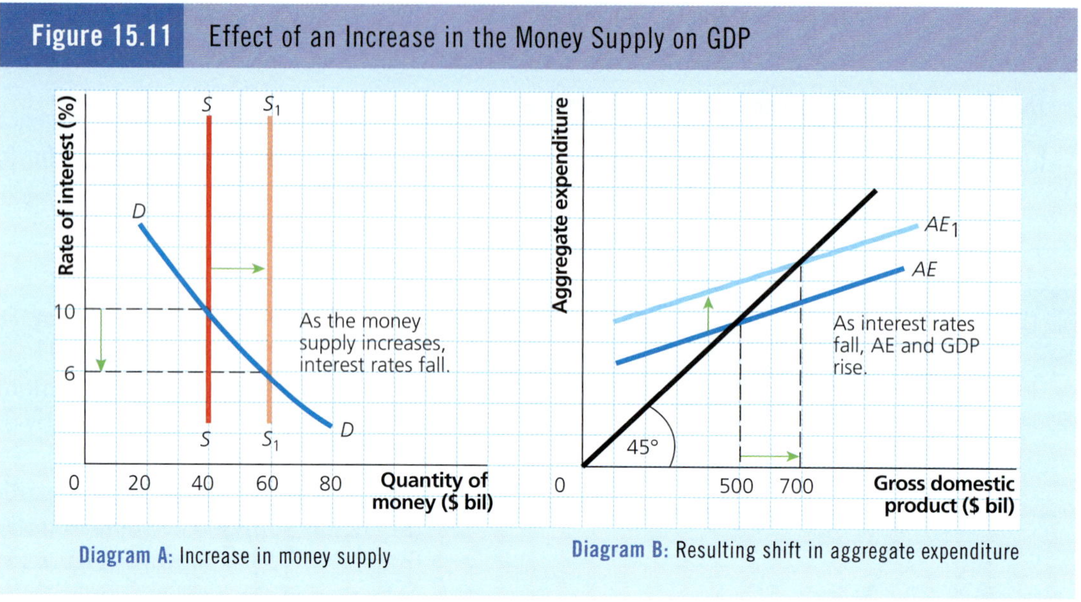

Diagram A: Increase in money supply

Diagram B: Resulting shift in aggregate expenditure

Effects of an Increase in the Money Supply on GDP Suppose that the demand for money curve is as shown in Diagram A of Figure 15.11. The quantity of money is $40 billion, and the equilibrium rate of interest is 10%. Suppose also that, under these conditions, the equilibrium level of GDP is $500 billion, as shown in Diagram B of Figure 15.11.

Now, let's see what happens when the monetary authorities increase the money supply from $40 billion to $60 billion. The money supply curve shifts to the right from *SS* to S_1S_1 as shown in Diagram A, and the rate of interest falls to 6%. Recall that a fall in the rate of interest leads to an increase in consumption and investment. This increase in consumption and investment causes the aggregate expenditure curve in Diagram B to shift upward from *AE* to AE_1, resulting in an increase in GDP from $500 billion to $700 billion.

An increase in the money supply causes the rate of interest to fall. The fall in the rate of interest increases consumption and investment, which, in turn, increases GDP.

Let us now investigate the effects of a decrease in the money supply.

Effects of a Reduction in the Money Supply on GDP Suppose that the demand for money, the supply of money, and the equilibrium rate of interest are as shown in Diagram A of Figure 15.12. Suppose further that the equilibrium level of GDP is $500 billion, as shown in Diagram B.

If the money supply is reduced from $40 billion to $20 billion, the supply curve shifts to the left from *SS* to S_0S_0. This reduction in the money supply results in an excess in quantity demanded (shortage), which forces the rate of interest up from 10% to 14%. As the rate of interest rises, the level of intended consumption and investment falls, resulting in a shift in the aggregate expenditure curve from *AE* to AE_0. The fall in desired aggregate expenditure leads to a reduction in GDP from $500 billion to $300 billion.

A reduction in the money supply causes the rate of interest to rise. The increase in the rate of interest reduces consumption and investment which, in turn, reduces GDP.

Figure 15.12 Effect of a Decrease in the Money Supply on GDP

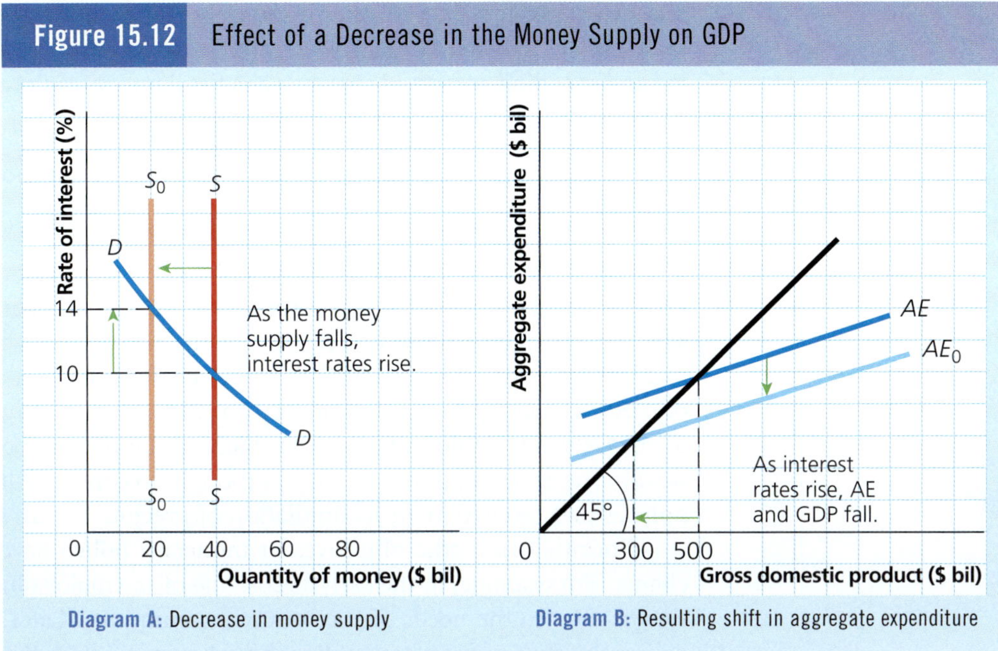

Diagram A: Decrease in money supply

Diagram B: Resulting shift in aggregate expenditure

Reading Comprehension

The answers to these questions can be found on MyEconLab at **www.myeconlab.com**. MyEconLab

1. According to the Keynesian model, how does an increase in the money supply affect GDP?
2. According to the Keynesian model, changes in the money supply affect GDP indirectly rather than directly. Explain.

LO 15.6 Discuss the meaning and objectives of monetary policy

The Meaning and Objectives of Monetary Policy

What exactly does monetary policy mean?

A policy is a course of action designed to achieve some desired objective. We defined monetary policy in earlier chapters as the manipulation of the money supply and interest rates by the central bank to achieve economic objectives. We can expand that definition as follows:

monetary policy the manipulation of the money supply and interest rates by the central bank to achieve economic objectives

> **Monetary policy** refers to the activities of the central bank (Bank of Canada, in this case) designed to bring about changes in the money supply, the availability of credit, and the level of interest rates in order to influence general economic activity.

We need to observe certain important points about this expanded definition: (1) the conduct of monetary policy in Canada rests with the Bank of Canada, (2) monetary policy has a desired objective (to influence general economic activity), and (3) monetary policy involves changes in the money supply and interest rates. Thus, changes in the money supply and interest rates do not constitute monetary policy unless initiated by the Bank of Canada. For example, if interest rates rise as a result of government borrowing and spending, we would view this as a fiscal policy result rather than monetary policy.

> Changes in the money supply and interest rates do not constitute monetary policy unless they have been initiated by the Bank of Canada.

What are the objectives of monetary policy?

Policies are designed to achieve objectives. Hence, the conduct of monetary policy presupposes one or more objectives that the policy hopes to accomplish. During the mercantilist period, when the public generally believed that a nation's wealth consisted of precious metals, standard monetary policy was limited to encouraging the inflow and discouraging the outflow of gold. The objective of monetary policy was to make the nation wealthy; because a nation's wealth was thought to consist of its stock of precious metals, policies that resulted in an accumulation of precious metals were actively pursued.

Since that time, the objectives of monetary policy have gone through periods of change. For example, in the early 1920s, one of the major objectives of monetary policy was to cater to the needs of the business community. Later, during World War II, the prime objective of monetary policy shifted from meeting the needs of business to satisfying the financial needs of the government.

What are today's economic objectives? Canada has certain economic objectives that most members of our society accept as desirable, and the government designs economic policies to achieve these objectives. The objectives of monetary policy are based on the objectives of the country's general economic policies. Ideally, most Canadians would like our economy to achieve the following goals:

1. Full employment
2. Price stability
3. Maximum growth of real output
4. Equilibrium balance of payments

Canada's economic performance would be considered exceptional if it could achieve these goals. However, each of these objectives needs to be examined.

Full Employment Full employment here should not be interpreted to mean a situation in which 100% of the labour force is employed. Given our economic system, at any given time some unemployment is unavoidable (e.g., frictional unemployment). Moreover, other factors, such as the institution of minimum wage legislation and labour union activity that can end up keeping wage rates above the market-clearing level, and employment insurance benefits that make it possible for some people to receive income without genuinely seeking or accepting employment, make it unrealistic to expect a zero rate of unemployment. Unemployment that results from the factors mentioned above is often referred to as natural unemployment. Accepting the unfeasibility of realizing a zero rate of unemployment, we use the term *full employment* to define the economic condition in which the unemployment rate is just equal to the natural rate of unemployment. In a situation of full employment, then, the only unemployment that exists is natural unemployment. For example, if the natural rate of unemployment is 7%, then full employment is defined as 93% of the labour force employed. If it is 6%, then full employment is defined as 94% of the labour force employed.

Closely associated with the objective of full employment is the objective of attaining and maintaining a level of real output that is at the full-employment level. Unemployment represents the existence of idle resources that could be used to increase the volume of real output. By the same token, once full employment is reached, it is extremely difficult to expand real output further on any long-term basis. In general, then, full employment and maximum real output are inextricably related. Ideally, our objective is for our economy to achieve and maintain its full-employment level of real output.

Price Stability Significant movements in the average level of prices are undesirable. Rapid increases in the price level have adverse effects on the economy. Such price increases can result in a misallocation of the economy's resources and a socially undesirable distribution of income. Precipitous price inflation (sharp decreases in the value of money) may cause people to be unwilling to accept money as a medium of exchange and cause them to revert to barter. At worst, the situation could degenerate into economic collapse, necessitating a complete reform of the entire monetary system.

Although it may be easy to see the adverse effects of inflation, it may be more difficult to see the adverse effects of deflation. This is probably due to the fact that we have witnessed increases in prices much more frequently than we have observed decreases in prices. Moreover, we tend to reason that when prices fall, purchasing power rises, so we are better off. But let us examine the matter a little more closely. Rapid reductions in prices may have adverse effects on businesses, causing them to cut back on the number of workers they hire. Deflation also adversely affects debtors because their debt now costs more than it did before. If prices are sticky downward (and they usually are), the forces that would normally bring about deflation of prices would instead cause a deflation of jobs, so that the situation is reflected in a recession.

A zero rate of inflation implies that the market rate of interest and the real rate of interest will be equivalent, and most economists would agree that this is a desirable economic condition; however, a target of a zero rate of inflation is probably idealistic. Realistically, policymakers would be happy if they could achieve a low (as opposed to zero) rate of inflation. An objective of reasonable price stability is more practical than a goal of complete price stability. In this regard, note that the Bank of Canada has set a 2% rate of inflation as its target.

Maximum Growth of Real Output Few, if any, Canadians would argue seriously against an improvement in the standard of living as a desirable goal. We expend time, energy, and money trying to improve our economic well-being. We want more goods and services, including more leisure time; therefore, we try to organize our economic lives to make this possible. It is indeed possible to allocate more goods and services to less wealthy groups and individuals in our society through redistribution of income, but, collectively, we cannot obtain more goods and services unless there is an increase in real output. Economic growth makes it possible for us to improve our standard of living. Today, economists realize that long-term economic growth is not an automatic process. Economic growth requires a consistent policy aimed at the expansion of real output.

An economy's productive capacity depends on the amount of human and nonhuman resources at its disposal and on its technology. These are often referred to as supply-side forces. But the availability of resources and appropriate technology do not guarantee that all of the economy's resources will be brought into the production process. Monetary policy can play an important role in regulating demand so that the economy's resources can be employed. A policy aimed at full employment is not necessarily consistent with one aimed at economic growth. For example, rapid economic growth might require substituting capital-intensive and labour-saving methods of production in place of labour-intensive methods. The substitution of capital for labour can result in unemployment. However, long-term expansion of real output does require the maintenance of a relatively high level of employment. After all, a high unemployment rate implies the existence of idle resources that could be put to use in increasing real output.

Equilibrium Balance of Payments The performance of the foreign sector of our economy can be evaluated in terms of its ability to maintain equilibrium in our balance of payments. You will see in a later chapter that it is not only internal balance (equilibrium in our domestic economy) that concerns our policymakers but also external balance. Associated with an equilibrium balance of payments is the objective of a steady exchange rate. The stability of the external value of its currency is an important economic objective for a country operating in a global economic environment in which the foreign sector is assuming increasingly greater significance. Indeed, one of the acknowledged functions of a central bank is to protect and control the external value of the currency.

Reading Comprehension

The answers to these questions can be found on MyEconLab at www.myeconlab.com. MyEconLab

1. What is monetary policy? Who conducts monetary policy in Canada?
2. It is easy to confuse monetary policy with fiscal policy. How can the confusion be avoided?
3. Give an example of a change in the rate of interest that would not be regarded as monetary policy.
4. What are the main objectives of monetary policy?

Lo 15.7 Discuss the tools of monetary policy and explain how monetary policy works

Specific Tools of Monetary Policy and How Monetary Policy Works

What specific tools are available to the Bank of Canada for influencing the money supply and interest rates?

The central bank has several specific tools for implementing monetary policy:

1. Open-market operations
2. Central bank advances and the bank rate
3. Switching government deposits and swap transactions
4. Purchase and resale agreements
5. Moral suasion

We will discuss each of these instruments in turn. You will observe that these tools will affect either the monetary base or the reserves of banks.

open-market operations the buying and selling of securities (bonds) by the central bank

Open-Market Operations **Open-market operations** refer to buying and selling securities (bonds) by the central bank. We have already seen from a study of the balance sheet of the central bank that government securities are the central bank's major asset, while its major liabilities are currency held by the public and bank reserves, which are the main components of the monetary base.

If the central bank wants to increase the money supply, it can purchase government securities on the open market. Holders of government securities will exchange their securities for money from the central bank. The assets and liabilities of the central bank will increase, and the monetary base will thus increase. The operation of the money-creation multiplier then causes the total money supply to increase even more than the increase in the monetary base. Open-market sales of government securities by the central bank have the opposite effect. By selling government securities, the central bank reduces its assets and liabilities at the same time, thus reducing the monetary base. Through the operation of the multiplier, the reduction in the monetary base causes an even greater reduction in the total money supply.

We must realize that open-market operations affect not only the money supply but also interest rates. When the central bank purchases securities in an attempt to increase the money supply, other things being equal, security prices will rise, which means that interest rates will fall. Similarly, when the central bank sells government securities, other things being equal, security prices will fall and interest rates will rise.

Central Bank Advances and the Bank Rate The commercial banks and other members of the Canadian Payments Association can borrow money from the central bank to augment their cash reserves. The rate of interest that the Bank of Canada charges on these loans and advances is called the **bank rate**. An increase in the bank rate makes it more expensive for institutional borrowers to use the lending facilities of the central bank. Accordingly, banks experiencing a shortage of reserves may call in some of their loans or liquidate some of their more liquid assets. As we have seen earlier, this action will result in a contraction of the money supply.

bank rate the rate of interest that the central bank charges on loans and advances to members of the Canadian Payments Association

Additionally, changes in the bank rate are interpreted by financial institutions as a signal by the central bank as to the course it would like interest rates to take. Hence, when the bank rate rises, lending institutions follow suit and raise their lending rates. They may also restrict their lending activities. When the bank rate falls, they lower their lending rates and also make credit more easily available.

Closely related to the bank rate is the overnight rate. This is the interest rate that major financial institutions charge when they lend overnight (or one-day) funds to other major financial institutions. The Bank of Canada sets a target for this rate, which is now referred to as the Bank of Canada's key policy rate. The use of this tool by the Bank of Canada will be discussed later in this chapter.

The Bank Rate and the Money Supply When the central bank changes the bank rate, other interest rates also tend to change. When interest rates change, the quantity of loans demanded changes, and this affects the money supply. Suppose that the central bank raises the bank rate so that market interest rates rise. With higher interest rates, people will tend to reduce their borrowing. They may also reduce their holdings of cash balances, converting non-interest-earning cash into interest-earning financial assets. This, of course, will reduce the money supply. Conversely, if the central bank reduces the bank rate, market interest rates will tend to fall. This fall in interest rates, other things being equal, will result in an increase in the amount of borrowing by households and firms. With banks granting more loans, the money supply will increase. Thus, by varying the bank rate, the central bank can ease or tighten money and credit to achieve its objectives.

We've heard about switching government's accounts and swap transactions. What are those?

Switching Government's Accounts The central bank can transfer government funds between the central bank and the commercial banks. If the central bank wants to increase bank reserves and thus increase the money supply, it can transfer funds from the government's account at the central bank to the commercial banks. The acquisition of new reserves by the commercial banks triggers the process of deposit creation and hence an increase in the money supply. The act of transferring government funds from the central bank to the commercial banks is referred to as a **redeposit** or **deposit switching**. A transfer of government funds from the commercial banks to the central bank, referred to as a **drawdown**, has the effect of reducing the money supply, because such an action causes the banks to lose reserves. Switching government accounts between both types of institutions has become a very important tool of monetary policy.

redeposit or deposit switching the act of transferring government funds from the central bank to the commercial banks

drawdown a transfer of government funds from the commercial banks to the central bank

Swap Transactions Akin to changing the location of the government's deposit accounts is the practice by the central bank of engaging in swap transactions with the Exchange Fund Account of the government. The Exchange Fund Account is an account in which the minister of finance holds foreign currencies. Suppose the Bank of Canada wants to increase the money supply. It may do so by initiating a swap. This involves purchasing foreign currency assets from the Exchange Fund Account, paying for them with Canadian dollars, and then correspondingly increasing the government's balance in Canadian dollars at the Bank of Canada. The newly acquired funds can then be transferred to the banks via the redeposit process discussed above; as a result, bank reserves increase.

What happens if the Bank of Canada decides to sell foreign currency assets back to the Exchange Fund Account?

If the Bank of Canada takes this action, it is called unwinding a swap. To pay for the foreign currency assets, the Exchange Fund Account arranges an advance from the Bank of Canada, which reduces the government's account at the Bank of Canada. The Bank of Canada replenishes the government's balance by transferring government funds from the chartered banks to the Bank of Canada. This effectively reduces the reserves of the chartered banks.

What are some of the advantages of using swap transactions as a tool of monetary policy?

As a tool of monetary policy, swap transactions have two main advantages. First, they can be implemented quickly. The Bank of Canada can initiate or unwind a swap at will. Second, the use of swap transactions has no direct impact on the financial market or on the foreign exchange market. This is because the swaps are with the Exchange Fund Account and do not involve transactions in either the money market or the foreign exchange market.

Purchase and Resale Agreements Among the most active tools of monetary policy are purchase and resale agreements. For more than 40 years now, the Bank of Canada has engaged in purchase and resale agreements (PRAs) with investment dealers or money market jobbers. These dealers agree to sell short-term government securities to the Bank of Canada and to repurchase them at a predetermined price. When investment dealers sell T-bills and short-term securities to the central bank, the cash reserves of chartered banks increase while the securities are held by the central bank. In 1985, the Bank of Canada introduced Special Purchase and Resale Agreements (SPRAs), offering securities on its own initiative. In 1986, the Bank of Canada initiated a new transaction called Special Sale and Repurchase Agreements (SSRAs) with chartered banks. With SSRA, the Bank of Canada can initiate sale and purchase transactions. Clearly, SSRAs are the opposite of SPRAs in terms of their operations. SSRAs and SPRAs are among the most frequently used instruments of monetary policy today.

moral suasion any persuasive tactic used by the central bank to secure the cooperation of the commercial banks

Moral Suasion **Moral suasion** is the term used to describe persuasive tactics used by the central bank to secure the cooperation of the commercial banks in achieving some objective of monetary policy.

The effectiveness of moral suasion as a tool of monetary policy depends to a great extent on the ability of the central bank to communicate its desire to the financial institutions and to convince them to act. Even though the number of banks in the Canadian banking system has increased considerably since 1980, when foreign banks were allowed to establish subsidiaries in Canada, the number is still relatively small, and the number of major banks in Canada has not been affected to any considerable extent. The compactness of the Canadian banking system makes communication between the Bank of Canada and the chartered banks and other financial institutions relatively easy. A few conferences, statements, memos, and communiqués are usually enough to get the Bank's message across to the other financial institutions.

If the Bank of Canada is pursuing a tight monetary policy, it attempts to obtain cooperation in pursuing appropriate lending and investment policies. If the Bank of Canada is successful in enlisting cooperation, all banks will restrict their lending and investment activities, and this will help the Bank of Canada to achieve its objective. If the Bank of Canada is pursuing a tight monetary policy, while the lending institutions are increasing their loans and investments, this will reduce the effectiveness of the Bank's tight monetary policy. If the Bank of Canada wants to increase the money supply in order to increase total spending and stimulate the economy, it can persuade the financial institutions to support its policy by increasing their lending and investment activities. The cooperation of the financial institutions will amplify the impact of the Bank's expansionary monetary policy. There are many instances in the history of Canadian banking when the Bank of Canada used moral suasion.

It must be noted that the use of moral suasion has not always had the desired effect. For example, in 1956, the Bank of Canada enlisted the support of the major finance companies in restricting consumer credit. The finance companies refused. As a result, the Bank of Canada suggested to the chartered banks that they reduce the credit limits of the major finance companies and thus limit their access to bank credit. It is unlikely that the Bank of Canada will exclude moral suasion completely from its arsenal of monetary policy weapons, but it is likely that moral suasion will be most effective when there is no perceived conflict between the objective that the Bank of Canada is trying to achieve and the profit-maximizing objective of the financial institutions.

How can monetary policy be used to combat unemployment?

We have already seen that changes in the money supply can affect output, employment, and the price level. We have also studied the various instruments available to the Bank of Canada for controlling the money supply and interest rates. We can now proceed to addressing the question regarding the use of monetary policy to combat unemployment.

> An expansionary monetary policy may be effective against unemployment, while a contractionary monetary policy may be effective against inflation.

Monetary Policy against Unemployment Let us assume that the economy is experiencing unemployment and that the Bank of Canada wants to use monetary policy to move the economy toward full employment. Figure 15.13 will help us to analyze the situation.

Diagram A shows that the economy is in equilibrium at a level of income of *Y*, which is below the full-employment level of *Yf*. In Diagram B, the equilibrium level of real output is *y*, where the aggregate demand and aggregate supply curves intersect. For simplicity, we have omitted the intermediate section of the aggregate supply curve.

To deal with this situation of unemployment, the Bank of Canada may increase the money supply and lower interest rates by using one or more of the instruments of monetary policy. The effect of this expansionary monetary policy is shown in Diagram A of Figure 15.13 by the upward shift of the aggregate expenditure line from *AE* to AE_1, and in Diagram B by the upward shift of the aggregate demand curve from *AD* to AD_1. The economy moves to full employment.

> The Bank of Canada can use an expansionary monetary policy to move the economy from a position of unemployment to one of full employment.

The occurrence of the 2008–2009 recession provides an excellent opportunity to see monetary policy at work in trying to deal with severe unemployment and a slowing economy. The relevant discussion is presented later in this chapter.

Figure 15.13 Monetary Policy to Combat Unemployment

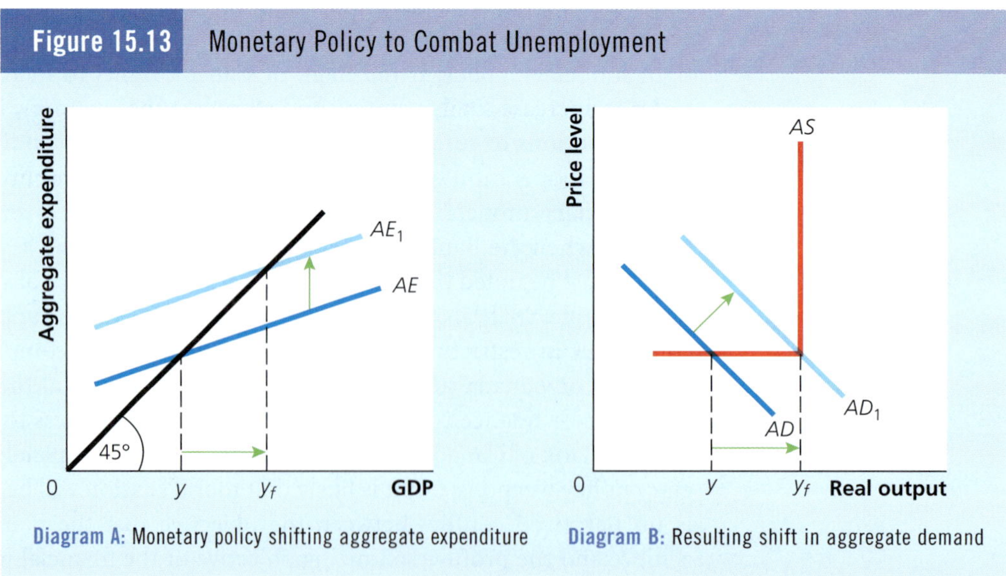

Diagram A: Monetary policy shifting aggregate expenditure **Diagram B:** Resulting shift in aggregate demand

Figure 15.14 Monetary Policy to Combat Inflation

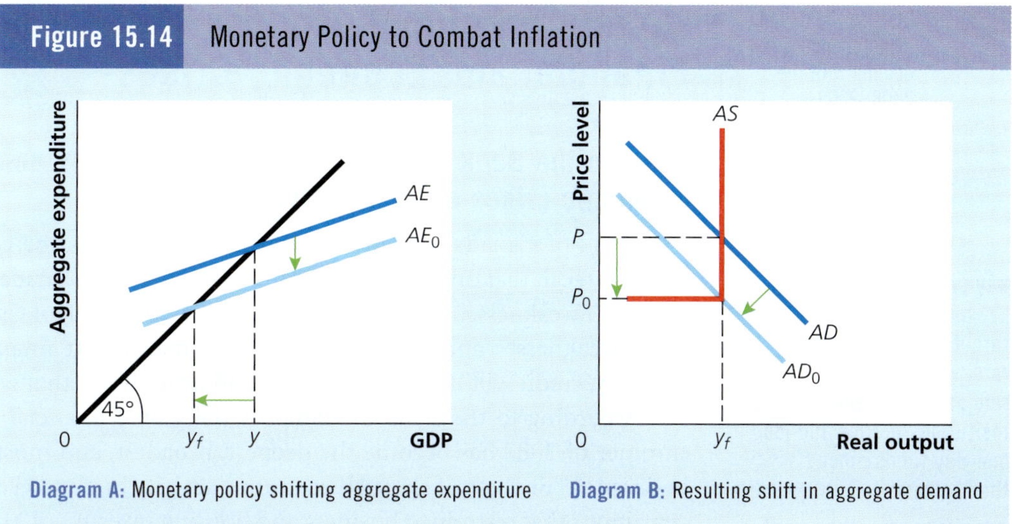

Diagram A: Monetary policy shifting aggregate expenditure **Diagram B:** Resulting shift in aggregate demand

How can monetary policy be used to combat inflation?

The Bank of Canada could follow an opposite procedure to that used to combat unemployment. Let's investigate.

Monetary Policy to Combat Inflation Assume that the economy is experiencing an inflationary period, as shown in Figure 15.14. In Diagram A, the inflationary situation is illustrated by the fact that aggregate expenditure exceeds full-employment output. In Diagram B, it is reflected in the fact that aggregate demand, *AD*, is higher than what is required to achieve full employment without inflation. In either case, the result is an increase in the price level.

The Bank of Canada can take action to relieve inflationary pressure by implementing a restrictive or contractionary monetary policy. Such a policy will reduce aggregate expenditure, as shown in Diagram A by the downward shift of the aggregate expenditure curve from *AE* to AE_0, or in Diagram B by the leftward shift in the aggregate demand curve from *AD* to AD_0. Equilibrium occurs at full employment, and the price level falls from the inflated level of *P* to P_0.

Reading Comprehension

The answers to these questions can be found on MyEconLab at www.myeconlab.com. MyEconLab

1. Explain how each of the following will affect the money supply:
   a. The Bank of Canada purchases securities on the open market.
   b. The Bank of Canada raises the bank rate.
   c. The Bank of Canada switches funds from the Bank of Canada to the commercial banks.
   d. The Bank of Canada undertakes a drawdown operation.
2. What is the effect of
   a. An open-market sale of securities on the rate of interest?
   b. A lowering of the bank rate on the money supply?
3. Discuss moral suasion as an instrument of monetary policy.
4. Briefly explain how monetary policy can be used to
   a. Curb inflation
   b. Reduce unemployment

LO 15.8 Discuss the role of monetary policy in dealing with the 2008–2009 recession

Monetary Policy Response to the 2008–2009 Financial and Economic Crises

How did the Bank of Canada respond to the financial and economic crises of 2008–2009?

key policy rate also the key interest rate or the target for the overnight rate, which is the interest rate at which major financial insitutions borrow and lend one-day funds among themselves

overnight rate the target interest rate or key policy rate set by the Bank of Canada for borrowing and lending among major financial institutions

transmission mechanism the process by which changes in the Bank's target interest rate or key policy rate affect the economy

The Bank of Canada, Canada's central bank, conducts the country's monetary policy. You will recall that one of the functions of the Bank of Canada is to support the financial system. If weaknesses exist in financial markets, the Bank of Canada may move to correct those weaknesses and strengthen financial markets. If financial markets are working properly, credit will flow to businesses and households that want to make expenditures.

According to the Bank of Canada, "the global financial turmoil that began in the summer of 2007 has become the deepest, broadest, and most persistent financial crisis in decades." Because of sluggish economic activity in Canada caused by tightening credit conditions that restrained business and housing investment, the Bank of Canada lowered its key policy rate. The **key policy rate**, also called the key interest rate or the target for the overnight rate, is set by the Bank of Canada and is defined as follows:

> The overnight rate is the interest rate at which major financial institutions borrow and lend one-day (or "overnight") funds among themselves.

Once the Bank of Canada perceived the economy to be in a recession or heading for one, it took swift action starting early in 2008. This monetary policy response, which the Bank referred to as "extraordinary" in its report on October 8, 2008, involved lowering its key policy rate 50 basis points. The "extraordinary" actions taken by the Bank of Canada to deal with the recession can be observed in changes in the target for the overnight rate presented in Table 15.1.

Table 15.1 Changes in the Target for the Overnight Rate (October 8, 2007 to January 18, 2011)

Date	Overnight Rate (%)
October 8, 2007	4.50
December 4, 2007	4.25
January 22, 2008	4.00
March 4, 2008	3.50
April 22, 2008	3.00
October 8, 2008	2.50
October 21, 2008	2.25
December 9, 2008	1.50
January 20, 2009	1.00
March 3, 2009	0.50
April 21, 2009	0.25
June 1, 2010	0.50
July 20, 2010	0.75
September 8, 2010	1.00

Source: Bank of Canada. **www.bankofcanada.ca/en/monetary-policy-introduction/key-interest-rate**

Note: As of January 18, 2011, the overnight rate was still at 1.00%.

You will notice that by June 2010, when the recession was considered to be over, the target for the overnight rate began to edge upward.

How does lowering the target for the overnight rate affect the economy?

This question relates to what economists refer to as the **transmission mechanism**—the process by which changes in the key interest rate affect the economy.

The key policy rate has an impact on other interest rates, thereby influencing the spending decisions of businesses and individuals. For example, when the Bank of Canada lowers its key policy rate, other interest rates fall. These lower interest rates stimulate consumer and business spending with a positive impact on employment and GDP.

Reading Comprehension

The answers to these questions can be found on MyEconLab at www.myeconlab.com. MyEconLab

1. Define the target for the overnight rate. How does this rate differ from the bank rate?
2. What kind of monetary policy did the Bank of Canada adopt as a response to the recession?
3. Explain how lowering the key policy rate affects employment and GDP.

LO 15.9 Discuss the effectiveness and limitations of monetary policy

The Effectiveness and Limitations of Monetary Policy

How effective is monetary policy in stimulating economic activity?

A significant part of the debate between monetarists and Keynesians surrounds the effectiveness of monetary policy. A great deal of attention will be given to this debate in the next chapter; for now, we will discuss two cases in which, theoretically at least, monetary policy will be ineffective.

The Case of the Liquidity Trap Some people have argued that a situation is possible in which increases in the money supply have very little or no effect in reducing the rate of interest. In such a situation, the liquidity preference curve is flat where it intersects the supply curve for money. The situation is illustrated in Figure 15.15.

liquidity trap a situation in which the rate of interest is so low that people prefer to hold large amounts of money over other forms of liquid assets

The liquidity preference (*LP*) curve, or the demand for money curve, and the money supply curve (*S*) intersect to determine the rate of interest, *r*. An increase in the money supply from *S* to S_1 has no effect on the rate of interest. This situation is called a **liquidity trap**. A liquidity trap defines an economic situation in which the rate of interest is so low that people prefer to hold large amounts of money over other forms of liquid assets.

Figure 15.15 The Liquidity Trap

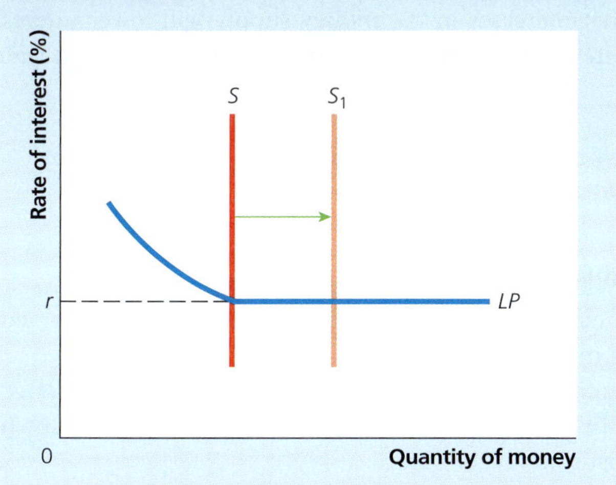

According to some economists, if the economy is in a liquidity trap, monetary policy will be ineffective as a means of stimulating economic activity. Because the liquidity trap occurs at very low rates of interest, and because interest rates have not seen such low levels for such a long time, most people consider the liquidity trap concept to be of theoretical interest only.

The steeper the liquidity preference curve, other things being equal, the more effective monetary policy will be.

The Case of Interest-Insensitive Investment Recall that in the Keynesian model, the money supply affects income and output: an increase in the money supply leads to a fall in the rate of interest, which in turn leads to an increase

Figure 15.16 Interest Rates and Investment

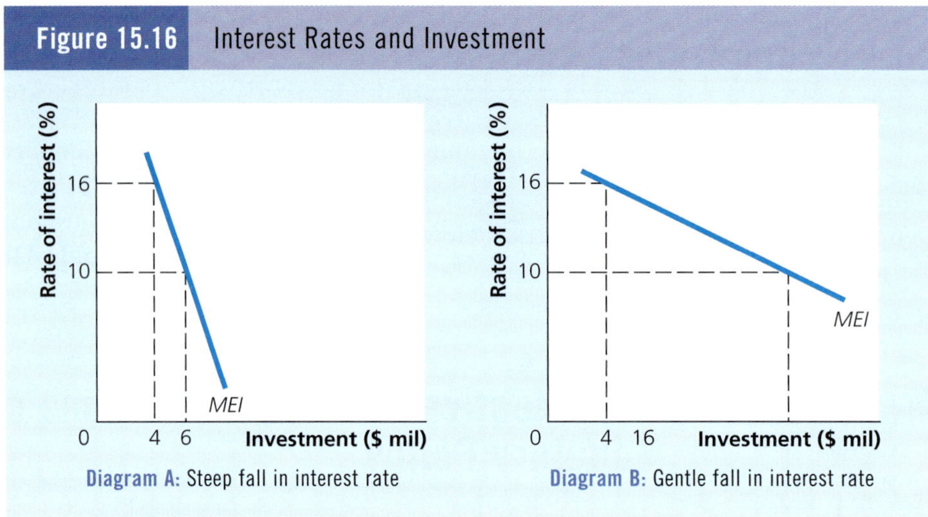

Diagram A: Steep fall in interest rate

Diagram B: Gentle fall in interest rate

in investment, which, via the multiplier, increases GDP. Using flow arrows, we can express the series of events as follows:

$$\Delta M\uparrow \rightarrow \Delta r\downarrow \rightarrow \Delta I\uparrow \rightarrow \Delta \text{GDP}\uparrow$$

where M = money supply, r = rate of interest, and I = level of investment.

The effectiveness of monetary policy, then, depends on the extent to which changes in interest rates affect investment. If the marginal efficiency of investment (*MEI*) curve (the investment demand curve) is relatively flat, a change in the rate of interest will have a greater impact on the level of investment than if the marginal efficiency of investment curve is steep. Figure 15.16 shows two investment demand curves: one relatively steep, the other relatively flat.

In Diagram A, a fall in the rate of interest from 16% to 10% results in an increase in investment from $4 million to $6 million. In Diagram B, an equivalent fall in the rate of interest has led to a much larger increase in investment—from $4 million to $16 million. In other words, investment is much more sensitive to interest rate changes in Diagram B than in Diagram A.

This analysis suggests that monetary policy is most effective when the liquidity preference curve is steep and the marginal efficiency of investment curve is flat. This combination of curves ensures that increases in the money supply will lower interest rates and that reductions in the rate of interest will stimulate investment and aggregate expenditure and output.

The flatter the marginal efficiency of investment curve, other things being equal, the more effective monetary policy will be.

What are the limitations of monetary policy?

Three instances (other than the liquidity trap and interest-insensitive investment) can be considered to be limitations of monetary policy.

First, during a recession, an expansionary monetary policy may prove to be ineffective. Although loans may be easily available, households and firms may not want to borrow money if they are pessimistic about the future.

Second, the problem of time lags discussed in connection with fiscal policy also applies to monetary policy. Keep in mind, however, that monetary authorities are able to act more swiftly than the makers of fiscal policy. But it is quite possible for the effects of monetary policy to be felt only after the need for such a policy has passed.

Third, a significant amount of investment may be financed out of retained earnings rather than through borrowing from bank and other lending institutions. The interest rate policies of the Bank of Canada may therefore have little or no effect on the investment decisions of firms.

Reading Comprehension

The answers to these questions can be found on MyEconLab at www.myeconlab.com. MyEconLab

1. Mention some of the limitations of monetary policy.
2. Under what circumstances will monetary policy be least effective in stimulating economic activity?
3. What is the liquidity trap? Why are economists today not terribly concerned about the liquidity trap?

Review

1. Review the learning objectives listed at the beginning of the chapter.
2. Have you accomplished all the objectives? One way to determine this is to answer the Reading Comprehension Questions at the end of each section. This will help you assess the extent to which you have accomplished the learning objectives.
3. If you have not accomplished an objective, review the relevant material before proceeding.

Key Points to Remember

1. LO 15.1 The crude quantity theory of money states that changes in the price level are due primarily to changes in the quantity of money. The assumptions that velocity is constant and that output remains constant at the full employment level are the main weaknesses of the crude quantity theory of money. The new quantity theory (monetarism) contends that there is a direct relation between the growth rate of the money supply and the growth rate of nominal income.
2. LO 15.2 he Keynesian theory of money identifies three reasons for holding money: (1) transaction purposes, (2) precautionary purposes, and (3) speculative purposes. People also hold money as a liquid asset.
3. LO 15.3, 15.4 The equilibrium rate of interest is determined by the intersection of the demand and supply curves for money. Other things being equal, an increase in the demand for money results in an increase in the rate of interest. A decrease in the demand for money results in a reduction in the rate of interest.
4. LO 15.4, 15.5 An increase in the money supply results in a fall in the rate of interest, an increase in investment, and an increase in GDP. A reduction in the money supply results in an increase in the rate of interest, a fall in investment, and a reduction in GDP.
5. LO 15.6 Monetary policy is the term used to describe the actions taken by the central bank to change the money supply and interest rates in order to achieve national economic objectives. The objectives of monetary policy are full employment, price stability, maximum growth of real output, and zero balance of payments.
6. LO 15.7 The specific tools available to the Bank of Canada for conducting monetary policy are open-market operations, central bank advances, the bank rate, switching

government deposits and swap transactions, purchase and resale agreements, and moral suasion. The overnight rate has become the key policy rate.

7. LO 15.7 An expansionary monetary policy can be used to move the economy toward full employment. A contractionary monetary policy can be used to reduce inflationary pressures.
8. LO 15.8 During the 2008–2009 recession, the Bank of Canada pursued a contractionary monetary policy by drastically reducing its key policy rate.
9. LO 15.9 A liquidity trap or an interest-insensitive investment curve can cause monetary policy to be ineffective. The problem of time lags also limits the effectiveness of monetary policy.

Economic Word Power

Bank rate (p. 395)
Drawdown (p. 396)
Equation of exchange (p. 378)
Key policy rate (p. 400)
Liquidity preference (p. 384)
Liquidity preference curve (p. 384)
Liquidity trap (p. 401)
Monetarism (p. 381)
Monetary policy (p. 391)
Money supply (p. 386)
Moral suasion (p. 397)
Open-market operations (p. 395)
Overnight rate (p. 400)
Precautionary demand for money (p. 382)
Quantity theory of money (p. 377)
Redeposit or deposit switching (p. 396)
Speculative demand for money (p. 383)
Transactions demand for money (p. 382)
Transmission mechanism (p. 400)
Velocity of circulation (p. 378)

Problems and Exercises

Basic

1. LO 15.1 Table 15.2 contains data on GDP and the money supply for a hypothetical economy. Complete the velocity column.

Table 15.2 Data on GDP and the Money Supply for a Hypothetical Economy

Year	GDP ($ bil)	Money Supply ($ bil)	Velocity
2000	350	60	
2001	375	63	
2002	378	68	
2003	380	74	
2004	383	78	
2005	384	84	
2006	387	90	

2. LO 15.1 In an economy at a certain time, the real GDP is $400 billion, the price index is 117, and the money supply is 110. Calculate the velocity of circulation.
3. LO 15.1 M is the quantity of money, V is the velocity of circulation, and Q is real GDP. If $M = 80$, $V = 3$, and $Q = 180$,
   a. Calculate P (the price level).
   b. If the quantity of money doubles, other things being equal, what will be the price level?
   c. What conclusion can be drawn about the relationship between the quantity of money and the price level?
4. LO 15.2 Identify the motive for holding money in each of the following cases:
   a. You keep $500 in a special chequing account to be used only in emergency situations.
   b. You keep a certain amount of money to pay your rent, buy groceries, and pay other bills.
   c. In anticipation of higher interest rates, you keep money to purchase bonds.
   d. You estimate that you will require $2000 for a trip to Alberta, but you take an extra $250.
5. LO 15.2 Determine whether each of the following is true (T) or false (F), other things being equal.
   a. Because cash is not an interest-earning asset, it is irrational to hold cash over and above what is required for current transaction purposes.
   b. The existence of credit cards increases the quantity of money held for precautionary purposes.
   c. The quantity of money held for transaction purposes depends on the level of income.
   d. If the rate of interest increases, other things being equal, the quantity of money demanded for speculative purposes will fall.

e. A fall in the rate of interest will shift the liquidity preference curve to the right.
f. A fall in the level of income, other things being equal, will shift the demand-for-money curve to the right.
g. Other things being equal, an increase in the money supply will shift the money supply curve to the right.
h. The monetary authorities can control the money supply and the rate of interest at the same time.

6. LO 15.7 Tndicate which among the following are tools of monetary policy:
a. Sales and purchases of government securities to and from the public by the Bank of Canada
b. Changes in taxes
c. The pursuit of a balanced budget change in spending
d. The bank rate
e. Redeposits and drawdowns
f. Moral suasion

7. LO 15.7 Indicate whether each of the following is true (T) or false (F):
a. An open-market purchase increases the money supply and lowers interest rates.
b. An open-market sale increases the money supply and raises interest rates.
c. Only chartered banks can borrow from the Bank of Canada.
d. An increase in the bank rate will tend to reduce the money supply.
e. An open-market purchase or sale will change the money supply by the amount of the open-market purchase or sale.
f. When the bank rate changes, other interest rates tend to follow suit.
g. A drawdown reduces the money supply.
h. The Bank of Canada cannot affect the money supply by initiating a swap.

8. LO 15.7 An economy is operating in the Keynesian range of the aggregate supply (*AS*) curve where the level of unemployment is cause for concern. Use the *AD–AS* model to show how monetary policy might be used to move the economy closer to full employment.

Questions in the Intermediate and Challenging sections cover several different concepts, and have not been organized by learning objectives.

Intermediate

1. Use the liquidity preference model to show how each of the following will affect the rate of interest:
a. The Bank of Canada increases the quantity of money.
b. The average level of income rises.
c. Because of economic uncertainties, people decide to hold more cash than previously.
d. The level of income rises at the same time that the quantity of money is increased.

2. Figure 15.17 shows two graphs. Diagram A shows that the demand and supply curves for money determine an equilibrium rate of interest of 12% in the money market. Diagram B shows that at a level of investment of $8 billion, the equilibrium level of income is *Y*. Show how an increase in the money supply (*Ms*) in Diagram A will affect the rate of interest and how the change in the rate of interest will affect the level of investment and equilibrium income in Diagram B.

3. Use the *AD–AS* model to illustrate why monetary policy might encounter problems in dealing with stagflation (simultaneous existence of inflation and unemployment).

Figure 15.17 Demand and Supply Curve and Level of Investment Curve

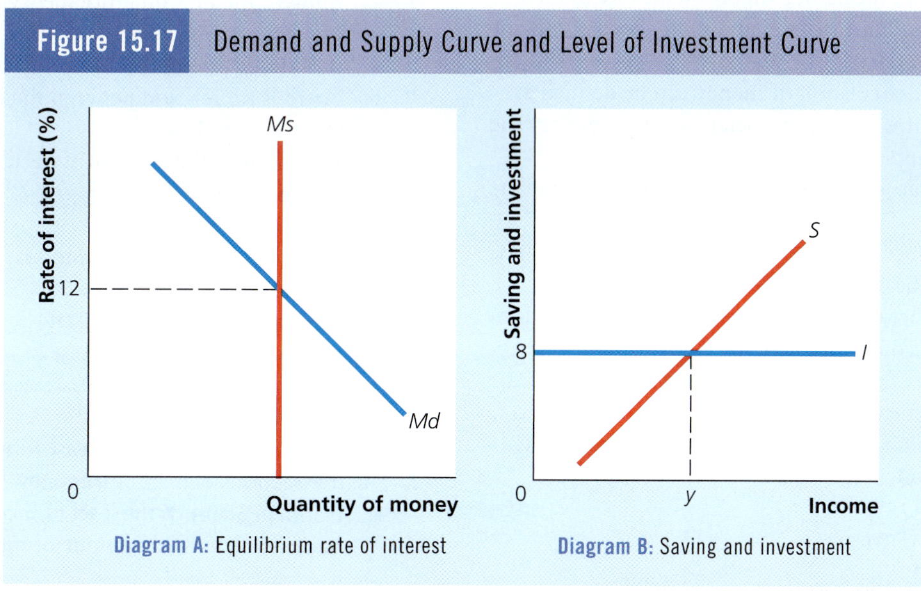

Diagram A: Equilibrium rate of interest

Diagram B: Saving and investment

4. Assume that the Bank of Canada implements an expansionary monetary policy by printing $50 billion, which it uses to buy government bonds from the public. Explain how such an action will affect each of the following:
   a. The rate of interest
   b. Bond holders
   c. Borrowers
5. Suppose that the Bank of Canada buys $5 million worth of bonds from a chartered bank. If banks keep a reserve ratio of 10%, what is the maximum impact that this transaction will have on the money supply?

Challenging

1. Present arguments in support of the view that the central bank has only limited influence over the rate of interest. Base your arguments on the Keynesian liquidity preference theory of interest rate determination.
2. Explain how you would go about disproving the validity of the crude quantity theory.
3. In the Keynesian model, monetary policy may not be effective in stimulating the economy. In the new quantity theory, monetary policy will be effective in stimulating the economy. Discuss.
4. Monetary policy is used more frequently than is fiscal policy. Suggest a plausible reason for this fact.

Study Guide

Self-Assessment

What's your score?

Circle the letter that corresponds with the correct answer.

1. Monetary theory deals with
   a. The factors affecting the demand for money
   b. The effect of the money supply on the rate of interest
   c. The effect of the money supply on the level of income
   d. All of the above
2. The velocity of circulation of money can be defined as
   a. The rate at which the monetary authorities vary the money supply
   b. The rate at which new money in injected into the economy
   c. The number of times, on average, that a dollar is spent in the course of a year
   d. The number of times that money is withdrawn from savings accounts in a year
3. If *M* represents the quantity of money, *V* represents the velocity of circulation, *P* represents the price level, and *Q* represents real GDP, which of the following is correct?
   a. $V = P \times Q$
   b. $V = P + Q$
   c. $V = Q \times P/M$
   d. $V = M/Q$
4. According to the crude quantity theory of money, an increase in the quantity of money will result in
   a. A decrease in the level of total spending
   b. A directly proportional increase in the price level
   c. A directly proportional decrease in prices
   d. None of the above
5. According to the new quantity theory of money,
   a. The economy's output will always be at its equilibrium level
   b. There is no relation between the quantity of money and the price level
   c. Variations in the velocity of circulation will be slight and predictable
   d. None of the above
6. According to monetarists, an increase in the quantity of money tends to
   a. Have a neutral effect on GDP
   b. Bring about a direct increase in total income
   c. Bring about an indirect increase in income through interest rates
   d. Bring about a direct decrease in total income
7. The transactions demand for money
   a. Is independent of the level of income
   b. Varies directly with the rate of interest

c. Varies directly with the level of income
d. None of the above

8. Monetarists and Keynesians agree that
a. Changes in the quantity of money do not affect interest rates
b. Interest rates have no effect on total spending
c. There is only one reason for holding money
d. Increases in the money supply will increase GDP

9. The opportunity cost of holding money is
a. The loss of convenience
b. Forgone interest income
c. Loss of the opportunity to make profitable investments
d. The liquidity that is sacrificed

10. The liquidity preference curve shows
a. An inverse relation between the level of GDP and the rate of interest
b. An inverse relation between the rate of interest and the quantity of money demanded
c. That the demand for money is unaffected by changes in income
d. None of the above

11. According to Keynesian theory, an increase in the demand for money, other things being equal, will result in
a. An increase in the rate of interest
b. A decrease in the rate of interest
c. A leftward shift in the demand curve for money
d. A vertical liquidity preference curve

12. The Government of Canada conducts monetary policy when it
a. Borrows money from the commercial banks
b. Raises taxes or introduces a new tax
c. Lends money to the central bank
d. None of the above

13. Which of the following is an objective of monetary policy?
a. Low unemployment
b. Low inflation
c. Economic growth
d. All of the above

14. Which of the following is true of the Bank of Canada?
a. It is so powerful that it can control the money supply and interest rates simultaneously
b. It can control the rate of interest but not the money supply
c. It can control the money supply but not the rate of interest
d. It can control either the money supply or the rate of interest, but not both simultaneously

15. The bank rate is
a. The rate of interest that the central bank charges on loans to members of the Canadian Payments Association
b. The rate of interest the government charges on tax arrears
c. The rate of interest that commercial banks charge their best customers
d. The rate of interest the federal government pays the central bank for lending money to the provinces

16. Specific tools of monetary policy include
a. Open-market operations
b. Moral suasion
c. Redeposits and drawdowns
d. All of the above

17. The Bank of Canada can increase the money supply and credit by
a. Purchasing government securities
b. Lowering the bank rate
c. Persuading banks to lower interest rates
d. All of the above

18. A contractionary monetary policy
a. Raises interest rates and reduces aggregate expenditure
b. Raises interest rates and increases aggregate expenditure
c. Lowers interest rates and reduces aggregate expenditure
d. None of the above

19. A liquidity trap exists when
a. The liquidity preference curve is vertical
b. The liquidity preference curve is horizontal
c. Interest rates are very high and people prefer not to hold money
d. None of the above

20. Monetary policy will be most effective when
a. The demand for money curve is flat and the investment demand curve is steep
b. The demand for money curve is flat and the investment demand curve is also flat
c. The demand for money curve is steep and the investment demand curve is also steep
d. The demand for money curve is steep and the investment demand curve is flat

Problems and Exercises (Use Quad Paper for Graphs)

Answers to these questions can be found on MyEconLab at www.myeconlab.com. MyEconLab

1. Table 15.3 gives data on the money supply and GDP.

Table 15.3 Money Supply and GDP Data

Year	GDP ($ mil)	Money Supply ($ mil)	Velocity
1	66 409	7 975	
2	72 586	8 323	
3	79 815	8 919	
4	87 215	9 396	
5	96 470	10 210	
6	102 324	11 129	

   a. Calculate the velocity of circulation of money and fill in the velocity column.
   b. In Year 4, $1 bought as much goods and services as $________ would have bought if spent once only.

2. Use the quantity theory of money to calculate the price level (P), if velocity (V) = 12, real output (Q) = $120 billion, and the quantity of money (M) = $20 billion. If M increases from $20 billion to $30 billion, find the new price level.

3. Show graphically the effect of a reduction in the money supply on the rate of interest, other things being equal.

4. State whether each of the following events will increase or decrease the amount of money that people want to hold:
   a. An increase in the level of income
   b. A fall in intended expenditures
   c. The increased use of credit cards
   d. A rise in the rate of interest

5. Illustrate graphically, by using the Keynesian model, that an increase in the money supply will result in an increase in gross domestic product.

6. Suppose that the Bank of Canada buys $5 billion worth of government bonds from bondholders. Explain the effect of this action on
   a. The rate of interest
   b. Expenditures of durable consumer goods
   c. Real investment spending

7. Explain why an open-market purchase of government securities of $10 million by the Bank of Canada will likely increase the money supply by more than $10 million.

8. Banks prosper when the economy is operating well, so it is in the banks' interests to ensure that the economy works well. There is therefore no need for a central bank. Discuss.

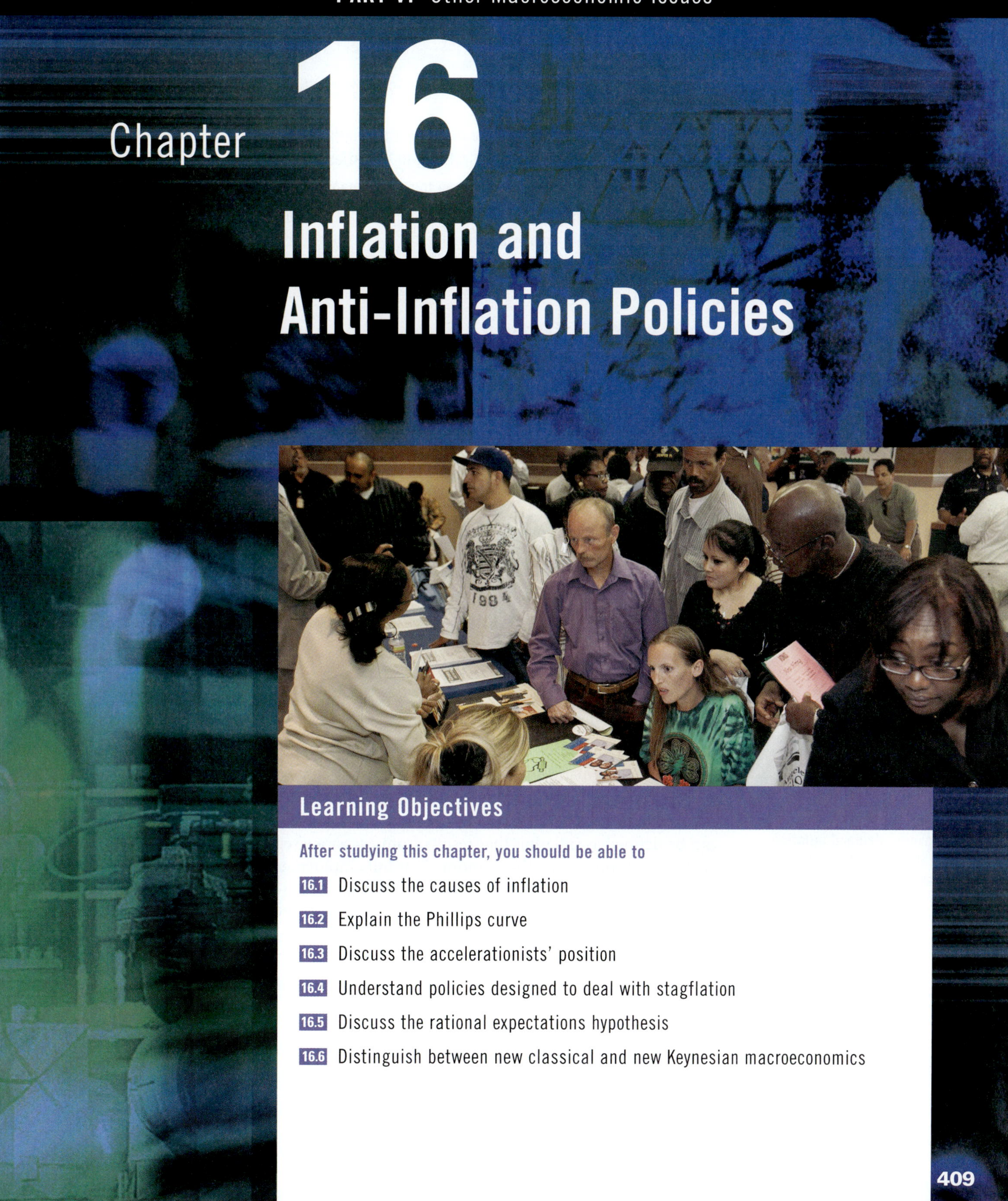

Chapter 16 Inflation and Anti-Inflation Policies

Learning Objectives

After studying this chapter, you should be able to

- 16.1 Discuss the causes of inflation
- 16.2 Explain the Phillips curve
- 16.3 Discuss the accelerationists' position
- 16.4 Understand policies designed to deal with stagflation
- 16.5 Discuss the rational expectations hypothesis
- 16.6 Distinguish between new classical and new Keynesian macroeconomics

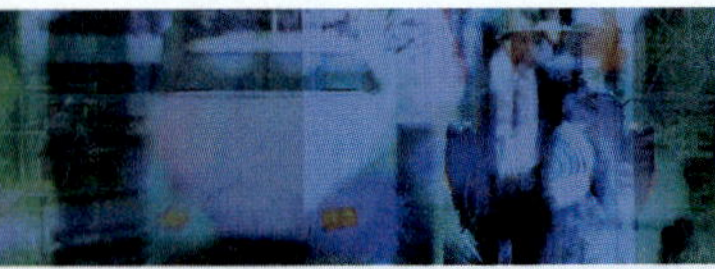

Assess Your Knowledge

MyEconLab

Answers to these questions can be found on MyEconLab at **www.myeconlab.com.**

1. Suppose most people anticipate that the rate of inflation will increase and are able to adjust their nominal income accordingly. How will this affect the rate of inflation?
2. Can an expansionary policy designed to reduce unemployment increase the rate of inflation?
3. How could the increase in the world price of oil as a result of the political upheaval in the Middle East affect employment in Alberta?

LO 16.1 Discuss the causes of inflation

Causes of Inflation

Before we discuss the causes of inflation, let us recall that, in Chapter 6, we distinguished between a one-time increase in the price level and a sustained increase in the price level. We defined inflation is a persistent increase in the average price level over time; it can be measured by the percentage change in a price index such as the CPI. We also pointed out that economic actors are concerned with how inflation affects their real income, that is, the purchasing power of their income. We showed that the percentage change in real income depends on the difference between the percentage change in money income and the rate of inflation.

When discussing inflation, we should consider changes in money wages, productivity, expectations, and the supply of money. These changes affect whether or not an initial increase in the price level will transform into a sustained increase in the price level.

What is demand-pull inflation?

Demand-Pull Inflation Demand-pull theories of inflation emphasize demand forces, an increase in the components of aggregate expenditure, such as excess spending caused by monetary expansion or government deficit spending. In terms of the models that you have studied, demand-pull inflation occurs when aggregate expenditure is so high, or when V is so high, that it exerts an upward pressure on the price level. In popular terminology, there is too much money chasing too few goods. Thus, **demand-pull inflation** can be defined as inflation that results from excess aggregate demand (or excess aggregate expenditure) when the economy is at full employment.

demand-pull inflation or excess demand inflation inflation that results from excess aggregate demand

Figure 16.1 illustrates demand-pull inflation. Suppose that the economy is in equilibrium at the full-employment level of real output, y_F, with the average price level at P. An increase in aggregate expenditure will cause the AD curve to shift to the right to AD1. The price level rises from P to P_1. The process of demand-pull inflation has been set in motion. Demand-pull inflation is also called **excess demand inflation** because it emphasizes excess aggregate demand.

Are there specific demand-pull theories of inflation?

Yes. Two popular theories of demand-pull inflation are the monetary theory and the budget deficit theory. Let us discuss each briefly.

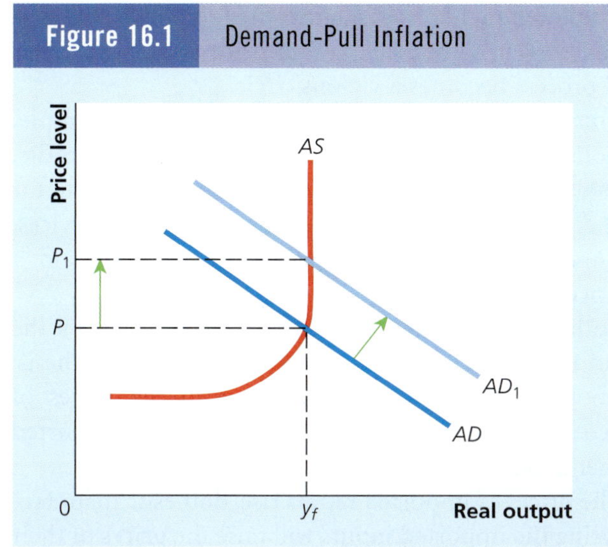

Figure 16.1 Demand-Pull Inflation

The Monetary Theory of Inflation When we discussed the quantity theory of money, we examined the relation between the quantity of money and the price level. According to the **monetary theory of inflation**, when the money supply increases at a rate faster than the increase in real output, it causes inflation. The theory suggests that people want to hold a certain amount of cash. An increase in the quantity of money means there is more money than households and firms would like to hold for different purposes. They will therefore spend the excess money balances on goods and services, causing the average level of prices to rise. Thus, the monetary theory of inflation concludes that inflation is caused by increases in the money supply.

If real output increases more quickly than the money supply, the increase in the supply of money will not result in inflation. It is only when the money supply increases faster than real output that the average level of prices rises.

monetary theory of inflation the theory that inflation is caused by increases in the money supply

budget deficit theory of inflation the theory that government deficit spending causes inflation

crowding-out effect the concept that increases in government spending lead to a reduction in private sector spending

The Budget Deficit Theory of Inflation The **budget deficit theory of inflation** says that government deficit spending causes inflation. The proponents of this theory argue that government deficits increase aggregate expenditure, which in turn results in inflation.

To a certain extent, the budget deficit theory of inflation is a variant of the monetary theory of inflation. Proponents of the monetary theory claim that government deficits are inflationary only if financed by printing money. They argue that if the deficit is financed by borrowing from households and firms, the increase in government spending will be offset by an equivalent reduction in spending in the private sector. The increase in government spending has displaced private spending. In other words, there will be a **crowding-out effect**, and there will be no increase in aggregate expenditure and hence no inflationary pressures. The crowding-out effect states that increases in government spending lead to a reduction in private sector spending.

What is cost-push inflation?

cost-push inflation or sellers' inflation inflation resulting from increases in wages and other supply-side factors

Cost-Push Inflation Whereas demand-pull theories of inflation emphasize demand forces as the main cause of inflation, cost-push theories of inflation, or **sellers' inflation** as it is often called, emphasize supply or cost factors as the dominant cause. **Cost-push inflation** is inflation that is caused by a decrease in the supply side of the economy, as a result of increases in wages and other supply-side factors. When wages increase, assuming no improvement in productivity; when other costs of production rise or firms increase prices, even when there is no increase in the cost of production, aggregate supply decreases, shifting the *AS* curve to the left, as indicated in Figure 16.2. The price level increases from P to P_1 and real output decreases from y_f to y_1.

According to cost-push theories, inflation can be caused by powerful unions or by powerful firms. The process is explained as follows. Unions demand higher wages for their members. Because unions are so powerful, that employers accede to their demands, even when there are no increases in productivity. Higher wages mean higher costs for firms. So to protect their profits, firms raise their prices. The higher prices lead unions

Figure 16.2 Cost-Push Inflation

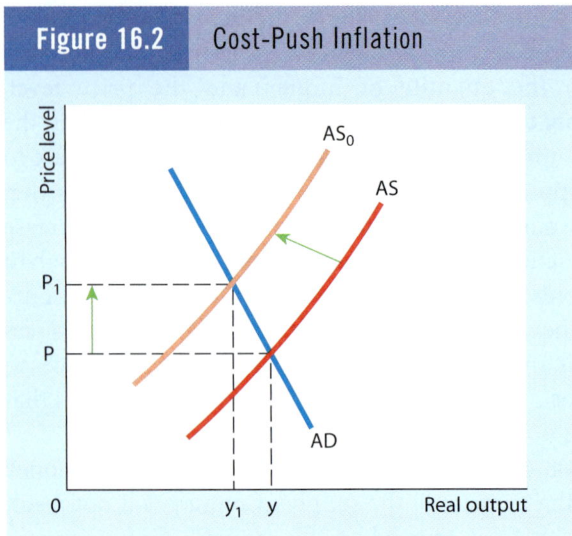

to demand even higher wages. Firms then respond by raising their prices even higher. This **wage-price spiral** continues and the process becomes a vicious circle.

Firms, too, can initiate the process. For example, monopolists can raise their prices to increase their profits. As a result, unions ask for higher wages to compensate for the higher prices workers have to pay for goods and services. This causes firms to raise their prices in response. Again, a wage-price spiral results.

Another variety of the cost-push family of inflation is the so-called **imported inflation**. According to this hypothesis, inflation can be caused by an increase in the prices of imported inputs or by increases in the prices of imported consumer goods.

If the prices of imported inputs rise, domestic manufacturers using the imported inputs will raise the prices of their products. Also, if there is inflation abroad, the prices of imported consumer goods will rise, which could cause the price of domestic consumer goods to increase, resulting ultimately in domestic inflation. Small open economies, such as the Canadian economy, are susceptible to imported inflation.

wage-price spiral the phenomenon of successive increases in wages followed by increases in prices followed by increases in wages

imported inflation inflation caused by increases in the prices of imported inputs

Figure 16.2 illustrates cost-push inflation. Suppose that the economy is operating at a level of real output of y with the price level at P. An increase in the firms' costs will cause the aggregate supply curve to shift from AS to AS_0.

Cost-push inflation results in the price level increasing from P to P_1. Note that cost-push inflation occurs even if the economy is operating below full employment.

An upward shift in the aggregate supply curve initiates cost-push inflation.

BUSINESS SITUATION 16.1

Your father runs a small business, importing products from the United States for sale in Canada.

How might inflation in the United States affect your father's business?

The answer to this Business Situation can be found in Appendix A.

Theories of demand-pull and cost-push inflation explain the initial causes of the increase in the price level; they don't explain the continuous increase in the price level. For the price level to continue rising, the money supply must increase. When the money supply increases, in response to the decrease in *AS*, the process is known as **validation**.

validation an increase in the money supply in response to the decrease in *AS*

Economists generally agree that an increase in the cost of production will result in inflation only if it is accompanied by an increase in the money supply. Consider the rate of inflation in Canada in the 1970s. Many economists cite this case as an example of cost-push inflation. The Organization of Petroleum Exporting Countries (OPEC) raised the price of oil significantly in 1974. Consequently, the price of oil and the prices of petroleum-related products increased. If these price increases had been offset by price reductions in other sectors of the economy, there would have been no increase in the average level of prices. Why were there no offsetting price reductions elsewhere in the economy? After all, given a certain amount of money, if we spend more on oil and products made from petroleum, then we have a smaller amount of our income to spend on other things. But if the monetary authorities validate cost-push inflation by increasing the money supply, then there will be overall increases in the price level. The increase in the supply of money increases aggregate demand, shifting *AD* to the right, as shown in Figure 16.1. This is what happened in 1974. It is in this sense that many economists claim that inflation is a purely monetary phenomenon.

Is there any other cause of inflation?

Economists have identified another type of inflation that they have referred to as expectational inflation. Let us discuss the concept briefly.

expectational inflation or inertial inflation inflation caused by the behaviour of buyers and sellers responding to expectations of inflation

Expectational Inflation **Expectational inflation**, also called **inertial inflation**, contains elements of both demand-pull and cost-push inflation. It is initiated by the behaviour of buyers and sellers responding to expectations of inflation. The expectational theory of inflation suggests that if people expect the rate of inflation to increase, they will tend to increase their current spending in order to avoid paying higher prices in the future. Graphically, once again, the aggregate demand curve in Figure 16.1 shifts to the right. This is the demand element of expectational inflation. There is also a supply (cost) dimension. If unions expect a higher rate of inflation, they will ask for wage increases that incorporate the expected rate of inflation. The increase in wages raises the cost of production, shifting the *AS* curve to the left in Figure 16.2. This increase in wages will cause firms to respond by raising the prices of their products, thus setting the wage-price spiral in motion.

Is inflation due mainly to demand-pull or to cost-push factors?

Economists disagree over the dominant cause of inflation. Some economists argue that all inflations originate from demand pressures. Other economists claim that inflation can originate from wage-push or price-push situations. Monetarists see monetary expansion as the prime cause of demand-pull inflation. For them, "Inflation is everywhere and always a monetary phenomenon." Neo-Keynesians view aggregate expenditure components, such as government spending and investment, as the main sources. However, most economists agree that once inflation has started, it tends to generate inflationary expectations and is often validated by monetary authorities, which fuel inflation and keep it going indefinitely.

In practice, determining whether a particular inflation is demand-pull or cost-push is quite difficult. What we observe are the increases in the average price level; we can't see what causes the increases. Consider the following scenario. An increase in government spending raises aggregate expenditure, which, in turn, increases the demand for labour. This increase in the demand for labour results in higher wages, which cause firms to raise prices. This starts the wage-price spiral. Thus, we have inflation. Is this inflation demand-pull or cost-push? It is demand-pull because it originated as a result of an increase in aggregate expenditure. But the inflation is also cost-push because the immediate cause of the increase in prices is the increase in wages.

Reading Comprehension

The answers to these questions can be found on MyEconLab at www.myeconlab.com. MyEconLab

1. What is demand-pull inflation?
2. What is cost-push inflation?
3. Discuss the process of validation.

Explain the Phillips curve

The Phillips Curve

What is the Phillips curve?

The coexistence of persistent high inflation and high unemployment in the 1970s was a relatively new phenomenon in the Canadian economy. Before 1950, many economists thought that unemployment and inflation could not exist simultaneously. They argued that inflation results from too much spending, while unemployment results from too little spending. By definition, too much spending and too little spending are mutually exclusive. Nevertheless, unemployment and inflation can coexist.

To help us better understand the important relationship between inflation and unemployment, we should first look at an important economic relationship—the Phillips curve. A.W. Phillips (1914–1975), a New Zealand economist, was among the first to call attention to the relationship between the rate of change in wages and the rate of unemployment. He explained this relationship as follows: During a period of high unemployment, competition among unemployed workers for jobs slows down wage increases. Workers are less likely to demand wage increases when there is a large surplus of unemployed people. Conversely, when unemployment is low, competition among employers for scarce labour services bids wages up. Unions are also in a strong position to demand wage increases for their members.

Phillips curve the curve showing the relationship between the wage rate and the rate of unemployment

Figure 16.3 The Phillips Curve

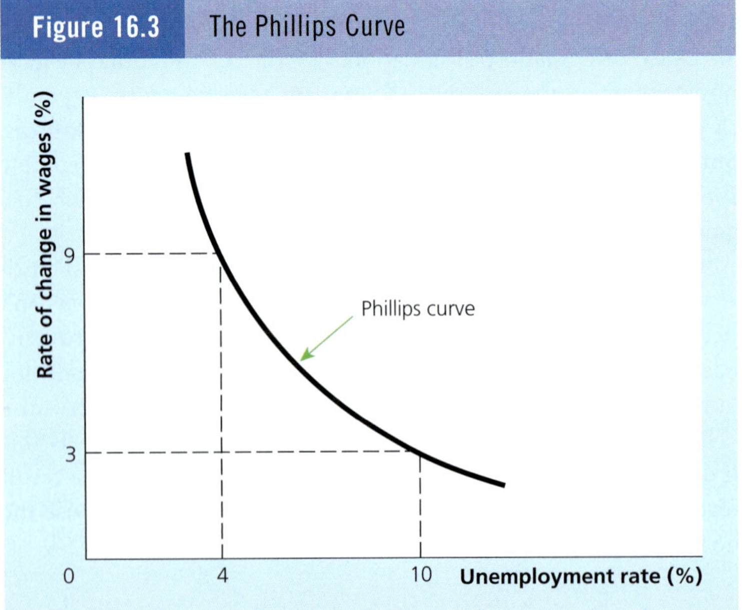

The higher the unemployment rate, the lower the rate of increase in wages will be; and the lower the unemployment rate, the higher the rate of increase in wages.

The inverse relationship between the rate of unemployment and the rate of change in wages can be presented graphically. A curve showing this inverse relationship between the rate of change in wages and the unemployment rate is called the **Phillips curve**, named after the economist who discovered the relationship. It is illustrated in Figure 16.3.

The curve shows the various combinations of unemployment rates and changes in wage rates that the economy can attain. It shows, for example, that when the unemployment rate is 10%, wages rise by 3%, and when the unemployment rate is 4%, wages rise by 9%.

Is it possible to proceed from the Phillips curve to a relationship between inflation and unemployment?

The Relation between Inflation and Unemployment You will recall that the cost-push theory of inflation implies a relationship between increases in wages and inflation. Specifically, it suggests that the percentage increase in wages is directly related to the rate of inflation. It shows when wages increase during a period of low unemployment the rate of inflation increases. Thus, by substituting the rate of change in the wage rate in the Phillips curve relation with the rate of inflation, we obtain a relation between inflation and unemployment. We have reached the following conclusion:

> The higher the rate of unemployment, the lower the rate of inflation will be; the lower the rate of unemployment, the higher the rate of inflation.

This inverse relationship between inflation and unemployment is illustrated in Figure 16.4.

The Phillips curve, strictly speaking, expresses the relationship between the rate of change in wages and the rate of unemployment. Today, however, when economists talk of the Phillips curve, it is the relationship between the rate of inflation and the rate of unemployment to which they usually refer. In the remainder of this chapter, we will follow this practice.

What do economists mean by the natural rate of unemployment?

natural rate of unemployment or NAIRU the rate of unemployment that is consistent with a constant rate of inflation; NAIRU stands for non-accelerating inflation rate of unemployment

The **natural rate of unemployment** is defined as the rate of unemployment that is consistent with price stability. It is the rate of unemployment that exists when there is full employment. In Chapter 6 we defined full employment as a situation in which there is only frictional and structural unemployment. Any given level of output is associated with a level of employment that is less than 100% of the labour force. In the long run, wages and prices adjust to clear the labour market. But there will still be some frictional and structural unemployment. Apart from frictional and structural unemployment, in long-run equilibrium, all those who want to find employment at the market-determined wage rate will be able to do so. Thus, in the long run, any unemployment over and above the frictional and structural unemployment could be considered voluntary.

The level of unemployment that prevails when the economy is in long-run equilibrium is referred to as the natural level of unemployment. It is natural in the sense that the economy will tend toward this level of output and employment in the long run. When the economy is in long-run equilibrium, there is no pressure for inflation to accelerate or decelerate. The rate of inflation will tend to be constant. Some economists refer to the rate of unemployment that is consistent with

Figure 16.4 Relationship between Inflation and Unemployment

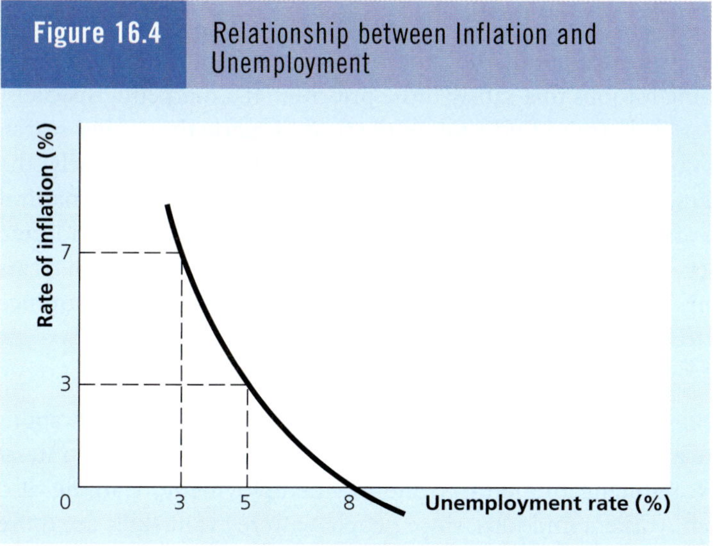

a stable rate of inflation—the non-accelerating inflation rate (NAIR)—as the natural rate of unemployment. Therefore, we can also define the natural rate of unemployment as the rate of unemployment that is consistent with a constant rate of inflation. This explains why the natural rate of unemployment is often referred to as the **NAIRU** (non-accelerating inflation rate of unemployment).

What is the natural rate of unemployment in Canada?

The term "natural" implies a fixed, unchanging, and even desirable rate of unemployment. But as Milton Friedman, the economist who introduced the term, says, "by using the term 'natural' rate of unemployment I don't mean to suggest that it is immutable or unchangeable." Empirical evidence in Canada and elsewhere shows there is no unique natural rate of unemployment below which, if the rate declines, inflation will accelerate. The natural rate of unemployment varies within a country and between countries. In Canada, in the 1960s, the rate of unemployment was low, but the rate of inflation also remained low. In the 1970s, Canada experienced a period of stagflation with high unemployment and high inflation. In the early 2000s, the rates of unemployment and inflation were relatively low in Canada. Because of the absence of a unique natural rate, some economists talk about a "time variant" natural rate of unemployment. There is no unique natural rate of unemployment for an economy.

What are the main factors that affect NAIRU?

The NAIRU is affected by a number of factors. During any period, some people will find jobs while others will lose or leave their jobs—the flows and stocks of the labour force discussed in Chapter 6. The rate of unemployment per period is determined by the rates at which people enter the labour force, find jobs, and lose or leave jobs. The higher the rates of labour force entry and job loss, the higher the rate of unemployment; the lower rate of labour force entry and the higher the rate at which workers find jobs, the lower the rate of unemployment. Any variable that reduces the rate of job loss and increases the rate at which workers find jobs on a long-term basis lowers the natural rate of unemployment. By the same logic, any variable that increases the rate of job loss and reduces the rate at which workers find jobs raises the natural rate of unemployment. Let us now examine some specific factors that affect the natural rate of unemployment.

Job Search People have priorities about the type of work they want, and they will expend their effort searching for jobs that satisfy those priorities. If a marketing specialist loses her job, she will most likely try to find a job in the field of marketing. If her search is unsuccessful, she will consider accepting a job offer in a related field. Clearly, the longer her job search takes, the longer she will remain unemployed. Thus, the natural rate of unemployment is affected by the tendency for unemployed workers to continue to search rather than to accept the first job offer. Searching for jobs is costly, both in terms of the time spent looking for work and forgone income, but employment insurance benefits reduce this cost to some extent.

Labour Market Information, Training, and Human Resource Planning Information about job vacancies for workers and the available workers for employers increases the rate at which workers find jobs, reducing the natural rate of unemployment. Training also increases the rate at which workers find jobs, since people with relevant skills are more likely to find jobs. Careful human resource planning, training, and development can be geared to meet the future needs of industry. Human resource planning could increase the rate at which workers find jobs and thus reduces the natural rate of unemployment.

Labour Force Growth If an increasing number of adults enter the labour force, then, other things being equal, it will be more difficult for the economy to absorb the additional entrants. Labour force growth reduces the rate at which workers find jobs and thus increases the natural rate of unemployment.

Employment Insurance Employment insurance benefits have prevented many unemployed workers from facing severe hardships. As stated earlier, the employment insurance benefits reduce the cost of searching for jobs. They also allow workers to find the jobs they would like to have and are best qualified for. But at the same time, the benefits reduce the rate at which workers find jobs. Because of employment insurance benefits, some unemployed workers may feel less pressured to search for jobs. They may also be more likely to refuse job offers that they consider to be unattractive. These tendencies reduce the rate at which workers find jobs. Moreover, knowing that they can receive employment insurance benefits if they lose their jobs, some workers may not be so hard pressed to hold on to their jobs. This tendency increases the rate of job loss. For all these reasons, we can conclude that employment insurance could increase the natural rate of unemployment.

Can we somehow summarize these factors and their effects on the NAIRU?

Let's do so in Table 16.1.

What is the implication of the trade-off between inflation and unemployment for government macroeconomic stabilization policy?

discomfort index or misery index the rate of inflation plus the rate of unemployment

Policy Implication Let us assume for the moment that the curve in Figure 16.4 is stable. If the government wants to reduce the rate of inflation from 7% to 3%, it can do so by implementing contractionary monetary or fiscal policies. The rate of unemployment, however, will rise from 3% to 5%. That is, lower inflation can be achieved only at the expense of higher unemployment. This, of course, is a real dilemma for policymakers. Because inflation and unemployment are serious economic problems, some people use the terms **discomfort index** and **misery index**, defined as the rate of inflation plus the rate of unemployment. But the two rates do not have the same impact on individuals. Most people would consider unemployment to be a more serious problem than inflation, especially if it is a moderate rate of inflation. Reducing the discomfort index is a tremendous task facing policymakers.

Table 16.1 Summary of Factors Affecting the NAIRU

Factors	Effect on the NAIRU
1. Job search	The willingness to prolong the job search process reduces the job-finding rate and therefore increases the NAIRU.
2. Labour-market information,	Human resource planning increases the job-finding rate and thustraining, and manpower planningreduces the NAIRU.
3. Labour-force growth	Labour-force growth reduces the job-finding rate and thus increases the NAIRU.
4. Employment insurance	Employment insurance reduces the job-finding rate, increases the rate of job loss, and therefore increases the NAIRU.

Is there a fixed trade-off between inflation and unemployment?

Almost 50 years ago, when the Phillips curve was popularized, economists thought that there was a relatively fixed trade-off between inflation and unemployment. They thought that the Phillips curve was stable. In the 1970s, however, they observed that the Phillips curve had shifted to the right. Referring to Figure 16.4, this means that when the inflation rate was 7%, the unemployment rate was more than 3%.

Many economists argued that the outward shift of the Phillips curve in the 1970s was due to supply-side shocks—a decrease in aggregate supply—such as the big increase in the price of oil, which shifted the aggregate supply curve to the left.

Is there a term for the simultaneous existence of inflation and unemployment? Is there any relationship between this phenomenon and aggregate supply?

stagflation the simultaneous occurrence of high rates of inflation and high rates of unemployment

Aggregate Supply and Stagflation The term **stagflation** has been used to describe the coexistence of inflation and unemployment. The word is made up of *stagnation* and *inflation.* Stagflation is therefore the simultaneous occurrence of high rates of inflation and unemployment.

We can use the aggregate demand–aggregate supply analysis that we developed earlier to explain simultaneous increases in the price level and decreases in real output. In Figure 16.5, *AD* and *AS* are the initial aggregate demand and aggregate supply curves.

Figure 16.5 Aggregate Supply and Stagflation

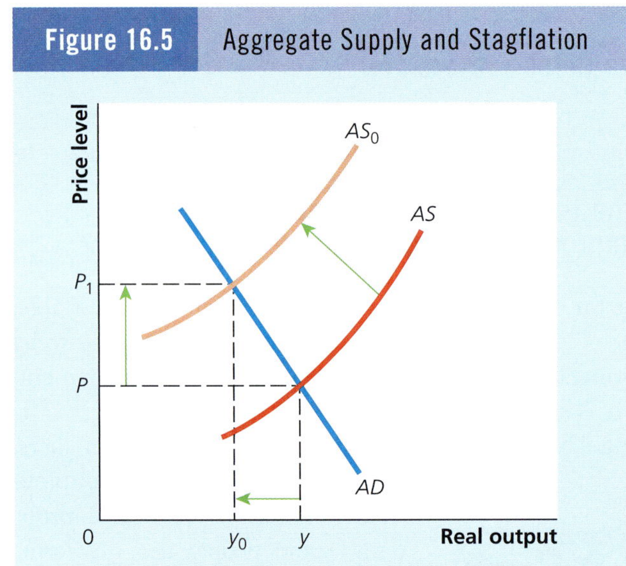

The initial equilibrium level of real output is y, and the price level is P. If the aggregate supply curve shifts from AS to AS_0, the level of real output falls from y to y_0, and the price level increases from P to P_1.

> An upward shift in the aggregate supply curve causes real output and employment to decrease and the price level to increase.

The aggregate demand–aggregate supply analysis points clearly to supply shifts as a cause of rising prices accompanied by falling employment and output—the phenomenon we have already referred to as stagflation. We must point out that not all economists accept the existence of a trade-off between inflation and unemployment, especially in the long run.

Reading Comprehension

The answers to these questions can be found on MyEconLab at www.myeconlab.com. MyEconLab

1. What does the Phillips curve indicate?
2. Discuss the natural rate of unemployment.
3. Is the natural rate of unemployment fixed?
4. What variables affect the natural rate of unemployment?

LO 16.3 Discuss the accelerationists' position

The Accelerationists and the Long-Run Phillips Curve

Why don't some economists accept the trade-off between inflation and unemployment?

According to several economists, including Milton Friedman (1912–2006) and Edmund S. Phelps (1933–), a stable trade-off between inflation and unemployment is valid only in the short run. These economists claim that there is no trade-off in the long run. They maintain that the long-run Phillips curve is vertical, as shown in Figure 16.6. Expansionary monetary and fiscal policies designed to reduce unemployment will result in accelerated inflation and only a temporary reduction in unemployment. For this reason, proponents of this view are called **accelerationists**. Accelerationists are economists who argue that there is no long-run trade-off between inflation and unemployment. They claim that attempts to keep employment below its natural level will simply accelerate inflation.

accelerationists economists who claim that attempts to keep unemployment below its natural level will simply accelerate inflation

Let us examine the argument of these economists. Suppose that the natural rate of unemployment is 7% in Figure 16.6, but policymakers attempt to reduce it to 4%, believing that 4% constitutes full employment. How does this affect unemployment and inflation? They will use expansionary monetary and fiscal policies to increase aggregate expenditure in the manner described in earlier chapters. Because the economy is already at its natural rate of unemployment, the increase in aggregate expenditure will cause the price level to rise. If nominal wages remain constant, then the increase in prices raises the profit margins of firms. Higher profits cause businesses to expand, hire more workers, and thus reduce the rate of unemployment from 7% to 4%. The economy thus moves from A to B along the short-run Phillips curve PC_1. The rate of inflation has risen from 0% at A to 3% at B. Policymakers have chosen to live with a 3% inflation rate in order to achieve a 4% unemployment rate. This analysis assumes that workers expect the future rate of inflation to be the same as the actual rate of inflation.

Figure 16.6 The Accelerationists' View of the Phillips Curve

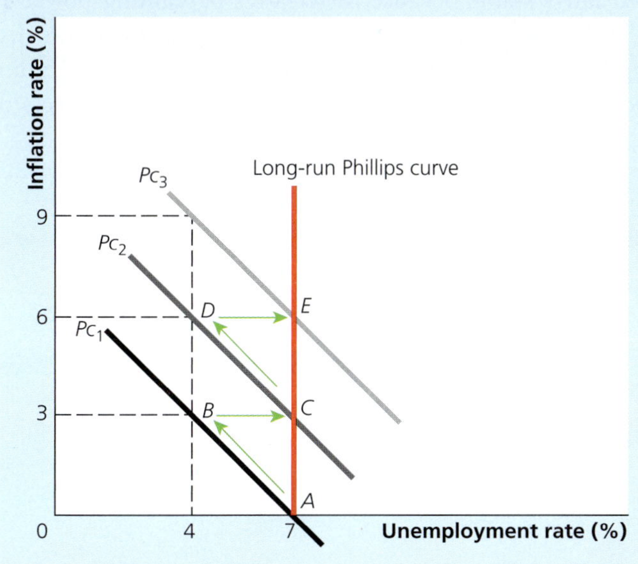

However, the accelerationists claim that the economy will not remain at *B* for long. That point represents a transitory position. Now that the rate of inflation has risen to 3%, workers adjust their expectations of inflation and demand higher wages to compensate for the loss in real wages caused by the increase in the price level. Workers demand and receive higher money wages, which reduce the firms' profits and cause them to reduce employment and output. The rate of unemployment therefore returns to its natural rate of 7%, but the inflation rate is still 3%. The economy is now at *C*. The short-run Phillips curve has shifted from PC_1 to PC_2.

With the unemployment rate again at 7%, the government once again tries to reduce it to 4% by using expansionary monetary and fiscal policies. The unemployment rate falls temporarily to 4%, but the increase in aggregate expenditure causes the rate of inflation to rise from 3% to 6%. The economy moves along the short-run Phillips curve PC_2 from C to D, as shown in Figure 16.6.

According to the accelerationists, the economy does not remain at D. As before, workers revise their inflationary expectations, and, as before, firms react by reducing employment and output. The unemployment rate returns to its natural rate of 7%, while the inflation rate remains at 6%, as shown by point E in Figure 16.6. The short-run Phillips curve shifts from PC_2 to PC_3. Thus, the policymakers' attempts to force unemployment below its natural rate have resulted only in raising the rate of inflation from 0% to 6%. According to the accelerationists, further attempts will just continue the spiral. Accelerationists therefore conclude that there is no long-run trade-off between inflation and unemployment. The long-run Phillips curve is vertical at the natural rate of unemployment.

> Accelerationists claim that attempts to use expansionary monetary or fiscal policies to push unemployment below its natural rate will result only in accelerated inflation.

Despite the proposition of the accelerationists, Canada had a period of a relatively low rate of unemployment and a low rate of inflation in the mid-2000s.

What variables explain the combination of the relatively low rate of unemployment and low rate of inflation in the mid-2000s?

The trade-off between the rate of unemployment and the rate of inflation, the Phillips curve, depends on productivity, monetary policy, expected inflation, and the relative bargaining power of workers. In the mid-2000s productivity grew significantly compared to the previous years. In 1992 the Bank of Canada adopted a target rule through which it attempted to control the rate of inflation at around 2% per year by following the appropriate monetary policy. The Bank of Canada was able to maintain the actual rate of inflation close to the target rate of inflation during this period. With the stable rate of inflation, both workers and firms adjusted their expectations of inflation to the target rate, resulting in wage stability. Some economists also argue that during this period, money wages remained fairly stable because the relative bargaining power of workers declined. The decline in the bargaining position of workers was due to the displacement of workers by technological change, the decrease in the rate of unionization in the labour force, the offshore outsourcing of production, and the other effects of globalization.

Reading Comprehension

The answers to these questions can be found on MyEconLab at www.myeconlab.com. MyEconLab

1. Discuss the acceleration hypothesis.
2. How do price expectations affect the Phillips curve?
3. What is stagflation?

LO 16.4 Understand policies designed to deal with stagflation

Policies to Deal with Stagflation

What policies that can be used to deal with stagflation?

If policymakers could shift the Phillips curve to the left, the economy could have either a lower unemployment rate without increasing the rate of inflation, or a lower rate of inflation without an increase in the unemployment rate. In other words, the discomfort index would be reduced. Figure 16.7 shows that by shifting the Phillips curve from position *A* to position *B*, policymakers can lower the unemployment rate from 12% to 5% while leaving the inflation rate at 4%. Figure 16.7 shows that if the Phillips curve shifts to the left, the unemployment rate will fall without increasing the rate of inflation.

To deal with the problem of stagflation, policymakers must adopt policies that shift the Phillips curve toward the origin. Among the factors that will cause a downward shift in the Phillips curve are greater mobility of labour, the development of relevant skills through education and training, better information about available jobs, and a reduction in inflationary expectations. All of these factors will tend to reduce unemployment without putting undue upward pressure on prices. Hence, the Phillips curve will shift toward the origin.

Are there any other ways of combatting stagflation?

Other ways of combatting stagflation are wage and price controls and tax-based incomes policies. Let us deal with each in turn.

wage and price controls or incomes policies restrictions imposed by the government to limit increases in wages and prices

Wage and Price Controls **Wage and price controls** are the direct intervention by government to limit increases in wages and prices. Such controls, sometimes referred to as **incomes policies**, were used in Britain as early as 1948. In August 1971, U.S. President Richard Nixon introduced wage and price controls in the United States; and in October 1975, Prime Minister Pierre Trudeau introduced them in Canada.

Figure 16.7 Phillips Curve and Unemployment

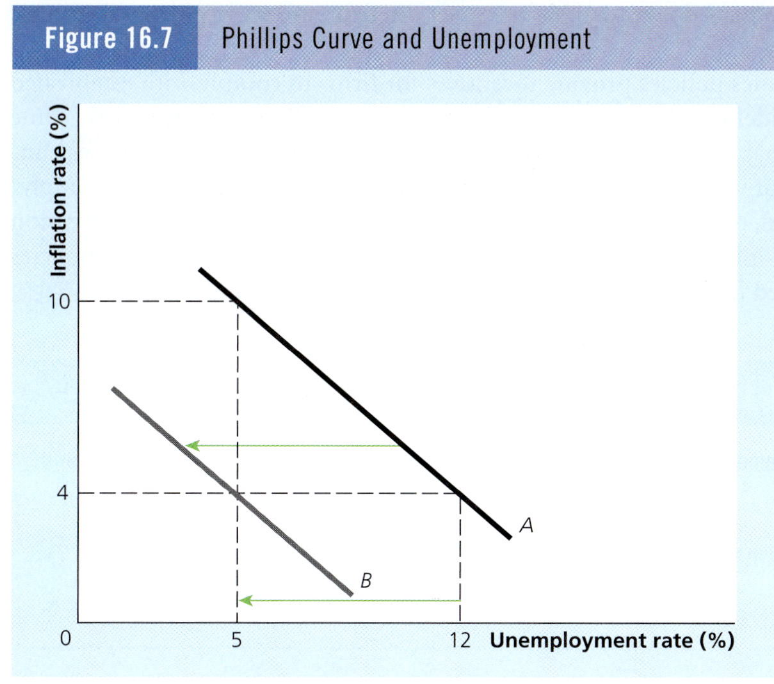

Wage and price controls are economic policy measures that impose a ceiling on wage and price increases to curb inflation.

Wage and price controls were not generally effective; prices continued to rise despite the restrictions. Those who support wage and price controls claim that the rate of inflation would have been higher had it not been for wage and price controls.

Do economists in general support wage and price controls?

In general, economists do not support wage and price controls. The main reason for the lack of enthusiasm is that such controls interfere with the efficient working of

Table 16.2 Illustration of Tax-Based Incomes Policy

Wage Increase Granted (%)	Corporate Income Tax Rate (%)
2	32
3	34
4	36
5	38
6	40
7	42
8	44

the price system, resulting in widespread misallocation of resources. Economists claim that the costs of administering the wage and price control programs often outweigh the benefits. These views notwithstanding, some economists contend that controls are necessary in certain circumstances. Let us turn now to tax-based incomes policies.

Tax-Based Incomes Policies Since the 1970s, some economists have suggested the use of **tax-based incomes policies** (TIPS) to increase the effectiveness of incomes policies. Tax-based incomes policies rely on tax incentives to encourage compliance with wage and price controls. There are two different but related forms of implementing this policy. In one form, the tax system is used as a stick to punish nonconformists. For example, the government might establish guidelines limiting wage and price increases at 5%. If firms grant wage increases or implement price increases in excess of the 5% guidelines, they would be penalized by increases in their corporate income tax rate.

tax-based incomes policies policies that use tax incentives to encourage compliance with wage and price controls

Table 16.2 illustrates how such a system might work where the customary corporate tax rate is 38%.

As the table shows, a company that grants wage increases of 5% will be taxed at the normal rate of 38%. But if it grants a wage increase of 7%, the tax rate will jump to 42%.

In the other form of tax-based incomes policies, the tax system is used as a carrot to provide incentive for employees and employers to limit wage and price increases. Let us assume again that the government establishes guidelines specifying a maximum increase of 5% in wages and prices. Under a carrot approach, employers and employees are given tax rebates if they operate within the guidelines. Thus, if a firm manages to keep its prices and wages down to a 3% increase, the firm and its workers will receive tax rebates.

Tax-based incomes policies provide incentives for firms to comply with established wage and price guidelines. However, they do have certain disadvantages. First, some economists claim that the implementation of tax-based incomes policies imposes considerable administrative costs. Second, some firms may experience hardship in complying with them. Third, union leaders may view tax-based incomes policies as an intrusion by the government into the collective bargaining process. Tax-based incomes policies have never been used in Canada, but they have attracted considerable attention.

BUSINESS SITUATION 16.2

A government decides to introduce a tax-based incomes policy. It will grant tax incentives for compliance with the wage and price guidelines.

How might such a policy adversely affect businesses?

The answer to this Business Situation can be found in Appendix A.

Reading Comprehension

The answers to these questions can be found on MyEconLab at www.myeconlab.com. MyEconLab

1. What are wage and price controls?
2. How do economists view wage and price controls?
3. What are the two ways of implementing a tax-based incomes policy?

LO 16.5 Discuss the rational expectations hypothesis

Rational Expectations Hypothesis

What is the rational expectations hypothesis?

In an earlier chapter, you learned that there is disagreement over supply-side economic policies. The controversy does not end there. One of the most controversial hypotheses in macroeconomics today is the rational expectations hypothesis (REH). To properly understand the theory of rational expectations, you should first grasp the notion of **adaptive expectations**. Quite succinctly stated, the adaptive expectations theory assumes that people form their expectations solely on the basis of the experience of the recent past. Thus, their expectations about inflation are based solely on past experiences with inflation. For example, if the rate of inflation were 3% last year, people would base their economic decisions on the expectation that the rate of inflation would be 3% this year. If the actual rate of inflation turns out to be different from the anticipated rate, then people will revise their expectations. Unions will revise their wage demands; and firms will revise their pricing decisions. According to the theory of adaptive expectations, people's expectations about the rate of inflation will be wrong most of the time. They will, in fact, be right only if the rate of inflation does not change. The theory of adaptive expectations therefore suggests that most people can be fooled most of the time.

adaptive expectations the hypothesis that people form their expectations solely on the basis of the experience of the recent past

The adaptive expectations hypothesis has been criticized on two counts. First, critics claim that it is unreasonable to assume people's expectations about the rate of inflation are formed only on the basis of past inflation rates. Other factors, such as anti-inflation policies, will affect people's inflationary expectations. Second, critics also claim that it is unreasonable to assume that most people can be fooled most of the time. They argue people are more rational than that.

rational expectations hypothesis the theory that, on average, people base their inflation expectations on their knowledge of policies and their effects

Rational Expectations The **rational expectations hypothesis**—a spin-off from monetarism—was developed mainly in response to the criticisms of adaptive expectations. This theory assumes that, on average, people base their inflation expectations on their knowledge of the economy and the effects of government policies. People generally understand the variables that affect inflation and use this information in forming their inflationary expectations. The rational expectations hypothesis therefore predicts that, on average, people's inflationary expectations and their subsequent decisions on wages and prices are correct.

Prominent rational expectations theorists include Robert Lucas (1937–), Thomas Sargent (1943–), and Neil Wallace (1939–). According to these economists, people's expectations and hence their decisions take into account the effects of government policies, which are known in advance. Rational expectations theorists also contend that markets are efficient. They argue that firms use all the available information, including the effects of government policies, to make decisions that will accomplish their objective of profit maximization. Similarly, they assert that workers base their wage demands in part on the consequences of government policies. Therefore, these economists conclude that the economy will achieve equilibrium at the level of full employment, that is, at the natural rate of unemployment. Unemployment above the natural rate is voluntary because workers know that they can find employment by accepting lower wages.

Is the theory of rational expectations rational?

Critics claim that the theory of rational expectations is hardly rational. They maintain that the inflationary process is extremely complex and that it is unreasonable to assume that people understand all the factors that determine inflation. It is also unreasonable to expect people to know precisely the effects of government policies. Franco Modigliani (1918–2003), winner of the 1985 Nobel Prize in Economics, was particularly critical of the rational expectations hypothesis. He claimed that the rational expectations hypothesis is not consistent with the evidence. It leads to the conclusion that unemployment should deviate only slightly from the natural rate, but, according to Modigliani, actual events refute this conclusion.

What is the implication of the rational expectations hypothesis for economic stabilization policies?

Let us assume that the economy experiences an unemployment rate of 12% and an inflation rate of 5%. Suppose policymakers decide to reduce unemployment with expansionary monetary or fiscal policies. How do the policies affect unemployment and inflation? According to the theory of rational expectations, firms and workers know the effects of these policies in advance. As a result of the policies, they expect the rate of inflation to increase. They also expect interest rates to rise. Accordingly, workers will demand wage increases to protect their real wage. With expectations of higher interest rates and higher wages, firms will raise prices, and will not find it profitable to undertake new investment projects. Expansionary monetary and fiscal policies will thus be ineffective. Monetary and fiscal policies, then, can be successful only if they come as complete surprises to people. The idea that monetary and fiscal policies will be ineffective if people have rational expectations is referred to the **policy irrelevance hypothesis**.

policy irrelevance hypothesis the proposition that monetary and fiscal policies will be ineffective if people have rational expectations

Reading Comprehension

The answers to these questions can be found on MyEconLab at www.myeconlab.com. MyEconLab

1. What is difference between adaptive and rational expectations?
2. Is government policy effective under the rational expectations hypothesis?
3. Can firms and workers predict with certainty the outcomes of government policies?

LO 16.6 Distinguish between new classical and new Keynesian macroeconomics

New Classical and New Keynesian Macroeconomics

What are the main features of the new classical macroeconomic model?

The New Classical Macroeconomic Model The *new classical macroeconomic model* is a macroeconomic model that assumes that wages and prices are flexible and macroeconomic adjustments are rapid. Because wages and prices adjust quickly, the economy moves quickly to the natural levels of employment and output. According to the new classical economists, if the price level is expected to rise, rational expectations will lead workers to immediately demand higher wages. At the same time, the expected higher production costs will cause aggregate supply to fall, resulting in an increase in price. Therefore, in the new classical model, wages and prices will adjust quickly.

The quick adjustment to a long-run equilibrium in the new classical macroeconomic model can be illustrated with the help of the *AD–AS* model. In Figure 16.8, *AD* and *SRAS* are the aggregate demand and short-run aggregate supply curves, respectively.

The economy is in a long-run equilibrium, consistent with the natural rate of unemployment, at the level of output indicated by y and at a price level of P. The long-run aggregate supply curve is *LRAS*. The long-run aggregate supply curve is vertical, because as long as wages are flexible (and the new classical economists assume that they are flexible in the long run), the economy will move to the natural employment level of output.

Let us assume that with the economy in this position, the Bank of Canada implements an expansionary monetary policy. As a result of the policy, the *AD* curve shifts to the right from *AD* to AD_1, and the economy moves to y_1.

The economy does not, however, stay at y_1. The expectation of higher prices causes workers and suppliers of other inputs to demand higher wages and prices for their inputs. This action raises the costs of production and shifts the short-run supply curve to the left from *SRAS* to $SRAS_0$. Immediately, the price level rises to P_1, and real output instantaneously returns to y. According to new classical economists, all these rapid adjustments take place automatically, such that activist macroeconomic stabilization policies are ineffective.

Figure 16.8 Adjustment in the New Classical Model

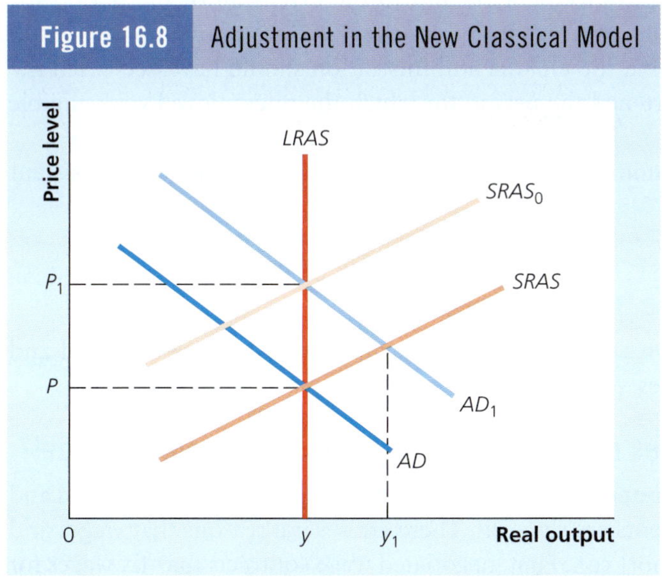

What do the new classical economists suggest the government do to reduce unemployment?

In general, new classical economists advocate little government intervention in the economy. These economists, just like the classical economists, argue that if unemployment is high, it is a short-run phenomenon. Given the flexibility of prices and wages, the forces of supply and demand will reduce unemployment until the economy reaches full employment. The only unemployment that will exist in the economy is frictional and structural unemployment. If there is persistently high unemployment, they attribute it to government policy, such as minimum wage legislation and employment insurance benefits. The new classicals assert that minimum wages discourage companies from hiring more workers. To support their claim, they cite studies that show that minimum wages reduce employment.

How do the new classical economists explain the impact of minimum wages on unemployment?

The new classical economists argue that when minimum wage rates are set above the equilibrium wage rate, the high wage rate creates unemployment. The effect of minimum wages on unemployment is higher in a recession than it is when the economy is expanding. When the economy is in a recession, the demand for labour decreases, shifting the demand curve to the left. The decrease in the demand for labour during a recession reduces the equilibrium wage rate, but the minimum wage is fixed at a higher level. At the minimum wage rate, the difference between the number of workers that firms wish to hire and the number of workers who are available to work increases. Because of the existence of minimum wages, the number of unemployed people in a recession is higher than it would have been under market conditions. Therefore, new classical economists conclude that minimum wages contribute to high unemployment, more so in a recession.

Some economists have described the 2007–2009 recession in the United States as the Great Recession because it was characterized by the deepest decrease in GDP, the longest recession, the second-highest rate of unemployment, and the longest duration of unemployment in the United States since the Great Depression. It was also the most internationally widespread recession since the Great Depression.

To reduce the rate of unemployment, new classical economists propose that the government should reduce minimum wages. For example, Gary Becker (1930–), a Nobel laureate and one of the well-known American economists at the University of Chicago, argued that to decrease the high level of unemployment in the 2007–2009 Great Recession, the Obama administration should have reduced minimum wages.

New classical economists also maintain that employment insurance benefits discourage workers from seeking employment. As evidence of the negative impact of employment benefits on the incentive to look for work, they cite the empirical evidence that shows that many unemployed workers find jobs just a few days before their benefits run out. Consequently, they suggest that the government should decrease the benefits in order to reduce the rate of unemployment. For example, Robert Barro (1944–), another Nobel laureate at Harvard University, suggested that the high rate of unemployment in the United States during the 2007–2009 Great Recession was partially attributable to the "generous" unemployment insurance benefits and to the extension of the period for eligibility to collect the benefits. In order to reduce the high rate of unemployment in the United States, he argued that the Obama administration should have decreased the benefits and should have shortened the period for which the unemployed were eligible to collect the benefits.

Clearly, new classical economists see government policy as the source of persistent high unemployment.

Are there other economists with a different view of how the government can influence unemployment?

Yes, there are. They are known as *new Keynesians:* economists who have accepted and extended J.M. Keynes's theories.

new Keynesian macroeconomic model macroeconomic model that assumes that wages and prices are rigid and that macroeconomic adjustment is sluggish

What are the main features of the new Keynesian macroeconomic model?

The **new Keynesian macroeconomic model** assumes that wages and prices are rigid and that macroeconomic adjustments are sluggish. There are several reasons that wages and prices may not adjust in the short run. First, negotiated wage contracts may fix wages for two to three years, and firms may enter into long-term contractual agreements with their suppliers to supply inputs at prearranged prices. Second, firms may find it more cost efficient not to change their prices. New price lists, new catalogues—new menus—may have to be printed following price changes. Such menu costs, as they are called, can deter firms from making short-run changes in prices. Third, firms may not follow marginal cost pricing; instead, they may use markup pricing. **Markup pricing** is a pricing formula in which firms charge consumers the cost of production plus an additional amount—a markup—to cover profit. The markup varies with industry, product differentiation, the size of firms, and economic conditions. Because of mark-up pricing and the pre-arranged agreements on the cost of inputs, firms may not reduce their prices in a recession. But new Keynesians accept the view that in the long run, wages and prices are flexible as time removes the rigidities imposed by contracts, menu costs, and markup pricing.

markup pricing a pricing formula in which firms charge consumers the cost of production plus an additional amount—a markup—to cover profit

The new Keynesian macroeconomic model is illustrated in Figure 16.9. The very short-run aggregate supply curve (*VSRAS*) is horizontal at a price level of *P*. Output can vary without affecting the price level. The economy is in full-employment equilibrium at a real output of *y* and a price level of *P*.

Let us now assume that aggregate demand falls from *AD* to AD_0. In the short run, the price level is not affected, but real output falls from *y* to y_0. The fall in aggregate demand causes firms to accumulate unintended inventories. They respond to this situation by cutting back production and laying off workers. Because wages and prices do not adjust, output remains unsold, and workers remain unemployed.

In the long run, however, wages and prices adjust downward. This results in lower costs of production, and, consequently, the very short-run aggregate supply curve shifts down from *VSRAS* to $VSRAS_1$, as shown in Figure 16.9. The price level falls from *P* to P_0, and output and employment increase until full employment is restored at *y*. Note that the new Keynesian model predicts that, in the long run, the economy will return to full-employment equilibrium. New Keynesian economists claim that when wages and prices adjust too slowly, activist policies should be used to move the economy more quickly to full-employment equilibrium.

What are the policy implications of the new Keynesian model?

Unlike the new classical economists, the new Keynesians argue that nominal wages and prices are not perfectly flexible. They maintain that the empirical evidence does not indicate that prices and wages decrease significantly in a recession.

They argue that prices and wages are inflexible mainly because of market rigidities. Firms are not entirely price takers; they control to a large extent how much they charge for their goods and services. This means, in a recession when demand is low, it may not be in the firms' best interest to lower prices. Similarly, firms may not be willing to reduce wages in a recession because of concerns with how a reduction in wages could affect the productivity and loyalty of their employees. Wages are also determined by long-term contracts. Labour unions could resist a decrease in wages. As a result, prices and wages tend to be "sticky"

Figure 16.9 The New Keynesian Model

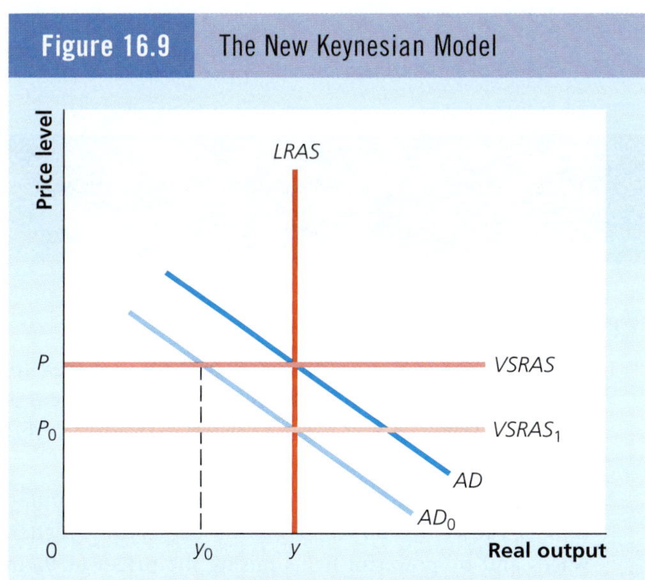

in a downward direction. Thus the new Keynesians conclude that the downward rigidity of prices and wages result in involuntary unemployment in a recession.

How do the new Keynesians assess the impact of minimum wages and employment insurance benefits on unemployment?

The new Keynesians, unlike the new classicals, are not convinced that minimum wages and employment insurance benefits have much impact on the labour market. They argue that the empirical evidence regarding the negative impact of minimum wages on employment is inconclusive. They concede that employment insurance benefits could influence the incentive to search for employment, but they assert that the main cause of unemployment in a recession is the decrease in aggregate demand. The policy recommendations of the new Keynesians are therefore radically different from those of the new classicals. They propose that the government should follow expansionary fiscal and monetary policies to reduce unemployment in a recession. For example, Paul Krugman (1953–) of Princeton University, another Nobel laureate and a prominent new Keynesian, advocated a larger "stimulus package," a larger amount of government spending, than was introduced by the Obama administration to reduce the high rate of unemployment in the United States during the 2007–2009 Great Recession. Other prominent New Keynesians, such as Joseph Stiglitz (1943–) of Columbia University and Robert Gordon (1940–) of Northwestern University, also supported higher government spending to deal with the situation.

Reading Comprehension

The answers to these questions can be found on MyEconLab at www.myeconlab.com. MyEconLab

1. Under the new classical model, how do minimum wages affect unemployment?
2. In the new classical model, how do employment benefits affect unemployment?
3. Under the new Keynesian model, what causes unemployment?
4. What kind of monetary policy and fiscal policy do the new Keynesians recommend for an economy in a recession?

Review

1. Review the learning objectives listed at the beginning of the chapter.
2. Have you accomplished all the objectives? One way to determine this is to answer the Reading Comprehension questions at the end of each section. This will help you assess the extent to which you have accomplished the learning objectives.
3. If you have not accomplished an objective, review the relevant material before proceeding.

Key Points to Remember

1. LO 16.1 Demand-pull inflation is due to increases in aggregate expenditure, which exert an upward pressure on prices. Demand-pull theories of inflation include the monetary theory and the budget deficit theory.
2. LO 16.1 The cost-push theory of inflation states that inflation is caused by powerful unions demanding higher wages and by powerful firms raising the prices of their

products. These actions produce an inflationary wage-price spiral. Cost-push theories of inflation include wage inflation and imported inflation.

3. LO 16.2 The Phillips curve expresses a relationship between the rate of change of wages and the unemployment rate. It is often used in the discussions of the trade-off between inflation and unemployment. Accelerationists claim that the inverse relationship between inflation and unemployment exists only in the short run. They argue that the long-run Phillips curve is vertical and that attempts to push unemployment below its natural rate will result only in accelerated inflation .
4. LO 16.3 The natural rate of unemployment is the rate of unemployment necessary for the economy to attain price stability. Factors affecting the non-accelerating inflation rate of unemployment (NAIRU) are job search, labour-market information and training, growth of the labour force, and employment insurance.
5. LO 16.4 The coexistence of inflation and unemployment is called stagflation. Stagflation can be explained by an upward shift in the aggregate supply curve. Policies to solve the problem of stagflation include promoting greater labour mobility, providing better labour market information, reducing inflationary expectations, and establishing incomes policies.
6. The rational expectations hypothesis suggests that government stabilization policies will be unsuccessful because households and firms will respond in a manner that will frustrate economic stabilization policies.
7. LO 16.6 The new classical macroeconomic model claims that wages and prices adjust quickly to move the economy to the natural levels of output and employment. Rational expectations and efficient markets result in the rapid adjustment of wages and prices. The new Keynesian macroeconomic model specifies that wages and prices are fixed in the short run so that the adjustment to the full-employment level of output is slow. In the long run, however, the rigidities will be removed and the economy will move to full employment.

Economic Word Power

Accelerationists (p. 419)
Adaptive expectations (p. 423)
Budget deficit theory of inflation (p. 411)
Cost-push inflation or sellers' inflation (p. 411)
Crowding-out effect (p. 411)
Demand-pull inflation or excess demand inflation (p. 410)
Discomfort index or misery index (p. 417)
Expectational inflation or inertial inflation (p. 413)
Imported inflation (p. 412)
Markup pricing (p. 427)
Monetary theory of inflation (p. 411)
Natural rate of unemployment or NAIRU (p. 415)
New Keynesian macroeconomic model (p. 426)
Phillips curve (p. 414)
Policy irrelevance hypothesis (p. 424)
Rational expectations hypothesis (p. 423)
Stagflation (p. 418)
Tax-based incomes policies (p. 422)
Validation (p. 412)
Wage and price controls or incomes policies (p. 421)
Wage-price spiral (p. 412)

Problems and Exercises

Basic

1. LO 16.1 Identify each of the following as demand-pull or cost-push inflation:
   a. The inflation is caused by excessive growth in the money supply.
   b. The inflation is caused by rapid wage increases.
   c. The inflation is caused by increases in the cost of imported goods.
   d. The inflation is caused by persistent government deficits.
   e. The inflation is caused by increases in production costs.
   f. The inflation is caused by monopolistic price hikes.
2. LO 16.2 Table 16.3 contains data on percentage changes in wages, money supply, and prices for the Canadian economy .
   a. Plot the relationship between wage increases and inflation (columns 2 and 4) either manually or by computer.
   b. Plot the relationship between the money supply growth and inflation (columns 3 and 4) either manually or by computer.
   c. Do the data seem to support the wage theory of inflation?
   d. Do the data seem to support the monetary theory of inflation?

Table 16.3 Changes in Wages, Money Supply, and Prices in Canada , 2005-2009

Year (1)	Wages (% change) (2)	Money Supply (% change) (3)	CPI (% change) (4)
2005	1.2	6.4	2.1
2006	2.4	10.2	1.9
2007	1.8	6.8	2.1
2008	1.7	12.8	2.3
2009	–2.4	13	0.3

Sources: Statistics Canada. *Table 282-0072 - Labour force survey estimates (LFS), wages of employees by type of work, North American Industry Classification System (NAICS), sex and age group, annual (current dollars unless otherwise noted)*, CANSIM (database), Using E-STAT (distributor) http://www.bankofcanada.ca/rates/indicators/key-variables.
Statistics Canada. Table 326-0021-Consumer Price Index (CPI), 2005 basket, annual (2002=100 unless otherwise noted), CANSIM (database), Using E-STAT (distributor).

3. LO 16.2 Table 16.4 contains data on percentage change in wages and the unemployment rate for Canada.

Table 16.4 Changes in Wages and Unemployment Rates in Canada, 2005-2009

Year (1)	Wages (% change) (2)	CPI (% change) (3)	Unemployment Rate (% change) (4)
2005	1.2	2.1	6.8
2006	2.4	1.9	6.3
2007	1.8	2.1	6
2008	1.7	2.3	6.1
2009	–2.4	0.3	8.3

Sources: Statistics Canada, Summary Tables, "Effective Wage Increases in Collective Agreements." Available online at www40.statcan.ca/l01/cst01/labor14.htm; Statistics Canada, Summary Tables, "Consumer Price Index, Historical Summary (1987 to 2006)." Available at www40.statcan.ca/l01/cst01/econ46a.htm; Statistics Canada, Summary Tables, "Labour Force Characteristics." Available online at www40.statcan.ca/l01/cst01/econ10.htm.

a. With percentage change in wages on the vertical axis and the unemployment rate on the horizontal axis, plot the relationship between the rate of change in wages and the unemployment rate either manually or by computer.

b. With the rate of inflation on the vertical axis and the rate of unemployment on the horizontal axis, plot the relationship between the rate of inflation and the rate of unemployment either manually or by computer.

c. Do your graphs support the Phillips curve theory?

4. LO 16.3 The questions below are based on Figure 16.10 of the Phillips curve. PC1 is the original Phillips curve.

Figure 16.10 Phillips Curve

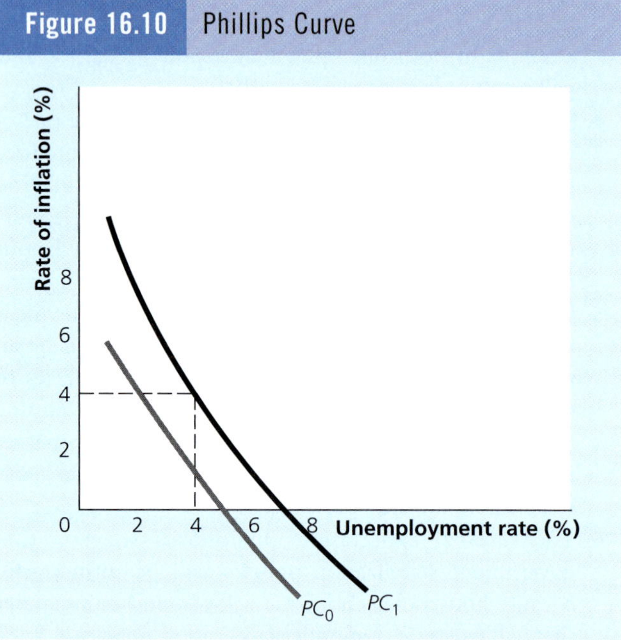

a. For the rate of inflation to be zero, what must be the unemployment rate?

b. If the authorities want a 4% rate of unemployment, what rate of inflation must they accept?

c. Suppose economic policy manages to shift the Phillips curve from PC_1 to PC_0. What rate of unemployment will now be possible with a 4% rate of inflation?

5. LO 16.2 Indicate whether each of the following is true (T) or false (F):

a. There is a direct relation between the length of job search and the natural rate of unemployment.

b. Typically, the Phillips curve is upward sloping because wages rates typically increase over time.

c. The greater the amount and quality of labour-market information, the higher will be the natural rate of unemployment.

d. Employment insurance increases the national rate of unemployment.

e. The Phillips curve can be useful when discussing or analyzing stagflation.

f. All economists now agree that there is a fixed trade-off between inflation and unemployment, and that the Phillips curve is stable.

6. LO 16.4 Use an *AD–AS* model to illustrate that demand-side policies face a dilemma when it comes to stagflation. What alternative policy might be effective against stagflation?
7. LO 16.4 A tax cut might affect both the demand and the supply sides of the economy. Explain with the help of an *AD–AS* model.

Questions in the Intermediate and Challenging Sections cover several different concepts, and have not been organized by learning objectives.

Intermediate

1. Which of the following is likely to be more effective in reducing unemployment and why?
   a. An increase in government spending financed by borrowing from the public
   b. An increase in government spending financed by borrowing from the central bank
2. It has been argued that supply-side tax cuts will reduce inflation. It has also been argued that inflation will accelerate because of the effects of the tax cuts on aggregate demand. How can these views be reconciled?

Challenging

1. The original Phillips curve expresses a relationship between the rate of change in wages and the rate of unemployment. The modern Phillips curve expresses a relationship between the rate of inflation and the rate of unemployment. What theory of inflation is implied to justify the change from the rate of change in wages to inflation?
2. Suppose that inflation has proceeded steadily over the past several years until it has now become a matter of concern that requires immediate attention. It has been determined that the inflation is of the demand variety. The government has the following two options:
   a. Announce publicly that it will use appropriate monetary and fiscal policies to deal with the inflationary situation.
   b. Conduct the appropriate monetary and fiscal policies with as little publicity as possible.

   Which of the above options is likely to be more effective and why? (Hint: Consider the rational expectations hypothesis.)

MyEconLab Visit the MyEconLab website at **www.myeconlab.com**. This online homework and tutorial system puts you in control of your own learning with study and practice tools directly correlated to this chapter's content.

Study Guide

Self-Assessment

What's your score?

Circle the letter that corresponds with the correct answer.

1. Inflation caused by too much aggregate expenditure is called
   a. Excessive inflation
   b. Demand-pull inflation
   c. Cost-push inflation
   d. Deficiency inflation
2. Demand-pull inflation can be caused by
   a. Excessive wage demands
   b. Price hikes by firms with enormous market power
   c. Rapid increase in the price of oil and other important inputs
   d. Rapid increases in the money supply
3. Inflation defined as too much money chasing too few goods is
   a. Demand-pull inflation
   b. Cost-push inflation
   c. Sellers' inflation
   d.N one of the above
4. Theories of inflation that emphasize increases in aggregate demand are called
   a. Price-push inflation
   b. Excess demand inflation

c. Wage inflation
d. None of the above

5. According to the monetary theory of inflation, the prime cause of inflation is
   a. Reductions in the money supply, which force interest rates up
   b. Reductions in government spending, which reduce taxes and increase overall spending
   c. Increases in the money supply, which lead to an increase in aggregate expenditure
   d. Increases in government spending, which reduce private sector spending
6. Which of the following is an example of cost-push inflation?
   a. Sellers' inflation
   b. Wage inflation
   c. Neither (a) nor (b)
   d. Both (a) and (b)
7. Cost-push inflation can be initiated by
   a. An upward shift in the aggregate supply curve
   b. A downward shift in the aggregate supply curve
   c. Severe reductions in the money supply
   d. None of the above
8. Government deficit spending can result in
   a. Cost-push inflation
   b. Demand-pull inflation
   c. Deficiency in aggregate expenditure
   d. None of the above
9. If there is significant unemployment and inflation at the same time, the inflation is likely to be of the
   a. Demand-pull variety
   b. Cost-push variety
   c. Seasonal variety
   d. None of the above
10. The simultaneous existence of inflation and unemployment is known as
    a. The business cycle
    b. The Phillips curve
    c. Stagflation
    d. Depression
11. If the aggregate supply curve shifts to the left,
    a. The price level will fall and real output will rise
    b. The price level will rise and real output will fall
    c. The price level and real output will both fall
    d. The price level and real output will both rise
12. According to the accelerationists,
    a. There is a stable long-run trade-off between inflation and unemployment
    b. The short-run Phillips curve is vertical
    c. The long-run Phillips curve is vertical
    d. None of the above
13. The imposition of wage and price controls is designed to
    a. Shift the Phillips curve to the left
    b. Deal with the problem of stagflation
    c. Reduce inflation without increasing unemployment
    d. All of the above
14. Tax-based incomes policies
    a. Provide incentives for firms to keep wage increases down
    b. Always result in rapid inflation
    c. Encourage unions to demand higher wages and firms to comply with the demand for higher wages
    d. All of the above
15. The adaptive expectations hypothesis states that
    a. Past inflation rates have no effect on people's inflationary expectations
    b. People incorporate anti-inflationary policies in their inflationary expectations
    c. People are quite adaptive and therefore do not have inflationary expectations
    d. People base their inflationary expectations solely on past experiences with inflation
16. Rational expectations theorists conclude that
    a. Stabilization policies will be extremely effective
    b. Stabilization policies will be ineffective
    c. Only fiscal policy will have any effect on economic activity
    d. None of the above
17. In the new classical macroeconomic model,
    a. Wages and prices are assumed to be fixed even in the long run
    b. Wages and prices are quite flexible and adjust quickly
    c. The long-run aggregate supply curve is horizontal
    d. None of the above
18. According to new classical macroeconomists,
    a. Monetary and fiscal policies must always be used to force the economy to long-run equilibrium
    b. Activist macroeconomic stabilization policies are unnecessary
    c. The price level and wages are inflexible in the short run
    d. The Phillips curve does not exist
19. Which of the following is a tenet of the new Keynesian macroeconomic model?
    a. Wages and prices may be rigid and may not adjust in the very short run
    b. In the long run, the economy will eventually return to full-employment equilibrium
    c. Negotiated wage contracts, small menu costs, and the practice of markup pricing may prevent wages and prices from being flexible
    d. All of the above

20. In the new Keynesian macroeconomic model,

a. The very short-run aggregate supply curve is vertical
b. The aggregate demand curve is upward sloping because of the rapid adjustment of wages and prices
c. The long-run aggregate supply curve is vertical
d. None of the above

Problems and Exercises (Use Quad Paper for Graphs)

Answers to these questions can be found on MyEconLab at www.myeconlab.com. MyEconLab

1. Table 16.5 gives data for the Canadian economy from 1986 to 2004. Study the data in the table and then answer the following questions.

Table 16.5 Canadian Economic Data 1999–2009

Year	% Change in M1	% Change in Real Output	% Change in CPI	Deficit (–) or Surplus (+) ($ mil)
1999	7.8	5.5	1.8	2 787
2000	12.3	5.3	2.7	6 999
2001	12.2	1.5	2.5	9 213
2002	6.2	3.0	2.2	7 348
2003	5.9	2.0	2.8	1 664
2004	9	3.0	1.8	2 126
2005	6.4	3.0	2.2	5 117
2006	10.2	2.7	2.0	9 541
2007	6.8	2.0	2.2	7 492
2008	12.8	–0.3	2.3	12 761
2009	13	–1.9	0.3	883

Sources: Statistics Canada, *Canadian Economic Observer* (Catalogue no. 11-210-XPB), pp. 6, 13, 43, 99; Statistics Canada, CANSIM, table 326-0021 and Catalogue nos. 62-001-X, 62-010-X, and 62-557-X. www40.statcan.ca/l01/cst01/econ46a.htm. Extracted March 23, 2011.

a. Do the data seem to support the monetary theory of inflation?
b. In 2000, 2001, 2008, and 2009, the rate of monetary expansion was relatively high, yet the rate of inflation in those years was relatively low. Is this a refutation of the monetary theory of inflation?
c. In 2008 and 2009, real output decreased by -0.3%, and -1.9%, respectively. What monetary policy measure would you have prescribed?
d. Do the data seem to support the budget deficit theory of inflation?

2. Suppose to combat inflation, the Canadian government introduces legislation forbidding wage settlements in excess of 4% annually. What type of inflation is assumed by the government?
3. Suppose that the government decides to fight inflation by raising interest rates and increasing taxes on disposable income. What type of inflation is assumed by the government?
4. Draw an aggregate demand–aggregate supply diagram and use it to explain how an increase in the price level and an increase in unemployment may occur simultaneously.
5. Draw a diagram to illustrate the view that stagflation in the 1970s may have been due, at least in part, to increases in the price of oil.
6. The United States is our largest trading partner. Explain how inflation in the United States might be imported into Canada.

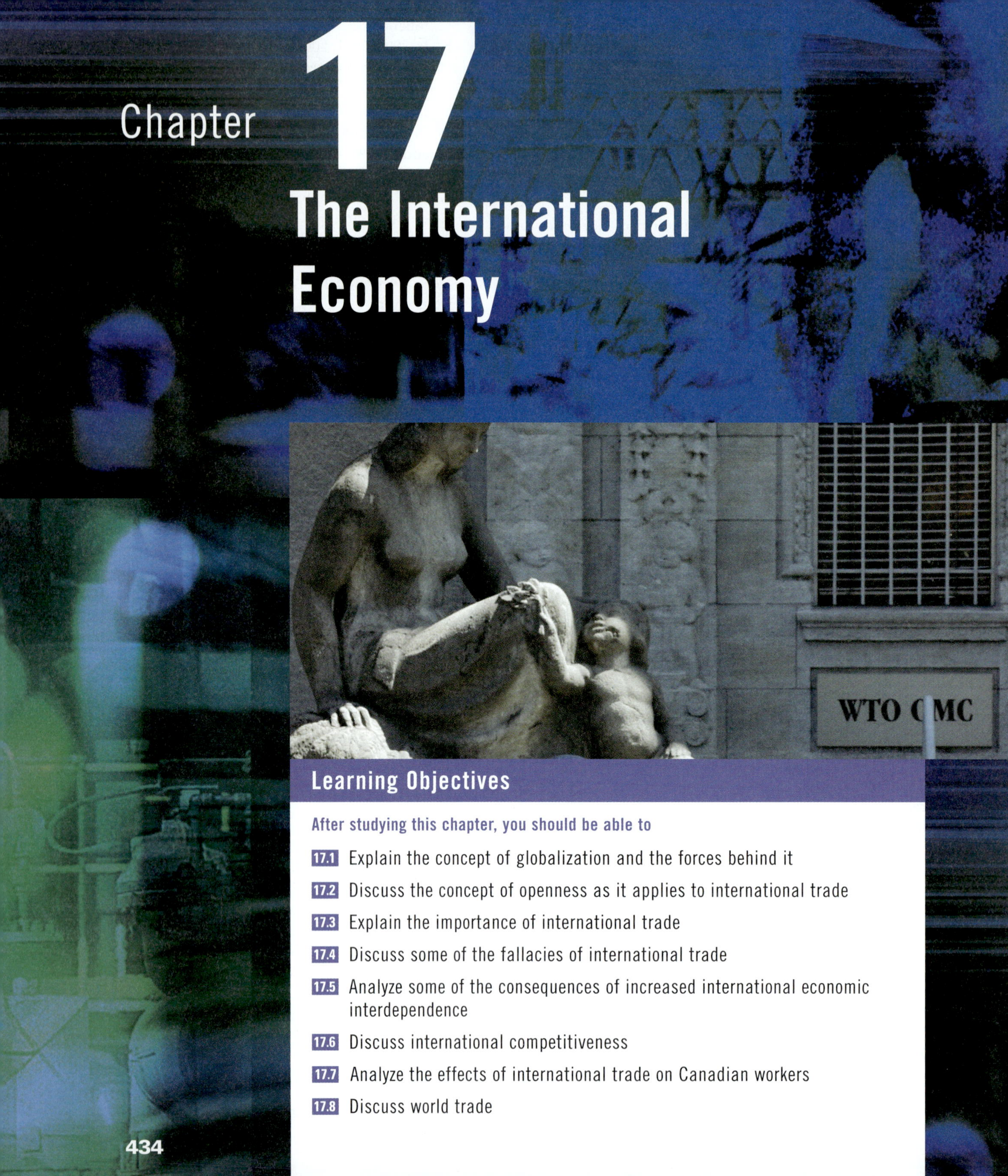

Chapter 17 The International Economy

Learning Objectives

After studying this chapter, you should be able to

- 17.1 Explain the concept of globalization and the forces behind it
- 17.2 Discuss the concept of openness as it applies to international trade
- 17.3 Explain the importance of international trade
- 17.4 Discuss some of the fallacies of international trade
- 17.5 Analyze some of the consequences of increased international economic interdependence
- 17.6 Discuss international competitiveness
- 17.7 Analyze the effects of international trade on Canadian workers
- 17.8 Discuss world trade

Assess Your Knowledge

MyEconLab

Answers to these questions can be found on MyEconLab at **www.myeconlab.com.**

1. What is globalization?
2. What is an open economy?
3. Is the following statement true or false? If two nations engage in international trade, one can gain only if the other loses.

LO 17.1 Explain the concept of globalization and the forces behind it

The Globalization of Economic Activity

We have heard the term *globalization* with increasing frequency over the past few years. What exactly is globalization?

globalization the increasingly rapid flow of capital, information, goods and services, communication, and people internationally

international trade the exchange of goods and services between countries

Some concepts are not easy to define even if we know what they mean. Globalization is one of them. However, we offer the following definition: **globalization** describes the increasingly rapid flow of capital, information, goods and services, communication, and people internationally. Globalization is related to **international trade**, the exchange of goods and services between countries.

Indeed, the term *era of globalization* is now being used to define our modern world. Some people see globalization as the internationalization of business, but this view places an unrealistic limitation on the applicability of the concept and ignores the political, social, and cultural dimensions of globalization.

Why has globalization proceeded at such a rapid pace?

There are three main driving forces behind globalization: (1) the political force, (2) the technological force, and (3) the economic and financial force.

trade liberalization the reduction or elimination of trade barriers among nations

tariff a tax on imported goods

The Political Driving Force Economic relations among sovereign nations have been facilitated by **trade liberalization** (the reduction or elimination of trade barriers among nations). Through rounds of multilateral trade negotiations, there have been significant reductions or complete elimination of import tariffs and other barriers. A **tariff** is a tax on imported goods. Countries that once placed high tariffs on international trade have now lowered these walls from double digits to low single digits. At the same time, most restrictions on quantities traded have been removed. These changes have provided an impetus for globalization.

The Technological Driving Force No force has propelled globalization more than technology. Information and telecommunications technology, such as the computer and the internet, and modern transportation systems have allowed decision makers to save a great deal of time and to overcome the limitations imposed by geography. The technological force has expanded the range of goods that can be produced, and developments in communication and transportation have brought people in different countries closer together for the purpose of trading.

The Economic and Financial Driving Force Over the years, international investment transactions have become increasingly liberal, and the development of international financial markets has facilitated international business transactions. These developments have fuelled international trade and globalization.

Reading Comprehension

The answers to these questions can be found on MyEconLab at www.myeconlab.com. MyEconLab

1. Briefly describe the condition to which the term *era of globalization* refers.
2. Discuss the forces that have fuelled globalization.
3. What role has technology played in the process of globalization?

LO 17.2 Discuss the concept of openness as it applies to international trade

The Openness of the Canadian Economy

What does openness mean in the context of international trade?

open economy an economy that engages in international trade

Let's begin by defining an open economy. An **open economy** is one that engages in international trade. The concept of openness is directly related to the concept of an open economy. *Openness* can be defined as the extent of involvement in international economic transactions. An economy with a relatively large foreign sector is more open than one with a relatively small foreign sector.

How dependent is the Canadian economy on international trade?

exports goods and services sold to foreign countries

A rough measure of the dependence of an economy on international trade is the ratio of its **exports** to its total output or GDP. Historically, the growth of the Canadian economy has been tied to foreign trade. During the colonial period, Canada exported mainly resources and imported finished goods. Today, the country is still heavily dependent on international trade. The now popular phrase of John Donne (1572–1631), "No man is an island, entire of itself," is certainly true of Canada as far as the international economy is concerned.

Canada's exports as a percentage of its GDP now stand at about 30%. We depend on world markets for the sale of our products, and many of the goods that we buy from foreign countries would be significantly more costly if we were to produce them domestically. Just imagine doing without your early morning orange juice or coffee—or paying the price if they were somehow produced in Canada instead!

How open is the Canadian economy compared with other major economies?

To answer that question, let's look at export/GDP ratios for a few selected countries. Table 17.1 contains the relevant data.

As the data show, Canada is more open than many other countries, including Brazil, China, Japan, and the United Kingdom, but it is also less open than Norway, the Netherlands, and Germany.

Table 17.1 Exports of Goods and Services as a Percentage of GDP, 2009

Country	Exports as % of GDP
Netherlands	66.3
Norway	49.6
Germany	45.3
Canada	30.5
Australia	23.7
France	23.6
Mexico	19.4
United Kingdom	18.5
Japan.	16.9
China	15.3
Argentina	11.4
Brazil	9.1
United States	8.6

Source: *The World Factbook*, Central Intelligence Agency.

Reading Comprehension

The answers to these questions can be found on MyEconLab at www.myeconlab.com. MyEconLab

1. How dependent is the Canadian economy on international trade? How can this dependence be measured?
2. "Canada's economy is one of the most open among industrial countries." Comment briefly.

LO 17.3 Explain the importance of international trade

The Importance of International Trade

It is obvious that international trade enables us to consume items that would be too costly or impossible for us to produce. Is there any other reason why international trade is important?

law of comparative advantage the general idea that trading partners can benefit mutually if each specializes in an activity in which it has a relative advantage

We can consider two main reasons for the importance of international trade. First, it allows nations to specialize in the production of things that they can produce at relatively low cost and then use the proceeds from these activities to purchase from abroad those things that they can produce only at relatively high cost. By so doing, the trading countries' joint output is higher than would be possible without specialization and trade. This notion is referred to as the **law of comparative advantage**. The law of comparative advantage is the general idea that trading partners can benefit mutually if each specializes in an activity in which it has a relative advantage.

Second, international trade increases competition, which in turn increases efficiency. Competition forces firms to be efficient or be forced out of the market. Competition from foreign producers provides a rather powerful incentive for domestic producers to reduce cost and improve quality. For example, stiff competition from Japanese auto manufacturers has resulted in better automobiles from North American auto manufacturers. Failure to at least keep up with the competition would result in loss of market share. Consequently, we are able to purchase reliable cars at reasonable prices.

Reading Comprehension

The answers to these questions can be found on MyEconLab at www.myeconlab.com. MyEconLab

1. Briefly explain the importance of international trade.
2. State the law of comparative advantage.

LO 17.4 Discuss some of the fallacies of international trade

Common Fallacies of International Trade

The previous section seems to argue against the idea that one trading partner can benefit only at the expense of another. Can you comment on this?

zero-sum game a situation in which one partner can gain only at the expense of the other

Your observation is correct. In fact, the erroneous belief that one trading partner can benefit only if another partner loses is one of the common fallacies of international trade. The truth is, trade is not a **zero-sum game**, where one can gain only at the expense of another. Both partners gain from international trade. Canada and Mexico, for example, are able to produce a larger joint output of wheat and coffee if Canada produces wheat and Mexico produces coffee. By specializing, Mexicans gain by purchasing wheat from Canada, using their revenue from coffee. Simultaneously, Canadians gain by using their revenue from wheat to purchase coffee from Mexico.

Are there other fallacious notions about international trade?

imports goods and services bought from foreign countries

It would be surprising if the fallacy of zero-sum trade were the only one in international trade. In fact, there are others. Let us consider the popular notion that a restriction on international trade saves jobs. Some people believe that by restricting foreigners from selling to us, we can promote employment at home. The truth is that a reduction in **imports**(goods and services bought from foreign countries) implies a reduction in the ability of foreigners to buy our goods and services. So our exports will fall, resulting in a possible loss of jobs in the exporting industries.

Another common fallacy is that exports stimulate domestic economic activity while imports depress the economy. This fallacy demonstrates a failure to recognize the inseparable link between imports and exports. The fact is, when Canadians import coffee from Mexico, it enables Mexicans to purchase our telecommunication devices. If Mexicans are prevented from selling to Canadians, then they will not be able to buy from Canadians. As a consequence, when our imports decrease, production and employment in our export industries will also decline.

Reading Comprehension

The answers to these questions can be found on MyEconLab at www.myeconlab.com. MyEconLab

1. Can all countries that engage in international trade benefit from trade?
2. Mention one popular fallacy about international trade.

LO 17.5 Analyze some of the consequences of increased international economic interdependence

Consequences of Increased International Economic Interdependence

What are some of the consequences of increased openness for the Canadian economy?

There is no doubt that the world economies have become increasingly interdependent. This interdependence is evidenced by the global impact of the financial crisis and the recession (2007–2009) that originated in the United States, and more recently by fears that the Greece economic crisis (2010) could spill over into other countries and could even spark a global crisis.

One of the consequences of increased international economic interdependence is increased vulnerability of the domestic economy to international disturbances. Imagine the effect of a prolonged Middle East war that disrupts the flow of Middle East oil to Canada. This would affect fuel prices in Canada. It must be pointed out, however, that there is another side to this coin. During periods of general shortages in Canada, domestic consumption may be satisfied from imports from the rest of the world.

economic policy a course of action designed to achieve an economic objective

Another consequence of increased openness is that it can dampen the effects of domestic **economic policy**. Economic policy is any course of action designed to achieve an economic objective. Suppose the government wants to stimulate domestic spending by reducing taxes, thereby leaving more money in the hands of Canadians. Because of the relative openness of the Canadian economy, a good portion of the resulting spending will go toward imported goods; thus, the impact on domestic spending will be reduced.

Reading Comprehension

The answers to these questions can be found on MyEconLab at www.myeconlab.com. MyEconLab

1. Increased openness has certain adverse consequences for an economy. What are some of these adverse consequences?
2. Make a case for increased economic cooperation among nations.

LO 17.6 Discuss international competitiveness

International Competitiveness

What does competitiveness mean and why are nations concerned about it?

Firms often advertise that their prices are competitive. They mean that their prices are not out of line with the prices for similar products in the marketplace. If a Canadian manufacturer can produce a better telecommunication device at a lower cost than a British manufacturer, then it is more competitive. We can define **competitiveness** as the extent to which a firm or an industry can compete with another in the marketplace on the basis of price or quality of product.

competitiveness the extent to which a firm or an industry can compete with another in the marketplace on the basis of price or quality of product

Nations are concerned about the competitiveness of their firms and industries for the simple reason that it is difficult for uncompetitive firms and industries to survive in the global marketplace. If North American auto manufacturers are uncompetitive, the Toyotas and the Hondas will drive them out of the market.

There seems to be a close relationship between competitiveness and productivity. Is there?

There certainly is! Let us think of productivity as output per worker. Consider two firms, A and B. If the productivity of the workers in firm A increases at a faster rate than that of the workers in firm B, then unit cost in firm A will decrease over time relative to unit cost in firm B. Thus, firm A will become relatively more competitive than firm B.

What are the main factors that affect a firm's or an industry's competitiveness?

Factors that affect competitiveness are

- Worker skills and motivation
- The level of technology at the firm's disposal
- The quantity and quality of its physical and financial resources
- The internal organizational structure
- Its scale of operation

To these must be added the nature of the economy's infrastructure (roads, water supply system, power supply, etc.) and public institutions, such as education and health.

How can we assess international competitiveness?

The competitiveness of a nation is much more difficult to assess than that of a firm or industry. The following facts underlie the difficulty of evaluating international competitiveness:

1. A nation can be competitive even if not all of its firms and industries are competitive
2. A nation can be competitive even if its imports exceed its exports, that is, even if it has a **balance of trade deficit**
3. The ability to create jobs does not necessarily make a nation competitive
4. Low wages do not necessarily make a nation competitive

balance of trade deficit the excess of imports over exports

A nation can be competitive in one area but not in another. For example, Canada is much more competitive than Bangladesh in the production of high-tech devices but much less competitive in the production of cane sugar. As a general rule, we can assess the competitiveness of a nation by its exports and its imports. If we export an item, we are relatively more competitive in that item than the country to which we export the item; and if we import an item, then the country from which we import the item is relatively more competitive than we are in that imported item.

Reading Comprehension

The answers to these questions can be found on MyEconLab at www.myeconlab.com. MyEconLab

1. What is the relationship between competitiveness and productivity?
2. Why are nations so concerned about competitiveness?
3. Mention three factors that affect competitiveness.

LO 17.7 Analyze the effects of international trade on Canadian workers

International Trade and the Canadian Worker

Do all workers gain from international trade?

Most, but not all, workers benefit from international trade. It allows workers as consumers to purchase goods that are cheapest. It also allows employers to use technology that increases employee productivity. As a country produces goods for export, it generates employment and income for workers in the exporting sector. Workers in such industries extol the virtues of international trade because they are aware that their jobs and standard of living depend on it.

But not all workers benefit from international trade, and some may actually be harmed, at least temporarily. Many Canadian workers feel threatened with a possible loss of their jobs because of cheap imports produced by lower-cost foreign workers, or because Canadian manufacturers may set up plants in foreign countries to take advantage of cheap labour and lax environmental standards. Other workers fear that immigrants from low-wage countries will offer to work for lower wages.

Reading Comprehension

The answers to these questions can be found on MyEconLab at www.myeconlab.com. MyEconLab

1. Is it true that imports into Canada will necessarily hurt Canadian workers?
2. Some workers benefit from international trade while others lose. Explain.

LO 17.8 Discuss world trade

World Trade

The importance of international trade has now been firmly established. Is there an organization whose main purpose is to promote trade among nations?

In fact, there is: the World Trade Organization (WTO). Before the establishment of the WTO in 1995, trade agreements were dealt with under the General Agreement on Tariff and Trade (GATT). The main objective of the WTO is "to help trade flow smoothly, freely and predictably." It is the only global international organization dealing with the rules of trade between nations. The WTO is headquartered in Geneva, Switzerland. In July 2008, some 153 countries were members of the WTO.

What exactly does the WTO do?

An official document of the WTO states that it

- Administers trade agreements between nations
- Acts as a forum for trade negotiations
- Settles trade disputes
- Reviews national trade policies
- Assists developing countries in trade policy issues, through technical assistance and training programs
- Cooperates with other international organizations

Where does Canada stand among the leading traders of the world?

Canada occupies a prominent position as a leading world trader. To hold the 11th position as an exporter and the 11th position as an importer is to rank highly among the largest trading countries of the world. Table 17.2 ranks the 20 leading world traders.

How does the rate of growth of world trade compare with the rate of growth of world output?

Under the GATT and the WTO, the rate of growth of world trade has outstripped the rate of growth of world output by a wide margin. This pattern has increased the degree to which national economies rely on international trade in overall economic activity. Nations now rely on international trade more than ever.

How large is the world economy?

The size of an economy can be considered from a variety of perspectives such as the size of its GDP, the size of its labour force, the size of its population, or the volume of its expenditure, depending on what one wants to capture. However, to provide some idea of the size of the global economy, we can look at certain key economic variables. Table 17.3 contains the relevant data. In addition to providing measures that give some indication of the size of the world economy, we provide a few other economic data about the world economy. In Table 17.3, we include data about the U.S. economy and the Canadian economy to serve as a benchmark for the data for the world economy.

Table 17.2 The Top 20 Leading Exporters and Importers, 2008

Rank	Exporters	Value (US $ bil)	Rank	Importers	Value (US $ bil)
1	Germany	1461.9	1	United States	2169.5
2	China	1428.3	2	Germany	1203.8
3	United States	1278.4	3	China	1132.5
4	Japan	782.0	4	Japan	762.6
5	Netherlands	633.0	5	France	705.6
6	France	605.4	6	United Kingdom	632.0
7	Italy	538.0	7	Netherlands	573.2
8	Belgium	475.6	8	Italy	554.9
9	Russian Federation	471.6	9	Belgium	495.5
10	United Kingdom	458.6	10	Korea, Republic of	435.3
11	Canada	456.5	11	Canada	418.3
12	Korea, Republic of	422.0	12	Spain	401.4
13	Hong Kong	370.2	13	Hong Kong	393.0
14	Singapore	338.2	14	Mexico	323.2
15	Saudi Arabia	313.4	15	Singapore	319.8
16	Mexico	291.7	16	India	293.4
17	Spain	268.3	17	Russian Federation	291.9
18	Taipei	255.6	18	Taipei	240.4
19	United Arab Emirates	231.6	19	Poland	204.3
20	Switzerland	200.3	20	Turkey	202.0

Source: International Trade Statistics, 2009. World Trade Organization, http://www.wto.org/english/res_e/statis_e/its2009_e/its09_world_trade_dev_e.pdf.

Table 17.3 The World Economy at a Glance, 2010

Item	World	United States	Canada
Population (billion)	6.77	0.31	0.03
Population growth rate (%)	1.13	0.97	0.82
Labour force (billion)	3.23	0.15	0.018
Unemployment rate (%)	8.8	9.6	8.0
Money stock ($ trillion)	22.4	1.74	0.05
Gross domestic product ($ tril)	74.43	14.72	1.33
Real GDP growth rate (%)	4.6	2.8	3.0
Exports ($ tril)	14.9	1.27	0.4
Imports ($ tril)	14.68	1.90	0.4
Public debt (% of GDP)	58.3	58.9	82.9

Source: CIA *World Fact Book*. https://www.cia.gov/library/publications/the-world-factbook/

The WTO is the organization that is concerned mainly with world trade. Are there other organizations that we should be familiar with in this context?

Yes. It would be helpful to know something about the United Nations Conference on Trade and Development (UNCTAD) and the International Monetary Fund (IMF). Let us begin with UNCTAD.

The UNCTAD was established in 1964. The organization is concerned with promoting the integration of developing countries into the world economy. According to UNCTAD:

> "The organization works to fulfil this mandate by carrying out **three key functions**:
>
> - It functions as a **forum for intergovernmental deliberations**, supported by discussions with experts and exchanges of experience, aimed at **consensus building**.
> - It undertakes **research, policy analysis and data collection** for the debates of government representatives and experts.
> - It provides **technical assistance** tailored to the specific requirements of developing countries, with special attention to the needs of the least developed countries and of economies in transition. When appropriate, UNCTAD cooperates with other organizations and donor countries in the delivery of technical assistance."

UNCTAD consists of 193 members, and Canada is a member of its Trade and Development Board.

What about the International Monetary Fund?

The IMF is an international organization of 187 countries. The main purpose of the IMF is to make sure that the international monetary system is stable. The international monetary system is the system of exchange rates and international payments that facilitates transactions between countries. According to the IMF, it:

> "promotes international monetary cooperation and exchange rate stability, facilitates the balanced growth of international trade, and provides resources to help members in balance of payments difficulties or to assist with poverty reduction."

Joining the IMF on December 27, 1945, Canada was one of its 37 original members.

Reading Comprehension

The answers to these questions can be found on MyEconLab at www.myeconlab.com. MyEconLab

1. How important is Canada on the world trading state?
2. Mention four of the world's leading exporters and importers.
3. Give some indication of the size of the world economy.
4. What is the role of the World Trade Organization?
5. What is the United Nations Conference on Trade and Development (UNCTAD) and what does it do?
6. What is the IMF and what is its main purpose?

Review

1. Review the learning objectives listed at the beginning of the chapter.
2. Have you accomplished all the objectives? One way to determine this is toanswer the Reading Comprehension Questions at the end of each section. This will help you assess the extent to which you have accomplished the learning objectives.
3. If you have not accomplished an objective, review the relevant material before proceeding.

Key Points to Remember

1. LO 17.1 National economies have become increasingly interdependent economically. International trade in resources, goods and services, and technology is now common practice in most countries.
2. LO 17.1 Globalization refers to the increasing flow of capital, information, and people among the countries of the world. It implies increased international economic interdependence. The main forces that have propelled globalization include trade liberalization; technological advances in computers, communication, information, and transportation; and the development of international financial markets.
3. LO 17.2 The Canadian economy is a relatively open economy. Its export to GDP ratio is about 38%. International trade has played, and continues to play, an important role in its economic progress.
4. LO 17.3 International trade is important because it permits a higher standard of living than would be possible without it. It also increases competition, which increases efficiency.
5. LO 17.4 Common fallacies of international trade include (1) the notion that one country can benefit from trade only if another country loses, (2) the idea that trade restrictions save jobs, and (3) the notion that exports are good while imports are bad for an economy.
6. LO 17.5 Increased international economic interdependence makes an economy vulnerable to disturbances abroad and may diminish the impact of domestic economic policy.
7. LO 17.6 Competitiveness refers to the extent to which the products of a firm or an industry can compete in the marketplace with regard to price and quality. A country's relative competitiveness can be assessed by its exports and its imports, because it will tend to export items in which it is relatively competitive and import those in which it is relatively less competitive.
8. LO 17.7 International trade benefits most workers in the long run but may harm some workers, especially in the short run.
9. LO 17.8 The World Trade Organization (WTO) promotes trade among nations and settles trade disputes among them. Canada ranks among the top 11 trading nations of the world. Germany, China, the United States, and Japan hold the top spots. Among other important international organizations are the United Nations Conference on Trade and Development (UNCTAD) and the International Monetary Fund (IMF).

Economic Word Power

Balance of trade deficit (p. 440)
Competitiveness (p. 440)
Economic policy (p. 439)
Exports (p. 436)
Globalization (p. 435)
Imports (p. 438)
International trade (p. 435)
Law of comparative advantage (p. 437)
Open economy (p. 436)
Tariff (p. 435)
Trade liberalization (p. 435)
Zero-sum game (p. 438)

Problems and Exercises

Basic

1. LO 17.1 Indicate whether each of the following would be classified as a political force (P), a technological force (T), or an economic force (E):
   a. International capital flows
   b. Growth of international financial markets
   c. Developments in international communication
   d. High-speed electronic information flow
   e. Trade liberalization
   f. The formation of trading blocs among nations
2. LO 17.2 State, giving reasons, whether the following statement is true or false: "The larger the volume of a country's exports, the more open its economy."
3. LO 17.3 List three specific benefits that Canada derives from international trade.
4. LO 17.4 Detect the error (if any) in the following argument: "Canada should restrict imports into the country because it is better for us to produce the imported items ourselves."
5. LO 17.6 Construct an example to show that uncompetitive industries in a global setting can be driven out of the market.

Questions in the Intermediate and Challenging Sections cover several different concepts, and have not been organized by learning objectives.

Intermediate

1. Present an argument to support the view that trade liberalization can adversely affect Canadian industries.
2. In 2007, countries A and B had the data shown in Table 17.4.

Table 17.4 Economic Data for A and B

Country	Exports ($ mil)	GDP ($ mil)	Export/GDP Ratio (%)
A	130.6	326.5	
B	180.7	602.3	

   a. Complete the export/GDP ratio column.
   b. Which of the two economies is more open?
3. Demonstrate that an economy can become more open even if the volume of its exports falls.

Challenging

1. In country A, capital is abundant, while in country B, labour is abundant. Assume that capital and labour are immobile between A and B. Show that trade between A and B will tend to equalize the prices of capital and labour in both countries.
2. Present an argument to convince Canadian workers that they can be made better off through international trade.

Study Guide

Self-Assessment

What's your score?

Circle the letter that corresponds with the correct answer.

1. Globalization refers to
   a. The distribution of trade to just a few global players
   b. The firm grip that the United States and its allies have on global trade
   c. The increasing pace of international exchanges of capital, information, and goods and services
   d. Attempts to create a single nation state in the world
2. Which of the following has been a significant factor in the globalization process?
   a. The erection of high tariff walls
   b. Technological advances
   c. Restrictions on the quantity of imports
   d. Wars and other disruptions in the world
3. A successful "buy Canadian" campaign by unions will *ultimately*
   a. Increase both imports and exports
   b. Increase imports but reduce exports
   c. Reduce imports and exports
   d. Reduce imports and increase exports
4. An open economy is one in which
   a. There are very few laws that control people's behaviour
   b. The open expression of personal opinions is not suppressed
   c. Passports are not required for travel
   d. None of the above
5. The openness of an economy can be measured by
   a. The size of the geographical space occupied by the country
   b. The extent to which its borders are guarded
   c. The size of the population
   d. The value of its exports divided by its gross domestic product
6. What percentage of its total production of goods and services does Canada export?
   a. About 7%
   b. About 40%
   c. About 55%
   d. About 15%
7. International trade is important because
   a. It enables us to consume items that would be too costly for us to produce
   b. It results in an increase in the joint outputs of trading partners
   c. It results in increased efficiency
   d. All of the above
8. According to the law of comparative advantage,
   a. Large countries take unfair advantage of small countries
   b. Large countries can benefit from international trade only at the expense of small countries
   c. The gains from trade will be relatively small
   d. None of the above
9. International trade tends to
   a. Increase competition
   b. Reduce competition
   c. Reduce efficiency
   d. Reduce productivity
10. Which of the following is a fallacy of international trade?
    a. One trading partner can benefit only at the expense of another
    b. A restriction on international trade saves jobs
    c. Exports stimulate the domestic economy while imports depress it
    d. All of the above
11. Which of the following is true?
    a. International trade is a zero-sum game
    b. International trade can benefit all traders
    c. International trade reduces specialization
    d. None of the above
12. Restrictions on imports will *ultimately* result in
    a. Expansion of exports
    b. Reductions in exports
    c. No impact on exports
    d. None of the above
13. Increased international economic interdependence may
    a. Expose the domestic economy to external disturbances
    b. Enable the domestic economy to obtain needed supplies during a period of general shortage in the domestic economy
    c. Dampen the effects of economic policy on the domestic economy
    d. All of the above
14. The extent to which the products of a firm or an industry can compete in the market with respect to price and quality is referred to as
    a. Competitiveness
    b. Marketplace adjustment
    c. Quality assurance
    d. None of the above

15. International trade will tend to
    a. Support uncompetitive firms
    b. Punish uncompetitive firms
    c. Punish competitive firms
    d. None of the above
16. Productivity and competitiveness are
    a. Inversely related
    b. Directly related
    c. Unrelated
    d. Identical concepts
17. Which of the following is likely to affect a firm's competitiveness?
    a. Workers' skills and motivation
    b. Available technology
    c. The quality of its resources
    d. All of the above
18. International trade will likely
    a. Benefit all workers in the short run
    b. Harm all workers both in the short run and in the long run
    c. Harm some workers in the short run and benefit most workers in the long run
    d. Benefit all workers both in the short run and in the long run.
19. Over the past few decades, world trade has
    a. Grown at a much slower rate than world output
    b. Grown at a much faster rate than world output
    c. Grown at about the same rate as world output
    d. Actually declined at an increasing rate
20. Where does Canada rank in world trade?
    a. 1st place
    b. 29th place
    c. About 35th place
    d. About 11th place
21. The WTO was established in
    a. 1939
    b. 1995
    c. 1944
    d. 2005
22. Which of the following is a function of the WTO?
    a. It administers trade agreements
    b. It reviews national trade policies
    c. It cooperates with other international organizations
    d. All of the above
23. Which of the following is *not* a key function of the UNCTAD?
    a. It settles trade disputes among nations
    b. It serves as a forum for international governmental deliberations
    c. It engages in research and data collection
    d. It provides technical assistance to developing countries
24. The main purpose of the IMF is to
    a. Maintain tariffs between countries
    b. Discourage the movement of capital among nations
    c. Ensure the stability of the international monetary system
    d. None of the above

Problems and Exercises (Use Quad Paper for Graphs)

Answers to these questions can be found on MyEconLab at www.myeconlab.com. MyEconLab

1. From the following list, determine which items would promote globalization and which would impede it, and then complete Table 17.5:

Table 17.5 Impediments and Promoters of Globalization

Impediments	Promoters

    a. High tariff walls
    b. Rapid economic growth
    c. Technological progress
    d. A philosophy of self-sufficiency
    e. Trade embargo
    f. Trade liberalization
    g Development of international financial markets
    h. Development of rapid transportation systems
2. In Table 17.6, list three fallacious arguments of international trade in the left column, and list the corresponding correct views in the right column.

Table 17.6 Fallacies and Correct View on International Trade

Fallacious Arguments	Correct Views

3. Which of the following groups of products would you expect Canada to import instead of producing for itself? Explain your choice.
    a. Cane sugar, coffee, tea, coconuts
    b. Iron, steel, aluminum, automobiles; computers, telephones, wood furniture, and McIntosh apples

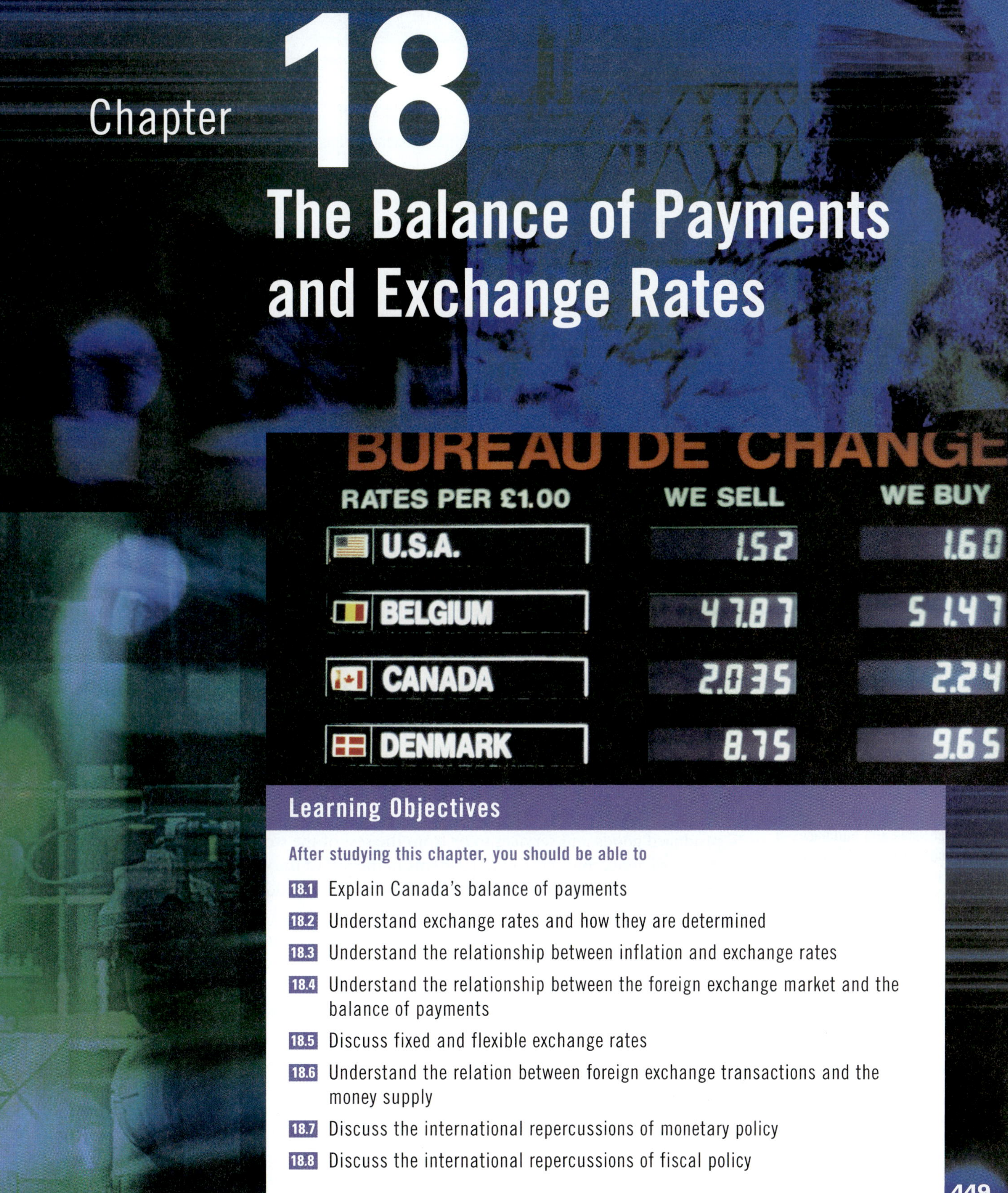

BUREAU DE CHANGE
RATES PER £1.00
WE SELL
WE BUY
U.S.A.
1.52
1.60
BELGIUM
47.87
51.47
CANADA
2.035
2.24
DENMARK
8.75
9.65

Chapter 18
The Balance of Payments and Exchange Rates

Learning Objectives

After studying this chapter, you should be able to

- **18.1** Explain Canada's balance of payments
- **18.2** Understand exchange rates and how they are determined
- **18.3** Understand the relationship between inflation and exchange rates
- **18.4** Understand the relationship between the foreign exchange market and the balance of payments
- **18.5** Discuss fixed and flexible exchange rates
- **18.6** Understand the relation between foreign exchange transactions and the money supply
- **18.7** Discuss the international repercussions of monetary policy
- **18.8** Discuss the international repercussions of fiscal policy

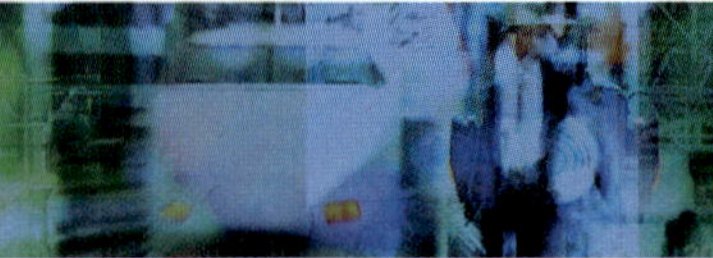

Assess Your Knowledge

MyEconLab

Answers to these questions can be found on MyEconLab at **www.myeconlab.com.**

1. What does a country's balance of payments show?
2. True (T) or false (F)? Canada's major economic transaction with the rest of the world involves exports and imports of goods and services.
3. Define *exchange rate.*
4. What do you think would happen to exports from Canada to the United States if the exchange value of the Canadian dollar fell from US$0.87 to US$0.82?

LO 18.1 Explain Canada's balance of payments

The Balance of Payments

What is the meaning of the balance of payments?

balance of payments a summary statement of international economic transactions

Economic transactions between Canada and the rest of the world are recorded in accounts called the balance of payments accounts. We can thus define the **balance of payments**as a summary statement of international economic transactions—that is, all transactions between residents of one country and residents in the rest of the world.

In recording entries in the balance of payments accounts, the procedure followed is that of recording transactions either as current account items or as capital account items. Accordingly, the balance of international payments is divided into two main parts: the current account and the capital account. Table 18.1 shows Canada's balance of international payments for 2010.

Some transactions result in the receipt of money by Canadian residents. Such transactions are "credit" entries and are therefore recorded with a plus sign (+) in the balance of payments. Transactions that result in the payment of money to foreigners by Canadian residents are "debit" items and are therefore entered with a minus sign (−) in the balance of payments.

current account a record of sales and purchases of currently produced goods and services to or from the rest of the world

Current Account The **current account** is a record of sales and purchases of currently produced goods and services to or from the rest of the world. Each year, Canadian residents sell goods and services to residents in the rest of the world. Canadian residents also buy goods and services from the rest of the world. In addition, they receive investment income from the rest of the world and make interest and dividend payments to the rest of the world. Transfer items are also included in the balance of payments. All these items are recorded in the current account section of the balance of payments. Let us examine these items a little more closely by looking at Table 18.1.

Exports and imports of goods constitute merchandise trade. Because exports result in a payment of money by foreign residents to Canadian residents, they are recorded as credit in the balance of payments. Imports, conversely, are recorded as debit because they lead to payment of money by Canadian residents to residents in the rest of the world. In 2010, Canada sold goods worth $404 543 million to the rest of the world, and purchased goods worth $413 110 million from the rest of the world. The difference

Table 18.1 Canada's Balance of International Payments, 2010

	Receipts (+) ($ mil)	Payments (−) ($ mil)	Balance ($ mil)
CURRENT ACCOUNT			
Total receipts	544 778	594 753	−49 976
Goods and services	474 632	506 508	−31 876
Goods	404 543	413 110	−8 567
Services	70 090	93 398	−23 309
Travel	16 263	30 382	−14 119
Transportation	11 364	21 492	−10 128
Other services	42 462	41 524	938
Investment income	61 430	77 093	−15 662
Direct investments	37 713	36 186	1 527
Portfolio investments	17 076	35 360	−18 284
Other investments	6 642	5 546	1 096
Transfers	8 715	11 153	−2 438
CAPITAL ACCOUNT			
Total capital and financial accounts, net flow			**55 546**
Capital account, net flow			**4 752**
Capital account, inflows			5 452
Capital account, outflows			−700
Financial account, net flow			**50 795**
Canadian assets, net flow			−97 496
Canadian direct investments abroad			−38 016
Canadian portfolio investments			−12 783
Foreign portfolio bonds			2 879
Foreign portfolio stocks			−13 220
Other Canadian investments			−46 697
Loans			−16 541
Deposits			−5 941
Official international reserves			−3 989
Other assets			−20 226
Canadian liabilities, net flow			148 291
Foreign direct investments in Canada			22 477
Foreign portfolio investments			116 239
Canadian portfolio bonds			95 747
Canadian portfolio stocks			17 353
Canadian money market			3 139
Other foreign investments			9 595
Loans			8 444
Deposits			65
Other liabilities			1 066
Statistical discrepancy			**−5 571**

Source (for Current Account): Statistics Canada. **http://www40.statcan.gc.ca/l01/cst01/econ01a-eng.htm**
Source (for Capital Account): Statistics Canada. **http://www40.statcan.gc.ca/l01/cst01/econ01b-eng.htm**
Extracted March 23, 2011.

balance of merchandise trade or balance of visible trade the difference between the value of goods exported and goods imported

balance of trade the difference between the value of a country's exports and the value of its imports

between total exports of goods and total imports of goods is called the **balance of merchandise trade** or the **balance of visible trade**.

In 2010, the merchandise trade balance was −$8567 million. When we include trade in services with trade in goods, we obtain the balance of trade. Services traded include tourist services, freight and shipping services, management, and insurance. We define the **balance of trade** as the difference between the value of a country's exports and the value of its imports

Is there any relationship between the balance of payments and GDP?

Indeed there is a link between the balance of payments and GDP. Recall that the expenditure approach to calculating the GDP can be expressed as

$$\text{GDP} = C + I + G + (X - M)$$

The last term $(X - M)$ in the above equation defines the balance of trade. It is what we referred to earlier in this text as net exports. Clearly, then, the balance of payments is linked to the GDP via the balance of trade or net exports.

A surplus in a country's balance of trade (i.e., a positive balance of trade) represents a debt owed to the country by the rest of the world. A deficit in a country's balance of trade (i.e., a negative balance of trade) represents a debt owed by the country to the rest of the world. Exports of goods and services from Canada totalled $474 632 million in 2010, consisting of $404 543 million worth of goods and $70 090 million worth of services. For the same period, imports of goods and services into Canada were valued at $506 508 million, consisting of $413 110 million worth of goods and $93 398 million worth of services. The balance of the trade in services was −$23 309 million.

Investment income is another major subheading in the current account section of the balance of payments. Canadian residents borrow funds from the rest of the world and also lend funds to the rest of the world. In 2010, Canadians received a total of $61 430 million as investment income in the form of interest and dividends. At the same time, they paid out a total of $77 093 in interest and dividends. The balance on this account was thus −$15 662. It is worth noting that for Canada, this investment account typically has a negative balance. In fact, the negative balance in this account is often a major contributor to Canada's current account deficit.

Why does Canada typically have a negative balance in its investment income account?

Investment income occurs as a result of investment in stocks and bonds. There is a substantial amount of foreign (mostly American) investment in Canada, so the foreign owners and lenders are paid dividends for their stocks and interest on their bonds. Canadian residents also have investments abroad, but the interest and dividends that they earn do not even come close to offsetting the interest and dividends paid to non-residents. This explains the huge deficit in the investment income account. Let's continue our analysis of the current account.

The next subcategory in the current account section of the balance of payments is transfers. Transfers include inheritances and immigrants' funds, personal and institutional remittances, withholding taxes, and official contributions. The funds that immigrants bring into Canada are recorded as a credit item under transfers. The funds that they send to their home country are recorded as a debit item. A withholding tax is a tax deducted from income payments to nonresidents. Official contributions include loans and grants made from Canada to foreign countries. In 2010, Canadians received a total of $8715 million as transfers, and paid out a total of $11 153 million. The balance on this account was −$2438 million. In 2010, the balance on the current account was −$49 976 million.

Capital Account Canada's trade with the rest of the world involves more than just trade in goods and services and the other items in the current account. It also involves trade in assets through international lending, borrowing, and investment. International purchases of stocks and bonds and direct foreign investments (such as the construction of factories abroad) are all recorded in the capital account. Whenever Canadian residents purchase or sell foreign assets, or whenever foreigners purchase or sell Canadian assets, the transactions are recorded in the **capital account**. The capital account is a record of international capital flows.

capital account a record of international capital flows

direct foreign investment the ownership or control of a business in a foreign country

portfolio foreign investment the purchase by foreigners of stocks and bonds whose term to maturity is more than one year

short-term capital flows the movement of financial assets whose term to maturity is less than one year

official reserves reserves held by a central bank to make international payments

special drawing rights (SDRs) deposits with the International Monetary Fund (IMF)

For convenience, we can classify the items in the capital account as longterm capital flows, shortterm capital flows, and changes in official reserves. Longterm capital flows include direct foreign investment and portfolio investment. **Direct foreign investment** is the ownership or control of a business in a foreign country. **Portfolio foreign investment** is the purchase by foreigners of stocks (shares) and bonds whose term to maturity is more than one year. Portfolio foreign investment does not imply ownership or control. **Short-term capital flows** refer to movement of financial assets whose term to maturity is less than one year.

The final item in the balance of payments to be discussed is official reserves. **Official reserves** are reserves held by a central bank to make international payments. They consist of gold, U.S. dollars, other major foreign currencies, and **special drawing rights (SDRs)**. Special drawing rights are deposits with the International Monetary Fund (IMF). They can be used as international money to settle indebtedness among nations.

The items in the capital account are arranged under two main subheadings in Table 18.1: Canadian assets (net flow) representing Canadian claims on nonresidents, and Canadian liabilities to non-residents (net flow). In 2010, claims on nonresidents totalled −$97 496 million, and Canadian liabilities on non-residents amounted to $148 291 million.

Note that when Canadians purchase foreign assets, the transaction is recorded as a debit item in the capital account because it results in an outflow of capital. Similarly, when foreigners purchase Canadian assets, the transaction is recorded as a credit item in the capital account because it results in an inflow of capital.

If there is a deficit in Canada's overall current and capital accounts, then the inadequacy must be made up by using reserve assets. Conversely, if there is a surplus in the overall current and capital accounts, the excess foreign exchange is added to Canada's foreign exchange reserves. The doubleentry system of bookkeeping used in recording the entries in the balance of payments means that the sum of all the credit items in the current and capital accounts, as well as the official settlements, must equal the sum of all the debit items. But because of estimation errors, there will be a discrepancy. The item in the balance of payments termed "statistical discrepancy" is designed to equalize the totals of debits and credits. Therefore, the balance of payments account always balances.

Reading Comprehension

The answers to these questions can be found on MyEconLab at www.myeconlab.com. MyEconLab

1. Give a brief account of the composition of a country's balance of payments.
2. Into which two main categories is the balance of payments divided? What does each section contain?
3. What is the difference between a balance of trade deficit and a current account deficit?
4. Explain why the balance of payments always balances.

LO 18.2 Understand exchange rates and how they are determined

foreign exchange market market in which foreign currencies are traded

exchange rate or foreign exchange rate the value of a country's currency in terms of another country's currency

flexible or freely fluctuating or floating exchange rate system an exchange rate determined by market forces

Exchange Rates

What is an exchange rate?

International economic transactions result in the payment of money by residents of one country to residents of another country. If a Canadian manufacturer exports goods to a customer in the United Kingdom, the Canadian manufacturer expects to be paid in Canadian dollars. Likewise, if a British supplier sells goods to a Canadian customer, the British supplier expects to be paid in British pounds. International trade therefore requires a mechanism through which the currency of one country can be converted into the currency of another country. The market in which foreign currencies are traded is called the **foreign exchange market**. The value of a country's currency in terms of another country's currency is called the **foreign exchange rate,** or simply the **exchange rate**. In other words, the exchange rate is the price of foreign currency.

Table 18.2 shows exchange rates for some of Canada's trading partners.

How is the exchange rate determined in the foreign exchange market?

The Foreign Exchange Market and Flexible Exchange Rates Figure 18.1 illustrates how the foreign exchange market determines the exchange rate. When a country decides to allow the market to determine the value of its currency, it is said to be on a **flexible** or **freely fluctuating** or **floating exchange rate system**. A flexible exchange rate is therefore an exchange rate determined by market forces.

Table 18.2 Prices of Various Currencies in Canadian Dollars, February 2011

Foreign Currency	Value in CDN $
United States dollar	0.976
United Kingdom pound sterling	1.927
Japanese yen	0.012
European euro	1.349
Mexican peso	0.085
Chinese renminbi (yuan)	0.501
Indian rupee	0.022
Brazil real	0.525
Australian dollar	0.996
Russian rouble	0.339

Source: Bank of Canada: **http://www.bankofcanada.ca/en/rates/exchange/daily-converter.html**

In Figure 18.1, we assume that the international traders are Canadians and British. The demand curve *DD* represents the demand for Canadian dollars by the British. There are three reasons that the British might want Canadian dollars (and thus supply British pounds on the foreign exchange market). First, they might want to buy Canadian goods. Because Canadian suppliers will expect payment in Canadian dollars, British importers of Canadian goods will need to purchase Canadian dollars on the foreign exchange market. Second, the British might want to invest in Canada. For instance, residents of Britain who want to buy shares in Canadian companies will need to convert their pounds into

Figure 18.1 Determination of Flexible Exchange Rates

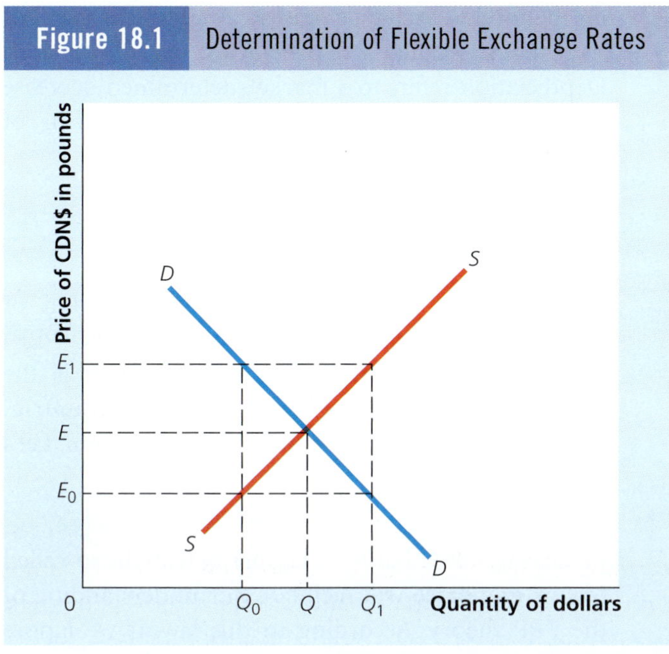

Canadian dollars for such investments. Finally, the British might want to hold Canadian dollars for speculative purposes. If they expect the value of the Canadian dollar to rise, they might increase their holdings of Canadian dollars in order to realize a capital gain.

Note that the demand for Canadian dollars by the British comes from the credit side of the balance of payments. The greater the number of pounds that have to be given up for Canadian dollars, the fewer dollars demanded by the British. The demand curve therefore slopes downward as shown in Figure 18.1.

The supply curve *SS* shows the supply of dollars by Canadians. Canadian residents supply Canadian dollars to the foreign exchange market for the same reasons that the British demand Canadian dollars. If Canadian residents want to purchase British goods or make investments in Britain or increase their holdings of British pounds for speculative purposes, they will require British pounds for these transactions. Note that the supply of Canadian dollars on the foreign exchange market comes from the debit side of the balance of payments. If the price of dollars (in terms of pounds) rises, Canadians will offer more dollars (buy more pounds). Therefore, the supply curve slopes upward, as shown in Figure 18.1.

At an exchange rate of E_1, Canadians are willing to supply $0Q_1$ Canadian dollars to the foreign exchange market, while the British want to buy only $0Q_0$. There is therefore a surplus of Canadian dollars on the foreign exchange market, which will force the exchange rate down. At an exchange rate of E_0, the quantity of dollars demanded by the British is greater than the quantity supplied by Canadians. This shortage of dollars on the market will bid the exchange rate up. The only exchange rate at which the quantity of dollars demanded equals the quantity supplied is *E*. Hence, the equilibrium exchange rate is *E*, where the demand and supply curves intersect, and the quantity of dollars traded is 0*Q*.

appreciation a market-determined increase in the value of a country's currency in terms of another country's currency

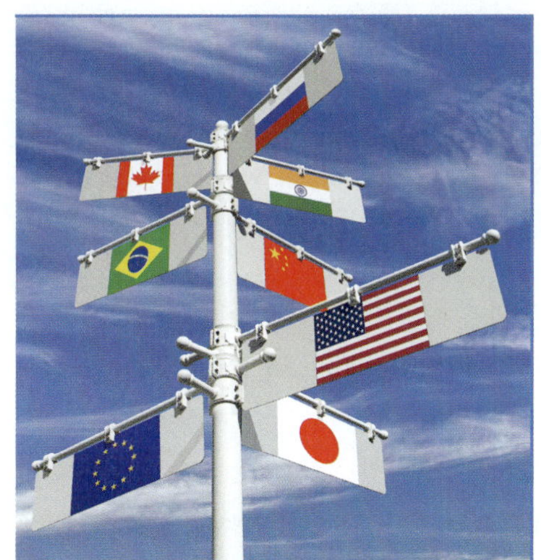

All these countries engage in international trade and are concerned with exchange rates.

What effect will an increase in the demand for Canadian goods have on the exchange rate?

We can now use the model of exchange rate determination to answer that question. If the foreign demand for Canadian goods increases, then foreigners will require more Canadian dollars to purchase Canadian exports. This increase in demand for Canadian dollars will shift the demand curve from *D* to D_1, as shown in Figure 18.2.

The increase in demand at an exchange rate of E results in a shortage of Canadian dollars on the foreign exchange market. Consequently, the exchange rate is bid up from *E* to E_1. This increase in the value of the Canadian dollar is called an **appreciation** of the Canadian currency. Appreciation refers to a market-determined increase in the value of a country's currency in terms of another country's currency. A fall in demand for Canadian goods would lower the value of the Canadian dollar

Figure 18.2 Effects of an Increase in Demand for Canadian Goods

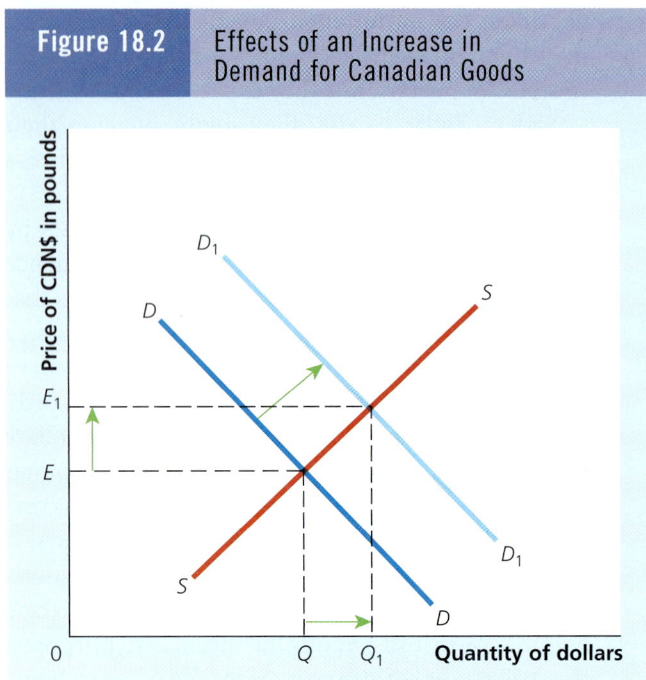

on the foreign exchange market. A fall in the value of a currency is called a **depreciation** of the currency. Depreciation refers to a market-determined decrease in the value of a country's currency in terms of another country's currency.

Is there an alternative method of determining the exchange rate?

An alternative approach to the determination of exchange rates is the purchasing power parity (PPP) theory approach. **Purchasing power parity** is the notion that the exchange rate between two countries will reflect the difference in prices between them. Let's examine this theory.

Purchasing Power Parity Familiarity with the so-called **law of one price** will facilitate our understanding of the PPP theory. According to this law, if we ignore transportation costs, customs duties, and other transaction costs associated with international trade, and if competition prevails, then the price of a good that is traded internationally will be the same wherever the good is traded. Thus, the law of one price states that the prices of traded goods should be the same everywhere after allowing for transportation and other transaction costs.

depreciation a market-determined decrease in the value of a country's currency in terms of another country's currency

purchasing power parity the notion that the exchange rate between two countries will reflect the difference in prices between them

law of one price the hypothesis that the prices of traded goods should be the same everywhere after allowing for transportation and other transaction costs

Why should the prices of traded goods be equalized?

Let us consider two neighbouring countries, Canada and the United States. According to the law of one price, the price of a CD player in Canada should be the same as an identical CD player in the United States. If the price were lower in the United States, Canadians would purchase their CD players in the United States instead of in Canada. Some traders might even find it profitable to buy CD players in the United States and sell them in Canada. Such transactions are referred to as *arbitrage transactions.* Arbitrage transactions would raise the price of CD players in the U.S. market and lower it in the Canadian market until the price was the same in both markets.

Now, to move from the law of one price to PPP is but a simple step. Let us assume that the cost of the CD player in Canada was CDN$400 while it was US$300 in the United States. Because, according to the law of one price, the price of the CD player must be the same in both countries, then

400 Canadian dollars = 300 U.S. dollars

That means that 1 Canadian dollar = 0.75 U.S. dollars. So the exchange rate between Canada and the United States should be

1 Canadian dollar for 0.75 U.S. dollar

The purchasing power parity (PPP) theory can be stated as follows:

> The purchasing power parity theory is the hypothesis that the exchange rate between two countries is that rate that equalizes the purchasing power of the currencies.

Example: A particular type of camera in Canada costs $500, whereas in Britain it costs £200. If the law of one price holds, what will be the exchange rate between Canada and Britain?

We know that

$$500 \text{ Canadian dollars} = 200 \text{ pounds}$$

$$\text{Therefore, } 1 \text{ Canadian dollar} = 200 \div 500 = £0.4$$

$$\text{or } £1 = 1 \div 0.4 = \$2.50$$

So the exchange rate would be 2.5 Canadian dollars per British pound.

The foregoing procedure for calculating the exchange rate can be summarized in a simple formula as follows:

$$E = P_f / P_d$$

where E is the exchange rate, P_f is the foreign price, and P_d is the domestic price. Applying this formula to the example, we get

$$E = 200/500 = 2/5$$

That is, the exchange rate is £2 to $5 or £1 to $2.5, as we calculated in the example.

A simple example of the use of the PPP theory to explain the determination of exchange rates is the Big Mac Index (BMI), popularized by *The Economist* magazine. The BMI looks at the price of hamburgers in McDonald's restaurants in various countries. If a Big Mac costs 3 U.S. dollars in the United States, and 2 pounds in Britain, then the PPP-determined exchange rate between the U.S. dollar and the British pound would be £2 for $3 or $1.5 per £1.

Does the PPP theory have any drawbacks?

Although the PPP theory is easy to understand and simple to use, it has some shortcomings. First, it applies only to goods that are traded internationally, mobile, and standardized. Second, it applies only when transportation and transaction costs are not significant. In fact, however, these costs can be quite significant. Just think of the shipping costs and insurance costs involved in buying a new car in Britain and then shipping it to Canada. Third, when there are barriers to trade (and there can be quite a few), the theory does not work. Finally, if markets are not competitive in the trading countries, the law of one price will break down, and the PPP theory will be invalid.

What are fixed exchange rates?

Fixed Exchange Rates Instead of allowing the forces of demand and supply in the foreign exchange market to determine the value of its currency, a country may decide to set its value in relation to some other country's currency. An exchange rate that is thus determined is said to be a **fixed exchange rate** or a **pegged exchange rate**. A fixed exchange rate is therefore an exchange rate that is fixed by the government at some specified level. For example, the Eastern Caribbean currency (the EC$) is currently set at 1 U.S. dollar for 2.7169 EC dollars.

fixed exchange rate or pegged exchange rate an exchange rate that is fixed by the government at some specified level

To maintain the exchange rate at its fixed or pegged value, the government enters the market and buys or sells foreign exchange. A country is said to *revalue* its currency if it raises the value of its currency in terms of another country's currency. It is said to *devalue* its currency if its lowers the value of its currency in terms of another country's currency. Note that the terms *appreciation* and *depreciation* apply to a regime of *flexible* exchange rates, whereas the terms **revaluation** and **devaluation** apply to a regime of *fixed* exchange rates.

revaluation the raising of the value of a country's currency in terms of another country's currency

devaluation the lowering of the value of a country's currency in terms of another country's currency

managed flexible exchange rate or dirty float an exchange rate that is neither totally fixed nor totally flexible

Are there any other alternatives to flexible or fixed exchange rates?

Managed Flexible Exchange Rate As an alternative to a fixed or completely flexible exchange rate, a country may adopt a **managed flexible exchange rate**. A **dirty float**, as it is also called, is an exchange rate that is neither totally fixed nor totally flexible. Instead, the government intervenes and manipulates the exchange rate so that it attains a level different from its market equilibrium level.

For example, if the market establishes a value of 85 cents U.S. for CDN$1.00, the Bank of Canada could intervene and prop up the Canadian dollar by selling U.S. dollars (buying Canadian dollars) on the foreign exchange market so that its value does not fall below, say, 90 cents U.S.

What is the relationship between the Canadian dollar and the U.S. dollar?

The value of the Canadian dollar in terms of the U.S. dollar has fluctuated over the years, sometimes rising above its U.S. counterpart. Over the past ten years, the value of the Canadian dollar averaged $0.89 U.S. Table 18.3 shows values of the Canadian dollar in terms of the U.S. dollar from 2000 to 2011.

real exchange rate the nominal exchange rate adjusted for differences in price levels in the trading countries

We discussed real and nominal GDP. Is there also a real exchange rate?

Yes. We have a nominal and a real exchange rate.

Table 18.3 Value of Canadian Dollar in Terms of U.S. Dollar, 2000–2011

Year	Value of CDN$ in terms of US$
2000	0.68
2001	0.65
2002	0.63
2003	0.71
2004	0.77
2005	0.83
2006	0.88
2007	0.93
2008	0.94
2009	0.87
2010 (April)	0.99
2011 (February)	1.019

Source: Bank of Canada: **www.bankofcanada.ca/exchange/cad-selected-currencies/#1EXM0102**

The Real Exchange Rate The exchange rate that we have been discussing so far is the nominal exchange rate. It is important for international traders to know the price of foreign currencies in terms of the domestic currency, that is, the nominal exchange rate. It is equally important for them to know how much a given unit of foreign exchange will purchase. This information requires knowledge of the real exchange rate. We know that a real variable is obtained by adjusting its nominal value for price level changes. Thus,

$$\text{Real GDP} = \text{Nominal GDP}/P$$

where P is the price level. Similarly, the **real exchange rate** is the nominal exchange rate adjusted for differences in price levels in the trading countries. Specifically, the real exchange rate (e) is defined as the nominal exchange rate (E) times the ratio of the domestic price level (P_d) to the foreign price level (P_f). That is,

$$e = E(P_d/P_f)$$

Example: If the nominal exchange rate is 2, the domestic price level is 3, and the foreign price level is 4, what is the real exchange rate?

$$\text{Given: } E = 2, P_d = 3, P_f = 4$$

$$\text{Then } e = E(P_d/P_f) = 2(3/4) = 1.5$$

Therefore, the real exchange rate is 1.5.

Can a country improve its balance of trade by changing its exchange rate?

Yes, it can. Let us suppose that a country has a large deficit in its balance of trade. It can improve the situation by devaluing its currency. By so doing, it will make its goods less expensive to foreigners. At the same time, it will make foreign (imported) goods relatively more expensive. Thus, by devaluing its currency, a country can stimulate its exports and discourage imports. This improves its balance of trade and may generate income and employment within the domestic economy. Recall that aggregate expenditure is $C + I + G + (X - M)$. A devaluation of the currency will increase the $(X - M)$ component of aggregate expenditure and thus stimulate output and employment.

Reading Comprehension

The answers to these questions can be found on MyEconLab at www.myeconlab.com. MyEconLab

1. With the help of a suitable diagram, explain how the exchange rate between Canadian dollars and Japanese yen is determined in the foreign exchange market.
2. Mention three different types of international transactions that give rise to a demand for Canadian dollars on the foreign exchange market.
3. What is the difference between the following pairs of concepts?
   a. Depreciation and devaluation
   b. Appreciation and revaluation
4. Explain the purchasing power parity (PPP) theory.
5. Explain how a country can use its exchange rate to improve its balance of trade.
6. Explain the effect of a depreciation of the Canadian dollar on its exports and imports.

LO 18.3 Understand the relationship between inflation and exchange rates

Exchange Rates and the Price Level

Is there a relationship between exchange rates and the price level?

A close relationship exists between exchange rates and price levels. Changes in exchange rates affect the price level, and changes in the price level affect the exchange rate. Let us examine each of these assertions.

The Effect of Changes in the Exchange Rate on the Price Level When the value of the Canadian dollar falls in terms of, say, the U.S. dollar, the prices of American imported goods rise. Canadian residents have to pay more for consumer goods imported from the United States. Moreover, a depreciation of the Canadian dollar in terms of the

U.S. dollar raises the prices of imported inputs from the United States and thus forces up production costs in Canada. The Canadian price level will therefore tend to rise when there is a depreciation of the Canadian dollar in terms of the U.S. dollar.

The exchange rate can affect the price level in another way. When the value of the Canadian dollar falls in terms of the U.S. dollar, Canadian goods become relatively cheap. Residents of the United States will tend to increase their purchases of Canadian goods and thus exert upward pressure on the price level. At the same time, the fall in the value of the Canadian dollar makes foreign goods more expensive. It is therefore likely that Canadian residents will substitute domestic goods for the relatively more expensive imported goods, thus putting further upward pressure on domestic prices.

> A fall in the external value of the Canadian dollar will tend to exert upward pressure on the Canadian price level.

Let us now examine the effect of changes in the price level on the exchange rate.

The Effect of Changes in the Price Level on the Exchange Rate Let us again consider Canada and the United States as our two trading economies. Figure 18.3 shows the foreign exchange market for Canadian dollars. *DD* and *SS* are the initial demand and supply curves. The equilibrium exchange rate is *E*. Suppose that the Canadian price level rises faster than the U.S. price level. Relatively higher prices in Canada will cause Canadian residents to switch from domestic goods and services to relatively cheaper U.S. imports. This means that the supply of Canadian dollars on the foreign exchange market will rise, as shown in Figure 18.3 by the shift of the supply curve from *SS* to S_1S_1.

At the same time, U.S. customers will substitute U.S. goods and services for the relatively more expensive Canadian goods. This decrease in the demand for Canadian goods will result in a decrease in demand for Canadian dollars by U.S. residents. The demand curve *DD* in Figure 18.3 shifts to D_0D_0. As a result of these changes, under a flexible exchange rate regime, the exchange rate will fall from *E* to E_0.

Figure 18.3 Effect of Changes in the Price Level on the Exchange Rate

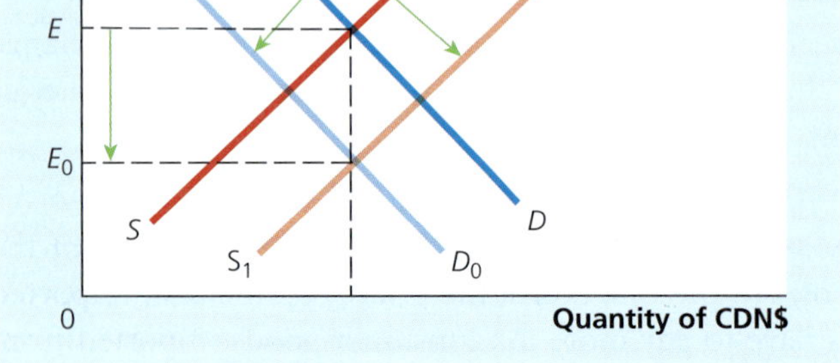

> Other things being equal, an increase in the average level of prices in Canada will result in a depreciation of the external value of the Canadian currency.

The analysis so far assumes that the exchange rate is flexible. If the exchange rate is fixed, the central bank will have to intervene to maintain the exchange rate at the desired level. But if the Canadian price level continues to rise faster than the U.S. price level, then the Canadian dollar will have to be devalued because Canada does not have an unlimited supply of foreign exchange.

Reading Comprehension

The answers to these questions can be found on MyEconLab at www.myeconlab.com. MyEconLab

1. What is the relationship between a country's exchange rate and its price level?
2. In what sense is the relationship between exchange rates and the price level a two-way relationship?

LO 18.4 Understand the relationship between the foreign exchange market and the balance of payments

Relationship between the Foreign Exchange Market and the Balance of Payments

How do changes in the balance of payments affect the exchange rate?

You may have suspected, intuitively, that there is a relationship between exchange rates and the balance of payments. The effect of changes in the balance of payments on the exchange rate depends on whether the exchange rate is flexible or fixed. Let us examine each case.

Flexible Exchange Rates and the Balance of Payments To facilitate this discussion, we will assume that there are only two countries in the world—Canada and the Rest of the World (ROW). We assume that, initially, the foreign exchange market is in equilibrium at an exchange rate of *E*, as shown bypoint *a* in Figure 18.4. We assume also that the balance of payments is in equilibrium.

Figure 18.4 The Foreign Exchange Market

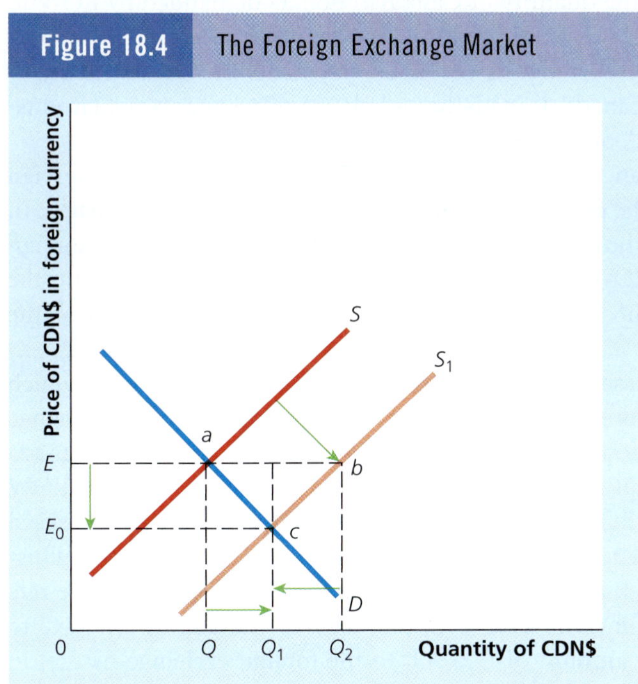

Now, suppose that average income in Canada rises so that Canadians import more goods and services from ROW. Canada will demand more ROW currency to pay for the increased imports, thus providing Canadian dollars in exchange for ROW currency. The supply of Canadian dollars will then increase, as shown in the shift in the supply curve from *S* to S_1 in Figure 20.4. Total payments to ROW will now exceed total receipts from ROW. Canada will have a deficit in its balance of payments account. The foreign exchange market moves from point *a* to point *b*.

Under a flexible exchange rate system, the excess quantity of Canadian dollars supplied ($b - a$) will lower the exchange rate. As the exchange rate falls, Canadian goods become more attractive to ROW, and goods from ROW become less attractive to Canadians. As Canadians reduce their imports of goods from ROW, the quantity of Canadian dollars supplied to the foreign exchange market decreases. There is a movement from point *b* to point *c*along the supply curve S_1. At this point, the market is again in equilibrium with

Figure 18.5 Fixed Exchange Rates and the Balance of Payments

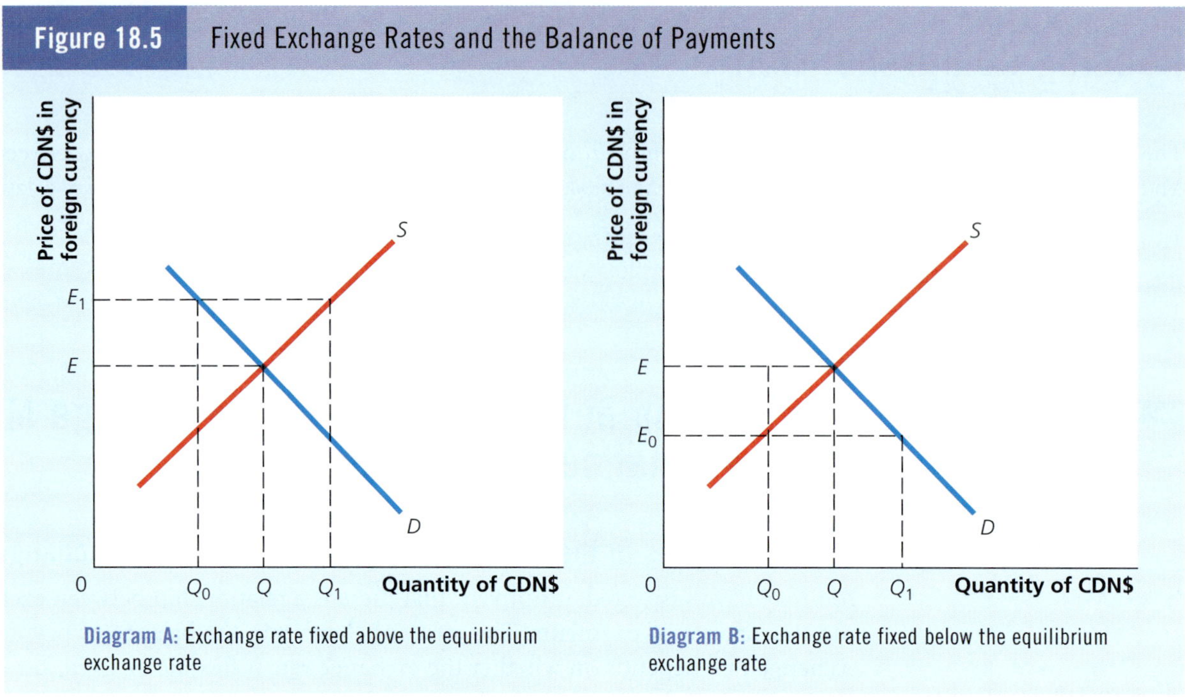

Diagram A: Exchange rate fixed above the equilibrium exchange rate

Diagram B: Exchange rate fixed below the equilibrium exchange rate

the exchange rate at E_0, and the balance of payments deficit is eliminated. Let us now examine the case of fixed exchange rates.

Fixed Exchange Rates and the Balance of Payments Let us assume that Canada fixes its exchange rate, with respect to the ROW currency, at E_1, which is above the equilibrium exchange rate, as shown in Diagram A of Figure 18.5.

At an exchange rate of E_1, the quantity of Canadian dollars demanded by ROW to make payments to Canada is Q_0. At the same time, the quantity of Canadian dollars supplied in exchange for ROW currency is Q_1. Thus, payments by Canada to ROW exceed payments by ROW to Canada. Canada has a balance of payments deficit illustrated by $Q_1 - Q_0$ in Diagram A of Figure 18.5.

In a regime of flexible exchange rates, the surplus of Canadian dollars on the foreign exchange market would cause the exchange rate to fall until the surplus is eliminated. In a fixed exchange rate regime, however, the Bank of Canada must enter the foreign exchange market and use its ROW currency out of its official reserves to buy up the surplus Canadian dollars. If the Bank's reserves are exhausted, a devaluation of the Canadian dollar will occur.

We will now examine the case in which Canada fixes its exchange rate at E_0, which is below the market equilibrium exchange rate of E (see Diagram B). At this exchange rate, the quantity of Canadian dollars demanded by ROW to make payments to Canada is Q_1. At the same time, the quantity of Canadian dollars supplied in exchange for ROW currency to make payments to ROW is Q_0. Thus, payments to Canada by ROW exceed payments to ROW by Canada. There is a surplus in Canada's balance of payments, illustrated by $Q_1 - Q_0$ in Diagram B of Figure 18.5. In order to prevent the exchange rate from being bid up to the equilibrium level of E, the Bank of Canada would have to supply Canadian dollars in the amount of $Q_1 - Q_0$ to the foreign exchange market in exchange for ROW currency. Canada's holdings of ROW currency would thus increase.

Reading Comprehension

The answers to these questions can be found on MyEconLab at www.myeconlab.com. MyEconLab

1. Briefly explain how changes in the balance of payments affect the exchange rate under a flexible exchange rate system.
2. Briefly explain how changes in the balance of payments affect the exchange rate under a fixed exchange rate system.

LO 18.5 Discuss fixed and flexible exchange rates

Exchange Rate Systems: The Debate

What are the advantages and disadvantages of flexible exchange rates?

One of the advantages of a freely fluctuating exchange rate is that no direct intervention is necessary to achieve equilibrium in the foreign exchange market. The exchange rate will adjust automatically to changes in demand and supply and thus maintain equilibrium. There is therefore no need to maintain foreign reserves in order to peg the exchange rate. A flexible exchange rate frees monetary policy so that it can be used in conjunction with fiscal policy to keep the economy operating at a high level of employment with relatively stable prices. Under a fixed exchange rate system, the central bank has to intervene in the foreign exchange market to maintain the fixed exchange rate. No such intervention is necessary under a flexible exchange rate regime.

A second advantage of a flexible exchange rate is that it helps to insulate a country against foreign inflationary pressures. Suppose that there is inflation in the United States while Canada is experiencing a period of stable prices. Canadian exports to the United States will rise as residents of the United States switch to relatively cheaper Canadian goods. Also, Canadian imports from the United States will fall as Canadian residents reduce the quantity of the relatively expensive U.S. goods demanded. The resulting increase in demand for Canadian goods will tend to increase prices in Canada. Under a fixed exchange rate regime, the money supply will be increased to maintain the pegged exchange rate, and, consequently, the U.S. inflation will tend to spill over into Canada. Under a system of flexible exchange rates, however, the exchange rate will rise and thus prevent Canadian prices from rising.

We turn now to the disadvantages of a flexible exchange rate system. First, the uncertainty associated with flexible exchange rates discourages international trade. It is important for international traders to know what they will pay for their imports and what they will receive for their exports. Trade cannot be expected to flourish in an environment of uncertainty and insecurity.

Another argument advanced against flexible exchange rates is that it may affect the economy adversely. For example, an appreciation of the Canadian dollar means that foreign goods become less expensive to Canadians. Lower-priced imports will then compete with Canadian-made goods, and consumers may buy foreign products instead of made-in-Canada products. This, in turn, may lead to reductions in income and increases in unemployment.

What are the advantages and disadvantages of fixed exchange rates?

Fixed exchange rates have the great advantage of certainty and security. International traders can arrange their transactions with confidence, knowing that prices and costs will not change in the interim. A serious disadvantage of a fixed exchange rate is that a country may be forced to adopt a monetary policy with undesirable domestic effects just to be able to maintain the exchange rate at its fixed level. For example, a restrictive monetary policy with high interest rates may be necessary to maintain the official level of the exchange rate. Such a policy, however, may result in high unemployment and low economic growth.

Is there a link between the exchange rate and the interest rate?

It is not too difficult to establish a link between the exchange rate and the interest rate. If interest rates in Canada are higher than interest rates in the United States, investors will purchase Canadian securities. To do so, they need Canadian dollars. This increase in demand for Canadian dollars will tend to raise the exchange value of the Canadian currency. If U.S. interest rates are higher than Canadian rates, then investors will purchase U.S. securities rather than Canadian securities. This will increase the value of the U.S. dollar relative to the Canadian dollar. The difference in interest rates between trading countries (the interest rate differential) can be expressed as

$$i_d - i_f$$

where i_d denotes the domestic interest rate and i_f denotes the foreign interest rate. Whenever the interest rate differential increases, Canadian securities become more attractive, and the demand for Canadian dollars increases, driving up the exchange value of the dollar.

Other things being equal, an increase in Canadian interest rates relative to interest rates abroad will increase the external value of the Canadian dollar.

Reading Comprehension

The answers to these questions can be found on MyEconLab at www.myeconlab.com. MyEconLab

1. What are the advantages and disadvantages of a flexible exchange rate system?
2. What are the advantages and disadvantages of a fixed exchange rate system?
3. Is there any relationship between a country's interest rate and its foreign exchange rate? Explain.

LO 18.6 Understand the relation between foreign exchange transactions and the money supply

Foreign Exchange Transactions and the Money Supply

How do foreign exchange transactions affect the domestic money supply?

The answer to this question depends on whether Canada is on a flexible or fixed exchange rate regime—that is, whether or not the Bank of Canada intervenes in the foreign exchange market to maintain a fixed exchange rate. Let us examine the effects in each case.

Flexible Exchange Rates Let us assume that the country is on a freely fluctuating exchange rate regime. To simplify the calculations and avoid needless complications, let us assume further that the Canadian dollar is on par with the U.S. dollar; that is, CDN$1 = US$1, and that there are no bank charges or commissions on transactions. If Miss Rose sells US$1000 to a Canadian bank and deposits the proceeds in her chequing account, her deposits (in Canadian dollars) at the bank increase by $1000. The bank then sells the US$1000 on the foreign exchange market to a buyer, Mr. Simon, who pays for the U.S. dollars with Canadian dollars drawn on his account. Mr. Simon's deposit account falls by CDN$1000. The combined effect of the foreign exchange transaction on the money supply is zero.

> Under a flexible exchange rate regime, foreign exchange transactions do not affect the domestic money supply because the central bank does not intervene.

Does the above conclusion hold under a fixed exchange rate regime?

That's an interesting question. Let's investigate.

Fixed Exchange Rates If the central bank does not intervene in the foreign exchange market, our result will not be affected. Under a fixed exchange rate regime, however, the central bank must often intervene to maintain a fixed exchange rate. Suppose that the Bank of Canada sells US$1 million to the chartered banks. We assume here also that the Canadian dollar is set at par with the U.S. dollar.

The chartered banks pay for the U.S. dollars by having their accounts at the Bank of Canada lowered by CDN$1 million. Hence, the cash reserves of the chartered banks fall. They reduce their lending activities and the money supply consequently falls. You should work through the effect on the domestic money supply of a purchase of U.S. dollars by the Bank of Canada. Note how closely the purchase and sale of foreign currency on the open market resemble the central bank's open market operations.

> A sale of foreign currency on the open market by the Bank of Canada reduces the domestic money supply. A purchase of foreign currency on the open market by the Bank of Canada increases the domestic money supply.

Reading Comprehension

The answers to these questions can be found on MyEconLab at www.myeconlab.com. MyEconLab

1. How do foreign exchange transactions affect the domestic money supply under a fixed exchange rate system? Would your answer be different for a regime of flexible exchange rates?
2. The effect of foreign exchange transactions on the domestic money supply depends on whether or not the central bank intervenes. Explain briefly.

LO 18.7 Discuss the international repercussions of monetary policy

Monetary Policy and Exchange Rates

What are the international repercussions of monetary policy?

Figure 18.6 Monetary Policy under Flexible Exchange Rates

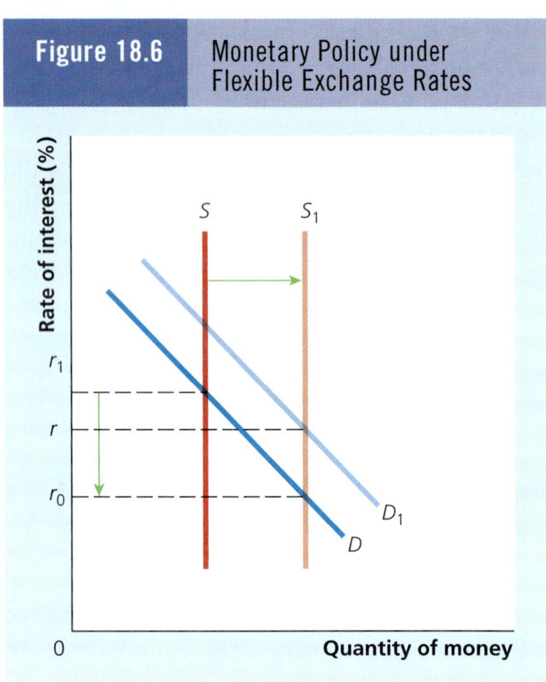

The international repercussions of monetary policy depend on whether the country is on a flexible or fixed exchange rate regime. Let us examine each case.

Flexible Exchange Rate Let us assume that the Canadian economy is experiencing a recession. Figure 18.6 shows the money market, with *D* and *S* representing the demand for and supply of money, respectively. The equilibrium interest rate is r_1. To stimulate economic activity, the Bank of Canada implements an expansionary monetary policy, increasing the money supply from *S* to S_1, as shown in Figure 18.6. As the money supply increases, the rate of interest falls from r_1 to r_0, as shown in Figure 18.6.

The fall in the rate of interest will stimulate aggregate expenditure and income, which will cause the demand for money to increase, as shown by the shift in the demand for money curve from *D* to D_1. (Note that it is not the fall in the rate of interest that shifts the demand curve, but the increase in income.) As a result, the rate of interest rises from r_0 to *r*, which is lower than the initial level of r_1.

Because Canadian interest rates are now lower than they were before the expansionary monetary policy, foreigners will find Canadian securities (bonds) less attractive than they were previously. Funds will flow out of Canada in search of higher yields elsewhere. The demand for Canadian dollars by foreigners will thus decrease, and the supply of Canadian currency will increase. The value of the Canadian currency will fall. As a result, Canadian goods will be relatively less expensive to foreigners, and foreign goods more expensive to Canadians. Canada's exports will rise and its imports will fall. The $(X - M)$ component of aggregate expenditure will rise, hence aggregate expenditure will rise. We can draw the following conclusion:

> If a country is on a flexible exchange rate regime, the effects of monetary policy will be amplified by international repercussions.

Fixed Exchange Rates Consider now what happens when the money supply is increased under a fixed exchange rate system. As in the case of a flexible exchange rate regime, an increase in the money supply causes interest rates to fall. This fall in interest rates, however, will not result in a fall in the external value of the Canadian dollar. The Bank of Canada will enter the foreign exchange market and sell foreign currency. This sale of foreign currency by the Bank of Canada reduces the money supply. Thus, the net increase in the money supply will be less than the initial increase. Furthermore, the expansionary monetary policy may push the domestic price level upward, resulting in a fall in Canada's exports and an increase in its imports. Hence, the $(X - M)$ component of aggregate expenditure falls, resulting in a fall in aggregate expenditure. We can draw the following conclusion:

If a country is on a fixed exchange rate regime, the effects of monetary policy will be dampened by international repercussions.

BUSINESS SITUATION 18.1

Odds & Ends is a small Canadian retail outlet that obtains most of its supplies from the United States. Interest rates in the United States are slightly lower than those in Canada, and the government is planning to stimulate the economy by expansionary monetary policy.

What decision should Odds & Ends make regarding orders from the United States to take advantage of the situation?

The answer to this Business Situation can be found in Appendix A.

Reading Comprehension

The answers to these questions can be found on MyEconLab at www.myeconlab.com. MyEconLab

1. How do international repercussions affect monetary policy under a flexible exchange rate regime?
2. Under a fixed exchange rate regime, an increase in the money supply causes interest rates to fall, other things being equal, but the fall in interest rates does not result in a fall in the external value of the Canadian dollar. Why not?

LO 18.8 Discuss the international repercussions of fiscal policy

Fiscal Policy and Exchange Rates

What are the international repercussions of fiscal policy?

Like monetary policy, the international repercussions of fiscal policy depend on whether the country is on a flexible or fixed exchange rate regime. Let us examine each case.

Flexible Exchange Rates Assume that the government adopts an expansionary fiscal policy, increasing government spending in an attempt to move the economy toward full employment. The resulting increase in aggregate expenditure and GDP will cause the demand for money to increase, pushing up interest rates. As interest rates rise, there will be some crowding out so that the expansionary impact of the fiscal policy will be lessened. But what about the international repercussions? Let's investigate.

The increase in domestic interest rates will cause capital funds to flow into the country to profit from higher yields. There will be an increase in demand for Canadian dollars and an increase in the supply of foreign currency. This will cause an increase in the external value of the Canadian dollar. Canadian exports will fall as Canadian goods will now be relatively more expensive to foreigners. Canadian imports will also tend to rise as foreign goods will now be relatively less expensive. The $(X - M)$ component of aggregate expenditure will fall; hence, the impact of the fiscal policy will be lessened. We can draw the following conclusion:

If a country is on a flexible exchange rate regime, the effects of fiscal policy will be dampened by international repercussions.

Fixed Exchange Rates Let us now assume that Canada is on a fixed exchange rate system and that the government increases its spending to reduce unemployment. Higher interest rates will result, and the demand for Canadian dollars by foreigners will rise. This increase in demand will exert upward pressure on the external value of the Canadian dollar. However, to maintain the fixed value, the Bank of Canada will enter the foreign exchange market and purchase foreign currency. This purchase of foreign currency will result in an increase in the domestic money supply, as discussed earlier. This increase in the money supply actually prevents interest rates from rising as high as they otherwise would and thus reinforces the effect of the expansionary fiscal policy.

If a country is on a fixed exchange rate regime, the effects of fiscal policy will be amplified by international repercussions.

Reading Comprehension

The answers to these questions can be found on MyEconLab at www.myeconlab.com. MyEconLab

1. How do international repercussions affect fiscal policy under a fixed exchange rate system?
2. The impact of fiscal policy is stronger under a fixed exchange rate system than under a flexible one. Explain briefly.

Review

1. Review the learning objectives listed at the beginning of the chapter.
2. Have you accomplished all the objectives? One way to determine this is toanswer the Reading Comprehension Questions at the end of each section. This will help you assess the extent to which you have accomplished the learning objectives.
3. If you have not accomplished an objective, review the relevant material before proceeding.

Key Points to Remember

1. LO 18.1 The balance of payments is a summary statement of all economic transactions between a country and the rest of the world. Transactions that result in the receipt of money from the rest of the world are entered as credit items, while those that result in the payment of money to the rest of the world are entered as debit items.
2. LO 18.1 The balance of payments is divided into two main parts: the current account and the capital account. The current account contains exports and imports of goods and services, receipt and payment of investment income, and transfers. The capital account contains purchases and sales of assets internationally. It also contains international borrowing and lending.
3. LO 18.2 The exchange rate is the rate at which one country's currency exchanges for the currency of another country. A country can adopt a flexible, a fixed, or a managed flexible exchange rate system. In a flexible exchange rate system, the exchange rate is determined by demand and supply in the foreign exchange market. In a fixed exchange rate system, the government pegs the exchange rate at a fixed value of some other country's currency. In a managed flexible exchange rate system, the exchange rate is allowed to fluctuate within a certain range.
4. LO 18.2 According to the purchasing power parity theory, prices of similar products will tend to be the same except for transportation costs and customs duties.
5. LO 18.5 Advantages of a flexible exchange rate system include automatic adjustment and insulation against foreign inflation. The disadvantages include uncertainty that impedes international trade and possible adverse effects on income and employment. A major advantage of fixed exchange rates is certainty of prices. A major disad-

vantage is that a country may be forced to adopt a policy that hurts the domestic economy.

6. LO 18.6 Foreign exchange transactions not involving the central bank have no effect on the domestic money supply. Under a fixed exchange rate regime, however, in which the central bank is involved, foreign exchange transactions affect the money supply in a similar manner to open market operations.
7. LO 18.8 Under a flexible exchange rate system, international repercussions magnify the effects of monetary policy. Under a fixed exchange rate system, international repercussions dampen the effects of monetary policy. Under a flexible exchange rate system, international repercussions dampen the effects of fiscal policy. Under a fixed exchange rate system, international repercussions amplify the effects of fiscal policy.

Economic Word Power

Appreciation (of currency) (p. 455)
Balance of merchandise trade or balance of visible trade (p. 452)
Balance of payments (p. 450)
Balance of trade (p. 452)
Capital account (p. 453)
Current account (p. 450)
Depreciation (of currency) (p. 456)
Devaluation (of currency) (p. 458)
Direct foreign investment (p. 453)
Exchange rate or foreign exchange rate (p. 454)
Fixed exchange rate or pegged exchange rate (p. 457)
Flexible exchange rate (p. 454) **also called freely fluctuating or floating exchange rate**
Foreign exchange market (p. 454)
Law of one price (p. 456)
Managed flexible exchange rate or dirty float (p. 458)
Official reserves (p. 453)
Portfolio foreign investment (p. 453)
Purchasing power parity (p. 456)
Real exchange rate (p. 458)
Revaluation (of currency) (p. 458)
Short-term capital flows (p. 453)
Special drawing rights (SDRs) (p. 453)

Problems and Exercises

Basic

1. LO 18.1 Indicate whether each of the following is a current account item or a capital account item:
   a. The amount spent by international tourists
   b. Direct investment abroad
   c. Direct investment by foreigners
   d. Imports into the country
   e. Exports from the country
   f. International loans
   g. Investment income
2. LO 18.1 Indicate whether each of the following is true (T) or false (F):
   a. The balance of payments is an inappropriate term because it hardly ever balances.
   b. Exports are recorded as credits while imports are recorded as debits.
   c. The current account deals with purchases and sales of currently produced goods and services internationally.
   d. There is absolutely no relationship between the balance of trade and the GDP. One is external, the other is domestic.
   e. Payment of interest and dividend income by Canada to the rest of the world is less than payment of these incomes to Canada from the rest of the world.
   f. Trade in current assets is recorded in the current account.
   g. Official reserves include gold, U.S. dollars, and other major foreign currencies.
   h. The exchange rate is the price of foreign currency.
3. LO 18.2 Consider the model of the foreign exchange market in Figure 18.7.

Figure 18.7 Foreign Exchange Market Model

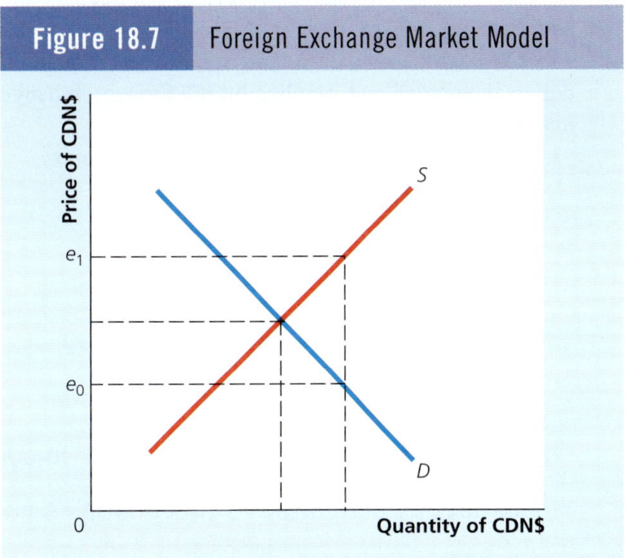

a. Explain what happens at an exchange rate of e_1.
b. Explain what happens at an exchange rate of e_0.

4. LO 18.2 Use graphs to illustrate how each of the following transactions will affect the foreign exchange market between Canada and a hypothetical country called Rest of the World (ROW):
   a. ROW increases its imports from Canada
   b. Canadians import more goods from ROW
   c. ROW invests in Canada
5. LO 18.2 Table 18.4 shows various values of the Canadian dollar in terms of U.S. funds. Calculate the value of the US$ in terms of CDN$ at the exchange rate given, and then complete the right-hand column.

Table 18.4 Value of Canadian Dollar in U.S. Funds

Value of CDN$ in US$	Value of US$ in CDN$
$0.90	
0.85	
0.80	
0.75	
0.70	

Questions in the Intermediate and Challenging Sections cover several different concepts, and have not been organized by learning objectives.

Intermediate

1. A certain type of laptop computer is sold in Canada for $800, while it is sold in Britain for £350. Assuming that the law of one price holds in this case, what will be the exchange rate between Canada and Britain?
2. If the nominal exchange rate is 2.5, the domestic price level is 3.5, and the foreign price level is 4.5, calculate the real exchange rate.
3. Table 18.5 contains data on the quantity of Canadian dollars demanded and supplied on the foreign exchange market.
   a. Plot the demand and supply curves on a graph.

Table 18.5 Supply and Demand Data for Canadian Dollars

Price of CDN$ in US$	Quantity of CDN$ Demanded ($ mil)	Quantity of CDN$ Supplied ($ mil)
1.05	150	210
1.00	160	200
0.95	170	190
0.90	180	180
0.85	190	170
0.80	200	160
0.75	210	150
0.70	220	140

   b. What is the equilibrium exchange rate?
   c. Show the effect of an increase in income in the United States that results in an increase in Canadian exports to the United States.

Challenging

1. X = exports and M = imports. In the past, a situation in which $(X - M) > 0$ was considered to be a favourable balance of trade, whereas a situation in which $(X - M) < 0$ was considered to be an unfavourable balance of trade. Why might a favourable balance of trade be unfavourable, while an unfavourable balance might be favourable?
2. "The rate at which one country's currency exchanges for the currency of another country (i.e., the exchange rate) is the best measure of the country's relative economic performance. For example, if the Canadian dollar is valued at 15% below the U.S. dollar, it means that the Canadian economy is 15% less efficient than the U.S. economy. If it is valued at 10% more than the U.S. dollar, it means that the Canadian economy is 10% more efficient than the U.S. economy; and if the Canadian dollar is at par with the U.S. dollar, then we can safely conclude that the Canadian and U.S. economies are equally efficient." Can you detect any error in the above argument?

Study Guide

Self-Assessment

What's your score?

Circle the letter that corresponds with the correct answer.

1. The balance of payments is
   a. The balance owing to foreign countries after imports have been paid for
   b. The balance due from foreign countries after partial payment has been made for imports
   c. A record of economic transactions with the rest of the world
   d. All of the above

2. The two main sections into which the balance of payments is divided are
   a. The revenue account and the capital account
   b. The domestic account and the foreign account
   c. The current account and the personal account
   d. The current account and the capital account

3. In which account would exports and imports of goods and services be recorded?
   a. The personal account
   b. The export/import account
   c. The domestic account
   d. The current account

4. In which account would direct foreign investment be recorded?
   a. The capital account
   b. The personal account
   c. The investment account
   d. The revenue account

5. Assume that Canada exports $50 000 worth of wheat to Hong Kong and imports $60 000 worth of handbags from Hong Kong. Then, we know that
   a. Canada will receive a net payment of $10 000 from Hong Kong
   b. Canada will make a net payment of $10 000 to Hong Kong
   c. Neither Canada nor Hong Kong has to make any payment because exports pay for imports
   d. None of the above

6. Which of the following is recorded in the capital account?
   a. Exports of goods and services
   b. Immigrants' funds
   c. Direct investment in Canada by foreigners
   d. Travel

7. Which of the following statements is correct?
   a. The balance of payments need not balance because exports and imports of goods and services may not be equal
   b. The current account always balances even if imports and exports of goods and services are not equal
   c. Exports are recorded with plus signs (+) in the capital account
   d. Imports of goods are entered with minus signs (−) in the current account

8. The foreign exchange rate is
   a. The ratio of a country's exports to its imports
   b. The amount of money it has to pay for a unit of foreign currency
   c. How much goods and services a unit of a country's currency will buy
   d. None of the above

9. If CDN$1.00 = US$0.98, then US$1.00 equals
   a. CDN$1.02
   b. CDN$0.98
   c. CDN$1.98
   d. None of the above

10. The demand curve for foreign currency slopes downward because
   a. Exports increase as the rate of inflation falls
   b. The higher the price of foreign currency, the less will be the quantity demanded
   c. The higher the price of foreign currency, the greater the amount of foreign currency that will be placed on the market
   d. None of the above

11. The equilibrium exchange rate of the Canadian dollar occurs where
   a. The foreign demand for Canadian dollars equals the supply of Canadian dollars by Canadians
   b. The value of the Canadian dollar equals the value of the foreign currency
   c. The quantity of Canadian dollars demanded by foreigners equals the quantity of Canadian dollars supplied by Canadians
   d. All of the above

12. According to the law of one price
   a. Once the equilibrium exchange rate is determined, it cannot be changed
   b. Each internationally traded item can have only one price

c. Once allowance is made for certain costs associated with trade, the price of an internationally traded item must be the same everywhere
d. None of the above

13. The law of one price is most closely related to
a. A fixed exchange rate
b. A flexible exchange rate
c. The purchasing power parity theory
d. A managed flexible exchange rate

14. Which of the following statements is correct?
a. Appreciation is to flexible exchange rates as revaluation is to fixed exchange rates
b. Devaluation is to flexible exchange rates as appreciation is to fixed exchange rates
c. Depreciation is to fixed exchange rates as appreciation is to flexible exchange rates
d. None of the above

15. If the Canadian dollar depreciates in terms of the U.S. dollar, we expect
a. Exports from Canada to the United States to fall
b. Imports to Canada from the United States to increase
c. Exports from Canada to the United States to increase
d. Canada to have a trade deficit

16. A country can reduce a large trade deficit by
a. Revaluing its currency
b. Discouraging exports
c. Encouraging imports
d. Devaluing its currency

17. An increase in average incomes in Canada is likely to
a. Increase imports and lower the exchange value of the Canadian dollar
b. Increase imports and raise the exchange value of the Canadian dollar
c. Lower imports and raise the exchange value of the Canadian dollar
d. Lower imports and lower the exchange value of the Canadian dollar

18. Under a flexible exchange rate system, a balance of payments deficit can be eliminated by
a. A fall in the exchange value of the currency
b. An increase in the exchange value of the currency
c. An increase in imports into the country
d. None of the above

19. Under a flexible exchange rate regime, a sale of foreign currency
a. Increases the domestic money supply
b. Reduces the domestic money supply
c. May increase or reduce the domestic money supply
d. Has no effect on the domestic money supply

20. If a country is on a fixed exchange rate system, the effect of an increase in the money supply, with international repercussions considered, will be
a. Amplified
b. Dampened
c. Zero
d. Uncertain

Problems and Exercises (Use Quad Paper for Graphs)

Answers to these questions can be found on MyEconLab at www.myeconlab.com. MyEconLab

1. How would each of the following transactions be recorded in Canada's balance of payments?
a. A shipment of wheat from Canada to Russia
b. An expenditure of $2000 by a Canadian couple vacationing on a Caribbean island
c. The establishment of a manufacturing company in Canada by a group of American investors
d. The transfer of a certain sum of money from a landed immigrant in Canada to a relative in a foreign country

2. Under which section of the balance of payments would each of the following be recorded?
a. A Canadian manufacturer buys inputs from a U.S. supplier.
b. Canadian farmers sell wheat to an importer from France.
c. The Bank of Montreal opens a branch in the Caribbean.
d. A German company builds a manufacturing plant in Alberta.
e. Canadian investors receive dividends from Japanese firms.
f. The Bank of Canada uses U.S. dollars to settle a deficit in the balance of payments.

3. Table 18.6 shows the quantities of Canadian dollars demanded and supplied on the foreign exchange market at various prices of Canadian dollars.

Table 18.6 Demand and Supply for Canadian Dollars on the Foreign Exchange Market

Price of CDN$ in US$	Quantity of CDN$ Demanded	Quantity of of CDN$ Supplied
1.10	100	180
1.05	110	170
1.00	120	160
0.95	130	150
0.90	140	140
0.85	150	130
0.80	160	120
0.75	170	110
0.70	180	100

a. Plot the demand and supply curves on a graph.
b. What is the equilibrium exchange rate?
c. Show the effect of an increase in income in Canada that results in an increase in imports of goods and services from the United States.

4. If the nominal exchange rate is 2.5, the domestic price level is 4, and the foreign price level is 5, what is the real exchange rate?

5. A certain brand of television set sells for $2000 in Canada, while it sells for $1600 in the United States. Assume that transportation and other transaction costs are zero. Use the purchasing power parity theory to calculate the exchange rate between Canada and the United States.

Appendix A Business Situation Answers

Chapter 1

1.1 John Adams faces the economic problem of scarcity. He has limited resources ($25 000), and he must decide whether he should use the money to increase his stock or do something else, such as buying a used delivery van.

1.2 The price at which the product would be sold and the quantity of the product to produce are microeconomic considerations. The others are macroeconomic considerations.

Chapter 1A

1A.1 A line graph would be appropriate to show the direct relationship between the number of calls and sales. She could put quarterly sales on the vertical axis and the number of calls per quarter on the horizontal axis, and then plot the points. The resulting upward-sloping line would illustrate her point.

1A.2 The 7% interest on $100 000 amounts to $7000. If he purchases inventories, he earns ($107 500 − $100 000) = $7500. He is better off using the money to purchase inventories.

Chapter 2

2.1 A production possibility curve is ideal for this illustration. It can be easily shown that a movement from one point on the curve to another involves giving up one type of ties for another.

2.2 If Maple Leaf Foods sells its products in the U.S. market, then a strong Canadian dollar would mean that Maple Leaf Foods products would become more expensive to Americans. Thus, sales in the U.S. market would decline and that could adversely affect Maple Leaf Foods profits.

Chapter 3

3.1 The consultant could have been thinking that the observed increase in the number of persons buying laptop computers could have been due to a lowering of the prices of laptops, and would therefore be an increase in quantity demanded rather than an increase in demand. To increase stock on the basis of a fall in price could be a mistake indeed. It is possible that the entrepreneur would be able to sell his increased stock only at greatly reduced prices—probably even at a loss.

3.2 Computers and flash drives are complements. By selling the computers at significantly reduced prices, the store will attract more people who want to purchase computers. As they purchase more computers, they will likely buy more flash drives as well.

Chapter 4

4.1 A pro-Keynesian government will address the unemployment situation by increasing government spending. This action will likely reduce unemployment, at least in the short run. With lower unemployment, wage rates will tend to increase. To avoid higher labour costs, the businessperson should hire the additional workers now rather than later.

4.2 The answer to this question depends largely on the sector in which the business operates. Certain sectors in the economy will recover quickly, and it would be wise for a business owner, in anticipation of higher levels of demand, to plan and prepare for this. However, other sectors are not recovering as quickly. Certain markets (for example, many export markets) have not recovered much at all, despite the rising levels of Canadian GDP.

Chapter 5

5.1 The manufacturer's decision regarding production levels should be related to its expected sales. Expected sales volume is a function of expected income. The manufacturer can look at recent GDP figures to observe any trend and, on that basis, decide on production levels.

Chapter 6

6.1 The claim that unemployment forces wages down and thus reduces production cost is valid. To suggest, however, that this cost reduction is beneficial to firms is to ignore the big picture. Unemployment exacts a toll not only on the unemployed but also on the economy and on the society as a whole. The reduction in the cost of labour that can result from unemployment must be measured against lost production, lost income, and lost sales. Lower labour costs mean very little if firms are unable to sell their output because of reduced incomes. Severe unemployment could so adversely affect businesses that widespread bankruptcies would ensue. You will see later that there are sounder grounds on which to base opposition to activist policies to reduce unemployment.

Chapter 7

7.1 When *AD* is lower, there is less demand for money. Low levels of demand for money cause the price of money to fall, hence interest rates fall. Generally, this kind of economic environment causes the Bank of Canada to pursue an "easy monetary policy" whereby they lower interest rates and make credit more readily available. This is the best environment for a business owner to make investments.

7.2 An increase in the aggregate quantity of goods and services purchased does not necessarily mean that there is an increase in aggregate demand. The manager will need to investigate the possible reason for the increase in purchases. If it results from a fall in the price level only, then there is no change in aggregate demand and a change in aggregate quantity demanded only. If it results, for example, from an increase in investment, an increase in government spending, or a reduction in taxes, then the change should be viewed as an increase in aggregate demand. If that is so, a price increase might be appropriate.

7.3 A reduction in business taxes means that, other things being equal, production costs will fall. Firms will then be able to produce more goods and services. As the total output of goods and services increases, other things being equal, the price level will fall.

Chapter 8

8.1 Small business owners all over Canada would be affected by this situation because of the effect that it had on the price of oil and the perceived threat to the supply of oil. The situation in Egypt, followed by a similar crisis in Libya, had a combined effect on the price of gasoline in Canada. In the 12-month period from April 2010 to April 2011 (during which these crises occurred) the price of gasoline in Canada rose by 30% (from approximately $1.00 per litre to $1.30). This high price of gasoline had a significant impact on business costs (think transportation) and affected small and large businesses alike.

8.2 An attempt to use fiscal policy to force an increase in real GDP will result only in a higher price level with no lasting change in real GDP. Knowing that prices in general will rise, you could be proactive and purchase your inputs before prices rise.

8.3 The effect of agricultural subsidies, or any form of tax policy which favours producers, causes the short-run aggregate supply curve (*SRAS*) to shift to the right. The effect that you should expect this to have on your business—in fact, upon your entire industry—is that these subsidies will lower your costs and thus increase the level of industry output, other things being equal. In the long run, the result is higher output levels and lower prices.

8.4 The specific answers to this question depend largely on the type of business that you are looking at. Generally, most responses will come in the form of reduce, re-use, and recycle, in efforts to reduce an environmental footprint.

Chapter 9

9.1 Undoubtedly, Select Printers will maintain a level of inventory that it considers to be desirable. A fall in the desired level of inventories and queues of retailers with unfilled orders are signals that output should be increased to retain inventories at their desired levels.

9.2 An increase in the saving rate suggests that, other things being equal, the equilibrium level of income and output will fall. With this fall in total income, total consumption would be expected to fall. This is certainly not good news for your uncle's business! You should advise your uncle to carefully monitor the situation to see if there is any impact on his particular business. He should, however, expect an increase in unplanned inventories, and should probably put any plans for expansion on hold.

Chapter 10

10.1 An increase in saving means that more funds are available for investment purposes. Businesses might see this as an opportunity to obtain investment funds at relatively low rates.

Chapter 11

11.1 The manager's decision depends on the effects of the expansionary fiscal policy. The expansionary policy will have the effect of increasing income, output, and employment. The cost of labour will likely rise as the rate of unemployment decreases. This being the case, the manager would be well advised to hire the additional workers before the implementation of the expansionary fiscal policy.

11.2 The government's program will affect the supply side of the economy, resulting in an increase in output and a reduction in the price level. Lower price levels and a greater real GDP will have implications for business decisions, such as sales volume, production costs, and employment of workers.

Chapter 12

12.1 The fact that the leading indicators turn upward is an indication that GDP will probably follow an upward trend. However, you would have to be careful about drawing any definitive conclusions; several events could occur to change the course of GDP. For example, a sudden decision by oil producers to double the price of oil would affect the course of GDP. Moreover, leading indicators are based on forecasts that may be inaccurate. As a business analyst, you would want to use other methods of forecasting and compare your results with those obtained from the leading indicators.

Chapter 13

13.1 The convenience of credit cards makes their use popular. The owner of the snowboarding equipment and apparel store must weigh the benefits from accepting credit cards (increased sales) against the cost of accepting them (the fee charged by the credit card companies). In the vast majority of cases, the benefits outweigh the costs.

13.2 If the Bank of Canada increases the rate of growth of the money supply in order to curb recessionary pressures, there is likely to be an increase in desired aggregate expenditure. People will loosen their spending in response to lower interest rates and the generally easier credit terms now available. This increase in desired aggregate expenditure culminates in higher total income and output levels. The now higher levels of aggregate expenditure trickle throughout the economy: businesses respond to the higher level of AE, quite often increasing production and hiring workers. The result is higher levels of employment.

Chapter 14

14.1 This is good news for you. The fact that the branch is 'over-reserved" means that it is in a position to grant loans.

14.2 The following options are available to you: (a) you can keep the excess reserves idle, (b) you can use them for loans, or (c) you can invest them in government securities. If you allow the funds to remain idle, you are losing interest income that the funds could have earned. Loans are risky when the economy is in a depressed state. You would want to be cautious about extending loans during such periods. Under the circumstances, the purchase of government securities would appear to be your best option. Government securities—treasury bills and bonds—are quite safe, and they also earn interest income.

Chapter 15

15.1 Businesses should expect a fall in interest rates after the expansion of the money supply. On this basis, businesses planning to contract loans for investment purposes will do well to postpone their plans until the Bank of Canada acts to increase the money supply. This decision will result in interest savings.

Chapter 16

16.1 Inflation in the United States will increase the cost of the items your father imports from that country. Your father can either leave his prices unchanged or increase them in response to increased costs. If he raises his prices, he may lose some business and this may negatively affect his profits. If he leaves his prices unchanged and absorbs the extra costs, his profits will also be negatively affected. In any event, inflation in the United States will adversely affect your father's business.

16.2 If labour productivity increases, workers expect to be rewarded with higher wages. Higher wages serve as an incentive for greater productivity. If employers deliberately keep wages low in order to comply with the wage guidelines established by the policy, workers can become frustrated and discouraged and unlikely to expend work effort. This can seriously affect business performance.

Chapter 18

18.1 If the government chooses to use monetary policy to stimulate the Canadian economy, the money supply will be increased, and the domestic interest rate will fall. This fall in the Canadian interest will reduce the interest rate differential between Canada and the United States. Consequently, the exchange value of the Canadian dollar will fall. With this information, Odds & Ends could purchase its supplies now at the existing rate and arrange for delivery at some future date.

Appendix B Answers to Study Guide Questions

Score

Give yourself one mark for each correct answer.

Interpretation

If you obtained a score of 80% or higher, you have a good understanding of the material covered in the chapter. However, you should review the sections dealing with the questions that you missed. If you obtained a score between 60% and 75%, you have a fair understanding of the material. You should study those sections dealing with your incorrect answers. A score below 60% means that you need to study the material again, paying special attention to your incorrect answers.

Chapter 1

Answers

1. c	2. d	3. b	4. b
5. b	6. b	7.c	8. b
9. b	10.d	11. c	12. c
13. b	14. b	15. b	16. c
17.c	18. d	19. d	20. c
21. a	22. d	23. c	24. a
25. a	26. c	27. c	28. d

Chapter 1A

Answers

1. b	2. c	3. d	4. d
5. c	6. c	7. c	8. d
9. a	10. b	11. a	12. d
13. c	14. c	15. c	16. a
17. b	18. c	19. b	20. b

Chapter 2

Answers

1. c	2. d	3. c	4. d
5. d	6. a	7. d	8. a
9. d	10. b	11. d	12. c
13. c	14. d	15. a	16. d
17. b	18. a	19. d	20. b

Chapter 3

Answers

1. d	2. c	3. b	4. a
5. c	6. d	7. c	8. b
9. c	10. d	11. c	12. b
13. a	14. c	15. b	16. c
17. a	18. d	19. d	20. a

Chapter 4

Answers

1. c	2. b	3. d	4. d
5. b	6. c	7. d	8. d
9. a	10. c	11. c	12. d
13. c	14. c	15. d	16. b
17. c	18. c	19. a	20. c

Chapter 5

Answers

1. d	2. b	3. d	4. d
5. b	6. c	7. d	8. b
9. c	10. d	11. d	12. b
13. b	14. d	15. b	16. c
17. b	18. d	19. d	20. d

Chapter 6

Answers

1. b	2. a	3. c	4. c
5. d	6. d	7. b	8. c
9. b	10. a	11. b	12. c
13. a	14. c	15. c	16. c
17. d	18. c	19. d	20. a

Chapter 7

Answers

1. d	2. d	3. a	4. d
5. c	6. b	7. d	8. b
9. a	10. a	11. c	12. b
13. c	14. d	15. a	16. c
17. a	18. b	19. b	20. a

Chapter 8

Answers

1. c	2. b	3. a	4. b
5. c	6. c	7. b	8. a
9. d	10. a	11. b	12. c
13. d	14. d	15. d	16. d
17. d	18. d	19. a	20. b

Chapter 9

Answers

1. b	2. d	3. c	4. c
5. c	6. b	7. d	8. b
9. b	10. b	11. b	12. d
13. a	14. a	15. c	16. c
17. c	18. d	19. c	20. d

Chapter 10

Answers

1. b	2. a	3. b	4. b
5. c	6. a	7. b	8. c
9. c	10. d	11. c	12. b
13. d	14. a	15. c	16. c
17. c	18. b	19. b	20. d

Chapter 11

Answers

1. c	2. d	3. c	4. a
5. b	6. d	7. b	8. d
9. c	10. b	11. c	12. a
13. d	14. c	15. a	16. a
17. c	18. d	19. d	20. d

Chapter 12

Answers

1. c	2. c	3. d	4. c
5. c	6. b	7. c	8. d
9. a	10. d	11. b	12. c
13. a	14. d	15. d	16. a
17. c	18. c	19. a	20. a

Chapter 13

Answers

1. c	2. c	3. d	4. b
5. c	6. d	7. b	8. c
9. d	10. a	11. a	12. c
13. c	14. c	15. d	16. d
17. d	18. a	19. a	20. c

Chapter 14

Answers

1. a	2. c	3. c	4. d
5. d	6. b	7. c	8. d
9. d	10. d	11. c	12. a
13. c	14. a	15. d	16. d
17. d	18. a	19. b	20. c

Chapter 15

Answers

1. d	2. c	3. c	4. b
5. c	6. b	7. c	8. d
9. b	10. b	11. a	12. d
13. d	14. d	15. a	16. d
17. d	18. a	19. b	20. d

Chapter 16

Answers

1. a	2.d	3.a	4.b
5. c	6. d	7. a	8. b
9. b	10. c	11. b	12. c
13. d	14. a	15. d	16. b
17.b	18.c	19. d	20. c

Chapter 17

Answers

1. c	2. b	3. c	4. d
5. d	6. b	7. d	8. d
9. a	10. d	11. b	12. b
13. d	14. a	15. b	16. b
17. d	18. c	19. b	20. d
21. b	22. d	23. a	24. c

Chapter 18

Answers

1. c	2. d	3. d	4. a
5. b	6. c	7. d	8. b
9. a	10. b	11. c	12. c
13. c	14. a	15. c	16. d
17. a	18. a	19. d	20. b

Glossary

Note: This comprehensive glossary lists the key terms and definitions included in the text and provides definitions for additional economic terms that you will encounter in your studies.

Acceleration principle The theory that an increase in income leads to an accelerated increase in investment

Accelerationists Economists who claim that attempts to keep unemployment below its natural level will simply accelerate inflation

Accelerator See *acceleration principle*

Activist policies Monetary and fiscal policy measures designed to influence the direction of the economy

Actual output The level of output actually produced by the economy

Actual rate of inflation The percentage rate at which the price level moves upward annually

***AD* shifters** Factors that cause the aggregate demand curve to shift; also called *demand-side shocks*

Adaptive expectations The hypothesis that people form their expectations solely on the basis of the experience of the recent past

Aggregate Total

Aggregate demand The total demand for all goods and services in the economy during a specific period; the various levels of real output that will be demanded at various price levels

Aggregate demand curve A graph that shows the relationship between the total amount of all goods and services that will be demanded at various price levels

Aggregate expenditure The total expenditure on the economy's output of goods and services

Aggregate income The sum of all income earned by resource suppliers in an economy during a period

Aggregate output The total amount of goods and services produced in an economy

Aggregate supply The total supply of all goods and services in the economy during a specific period; the various quantities of output that will be supplied at various price levels

Aggregate supply curve The curve showing the relation between the total output of all goods and services that will be produced and the average level of prices

Aggregation problem The problem encountered in aggregating (adding up) individual units to arrive at a single total

Appreciation (of currency) A market-determined increase in the value of a country's currency in terms of another country's currency

***AS* shifters** Factors that cause the aggregate supply curve to shift; also called *supply-side shocks*

Asset Anything of value that is owned by an economic unit

Assumptions Statements of the conditions under which a model will work

Automated teller machines (ATMs) Banking machines that facilitate transactions electronically

Automatic fiscal policy Fiscal policy measures that are built into the economy; also called *automatic (built-in) stabilizers*

Automatic stabilizers See *automatic fiscal policy*

Autonomous consumption Consumption that does not depend on income

Autonomous government spending Government purchases that are independent of the level of income

Autonomous investment Investment that does not vary with income

Average propensity to consume (*APC*) The fraction of total income that goes into consumption ($APC = C/Y$)

Average propensity to save (*APS*) The fraction of total income that is saved ($APS = S/Y$)

Bad money Money whose face value exceeds its commodity value

Bads Things that are unwanted and do not give any satisfaction

Balance of merchandise trade The difference between the value of goods exported and goods imported; also called *balance of visible trade*

Balance of payments A summary statement of international economic transactions

Balance of trade The difference between the value of a country's exports and the value of its imports

Balance of trade deficit The excess of imports over exports; also called *trade deficit*

Balance of trade surplus The excess of exports over imports; also called *trade surplus*

Balance of visible trade See *balance of merchandise trade*

Balance sheet A statement of assets, liabilities, and owners' equity or capital

Balanced budget A condition in which government spending equals tax revenues

Balanced budget change in spending The condition in which a change in government spending equals the change in taxes

Balanced budget multiplier The number that when multiplied by the change in government spending yields the change in equilibrium income when $G = T$

Balanced budget theorem Theory which states that if government spending and taxes increase by the same amount, the resulting increase in income will equal the increase in government spending

Bank Act Federal legislation that governs the operations of the chartered banks

Bank multiplier See *deposit expansion multiplier*

Bank of Canada Act Federal legislation that established the Bank of Canada in 1934

Bank of Canada notes Paper currency issued by the Bank of Canada

Bank rate The rate of interest the central bank charges on loans to members of the Canadian Payments Association

Banking system The association of the central bank and the chartered banks as part of a larger financial network

Bar graph A vertical or horizontal graph with categories on one axis and the value assigned to each category measured on the other axis

Barter The direct exchange of goods and services for other goods and services, without the use of money

Base period See *base year*

Base year A year chosen as a reference point against which other years are measured; also called *base period*

Basic economic problem The scarcity of resources relative to wants

Basic sectors of the economy Household sector, producing sector, and government sector

Better measure of economic well-being (BMEW) GDP plus non-marketed goods and services plus under-the-table transactions minus environmental damage

Bond Interest-earning evidence of debt issued by a government or corporation, which pays interest to the lender for a specified period and the principal when the loan matures

Boom A period of economic expansion

Branch banking system A banking system based on relatively few banks with many branches

Break-even level of income The level of income at which consumption equals income or saving is zero

Budget deficit The condition in which government spending is greater than tax revenues

Budget deficit theory of inflation The theory that government deficit spending causes inflation

Budget philosophy A general view concerning budget policies

Budget surplus The condition in which government spending is less than tax revenues

Built-in stabilizers See *automatic fiscal policy*

Business cycles Alternating periods of economic expansions and contractions;also called *economic fluctuations* and *business fluctuations*

Business fluctuations See *business cycles*

Bust A period of economic contraction

Caisse populaire A financial institution organized on the principle of the cooperative

Canada Deposit Insurance Corporation (CDIC) A federal Crown corporation established in 1967 that insures bank deposits up to $100 000, in the case of bankruptcy at a participating bank

Canadian Payments Association (CPA) An association that facilitates transfers between financial institutions

Capacity utilization rate Shows the degree to which firms use their factories and machinery

Capital Produced means of production; the productive factor of production defined as all human-made means of production; it includes the stock of machinery, equipment, buildings, human skills, and so on

Capital account A record of international capital flows

Capital consumption allowance An allowance made for the depreciation of the economy's capital stock during production

Capital flows Movement of capital, usually between international economic entities

Capital–output ratio The ratio of the value of capital stock to the value of annual output

Cash (currency) drain Withdrawal of currency from the banking system by the public

Cash reserve ratio The ratio of a bank's cash to its deposits

Central bank An institution whose function is to act as banker to the commercial banks and the government, and to ensure the efficient working of the country's monetary system

Ceteris paribus Other things being equal; allows for the investigation of the effects of one variable while assuming that others remain constant; also called *other things being equal assumption*

Chained Price Index for Consumption (CPIC) An index based on the consumption expenditures reported in the national income accounts

Chartered bank A financial institution operating under federal charter; it accepts deposits and makes loans and investments; also called *commercial bank*

Cheque An instrument authorizing a financial institution to pay a specific amount at a specific time from a specified account

Chequing accounts Bank deposits that are transferable by cheque

Choice The ability to decide between one thing and another when the means to obtain both are not available

Circular flow An economic model that shows the flow of resources, goods and services, expenditures, and income between sectors of the economy

Classical economic models Pre-Keynesian economic models that emphasized the market forces of demand and supply

Classical economists Eighteenth-, nineteenth-, and early twentieth-century economists who argued that the economy would automatically achieve full employment if wages and prices were flexible

Classical range The vertical section of the aggregate supply curve that represents output at its maximum

Clearing house system The mechanism through which the net indebtedness between financial institutions is determined

Closed economy An economy that does not engage in foreign trade

Coincidental indicators Variables that coincide exactly with the business cycle

Commercial bank See *chartered bank*

Commodities Goods and services together

Commodity money Any item that serves both as a medium of exchange and as a commodity

Competitiveness The extent to which a firm or industry can compete with another in the marketplace on the basis of price or quality of product

Complements (in production) Goods such that the production of one implies the production of the other; also called *joint products*

Concave curve A curve bowed outward from the origin

Constant Anything that remains unchanged

Constant prices Values expressed in terms of the prices existing in a given (base) year

Consumer price index (CPI) An index that measures the level of the prices of consumer goods and services

Consumption The use or purchase of consumer goods and services to satisfy wants

Consumption curve A curve that shows the relation between consumption and income

Consumption function An equation expressing the functional relation between consumption expenditure and its determinants

Consumption schedule A table showing the relationship between total consumption and total income

Contractionary fiscal policy Decreases in government spending and increases in taxes that result in a reduction in aggregate expenditure

Convex curve A curve bowed toward the origin

Core CPI See *core rate of inflation*

Core inflation A measure of inflation using the core CPI

Core rate of inflation The rate at which core inflation changes; excludes volatile prices such as prices of gasoline and some food items; also called *core CPI*

Corporate income tax A tax on the profits of corporations

Correlation A relationship between variables; variables are correlated if they change together

Cost A payment for the inputs used to produce goods and services

Cost of living The amount of money that must be paid to obtain goods and services

Cost-benefit approach An analysis in decision making that involves the comparison of costs and benefits

Cost-plus pricing A pricing strategy in which firms determine price by adding a certain percentage markup on cost; also called *markup pricing*

Cost-push inflation Inflation resulting from increases in wages and other supply-side factors; also called *sellers' inflation*

Countercyclical policy Government policy designed to work against the business cycle to achieve economic stability

Credit A receipt of payment

Creeping inflation Relatively mild or moderate inflation (less than 8% annually)

Crowding-out effect The concept that increases in government spending lead to a reduction in private sector spending

Currency The notes and coins that serve as a country's medium of exchange; also called *hand-to-hand money*

Current account A record of sales and purchases of currently produced goods and services to or from the rest of the world

Current account balance Total current receipts from foreigners minus total payments to foreigners

Current GDP Gross domestic product measured in current (as opposed to constant) dollars; nominal GDP

Current income hypothesis The proposition that consumption depends on current income

Cyclical unemployment Unemployment that arises because of declines in aggregate expenditure and aggregate output, such as during recessions

Cyclically balanced budget The budget philosophy that supports budget deficits during recessions to be financed by budget surpluses during expansions

Debentures Bonds secured by the creditworthiness of the borrower rather than by specific assets

Debit A withdrawal or subtraction; a recording of debts

Debit cards Cards that electronically transfer funds from the customer's account to the merchant's account

Debt monetization The process by which banks create money when they extend loans

Decision lag The time that elapses between the recognition of a problem and the decision to act

Deficit The condition that exists when spending exceeds income

Deficit financing The methods used to finance a budget deficit

Definition A set of words that explain the meaning of a term or concept

Deflation A sustained decrease in the average level of prices

Deflationary gap The amount by which aggregate expenditure falls short of aggregate output at full employment; also called *recessionary gap*

Demand The various quantities of a good or service that people are willing and able to buy at various prices during a specific period

Demand curve A downward-sloping curve showing the inverse relationship between price and quantity demanded

Demand deposits Bank deposits that can be withdrawn without prior notice

Demand function An equation expressing the relationship between price and quantity demanded

Demand schedule A table showing the inverse relationship between price and quantity demanded

Demand shifters The non-price determinants that shift the demand curve

Demand-pull inflation Inflation that results from excess aggregate demand; also called *excess demand inflation*

Demand-side economics Macroeconomic theory and policy that focus on aggregate expenditure as a way of promoting full employment and price stability

Demand-side shocks Factors that cause the aggregate demand curve to shift; also called *AD shifters*

Dependent variable The variable that is being explained; a variable whose value is determined by the value of some other variable

Deposit expansion multiplier The number by which an initial bank deposit is multiplied to arrive at the resulting total deposits; also called
money multiplier or ***bank multiplier***

Deposit multiplier The amount of increase in the money supply that can result from an initial increase in bank reserves; the maximum deposit multiplier is the reciprocal of the desired reserve ratio

Deposit switching The act of transferring government funds from the central bank to the commercial banks; also called *redeposit*

Depreciation (in national income accounting) The wear and tear of the capital stock during production; also called *capital consumption*

Depreciation (of currency) A market-determined decrease in the value of a country's currency in terms of another country's currency

Depression An economic period characterized by low economic activity and severe unemployment

Derivative deposit A deposit that is created by a bank when it extends a loan; also called *secondary deposit*

Desired reserves The minimum amount of reserves that banks desire to hold

Devaluation (of currency) The lowering of the value of a country's currency in terms of another country's currency

Direct foreign investment Ownership or control of a business in a foreign country

Direct relation The relation that exists between variables that increase or decrease together; the variables move in the same direction

Dirty float See *managed flexible exchange rate*

Discomfort index The rate of inflation plus the rate of unemployment; also called *misery index*

Discouraged workers Workers who have abandoned the search for jobs because they are unable to find work

Discretionary fiscal policy Deliberate changes in government spending and taxes to achieve desired economic objectives

Disposable income After-tax income that an individual can spend or save

Dissaving A situation in which current consumption exceeds current income, so that saving is negative

Dividends Payments made to shareholders of corporations; the reward for capital

Double coincidence of wants A situation in which a buyer finds a seller who has what the buyer wants and who wants what the buyer has

Double counting Counting an item more than once when measuring GDP

Drawdown A transfer of government funds from the commercial banks to the central bank

Durable good A good that is intended to last for a long time (arbitrarily, more than a year)

Econometrics The use of statistical methods to test economic hypotheses

Economic fluctuation See *business cycles*

Economic forecast The assignment of a future value to a variable

Economic growth An increase in a country's real GDP

Economic model A simplification of economic reality

Economic policy A course of action designed to achieve an economic objective

Economic prediction A statement of the general direction of a variable resulting from the fulfillment of certain conditions

Economic system A set of mechanisms by which a society accomplishes the task of producing goods and services to satisfy wants

Economic theory (model) A simplified version of reality designed to capture the important features of the relationship being studied

Economics The social science that studies how people use limited means to satisfy their unlimited wants

Economy An entity within which production, consumption, and exchange take place

Effect lag The time necessary for economic policy to have an effect on the targeted variable or variables; see *impact lag*

Electronic funds transfer system (EFTS) A system whereby funds can be transferred instantly between accounts

Empirical Descriptive, as in observed, measured, and recorded

Employment rate Indicates the percentage of the labour force that is employed

Endogenous variable A variable whose value is determined within a given model

Entrepreneur An individual who assumes the risk of organizing resources into production with the objective of producing a good or service for sale at a profit

Entrepreneurship The organization of land, labour, and capital into production; the risk-taking aspect of business decision making

Equation of exchange An expression that equates the product of the quantity of money and the velocity of circulation (*MV*) and the product of the price level and real output (*PQ*)

Equilibrium A situation in which change is unlikely to occur; a state of balance

Equilibrium income The level of income at which aggregate expenditure equals aggregate output

Equilibrium level of real GDP The level of real GDP at which the *AD* and *AS* curves intersect

Equilibrium price The price at which quantity demanded equals quantity supplied; there is no tendency for this price to change

Equilibrium price level The price at which quantity demanded equals quantity supplied

Equilibrium quantity The quantity traded (bought and sold) at the equilibrium price

Euro The official currency of the Euro Area; now used by 15 European Union countries

Eurodollars U.S. dollars deposited on foreign banks as well as on foreign branches of U.S. banks

Ex ante Before the fact; planned or intended

Ex post After the fact; actual or realized

Excess demand inflation See *demand-pull inflation*

Excess quantity demanded See *shortage*

Excess quantity supplied See *surplus*

Excess reserves Cash reserves held in excess of the desired cash reserves

Exchange rate The value of a country's currency in terms of another country's currency; also called the *foreign exchange rate*

Exogenous variable A variable whose value is determined by factors outside a given model

Expansion The phase of the business cycle characterized by an increase in employment, income, and economic activity in general; also called *recovery*

Expansionary fiscal policy Increases in government spending and increases in taxes that result in an increase in aggregate expenditure

Expectational inflation Inflation caused by the behaviour of buyers and sellers responding to expectations of inflation; also called *inertial inflation*

Expenditure and income equation An equation that shows the equality between injections into and withdrawals from the income stream

Expenditure approach A method of calculating GDP that involves measuring the total amount spent on the economy's total output of goods and services

Exports Goods and services sold to foreign countries

External balance Equilibrium in the foreign exchange market

External balance curve Curve showing external balance in the foreign exchange market

External debt A debt owed to a foreign entity

Factor market The market in which factors of production are bought and sold; also called *resource market*

Factors of production Resources used to produce goods and services

Fallacy of composition The assumption that what is true of the part must also be true of the whole

Federal debt The amount of money the federal government owes its creditors

Fiat money Legal tender money that is not backed by gold or any other precious metal

Fiduciary Relating to trust

Fiduciary monetary system Monetary system based on trust or confidence

Final product A good or service intended for final use and not intended for resale or further processing

Financial capital Money, as opposed to real capital (machinery, equipment, tools, etc.)

Financial intermediaries Financial institutions that accept funds from savers and lend them to borrowers, thus serving as a go-between for savers (lenders) and borrowers

Fine tuning Controlling some of the ups and downs of the economy by minor adjustments in economic policy

Firms The economic sector that makes decisions about what resources to purchase and how the resources will be used to produce goods and services; the economic unit that transforms inputs into output

Fiscal drag Phenomenon in which automatic stabilizers prevent the economy from recovering from a recession

Fiscal policy The use of government spending and taxes to regulate economic activity; changes in government spending and taxes designed to influence aggregate demand

Fixed exchange rate An exchange rate that is fixed by the government at some specified level; also called *pegged exchange rate*

Flexible exchange rate system An exchange rate determined by market forces; also called *freely fluctuating exchange rate system* or *floating exchange rate system*

Floating exchange rate system See *flexible exchange rate system*

Flow A change in a stock over time

Flow variable The change in a stock variable during a period

Foreign aid Financial assistance to certain countries to promote economic development

Foreign currency See *foreign exchange*

Foreign exchange The currency of another country; also called *foreign currency*

Foreign exchange market Market in which foreign currencies are traded

Foreign exchange rate See *exchange rate*

Foreign trade effect The impact of changes in the price level on exports and imports and thus on the quantity of real GDP demanded

Fractional reserve banking system A banking system in which banks keep only a fraction of their deposits in cash reserves

Free good A good that is so plentiful that even at a price of zero, the quantity available exceeds the quantity demanded

Free lunch Additional output produced without sacrificing the production of any other good or service

Freely fluctuating exchange rate system See *flexible exchange rate system*

Frictional unemployment Unemployment that results from people moving between jobs or entering or re-entering the labour force

Full employment A condition that prevails when the only unemployment is frictional and structural unemployment

Full-employment budget The position of the budget if the economy were at full employment

Full-employment income/output The economy's output at full employment; also called *potential GDP*

Full-employment surplus The difference between government revenues and expenditures at the full-employment level of income

Function An expression of a relation among variables

Functional finance The intentional use of deficits and surpluses to achieve desired economic objectives

Functional notation A mathematical tool for expressing relations among variables

Functional relationships Cause-effect relationships among variables

Fundamental psychological law The notion that people increase their consumption as their income increases but by less than the increase in income

Galloping inflation Relatively rapid inflation, usually in the double digits

GDP deflator An index that measures the average level of prices; also called *implicit price deflator*

General equilibrium analysis A method of analysis that studies the effects of a variable in different markets

Generalized multiplier The multiplier that results from considering all withdrawals; the reciprocal of the marginal propensity to withdraw

Globalization The increasingly rapid flow of capital, information, goods and services, communication, and people internationally

Good money Money whose face value equals its commodity value

Goods Tangible things that satisfy wants

Goods and services market See *product market*

Government purchases Expenditures on goods and services by all levels of government

Government sector The sector of the economy that involves government purchases of goods and services; production decisions are made by government or government agencies; also called *public sector*

Government securities Government bonds and other instruments of debt issued by the government to finance its debt

Government spending multiplier The ratio of the change in income to the change in government spending that causes it

Government transfer payments Payments made by the government that do not represent payments for productive services (e.g., employment insurance payments, welfare payments, old age security payments)

Graph A geometric (diagrammatic) representation of information

Great Depression A period of severe economic slump lasting 10 years, from 1929 to 1939

Green revolution The tremendous increases in agricultural yields

Gresham's law The hypothesis that bad money will drive good money out of circulation

Gross domestic product (GDP) The market value of all final goods and services produced in an economy during a specific period

Gross investment The total expenditure on investment goods; the sum of net investment and capital consumption allowance

Gross national product (GNP) The market value of all final goods and services produced by a country's nationals and their resources during a period

Growth rate The percentage change in a country's real GDP per capita (The growth rate is a general term that can apply to any variable. The percentage change in a country's real GDP would be the growth rate of real GDP per capita.)

Hand-to-hand money See *currency*

High-powered money New reserves that allow banks to grant loans and expand deposits

Households The economic sector that makes decisions about what resources to sell and what goods and services to buy

Human capital Education, training, skills, health, and so on, that improve the quality of labour

Human Development Index (HDI) A composite index designed to measure human well-being in a country

Hyperinflation An excessively high rate of inflation, usually 100% or more annually; also called *runaway inflation*

Hypothesis A statement of suspected relationships among two or more variables

Impact lag The time that elapses between the implementation of a decision and its effects on the economy; also called *effect lag*

Implementation lag The time that elapses between the decision to act and the implementation of the decision

Implicit price deflator See *GDP deflator*

Imported inflation Inflation caused by increases in the prices of imported inputs

Imports Goods and services bought from foreign countries

Income and employment theory See *macroeconomic theory*

Income approach A method of calculating GDP that involves measuring the total income generated in the process of producing the economy's goods and services

Income effect The effect on quantity demanded caused by the change in purchasing power resulting from a change in price

Income gap The difference between the potential output and the actual output of an economy; the difference between the equilibrium level of income and the full-employment level of income; also called the*output gap*

Income (output) gap The difference between full-employment income (output) and actual income (output)

Income-expenditure model The simple Keynesian model of income determination in which the aggregate expenditure and the aggregate output (45-degree) lines intersect to determine the equilibrium level of income

Incomes policies Actions taken by the government to control wages and prices to achieve economic objectives

Independent goods Goods that are not related

Independent variable The variable that provides the explanation; it causes changes in the dependent variable

Index numbers Numbers that measure the levels of variables; for example, price index numbers measure the level of prices

Indirect business taxes Taxes other than income taxes imposed on businesses; examples are property taxes and sales taxes

Induced consumption The portion of consumption that depends on the level of income

Induced investment Investment that varies with the level of income

Inertial inflation See *expectational inflation*

Inferior goods Goods for which demand decreases as income increases and for which demand increases as income falls

Inflation A sustained increase in the average level of prices over time; a persistent increase in the cost of living

Inflationary gap The amount by which desired aggregate expenditure exceeds aggregate output at full employment

Initial deposits Deposits that deposit-taking institutions sell for cash; also called*primary deposits*

Injections Any income or expenditure such as investment and government spending that is pushed into the income-expenditure stream

Interest The reward for capital; the payment for borrowed money

Interest and dividends Income from capital

Interest rate effect The impact of changes in interest rates on consumption and investment and thus on total spending

Interest spread The difference between the interest rate that banks charge for loans and the interest rate they pay their depositors

Intermediate products The outputs of one firm that are used as inputs by other firms or businesses

Intermediate range The upward-sloping section of the aggregate supply curve that represents high price levels

Internal balance A situation in which aggregate expenditure equals aggregate output at full employment; it represents equilibrium in the domestic economy

Internal debt A debt that a nation owes to its citizens

International trade The exchange of goods, services, and resources between countries

Inventories Stocks of finished and semi-finished goods and raw materials kept by a firm

Inventory cycles Economic fluctuations caused by changes in inventory investment

Inverse relation The relation that exists between variables such that as one increases, the other decreases, and vice versa; the variables move in opposite directions

Investment Expenditure on capital goods

Investment function An equation expressing the relationship between investment spending and its determinants

Invisible hand The term used by Adam Smith to describe the free market mechanism

Joint products See *complements (in production)*

Key interest rate See *key policy rate*

Key policy rate The interest rate at which major financial institutions borrow and lend one-day funds among themselves; see also *key interest rate, overnight rate,* and *target for the overnight rate*

Keynesian cross The 45-degree diagram showing aggregate expenditure and aggregate output

Keynesian economics Economics based on the premise that total output is determined by total spending; it emphasizes the demand side of the economy

Keynesian expenditure model A macroeconomic model that emphasizes aggregate expenditure, with the assumptions of a constant price level and unemployed resources

Keynesian model A model of the economy that emphasizes demand-side factors as determinants of output and employment, and the importance of fiscal policy as a means of stimulating the economy

Keynesian range The horizontal section of the aggregate supply curve that represents high unemployment and low real GDP

Keynesian theory of unemployment This theory of unemployment states that unemployment can be caused by low aggregate expenditure

Labour Human physical and mental efforts

Labour force The sum of all employed people and all unemployed people who are willing and able to work

Labour force participation rate The labour force expressed as a percentage of the adult population; also called *participation rate*

Laffer curve A curve showing the relationship between tax revenues and tax rates

Lagging indicators Variables that turn downward after the peak and upward after the trough

Land All natural resources

Law of comparative advantage The general idea that trading partners can benefit mutually if each specializes in an activity in which it has a relative advantage

Law of demand A statement of the inverse relationship between price and quantity demanded

Law of increasing opportunity cost The phenomenon of increasing unit cost as an economy increases its production of a commodity

Law of one price The hypothesis that the prices of traded goods should be the same everywhere after allowing for transportation and other transaction costs

Law of supply A statement of the direct relationship between price and quantity supplied: other things being equal, as the price of an item falls, the quantity supplied will also fall, and vice versa

Leading indicators Economic variables that turn downward before the cycle peak and upward before the trough

Leakage See *withdrawal*

Legal tender Money that must legally be accepted if offered as payment to settle debt

Lender of last resort The central bank's function of advancing loans to financial institutions

Less developed country (LDC) A country with a relatively low per capita real income

Liability The amount owed to a creditor; a debt

Liquid asset Any asset that can easily be converted into cash without much capital loss

Liquidity The ease with which an asset can be converted into cash with minimal loss

Liquidity preference The desire to hold money rather than less liquid interest-earning assets

Liquidity preference curve The curve showing the inverse relationship between the quantity of money demanded and the rate of interest

Liquidity preference schedule A table showing the relation between the quantity of money demanded and the rate of interest

Liquidity trap A situation in which the rate of interest is so low that people prefer to hold large amounts of money over other forms of liquid assets

Long run A situation in which firms are unconstrained by fixed factors and therefore can vary all their inputs and adjust fully to market conditions

Long-run aggregate supply (*LRAS*) curve A vertical line representing the economy's potential real GDP in the long run at full employment

Long-run macroeconomic equilibrium The condition that exists when the economy's *AD* curve and its *LRAS* curve intersect, which occurs at the full-employment level of real GDP

Lump-sum tax A fixed tax that is independent of the level of income

M1 A measure of the money supply consisting of currency and demand deposits

M1A A measure of the money supply consisting of M1 plus daily interest chequable and non-personal term deposits

M2 A measure of the money supply consisting of M1A, other notice deposits, and personal term deposits

M2+ A measure of the money supply consisting of M2, deposits at trust and mortgage loan companies and credit unions and caisses populaires, life insurance company individual annuities, personal deposits at government-owned savings institutions, and money market mutual funds

M3 A measure of the money supply consisting of M2, mutual funds, and Canada Savings Bonds

Macroeconomic policy Deliberate government action taken to achieve economic objectives

Macroeconomic theory A model or theory that explains how the macroeconomy functions; also called *income and employment theory*

Macroeconomics The branch of economics that studies the behaviour of broad economic aggregates

Managed flexible exchange rate An exchange rate that is neither totally fixed nor totally flexible; also called *dirty float*

Marginal A concept widely used in economics to mean incremental, extra, or additional

Marginal efficiency of investment (*MEI*) curve A curve on a graph showing the relation between the rate of interest and the level of investment

Marginal efficiency of investment (*MEI*) schedule A table showing the relation between the rate of interest and the level of investment

Marginal propensity to consume (*MPC*) The fraction of extra income allocated to consumption; a change in consumption resulting from a change in income; *MPC* = Δ*C*/Δ*Y*; mathematically, it is the slope of the consumption curve

Marginal propensity to import The fraction of extra income that is spent on imported goods and services; it is expressed as Δ*M*/Δ*Y*, where *M* represents imports

Marginal propensity to save (*MPS*) The fraction of extra income allocated to saving; a change in saving resulting from a change in income; *MPS* = Δ*S*/Δ*Y*; mathematically, it is the slope of the saving curve

Marginal propensity to withdraw (*MPW*) The fraction of extra income allocated to saving, taxes, and imports; *MPW* = Δ*W*/Δ*Y*

Marginal tax rate (*MTR*) The fraction of extra income that is paid in taxes; *MTR* = Δ*T*/Δ*Y*

Market The mechanism that facilitates the buying and selling of resources and goods and services

Market condition The relationship between quantity demanded and quantity supplied

Market-size effect The effect on quantity demanded caused by a change in the number of buyers in the market as a result of a change in price

Markup pricing A pricing formula in which firms charge consumers the cost of production plus an additional amount—a markup—to cover profit; see *cost-plus pricing*

Measure of value An item used to evaluate the value of something; one of the functions of money; see also *unit of account*

Medium of exchange Any item that is used to effect a purchase or a sale

Merchandise trade Exports and imports of goods

Microeconomics The branch of economics that studies the behaviour of individual economic units; also called *price theory*

Misery index See *discomfort index*

Mixed economy An economy that has a mixture of free enterprise and central decision making

Model A simplified version of a more complex system of relationships; sometimes called a theory

Monetarism The school of thought that claims that changes in the money supply are the major cause of economic fluctuations and that macroeconomic stability can be achieved by a steady increase in the money supply

Monetary aggregates Different measures of the money supply

Monetary policy Action taken by the central bank to change the money supply and interest rates to achieve economic objectives

Monetary theory The study of the demand for and supply of money and their effects on the economy

Monetary theory (of business cycle) The hypothesis that economic fluctuations are caused by changes in the availability of money and interest rates

Monetary theory (of inflation) The theory that inflation is caused by increases in the money supply

Money Anything that is generally accepted as final payment for goods and services

Money aggregates Different measures of the money supply

Money flows Flows of income and expenditures in monetary terms

Money multiplier See *deposit expansion multiplier*

Money supply The total quantity of money supplied at various rates of interest

Moral suasion Any persuasive tactic used by the central bank to secure the cooperation of the commercial banks

Multiplier The number by which a change in spending is multiplied to arrive at the change in income; the ratio of the change in income to the change in autonomous spending that generates the change in income; the multiple by which income increases as a result of an increase in autonomous spending

Multiplier effect The ultimate change in equilibrium income is greater than the change in spending that caused it

NAIRU Non-accelerating inflation rate of unemployment; see also *natural rate of unemployment*

National debt The amount the government owes its creditors; also called *public debt*

National income The total income earned for factor services by the owners of the factors of production

National income accounting The process of collecting, measuring, and recording data on the economy's output

Natural rate of unemployment or NAIRU The rate of unemployment that is consistent with a constant rate of inflation

Near bank A financial institution (such as a credit union, trust company, or mortgage loan company) that is not a chartered bank but accepts deposits from the public

Near money Highly liquid assets that can be easily converted into currency or demand deposits without any appreciable loss of value

Negative slope The slope of a declining curve

Net capital formation (net investment) The difference between total (gross) investment and replacement investment; investment that increases the capital stock; also called *net investment*

Net domestic income at factor cost The total income earned by the factors of production

Net domestic product at basic prices An aggregate measure consisting of all factor incomes plus taxes on the factors of production

Net export function The relation between net exports and the level of income

Net exports The difference between a country's sale of exports and its purchase of imports

Net investment See *net capital formation*

Net national income at factor cost The total income earned by a country's factors of production

Net national product (NNP) Gross national product minus capital consumption allowance

New classical economists Economists who emphasize wage and price flexibility and believe in rapid macroeconomic adjustment

New classical macroeconomic model Macroeconomic model that assumes that wages and prices are flexible and macroeconomic adjustment is rapid

New Keynesian economists Economists who accept and extend the ideas of Keynes, who emphasize wage and price inflexibility and believe that markets can fail to adjust

New Keynesian macroeconomic model Macroeconomic model that assumes that wages and prices are rigid and that macroeconomic adjustment is sluggish

Nominal GDP GDP expressed in current dollars

Nominal income Income expressed in current dollars

Non-merchandise transactions (invisibles) Services, investments, and transfers, as noted on the current account section of the balance of payments

Normal goods Good for which demand increases as income increases and for which demand falls as income falls

Normative economics Explains how the economy should work

Normative statements Statements about what ought to be

Notice deposits Interest-earning deposits subject to notice before withdrawal

Occam's razor The idea of stripping away unnecessary details from what is being studied and focusing only on what is immediately relevant

Office of the Superintendent of Financial Institutions The principal regulatory body that supervises financial institutions

Official Development Assistance (ODA) Foreign developmental aid channelled through Canadian International Development Agency (CIDA)

Official reserves Reserves held by a central bank to make international payments

Okun's law The assertion that real output falls by 3% for every 1% that the unemployment rate rises

Open economy An economy that engages in international trade

Open-market operations The buying and selling of securities (bonds) by the central bank

Opportunity cost The alternative that is sacrificed when a choice is made

Optimal labour force The labour force that is consistent with maximum real GDP per worker

Origin The point of intersection of the vertical and horizontal axes

Other things being equal assumption See *ceteris paribus*

Output gap The difference between the potential output and the actual output of an economy; also called the *income gap*

Outputs The goods and services produced by the factors of production

Overall balance The condition that exists when the domestic economy and the foreign sector are in equilibrium simultaneously

Overnight rate The target interest rate or key policy rate set by the Bank of Canada for borrowing and lending among major financial institutions; see also *key interest rate, key policy rate*, and *target for the overnight rate*

Paradox of saving See *paradox of thrift*

Paradox of thrift The apparent contradiction in the fact that an increase in intended aggregate saving results in a decrease in actual saving; also called *paradox of saving*

Participation rate See *labour force participation rate*

Payments system A set of arrangements that facilitate the exchange of goods and services

Peak The phase of the business cycle in which economic activity has reached its highest point

Pegged exchange rate See *fixed exchange rate*

Per capita income Total income divided by total population

Permanent income hypothesis The hypothesis that current consumption depends significantly on permanent (average long-term) income

Personal disposable income Personal income minus personal taxes and personal transfers to the government

Personal income The total income of individuals from all sources before personal income taxes are paid

Personal income taxes Taxes paid by individuals based on income

Personal saving The part of disposable income not spent on consumer goods and services

Phillips curve The curve showing the relationship between the wage rate and the rate of unemployment

Physical capital Manufactured resources used to produce goods and services

Pie chart A circular graph whose pieces add up to 100%

Planned investment Intended expenditure on capital goods

Planned saving The amount that income earners intend to save out of their incomes

Policy irrelevance hypothesis The proposition that monetary and fiscal policies will be ineffective if people have rational expectations

Political business cycle Business cycle that is caused by changes in government spending and taxes to achieve political rather than economic ends

Population explosion Rapid population growth, particularly in less developed countries

Portfolio foreign investment The purchase by foreigners of stocks and bonds whose term to maturity is more than one year

Portfolio investment The purchase of securities whose term to maturity is more than one year

Positive economics Explains or describes how the economy works

Positive slope The slope of a rising curve

Positive statements Statements about what is

Post hoc fallacy The erroneous conclusion that one event causes another simply because it precedes the other

Potential GDP The economy's output at full employment; also called *full-employment output*

Potential gross domestic product The level of GDP that an economy could produce if full employment existed

Precautionary demand for money The desire to hold money for unexpected contingencies

Price Value expressed in terms of money; the amount of money paid for a unit of a commodity

Price indexes Numbers that measure changes in prices over time

Price level The average level of prices as measured by an appropriate price index

Price mechanism The market system in which prices determine the production and distribution activities in an economy

Price system A system of prices and markets that determines what to produce, how to produce, and for whom to produce

Price theory See *microeconomics*

Primary deposits See *initial deposits*

Primary reserves Bank reserves held in cash

Prime rate The rate of interest that banks charge their most creditworthy customers

Private debt A debt owed by households or firms to other households or firms

Private sector The household sector and the private business sector; the non-public sector

Private transfer payments Transfers of purchasing power from one individual or group to another for which no goods and services are produced

Producer price index An index that measures changes in the prices of primary goods

Producer sovereignty The concept that producers decide what to produce and then convince consumers to buy it

Producers See *firms*

Product market The market in which goods and services (products) are bought and sold; also called *goods and services market*

Production possibilities (p-p) curve A graph showing all combinations of goods and services that can be produced if all resources are fully employed and technology is constant; also called *production possibility (p-p) boundary, production possibility (p-p) frontier*, and *transformation curve*

Production possibilities (p-p) schedule A table showing various combinations of goods and services that can be produced with full utilization of all resources and a given state of technology

Production possibility (p-p) boundary See *production possibility (p-p) curve*

Production possibility (p-p) frontier See *production possibility (p-p) curve*

Production possibility (p-p) point A combination of goods or services that an economy can produce

Productive efficiency The situation that exists when an economy cannot increase its production of one commodity without reducing its production of some other commodity

Productive inefficiency The situation that exists when it is possible to produce more of one commodity without producing less of some other commodity

Profit Income from entrepreneurship; the difference between total revenue and total cost

Progressive tax system A system in which the tax rate increases as income increases

Property tax A tax levied on property, usually on real estate

Proportional tax system A system in which the taxrate remains constant as income rises

Public debt See *national debt*

Public investment The purchase or production of new capital goods by the government

Public sector See *government sector*

Purchasing power The ability to purchase goods and services

Purchasing power parity The notion that the exchange rate between two countries will reflect the difference in prices between them

Quantity demanded The quantity that people will be willing and able to buy at a specific price

Quantity theory of money The theory that states that changes in the price level are due to changes in the quantity of money

Rate of inflation Rate of change of the average level of prices

Rational expectations hypothesis The theory that, on average, people base their inflation expectations on their knowledge of policies and their effects

Real business cycle The theory that the business cycle is caused by supply-side shocks

Real capital Capital goods, such as buildings, tools, and equipment; not money capital

Real exchange rate The nominal exchange rate adjusted for differences in price levels in the trading countries

Real flows Flows of real, physical goods, services, and resources

Real GDP per capita A measure of GDP that accounts for changes in the population

Real gross domestic product Gross domestic product expressed in constant dollars

Real income Nominal income adjusted for the rate of inflation

Real per capita output Real GDP divided by the population

Real wage The wage measured in terms of constant dollars

Real wealth effect The impact of changes in the price level on real wealth and thus on the quantity of real GDP demanded

Recession A phase of the business cycle characterized by a general downswing in economic activity

Recessionary gap See *deflationary gap*

Recognition lag The time that elapses before a problem is fully recognized

Recovery See *expansion*

Redeposit See *deposit switching*

Relative price The ratio of two absolute prices; the price of one good expressed in terms of the price of another good

Rent Income from land

Reserve ratio The ratio of cash reserves to total deposits

Reserve requirement The amount that commercial banks were legally obliged to keep in cash or as deposits at the central bank; no longer in effect

Resource market See *factor market*

Resources The things used to produce goods and services

Retained earnings Profits that are not distributed to shareholders; also called *undistributed profits*

Revaluation (of currency) The raising of the value of a country's currency in terms of another country's currency

Robin Hood effect The redistribution of income from high-income earners to low-income earners, thereby increasing total consumer spending

Rule of 70 A formula for determining the number of years required for a number to double for a given rate of change

Runaway inflation See *hyperinflation*

Saving That part of disposable income that is not spent on consumer goods and services

Saving curve A graph that shows the relationship between saving and income

Saving function A mathematical expression of the relationship between saving and income

Saving schedule A table that shows the relationship between saving and income

Savings deposits Deposits that earn interest in financial institutions

Say's law The assertion that the production of goods and services creates a market for those goods and services (supply creates its own demand)

Scarcity The situation that exists when resources are inadequate to produce all the goods and services that people want

Schedule A banks Canadian-owned banks

Schedule B banks Foreign-owned banks

Science A particular method of acquiring knowledge that involves observation, measurement, and testing; also refers to the knowledge acquired through the process; see also *scientific method*

Scientific method See *science*

Seasonal unemployment Unemployment caused by seasonal variations

Secondary deposit See *derivative deposit*

Secondary reserves Liquid assets, such as currency, day-to-day loans, treasury bills, and call and short loans, held as reserves

Secular decline in the price level A persistent decline in the average level of prices over time

Selective controls Controls designed to affect certain industries or sectors of the economy, but not the whole economy directly

Sellers' inflation See *cost-push inflation*

Services Intangible things that satisfy wants

Short run A situation in which firms cannot vary all their inputs or productive resources; thus, they operate with some fixed costs

Shortage A situation in which quantity demanded exceeds quantity supplied; also called excess quantity demanded

Short-run aggregate supply curve A graph that shows the various quantities of real GDP that will be supplied at various price levels in the short run

Short-run aggregate supply The various quantities of real GDP supplied at various price levels, other things being equal

Short-run Phillips curve A curve illustrating the inverse relationship between inflation and unemployment in the short run

Short-term capital flows The movements of financial assets whose term to maturity is less than one year

Slope (of a curve) The steepness or flatness of a curve; the upward or downward inclination of a curve

Slope of a linear curve The vertical distance divided by the horizontal distance; slope is Δ*Y*/Δ*X*

Slope of a non-linear curve (at a point on the curve) The slope of the line drawn tangent to the curve at the given point

Social science Any discipline that studies human behaviour

Socialism An economic system in which the state owns and controls the resources of the economy

Socialistic system See *command economy*

Special drawing rights (SDRs) Deposits with the International Monetary Fund (IMF)

Speculative demand for money The desire to hold money in anticipation of movements in the prices of financial assets

Stabilization policies Actions taken by the government and the central bank to promote economic stability

Stagflation The simultaneous occurrence of high rates of inflation and high rates of unemployment

Statistics Canada The special federal government agency responsible for collecting and publishing national economic and social statistics

Stock A quantity existing at a particular time

Store of value Money or other assets put away for future use; also called *store of wealth*

Store of wealth See *store of value*

Structural unemployment Unemployment that is caused by a mismatch between the types of skills that unemployed workers possess and the types of workers that employers would like to hire

Substitute A good that can be used in place of another

Substitutes (in production) Goods that are produced as alternatives to each other

Substitution effect The effect on quantity demanded caused by people switching to or from a product as its price changes

Supply The various quantities of a good or service that sellers are willing and able to offer for sale (place on the market) at various prices during a specific period

Supply curve An upward-sloping curve showing the direct relationship between price and quantity supplied

Supply function Equation expressing the relationship between price and quantity supplied

Supply schedule A table showing the direct relationship between price and quantity supplied

Supply shifters The non-price determinants that shift the supply curve

Supply shocks Events that affect aggregate supply

Supply side The production or cost side of the economy

Supply-side economics An approach to economics that stresses supply or cost factors, such as technology, incentives to work, save, and invest

Supply-side policies Policies designed to influence real GDP and the price level by shifting the *AS* curve

Supply-side shocks See *AS shifters*

Surplus A situation in which quantity supplied exceeds quantity demanded; also called *excess quantity supplied*

Sustainable development *Development that meets the needs of the present without compromising the ability of future generations to meet their own needs*

Target for the overnight rate See *key policy rate*

Target reserve ratio The fraction of demand deposits that chartered banks hold as cash reserves

Tariff A tax on imported goods

Tax A compulsory payment imposed by a government

Taxable income The portion of income on which income tax payable is calculated

Tax-based incomes policies (TIPS) Policies that use tax incentives to encourage compliance with wage and price controls

Technological unemployment A type of structural unemployment caused by the introduction of labour-saving equipment or methods of production

Theory A testable hypothesis about the way in which variables are related; sometimes called a model

Token money Money whose face value exceeds its commodity value

Trade deficit See *balance of trade deficit*

Trade liberalization The reduction or elimination of trade barriers among nations

Trade surplus See *balance of trade surplus*

Transactions demand for money The desire to hold money for transactions purposes

Transfer payments (transfers) Payments that do not represent compensation for goods or services

Transformation curve See production possibility (p-p) curve

Transmission mechanism The process by which changes in the Bank's target interest rate or key policy rate affect the economy

Treasury bill (T-bill) A security sold by the government with a promise to pay a certain amount within a short time, usually from 30 to 90 days

Trough The lowest point in the business cycle

Underemployment A situation in which workers accept low-paying jobs or part-time jobs because they cannot find a full-time job consistent with their qualifications

Underground economy All economic activities that are not reported to government and on which no taxes are paid

Undistributed profits See *retained earnings*

Unemployment An economic condition that exists when workers are without jobs even though they are willing and able to work

Unemployment rate The number of working-age Canadians actively seeking employment (yet unemployed) expressed as a percentage of the labour force

Unit banking system A banking system with many independent banks with no branches

Unit of account The common unit for expressing the value of goods and services; also called *measure of value*

Validation An increase the money supply in response to the decrease in *AS*

Value added The difference between the value of the output and the cost of the inputs

Variable Anything that changes

Velocity of circulation (of money) The number of times, on average, that a unit of money is spent per year

Wage and price controls Restrictions imposed by the government to limit increases in wages and prices; also called *incomes policies*

Wage-price spiral The phenomenon of successive increases in wages followed by increases in prices followed by increases in wages

Wages and salaries Income from labour

Wealth (net) The value of assets minus liabilities

Wholesale price index A price index that measures the level of the prices of primary goods

Withdrawal Any income or expenditure taken out of the income-expenditure stream, including savings, taxes, and imports; also called *leakage*

Zero-sum game A situation in which one party can gain only at the expense of another

Photo Credits

P. 1 © mediaphotos/iStockphoto; p. 8 © aaronpeterson.net/Alamy; p. 47 © Lucenet Patrice/age fotostock/Maxx Images; p. 60 © Jupiterimages; p. 69 Brendan Howard/Shutterstock.com; p. 78 © Lars Christensen/Shutterstock; p. 112 Paul Popper/Popperfoto/Getty Images; p. 114 Tim Gidal/Picture Post/Getty Images; p. 125 THE CANADIAN PRESS/Sean Kilpatrick; p. 136 © PCL/Alamy; p. 157 REUTERS/Philimon Bulawayo; p. 185 AP Photo/Mohammed Abu Zaid; p. 212 AP Photo/Francois Mori; p. 234 © Rick Friedman/Corbis; p. 244 © Bettmann/CORBIS; p. 263 Rick Lewis/Shutterstock; p. 281 THE CANADIAN PRESS/Adrian Wyld; p. 295 Sascha Burkard/Shutterstock; p. 313 Viktor1/Shutterstock; p. 331 THE CANADIAN PRESS/Fred Chartrand; p. 334 Toi Mine/Wikipedia; p. 339 Elder Vieira Salles/Shutterstock; p. 349 © TheStoreGuy/Alamy; p. 351 Rick Eglinton/GetStock.com; p. 376 Bain News Service, New York/US Library of Congress; p. 381 © Roger Ressmeyer/CORBIS; p. 409 AP Photo/Damian Dovarganes/CP Images; p. 434 AP Photo/Anja Niedringhaus/CP Images; p. 449 John Foxx/Thinkstock; p. 455 SVLuma/Shutterstock.

Index

Key terms and their page references are in boldface.

D

H

I

Manufactured by Amazon.ca
Bolton, ON